W9-BWH-239

THE ROUTLEDGE COMPANION
TO RELIGION AND FILM

The Routledge Companion to Religion and Film brings together a lively and experienced team of contributors to investigate the ways in which this exciting discipline is developing. Divided into four parts, the *Companion*:

- analyzes the history of the interaction of religion and film, through periods of censorship as well as appreciation of the medium
- studies religion-in-film, examining how the world's major religions, as well as postcolonial, Japanese and new religions, are depicted by and within films
- uses diverse methodologies to explore religion and film, such as psychoanalytical, theological, and feminist approaches, and audience reception
- analyzes religious themes in film, including redemption, the demonic, Jesus or Christ-figures, heroes and superheroes
- considers films as diverse as *The Passion of the Christ*, *The Matrix*, *Star Wars*, and *Groundhog Day*

This definitive handbook provides an accessible resource for this emerging field and is an indispensable guide to religion and film for students of religion, film studies, and beyond.

John Lyden is Professor and Chair of the Religion Department at Dana College in Blair, Nebraska. He is the editor of *Enduring Issues in Religion* (1995) and author of *Film as Religion: Myths, Morals, and Rituals* (2003)

THE
ROUTLEDGE COMPANION
TO RELIGION AND FILM

Edited by
John Lyden

Routledge
Taylor & Francis Group

LONDON AND NEW YORK

First published 2009 by Routledge

2 Park Square, Milton Park, Abingdon, Oxon. OX14 4RN

Simultaneously published in the USA and Canada by Routledge
711 Third Avenue, New York, NY 10017

Routledge is an imprint of the Taylor & Francis Group

© 2009 John Lyden for selection and editorial materials. The contributors for
their contributions.

Typeset in Goudy Oldstyle Std 10.5/13pt by Fakenham Photosetting Limited

All rights reserved. No part of this book may be reprinted or reproduced or utilized
in any form or by any electronic, mechanical, or other means, now known or
hereafter invented, including photocopying and recording, or in any information
storage or retrieval system, without permission in writing from the publishers.

British Library Cataloguing in Publication Data
A catalogue record for this book is available from the British Library

Library of Congress Cataloging-in-Publication Data
The Routledge companion of religion and film/edited by John C. Lyden.
p. cm.
Includes bibliographical references and index.
1. Motion pictures--Religious aspects. 2. Motion pictures--Moral and ethical aspects.
1. Lyden, John, 1959–
PN1995.5.R68 2009
791.43'682--dc22
2008043723

ISBN13: 978-0-415-44853-6 (hbk)

ISBN13: 978-0-415-60187-0 (pbk)

To my wife Liz, for all her support, love, and encouragement

CONTENTS

List of illustrations   x
Notes on contributors   xi

Introduction
John Lyden   1

PART I
**History of the interaction between religion and film: focus on
Western Christianity**   11

1 Silent cinema and religion: an overview (1895–1930)
   TERRY LINDVALL   13

2 The era of censorship (1930–1967)
   ANDREW QUICKE   32

3 The Roman Catholic Church and cinema (1967 to the present)
   PETER MALONE   52

4 Modern Protestant approaches to film (1960 to the present)
   BRYAN STONE   72

PART II
Depictions of and by religious practitioners in films   89

5 Judaism
   MELANIE J. WRIGHT   91

6 Christianity
   CRAIG DETWEILER   109

7 Islam
   AMIR HUSSAIN   131

8 Hinduism
   RACHEL DWYER   141

9 Buddhism
   FRANCISCA CHO   162

10 Postcolonial religious syncretism: focus on the Philippines, Peru,
   and Mexico
   ANTONIO D. SISON   178

11 Religion in Japanese film: focus on *anime*
   JOLYON BARAKA THOMAS   194

12 New religious movements
   PAUL THOMAS   214

PART III
Academic approaches to the study of Religion and Film   235

13 Feminism
   GAYE WILLIAMS ORTIZ   237

14 Audience reception
   CLIVE MARSH   255

15 Cultural theory and cultural studies
   GORDON LYNCH   275

16 Psychoanalysis
   KENT L. BRINTNALL   292

17 Theological approaches
   ROBERT K. JOHNSTON   310

PART IV
Categories applicable to religion and film studies   329

18 Narrative
   ROY M. ANKER   331

19 Redemption
   CHRISTOPHER DEACY   351

20 Apocalyptic
   CONRAD OSTWALT   368

CONTENTS

21 Heroes and superheroes
ROBERT JEWETT and JOHN SHELTON LAWRENCE   384

22 Horror and the demonic
DOUGLAS E. COWAN   403

23 Jesus and Christ-figures
ADELE REINHARTZ   420

24 Iconography
DIANE APOSTOLOS-CAPPADONA   440

25 Sacrifice
JON PAHL   465

26 Ethics
JOLYON MITCHELL   482

Index   501

ILLUSTRATIONS

The following were reproduced by kind permission.

10.1 Still from *Santa Santita*, dir. Laurice Guillen (2004). Courtesy Tony I. Gloria and Tito Velasco, Unitel Pictures, Philippines 184

21.1, 21.2 Stills from *From the Manger to the Cross* (1912). Courtesy Kalem Company 386–7

24.1 Henry Ossawa Tanner (1859–1937), *The Savior* (ca. 1900–5). Oil on wood, 29⅛ × 21¾ in. Smithsonian American Art Museum, Washington DC © 2006. Photo Smithsonian American Art Museum/Art Resource/Scala, Florence 445

24.2 Gustave Doré (1832–83), *Jesus and the Woman Taken in Adultery*, from the *Doré Bible Illustrations* for John 8:3–5. Courtesy www.creationism.org 452

24.3 James Tissot (1836–1902), *What Our Savior Saw from the Cross*, illustration for *The Life of Christ* (ca. 1886–96). Gouache on paperboard. Brooklyn Museum of Art, New York, USA/The Bridgeman Art Library 454

24.4 Michelangelo Merisi da Caravaggio (1571–1610), *The Taking of Christ* (1602). Society of Jesus of Ireland on loan to the National Gallery of Ireland, Dublin. Photograph courtesy of the National Gallery of Ireland 457

24.5 Matthias Grünewald (ca. 1475–1528), *Isenheim Altar: Crucifixion*. Colmar, Musée d'Unterlinden. © 1996. Photo Scala, Florence 458

24.6 Matthias Grünewald, *Isenheim Altar: Crucifixion*, detail. Colmar, Musée d'Unterlinden © 1996. Photo Scala, Florence 459

CONTRIBUTORS

Roy M. Anker is Professor of English at Calvin College, Grand Rapids, Michigan. He is the author of *Catching Light: Looking for God in the Movies* (2005) and writes regularly about film for a number of periodicals.

Diane Apostolos-Cappadona is Adjunct Professor of Religious Art and Cultural History at Georgetown University. Her research combines religion, art, cultural history, and gender studies, and she has published numerous essays on the use of classic art in film, especially in the representation of biblical women.

Kent L. Brintnall is an Assistant Professor of Religious Studies at the University of North Carolina at Charlotte. His research focuses on visual culture and constructions of masculinity. His first book, Ecce Homo: *The Male-Body-in-Pain as Redemptive Figure*, is forthcoming from University of Chicago Press.

Francisca Cho is Associate Professor of Buddhist studies at Georgetown University. She is the author of *Embracing Illusion: Truth and Fiction in the* Dream of the Nine Clouds (1996) and *Everything Yearned For: Manhae's Poems of Love and Longing* (2005) as well as articles on Buddhism and film, and religion and science.

Douglas E. Cowan is Associate Professor of Religious Studies and Social Development Studies at Renison University College, University of Waterloo, Canada. He is the author of numerous books and articles, including *Sacred Terror: Religion and Horror on the Silver Screen* (2008).

Christopher Deacy is Lecturer in Applied Theology at the University of Kent. His publications include *Screen Christologies: Redemption and the Medium of Film* (2001), *Faith in Film: Religious Themes in Contemporary Cinema* (2005), and *Theology and Film: Challenging the Sacred/Secular Divide* (coauthored with Gaye Ortiz, 2008).

Filmmaker **Craig Detweiler**, PhD, co-directs the Reel Spirituality Institute for Fuller Theological Seminary's Brehm Center. Detweiler's books include *A Matrix of Meanings: Finding God in Pop Culture* (2003) and *Into the Dark: Seeing the Sacred in the Top Films of the 21st Century* (2008). He also made the award-winning comedic documentary *Purple State of Mind* (2007).

Rachel Dwyer is Professor of Indian Cultures and Cinema at SOAS, University of London. Her recent books include *100 Bollywood Films* (2008), *Filming the Gods: Religion and Indian Cinema* (2006), and *What do Hindus Believe?* (2008).

Amir Hussain is an Associate Professor in the Department of Theological Studies at Loyola Marymount University in Los Angeles. He teaches courses on world religions and specializes in Islam and Muslim communities in North America. He is the author of *Oil and Water: Two Faiths, One God* (2006).

Robert Jewett is Professor Emeritus at Garrett-Evangelical Seminary and currently Guest Professor of New Testament at University of Heidelberg in Germany. He has written *St. Paul at the Movies* (1993) and *St. Paul Returns to the Movies* (1999). With John Shelton Lawrence he coauthored *The American Monomyth* (1977), *The Myth of the American Superhero* (2002), *Captain America and the Crusade against Evil* (2003), and the popular culture essay for *The Oxford Handbook of Eschatology* (2008).

Robert K. Johnston is Professor of Theology and Culture and Co-Director of the Reel Spirituality Institute at Fuller Theological Seminary. His recent writings in theology and film include *Reframing Theology and Film* (2007, editor), *Reel Spirituality* (2006, 2nd edition), *Useless Beauty* (2004), and *Finding God in the Movies* (2004, coauthor with Catherine Barsotti).

John Shelton Lawrence, currently living in Berkeley, is Emeritus Professor of Philosophy at Morningside College. With Robert Jewett he coauthored *The Myth of the American Superhero* (2002), *Captain America and the Crusade against Evil* (2003), and the popular culture essay for *The Oxford Handbook of Eschatology* (2008).

Terry Lindvall occupies the C. S. Lewis Chair of Communication and Christian Thought at Virginia Wesleyan College, publishing works on the historical interface between film and religion including *Sanctuary Cinema* (2007) and *The Silents of God* (2001), and presently exploring religion and satire.

John Lyden is Professor and Chair of Religion at Dana College. He is the author of *Film as Religion: Myths, Morals, and Rituals* (2003) and numerous articles on religion and film. He is currently the Chair of the Religion, Film, and Visual Culture Group of the American Academy of Religion.

Gordon Lynch is Professor of Sociology of Religion and Director of the Centre for Religion and Contemporary Society at Birkbeck College, University of London. His previous books include *Understanding Theology and Popular Culture* (2005) and *The New Spirituality: An Introduction to Progressive Belief in the Twenty-First Century* (2007).

Peter Malone has been reviewing films since 1968. In 1998 he was elected World President of the International Catholic Organization for Cinema (OCIC) and its successor SIGNIS, World Catholic Association for Communication (2001–5). His books include *Movie Christs and Antichrists* (1990) and *Through a Catholic Lens: Religious Perspectives of 19 Film Directors from Around the World* (2007).

Clive Marsh is Principal of the East Midlands Ministry Training Course, an Honorary Fellow in the School of Education, and teaches theology and film in the Department of Theology and Religious Studies at the University of Nottingham (UK). His publications include *Christ in Focus* (2005), *Christ in Practice* (2006), and *Theology Goes to the Movies* (2007).

Jolyon Mitchell is Senior Lecturer at New College, Edinburgh University. A former BBC World Service Producer, his recent publications include *Media Violence and Christian Ethics* (2007) and *The Religion and Film Reader* (2007, as co-editor with Brent Plate).

Gaye Williams Ortiz teaches Communication Studies at Augusta State University, Augusta, Georgia. Her publications include (with Clive Marsh) *Explorations in Theology and Film* (1997) and *Theology and Film: Challenging the Sacred/Secular Divide*, written with Christopher Deacy (2008).

Conrad Ostwalt is Professor of Religious Studies and Chair of the Philosophy and Religion Department at Appalachian State University. His publications include *After Eden* (1990), *Screening the Sacred* (1995, ed., with Joel Martin), *Love Valley: An American Utopia* (1998), and *Secular Steeples: Popular Culture and the Religious Imagination* (2003).

Jon Pahl is Professor of the History of Christianity in North America at the Lutheran Theological Seminary at Philadelphia. He has written *Shopping Malls and Other Sacred Spaces* (2003), *Youth Ministry in Modern America* (1999), and *Blessed Brutalities: The Religious Origins of American Empire* (NYU, forthcoming).

Andrew Quicke is Professor of Cinema Television at the School of Communication and the Arts, Regent University. He spent twenty-five years writing, directing, and producing for BBC television, Reuters Visnews, Clearview International cable television, and his own film company, Kensington Film Services. His publications include (with Andrew Laszlo) *Every Frame a Rembrandt: Art and Practice of Cinematography* (2000).

Adele Reinhartz is Professor in the Department of Classics and Religious Studies at the University of Ottawa (Canada). She is the author of *Scripture on the Silver Screen* (2003) and *Jesus of Hollywood* (2007). Her main areas of research are the Gospel of John, early Jewish–Christian relations, feminist criticism, and the Bible and film.

Antonio D. Sison, CPPS, teaches Theology and World Cinema at the Catholic Theological Union in Chicago. He is author of *Screening Schillebeeckx: Theology and Third Cinema in Dialogue* (2006). A digital filmmaker, Sison presented his film *ICHTHUS* at the American Academy of Religion (AAR) conference in 2008.

Bryan P. Stone is the E. Stanley Jones Professor of Evangelism at Boston University School of Theology. He is the author of, among other works, *Faith and Film: Theological Themes at the Cinema* (2000).

Jolyon Baraka Thomas is a PhD student in Religion at Princeton University. He wrote his MA thesis (University of Hawai'i, 2008) on religion, *manga*, and *anime*, and his primary research interests are religion and civil society and the definition of religion in modern Japan.

Paul Brian Thomas is Assistant Professor of Religious Studies at Radford University. His research interests include the appropriation of ancient religious narratives in new religious movements. He has authored articles on the appropriation of Ishtar in modern Goddess worship and is currently examining the appropriation of biblical narratives by UFO-related religions.

Melanie J. Wright is a Lecturer in Religious Studies at the Open University, UK. She is the author or editor of numerous articles and five books including *Religion and Film: An Introduction* (2007) and *The Religious Roots of Contemporary European Identity* (co-edited with Lucia Faltin, 2007).

INTRODUCTION

John Lyden

It is a truism to state that the field of Religion and Film is still very young. Motion pictures themselves are only a little over a century old, and the academic study of film dates to some scholarship of the 1950s, but film studies as an academic field did not begin to appear in universities until a decade or two later. The study of Religion and Film, as an academic field, began to produce scholarship in the 1970s, but it has only been since the 1990s that the field began to grow at its current rapid pace. Evidences for this include: an increased number of books on the subject being published and purchased; more scholarly interest in the field (such as the American Academy of Religion Group on Religion, Film, and Visual Culture); professional conferences focused on the topic; more classes taught on the subject, both at the undergraduate and graduate levels; and doctoral degrees with a focus on Religion and Film being granted at an increased rate.

As the field of Religion and Film has developed, it has made use of the methodological approaches of its parent disciplines, which include not only film studies and religious studies, but more specifically theology, biblical studies, comparative religion, philosophy, psychology, anthropology, sociology, literary analysis, and cultural studies, to name a few. These diverse viewpoints that represent the range of the field show why it is difficult to define the parameters of the emerging discipline of Religion and Film, in terms of either methodology or subject matter. What unites scholars writing in this area is a shared interest in the topic, although each has their own area of expertise. Many of us came to this interest from an entirely different discipline, but we have applied our knowledge and expertise to this new field and have found ways to contribute. Others are trained in disciplines more obviously related to the subject, and include filmmakers as well as those trained in such disciplines as film theory, art history, and popular culture.

This diversity is both a challenge and a strength to the discipline of Religion and Film. It is a strength in that there exists such a wide array of knowledge and methodologies to draw from, and this background has tremendously enriched the breadth of the field, as the range of contributors to this volume shows. It is also a challenge, however, because it is harder to synthesize conclusions about the field or summarize its direction and foci. This volume does not seek to impose any unity on the field which does not exist, but rather to introduce the reader to the field in its multifaceted nature. What emerges is a picture of a dynamic and exciting discipline that touches on multiple topics of interest to anyone who wants to understand religion or popular culture or their intersection. There is a good deal of dialogue in these pages also, as the contributors frequently comment critically on each other's work, with the aim of seeking to bring us all closer to an adequate understanding of the subject. This means that these essays do not only summarize existing scholarship or directions, but make constructive suggestions on new directions that may be followed, and in a number of ways these suggest creative syntheses of the existing approaches. The organization of a volume of this sort could be undertaken in any number of ways, obviously, and any format will undoubtedly leave some things out that might have been included. It is for this reason that this volume does not seek to summarize everything that has occurred or is occurring in the field, but to highlight some of the more significant ideas and ways of approaching Religion and Film, which can also illuminate some of the directions that may be undertaken by future research.

The book is organized into four groups of essays, each with a distinct focus. Below, I attempt to clarify the focus of each section, the reason for inclusion of particular topics, and a summary of what each of these includes.

History of the interaction between religion and film

The first set of essays speaks to the history of the interaction between religion and film. This set of essays focuses on Western Christianity as one place where there has been considerable tension as well as dialogue between the emerging film industry and the institutional churches. Clearly, one could look to other religious contexts and their interaction with cinema. The reasons for focusing on Western Christianity are threefold. First, the commercial center of the motion picture industry has from its inception been in the West, and it is from here that its cultural influence has been most clearly felt. Second, there has been more written about this particular interaction due to the fact that film scholarship has developed most clearly in the West as well. Third, this particular interaction highlights the conflicts which can arise between the two, as it is a history colored by efforts at censorship as well as rapprochement. Western Christianity's history has at times included an iconoclasm that fears images and their powers of influence. This history surfaced in various ways as churches dealt with the development of motion pictures. Other arts presented similar challenges, but the almost uncontrollable emotional appeal of the cinema clearly created a set of challenges that came at Christianity before it was ready to fully address them.

Terry Lindvall's chapter first gives the background of how early silent films were received by Christians, and how Christians interacted with this new cultural medium. He points out that the silents often had religious themes and content, whether they were created by Christians or not, as they sought to attract religiously oriented filmgoers. Many Christians did not initially perceive the cinema as a threat to Christian values (as it was often understood later), but rather as an opportunity to convey Christian stories and values to a wider audience in an immediate and effective way. Christian groups tried their hand at making films, although budgetary constraints and ambivalence about the medium prevented this from becoming entirely successful. Toward the end of the silent era, efforts by church leaders to censor films they considered objectionable set the stage for the next period of interaction.

Andrew Quicke's chapter covers the period which begins with the early sound pictures and soon created the Hays Office and its "code" that provided the standards for censorship of films for the next four decades. He shows that while both Roman Catholics and Protestants were involved in the efforts to censor film content and so make it acceptable to Christians, it was the Catholic leaders who exerted the most influence over censorship. Arguments over what should or should not be shown in a film reflected different evaluations of the morality of the movies, based on diverse religious and moral standards. As the Catholics took control of this process, Protestants felt marginalized, and often disagreed with the censorship decisions that reflected a more Catholic than Protestant understanding. This was particularly clear when Catholic leaders condemned films that depicted Protestant clergy (including Martin Luther) positively, even though there was no morally objectionable content in them. The era of censorship came to an end when both Protestants and Catholics came to recognize the moral and artistic value of films that did not conform to the standards of the Hays Office code.

Peter Malone's chapter details the ways in which the relationship of Roman Catholics to films changed after censorship collapsed. As a key participant in decisions about cinema within the Roman Catholic Church in these years, he has witnessed firsthand the changes that have taken place in the past four decades in the relationship of Catholics to film. He details the way in which the Church has developed a much more productive relationship to cinema through its evaluation of the positive values and messages of movies. While controversies continue in the evaluation of some films, he also notes that differences in cultural sensitivities result in diverse evaluations by Catholics around the world.

Finally, Bryan Stone writes about modern Protestant approaches to film. He shows that there is also great diversity here, but that in general there has been greater appreciation of cinema than in the era of censorship. Many Protestants favor media literacy approaches which encourage people to view questionable movies critically rather than refrain from viewing them at all. There have also been films that have been condemned and boycotted by some groups, of course, reflecting how some conservative Protestants view popular culture as a threat to "Christian values." There is also a Protestant film industry which, while generally not producing huge revenues, has had an impact through the production of films like the *Left Behind* series.

This section as a whole shows that there have always been conflicts between religious and filmic perspectives, but also that there has been appreciation of shared interests and values. Films have been perceived as a useful medium for religious perspectives as well as a dialogue partner for religions as they encounter culture. It is also the case that one could find some of the same relationships between Religion and Film in contexts other than Western Christianity, and the next section deals with diverse religious contexts and their relationship to film.

Depictions of and by religious practitioners in films

This section presents the way in which eight religious traditions have been depicted in film. This includes both the explicit portrayal of religious people and activities in films as well as the depiction of the values and ideas of those traditions. Films may present religious ideas explicitly or implicitly, and in this way express a religious perspective associated with a historic religion even when it is not always identified as such. The filmmakers may also identify themselves as religious, or not, but frequently they draw from the religious traditions of their countries even when they have a more secularized perspective themselves. Films also often represent religious groups in distorted or prejudicial ways, and the study of religious depictions in film therefore requires us to deconstruct the images that are often used to marginalize or condemn religious groups.

Melanie Wright's chapter on Judaism notes that we should avoid essentializing "Jews" or "Judaism" as if there were one thing to which such terms refer. The anti-semitic claim that "the Jews" control Hollywood is a case in point; filmmakers, actors, and movie executives of Jewish religious or ethnic background represent a wide range of perspectives and are not defined simply by being Jewish. It is also worth noting that the presence of significant numbers of Jews in the film industry did not diminish the extent to which depictions of Jewish religious life were often negative. This was not only because films catered to Christian antisemitism, but also because many Jewish filmmakers were themselves highly secularized and had a very critical view of the tradi-tional Jewish religious life they had abandoned. Wright finds that images of Judaism have often been stereotypical caricatures that viewed Jewish religion nostalgically as an obsolete relic in the modern world, but she also finds some promise in newer filmic images of Judaism which attempt to show its ongoing life and diversity.

Craig Detweiler's chapter on Christianity delves into the near-omnipresence of Christian imagery and concept in film, which is largely a result of the dominance of Western cinema (mentioned already) and the prevalence of Christian themes in it. This obviously includes biblical epics and stories of Christian saints, clergy, and missionaries, but it also includes Christ-figures, images of the end of time, and stories of redemption. Whether filmmakers in the West are Christian or not, they can hardly help drawing on these notions which are ingrained in Western cultural vocabulary. Detweiler also shows how filmmakers outside of Hollywood have expressed Christian ideas of redemption and transcendence, concepts that will be taken up again in the final section of essays.

Amir Hussain's chapter on Islam deals with the large number of negative depictions of Muslims found especially in US cinema, both before and after September 11, 2001. Hollywood films both reflect and reinforce the basic misunderstanding and stereotyping of Muslims that are so prevalent in US culture today. Positive images of Islam are almost impossible to find in the West, but films from predominantly Muslim countries do offer alternatives. We can see clearly that the culture in which a film is made expresses the religious prejudices of the majority, and in this way it may serve as an instrument that reinforces hegemonic judgments on that which has been deemed dangerous or alien.

Rachel Dwyer's chapter on Hinduism points out that Indian cinema has been religious since its inception, full of devotional films to gods and goddesses as well as retellings of Hindu mythology. Even Indian filmmakers who define themselves as nonreligious cannot help but incorporate into their films the religious imagery and concepts of their cultural background (much like the way secular filmmakers in the West make use of Christianity). India also has a strong secular presence blended with tremendous religious diversity, even within the so-called religion of "Hinduism" itself (which easily defies definition to the point that many would say that a religious tradition by this name does not really exist). In any case, the history of Indian cinema is rich with religious symbolism that can be mined again and again by filmmakers and their interpreters.

Francisca Cho's chapter on Buddhism begins with the question of why Buddhists might have a certain affinity for film. Unlike the sometimes iconoclastic religions of the West which may be suspicious of images, or the iconophilic traditions of Hinduism, Buddhism sees a connection between film and life in that both are impermanent and illusory, without lasting substance or essence. Cho develops a Mahayana Buddhist semiotics which suggests that there is no difference between illusion and reality, samsara and nirvana, the world and the goal. Reality is found in the illusion for it is no different from it; in this way, film is a perfect medium for expressing Buddhist concerns, not because it points "beyond" itself, but because it shows the interconnection and ultimate identity of what we call reality and illusion, Buddha and world, religious and secular. Cho shows how the iconography and narrative of Buddhist films demonstrate this dialectic and therefore express the Buddhist worldview.

Antonio D. Sison's chapter deals with cultures that are the product of colonialism and postcolonialism in which religious symbols of the colonial powers have been blended with precolonial religion. He chooses examples from the cinema of the Philippines, Peru, and Mexico to demonstrate how in these different cultural settings religious syncretism has informed and been expressed in the local cinema. In each case, tensions between colonial and precolonial religion are present, but also blend into a whole that marks a distinctive religious experience. Sison shows how indigenous people both incorporate and challenge the ideas of their conquerors and so are able to express and preserve their cultural memory of struggle and survival through film.

Jolyon Baraka Thomas writes about Japanese religion in film and in particular the use of religious themes in *anime*. Religion in Japan is notoriously hard to define due to the fact that most Japanese people do not claim formal religious membership but still participate in practices that seem "religious." This is a testament to the incorporation of religious ideas, attitudes, and behaviors which come from a variety of sources (Shinto, Buddhist, and other) that together form a set of traditions from which most Japanese people draw. This syncretism is shown in Japanese *anime* that fuse elements of multiple religious sources in creative retellings. These stories may have aesthetic or didactic purposes, or both, but they are in any case expressive of the religious elements in a very popular form of modern cinema.

Paul Thomas writes about the depiction of New Religious Movements in film, and as is the case with Islam, the depiction tends to be almost totally negative. This is clearly due to the marginalized character of New Religions in most societies and the perceived need to de-legitimize them. Utilizing a Gramscian analysis of culture, Thomas shows how the dominant group assures its hegemony through its depiction of these minority religions as aberrant and dangerous in their alleged opposition to shared cultural values. Although most NRMs are not violent and do not engage in coercive "brainwashing" techniques, films depict them this way, and viewers assume that all NRMs conform to the filmic description. This is perhaps one of the clearest examples of film's power to reinforce ideology, especially when it comes to the suppression of nonconformist religious views.

Academic approaches to the study of Religion and Film

The next section deals with the various methods that have been used in the study of Religion and Film, assessing both their history and their prospects for their future. As has been noted, this is a very young and very diverse field, so there is a plurality of methods all of which are in a process of development.

Gaye Williams Ortiz summarizes the history and current status of feminist approaches to Religion and Film. As an interdisciplinary field, feminism has influenced the study of Film as well as the study of Religion and Theology, as both have utilized ideological analysis of the construction of gender and gender relations throughout the history of culture and religion. The history of how women have been represented in film, as well as the history of female spectatorship, provide rich resources from which to discuss how film has been used to reinforce hegemonic gender relations as well as how women may attempt resistance. Newer frontiers include an appreciation of nonwhite and non-Western women's perspectives, the use of queer and lesbian theory, and the analysis of interactive video technologies and their significance for women. Religion and Film as a field will continue to be informed by feminist ways of understanding ideology, popular culture, gender, representation, and spectatorship (to name only a few relevant categories).

Clive Marsh considers the value of audience reception theory for the study of Religion and Film. These approaches examine the role of the viewer in the conscious appropriation of meaning in a film through the (not always articulated) choices that they make as they consume popular media. The consumption may involve ritual activities that parallel religious activities, as communities of fans develop a range of meanings present in their filmgoing experience. Films may affect individual beliefs, values, and action, and so alongside traditional religions they contribute to the ways individuals make meaning and choose what they value. Marsh argues that cinema is never only ideology, as viewers are actively involved in how they receive and make use of film – just as they are with their religious commitments.

Gordon Lynch's chapter focuses on the value of the methods of cultural studies and cultural theory for the study of Religion and Film. Cultural theory pays attention to the ways in which power structures are transmitted and reinforced through cultural products, including films. Cultural studies as an empirical discipline has made use of cultural theory and developed its insights to include more attention to the ways in which the reception of culture may involve competing systems of values, as the dominant ideology collides with attempts to resist it through alternative interpretations. As such, these methods recognize the ways in which consumers influence media producers (through their perceived market demand) but also how media shapes consumer choices through marketing. Processes of production, consumption, and regulation all contribute to the ways in which films are received and interpreted, and the religious import and reception of films cannot be understood without attention to these.

Kent Brintnall's chapter discusses the continued relevance of psychoanalytic approaches to Religion and Film. Although such approaches have often been criticized as speculative and nonempirical in their assumptions about the "meaning" of films, Brintnall argues for the heuristic usefulness of such approaches in the interpretation of films, and seeks to develop psychoanalytic approaches beyond their heterosexist roots. Beginning with a summary of Freud's and Lacan's concepts of desire, subjectivity, and sexual difference, Brintnall summarizes and critiques the history of psychoanalytic approaches to film. In particular, he points out how spectatorship theory has ignored gay and lesbian viewers, focusing instead on how it is believed heterosexual men and women see movies. Brintnall concludes that psychoanalytic approaches remain essential to the study of Religion and Film (e.g., *The Passion of the Christ*) as they can uncover ideological dimensions of filmic reception that would otherwise remain hidden.

Robert Johnston's chapter discusses theological approaches to Religion and Film. He notes the range of approaches that have existed – from total rejection of film to an acknowledgment of divine encounter in it – and the fact that these parallel the approaches to culture that have always existed for theology. He also notes that theology has meant many things, from contemplation to reflection to faithful practice, and films have been understood to be useful material for all three tasks. He concludes by noting that theological approaches have entered into dialogue with the other approaches discussed in this section, and that they now more consciously seek to overcome the narrowness present in earlier theological approaches, viz.: the restricted focus on Western culture and film; treating film mainly as "text"; and a tendency to ignore noncognitive dimensions of cinematic appropriation.

Categories applicable to religion and film studies

This final section of the book includes a series of essays on various topics that have been important to the field of Religion and Film. As such, it does not claim to be exhaustive or authoritative; other topics could be chosen, but these are representative of a range of issues that are often discussed and which remain relevant. These topics, drawn from religious studies, can be applied to the study of film and so show the applicability of concepts from one discipline to another. Each illuminates important ideas in the field that will continue to have relevance. In particular, they suggest a dialogue between religious and filmic understandings of these concepts, which provides opportunities for uncovering similarities and differences between them.

Roy M. Anker's chapter on narrative deals with the question of how to understand the way in which films tell stories, and how this relates to the way in which religions tell stories. Even given the difficulties in representing the objects of religious faith, filmmakers have often succeeded in expressing religious content precisely because they have resisted straightforward "literal" depictions of these ideas. Different varieties of realism, parabolic narratives, mythological fables, and visually arresting meditative styles of filmmaking have all been used to engage the transcendent. Anker suggests that films are at their most profound and religiously significant when they act to redeem ordinary reality, reinvesting it with meaning and purpose.

Christopher Deacy's chapter on redemption analyzes the extent to which films may be said to provide "redemption" in ways that are analogous to how religions (especially Christianity) claim to do so. Although filmic redemptions usually transpose religious notions to a secular context, this does not erase the similarities between them, and it may also point to the religious necessity of secularizing redemption – placing it in the world we know and live in. Even escapist films may provide images of transforming hope that are akin to those offered by religions, and for this reason it is essential that the dialogue between religious and filmic representations of ideas continues.

Conrad Ostwalt considers the applicability of the concept of apocalyptic to film, and suggests that the term is often used in ways that diverge from the traditional religious understanding of the concept. Secular versions of "apocalyptic" may include plots dealing with the destruction of the world, but this does not mean that they have translated the essential elements of religious apocalyptic, including a struggle with evil in which divine sovereignty is established. Ostwalt suggests a distinction between films that seek to depict traditional religious apocalyptic and those that suggest a secular apocalypse which is often both caused and prevented by humans. A comparison of these reveals how our fears about and faith in technology parallel and yet differ from traditional religious faith.

Robert Jewett and John Lawrence's chapter on heroes and superheroes discusses how the religious concept of the hero has been developed in film, especially in American cinema. Filmic versions of biblical heroes like Moses alter the scriptural depiction to highlight them as virile and masculine although at the same time ascetic. The American version of the hero sacrifices family and sexuality to save others, defending their freedom, often through the use of violence. Although not all films follow this pattern, the vast majority of Hollywood films have reinforced this American myth of a hero who safeguards freedom by violent action, showing how powerfully film can transform traditional religious ideas into political ideology.

Douglas E. Cowan's chapter on horror and the demonic points out that, far from being empty of religious content or reference, the filmic genre of horror frequently draws on religious concepts of evil supernatural or demonic forces. Such films suggest the reality of this "unseen order" and may represent (however inaccurately) religions that worship spirits and gods other than the God of Western monotheism. In Cowan's view, this shows the persistence in the modern (allegedly secularized) world of a range of fears: of change in the sacred order, death, evil, sexuality, sacred places, and religious fanaticism. This demonstrates how films relate to beliefs about the supernatural that are often viewed as superstitions, but which for many people comprise a central part of their religious experience.

Adele Reinhartz examines the use of Jesus and Christ-figures in films, which include efforts both to depict the Jesus of the Bible and to create "Christ-figures" who are in some way analogous to Jesus. Jesus films, like all retellings of scripture, reflect the values of the times in which they are made through, for example, the introduction of political context that makes his times seem similar to our own. Christ-figures are also used to convey a variety of messages, as characters are imbued with traits that viewers will link to Jesus; for example, a mysterious charismatic figure challenges the authorities and suffers for it, providing some sort of redemption that endures beyond his or her death. These stories also seek to imbue solutions to contemporary concerns with biblical authority, reflecting again the tendency of popular culture to draw on traditional religion and remake it in the image of modern values and ideologies.

Diane Apostolos-Cappadona analyzes the use of religious iconography in film and so brings the history of religious art into dialogue with cinema. Filmmakers have very intentionally recreated religious scenes from famous paintings, and viewers resonate with these familiar images even when they cannot consciously identify their source. Cinematography, for example, is based in part on classic paintings (such as those of Caravaggio) that pioneered the use of light and shadow. More than this, however, film as an art form evolved out of previous art forms such as painting, and so is in a real sense dependent on it. Our "seeing" of religious films is based on a history of seeing religious images in art and how we respond to them. Apostolos-Cappadona makes a clear argument that, to understand the depiction of religion in film, we need to understand film's prehistory in religious art.

Jon Pahl's chapter discusses the concept of sacrifice and how it has developed in cinema. Films have both critiqued and justified sacrifice, but the latter are more common, especially among US films that have defended the necessity of sacrifice to safeguard American purity. Pahl analyzes a number of films to show how sacrificial imagery has been used ideologically by filmmakers in ways that seldom acknowledge the religious heritage of these ideas. These films legitimize torture and violence not only as politically expedient but as essential to the preservation of the social order. Religious analysis of these films can highlight this ideology and point to the ways in which religious concepts have been put in the service of racism, misogyny, and nationalistic violence.

Jolyon Mitchell's chapter discusses ethics in film. Although the early history of film (as we have seen) was marked by criticisms of film for its alleged immorality, more recently films have become viewed as a site for ethical consideration of moral issues. Mitchell considers both how films have represented ethics and how they have contested ethics. It proves difficult to represent the gradual development of virtue or the complexity of ethical reasoning in film. Films can, however, become "catalysts for ethical reflection" when they suggest questions about the contested ethics of violence, competing virtues, justice, or duty. In this way films share the interest that religions have in ethical questions and the attempt to answer them.

Conclusion

This volume can only begin to represent the diversity of issues and methods that exist in the study of Religion and Film. As this field develops, these directions will be deepened even as newer ones emerge. This book can provide the reader some structure with which to approach the field. It is also worth noting that each essay includes a bibliography and filmography, and often suggestions for further reading; readers will find more than enough resources to go deeper into any particular area of interest. It is hoped that the next generation of Religion and Film scholars will take this as a starting point to develop their own approaches, and that these essays will provide a necessary orientation to that task.

I cannot conclude without thanking those who helped make this book possible. Lesley Riddle and Amy Grant at Routledge Publishers gave invaluable assistance in the development of the project from its inception to its completion. A number of scholars – too many to mention by name – helped me to find the right authors for each chapter by making suggestions of persons to contact, which often led to another contact. Without their assistance, I do not believe this volume would be as strong as it is, as the authors are truly experts on their topics due to their previous related research. I must also thank the authors themselves, who worked hard to please me, even when I demanded a great deal in terms of detail, clarity, and analysis. They have created essays of outstanding quality that I believe will make this book well worth reading for a long time. Lastly, I must thank my family for putting up with my endless hours at the computer, editing text and sending emails around the globe. My love and gratitude go particularly to my wife Liz, who has been so supportive of all my scholarship and has understood the value it holds for me.

Part I

HISTORY OF THE INTERACTION BETWEEN RELIGION AND FILM: FOCUS ON WESTERN CHRISTIANITY

1
SILENT CINEMA AND RELIGION: AN OVERVIEW (1895–1930)

Terry Lindvall

The monk quietly and patiently fiddled with his toy. In 1646, Father Athanasius Kircher had experimented with mirrors and light and discovered a process whereby he could project images on the monastery wall or even on billows of smoke. He called his invention a magic lantern, a novelty that entertained his fellow monks, that is until he playfully contrived to show phantasmagoric images of devils and demons to his zealously pious audience. In danger of being exorcised or tortured, he did what any good schoolman would do: publish rather than perish. Thus he wrote his *Magnus Ars Umbra et Lucis*, the *Great Art of Shadow and Light*, that explained how he had taken principles of God's natural world and concocted the whole experiment (Godwin 1979). He continued to dabble in his suspect art, but with considerably less publicity.

The connection between a religious cleric and projected images would culminate over 200 years later, when an Episcopal priest and amateur chemist, rector Hannibal Goodwin, was tinkering with chemicals and gave birth to celluloid strips. Early churchmen would point to this cleric and urge religious artists to emulate his use of a new medium for the Kingdom of God. For example, in 1916, the Reverend Chester S. Bucher would ask:

> Jesus used a lost coin, a dead sparrow and a little child as object lessons. Beecher auctioned off a slave girl in a Plymouth pulpit. Wilberforce made them shudder when he held up the chains of Africans and dropped them with a clanking thud on the floor. Why should the churches disregard this great potential asset, especially since it was a clergyman, the Rev. Hannibal Goodwin, who was the inventor of the flexible film that made motion pictures possible? (Bucher 1916: 1825)

The relations between silent American film and religion in general and Christianity in particular began tentatively, but with a remarkable openness to a visionary rapprochement. The relationship was not, as some historians have painted it, extensively negative or hostile. It was in the early years, at worst, ambivalent, and at best, downright optimistic.

By the end of the silent era, Hollywood producer Paul Bern still acknowledged the Church as a determining foundation of the film industry, much like it had been during the creative structuring of cathedrals. In a lecture at the University of Southern California on 6 March 1929, Bern pointed out that early films followed the pattern set down by historical church drama, such as in the Miracle and Morality plays, in which, he observed, "various characters, so that they might be easily understood by the simple audiences which saw them were named Envy, Sin, Lust, Weakness, Love (something like the pictures of today)" (Tibbetts 1977a: 67).

In the intervening years between 1896 and 1927 the interface between religion and silent moving pictures would prove a fertile, rocky, and important ground for the sowing and reaping of religion in cinema. In his anecdotal and revisionist history of early film history, A Million and One Nights, Terry Ramsaye opined that early film presented a dangerous rival to moral leaders as worldly amusements that might tempt parishioners astray (Ramsaye 1926). During the time of his writing in the mid-twenties, filled with the controversies of Hollywood scandals and theological rifts between modernists and fundamentalists, moving pictures would indeed become an arena of debate. However, other documents present a much more complex and nuanced set of relationships between religious groups and the silent American cinema during the first two decades. American movies would in fact propagate various themes and icons of religion, especially Protestant Christianity.

Key early narratives centered upon the familiar stories of the Bible. The importation of the Oberammergau Passion Play found ready and receptive audiences, particularly in churches (Gunning 1992). The French Roman Catholic publishing house La Bonne Presse saw fit in 1897 to reproduce the famously pious Horitz narrative on the back lots of Paris rather than in Bohemia. In 1898, the same year that Pope Leo XIII granted permission for W. K. L. Dickson to film His Holiness at the Vatican so that his pontifical blessing could be conveyed to congregants in America, a series of religious subjects debuted in the United States. Churches frequently served as sites of sanctuary cinemas, so much so that in 1910 Pope Pius X stopped the desecrating practice of charging money for showing biblical spectaculars in Roman Catholic churches. Tableaux versions of the filmed passion play would premiere in January 1898 on Broadway with full orchestra to rave reviews, drawing together elite cultural groups and various religious leaders.

Where films had gone like John Wesley's itinerant preaching out into the countrysides and fairgrounds, various evangelists exploited the new medium for revival services. The consensus was that the Kingdom of God had nothing to fear from this instructional and inspirational tool. In fact, a former corporation lawyer and New York journalist (two occupations of which he repented), Colonel Henry H. Hadley, was converted and found that he could combine dramatic showmanship with evangelism, particularly in his obsession to illustrate the iniquities of hard liquor. When he viewed a photoplay version of the passion play, he obtained a print as an illustrative accessory for his camp meetings in merry-go-round gospel tents in Atlantic City and Ocean Grove, New Jersey.

Hadley prophesied that these "pictures are going to be a great force. It is the age of pictures; these moving pictures are going to be the best teachers and the best preachers in the history of the world. Mark my words: there are two things coming, prohibition and motion pictures. We must make people think above the belt" (Ramsaye 1926: 375). Thousands attended his spectacular revivals that combined movies with music (*Ave Maria, O Holy Night*, etc.) to draw in crowds to hear and see the Gospel message. It was the beginning of a movement that was to embrace the possibilities of enabling the eyes to see the wonders of God.

Passion plays baptized the medium with their holy sights and biblical scenes. Pathé director Ferdinand Zecca coordinated a colored tinted feature in the early twentieth century while, in 1912, Kalem director Sidney Olcott's *From the Manger to the Cross* (1912) generated an even greater sense of credibility with its authentic locations in Palestine and Egypt functioning as key sites of piety for both Protestant and Roman Catholic audiences. Even when trickster producer Sigmund Lubin shot his own version of the Oberammergau drama on a Philadelphia rooftop, with the actor for Peter often on a binge and other disciples playing dice, crowds would flock to storeroom chapels to see the film. (And when the pianos were added, so were the hymns.) In these films one not only heard of God but also could now see Him starring and making cameos in films. Illiterate audiences around the world could be simultaneously instructed and entertained through these technological signs and wonders.

A moral Methodist filmmaker

The emergence of a director like Biograph's D. W. Griffith ushered in an era of Victorian religion, one emphasizing respectability, tradition, Southern chivalry, and deep sentiment, especially toward the home and mothers. While developing a grammar for the cinema (of close-ups, parallel editing, lighting, and many other devices he claimed to have invented), he also shaped the moral imagination of early film audiences. Griffith, the archetypal director of the early silent films, defined his purpose as to make his audience see.

In many ways, Griffith centered on the sanctity of the religious home. Rooted in the narrative action and social morality of Charles Dickens, Griffith sought to reinvigorate middle-class mores with high culture, demonstrating that beauty is the handmaiden of truth. With Protestant reformers Washington Gladden and Walter Rauschenbusch emphasizing the plight of the poor, Griffith would echo their diatribes, castigating the greed of financial speculators in such films as *A Corner in Wheat* (1909). The photoplay paralleled the Progressive movement with many of the same concerns. For Griffith, the camera was a "God given means for communicating." Historian Lary May pointed out that "such a power allowed the director to work like those revivalist preachers he must have heard as a child. Using images of sin and salvation, he might provide an experience that could convert the soul from evil to good. In fact, Griffith saw himself as a secular preacher, spreading the Word far beyond that Methodist

Church in La Grange" (May 1980: 72–3). In *A Drunkard's Reformation* (1909), an abusive father and husband is shown the evil of his way not through preaching but when he accompanies his daughter to a stage production where his vices are dramatically re-presented in a moral melodrama, suggesting that the theatre and movies could reform erring sinners more effectively than sermons (Gunning 1988).

Two important stylistic marks shaped Griffith's visual sermons films. The first was what May defined as his Southern Methodist upbringing that would emphasize both a traditional moral order and an abiding sentimental concern for the poor and downtrodden. Second, Griffith was haunted by a sort of Christ consciousness, where Jesus would make cameos in films ranging from *The Avenging Conscience* (1914) to *The Birth of a Nation* (1915), culminating in the fourth narrative episode of *Intolerance* (1916). Yet Griffith also had an ingrained reaction to humbuggery in religion. Religious women in *The New York Hat* (1912) gossip so much that they almost ruin the reputations of a young woman (Mary Pickford) and the local minister (Lionel Barrymore). In *Intolerance*, Griffith attacks self-righteous reformers and smug, hypocritical "uplifters" when he adds an inter-title that reads: "When women cease to attract men they often turn to Reform as a second choice." Under the guise of reform, Pharisee Uplifters practiced intolerance toward others. In his *The Reformers* (1913) the prissy and prune-faced League of Civic Purity assert their political power in stopping drinking, smoking, blackfaced vaudeville skits, terpsicord dancing, and Shakespeare's *Othello* and *Macbeth* in Pictures in the name of Progressive reform. In *Way Down East* (1920), priggish church people send Lillian Gish out into the freezing ice floes to an almost certain death. In *The Reformers*, a character whose own children have strayed even makes a vaudeville audience sing "Lead Kindly Light for I am Far from Home." Griffith demonstrates his ill-advised efforts as instead of beer and fellowship in the taverns, there is now bootleg whiskey in the streets.

Not only was Griffith's style marked by Victorian dualism and respectability, but Griffith's eschatology leaks through his films (Holloway 1977). Millennialism infused some of his films, particularly his *Birth of a Nation*, in which all Aryans gathered together in an antebellum South. When he was directing Lillian Gish and she insouciantly called them flickers, Griffith reproved her: "never call them flickers, as they will usher in the Millennium" (May 1980: 72). For Griffith, everyone could understand the silent image, direct, and concrete; it was a "universal language" (Gish and Pinchot 1969). For such visionaries, film communicated directly through the eyes, the windows of the soul, and could thus transport viewers to a more spiritual realm of existence. In 1919, Griffith addressed thousands of Methodists at their Columbus Ohio Centenary and motivated them to adopt moving picture projectors and use them for teaching, preaching, and worldwide mission work (Lindvall 2007).

Religious prophets and the movies

During the period Griffith was working out his moral religion, church leaders debated the dangers of "worldly amusements." While some found the theaters as the devil's workshop and a menace (even more so in the 1920s after the Hollywood scandals), many more religious leaders commended films for beneficial church use. As early as 1910, the *Congregationalist and Christian World* periodical devoted two issues to argue for a case for motion pictures as "a modern force for brotherhood" (Anderson 1910: 46). Editor George J. Anderson summoned the reputable genius of Thomas Edison to speak to his readers on the educational and religious opportunities provided by this novel medium.

One Congregational minister and apologist who saw the potential of the film both to battle Satan ("seize his guns and turn them upon him" as K. S. Hover wrote in 1911) and to articulate a vision for the Church was the Reverend Herbert A. Jump. Jump penned a classic essay in 1911 entitled "The Religious Possibilities of the Motion Picture" (Jump 1911). It would be the first significant document reflecting on the religious and cultural potential of film. For example, whereas numerous civic leaders were concerned with the boxing-film genre as detrimental to social order, Jump found a biblical model for such films, in that the Apostle Paul had used boxing images drawn from the brutal Roman arena games to express theological ideas.

Jump recommended Jesus' parable of the Good Samaritan as the ideal model for Christianity to speak to all people. He saw it as a dramatic sermon-story that shared certain characteristics with the motion picture. It was taken from contemporary sources, not from the Bible of Jesus' day. Like the western, it contained violence and provided an exciting robber adventure. And like the later films of the "good/bad man" William S. Hart, Jesus' parable introduced morally dubious examples – such as hypocritical religious leaders – and left them intact even at the end of the narrative. In fact, regarding the robbers themselves, Jump observed that "not only did the story give a most realistic description of precisely how they perpetrated the cowardly crime of violence, but it leaves them victorious in their wickedness, scurrying off with their booty, unrepentant of their sins, probably chuckling at the folly of the traveler." It only needed a zesty new title such as "The Adventures of the Highwaymen" to sell and draw in the boys who would not visit Sunday school classes (Lindvall 2001: 55).

During this decade, another religious voice opined a religious vision for the movies, this time a poet. Vachel Lindsay had initially wanted to become a Christian cartoonist, but emerged as a progressive poet out of a fundamentalist Disciples of Christ background; however, he broadened into a more syncretistic advocate for Buddha as much as Jesus. Crunden described him as "almost too Christian to be a good progressive, since he displayed an uncharacteristic pessimism about progress and human nature" (Crunden 1982: 100). His "Abraham Lincoln Walks at Midnight" shaped the president as a Christ-figure, a precursor to Griffith's work. Two contrasting works by Lindsay on film mark the waxing and waning of religious influence in the silent film era. His optimistic work, *The Art of the Moving Picture* (published in 1915), saw Edison as the new Gutenberg, ushering in a flowering period of creative energy and moral evangelism. Wandering from the sectarian world of a mother who served in religious missionary work, he found in art a "better vocation to express Christ" (Lindsay 1970: xi). Yet even Lindsay, with early religious fervor and sanguinity, brightened by his Swedenborgian denial of the negative forces of human nature and institutions, could not cope with the decline of his own poetic and ethical influence in the wilder days of the 1920s. A second book of film criticism, *The Progress and Poetry of the Movies*, written for publication around 1925, looks more gloomily and desperately at the emerging mass-produced, consumerist entertainment culture (Lindsay 1995). The truly Progressive and democratic evangelist Lindsay saw the industry being overrun by the malicious "Soul of the Spider" rather than enlightened by the spiritual grace of the "soul of the Butterfly." The photoplay in this decade between 1915 and 1925 lost its religious soul and discovered Mammon.

To Lindsay, the visual signs of film had both literal (naturalistic) and symbolic (spiritual) sides. These angles parallel his parents' professions: his father in medicine and his mother in religious missionary work. Just before the turn of the century, he left a sectarian college to follow a fresh and promising vocation in which he could "express Christ." He wrote to his parents: "Now that I have found it must be Art, I must learn to preach my purpose into other artists" (Lindsay 1970: xi). Like the Harvard psychologist Hugo Munsterberg, Lindsay went forth to proclaim and spread the gospel of Beauty. As an avid Anti-Saloon League member, Lindsay praised film for having edged out the saloon in popularity and for bringing the family back together. He saw himself as the apologist, poet, and evangelist of a cultural art that could change society for the good, particularly as a means to abolish the saloon (Lindvall 2008).

This evangelist with charisma, a propagandist with vision, lavished reflections and praise on the pictures of the screen. One entire chapter was devoted to "The Picture of Religious Splendor" with two memorable examples updated in his 1922 version: William Vaughn Moody's play *The Faith Healer* and the commercial film *The Miracle Man* (1919). "Not until the religious film is taken out of the commercial field, and allowed to develop unhampered under the Church and the Art Museum, will the splendid religious and ritualistic opportunity be realized" (Lindsay 1970: 6).

Western films as sacred texts

The genre that lent itself most expediently to unequivocal religious sensibilities was the western. The inclusion of religious themes and symbols in western films drew in Protestant audiences, with their emphases upon a Calvinist doctrine of sin in the heroes and the necessary repentance of the individual, with significant personal and social change. While other genres, particularly the passion play attractions and the melodrama, mapped out middle-class religious concerns through various iconographic signposts (e.g., Bible stories, inclusion of clergy, concern for the poor, cameo appearances by Jesus Christ Himself, etc.), key western films functioned in unabashedly explicit ways to proclaim Protestant perspectives, such as in the individual conversions of sinners convicted by reading of the Bible (often in the films of G. M. "Broncho Billy" Anderson or William S. Hart, frequently with a bottle of whiskey right next to the convicted sinner wrestling with his faith).

The heroes of these silent westerns became, in Henry Wadsworth Longfellow's words, commensurate with America's "mountains and our rivers ... altogether shaggy and unshorn, that shall shake the earth, like a herd of buffaloes thundering over the prairies." They were good/bad guys whose hearts knew what was irresistibly right and were turned from their wicked ways to become sacrificial saints. These frontiersmen inhabited the spectacular landscape of the plains and mountains, and conflated human figures with majestic landscapes and religious visions of the American myth.

The first cowboy movie hero was G. M. "Broncho Billy" Anderson, a somewhat bumbling and unlikely star. Yet this Robin Hood character produced and starred in over 300 one- and two-reel films between 1908 and 1915 that according to one critic held up the moral values of our "Christian society. In the conflict of Good and Evil, the Good is invariable held up as right. On the side of Good are honesty, loyalty, sympathy for the oppressed, respect for just law, and, if it is occasioned in the story, love of children and respect for religion" (Elkin 1950: 77). The narrative structure often involved self-sacrifice, redemption, and even martyrdom for the sake of others.

In the middle of the decade, Broncho Billy was replaced by a new popular cinematic hero, William S. Hart. His religious films require an essay of their own. Yet both cowboys were men of the saddle, and men transformed by faith. Conservative Calvinism, in its waning days of influence in the teens, found itself translated into the visual sermons of western cinema. Like John Bunyan's solitary pilgrim, the lonely cowboy found his natural state to be solitude. He would ride through a rough world of evil and injustice, and survive because he rightly assessed this fallen nature of existence. Hart was the grim, rugged Puritan, who wrestled not only against the winds and rains of nature but also against the darker nature of himself and his fellow human beings, even the religious ones.

In 1915 and 1916, the top two box office stars in America as voted by the annual Quigley Publications Poll were Mary Pickford and William S. Hart. While Pickford was America's Sweetheart with flowing golden curls, Hart was the classic good/bad man of silent American cinema, a stoic stone-faced cowboy as taciturn as the desert, and a spiritual descendent of Broncho Billy. In his autobiography, Hart acknowledged his personal education as grounded in the sermons of nonconformist preachers and the family readings of Charles Dickens' moral melodramas. His theatrical career culminated in portrayals of a muscular Messala in a 1899 production of *Ben Hur*, the titular role in *The Christian*, and the wild, devilish "mean skunk" of a cowboy in *The Squaw Man*. As such, his own fundamentalist melodramas were worked out under the "eye of a judging but merciful Deity" (Koszarski 1980: ix).

Hart often portrayed a sinful maverick hounded by the grace of God. Crosses, prayers, Bibles, and religious visions dotted the black and white landscapes of his films. The actor's austere physical presence and personal charisma in the role of the good/bad man cemented an enduring icon of Puritan virtues and Calvinist stoicism in an untamed wilderness.

Other directors were inspired to speak their religious convictions onto the screen. Where Griffith saw "man made in the image of God," but ruined by Satan as the source of all evil and misery (or as Richard Meyer points out, owing to his almost dualistic Southern Fundamentalism, in which "Christ in Heaven is pitted against the Devil in Hell" [Meyer 1967: n.p.]), another, young, and even naïve director, King Vidor, opted for the optimistic view of human nature as fundamentally good, honest, and strong. His early exposure to the cultic teachings of Mary Baker Eddy left him a lifelong adherent to Christian Science. The murky alloy of mysticism and self-help, of the superiority of mind over matter, appeared in his 1918 feature scenario, "The Turn in the Road," which the *New York Times* described as "frankly a preachment."

In the January 1920 issue of *Variety*, director King Vidor, still quite fresh in his visionary sense of a sacred vocation, published his "Creed and Pledge" as a filmmaker. He affirmed that he wished his films to carry a message to humanity that would help free it from the "shackles of fear and suffering." He also promised not to produce anything untrue to human nature, anything that would injure anyone, nor anything "unclean in thought or action." As a preview of the later Hays code, he insisted that he would not "deliberately portray anything to cause fright, suggest fear, glorify mischief, condone cruelty or extenuate malice" (Vidor 1920: n.p.). Drawing up "the inexhaustible source of Good," he asserted that such principles would guide his filmmaking. Yet even Vidor saw the hypocrisy of what he wrote. More than fifty years later in an interview with the Directors Guild, he commented:

> I might have been stupid enough in my first few pictures to put out a creed that I wouldn't make pictures with violence or sex ... It was an advertisement, you know ... Right after it came out in the paper, I got arrested for playing poker in a sixty-cent game. The headlines were pretty awful. It didn't go with ˙ this idealistic statement. (Durgnat and Simmon 1988: 31)

The act of publicizing a moral creed may have stirred nary a ripple in a religious periodical, but for a virile film director to shout from the headlines of a trade magazine that he would forego sex and violence in his films was a burst of inspired idealism. The passion for virtue may have been quenched and subverted in the shooting of his western religious adventure, *Sky Pilot* (1921), not so much regarding the moral content of the film, but in Vidor's extramarital affair with his star, Colleen Moore. As one wag put it, "sinning has a way of changing one's view of sin." Vidor's own moral impropriety signaled the decline and denial of his creed. One could not preach what one did not practice. Vidor's life thus prefigured his art over a decade later, when he directed a story of temptation, sin, and salvation with an all-black cast in *Hallelujah* (1929).

By the end of the 1910s and the early 1920s the relationship between the Church and Hollywood began to change. Film audiences had changed as well, with a contrast of tastes. One group wanted more "sophisticated" films while the other wanted a return to more traditional values. Tom Forman's *Shadows* (1922) starring Lon Chaney (the man of a thousand faces) as a Chinese laundryman, Yen Sin, struck a chord among religious audiences. The story follows a young minister who arrives at a fishing village the same time immigrant Yen Sin is washed ashore from an apparent shipwreck. The minister proceeds to marry a local widow and tries to convert Yen Sin to Christianity. While respecting the minister, Yen Sin is not impressed with the hypocritical Christianity he sees in the town's church people and continually refuses the minister's appeals. A rival suitor attempts to dishonor the minister in the sight of his bride by blackmailing him into thinking that her first husband is still alive. Yen Sin is able to expose the culprit and informs the minister of the deception. Yen Sin fully expects the minister to take revenge on the blackmailer, but instead the minister forgives him in an act of Christian charity. Witnessing such a sincere act of forgiveness convinces Yen Sin of the truth of Christianity. In response, he accepts the minister's God as his own. Robert Sherwood included this film in his book *The Best Moving Pictures of 1922–1923* and declared it a picture filled with "finer and better" things (Sherwood 1923: 27).

The apotheosis of this trend was undeniably George Loane Tucker's *The Miracle Man*, lauded as great entertainment and the apex of uplifting thought. For contemporary critic Benjamin Prager, it revealed "the power of faith, the basis of all religion, and in its revelation enthralled a nation and gave it a deeper understanding of the spiritual forces that govern life." It proved not only an artistic triumph but a financial success as well.

One director epitomized the schizophrenic duality of a post-Victorian society, where on the one hand spectators furtively wished to see what they considered sinful and taboo, and on the other, wanted to preserve their own sense of righteous respectability in the process. The director who most challenged traditional middle-class mores and then pandered to them with debauchery was the great showman, Cecil B. DeMille. He was faithfully aided by his paramour, screenwriter Jeanie MacPherson, who scripted his comedies like *Don't Change Your Husband* (1919), and was credited with his religious epics, *The Ten Commandments* (1923) and *The King of Kings* (1927). An Episcopal lay minister, DeMille's curious relationship with religious topics explored reincarnation (*The Road to Yesterday*) as much as a generic liberal Protestantism. DeMille would be identified as the sensational director who splashed equal amounts of sex, sadism, and spurious piety into his films (Maltby 1990).

This audience duality seemed to be satisfied by his productions that flaunted sinfulness for six reels and then set all things righteous in the seventh. A prime example of this duality is Cecil B. DeMille's *Manslaughter* (1922), offering everything from a Roaring 20s party which transposes into a Roman-era orgy, to the very sincere and believable religious conversion of its two main characters. One conversion is initiated by remorse and the desire to help humanity, and the other by the love of a good woman. This story, taken from a novel by Alice Duer Miller, follows DeMille's model of depicting riotous life for six reels and then, in the final reel, repentance and redemption (or judgment). He received especially strong criticism for the excesses of the Roman debauchery which he compared with the lifestyle of the frivolous and well-to-do youth of the 1920s. Despite its criticism, the film managed to make $1,200,000.

DeMille, however, managed to produce the two most enduring religious spectacles of the silent era, *The Ten Commandments* (1923) and *The King of Kings* (1927), easily overshadowing films like Michael Curtiz's *Noah's Ark* (1928). DeMille remade the biblical narratives in the images of a Jazz Age director, full of sex and spectacle and plastic piety. He would also chastise the Church for its lack of global vision in failing to use film as a universal language – in particular, he stressed its capacity to create an international image of the US as the world's savior:

Pictures are the greatest factor in the world for uniting the races and the nations. Pictures speak an international language that everybody can understand. Say a Japanese jingo goes in to see an American picture. He sees a mother with a poor sick baby. An American doctor is trying to help her. His heart warms to that picture, and he says, "After all these Americans are not half bad!" You church people are always talking about the international mind. The pictures are the strongest medium to produce that international mind. (Stidger 1932: 14–15)

Comedies of grace

Actors as well as directors shaped religious sensibilities. Two of the most well-known and well-loved stars were haunted by religion in their personal lives and films. Historian Constance Kuriyama identifies the roots of Charlie Chaplin's fusion of pathos and comedy in two items: severe bouts of depression stemming from an impoverished and transient childhood and a "Christ-fixation" (Kuriyama 1992: 30). In fact, in his first feature film, *The Kid* (1921), Chaplin portrays an unwitting (and unwilling) Christ-like figure who adopts a discarded child and raises him with love. At one point, having lost the Kid (much like Chaplin had recently lost his own first child), he searches Heaven for him, a reflection of his own longing. The Mother of the Child ("whose only sin is motherhood") is framed by a halo-like effect and shown with a non-diegetic insert of Christ carrying His cross up Calvary (Maland 1989: 57).

He does satirize religious hypocrisy in *The Pilgrim* (1923), where convict Charlie disguises himself as a chaplain, stealing a minister's clothing to hide out in a church in Devil's Gulch. Welcoming him as the new minister, the deacons (one with a whiskey bottle in his back pocket) set him up to preach his first sermon. He pantomimes in true vaudeville fashion the underdog sermon of David and Goliath and awakens a bored young boy in the front pew to the adventure of the Bible. As such, he both condemns the hypocrisy of religious people and celebrates appealing Bible stories.

In the era of the Social Gospel, Chaplin's concern for the poverty, crime, and moral decline of the inner city is reflected in his *Easy Street* (1917). The film opens with Charlie asleep on a stoop outside the Hope Mission, similar to a Salvation Army station. He "hears" angelic singing and enters the mission. Through the efforts of the minister and a pretty girl mission worker (Edna Purviance), Charlie is reformed and decides to become a policeman in order to help clean up Easy Street. After a number of humorous battles with the tough guy (Eric Campbell) involving a lamppost and a cast-iron stove, Charlie is eventually able to clean up the street and creates the *New* Hope Mission, where the Gospel message has reformed not only him, but his community. While some critics consider the film an ironic comment on moral uplift, suggesting that hope and reality are irreconcilable, the positive role of the mission worker points otherwise (Mast 1979: 82). The presence of Salvation Army workers would often be responsible for the reformation of disreputable characters, such as in Douglas Fairbanks' *Flirting with Fate*, in which an assassin is converted at such a mission and so is prevented from killing his target (Fairbanks).

While not a believer in religion, Chaplin yet confessed to being fascinated by Christ and the New Testament (although finding the Hebrew Bible full of "horrific cruelty degrading to the human spirit" [Chaplin 1964:134]). His emphasis, however, was rooted in a religion that included love and pity for the poor, the weak and children, forgiveness for an adulterous woman, hatred of hypocrisy, and an affinity to the humanity of Jesus Christ, particularly reflected in Georges Rouault's expressionist harlequin figure of God. At one point, as he was producing *The Circus* (1928), Chaplin acknowledged that he wished to film the life of Christ: "If I could produce a film on the story of Jesus, I would show him welcomed with delirious joy by men, women, and children; they would throng round him in order to feel his magnetism. Not at all as a sad, pious, and stiff person, but a lonely man who has been the most misunderstood of all time" (Chaplin 1964: 134). Chaplin envisioned Jesus as the Tramp, unabashedly remaking God in his own image.

Along with Chaplin, America's Sweetheart, Mary Pickford, dominated the movie industry both as an actress and as a professional member of the original United Artists Studio. Raised by an Irish Catholic mother and a Methodist father, Gladys Smith sculpted a career as a spunky, independent, and pious woman/child, whose films celebrated an undeniably religious atmosphere with a frisky twist. In *Tess of the Storm Country* (1922), Mary selflessly adopts the illegitimate child of a woman whose church family would be scandalized and raises her as her own. When the baby becomes sickly, she marches into the church to demand that the child be baptized before she dies. Standing up against the hypocritical elders, she washes the child's hot brow with holy water in the midst of a church service (Windeler 1974: 83).

In the Dickensian *Sparrows* (1926) or sunshiny *Rebecca of Sunnybrook Farm* (1917), she is the very model of sheer spunk, honest piety, lively mischief, and savvy wit. In Pickford, goodness did not mean saccharine or treacly. As Julia Marlowe wrote, "it takes a greater artist to make a good woman sympathetic and thrilling than to make a base woman sympathetic and thrilling." She made goodness exciting (Marlowe 1955: n.p.).

In an interview with historian Kevin Brownlow, Pickford reflected on her trajectory through the course of cinema: "I always tried to get laughter into my pictures. What do people go to the movies for? An emotional exercise. And no preachment" (Brownlow 1968: 134). Yet her movies celebrating a lost innocence were packed with sermons. Attending a passion play three times, "Veronica's Veil," in St. Joseph's auditorium, West Hoboken, Pickford explained to one of the directors, Father Conrad, that her purpose was to study the atmosphere in which a religious play is produced, as she hoped shortly to film a biblical photo drama (Brownlow 1968: 134).

America's Sweetheart sprinkled her films with devout images of prayer. In *Little Annie Rooney* (1925), she leads her Irish cop father and brother in prayer, putting her father's newspaper aside and slapping her brother when he tries to sneak some turkey during the grace. (Buster Keaton used prayer similarly in *Our Hospitality* [1923], when he has entered the household of the Canfields, the nemeses of his own Tennessee family, and everyone watches and prays with one eye open.) Playing a little Irish Catholic girl in trouble for a bit of mischief, she crosses herself just before meeting her father for a reprimand. Later in the same film, she joins in Jewish prayers, still crossing herself. Her brother shoots a man she has a crush on, and the victim needs an emergency blood transfusion. Mary offers her own blood. The journalist sees "a peach of a story: can you beat that? She thought *she was giving up her life for his.*" The biblical sermon was evident.

The sermon is even more direct in her 1926 Gothic thriller, *Sparrows*, the title taken from the Gospel story of Jesus promising to watch over His little ones more than the birds of the air. As the caretaker of a group of orphans held captive on a Baby Farm in the swamp, tyrannically governed by the devil's own Mr. Grimes, she appeals to God for rescue, sending a kite for help, praying "Lord, it's us again." While the Lord's answers to prayer are often "no," Mary persists in seeking His help, against the quicksand, alligators, and other dangers of the swamps. The film poignantly shows the death of one infant, held gently in Mary's arms throughout the night. As Mary rests and prays, the wall of the barn dissolves and we see Jesus, the Great Shepherd, tending His sheep. He walks over and takes the baby from Mary's arms and returns to His flock. Mary, eyes brimming with tears, looks up and nods, understanding that God has taken the child home.

Within two years, the actress Pickford shined in a brief apotheosis as a luminescent Virgin Mary in her appearance in Douglas Fairbanks' amazingly Roman Catholic film *The Gaucho* (1928). She is no longer the icon but the star object of Fairbanks' narrative; she brings healing and hope to the oppressed common people of an exotic Argentine locale, establishing a City of the Miracles. Thus Mary Pickford is introduced in a chapter aptly entitled "The Gods Arrive" in Lloyd Morris' *Not So Long Ago*, a social history of the automobile, the radio, and the motion picture. Morris sees the movies' democratic fables of rags to riches, their Horatio Alger myth, taking on a frisky feminine mystique under Mary's influence, as in *The Hoodlum* (1919), in which she plays the Little Evangelist. For Morris, Mary's inspirational appeal as one pure of heart ascending into grace could be likened to the buoyant exhortations of religious boosters like Dr. Russell H. Conwell or the emerging Pentecostals. Both Mary and the boosters inspired the emotions with hope and enthusiasm. Essentially, Morris argued, Pickford's films were a "series of parables that expounded Miss Pickford's heartening gospel" (Morris 1949: 85), the new sermons of a distinctly American religion, honoring celebrity, individualism, humanism, and Mammon. Yet Mary also connected with religious leaders in a progressive age with her films' deep concern for the downtrodden and the poor.

Religious leaders and Hollywood stars would join for baseball games to raise charity funds. From such sporting events one sees an amiable relationship between one particular religious leader and the film industry. A reason for this friendly camaraderie could be because Billy Sunday and Douglas Fairbanks had so much in common: they looked surprisingly alike, they acted with the same aggressive enthusiasm, and they both had a message to communicate (Lindvall 2008). For Sunday it was the "good news of Jesus Christ," and for Douglas Fairbanks it was what John Tibbetts called a "practical idealism known as the 'Social Gospel'" (Tibbetts 1977b: 41). Many of Fairbanks' moving pictures were referred to as 'sermon' films and all preached a similar message of optimism and enthusiasm – an early rendition of Norman Vincent Peale's positive thinking – *The Habit of Happiness* (1916), *Mr. Fix-It* (1918), *He Comes Up Smiling* (1918), *When the Clouds Roll By* (1919), *The Nut* (1921), and "the ultimate expression of this philosophy," *Down to Earth* (1917). Sunday and Fairbanks were entertainer/preachers. Their messages might have been different in intensity and focus, but they both used their respective media to communicate "a modified kind of Social Gospel" (Tibbetts 1977b: 40).

Handmaidens of theology

The greatest scenario writers of the era were women, and religious women at that. Both Anita Loos and Frances Marion married seminarians. Jeanie MacPherson, although allegedly Cecil B. DeMille's mistress, scripted both *The Ten Commandments* and *The King of Kings* for the director of religious spectacles, even sharing screen-writing credit with the Gospel writers. June Mathias negotiated the productions of *The Four Horsemen of the Apocalypse* (1921) (furthering the career of screen lover Rudolph Valentino) and *Ben Hur* (1925). The first narrative director has frequently been said to be Roman Catholic director Alice Guy Blache. However, the first American-born female filmmaker, Lois Weber, exhibited a missionary zeal to make films that would reform society and preach good news.

While working in Pittsburgh industrial slums, singing hymns on street corners, Weber realized the need to evangelize and work for social change. In a speech to the Woman's City Club of Los Angeles, she reflected that: "during two years of church army work, I had ample opportunity to regret the limited field any individual worker could embrace even by a life of strenuous endeavor. Meeting with many in that field who spoke strange tongues, I came suddenly to realize the blessing of a voiceless language to them" (Slide 1996: 35). Weber received a call to carry out the idea of missionary pictures, following her uncle's advice: "As I was convinced the theatrical profession needed a missionary, he suggested that the best way to reach them was to become one of them, so I went on the stage filled with a great desire to convert my fellowman" (Kay and Peary 1977: 147). As she envisioned the cinema's potential to dramatize a moral issue, she found the most strategic outlet for her emotions and ideals. "I can preach to my heart's content; and with the opportunity to write the play, act the leading role, and direct the entire production. If my message fails to reach someone I can only blame myself." Her Social Problem films ran the gamut from anti-saloon films (*Hop, the Devil's Brew*, 1916), diatribes against child labor, capital punishment, and the insufficient pay for teachers (*The People vs. John Doe* [1916], *Shoes* [1916], *The Blot* [1921]), and a powerful anti-abortion and pro-birth control film, *Where Are My Children?* (1916), dramatically showing the abhorrent act of destroying unborn babies by selfish parents. Historian Sloan described the fountain of her thought as springing from "a curious combination of the Progressive notion of 'uplift,' optimistic reformism, and a Victorian sense of religious responsibility" (Sloan 1988: 90).

Sanctuary cinema

Historically, the Church has frequently wrestled with the invention and expansion of the arts, alternatively viewing it as an interloper, competitor, or handmaiden (Anon. 1920: 46–7). Informing the early reception of silent movies in America was the cultural hegemony of Protestants and, by the end of the era, the emerging influence of Roman Catholics. Churches and religious groups had made use of magic lanterns and stereopticons during the decades before film; thus, many were primed for the diffusion of new technology, finding it as an effective tool for teaching, preaching, and missionary work. It was also touted as a wholesome alternative to the saloon and the brothel. As early as 1910, it was viewed by the *Congregationalist* magazine as a "modern force for brotherhood" (Anderson 1910: 46).

While many did find the movies suspect, especially in their portrayal of crime and violent sports like boxing, liberals and conservatives alike investigated novel ways to use movies, inaugurating an era of Sanctuary Cinema, where churches not only exhibited films for youth and evangelism, but eventually got into the movie-making business. K. S. Hover reported that films were a vehicle for uplifting humanity and becoming a "new enemy of Satan." The film projector was as necessary a piece of church equipment as a "janitor, an organ or the heavy and depressing looking pews of oak" (Hover 1911: 86). For some, movies were the most effective sermons.

Up until the early 1920s, the primary concern with movies, as with most amusements of the day, was the Sunday issue, the breaking of the Sabbath rest. However, writers for periodicals like the *Moving Picture World*, such as the Reverend E. Boudinot Stockton in his regular column "The Pictures in the Pulpit," recommended specific religious pictures and relevant biblical texts for Sunday showings (Lindvall 2001: 79–92). One liberal churchman, writing for *Photoplay* magazine, averred that Jesus would approve of the movies because the Lord was for anything that made people happy (Grant 1920). Others saw that culture was being sacralized; it was beginning to provide the stories, the rituals, the mores, and the styles for the young. Another problem with the movies was its essential nature as a profit-making business. Even as the Federal Council of Churches sanctioned the potent use of movies for spirituality and reform, others were wondering if it were not just a secular wedge into the lives of young people. Films were seductive, a sort of twilight amusement.

Yet in the summer of 1919, at the Centenary of the Methodist Episcopal Church in Columbus, Ohio, hundreds of films were shown to tens of thousands of pastors and religious leaders, with many returning to their churches to institute movies (Lindvall 2001; 2007). In 1920 Eastman Kodak contributed 2,000 projectors to Presbyterian churches. Various religious organizations, such as the *Christian Herald Magazine*, were primed to produce religious products. The *Literary Digest* suggested that the Church was "wresting another weapon from the devil and converting it to its own purpose" (Anon. 1920: 46). Film was becoming a handmaiden to theology.

Twilight of the religious cinema

However, in 1921, when scandals broke out in Hollywood and more sophisticated postwar films were emerging, cries for censorship mounted. Concerns about Sunday showings were abetted by the increase of mature subjects and titillating images. Religious characters were depicted as hypocrites. A division between modernists and fundamentalists created tension about movies, as conservatives viewed cinema as the devil's tool. To counter such a diabolical tendency, the motion picture producers hired Presbyterian elder Will H. Hays to be their Hollywood czar, to oversee the moral and religious content of the film industry. Church leaders, particularly Roman Catholics and many disgruntled Protestants, questioned and rejected the professional leadership of Hays (Black 1997; Skinner 1993; Walsh 1996). The *Christian Century* concurred with Roman Catholics in their mutual frustrations about getting better pictures. Praising the committed stand of the Roman Catholic boycott proposal ("Catholics are not likely to be fooled again"), the periodical sought to rally general Protestant support by distancing themselves from "the wishy-washy attitude of much Protestant leadership," namely Hays (Anon. 1934a: 652; Anon. 1934b: 822). Hays had boasted in his memoirs that he enabled the film industry to render a unique service to worldwide religion. At the 1926 Chicago Eucharistic Congress, he envisioned the breaking of all national and religious boundaries in bringing about an adoration of God through film:

> Now comes to the service of this magnificent purpose this great new instrument; with the motion picture, the Eucharistic Congress will go to the farthest corners of the earth, carrying the message of faith, the voice of religion. Men of all languages, of all races, may draw from it inspiration and understanding. Where thousands saw, now millions will see – hundreds of millions. (Hays 1929: 376)

Fred Eastman, professor of religious literature and drama at Chicago Theological Seminary, soundly castigated Hays as Hollywood's sop to the churches: "Certainly it was naïve to believe that the industry pays him a salary reputed to be double that of the President of the United States for the purpose of cleaning up the pictures. It is much more likely that that salary is paid for the purpose of protecting and increasing the profits of his employers." For these churchmen, the "old, sure-fire Hays hokum" no longer worked (Eastman 1931: 19; Anon. 1932: 725).

A letter printed in the liberal Episcopal *Churchman* from Maude M. Aldrich, field secretary of the Federal Motion Picture Council in America, indicated that Hays exploited his church connections to protect his cronies "from undesired scrutiny and the threat of remedial action" (Anon. 1930: 325). In February 1924, a National Motion Picture Conference was held in Washington DC in which motion picture interests were not seen as being reformed as promised by the Presbyterian elder; thus a recommendation by churchmen addressed the pending Updyke Bill for federal regulation of films. By 1929, the *Churchman* carried on a crusade against what they saw as the Hays methods of bamboozling the public. "Church people for many years were asinine enough to fall for Mr. Hays' pious remarks in speeches before church groups and women's clubs. At last they have Will's number written inside their hats" (Anon. 1934c: 409). Numerous Protestant denominations, aroused to a high pitch of enthusiasm by what they saw as a battle against filth and depravity, made common cause with the Catholics. Other religious and social organizations, including noted Jewish leaders, endorsed the campaign, providing both vocal and economic support for its international application (Anon. 1934d: 20; 1935: 18).

Hays, the alleged moderator of movie morals, had not been able to clean up the business himself, so Catholics and Protestants in the Federal Council of Churches united to take control. What this meant for the Christian film industry was that the focus of religious concerns was altered from making movies to critiquing and policing them. The seemingly corrupting influence of Hollywood on American morality, as propagated by Henry James Forman's dubious summary of the Payne Studies in the early 1930s on the influence of the movies on the minds and character of children, summoned forth crusaders to ferret out evil and scold those who exploited the medium for their own gain or perversity. The Church sought various means to combat the laxity of Hays' alleged reforms and take authority over the vacuum of moral leadership.

Vanity Fair, with tongue firmly implanted in cheek, touted the Federal Council of Churches as finally attending to motion pictures, primarily through their own missionary, Presbyterian elder Will B. Hays. He was known for making pious speeches, winding up with "God's in His heaven; All's right with the world." Hays' rules forbade ridicule of clergy, which Alva Johnston found "an absurd invasion of the rights of churchmen who are as much entitled as any others to the moral tonic and wholesome discipline of satire." So, too, another prescription by the czar of the movies was suspect, as he required that constituted authorities and the rule of law must always triumph over law-breakers, "a rule which would require the director to throw the sympathy with the lions as against the Christians in *Ben Hur*" (Johnston 1931: 84).

For critic Alva Johnston, the cinema craved the Church's approval, believing that it still enjoyed a dangerous amount of health. But the Church would perform its greatest service, if "it would teach Hollywood by example rather than precept. Let the Federal Council or some other religious group produce a pious epic that grosses a million dollars. Everyone knows what imitators the magnates are: there will be an immediate stampede to dramatize purity and sanctity. It would be better still if the church would produce a series of masterpieces; three or four super pictures could be made from the money now sunk in one cathedral." He concluded, "The enormous mileage of empty pews in the churches of America suggests that it is impossible to run a religion without a villain. Perhaps the church, after all, has more to learn from Hollywood than to teach it" (Johnston 1931: 84).

The final amen to the silents

Warner Brothers' inaugural talking film of 1927, *The Jazz Singer*, traced the religious trajectory of Jakie Rabinowitz, a Jewish cantor's son, from the faith and orthodox tradition of his fathers to a new existential religion, that of theatrical entertainment. Arguing against going back to the synagogue to sing the prayers for his dying father, Jakie shouts, "We in the show business have our religion too – on every day – the show must go on." At the end of the film, the jazz singer has left the synagogue behind and performs on the stage of the new secular temple, "singing to *his* god" (Schuchardt 2006: 49). Such films augured the changing religious values of society, and the Hollywood industry became a repository of alternative religious expressions and visions. It became, in Kenneth Anger's classic description, Hollywood Babylon, a factory of idols. Unfortunately, the Church's films could not compete with either the slick professional entertainment of Hollywood or with the mythic appeals of violence, adventure, success, and romance as a means to salvation. As critic Margaret Miles suggests, the Christian churches had "relinquished the task of providing life-orienting images" and thus the secular film culture filled the void (Miles 1985: 152).

Bibliography

Anderson, G. (1910) "The Case for Motion Pictures, Part I," *Congregationalist and Christian World* 95 (29) (9 July).

Angly, E. (1934) "Boycott Threat is Forcing Movie Clean-Up: Movement Initiated by Roman Catholics, and Approved by Other Churches, Bringing Results," *Literary Digest* (7 July).

Anonymous (1920) "The Motion Picture as a 'Handmaid of Religion,'" *Literary Digest* 64.

—— (1925) "Church Pictures Are Assured," *The Church, the Child and the Motion Picture* 1 (4) (October).

—— (1930) "Will Hays and the Presbyterians," *Christian Century* 47.

—— (1932) "The Presbyterians Seem Fed Up with Elder Hays," *Christian Century* (8 June).

—— (1934a) "The Catholic Crusade for Better Movies," *Christian Century* 51 (16 May).

—— (1934b) "The Movies Last Chance," *Christian Century* 51 (20 June).

—— (1934c) "The Church and the Movies," *The Nation* 139 (3614) (10 October).

—— (1934d) "Legion of Decency Campaign Intensified," *Literary Digest* 118 (20) (22 December).

—— (1935) "New Move for Screen Reform," *Literary Digest* 119 (19 January).

Black, G. (1997) *The Catholic Crusade against the Movies, 1940–1975*, Cambridge: Cambridge University Press.

Brownlow, K. (1968) *The Parade's Gone By . . .*, New York: Knopf.

Bucher, C. S. (1916) "Preaching by Pictures: Screen Sermons," *The Advance*.

Chaplin, C. (1964) *My Autobiography*, New York: Simon and Schuster.

Crunden, R. (1982) *Ministers of Reform: The Progressives' Achievement in American Civilization, 1889–1920*, New York: Basic Books.

Durgnat, R. and Simmon, S. (1988) *King Vidor: American*, Los Angeles: University of California Press.

Eastman, F. (1931) "What Can We Do about the Movies?," *Parents Magazine* 6 (19).

Elkin, F. (1950) "The Psychological Appeal of the Hollywood Western," *Journal of Educational Sociology* 24.

Gish, L. and Pinchot, A. (1969) *The Movies, Mr. Griffith, and Me*, Englewood Cliffs, NJ: Prentice-Hall.

Godwin, J. (1979) *Athanasius Kircher: A Renaissance Man and the Quest for Knowledge*, London: Thames and Hudson.

Grant, P. S. (1920) "If Christ Went to the Movies," *Photoplay Magazine* 17 (4).

Gunning, T. (1988) "From the Opium Den to the Theatre of Morality: Moral Discourse and the Film Process in Early American Cinema," *Art and Text*.

—— (1992) "Passion Play as Palimpsest," in *Une invention du diable?*, Lausanne: Éditions Payot Lausanne et Quebec, Presses de l'Univ. Laval.

Hays, W. H. (1929) *See and Hear*, New York: Doubleday/Doran.

Holloway, R. (1977) *Beyond the Image*, Geneva: World Council of Churches.

Hover, K. S. (1911) "Motography as an Arm of the Church," *Motography* 5 (5).

Johnston, A. (1931) "Hollywood Gets Religion," *Vanity Fair* 27.

Jump, H. (1911) "The Religious Possibilities of the Motion Picture," *Film History* 14 (2) (2002): 216–28.

Kay, K. and Peary G. (1977) *Women and the Cinema*, New York: Dutton.

Koszarski, D. (1980) *The Complete Films of William S. Hart*, New York: Dover.

Kuriyama, C. (1992) "Chaplin's Impure Comedy – the Art of Survival," *Film Quarterly* 45 (3) (Spring).

Lewis, K. (2002) "Rev. Herbert Jump and the Motion Picture," *Film History* 14 (2).

Lindsay, V. (1970) *The Art of the Moving Picture*, New York: Liveright.

—— (1995) *The Progress and Poetry of the Movies*, ed. M. Lounsbury, Lanham, MD: Scarecrow Press.

Lindvall, T. (2001) *The Silents of God: Selected Issues and Documents in Silent American Film and Religion*, Metuchen, NJ: Scarecrow Press.

—— (2002) "The Organ in the Sanctuary: Silent Film and Paradigmatic Images of a Suspect Clergy," in D. S. Claussen (ed.) *Sex, Religion and Media*, Boulder, CO: Rowman and Littlefield.

—— (2007) *Sanctuary Cinema*, New York: New York University Press.

—— (2008) "Sundays in Norfolk: Toward a Protestant Utopia through Film Exhibition in Norfolk, Virginia, 1910–1920," in M. Stokes (ed.) *Going to the Movies: Hollywood and the Social Experience of Cinema*, Exeter: University of Exeter Press.

Maland, C. J. (1989) *Chaplin and American Culture*, Princeton: Princeton University Press.

Maltby, R. (1990) "The King of Kings and the Czar of All the Rushes: The Propriety of the Christ Story," *Screen* 31.

Marlowe, J. (1955) *Mary Pickford, Sunshine and Shadow*, London: Doubleday.

Mast, G. (1979) *The Comic Mind: Comedy and the Movies*, Chicago: University of Chicago Press.

May, L. (1980) *Screening Out the Past: The Birth of Mass Culture and the Motion Picture Industry*, New York: Oxford University Press.

Meyer, R. (1967) "D. W. Griffith," *Film Comment* (Fall/Winter).

Miles, M. (1985) *Image as Insight: Visual Understanding in Western Christianity and Secular Culture*, Boston: Beacon Press.

Morris, L. (1949) *Not So Long Ago*, New York: Random House.

Prager, B. (1920) "Popularity of Semi-Religious Picture Fast Increasing," *Moving Picture World* (9 October).

Ramsaye, T. (1926) *A Million and One Nights: A History of the Motion Picture through 1925*, New York: Simon and Schuster.

Schuchardt, M. (2006) "Cherchez la Femme Fatale: The Mother of Film Noir," in Mark Conrad (ed.) *The Philosophy of Film Noir*, Lexington, KY: University Press of Kentucky.

Sherwood, R. E. (1923) *The Best Moving Pictures of 1922–1923*, Boston: Small, Maynard.

Skinner, J. (1993) *The Cross and the Cinema*, Westport, CT: Praeger.

Slide, A. (1996) *The Silent Feminists*, Metuchen, NJ: Scarecrow Press.

Sloan, K. (1988) *The Loud Silents: The Social Problem Film*, Urbana, IL: University of Illinois Press.

Stidger, W. (1932) "Taming the Movies: The Story of Cecil Blount DeMille, the Man Who Made 'The King of Kings' and 'The Ten Commandments,'" *Christian Herald*.

Tibbetts, J. C. (ed.) (1977a) *Introduction to the Photoplay*, Kansas: Shawnee Mission National Film Society.

—— (1977b) *His Majesty the American: The Cinema of Douglas Fairbanks*, Cranbury, NJ: Barnes.

Vidor, K. (1920) "Creed and Pledge," *Variety*.

Wagenknecht, E. (1962) *The Movies in the Age of Innocence*, Norman, OK: University of Oklahoma Press.

Walsh, F. (1996) *Sin and Censorship: The Catholic Church and the Motion Picture Industry*, New Haven, CT: Yale University Press.

Windeler, R. (1974) *Sweetheart: The Story of Mary Pickford*, New York: Praeger.

Filmography

The Avenging Conscience (1914, dir. D. Griffith)
Ben Hur (1907, dir. S. Olcott)
Ben Hur (1925, dir. F. Niblo)
The Birth of a Nation (1915, dir. D. Griffith)
The Blot (1921, dir. L. Weber)
The Circus (1928, dir. C. Chaplin)
A Corner in Wheat (1909, D. Griffith)
Don't Change Your Husband (1919, dir. C. DeMille)
Down to Earth (1917, dir. J. Emerson)
A Drunkard's Reformation (1909, D. Griffith)
Easy Street (1917, dir. C. Chaplin)
The Faith Healer (1922, dir. W. Moody)
Flirting with Fate (1916, dir. C. Cabanne)
The Four Horsemen of the Apocalypse (1921, dir. R. Ingram)
From the Manger to the Cross (1912, dir. S. Olcott)
The Gaucho (1928, dir. F. Jones)
The Habit of Happiness (1916, dir. A. Dwan)
Hallelujah (1929, dir. K. Vidor)
He Comes Up Smiling (1918, dir. A. Dwan)
The Hoodlum (1919, dir. S. Franklin)
Hop, the Devil's Brew (1916, dir. L. Weber)
Intolerance (1916, dir. D. Griffith)
The Jazz Singer (1927, dir. A. Crosland)
The Kid (1921, dir. C. Chaplin)
The King of Kings (1927, dir. C. DeMille)
Little Annie Rooney (1925, dir. W. Beaudine)
Manslaughter (1922, dir. C. DeMille)
The Miracle Man (1919, dir. G. Tucker)
Mr. Fix-It (1918, dir. A. Dwan)
The New York Hat (1912, dir. D. Griffith)
Noah's Ark (1928, dir. M. Curtiz)
The Nut (1921, dir. T. Reed)
Oberammergau Passion Play (1898, dir. H. Vincent)
Our Hospitality (1923, dir. J. Blystone)
The People vs. John Doe (1916, dir. L. Weber)
The Pilgrim (1923, dir. C. Chaplin)
Rebecca of Sunnybrook Farm (1917, dir. M. Neilan)
The Reformers (1913, dir. D. Griffith)
The Road to Yesterday (1925, dir. C. DeMille)
Shadows (1922, dir. T. Forman)
Shoes (1916, dir. L. Weber)
The Sky Pilot (1921, dir. K. Vidor)
Sparrows (1926, dir. W. Beaudine)
The Ten Commandments (1923, dir. C. DeMille)
Tess of the Storm Country (1922, dir. J. Robertson)
Way Down East (1920, dir. D. Griffith)
When the Clouds Roll By (1919, dir. V. Fleming)
Where Are My Children? (1916, dir. L. Weber)

2

THE ERA OF CENSORSHIP (1930–1967)

Andrew Quicke

Introduction

The thirty-seven-year era of censorship is one of the strangest in the history of American film, because a handful of articulate Catholics were able to muzzle an entire industry, using a powerful pressure group, the Legion of Decency, to advance their views. Much has been written about the Catholic Church's contribution to the formation and policing of the Production Code Administration in 1930 (PCA). The Catholics were not alone in demanding censorship of motion pictures; the Protestant Federal Council of Churches was actively demanding federal legislation during the 1920s. Many Protestant churches supported the aims of the (Catholic) Legion of Decency in the 1930s, and welcomed the tough approach to code enforcement adopted by Catholic Joseph Breen when he became the director of the PCA.

However, during the 1940s, Protestant attitudes to Hollywood became increasingly friendly; and Hollywood films received favorable reviews in the pages of denominational newspapers like the *Christian Herald* and *Christian Advocate*. In the postwar years the Protestant churches were much more in tune with postwar social attitudes, and began to disagree with the Legion of Decency over a wide range of issues. In addition the popularity of imported Italian movies not required to submit to PCA classifications led to dissension within Catholic ranks. Finally censorship battles led the Supreme Court to award motion pictures protection under the First Amendment in 1952. Unlike the Catholic Church and the Legion of Decency, the Protestant churches enjoyed a friendly relationship with Hollywood studio heads like Jack Warner of Warner Brothers, and Spyros Skouras of Twentieth Century Fox. In postwar years Protestants also took the lead in the production of 16mm nontheatrical films made specifically for the church market, as movie nights became an important part of church activities. The subjects covered ranged widely from worship to teen dating. All these factors led to the eventual demise of both the Production Code Administration and the Legion of Decency by the mid-1960s.

Origins of movie censorship in the USA

From the earliest days of the industry, religious leaders and reformers recognized the power of movies. Moralists of every religious and political persuasion became convinced that since films could portray taboo subjects like sex and politics, they would powerfully influence the moral and political behavior of their viewers, and particularly their younger viewers.

Films had faced censorship issues from 1907, when the City of Chicago passed the first moving picture ordinance. "Chicago vested control of its movie screens in its police commissioner, who in turn was empowered to hire such censors as he saw fit" (Wittern-Keller 2008: 22). Other big cities introduced censorship laws of their own; by 1915 individual cities united to join the National Board of Review of Motion Pictures. That same year of 1915 brought the first Supreme Court decision on movie censorship, when the Mutual Film Corporation of Ohio objected to paying the State of Ohio a fee to have their movies licensed and took their case to the Supreme Court. To their dismay the Court unanimously rejected their case: Justice Joseph McKenna wrote that the guarantees of free opinion and speech could not be obtained for the theater, the circus, or the movies because "they may be used for evil" (US Supreme Court 1915: 238).

In 1922 a series of Hollywood sex and drug scandals among Hollywood actors and producers created a public relations crisis for the film industry. The studios, seriously worried by the threat that government might step in to regulate movies, formed the Motion Picture Producers and Distributors of America (MPPDA) in 1922, and chose as president of this new organization Will Hays, a staunch Presbyterian and former Postmaster General under President Harding. In 1924 Hays produced what he called "the Formula," new rules which required all studios to submit to his office a synopsis of every story which was being considered for production. Yet church papers continued their criticism of Hollywood films despite this censorship (Moley 1945: 59–63).

Throughout the 1920s various women's and Protestant groups continued to call for government regulation of the industry (Jowett 1976: 10–17). One of the most powerful was the Federal Motion Picture Council (FMPC), an alliance between Presbyterian ministers and the Women's Christian Temperance Union. The FMPC were supported by Christian journals like the nondenominational *Christian Century*. Objecting to certain films on moral grounds, they aimed to outlaw block booking which, they claimed, forced exhibitors to show immoral films. They supported legislation in Congress to form a Federal Censorship Board as suggested in the Upshaw Bill of 1928 and the Brookhart Bill of 1929, which also proposed a ban on block booking; both bills failed to find support in Congress.

The birth of Catholic censorship

The birth of the "talkies" in 1927 led to church demands for still tighter regulation covering the use of language. Hays, worried about ever growing calls by church newspapers for tougher censorship, looked for a stricter set of rules. Extraordinarily, these regulations that would control a multimillion-dollar industry for thirty years were written by three little-known Catholics. The first was Martin Quigley, a staunch lay Catholic with very conservative views that led him to oppose any attempt by movies to discuss either political or social subjects. He wrote lengthy editorials about the decay of movie morality in his trade paper the *Motion Picture Herald*. Paradoxically Quigley opposed federal censorship and supported industry abuses like the block-booking system, which permitted the studios to force theater owners to show any movies they were sent without the chance to preview them. Here he was at odds with the Protestant lobby and the Federal Motion Picture Council, who wanted to eliminate block booking, because it could force theater owners to exhibit movies which they might consider unsuitable for their local audience. Quigley never attempted to cooperate with Protestants, and in later years his hostility to them led him to work actively to discourage Catholics from viewing any films about Protestants such as *One Foot in Heaven* (1941) and *Martin Luther* (1953). Arrogant and argumentative, he ruthlessly attacked equally in print or in private any Catholic who dared to disagree with his reactionary views.

Quigley and his local Catholic Jesuit priest, Father Fitz-George Dineen, decided that a code of behavior for the film industry was vitally important. Quigley then met with the powerful Cardinal Mundelein to persuade him that such a code could force Hollywood to reform, if it were backed by the Catholic Church with its 20 million members and its own Catholic newspapers. Father Dineen suggested that another Jesuit, Father Daniel Lord of Saint Louis University and editor of the Catholic newspaper *Queen's Work*, be brought in as the third member to draw up the code (Black 1998: 11). When Lord and Quigley wrote their code and took it to Will Hays at the MPPDA, he was delighted that someone had stepped in to solve his problems: "My eyes nearly popped out when I read it. This was the very thing I had been looking for" (Hays 1955: 439).

It is possible to speculate that the code might never have been put into force had the Great Depression not adversely affected movie ticket sales. But already declining revenues and the threat of a Catholic-inspired movie boycott enabled the Presbyterian movie supremo Will Hays to introduce the Catholic-authored code in 1930. Hays convinced his studio heads in New York that the new code would be good for business; his motivation was in sharp contrast with that of its authors Daniel Lord and Martin Quigley, who were convinced that if Hollywood and the movie industry could get together and promote a higher moral good, then a better society would result.

On the West Coast the producers in Hollywood were horrified by Lord's code. Irving Thalberg, Head of Production at MGM, B. P. Schulberg of Paramount, Jack Warner of Warner Brothers, and Sol Wurtzel of Fox all rejected Lord's censorship proposals, claiming that their films were simply "one vast reflection of every image in the stream of contemporary life" (Hays 1955: 439-43). Historian Robert Sklar sees the conflict between the film studios and the churches in more sociological terms: the ultimate industry acceptance of self-censorship by the Production Code Administration was "not simply the grudging acceptance of immigrant entrepreneurs to hostile demands for conformity by Conservative, old-line Americans. It was part of a much broader cultural warfare, – a series of struggles over power and purpose in American society – that preceded and transcended the movie business" (quoted in Couvares 1996: 4).

Hoping to please the increasingly vociferous Catholic lobby, Will Hays hired Joseph Breen, a deeply convinced, virulently anti-Jewish, articulate Catholic polemicist as his public relations consultant. Breen's appointment would lead later to his selection as director of the Production Code Administration. Now that historians like Black have been given access to the PCA and Legion of Decency archives, it is possible to know how Joseph Breen described the situation to a Catholic friend and adviser, Father Wilfred Parsons. He wrote that perhaps Will Hays thought "these lousy Jews out here would abide by the code's provisions, but if he did he should be censured for his lack of proper knowledge of the breed." He described Jewish studio heads as "dirty lice" and "the scum of the earth" (Black 1998: 20).

By 1933 the cause of censorship articulated by the two Catholics Father Daniel Lord and Martin Quigley was strengthened by the fact that no less than forty national organizations had passed resolutions condemning the film industry for its lack of moral standards. In spring 1933 a sensational book entitled *Our Movie-made Children* had suggested that 72 percent of all movies were unfit for children (Forman 1933: 1–100). Churches of every denomination were worried about Hollywood's immoral films. Quigley's next move was to have Monsignor Amulet Cigognani, the Pope's new apostolic delegate to the United States, demand Catholic action against the movies. This call led to the Catholic bishops appointing an Episcopal Committee on Motion Pictures. Under the advice of Father Daniel Lord, coauthor of the 1930 code, the Episcopal Committee proposed the formation of an entirely new Catholic pressure group which would claim to represent all Christians, Protestants included; its name was to be "The Legion of Decency." The task of the Legion was to create a pressure group that would call for the boycott of offensive films and would support self-regulation and conformity with the Production Code (Facey 1974: 45). In December 1933, under pressure from the Legion, Will Hays named Joseph Breen as director of the Production Code Administration. The PCA often was and still is referred to as the "Hays Office," which obscures the fact that it was the fervently Catholic Joseph Breen, not the mild Presbyterian Will Hays, who took up the day-to-day duties of director running the office of the PCA. Breen lost no time in enforcing his right to censor all screenplays submitted to the PCA. His decree that every film had to show moral compensating values for any evil that might be shown amounted to an attempt at Catholic social engineering. He demanded that all films were to encourage social spirit and patriotism (Black 1998: 23).

Breen's method of censorship had four stages; first, the PCA censored the screenplay; second, it checked up on location that the script was being followed during filming; third, it examined the first release print, and then finally the PCA sent the film to the Legion of Decency in New York. This fourth stage was outside the PCA remit, but became the standard procedure. At the Legion the films were seen by a team of women led by Mrs. Mary Looram, Head of the Motion Picture Bureau of the International Federation of Catholic Alumnae (IFCA), a Catholic women's organization. Together the Legion and the IFCA issued a four-part rating system as follows:

A1 Unobjectionable for general patronage
A2 Unobjectionable for adults
B   Objectionable in parts
C   Condemned (Black 1998: 25)

Film historian Mark Vieira suggests that the Legion of Decency was not so much an organization as it was a manifestation of Catholic will. Every American Catholic had to sign a pledge card which read as follows:

> I wish to join the Legion of Decency, which condemns vile and unwholesome moving pictures. I unite with all who protest against them as a grave menace to youth, to home life, to country and religion. I condemn absolutely those salacious motion pictures which, with other degrading agencies, are corrupting public morals and promoting a sex mania in our land. I shall do all I can to arouse public opinion against the portrayal of vice as a normal condition of affairs, against depicting criminals of any class as heroes and heroines, presenting their filthy philosophy of life as something acceptable to decent men and women ... Considering these evils, I hereby promise to remain away from all motion pictures except those which do not offend decency and Christian morality. (Vieira 1999: 172)

By mid-1937 the Catholic lobby totally dominated Hollywood film content. Breen's PCA worked so closely with the Legion of Decency that studios themselves pre-censored nearly everything they sent to the Production office. The result was that the vast majority of films were able to be classified either A1 (equivalent to today's G rating) or A2 (roughly equivalent to today's PG rating). Only thirty-two of the PCA-approved films were given the B license as adult fare (roughly equivalent to today's PG13 rating) and no film from any major studio was banned altogether, that is, given a "C for condemned" rating.

The Protestant reaction to the Production Code

At no point were Protestant church people involved in the decisions of the Legion of Decency, nor were Protestants involved in PCA decisions, though Geoffrey Shurlock, Breen's deputy and later his successor, was in fact an Episcopalian from England and more moderate in his judgments.

The Protestant churches' response to Hollywood excesses, however, had always been more muted than the Catholic reaction that had led to the formation of the Production Code. There were three reasons for this. First, denominational loyalties were strong, and Baptists, Lutherans, Methodists, and Congregationalists did not normally work closely together at the national level. In 1934 the Methodist Movement for Better Movies produced a pledge card which began: "I wish to join with other Protestants, co-operating with Catholics and Jews, in condemning vile and unwholesome moving pictures" (*Methodist Movement* 1934: 704). Dr. Fred Eastman of Chicago Theological Seminary was more critical; he wrote "we want more than decency. Decency is at best a negative thing. It means only the absence of dirt. A picture can be decent, and still be inane, trashy, essentially dishonest in its portrayal of human values" (Eastman 1934: 656). While there is evidence that many Protestant churches at first subscribed to the Legion of Decency's approach, their tacit support slowly faded as the Legion became increasingly hostile to films that featured Protestant ministers, especially in the postwar years.

The second reason that Protestants responded less strongly to Hollywood was that they had always put more interest into making movies of their own, even though the invention of talking pictures in 1927 largely put a stop to church filmmaking for a while. Not only was the cost of shooting high, but also few churches had 16mm sound projection equipment. But since interest in making Protestant movies for church remained strong, two Protestant organizations were founded to develop such motion pictures. The first group, the Religious Motion Picture Foundation of New York City (often known as the Harmon Foundation), issued a booklet entitled *How to Stimulate Great Activity in your Church through Motion Pictures*. Their eight-point recommendations included a budget for motion pictures in the church's annual budget, regular movie shows, and special movie nights for families and young people. Their ambitions were ably supported by Dr. Paul H. Veith of Yale University Divinity School who held a series of Motion Picture Practicums in the summer vacations during the 1930s. This view that movies were a good source of education as well as entertainment was more common in Protestant than Catholic circles (Lindvall 2007: 163). The second group was the Committee on Motion Pictures of the Federal Council of Churches who published a booklet entitled *Source Material on Motion Pictures for Pastors*. This second group sponsored a conference on 13 July 1934 to consider Protestant cooperation with the Legion of Decency, and voted unanimously to urge the Protestant Church to cooperate with the Legion (Johnson 1934: 139). One year later the editors of *Educational Screen* wrote that "An important bi-product of the 'decency' movement has been the rapid acceleration of constructive study of and experimentation with motion picture in our educational, public welfare and church life" (Brady 1935: 289).

The last reason for the more muted reactions to Hollywood's perceived immorality in the 1930s by the Protestant churches arose because the churches lacked an industry trade publication like the *Motion Picture Herald*, owned by the fervent Catholic Martin Quigley, who never ceased to promote his ultra-conservative views. In contrast to Quigley, by the 1940s, Dr. Daniel Poling of Philadelphia, editor of the newspaper the *Christian Herald*, began both to befriend Hollywood and to advance the making of movies for churches. The *Christian Advocate* also took up befriending Hollywood after the outbreak of the Second World War. Quigley's diatribes became so increasingly anti-Protestant that he lost any support the Catholics might have enjoyed from Protestant circles. Eventually a leading Catholic, Monsignor Little of the Legion of Decency, could tell his subordinate Bishop McNulty, also of the Legion of Decency, that Quigley suffered from a "form of megalomania and that unless he personally made all the important decisions he would remain unhappy until his dying day" (Black 1998: 197).

The Protestant reaction to the Legion of Decency

The *Christian Herald* became the most active Protestant newspaper that regularly wrote about movies and their use in Protestant churches. At first the paper had supported Joseph Breen and his ruthless application of the Production Code, even recommending that Breen be given an Oscar for his work. Guest writer on the *Christian Herald* Clarence Hall gives an amusingly accurate description of the Breen regime:

> The Catholic High Command, through the Legion of Decency, dealt the film industry a body blow with a sweeping boycott, and the Protestants, through the Federal Council of Churches of Christ in America, began to live up to their name with loud and continuing protesting. Breen's reign of dictatorship officially began on July 15, 1934. In the first six months of the Breen regime more pictures were sent back to the producers for retakes, remakes or just plain junking than had ever been questioned in the previous half dozen years. Broadway gagmen began to refer to Breen as the banishing American, and pictures passing the Code tests were said to have been "Breened." (Hall 1940: 16, 18)

By September 1940, Protestant writers were seriously critiquing the Catholic attack on everything to do with Hollywood. In the *Christian Herald*, motion picture commentator Howard Rushmore wrote, "There comes a time when even a movie critic feels that Hollywood too long has taken the blame for all forms of national calamities, including surrealism, bathing beauties, communism and Jesse James. Patiently, if not too courageously, the film capital has tried to give the public what Hollywood thinks Mr. & Mrs. America want (and ought) to see" (Rushmore 1940: 44).

The *Christian Herald* editor-in-chief Dr. Daniel Poling published a string of articles that praised Hollywood for its contribution to the war effort, singling out Warner Brothers' movie *Pastor Hall* (1940) as a truly magnificent film telling the story of a middle-aged pastor in Germany who challenged the Nazi philosophy. Jack Warner, Head of Production at Warner Brothers, was quick to respond to favorable reviews from the Protestant press. He wrote a fulsome letter to Poling asking for advice and help with his next film, which was to be about a Protestant pastor in the USA. He wrote:

> Warner Bros. are planning to produce on the screen Hartzell Spence's remarkable book about the life of his father *"One Foot in Heaven"* ... We of Warner Bros. like to think that certain films produced by us in recent years have contributed not only to the prestige and standing of the motion picture industry, but also to the inculcation throughout its world-wide audiences of standards of living and thinking, of justice, tolerance and democracy, which were never more needed than today. One field however of the highest importance remains as yet untouched by the screen. That is the life of the Protestant minister in the American community – his ideals, his problems, his

influence upon the men and women among whom he lives. No class of men has played a more powerful and dynamic role in the up building of American civilization than these devoted men of God ... We want to make *One Foot in Heaven* a picture worthy of its theme. We want it to be a permanent tribute by the American picture industry to one of the noblest types of American life and character. Can the *Christian Herald* help us to obtain this advice and wise counsel? (Warner 1940: 70)

Significantly, this letter shows that the Protestant approach of praising rather than condemning Hollywood studios was beginning to bring a type of cooperation between Jewish-led studios and the Protestant churches undreamed of by the antisemitic Legion of Decency, who only condemned, never praised, movies. Poling's reply to Jack Warner's flattering approach was a masterpiece of bridge building between those of his readers who loved Hollywood and those who disliked it. He wrote, "We could ignore [Jack Warner's approach] as though movies did not exist. We could refuse the invitation and assume a negative attitude entirely, or we can accept the invitation and make an earnest effort to render 16 million young Protestants and millions of others a constructive service" (Poling 1941a: 12). Poling formed an advisory board for Warner Brothers which included Episcopal, Methodist, Presbyterian, and Baptist ministers. All went well; when the film *One Foot in Heaven* (1941) was released Poling was delighted, writing, "In our opinion it is a milestone in the history of the motion picture" (Poling 1941a: 1). He was deeply disappointed when a Catholic bishop chose to warn his congregation to stay away from the film because the film's subject was a Protestant minister. Poling suggested that any *Christian Herald* reader could approve of such Hollywood product as *The Great Commandment* (1939), *Meet John Doe* (1941), *Sergeant York* (1941), *How Green Was My Valley* (1941), and of course *One Foot in Heaven* (1941). Later the *Christian Herald* praised movies like *The Keys of the Kingdom* (1944), *Till We Meet Again* (1944), and *Going My Way* (1944).

The pro-Hollywood stance of Protestants became even more marked as the war continued. In 1944 under the heading "What's Right with the Movies?," columnist Roscoe Gilmore Stott confessed: "A friend asked me point blank whether I would want my Christ to see me coming out of a motion-picture theater? [I replied] No, I am not ashamed to be seen coming out of a motion-picture theater" (Gilmore Stott 1944: 33). Ten years after Martin Quigley and Father Daniel Lord had been instrumental in the formation of one of the most successful of all movie pressure groups, Gilmore Stott acknowledged that the Protestant churches have "wealth, prestige, [and] leadership," and asked why Protestant churches should not have as effective a league for fighting for the highest of picture morals as any other group (Gilmore Stott 1944: 75). Copying the Catholic women's role in the Legion of Decency, the *Christian Herald* took the lead in forming "a militant Protestant voice," named the Motion Picture Council of Protestant Women (MPCPW), in February 1945 (Poling 1945: 37). This group of Protestant women produced regular reviews for the *Christian Herald* under the heading "Movie of the Month," and then created a competition for readers to write in with their suggestions for "The Movie of the Year." Hollywood studios responded by advertising their new movies with the MPCPW "Movie of the Year" designation. The *Christian Herald* even produced a bulletin board holder to hold the "picture of the month" clipping, free for any church that asked for one (*Christian Herald* 1946: 59).

In March 1946 the Motion Picture Council of Protestant Women changed its name to the Protestant Motion Picture Council (PMPC). Columnist Jimmie Fiddler claimed rather more for this new organization than it would actually achieve, when he wrote, "The Protestant Motion Picture Council [is] a very powerful organization [that] will act on behalf of Protestant churches much as the Legion of Decency now functions for the Roman Catholic Church" (Fiddler 1946: 61). This claim was to be unfulfilled because the PMPC had neither friends at the Production office, nor a newspaper like the *Motion Picture Herald* run by an industry insider like Martin Quigley. Also in 1946, a second organization, the Protestant Film Commission, was created, tasked with the special duty of co-coordinating efforts to produce church films suitable for a variety of Protestant denominations. All "Picture of the Month" reviews in the *Christian Herald* now stated that their film reviews and ratings came from "The Protestant Motion Picture Council cooperating with The Protestant Film Commission."

In the postwar years friendly relations between Hollywood and Protestants continued. In March 1950 the *Christian Advocate* reported that "official representatives of the Methodist Church cooperated with William H. Wright in the production of MGM's *Stars in My Crown*" (1950) (Spencer 1950: 318). Twentieth Century Fox created a special unit under an Episcopal professor, John Adams, to produce films for church use. *I'd Climb the Highest Mountain* (1951) was based on the book *A Circuit Rider's Wife* by Cora Harris. The President of Twentieth Century Fox, Spyros Skouras, believed that "the motion picture industry in general, and our company in particular, can and should perform a service for the religious community by providing it with films of high quality on religious subjects" (Skouras 1951: 10).

Protestant Church movies

During the war the army, navy, and air force made a large number of training films on 16mm film, shown to troops serving in different theaters of the war across the world. More churches thus came to accept that movies had a teaching as well as an entertaining role. When after the war there was a surplus of 16mm equipment, it was sold off cheaply to anyone, including churches; those who had sponsored the formation of the Protestant Film Commission were now anxious that a central body should start producing quality interdenominational films for Protestant parishes.

Columnist Paul Heard of the *Christian Herald* was delighted: "Taking a leaf from the armed forces' book, The Protestant Film Commission is now planning the production of non-theatrical films that will attempt the same kind of job for the church: viz, to so dramatize the teachings of Christianity, and so employ the tested techniques, as to stimulate the masses of American people toward Christian attitudes and action" (Heard 1946: 103). The PFC did produce well-made nondenominational 16mm movies of its own, distributed by Lutherans and Methodists, and glowingly reviewed in the pages of the *Christian Herald* and *Christian Advocate*. But the task of fully developing the new market for 16mm church films fell to three highly gifted individuals, Episcopalian Dr. James Friedrich, Pentecostal Carlos Baptista, and Dr. Irwin Moon of the Moody Institute of Science.

Dr. James Friedrich, an Episcopal priest appointed to the Los Angeles diocese, determined to produce quality Bible-based movies. He said, "I have seen the pictures that have been produced in the name of religion, and they were most discouraging. I felt that unless we could get the quality of a theatrical film into a religious film, it would be futile to try and present religion on the screen, as it would only reflect to the detriment of the church" (Lindvall and Quicke 2008: 48). Using the old Selznick Studios in Burbank, he produced high-quality black and white Bible parable films, and two longer series, *The Life of St. Paul* (1948–51) and *The Living Christ* (1951–7). The Audio-Visual Resource Guide wrote that "the imagination, sensitivity and creativity of the producer and director are evident in each film" (Hess 2000: 165). Friedrich's aims were to edify and educate the Church, to enhance interest in civic affairs, to promote missions work, and to evangelize. His films were widely distributed by the major Protestant denominations, particularly Methodists and Baptists (Lindvall and Quicke 2002: 7–11).

Carlos Baptista was a piano salesman from Venezuela who developed a number of unsubtle evangelistic films, beginning with *The Story of a Fountain Pen* (1939, 1941). With so few church movies available, his production company (entitled Scripture Visualized Institute) flourished for a time. His most interesting films were animated productions; his best achievement was a full-length animated version of *The Pilgrim's Progress* (1946). His company also manufactured the Miracle 16mm projector which was much lighter than its rivals and was guaranteed to project "Until the Lord Returns." Sadly, the cost of development ultimately proved too high and his company fell into bankruptcy (Lindvall and Quicke 2002: 2–6).

The third of the creative producers was pastor of a Los Angeles church, the Rev. Dr. Irwin Moon, a scientist, minister, and filmmaker at the Moody Institute of Science in Chicago, who managed to show that science was the tool whereby God's mysteries of His created world could be revealed. Irwin Moon made the best science films available, shown to millions in school classrooms and in the armed services as part of character-formation training. *God of Creation* (1946) was Moon's first movie, in which he used full color and time-lapse photography to reveal "God's hidden miracles" within the natural order. His films pointed to underlying spiritual realities, seeking to find transcending patterns behind growing things. In all, eighteen *Sermons from Science* films were made over the course of the next three decades. The well-financed (Protestant) Moody Institute of Science saw their work as an effective way to permeate non-Christian institutions like public schools and the military; overseas film prints were circulated in Russia and other Eastern bloc countries (Lindvall and Quicke 2002: 11–14).

The 1960s saw growth in movies made for Protestant churches by evangelical filmmakers; Ken Anderson made some worthy evangelistic films; Billy Zeoli, later chaplain to President Gerald Ford, masterminded his Gospel Films company into a position where it dominated evangelical church film distribution throughout the

United States. Billy Graham's in-house film company Worldwide Pictures distributed its big-budget films made in its own Hollywood studio, not only to churches but to movie theaters and later to television. One of the Worldwide Pictures advertisements for pastors claimed, "A Worldwide Pictures film showing is starting somewhere in the world every nineteen minutes around the clock." Their most successful production was *The Hiding Place* (1975) about the Dutch Ten Boon sisters who were sent to a Nazi concentration camp.

During the 1950s and 1960s, films made by the different Protestant denominations for their own churches flourished. The Baptists had their own film company, Boardman Films in Nashville, as did the Methodists; both denominations organized their own production networks though their bookshop chains. Presbyterians, Episcopals, and Lutherans also made denominational films. In contrast Gospel Films and Family Films made nondenominational Protestant films for distribution to any church that wished to show them. During this same time period there were Protestant film libraries across America, allied together under their own trade organization, the Christian Film Distributors' Organization (CFDA). Sadly, by the 1980s, rising costs and the growth of videocassette distribution competing for scarce dollars killed these enterprises. Some 1,500 of these forgotten 16mm films are now archived in the Regent University Library in Virginia Beach.

Catholic censorship loses support

After the Second World War, the tacit assumption in Hollywood that the Legion of Decency spoke not just for Catholics but for all Christians finally evaporated. One "Picture of the Week" reviewer complained that "whenever a drama with a religious background is used, almost invariably the hero has turned out to be a Catholic priest. Not that we have anything against having our Roman brethren well depicted ... it is just that in a land predominantly Protestant, it seems a bit out of balance to have religious pictures go Catholic by ten to one. And, whether Hollywood realizes it or not, that unbalance has made a great many Protestants good and mad" (*Christian Herald* 1948: 82).

For the whole of the previous decade 1935–45, for commercial reasons the Hollywood studios had chosen not to fight the censorship of the Catholic-promoted Legion of Decency and the Production Code Administration; their box office receipts remained good throughout the years 1937 to 1946 in spite of censorship. In 1947 movie audiences, wanting more from their films, and because of demographic changes, began to shrink drastically; but no studio wanted to challenge the Production Code Administration, because to do so would have revealed clearly that the MPPDA was a tightly controlled monopoly, already under investigation by the Justice Department for restraint of trade. When the Supreme Court did declare the movie industry an illegal monopoly in May 1948 in the so-called Paramount Decision, their judgment "broke the production-distribution-exhibition chain which had prevailed in the United States for decades" (Draper 1999: 199).

The Paramount divorcement decision not only broke the power of the studios to control what was exhibited; it also broke the power of the Production Code

Administration. So long as the studios had refused to allow the theaters to show any movie which did not have the Production Code Administration seal of approval, they effectively excluded independent filmmakers from exhibiting in American theaters. Once the theaters became independently owned, they could choose to exhibit any films they liked, with or without the PCA seal. When later in 1952 Supreme Court Justice Douglas stated, "We have no doubt that moving pictures, like newspapers and radio, are included in the press whose freedom is guaranteed by the First Amendment," the Catholic censorship of the movies was doomed to fail (Carmen 1966: 45).

The arrival of uncensored Italian films

In contrast to the 1930s, when all the churches agreed that movie censorship was necessary, in the late 1940s and 1950s, there was "deep disagreement about the proper role of film in society" (Draper 1999: 187). The first crack in the façade of PCA and Catholic unity over what was appropriate film material appeared when the Italian Catholic director Roberto Rossellini released his trilogy of films on the American market during 1946 to 1948. Though the first film, *Rome, Open City* (1945), showed not only drugs and lesbianism, but also a friendship between a Catholic priest and a communist leader, the only cuts required by the PCA were of a child on a chamber pot and scenes of the heroine's pregnancy, in spite of the PCA rules requiring avoidance of political and indecent subjects.

When another Italian director, Vittorio De Sica provided a vastly popular film *The Bicycle Thief* (1948) which received a warm welcome from the critics, Breen as censor refused it a PCA seal because of one scene in which a small boy tried to urinate. The distributor Joseph Burstyn appealed Breen's decision to the studio's trade organization, renamed in 1945 the Motion Picture Association of America (MPAA) when Will Hays retired. The MPAA upheld Breen's decision, but three of the major movie theater circuits flouted the MPAA rules and showed the film to crowded houses without the PCA seal of approval (Leff and Simmons 1990: 155–6). Although their defiance was a setback for Breen and the PCA, Breen was determined to resist what he regarded as immoral foreign movies being shown in the USA.

The Catholic Church and the PCA did not expect that in 1950 a short film by Catholic Roberto Rossellini called *The Miracle* (1948), shown as part of a trilogy entitled *The Ways of Love* (1950), would deliver three mortal blows to the cause of Catholic censorship. This film blew away any support they had derived in past years from the Protestant churches, caused the US Supreme Court to give First Amendment privileges to all motion pictures, and permanently damaged the Legion of Decency. *The Miracle* is a forty-minute film without crime, nudity, or suggestive clothing; the simple-minded young heroine, played by Anna Magnani, believes that she has met St. Joseph and he is the father of her child. The film, passed by both the Italian censorship board and the New York State censorship board, opened quietly in New York City on 5 December 1950, but eleven days later the Legion of Decency gave it its harshest rating, C for "condemned." The Legion's executive secretary demanded that the New York City Commissioner, a loyal Catholic called McCaffrey, ban the film.

McCaffrey did so, calling it "officially and personally blasphemous"; he "felt there were hundreds of thousands of citizens whose religious beliefs were assailed by the picture" (Draper 1999: 186). The distributor Joseph Burstyn challenged McCaffrey's authority to ban a film already approved for public exhibition by the New York State censorship board; the US Supreme Court ruled in favor of Joseph Burstyn (Black 1998: 85).

Movies gain First Amendment protection

Suddenly the Catholic Church was thrown into a battle in the courts; they would have been wise to avoid it since, so long as motion pictures were not protected by the First Amendment, censorship could continue. Cardinal Spellman used his papal authority to call on all American Catholics to boycott any theater which showed *The Miracle*, writing that Catholics were the guardians of the moral law. This statement angered Protestant clergyman Karl Chworowsky, who replied from his pulpit, "I resent a public statement calling the Catholics of the nation 'the guardians of the moral law' and I further and deeply resent the insinuation of the Cardinal that everyone refusing to share his opinions regarding seeing the movie *The Miracle* is thereby classified as an 'indecent person'" (Draper 1999: 193). At first Spellman's pronouncement that seeing the movie was classified as a mortal sin seemed to be working; Catholics rallied to his call, and over a thousand men and women picketed the theater, shouting abuse at the many who came to buy tickets. Martin Quigley in the *Motion Picture Herald* labeled the film as communist. Then the New York Board of Censors revoked its license to show *The Miracle* on the grounds that New York law demanded "men and women of all faiths respect the religious beliefs held by others" (Black 1998: 97). *The Miracle's* distributor Joseph Burstyn promptly appealed to the United States Supreme Court, and the battle over film censorship finally came into the open.

There were two separate issues before the US Supreme Court. One was whether government licensing of films before exhibition was constitutional; more specifically, a question arose as to the constitutionality of a New York Supreme Court ban. Acting for distributor Joseph Burstyn was the brilliant attorney Ephraim Loudon, who argued that film communicates ideas and is therefore entitled to the "privileges, immunities, and freedom guaranteed the press by the Constitution." He went further, to argue that the State of New York by requiring that a film be licensed before exhibition was violating the essence of the First Amendment. While he agreed that an exhibitor of obscene films could be prosecuted under existing criminal law, the requirement of prior licensing was unconstitutional (Black 1998: 97–102).

Attorney Loudon hammered home the fact that this controversy had been created by the Catholic Church alone, not the other Christian churches. He also ridiculed the New York State censorship board's suggestion that the film was sacrilegious, citing hundreds of letters from ministers and church members who found no offense in the movie. The MPAA refused to give an opinion, because they did not wish to reveal themselves as a monopoly. All the freedom pressure groups, including the American Civil Liberties Union, and the Authors League of America supported freedom from censorship for movies.

The Supreme Court gave a unanimous decision to overturn the New York Court of Appeals decision, stating their opinion that movies like books, magazines, and newspapers were all sold for profit, but that did not "prevent them from being a form of expression whose liberty is safeguarded by the First Amendment" (Devol 1982: 275). On the issue of sacrilege, the Supreme Court felt that it was no concern of government "to suppress real or imagined attacks upon a particular religious doctrine, whether they appear in publications, speeches or motion pictures" (Devol 1982: 276–7). The Court had thus ruled that all state and municipal censorship boards were also unconstitutional, because they permitted sacrilege as a cause for censorship.

The Legion of Decency becomes a purely Catholic pressure group

For seventeen years, from 1935 to 1952, the Legion of Decency had been able to suggest that it enjoyed the support of many different religious organizations that approved of motion picture censorship on religious and moral grounds. The affair of *The Miracle* led to the exposure of the Legion as a purely Catholic pressure group, since Protestants saw nothing sacrilegious or immoral in the story of a simple Italian peasant girl, and asked why such a harmless forty-minute short should produce pickets and vicious boycotts.

Catholics as well as Protestants criticized their Church; a Catholic publication, *Commonweal*, gave the opinion, "Catholics obey the voice of the church, it is a free act; to pressure or force, even indirectly, others who do not believe, into the same kind of obedience is to ask for servility" (Black 1998: 133).

Another clash over censorship occurred when in 1949 independent producer Charles Feldman bought the rights to Tennessee Williams' play *A Streetcar Named Desire*, which featured homosexuality, nymphomania, and rape. Breen and his Production Code Administration insisted on altering the end of the movie before they would issue a PCA seal. Then, as was their invariable practice, they forwarded the amended film to the Legion, where it shocked Father Patrick Masterson (spokesman for the Legion), Mary Looram, and Martin Quigley. The three informed Warner Brothers that *A Streetcar Named Desire* (1951) would be condemned if certain scenes were not eliminated. Warner Brothers, worried that director Elia Kazan and writer Tennessee Williams would object if they knew about religious censors cutting their work, secretly hired Martin Quigley to make the cuts required by the Legion. Furious, director Kazan went to New York to complain. Father Masterson of the Legion told Kazan that he was not a censor and that the Legion simply classified films, which was transparently untrue. Kazan then went to Quigley to question why the Catholic Church should enforce its set of moral values on all Americans; Quigley first claimed that what was important was "the preeminence of the moral order over artistic considerations," and then added that the Legion censored according to the Ten Commandments (Kazan 1988: 435).

Catholics and *Martin Luther* (1953)

The Protestant churches were by now less than enthusiastic toward the Legion of Decency, and their opinions turned to outright hostility when the Legion then attacked a low-budget movie on the life of Martin Luther, which had been paid for by six different Lutheran organizations throughout the USA. The PCA under Joseph Breen gave *Martin Luther* (1953) their seal of approval, and film critics like Bosley Crowther of the *New York Times* termed it a "fully responsible job" (Crowther 1953: 22). Protestant publications like the *Christian Herald* and the *Methodist Recorder* were delighted with the film, and urged their readers to see it. By the end of its first run *Martin Luther* had earned $5 million on an investment of $700,000. But the Catholic Church and the Legion of Decency seemed not to have forgiven Martin Luther for starting the Reformation 400 years earlier. Catholic publications attacked the film as bad theology and faulty history; one Legion member stated that the film "not only teaches heresy but bears false witness against the Catholic Church's teaching" (Skinner 1993: 63). The Legion could not condemn the film with a C categorization, since there was no sexual or political content, so they gave it a "separate classification" instead. Catholic priests were much harsher than was the Legion of Decency in their condemnation of the movie, while William Mooring in the Catholic publication *Tidings* stated: "If *Martin Luther* had been made by pro-communists for the purpose of launching an attack upon the Catholic Church, it could not very well have been contrived with greater subtlety nor with more characteristic style" (Skinner 1993: 64).

The *Martin Luther* case harmed Catholic–Protestant Church relations severely. Prominent writer and columnist Arthur Schlesinger Jr. suggested that many of the PCA rules were idiotic. Martin Quigley, who refused to consider any criticism of the code he had coauthored, claimed again that the rules were based on the Ten Commandments, and that Schlesinger had created a shadow of anti-Catholic bigotry. Schlesinger replied that the Ten Commandments were statements of profound moral principles, not niggling details, and asked whether Quigley imagined "the literature and art of the world would have been improved if all writers and artists had been compelled throughout history to work under the principles of the Hollywood Production Code" (Black 1998: 135).

The papal bull *Miranda Prorsus*

In 1957 the Legion of Decency was again attacked but from a surprising quarter, the Vatican itself. It is clear that Pope Pius XII's new approach to postwar cinema as suggested in the papal bull *Miranda Prorsus* was at variance with the Legion of Decency's hard-line approach. At the January 1957 meeting of the Organisation Catholique International du Cinéma (OCIC) in Havana, Cuba, the subject chosen was *The Promotion of Good Films and the Grouping of Cinematographic Culture*. Pope Pius XII sent a message to be read to delegates, praising the cinema "as a privileged instrument" given to man by God that could "elevate" man if correctly used. Since most of the delegates present already considered the Legion of Decency to be out of touch with modern cinema, they derided the Legion representative Monsignor Little when he spoke of how the Legion of Decency and the PCA worked together to provide a "voice for morality" and "compensating moral values" in American film. A Belgian Dominican monk ridiculed Little's assumption that by inserting "compensating moral values" he had "punished sin" and "disposed of it" (Vizzard 1970: 252, 254). The Monsignor did not know what to say and resigned his chairmanship of the committee the next day.

Taking his cue from the Pope, Archbishop William Scully, Chairman of the (Catholic) Episcopal Committee on Motion Pictures, praised the Havana conference for encouraging Catholics to form study groups "dedicated to the analysis and criticism of motion pictures" (Scully 1957: 726-7). The Legion added two new classifications after the Havana conference: the A2 category would be relaxed to include movies for adolescents and adults, and the new A3 category would be for adults only. The B category was reserved for films that were "morally objectionable."

The decline and fall of the Legion of Decency

In contrast to the Legion's hard-line stand, younger Catholic priests discerned much valuable moral teaching that could be derived from the portrayal of sinful situations. New councilors replaced Mrs. Looram's team of now-old women who had given so many years of faithful service in the cause of decency. The papal bull *Miranda Prorsus* led to Catholic universities now teaching classes on film criticism. The Catholic Church had finally recognized what Martin Quigley and Father Lord had not accepted, that is, that adult themes in movies would not necessarily corrupt adult viewers.

The end of the Legion came in the mid-sixties, as Protestant Christians joined in the general secular trend to liberalize movie classifications. The movie that actually broke the Legion's powers of censorship was *The Pawnbroker* (1964), a tragic tale of Sol Nazerman, a Jewish man who escaped the Holocaust but could never forget how the Nazis tortured, defiled, and murdered his wife. "The final version of the movie contained two nude scenes; a modest shot of Nazerman's wife at the camps, and a bold one of a Negro prostitute who bared her breasts for the pawnbroker" (Leff and Simmons 1990: 251). PCA censor Geoffrey Shurlock admired the picture, but unfortunately the code's ban on nudity left him no room for maneuver; he had to ban the picture. So producer Eliot Landau appealed to the MPPDA Production Code Review Board, who granted *The Pawnbroker* a special exemption, providing certain scenes were shortened. The film was then selected by the United States Information Agency and the Hollywood guilds as the official entry to the Berlin Film Festival in 1964.

On the one hand, Monsignor Little for the Legion of Decency informed the producers that the film was condemned by the Legion "ipso facto" because it contained nudity, and this MPPDA exemption would "open the door to substantial abuse in future American motion picture production" (Leff and Simmons 1990: 253). On the other hand, the liberal Catholic press saluted the picture and strong support also came from the Protestant press. The Protestant *Christian Century* gave *The Pawnbroker* a rave review; it was "about pain and sin ... a unique expression of modern life" (Boyd 1965: 942–3). The Legion's condemnation of *The Pawnbroker* was a serious mistake because it drew the accusation that this was not only evidence of Catholic insensitivity over the Holocaust, but worse, suggested that the Legion was antisemitic (Black 1998: 228).

The Legion tried to recover its power over the film industry but the world had changed. The final straw was placed on the camel's breaking back when Warner Brothers bought the film rights to Edward Albee's Broadway play *Who's Afraid of Virginia Woolf?* and cast superstars Richard Burton and Elizabeth Taylor to play the leads. In the days of Joseph Breen's full censorship, this portrait of a marriage made in hell would have been condemned immediately; now in 1966 scenes of casual sex and drinking were overlooked. What was harder to accept for both the PCA and the Legion was the uncensored language. "In addition to seven 'bastard's' and five 'son-of-a-bitch's', Shurlock and associates counted over fifteen 'goddamn's, thirteen references to Christ, and such piquant anatomical phrases as 'ass' and 'right ball,' 'angel boobs' and 'melons bobbling'" (Leff and Simmons 1990: 243–4). Geoffrey Shurlock, by now seventy and tired, knew he must refuse the PCA seal of approval on account of the language, but he encouraged Jack Warner to appeal to the MPAA. Under its new chairman Jack Valenti, the MPAA recommended an exemption from Production Code rules for *Who's Afraid of Virginia Woolf?* (1966) (Leff and Simmons 1990: 261). Across New York at the Legion offices, renamed the National Catholic Office for Motion Pictures (NCOMP) in 1965, Father Sullivan invited some ninety consultants to view the movie; only eighteen voted to condemn it. The NCOMP finally decided to grade it A4 when Warner Brothers agreed to refuse admittance to anyone "under the age of 18 unless accompanied by his parent." The final Catholic legacy to Hollywood was to be the acceptance by the film industry of an age-based rating system which, though modified, still endures in 2008.

Suddenly the solution to the discord challenging the successive presidents of the MPAA became crystal clear. Though the film industry had fought for generations to avoid age restrictions for film theaters, it had at the same time demanded increasingly adult themes, more sex, and more violence. When Valenti's new Code and Ratings system, based on the age of those attending movies, was announced in 1966 and finally introduced in 1968, the Catholic code of Martin Quigley and Father Lord was dead. Few would mourn its passing; adults were now free to see movies with adult themes.

What harm did the code do to the American movie industry? Probably in the prewar years it did none, because the code's provisions were in tune with what the American public and American churches were prepared to accept. But after the Second World War the Protestants found the code biased against non-Catholic themes, while freethinkers regarded its anachronistic rules as absurd. By its very censorship the Legion demonstrated that it had always been male chauvinist, antisemitic, socially conservative, intolerant, and ready to enforce its code ruthlessly. On occasion Catholic Knights of Columbus members aggressively picketed the theaters where Legion-proscribed movies were shown. The Legion's power was fatally undermined by the Supreme Court's decision to give movies First Amendment protection in 1952; even so, ten years passed before the Legion could truly realize that its time had passed for ever.

Those who favor censorship, both then and now, insist that movies affect behavior, and that movies can harm society; back in 1915 the Supreme Court itself thought movies could be an evil influence. But others have always supported "the free market of ideas and amusements" (Couvares 1996: 4), and nearly forty years later the Supreme Court decided that movies were to be protected by the First Amendment. The thirty years of censorship represented a victory for conservative morality, yet those Catholics and Protestants who attacked Hollywood were not trying to wreck the movie industry; rather, they wanted to assert their own cultural and moral power to control what the public saw, in order to stem immorality and promote change for the better in society. The Jewish owners of the studios, wanting both profit and respectability, were able to agree to the limitations imposed by the PCA and the Legion. Film censorship was part of a much broader cultural warfare – a series of "struggles over power and purpose in American society" (Sklar 1975: 4). Today we recognize the contest between filmmakers and censorship boards as part of the culture wars. Because both religion and film are concerned with how we live our lives, we must recognize, if not admire, those on either side of the censorship divide who cared so much for what they believed for over thirty years.

Bibliography

Black, G. D. (1998) *The Catholic Crusade against the Movies 1940–1975*, Cambridge: Cambridge University Press.

Boyd, M. (1965) *Christian Century* 82 (28 July): 942–3.

Brady, M. (1935) "The Church Field: A New Era for the Church," *Educational Screen* (December): 289–90.

Carmen, I. H. (1966) *Movies, Censorship and the Law*, Ann Arbor: University of Michigan Press.

Christian Advocate (1950) Report (16 November): 1426.

Christian Herald (1945) "A Militant Christian Voice" editorial (February): 37.

—— (1946) "We have One for Your Church" unsigned (March): 59.

—— (1948) "Picture of the Month: Film Reviews and Ratings from the Protestant Motion Picture Council: Review of *The Tender Years*" (February): 82.

Couvares, F. G. (ed.) (1996) *Movie Censorship and American Culture*, Washington DC: Smithsonian Institution Press.

Crowther, B. (1953) Review of "Martin Luther," *New York Times* (10 September): 22.

Devol, K. S. (ed.) (1982) *Mass Media and the Supreme Court*, 3rd ed., Mamaroneck, NY: Hastings.

Draper, E. (1999) "Controversy Has Probably Destroyed Forever the Context: *The Miracle* and Movie Censorship in America in the 1950s," in M. Bernstein (ed.) *Controlling Hollywood: Censorship and Regulation in the Studio Era*, New Brunswick, NJ: Rutgers University Press: 186–93.

Eastman, F. (1934) "For Decent Movies" editorial, *Christian Advocate* (26 July): 656.

Facey, P. W., SJ (1974) *The Legion of Decency: A Sociological Analysis of the Emergence and Development of a Social Pressure Group*, New York: Arno Press.

Fiddler, J. (1946) "Hollywood Hears from the Protestants," *Christian Herald* (June): 61.

Forman, H. (1933) *Our Movie-made Children*, New York: MacMillan.

Friedrich, J. (1947) National Council of Churches Broadcasting & Film Commission interview with James K. Friedrich. Green Lake, WI: Fourth International Film Workshop, 1947 in Billy Graham Center Archives, Collection 327, Wheaton College Illinois.

Gilmore Stott, R. G. (1944) "What's Right with the Movies?," *Christian Herald* (October): 33–4, 74–6.

Hall, C. (1940) "An Oscar for Joe," *Christian Herald* (April): 16, 18, 44.

Hays, W. (1955) *The Memoirs of Will H. Hays*, Garden City, NY: Doubleday.

Heard, P. (1946) "One Way to Avoid Film Censorship," *Christian Herald* (November): 103.

Hess, B. (2000) "Between Scylla and Charybdis: A Look At Two Christian Film Companies." Thesis, Virginia Beach: Regent University.

Johnson, R. (1934) "The Church Field," *Educational Screen* (September): 139.

Jowett, G. (1976) *Film: The Democratic Art*, Boston: Little, Brown.

Kazan, E. (1988) *A Life*, New York: Knopf.

Leff, J. L. and Simmons, J. L. (1990) *The Dame in the Kimono: Hollywood, Censorship and the Production Code from the 1920s to the 1960s*, New York: Weidenfeld.

Lindvall, T. (2007) *Sanctuary Cinema: Origins of the Christian Film Industry*, New York: New York University Press.

Lindvall, T. and Quicke, A. (2002) "The Christian Film Industry." Thesis, Virginia Beach: Regent University.

—— (2008) "Film: From Church Reels to Digital Media," in Q. Schultze and R. Woods (eds) *Understanding Evangelical Media: The Changing Face of Christian Communication*, Grand Rapids, MI: InterVarsity Press: 58–70.

Lord, D. (1955) *Played by Ear*, Chicago: Loyola University Press.

Methodist Movement (1934) "For Movie Betterment" editorial (16 August): 704.

Moley, R. (1945) *The Hays Office*, New York: Bobbs-Merrill, New York.

Nicola, J. D. (1966) "Virginia Woolf: The Making of a Film Rating," *Ave Maria* 104 (27 August): 7–11.

Poling, D. (1941a) "One Foot in Heaven" Advisory Committee on the Production of One Foot in Heaven, *Christian Herald* (6 October): 12.

—— (1941b) "An Open Letter to Our Friends," *Christian Herald* (December): 1.

—— (1945) "A Militant Protestant Voice," *Christian Herald* (4 February): 37–8.

Rushmore, H. (1940) "Motion Picture Commentator," *Christian Herald* (September): 44.

Scully, W. A. (1957) "The Movies: A Positive Plan," *America* 96 (30 March): 726–7.

Skinner, J. (1993) *The Cross and the Cinema: The Legion of Decency and the National Catholic Office for Motion Pictures, 1933–1970*, Westport, CT: Praeger.

Sklar, R. (1975 rev. 1994) *Movie-Made America: A Cultural History of American Movies*, New York: Vintage.

Skouras, S. (1951) *Christian Advocate* (27 December): 10.

Spencer, H. (1950) "The Methodist Church and MGM," *Christian Advocate* (9 March): 318.

US Supreme Court (1915) 236 US230. *Mutual Film Corporation v. Ohio Industrial Commission*, 236 US230: 238

Vieira, M. A. (1999) *Sin in Soft Focus: Pre-code Hollywood*, New York: Harry N. Abrans.

Vizzard, J. (1970) *See No Evil: Life Inside a Hollywood Censor*, New York: Simon and Schuster.

Warner, J. L. (1940) letter to *Christian Herald*, 5 November (February 1941): 70.

Westin, A. F. (1961) *Miracle Case, the Supreme Court and the Movies*, Alabama: University of Alabama Press.

Wittern-Keller, L. (2008) *Freedom of the Screen*, Lexington, KY: University of Kentucky Press.

Filmography

The Bicycle Thief (1948, dir. V. De Sica)
God of Creation (1946, dir. I. Moon)
Going My Way (1949, dir. L. McCary)
The Great Commandment (1939, dir. I. Pichel)
The Hiding Place (1975, dir. J. Collier)
The Hoodlum Saint (1946, dir. N. Taurog)
How Green Was My Valley (1941, dir. J. Ford)
I'd Climb the Highest Mountain (1951, dir. H. King)
The Keys of the Kingdom (1944, dir. J. Stahl)
The Life of St. Paul series (1948–51, dir. J. Coyle)
The Living Christ series (1951–7, dir. J. Coyle)

Martin Luther (1953, dir. I. Pichel)

Meet John Doe (1941, dir. F. Capra)

The Miracle (Il miraculo) (1948, dir. R. Rossellini: US release 1950 as part of *The Ways of Love*)

One Foot in Heaven (1941, dir. R. Lord and I. Rapper)

Open City (Roma, città aperta, aka Rome, Open City) (1945, dir. R. Rossellini)

Pastor Hall (1940, dir. R. Boulting)

The Pawnbroker (1964, dir. S. Lumet)

The Pilgrim's Progress (1946, dir. C. Baptista)

Quo Vadis (1951, dir. M. LeRoy)

Rome, Open City (1945) see *Open City*

Sergeant York (1941, dir. H. Hawks)

The Song of Bernadette (1943, dir. H. King)

Stars in My Crown (1950, dir J. Tourneur)

The Story of a Fountain Pen (1939, 1941, dir. C. Baptista)

A Streetcar Named Desire (1950, dir. E. Kazan)

Till We Meet Again (1944, dir. F. Borzage)

The Ways of Love (1952) comprising *A Day in the Country* (1946, dir. J. Renoir), *Jofroi* (1946, dir. M. Pagnol) and *The Miracle* (1948, dir. R. Rossellini)

Who's Afraid of Virginia Woolf? (1966, dir. M. Nichols)

3

THE ROMAN CATHOLIC CHURCH AND CINEMA (1967 TO THE PRESENT)

Peter Malone

Prologue

Venice, September 1964. The Catholic Jury for OCIC, Organisation Catholique Internationale du Cinéma, has awarded its prize to Marxist novelist and director Pier Paolo Pasolini, for his *Gospel According to St. Matthew*.

Venice, September 1968. The OCIC Jury has again awarded its prize to Pasolini, this time for *Teorema*. This decision evokes protests and condemnations of OCIC, including Vatican complaints. An angry Pier Paolo Pasolini decides to return his first award. The situation is made more complex by another OCIC Jury award, to John Schlesinger's *Midnight Cowboy* at the 1969 Berlin Film Festival. The president of OCIC, Jean Bernard, attends many meetings during 1969 to assuage the controversy and ensure the continued work of OCIC as a recognized Catholic organization for cinema. Ultimately, he succeeds and OCIC survives.

Leading up to the 1960s

The 1960s was an era of change in all aspects of life in the West. This was true for the Catholic Church. In January 1959, Pope John XXIII convened a worldwide "ecumenical" council. The preparations lasted over three years. The Council finally opened on 11 October 1962 and continued during the next four northern-hemisphere autumns, drawing to a close on 8 December 1965. While significant changes came about in liturgy, in development of biblical studies, in a more accessible language for church teaching and documents, there were repercussions for communications and media. In fact, the first document discussed, *Inter Mirifica* (Amongst the wonderful things ...), was a brief document on Social Communications. For church renewal and updating there was a more authoritative document, *Gaudium et Spes* (Joy and hope), discussed extensively in 1964 and 1965, promulgated in 1965. One of its aims was to alert the Catholic Church, worldwide, to be aware of the "signs of the times" and respond pastorally to these signs. This more open perspective coincided with changes in cinema production and more "adult" themes and treatment in movies, especially from the United States.

The initial Catholic response to cinema at the beginning of the twentieth century was favorable, although in 1912 Pope Pius X ordered churches themselves not to be used for screenings. Church authorities tend to be wary of media and to be protective of their members. This has been less the case in Europe than in the United States. Europe, with its long visual-arts tradition, was far more accepting of serious themes and treatment. While some national offices followed the lead of the United States and issued suitability lists for films (sometimes with penalties for disobeying and exhortations against the cinema), the approach to cinema in Europe by Roman Catholics was more positive, including an interest in distribution and exhibition of good films, critical review and essays, and even a desire to make films (which in fact was beyond their available financial means) (Molhant 2000).

This led to the formation in 1928 of OCIC in the countries of Western Europe, centered in Belgium. Gradually extending its membership and holding international meetings during the 1930s, it had become a substantial Catholic film organization by the outbreak of the Second World War. However, the Nazi invasion of Belgium led to the occupation of the General Secretariat. The Secretary General, Fr. Jean Bernard, was interned in Dachau for critical writing against the Nazi regime (Bonneville 1998). An episode in 1942 where he was released to go to his native Luxembourg to talk with the archbishop about German superiority and his subsequent return to the concentration camp was the subject of Volker Schlöndorff's *Der Neunte Tag* (2004).

Americans, on the other hand, are descended from religious refugees from Europe, especially Christian nonconformists of the seventeenth and eighteenth centuries, reinforced by the Irish and Italians from the nineteenth century and escapees, especially Jewish middle Europeans, fleeing Cossacks and other persecutors. Calvinist predestination theology as well as tenets of Puritan behavior also crossed the Atlantic to give American culture an overt religious perspective and, frequently, a moralizing perspective. This was manifest in the writing of the Motion Picture Code (with strong Catholic contributions from Martin Quigley and Fr. Daniel A. Lord SJ). It was even more manifest in the development and thirty-year existence of the Legion of Decency. In 1968, Jack Valenti was the first president of the Motion Picture Association of America, the body designated to classify and censor movies, which inherited these stances.

To make the point: an archbishop from the United States, interviewed after seeing the Coen Brothers' *O Brother Where Art Thou* (2000), immediately stated that there was nothing objectionable in it – and then added that he had enjoyed it. A European response would have emphasized the enjoyment, later adding, if necessary, some moral or aesthetic limitations.

Already in 1953, director Otto Preminger had challenged the code by including the words "virgin" and "pregnant" in his mild comedy *The Moon is Blue*. In 1966, he was still being provocative with a suggestive phallic scene in *Hurry Sundown* where Jane Fonda is fondling a saxophone. Meanwhile in Europe, Preminger had been awarded a papal medal in 1963 for *The Cardinal*, which was screened for many of the bishops attending the Vatican Council.

The years 1966 and 1967 were pivotal for rethinking stances on the code and the Legion, and on how issues of language, sexuality, and violence were to be judged for classifying films. Troubled by Billy Wilder's cheeky thumbing his nose at standards with *Kiss Me Stupid* (1964) (Wilder reshooting some scenes to comply with the Legion) and the baring of breasts by a woman in Sidney Lumet's powerful and Oscar-nominated *The Pawnbroker* in 1964, reviewers for the Legion were trying to find more appropriate norms for classifying the movies.

The studios were also anxious and the story is told of how Warner Brothers were cautious about Mike Nichols' *Who's Afraid of Virginia Woolf?* (1966) but risked a screening for Fr. Patrick O'Sullivan SJ and other Catholic reviewers. This group praised the film and introduced a new category to their classifications, "A IV, Morally unobjectionable for adults, with reservations." (Warner Brothers in Australia were shrewd in one of their taglines for the movie – though it was not at all prophetic – "will never be shown on TV.") Some commentators were alarmed and declared that the floodgates had been opened. Of course, they were not entirely wrong, but the challenge to the Catholic Church was how to respond to these changes in a credible as well as pastoral way.

Official Catholic policy

To gauge the Catholic response to cinema, it is important to look at the statements and stances of church officials as well as to look at the practice of the Church.

In 1936, Pope Pius XI's encyclical letter *Vigilanti Cura* (With vigilant care) was the first to address the cinema, forty years after the first Lumière Brothers' screenings. The title of the letter indicates the protective attitude against morally dubious material. The Pope endorsed the work of the Legion of Decency. However, the text showed an appreciation of the impact of cinema, referring to story and images as "more effective than abstract reasoning" (no. 23). Twenty-one years later, Pius XII wrote the second encyclical on cinema, *Miranda Prorsus* (Those very remarkable technical inventions). In this letter, he encouraged the study of cinema and the appreciation of how cinema has its own "language" of communication (no. 57). (Because of the focus on understanding the moving image, this should perhaps be called "visuacy".) Pius XII was interested in both the arts and scientific development and regularly received representatives of these worlds in private and group audiences after the Second World War.

This was the setting for the Vatican II document *Inter Mirifica* (1963), which led to the establishing in 1964 of a Vatican department for Social Communications which would become the current Pontifical Council for Social Communications. Paul VI, in the spirit of the Council, issued his first encyclical letter in 1964. Its topic was the range of dialogue between the Church and the world, *Ecclesiam Suam* (His, i.e., Christ's, Church).

One of the immediate consequences of *Inter Mirifica* was the establishing of the Pontifical Commission for the Instruments of Social Communication (later the

Pontifical Council for Social Communications) and the annual World Communications Day to be observed throughout the whole Church. The first was in May 1967 and this has continued through the papacies of Paul VI (†1978), John Paul II (†2005), and Benedict XVI. The Pope issues a special statement for that day, taking up a relevant media theme (Eilers 1993).

The Pontifical Council for Social Communications produced a long document in 1971, a Pastoral Instruction, *Communio et Progressio* (The unity and advancement ...), the kind of document that many had hoped the Vatican Council itself might have written. It covered all contemporary media. In its sections on cinema, one of the directions it emphasized and encouraged was the "spiritual" dimension of cinema (nos. 142, 144). As will be seen later, this was a direction which had been emerging in Catholic practice in the mid-1960s.

Another activity of the Pontifical Council for Social Communications has been the production of booklet-size studies of media and morals on topics such as advertising and the internet. In 1989, they issued a document on violence and pornography. In 2003, a process began for a document on cinema and spirituality written for "the multiplex audience" to help appreciate the values in popular cinema but the document did not eventuate.

In 1992, to celebrate twenty years since *Communio et Progressio*, the Pontifical Council issued a pastoral document on the media, *Nostra Aetate* (Dawn of a new era), acknowledging the changes (for example, the proliferation of video recorders and players) since 1971. This document also set out a media pastoral plan and urged its implementation by all dioceses and religious institutions – which has been, as Shakespeare shrewdly said of human behavior, more honored in the breach than the observance. However, as regards cinema, many bishops conferences do have a ratings and classifications system while many websites and Catholic newspapers, magazines, and bulletins run film reviews.

While John Paul II did not write an encyclical letter on cinema, his outlook on media was very positive. He had written plays and acted and enjoyed the media coverage of his pontificate. He also enjoyed film screenings in the Vatican which included Roberto Benigni's *La vita è bella* (1997) and Polish films like Wajda's *Pan Tadeusz* (1999) and Jerzy Kawalerowicz's *Quo Vadis?* (2001). On the occasion of the screening of the American television movie *Jesus*, at the Festival of the Third Millennium in Rome in 1999, the Pope received the stars, Jeremy Sisto, Jacqueline Bisset, and Gary Oldman, in an audience. In his first year as Pope, Benedict XVI attended a screening of the Italian film, *Pope John Paul II* (2005), where he met the stars, Jon Voight and Cary Elwes.

John Paul II's approach was to refer to media as "gifts of God." His last published document, February 2005, was a look at contemporary media and technology, *Il Rapido Svilluppo* (The rapid development ...). Benedict XVI, like John Paul II, always receives members and consultors during the annual assembly of the Pontifical Council and always gives an address and an exhortation on a topical media subject. There is always a screening during the assembly. Recent films have included *2001: A Space Odyssey* (1968), *La stanza del figlio* (2001), *The Emperor's Club* (2002), *The Passion of the Christ* (2004), and *The Chronicles of Narnia: The Lion, the Witch and the Wardrobe* (2005).

In this age of rapid development and public relations, producers of religious films have been keen on obtaining Vatican endorsement for their productions. There was the story of John Paul II's alleged viewing of *The Passion of the Christ* and his remark, "it is as it was," subsequently denied by officials. The producers of *The Nativity Story* had a coup in holding the premiere in the Paul VI hall in the Vatican, in November 2006. Pope Benedict was to leave for a visit to Turkey the next day (where he would be photographed praying with an imam in the Blue Mosque) and did not come but Cardinal Bertone, the Secretary of State, did attend.

One of the repercussions of the release of *The Passion of the Christ* (2004) was that many bishops conferences issued statements on the film and included comment in their newspapers and on their websites. There was even more comment and website information with the 2006 release of *The Da Vinci Code*. While Archbishop Amato of the Congregation for the Doctrine of the Faith spoke out against the film, many bishops conferences took a more balanced approach, acknowledging the inaccuracies of the plot but offering positive information about viewing the film and opportunities for finding out more objective information.

OCIC (and since 2001 as SIGNIS, the World Catholic Association for Communication) has also contributed to this kind of assessment of controversial films. The president, Peter Malone (1998–2005), released statements on films ranging from *Amen* (2002) and *The Magdalene Sisters* (2002) to *Kingdom of Heaven* (2005), *The Exorcism of Emily Rose* (2005), and *Elizabeth: The Golden Age* (2007), many of which were taken up by the bishops conferences and the websites of Catholic organizations.

Catholic approaches from the 1960s to the present

Many film students and enthusiasts were encouraged by the 1960s emphasis on "the signs of the times" and the Church's move toward dialogue. The reflection coming from Europe focused on serious cinema and its meanings, with appreciation courses and cineforum discussion on the films of directors like Ingmar Bergman. Anecdotally speaking, the present author attended training sessions on film in Rome by Enrico Baragli SJ who contributed, along with Jean Bernard and other media experts, to *Inter Mirifica* and who published collections of Vatican documents on the media, as well as participating in cineforum meetings conducted by the Salesians on Bergman's *Through a Glass Darkly* (1961) and Pasolini's *Gospel According to St. Matthew* (1964). However, at a cineforum at Rome's Propaganda Fidei College (for seminarians from Africa and the Pacific) which screened *Becket*, students were told at the start that some cuts had been made because the scenes were "beneath human dignity." When *Becket* screened later that year (1965) at the Oratorio San Pietro, adjacent to the then Holy Office, where clerics could see contemporary films because they were forbidden to go to regular cinema screenings, it emerged that there were forty-five minutes cut, the complete first half of the film about Becket's "worldly" life.

At the same time, Father Karel Truhlar SJ was conducting courses at the Gregorian University on the surprisingly titled *Theologia Recreationis* (Theology of recreation), which included reflection on the spirituality of cinema and its philosophical and biblical foundations. This thinking led to the establishment of periodicals, journal articles, and associations, for the exploration of theological themes in cinema, especially in continental Europe, which still flourish.

In the English-speaking world, a breakthrough came in 1960 with the publication of *The Image Industries* by William Lynch SJ. He had also published *Christ and Apollo* which brought the insights of theology into the study of literature. *The Image Industries* was quite exhilarating at the time. While literature was respectable, many (most?) saw the movies as a medium simply for entertainment and, therefore, not to be taken so seriously. By applying aesthetic, moral, and theological thought to popular, and contemporary, cinema (e.g., Billy Wilder's acerbic *The Apartment*, which won the Oscar for Best Film of 1960), film students as far away from the United States as Australia began to follow Lynch's leads.

Groups within the Church who were influenced by the Jocist movement – the Young Christian Workers of the 1920s, established by Canon Joseph (later Cardinal) Cardijn in Belgium with its process for Catholic Action of "See, judge, act" – applied these principles to cinema. The British periodical *Focus* (1948–58) contained reviews that blended European reflection on issues with the classifications influenced by the Legion of Decency. Booklets by Father Fred Chamberlin, Young Christian Students chaplain in Melbourne, Australia, entitled *Films and You* (1950) and *You and the Movies* (1952) enabled young Catholics to view the popular films they were seeing in greater depth.

The period of the mid-1960s to the mid-1970s was both challenging and fruitful for Catholic thinking, speaking, and writing about cinema. Of particular importance was the work of a group of young Catholics in Chicago, especially Henry Herx, who was later director of the US Bishops office on film, and Ron Holloway who has since spent decades in Europe promoting this kind of reflection, especially in German cinema. They wrote articles, compiled discussion material, conducted seminars – and excited young filmgoers at home and abroad. John R. May's chapter surveying writing in English during this period in *New Images of Religious Film* offers specific comment on many of the writers of the times and their books and articles. He indicated five different approaches taken by these writers.

John May's typology of approaches to film

The first approach is titled *Discrimination* (also *Heteronomy*). It is a morality-based approach to appreciating film. May quotes Harold Gardiner in this regard, "the total artistic judgment, the complete critical evaluation, of a work of art includes a moral dimension" (May 1997: 20). An important question raised here is the extent to which an alleged moral responsibility may police freedom of expression. May cites Michael Medved's 1992 polemic against Hollywood, a political and frequently generalizing look at the US movie industry, *Hollywood vs. America: Popular Culture and the War on Traditional Values*, as an example of this approach (May 1997: 21). May finds this approach important to examine, but also finds that the pressure from concerned parents and those alarmed by what they perceive as permissiveness in films leads to many pragmatic decisions which involve a moralizing injunction about suitability – rather than a deeper moral evaluation which is concerned with the context of the issues presented in films.

May's second approach is called *Religious Visibility*, a reference to films with specifically religious subjects and treatment. This is a tricky area because many earnest commentators automatically applaud films which are explicitly religious with discussions on the spiritual dimensions of, say, DeMille's *King of Kings* (1927) and Dreyer's *Passion of Joan of Arc* (1928), of Bing Crosby's priest in *Going My Way* (1944) or the priest in Bernanos' *Diary of a Country Priest* (1950). The question is, are films with a "religious" subject matter necessarily religious? Is it always the case that Catholic filmmakers make Catholic films? An interesting complex example is *The Last Temptation of Christ* (1988), based on the novel by Orthodox Christian Nikos Kazantzakis, with a screenplay by post-Calvinist Paul Schrader, and directed by New York Italian American Catholic Martin Scorsese. To what extent is this a Catholic or even a Christian film?

Religious Dialogue is May's third approach, in which the viewer brings a moral and religious perspective to a film. The aim is to discern in what ways the film is implicitly religious and what its moral and human/humane values are. This opens up the possibility of dialogue between religious and secular critics and filmmakers in their pursuit of a common humanity and morality. This approach is particularly valued in Europe, encompassing intense dialogue with such directors as Andrei Tarkovsky, Wim Wenders (especially for *Wings of Desire* [1987]), and Krzysztof Kieslowski (and his *Three Colours* trilogy [1993–4]).

The fourth approach is *Religious Humanism* (or *Theonomy*). May quotes Neil Hurley (May 1997: 25) and concludes that his emphasis on discerning the values and human themes in films is a significant way to interpret cinema. It encourage audiences to deepen their "spiritual" more than their "religious" response. Here May is quoting Ronald Holloway (May 1997: 26). Some of the books that were written by the present author during that period are listed in this category. May singles out an approach in these books that seeks "the harmony between Christian and basic human attitudes" (May 1997: 26). This is a dialogue that emphasizes a meeting of hearts, minds, and imaginations rather than a polemical approach to movies.

May has much more to say about his fifth approach, *Religious Aesthetics* (or *Autonomy*). The previous approaches had focused on religion, values, and themes, always acknowledging that there was a specific cinema aesthetic. May notes that in the 1980s writers began to explore more philosophical implications of the cinema experience in terms of art and human consciousness. They were "discerning the holy within the real" (May 1997: 29). The value of this approach is that it respects the distinctive "language" of cinema without imposing any Christian perspective. One of the consequences, however, is that it also moves the discussion to what is, unfortunately (and sometimes derogatorily), referred to as "art-house cinema." This approach appeals especially to Europeans and to academic film analysts around the world. The more pragmatic approach of the English empirical tradition respects theory but is more interested in the practical applications of that theory. They think that this aesthetic approach to "cinema" too often moves the discussion away from "the movies" which most audiences watch.

The role of OCIC/SIGNIS

As explained earlier, OCIC, L'Organisation Catholique Internationale du Cinéma, was established in 1928. The Second World War prevented any growth in the organization. However, after the war, the president, Abbé Brouhée, suddenly died and the secretary general, Father Jean Bernard, who had recuperated from his years in Dachau, succeeded in 1947. He was to remain president for twenty-five years. During his time in office, he consolidated the organization in Europe and extended the activities of OCIC to participation in film festival juries.

The new juries meant that criteria had to be established for assessing films for awards. The basic criteria were: quality filmmaking and positive values in harmony with the Gospel message. One early criterion was that a film coming from a communist country could not win an award but soon the films from Eastern Europe challenged that criterion and it was dropped. Because the criteria were determined in Europe, there was a more open approach to the films than in the United States, where evaluations were influenced by the Legion of Decency classifications and the need to state briefly and explicitly the nature of offending sequences. This came to a head in the controversy over *Teorema* in 1969 and the need for clarifying the ways to assess a film morally.

Father Bernard was able to finish his presidency with OCIC once more in good standing in the Church. His successor, Monsignor Lucien Labelle, from Montreal, was an administrator and consolidated the workings of the organization. It was during his presidency that OCIC joined with the Protestant organization Interfilm to form ecumenical juries. The first was in Locarno in 1973 (Zanussi's *Illumination* won the award) and the second in Cannes in 1974 (with the prize going to Fassbinder's *Fear Eats the Soul*). This collaboration developed over the subsequent thirty years with thirteen ecumenical juries by 2007, the most recent being established in 2007 at the Golden Apricot Festival in Yerevan, Armenia.

Even though Protestant members of the juries had differing theologies from the Catholic members, there has been little difficulty in coming to mutually satisfying decisions. There is often more difficulty in discussions because of quite different cultural traditions irrespective of church affiliation. For example, jurors from the English-speaking tradition sometimes have difficulty with the narratives, storytelling, and pace of films from Eastern Europe.

At this time bonds strengthened between OCIC and Unda (the International Catholic Organization for Radio and Television). Another 1970s development was the emphasis on small media and grassroots media (like street theatre in India). Video production and distribution was about to become commonplace and discussions were held about which organizations took responsibility for the different media. Unda took on video production but video distribution went to OCIC. By 1980, especially through the efforts of Father Ambros Eichenberger OP, vice-president of OCIC, who had been able to extend membership to Asian countries, Africa and the Pacific, a joint assembly was held in Manila. During the 1980s, with Father Eichenberger as president, there was much discussion and both enthusiasm and hesitation about the two associations merging. This continued into the 1990s, especially driven by the new secretary general of OCIC, Robert Molhant, who worked in the post from 1979 to 2005. Eventually, a straw vote was taken at the OCIC and Unda assemblies in Prague 1994. The result was against a merger.

However, the realities of cross-media work and the economies of having two Catholic audiovisual organizations (the Catholic Union of the Press opted for its own separate identity) led to negotiations during 1995–7. The two boards voted that the organizations should merge. This was ratified almost unanimously at the assemblies held in Montreal in 1998.

In 2006, Robert Molhant, who had been so active a man of initiatives and organization, reflected on his years as secretary general and the directions of OCIC under the three presidents he served with. The first was Ambros Eichenberger, a German Swiss Dominican priest, president from 1980 to 1990. He was a journalist as well as a film scholar. He broadened the horizons of OCIC beyond Europe to Asia, Africa, and the Pacific. He also supported filmmakers in the Eastern bloc. His successor, Fr. Henk Hoekstra, a Dutch Carmelite priest, president from 1990 to 1998, was a media lecturer but had a strong interest in the spirituality dimensions of cinema and contributed to manuals for seminaries in Africa as well as materials for cinema and spirituality in Latin America. He was succeeded by Peter Malone, an Australian Missionary of the Sacred Heart priest, president from 1998 to 2001. He moved OCIC into consideration of mainstream cinema along with art-house cinema and was concerned with the developments in classifications and consumer advice rather than censorship as well as the pastoral dimensions of moviegoing and discovering the values in the wide gamut of films. Each of these men contributed a chapter to John May's *New Images of Religious Film* and their perspectives there illustrate what they contributed to the life of OCIC. Ambros Eichenberger wrote on "Approaches to Film Criticism" (May 1997: 3–16), Henk Hoekstra on "Film Education in a Christian Perspective: Some Contemporary Approaches" (181–96), and Peter Malone on "Jesus on our Screens" (57–71).

Peter Malone and the OCIC Board inherited the OCIC and Unda decision to merge. For three years, the executives of both organizations, the joint boards, and the world membership followed a plan and a timeline to develop aims and objectives, structures and memberships, finances and statutes so that in November 2001, the two organizations did merge, forming SIGNIS, the World Catholic Association for Communication. SIGNIS is not an acronym. Anyone who has worked with an international group will know that acronyms are almost impossible because of the placement of nouns and adjectives and perceived verbal infelicities! It seems *signum* is Thai for breast. Eastern Europeans did not want any name with "Com" in it. SIGNIS arose from a slip of the white-board pen as Robert Molhant wrote up the potential names and, with Sign and the Latin word for fire in mind (*ignis*), he wrote SIGNIS. SIGNIS became the name of the organization, and Peter Malone was elected its first president (2001–5).

This meant that cinema took its place amongst all the SIGNIS priorities: radio, television, video production, IT, media education, and media advocacy. The cinema desk continues with Peter Malone and Guido Convents, an expert in African cinema, who has worked for OCIC and SIGNIS since 1987.

The Catholic Church, OCIC/SIGNIS, and film festival juries

A significant way of assessing the Catholic approach to cinema is to look at the sixty years of its presence in film festivals including the "A list" festivals (e.g., Cannes, Berlin, Venice, Montreal, San Sebastian, Karlovy Vary, Locarno), the middle list of festivals (e.g., Mannheim, Fribourg, Amiens), and emerging festivals (e.g., Seville, Las Palmas, Bratislava). There are many Latin American juries in such cities as Buenos Aires, Havana, and Quito. SIGNIS is present in the African film festival of Fespaco (in Ougadougou, Burkina Faso), in Zanzibar, in Hong Kong, and in Dhaka, Bangladesh. SIGNIS collaborates with Muslim members at the Fajr Festival in Tehran and in an interfaith jury in Brisbane, Australia. Significantly, there is no SIGNIS jury in the United States. However, the Catholic Academy of Communication Arts Professionals, the US branch of SIGNIS International, has been making its own film awards, the Gabriels, since 2001. The large Los Angeles-based association Catholics in Media also makes annual film awards. Many offices have been making national cinema awards for a long time, including Japan, Taiwan, Canada, India, and Australia. There have been no ecumenical juries in Italy, Spain, or the Latin American countries. With the dominance of Catholicism in these countries, there has been little felt need for ecumenical collaboration.

An important part of recovering cinema dynamism in Europe after the Second World War was the establishing of world festivals of cinema. Before the outbreak of the war, Venice had hosted a festival but it was strongly influenced by Mussolini's fascism. Venice was renewed after the war but a new venue for a new festival was needed. The decision was for southern France and Cannes. Festivals increased in number during the 1950s with Berlin, Melbourne, and San Sebastian. They have been increasing, as they say, exponentially, and continue to do so at this moment.

With Father Jean Bernard as president of the reestablished OCIC and with the vision of Andrei Ruszowski, OCIC dialogued with festival authorities and began to be accepted as putting forward autonomous juries. The other group to do this was FIPRESCI (the International Federation of Film Critics). In recent years, SIGNIS and FIPRESCI have been hosting several joint awards functions.

The first OCIC jury, in Venice 1948, made its awards to two American films, John Ford's *The Fugitive* (based on Graham Greene's novel *The Power and the Glory*) and Fred Zinnemann's moving postwar drama *The Search*. The first OCIC jury was established in Cannes in 1952, in Berlin in 1953. The complete list of OCIC and SIGNIS awards is available on the SIGNIS website and most cinema buffs have been impressed with the quality of so many of the films chosen for awards. Many of them are still regarded as classics; for example, awards from the 1950s include *La strada* (1954), *On the Waterfront* (1954), *Pather Panchali* (1955), *Twelve Angry Men* (1957), *The Nights of Cabiria* (1957), and *He Who Must Die* (1957). It can be noted that these films are not merely "nice" films. They explore the depths of human experience and are not afraid of presenting evil and the need for redemption.

As mentioned in the prologue to this chapter, trouble struck after twenty years, in 1968–9, with the award to *Teorema* (1968) followed by *Midnight Cowboy* (1969). With Vatican complaints, including some from Pope Paul VI, the issues took some time and much discussion to resolve (Bonneville 1998: 114–30).

The *Teorema* problems raised a question with which many of the Catholic writers were grappling at that time. It is not sufficient merely to focus on "what" is presented and be alarmed if issues of grave and scandalous morality are the subject of a film. After all, if that criterion were applied, there are large chunks of the Jewish scriptures that would have to be excised. The important question is the "how" question: how are these issues presented? Vile subjects need not be presented vilely.

It has long been part of Catholic theology that there are criteria for serious, "mortal," sins. For a person to commit a mortal sin, it not only must be a serious, grave matter, but what is required is a full knowledge and understanding of what is being done as well as a full consent of a will that is not impaired by any impediment. This is required pastoral practice for a priest hearing confessions. There is some parallel in the requirements for a valid consent in marriage or for ordination, that there be no fear or force in the making of the commitment. These are examples of the "how" question that must be answered to properly assess the morality of a situation or a film.

This requires what might be called a "delicacy of sensitivity" (parallel with Catholic moral theology's "delicacy of conscience") in assessing the moral perspective of the film. There is a great need to remember that the film is not complete until the final credits have rolled. But, along with the fine-tuning of a delicate sensibility, there is a need for a "robust" sensitivity which does not wilt in the face of the evils and suffering in our world. A delicate sensitivity must not be fragile or it will be easily shattered. At the same time, a robust sensitivity cannot become crass, or it will entail a loss of sensitivity which possesses little or no capacity for moral discernment. Government offices for classification, alert to these nuances, have been relying in recent decades on norms which are based on current acceptable (though fluid) community standards.

The crisis of 1968 led to a fuller awareness of moral sensibility concerning films. This was absorbed into the approach to judging films for OCIC/SIGNIS/ecumenical awards. For ecumenical juries, half the members are nominated by Interfilm, half by OCIC/SIGNIS. Presidency of the jury is taken in turns by the two organizations. Events associated with the ecumenical juries have developed over the years. In Cannes, there is a "Stand of the Ecumenical Jury" in the Festival Market. There is separate worship on the Sunday followed by a group aperitif in the street. At times there have been joint press conferences and round-table discussions. There is always an Ecumenical Prayer Service open to the festival and to all denominations in Cannes. There are also Ecumenical Services in Berlin and in Locarno. Ecumenical dialogue in the context of cinema, the arts, and imagination leads to friendship and meeting of minds according to the particular denominational traditions.

There were no recorded jury problems during the 1970s or the 1980s, but problems resurfaced beginning in the 1990s. Venice seems to have a historical role in raising controversy. In 1993, the vote for the award was between Kieślowski's *Three Colours: Blue* and Australian Rolf de Heer's *Bad Boy Bubby*. An Italian member of the jury considered *Bad Boy Bubby* unworthy of consideration and complained to the festival directors that it was "unethical and beastly." With the vote, however, the prize went to *Blue* and a commendation to *Bubby*. Difficulties in discussion occurred in Venice in the first half of the 1990s with winners *Daens* (1992) (about a nineteenth-century worker priest), *Before the Rain* (1994) (including a Balkans' conflict setting), and Abel Ferrara's gangster film *The Funeral* (1996).

The 1993 theological discussions sponsored by the Gregorian University in Rome were held at Cavaletti. Another of Ferrara's films, *Bad Lieutenant* (1992), was the subject of debate (as was *Bad Boy Bubby*). A useful term was introduced to explain why approval could be given to these films. The term came from the opening of Psalm 130, "De Profundis" (used by Oscar Wilde for his poem-letter of the same name): "Out of the Depths I cry to you, O Lord. Lord, hear my voice." A *De Profundis* film shows the human condition in all its ugliness and desperation: men and women crying out in agony without knowing whether anyone, human or divine, can hear their voices. We know that life is a search for God and that many search in byways rather than highways and find themselves, not infrequently, in dead ends. The portrayal of these searches may be ugly, but they are still searches for the transcendent and for God. A question was raised whether awards to these films would scandalize "the faithful." As too many Hollywood screenplays say, "That's a chance we'll just have to take."

In more recent years, especially with television series and soap opera dramas, SIGNIS has had to look at many more films which we might describe as popular and "surface-oriented." They make us realize that God is not only sought out of the depths but also out of the shallows of life. This means appreciation of not only *De Profundis*, "Out of the Depths" films, but also what one might call, "Out of the Shallows" films. These discussions have stood juries in good stead since, in such decisions as Cannes 1999 with Almodóvar's *All About My Mother* receiving the Ecumenical Prize and in Venice 2002 with the Korean film *Oasis* winning the SIGNIS Prize.

The number of SIGNIS juries has increased in recent years. Many festivals have found they have severe budget restraints so new juries tend to have only three members and new ecumenical juries consist of an Interfilm member, a SIGNIS member, and a third juror from the host country.

In 2002, after a delegation from the Iranian government and film industry visited the Vatican, an invitation was extended for Catholics to attend the Fajr Film Festival in Tehran. Peter Malone, as president of SIGNIS, represented the Church. The welcome was so cordial that he proposed an interfaith jury with two Muslims and two Catholics to award prizes to the Iranian films in competition. The proposal was quickly accepted and SIGNIS' first interfaith jury was established (soon followed by another in Brisbane where there is always a SIGNIS member and two members from any other faith). The year 2008 saw the first interfaith jury in Dhaka.

Another feature of festivals today is an increasing number dedicated to spirituality or with a significant section on Spirituality Cinema. The Religion Today festival based in Trento, Italy, which has traveled as far afield as Tunis, Jerusalem, São Paulo, and Dhaka, was a pioneer in 1997. The Infinity Spirituality Festival opened in Alba, Italy, in 2002. Fajr also set up a Spirituality Cinema section for its festival in 2005 with an international jury which has included directors Krzysztof Zanussi, Volker Schlöndorff, and Agnieszka Holland.

OCIC and SIGNIS have long held that the organization should be a bridge between the Catholic Church and the professional world of cinema. The acceptance by the major festivals of juries, the repute of the jurors, and the quality of the awards has given the Church greater credibility. Another bridge in Latin America is SIGNIS giving, since 1998, yearly post-production monetary awards to Latin American directors (three $30,000 awards to features, fiction, or documentary, and $10,000 to a short film). The festivals in Toulouse and San Sebastian then feature these films.

Response to controversies

One way of gauging the Catholic attitude toward cinema since 1967 is to look at sample controversies and how the Church responded. Mention has been made already of the response to *The Passion of the Christ* (2004) and *The Da Vinci Code* (2006).

On the whole Catholics did not take to the streets in the past, although Cardinal Spellman asked the faithful to rally round and go out to publicly protest *The French Line* (1954, with Jane Russell) and the film version of Tennessee Williams' *Baby Doll* (1957). Ordinarily, the reaction in the United States was to impose an Objectionable or a Condemned rating from the Legion of Decency. (At the beginning some bishops imposed a penalty of mortal sin on those who attended some nominated films.)

Monty Python's *Life of Brian* (1979) was an interesting case. The Python team has gone on record many times to say that they were not intending a blasphemous mockery of the Gospels. They defended the film as a spoof of biblical and costume movie epics against public attacks by Malcolm Muggeridge and Anglican bishop Mervyn Stockwood. The film could not be shown on British television until 1999.

However, the main source of dissatisfaction and protest against *Life of Brian* came from North America. The US bishops conference gave it an O, Offensive rating, with the short review:

☐ **Life of Brian** – Monty Python movie about a hapless fellow named Brian, a contemporary of Jesus, who is mistaken for the Messiah and eventually crucified by the Romans. The nihilistic, anything-for-laughs thrust of director Terry Jones's comedy deliberately exploits much that is sacred to Christian and Jewish religious tradition. Especially offensive is the mocking parody of the crucifixion scene (O). (USCCB 1979)

Meanwhile, in Australia, responding to a few Catholic protests, the director of the Australian Catholic Film Office, Father Fred Chamberlin, went to see the film and reported that he "laughed unashamedly." This was the reaction of most Australian Catholics. This seems to indicate that some "moral stances" are really "sensibility stances," even differences in senses of humor, and that it is dangerous to generalize about Catholic responses to particular films.

This was much more evident in the late 1980s with the release of Martin Scorsese's *The Last Temptation of Christ* (1988). American evangelical indignation was rife before anyone had seen the film. Demonstrations were organized, including one to Universal Studios in Hollywood to petition the burning of the negative (with, it is said, 25,000 protestors traveling in 15,000 cars all of which parked – and paid – in the Universal lot).

Many Catholic groups on hearing the reports of these protests and vigorous denunciations of the film followed suit, including some Vatican offices. A wave of anger spread over the northern hemisphere before the release of the film. The US bishops conference short review read:

☐ **Last Temptation of Christ, The** – Deeply flawed screen adaptation of the Nikos Kazantzakis novel probing the mystery of the human nature of Jesus Christ, the Son of God, fails because of artistic inadequacy rather than anti-religious bias. Director Martin Scorsese's wrong-headed insistence on gore and brutality, as well as a preoccupation with sexual rather than spiritual love, is compounded by screenwriter Paul Schrader's muddled script, shallow characterizations and flat dialogue delivered woodenly by William Dafoe in the title role. Excessively graphic violence, several sexually explicit scenes and some incidental nudity (O). (USCCB 1988)

To return to the other side of the world again. The head of the Australian Office of Classification of Film and Literature was a Catholic. In view of the protests, he suggested that the distributors offer screenings of *Last Temptation* to representatives of all the churches in each state before the office gave it a classification and to gauge whether the churches thought the film "blasphemous." Only one churchman, a sponsor of Mary Whitehouse's Festival of Light, considered the film blasphemous. The Catholic Church participated and contributed balanced comment. The film received an M (15+) classification except for Queensland where it received an R (Restricted, 18+) and the film was calmly screened, reviewed, and attended, the only picketers being a group of extreme Greek Orthodox communities. This provided an object lesson in how to deal more circumspectly with controversy – after the film was actually viewed.

The distribution of *Priest* (1995) fared well in most countries. The main difficulties were in the United States and the Philippines (where Cardinal Sin was advised to make a public condemnation, sight unseen). At the time of its screening at the 1994 London Festival, the Catholic writer, Jimmy McGovern, met with church representatives to discuss the film and its issues. After its screening in Panorama at the 1995

Berlin Film Festival, OCIC president Henk Hoekstra discussed the film with the Catholic members of the ecumenical jury who wrote an OCIC statement to help Catholics respond to the issues of priesthood, celibacy, sexual orientation, child abuse, and the confidentiality of the seal of the confessional. It was read out by the German media bishop at the Ecumenical Service during the festival. A number of bishops conferences, especially in Europe, held screenings and the film was seen and fruitfully discussed.

The film was released provocatively in the US during Lent and bombs were exploded in some New Jersey cinemas. Cardinal O'Connor said that he took advice from experts and declared that it was one of the worst films that "had ever rotted on the silver screen."

Despite the pressure of protests, the US bishops conference reviewer tried to offer a balanced guide for audiences, this time not using the O Offensive classification but rather the A IV, Unobjectionable for Adults with Reservations:

> ☐ **Priest** – Flawed British drama probes the conflict between religious ideals and human frailties in a story set in a working-class Catholic parish where a young curate tries to live a life of celibacy, yet initiates several homosexual encounters, partly out of torment at his helplessness in stopping a case of incest revealed in confession. Director Antonia Bird provides a credible picture of a lonely priest in a busy parish, though its emphasis on his struggles with his own sexuality strangely lacks any notion of sin and the ambiguous ending in an emotionally powerful scene of reconciliation leaves matters unresolved. Serious treatment of a very troubling subject, depictions of homosexual acts and occasional crude language (A–IV). (USCCB 1995)

Quoting the US classification reviews indicates that year by year Catholic commentators have been trying to work with a keener delicacy of sensitivity toward the films themselves and to the perceived need for guidance of consumers. However, an indication that problems are perennial was the reaction to the classification given to *Brokeback Mountain* (2005). The film was given an L (Limited) classification (the revamped A IV) but a vitriolic website campaign and some vicious attacks on the reviewer led to an official change to the classification, moving it to O (Offensive).

The American situation seems to be quite different from much of the rest of the world. At the end of 2007, William Donohue of the Catholic League for Civil and Religious Rights, which has targeted films for years, especially via the media and chat shows which ensures controversy and publicity, set the League's sights on the film version of Philip Pullman's *The Golden Compass*. Months before the release of the film, the League campaigned on its website against the dangers of Pullman's atheistic approach and his alleged desire to kill God. They published a booklet, "*The Golden Compass*: Agenda Unmasked," distributing it extensively through American parishes and schools and beyond. Despite reassurances that the film was "toned down," William Donohue complained that the film would lead children to read the books, "a recipe for atheism." The booklet and the numerous emails of warning sent worldwide alarmed many Catholics and Christians. This kind of scaremongering crusade finds little official favor in the Catholic Church except when unsolicited material is taken on face value. This is polemic which reinforces stances rather than a dialogue which seeks some meeting of minds and hearts. It also indicates an attitude that adult Catholics are not able to deal intelligently with challenges to their faith and may be easily prone to lose it.

A final example from 2002, from the Philippines. In 2000, the bishops conference's Office for Women was commissioned to set up a church classifications body. This was well prepared by seminars and training, mainly for women reviewers, through a group called CINEMA (Catholic Initiative for Enlightened Cinema Appreciation). At first mocked by the press as a Catholic pressure group, CINEMA soon won respect for its thoughtful reviews and classifications. The local Filippino film *Toro* (2000) (released in the Philippines as *Live Show*), a film about young Filipinos involved in live sex acts for customers and parties, was screened at the Berlin Film Festival in 2000 with the director stating that his film would be prohibited from being screened at home by the Church. In 2001 it was released amid strong protest. The president of the Philippines, Gloria Arroyo, withdrew the film from theatrical distribution (but not from video distribution). CINEMA had reviewed the film, classified it for a 21+ audience, and noted its angry moral perspective about sexual abuse in the Philippines. The CINEMA group was immediately condemned by government aides and insulted by many clergy. The bishop in charge advised quietly waiting out the crisis. He was right. CINEMA looked at the film again and, despite a number of the group finding the film distasteful, reaffirmed their classification. In fact, CINEMA survived and some of the protestors were later discredited. This is not to say that *Live Show* was essential viewing, but it indicates that a more mature approach to film is more constructive than mere vociferous crusade and polemic.

Directions

In recent decades, the Catholic hierarchy and clergy have been the subject of strong criticism in their handling of sexual abuse cases by clergy and by employees of Catholic institutions. This has undermined the credibility of the Church and the Gospel message in many quarters. There has been criticism of lack of compassion on the part of the Church, of the handling of the transfer of offending priests, and cover-up of scandals. While other English-speaking countries had to face this in the 1990s, it was only in 2002 that the crisis reached the headlines in the United States.

This has become the subject of a number of films. Already in 1990, *Judgment* was aired on cable television. It dramatized a 1980s case in Louisiana. More recently, Showtime produced a drama based on the situation in Boston with Father John Geoghan, *Our Fathers* (2005), and how Cardinal Bernard Law handled the investigation. *Deliver Us from Evil* was a 2006 Oscar-nominated documentary on Father Oliver O'Grady and his abuse in California. There were fiction features coming from Ireland and the United Kingdom: *The Magdalene Sisters* (2002) and *Song for a Raggy Boy* (2003). Mexico released *The Crime of Father Amaro* (2002). This is a reality the

Catholic Church has to live with. These films can serve as a telling examination of conscience.

However, it is interesting to note a more mature approach in the presentation of Church and of clergy in contemporary features. The crises have sharpened audience critical responses but it has meant that films like *Keeping the Faith* (2001) and *Shooting Dogs* (2006) (US title: *Beyond the Gates*) have reaffirmed the strengths of the priesthood.

One of the most important trends in the Catholic Church's approach to cinema is in the process of maturing the expression of classification and consumer advice. This trend can be evaluated in the pastoral letter issued by Cardinal Roger Mahoney of Los Angeles in 1992. It is a quite comprehensive overview of an approach to film, acknowledging both the aesthetic and the moral dimensions and taking the stand that censorship for adults should be minimal while children must be ensured protection from damaging material.

Sometimes this requires a "delicacy" of sensitivity on the part of the classifier which acknowledges moral fine-tuning along with a robust realism in facing the harsher realities of human experience. Harry Forbes, director of the American Bishops Conference Office for Film and Broadcasting, rightly refers in his review of *Black Snake Moan* (2007) to "the finest of lines between what is morally objectionable and dramatically valid." This means acknowledging that there is some truth in Flannery O'Connor's remark that the approach of many Catholics to moral issues in the arts is the equivalent of a fifteen-year-old schoolgirl. The Catholic moral sense needs to develop a mature and adult delicacy and robustness of sensitivities.

Encouraging signs include intellectual, spiritual, and pastoral developments. Intellectually, the increasing number of courses in film studies in Catholic universities and colleges leads to a cinema-literate group which can discuss and publish on religious and cinema questions. Publishers' lists have an increasing number of religion and faith-oriented books. The present author edited *Through a Catholic Lens: Religious Perspectives of Nineteen Film Directors from around the World*, which included studies of directors who have a Catholic background and subtext to the films they write and direct. Directors included Buñuel, Almodóvar, Malle, Arcand, and, from the United States, directors as different as John Sayles, Mel Gibson, and Kevin Smith. Since 1995, Interfilm and OCIC/SIGNIS have held a number of ecumenical conferences on cinema, celebrating the centenary of cinema and, most recently in Edinburgh, 2007, "Peacemaking, Conflict and Reconciliation in Film." The Edinburgh conference drew fifty participants from twenty-three different countries, religious, academics, producers, and students.

Spiritually, the ecumenical dimension has been developed in the United States, especially with such events as the annual City of Angels Festival which brings Christians from all churches together to watch films on a set theme ("The Road Journey," "The Work of the Spirit," "Myths and Heroes," "And Justice for ... All?"), to discuss them and to explore the issue of what Catholics can learn from Protestants and Protestants from Catholics in terms of film, faith, words, and images, that is, incarnational theology. A 2006 panel question was "Are horror films Catholic?" This elicited the response that classic horror films are.

Books and articles on cinema and spirituality are proliferating as are websites, with European writing tending toward the theoretical, knowledge for its own sake, while American writing is more interested in the practical and pragmatic applications. A project initiated by German Hans Jüergen Feulner examines the dramatizing of rituals (primarily but not exclusively Christian) in films both popular and art-house, which holds more appeal for European sensibilities.

Pastorally, the American practical approach to cinema and spirituality has led to many books being written by Catholics and Protestants alike, particularly linking popular films to the Creed, to Pauline themes, to the suffering and death of Jesus, illustrating the *Spiritual Exercises* of St. Ignatius, or material for prayer, retreats, and for sermons, like *Finding God in the Dark* by John Pungente and Monty Williams, and Richard Leonard's *Movies that Matter*. In the Catholic tradition, there is the *Lights Camera Faith* series by Peter Malone and Rose Pacatte which offers dialogue between a film and the liturgical readings for the three-yearly cycles as well as for the Ten Commandments and the Beatitudes and Deadly Sins. These books offer opportunities for film and film-clip watching in homes, classrooms, groups, and in liturgy preparation.

Other publicized activities include the American National Film Retreat and, in Romania since 2005, a conference by SIGNIS with UNICEF collaboration, called "Facing Children," an opportunity to reflect on children's rights through feature and documentary film and discussion, giving a "face to the faceless."

Any current report on the approach of the Catholic Church to cinema will be only an interim report. This present interim report comes at a time of positive engagement of the Church with cinema.

Bibliography

Bonneville, L. (1998) *Soixante-dix ans au service du cinéma et de l'audiovisuel*, Quebec: Fides.

Eilers, F.-J. (1993) *Church and Social Communication: Basic Documents*, Manila: Logos.

Johnston, R. (2000) *Reel Spirituality: Theology and Film in Dialogue*, Grand Rapids, MI: Baker Academic.

Leonard, R. (2006), *Movies that Matter*, Chicago: Loyola Press.

Lynch, W. (1960) *The Image Industries*, New York: Sheed & Ward.

—— (2004) *Christ and Apollo: The Dimensions of the Literary Imagination*, Wilmington, DE: ISI Books.

Malone, P. and Pacatte, R. (2001–8) *Lights, Camera . . . Faith! A Movie Lectionary, Cycles A, B, C; The Ten Commandments; Beatitudes and Deadly Sins*, Boston: Pauline Media.

May, J. (1997) *New Images of Religious Film*, Kansas City: Sheed & Ward

Medved, M. (1992) *Hollywood vs. America: Popular Culture and the War on Traditional Values*, San Francisco: Harper Collins.

Molhant, R. (2000) *Catholics in the Cinema: A Strange History of Belief and Passion, Beginnings: 1895–1935*, Brussels: OCIC.

Pungente, J. and Williams, M. (2005) *Finding God in the Dark*, Boston: Pauline Media.

United States Conference of Catholic Bishops, Office for Film and Broadcasting, Archived Movie Reviews. *Life of Brian* (1979). Online. Available HTTP: <http://www.usccb.org/movies/l/lifeofbrian1979.shtml> (accessed 31 August 2008).

—— *The Last Temptation of Christ* (1988). Online. Available HTTP: <http://www.usccb.org/movies/l/lasttemptationofchristthe1988.shtml> (accessed 31 August 2008).

—— *Priest* (1995). Online. Available HTTP: <http://www.usccb.org/movies/p/priest1995.shtml> (accessed 8/31/08).

Filmography

All About My Mother (1999, dir. P. Almodóvar)
Amen (2002, dir. C. Gavras)
The Apartment (1960, dir. W. Wilder)
Baby Doll (1957, dir. E. Kazan)
Bad Boy Bubby (1993, dir. R. de Heer)
Bad Lieutenant (1992, dir. A. Ferrara)
Becket (1964, dir. P. Glenville)
Before the Rain (1994, dir. M. Manchevski)
Black Snake Moan (2007, dir. C. Brewer)
Brokeback Mountain (2005, dir. A. Lee)
The Cardinal (1963, dir. O. Preminger)
The Chronicles of Narnia: The Lion, the Witch and the Wardrobe (2005, dir. A. Adamson)
El crimen del Padre Amaro (2002, dir. C. Carrera)
The Da Vinci Code (2006, dir. R. Howard)
Daens (1992, dir. S. Coninx)
Deliver Us from Evil (2006, dir. A. Berg)
Diary of a Country Priest (1950, dir. R. Bresson)
Elizabeth: The Golden Age (2007, dir. S. Kapur)
The Emperor's Club (2002, dir. M. Hoffman)
The Exorcism of Emily Rose (2005, dir. S. Derrickson)
Fear Eats the Soul (1974, dir. R. Fassbinder)
The French Line (1954, dir. L. Bacon)
The Fugitive (1948, dir. J. Ford)
The Funeral (1996, dir. A. Ferrara)
Going My Way (1944, dir. L. McCarey)
The Golden Compass (2007, dir. C. Weitz)
The Gospel According to St. Matthew (1964, dir. P. Pasolini)
He Who Must Die (1957, dir J. Dassin)
Hurry Sundown (1966, dir. O. Preminger)
Illumination (1973, dir. K. Zanussi)
Jesus (1999, dir. R. Young)
Judgment (1990, dir. T. Topor)
Keeping the Faith (2001, dir. E. Norton)
The King of Kings (1927, dir. C. DeMille)
Kingdom of Heaven (2005, dir. R. Scott)
Kiss Me Stupid (1964, dir. W. Wilder)
The Last Temptation of Christ (1988, dir. M. Scorsese)
Life of Brian (1979, dir. T. Jones)
The Magdalene Sisters (2002, dir. P. Mullan)
Midnight Cowboy (1969, dir. J. Schlesinger)
The Moon is Blue (1953, dir. O. Preminger)
The Nativity Story (2006, dir. C. Hardwicke)
Der Neunte Tag (2004, dir. V. Schlöndorff)
The Nights of Cabiria (1957, dir. F. Fellini)
Oasis (2002, dir C. Lee)
O Brother Where Art Thou (2000, dir. J. and E. Coen)
On the Waterfront (1954, dir. E. Kazan)
Our Fathers (2005, dir. D. Curtis)
Pan Tadeusz (1999, dir. A. Wajda)
The Passion of the Christ (2004, dir. M. Gibson)
The Passion of Joan of Arc (1928, dir. C. Dreyer)
Pather Panchali (1955, dir. S. Ray)

The Pawnbroker (1964, dir. S. Lumet)
Pope John Paul II (2005, dir. J. Harrison)
Priest (1995, dir. A. Bird)
Quo Vadis? (2001, dir. J. Kawalerowicz)
The Search (1948, dir. F. Zinnemann)
Shooting Dogs (*Beyond the Gates*) (2006, dir. M. C. Jones)
Song for a Raggy Boy (2003, dir. A. Walsh)
La stanza del figlio (2001, dir. N. Moretti)
La strada (1954, dir. F. Fellini)
Teorema (1968, dir. P. Pasolini)
Three Colours trilogy (1993, 1994, dir. K. Kieślowski)
Through a Glass Darkly (1961, dir. I. Bergman)
Toro (*Live Show*) (2000, dir. J. Reyes)
Twelve Angry Men (1957, dir. S. Lumet)
2001: A Space Odyssey (1968, dir. S. Kubrick)
La vita è bella (1997, dir. R. Benigni)
Who's Afraid of Virginia Woolf? (1966, dir. M. Nichols)
Wings of Desire (1987, dir. W. Wenders)

Further reading

Black, G. (1994) *Hollywood Censored: Morality Codes, Catholics, and the Movies*, Cambridge: Cambridge University Press.

Blake, R. (2000) *Afterimage: The Indelible Catholic Imagination of Six American Filmmakers*, Chicago: Loyola.

Keyser, L. and Keyser, B. (1984) *Hollywood and the Catholic Church: The Image of Roman Catholicism in American Movies*, Chicago: Loyola.

Lyden, J. (2003) *Film as Religion: Myths, Morals, and Rituals*, New York: New York University.

Malone, P. (ed.) (2007) *Through a Catholic Lens: Religious Perspectives of Nineteen Film Directors from around the World*, New York: Rowman and Littlefield.

—— (2008) *Film and Faith*, Manila: Communications Foundation for Asia.

—— (2009). *Film, Faith and Church*, Manila: Communications Foundation for Asia.

—— (2009). "Catholicism and Cinema,". in W. Blizek (ed.) *Companion to Religion and Film*, New York: Continuum Press.

Molhant, R. (2000) *OCIC Awards at Film Festivals and Grand Prix*, Brussels: OCIC.

Pacatte, Rose (2007) "Shaping Morals, Shifting Views: Have the Rating Systems Influenced How (Christian) America Sees Movies?," in R. Johnston (ed.) *Reframing Theology and Film*, Grand Rapids, MI: Baker Academic.

Skinner, J. (1993) *The Cross and the Cinema: The Legion of Decency and the National Catholic Office for Motion Pictures, 1933–1970*, Westport, CT: Praeger

Walsh, F. (1996) *Sin and Censorship: The Catholic Church and the Motion Picture Industry*, New Haven and London: Yale University Press.

4
MODERN PROTESTANT APPROACHES TO FILM (1960 TO THE PRESENT)

Bryan Stone

The story of Protestantism and its relationship to film is as complex and varied as Protestantism itself. While some Protestants have been particularly cautious about or even antagonistic toward Hollywood, others have actively pursued constructive and close engagement with the film industry. Theologically, Protestant responses to film have likewise represented a range of possibilities including those that exhibit a primary concern for whether a film upholds traditional religious and moral values to more dialogical, transformative, or even sacramental approaches that seek to learn from or appropriate the insights and aesthetic vision of a film.[1] If Protestant responses to film are diverse as compared with one another, they also exhibit a tremendous diversity across time. As compared with Roman Catholicism or Eastern Orthodoxy, one might well speak in more general terms of a characteristically "Protestant" attitude that has tended to distrust the image in favor of the word. But today it is fairly difficult to identify a single, monolithic set of approaches to film that is distinctively Protestant; indeed, this earlier Protestant iconoclasm has increasingly given way to a variety of creative interactions with film and a more willing embrace of the medium in the post-Hays code era (after 1960), which is the focus of this essay.

From censorship to the ratings system

Protestants once dominated local, state, and national censorship boards and played a critical role in the creation and implementation of production codes, thereby attempting to force Hollywood to make "good" films. But Protestant institutional power began to retreat in the 1960s at the same time as major changes were being implemented in the film industry. The Hays Production Code, which closely guarded conventional morality, was abandoned in 1968 in favor of the new Motion Picture Association (MPA) film rating system, which categorized films in relation to their suitability for younger audiences as either G (general), M (mature), R (children under seventeen not admitted without parent), or X (no one under seventeen). Rather than a censorship board approving or disapproving of a film, the film industry would now regulate itself by giving advance cautionary warnings to parents and allowing them to decide what their children would see.

The Protestant Film Commission (also known as the Protestant Film Office) had been organized in 1946 and had participated in approving Hollywood film scripts under the Hays code. Throughout the 1940s and 1950s, Protestants were well aware of and often vexed by the reality that far more images of Catholic priests than Protestant clergy appeared in films. In addition to raising money for the production of religious shorts and documentaries, one of the aims of the Protestant Film Office was "to flavor Hollywood's movie output with as much Protestant salt as possible" (*Time Magazine* 1946). The Protestant Film Office, however, was closed in 1966, just prior to the closure also of the influential Catholic Legion of Decency in 1968. The Protestant Film Office was in reality the West Coast office of the Broadcasting and Film Commission (BFC) of the National Council of Churches (founded in 1950), and the work of that office would now be continued through the East Coast headquarters of the BFC, which was renamed the Communication Commission in 1975. As an ecumenical association, the National Council of Churches (NCC) was originally composed of Protestant mainline and Orthodox denominations. The NCC has been viewed with suspicion by many evangelical Protestants, who have long disagreed with what they judge to be its more liberal leanings (there exists, therefore, a corresponding federation called the National Association of Evangelicals). Through the BFC and its successor bodies, the NCC has, over the decades, tried to take a more constructive relationship to media and culture as well as a noncensorship approach in its attempts to influence film.

From its inception, the NCC focused primarily on creating and promoting Protestant television programming in the United States, but it also gave significant attention to print media, radio broadcasting, and, of course, film. It continued to offer the film studios script advisement in relation to scenes or language that were considered offensive, and in 1963 it began to give awards to filmmakers in order to educate the Church around film appreciation and discrimination, with the hope also of influencing the industry by encouraging high-quality films. In 1967, the awards were offered jointly with the National Catholic Office for Motion Pictures (Trotter 1969: 268). Though the criteria for awards were revised over the years, the following 1968 statement gives a sense for how and why the awards were given:

> The Broadcasting and Film Commission of the NCC may make awards annually to films of outstanding merit that, within the perspective of the Christian faith, also (1) portray with honesty and compassion the human condition – including human society in its cultural environment – depicting man in the tension between his attempt to realize the full potential of his humanity and his tendency to distort that humanity; and (2) portray the vitality, tragedy, humor, and variety of life in such a way as to provide entertainment value appropriate for family viewing and general audience appeal; and (3) present subject matter which, in terms of form and content, will

fire the mental, moral and existential development of youth. (Trotter 1969: 268)

Film awards were given in the categories of (1) for mature audiences, (2) for youth, and (3) for family viewing. The award given by the BFC to the controversial *The Pawnbroker* in 1965 was particularly significant and demonstrated that a new day had dawned, at least among mainline Protestants, who were increasingly interested in films that laid bare the truth about the human condition and offered serious and realistic, even if intense and gritty, portrayals of the world, rather than merely sentimental films simply because they did not offend (Berckman 1980: 297). But while the awards may have helped produce greater audience turnout for some individual films the BFC deemed superior, ultimately they were abandoned in 1973, as the industry was apparently unmotivated by the awards in rethinking its products.

Though the MPA ratings system was initiated in 1968, the movement from censorship boards to a self-regulated ratings system neither materialized overnight nor did Christians accept this shift unambiguously or without a struggle. In 1972, the BFC and the Catholic film office withdrew their endorsement of the MPA ratings system because of several perceived inadequacies. MPA leader Jack Valenti and National Association of Theater Owners representative Julian Rifkin visited the BFC, making a plea for the Commission to reendorse the ratings system. They described the previous withdrawal of endorsement as a "serious blow" to freedom in the United States and as an action that might well move society back to an era of censorship (Wall 1974b).

Their fears were not ungrounded. In the early 1970s, the Supreme Court had given censorship powers back to local authorities, and by the middle of the decade as many as two-thirds of all state legislatures were considering censorship laws for motion pictures shown in their states. Without the support of the mainline churches, it was difficult for the film industry to argue for its own self-regulation to a growing list of state legislative committees debating censorship bills (Wall 1975). What the film industry could and did do in relation to the BFC is appeal to the higher value of artistic liberty and freedom of speech since, as *Christian Century* editor James Wall put it, the suppression of freedom was "hated by Protestants almost as much as – or in some cases more than – dirty movies" (1974a). Indeed, as Lynn Schofield Clark argues, citing the work of N. J. Demerath III, whatever institutional decline we may observe in liberal Protestantism since 1960, one may nonetheless affirm its "cultural victory" in terms of widely shared values such as "individualism, freedom, pluralism, tolerance, democracy, and intellectual inquiry" (Schofield Clark 2002: 7).

While the NCC did not wish to return to censorship or give support to vigilante moral policing on the part of local and state boards, it nonetheless continued to find the MPA system woefully inadequate. William Fore, BFC executive from 1964 to 1989, argued that (1) a truly helpful and educational ratings system should evaluate films contextually to evaluate their emotional impact on young people rather than on the basis of a rigid set of guidelines that stipulate what a film can get by with so that compliance is focused on individual and isolated phrases or scenes, (2) the film industry had not done an adequate job in educating the public about the system, and

(3) compliance by local theaters was still voluntary and not uniformly administered (Wall 1974a; 1974b). Though Protestants from the BFC would not reendorse the ratings system until the reforms they sought were implemented, they committed themselves to work closely with the film industry during this period of transition. While the relationship between the film industry and the BFC varied from something more like a boxing match to that of a standoff at times, there were several points of contact that made for an ongoing constructive conversation between the two. On the one hand, the NCC rejected censorship, which meant it would have to tolerate the inadequacies of a ratings system. On the other hand, since the film industry still needed the Church's endorsement of its system, it would have to take church criticism seriously (Wall 1974b). In an October 1974 editorial, Wall summarized the Protestant position – or at least the position of many mainline Protestants – as follows: "The motion picture is an art form – admittedly commercial – and it cannot be regulated by the government as a product. It can survive and grow only in an atmosphere of freedom" (1974c).

The cinema comes "home"

By the 1980s, the rise of cable television and the easy availability of Hollywood movies through video rental stores posed new challenges and provoked new responses from Protestants. Conservative Protestants had long spoken out against the evils of television and cinema, with some denominations, like the Assemblies of God, the Church of the Nazarene, the Free Methodist Church, and the Christian Reformed Church, instructing their members to avoid attendance of the cinema altogether. But Hollywood had found new inroads into the lives and homes of Christians. The motion picture theater was now as close as the remote control.

With easier and greater availability of home movie-viewing, film purchasing, and film rental, those denominations that had once insisted on wholesale abstinence from the cinema were now forced to rethink or more fully texture their prohibitions. The dissonance, if not hypocrisy, of refusing to watch films at the cinema while watching them six months later on HBO or network television (while simultaneously building a personal video library!) finally became untenable. Some Protestant denominations, such as the Christian Reformed Church, which as far back as 1928 had warned against movie theater attendance or being employed in the industry (Romanowski 1995: 52–3), had already begun to reconsider the relationship of the Church and film. In 1964 the Christian Reformed Church appointed a committee to examine the matter and in 1966 adopted declarations on "The Church and the Film Arts." The declaration considered film a "legitimate cultural medium" rather than merely an amusement and urged discernment instead of abstinence by Christians. Its present denominational statement is typical of many conservative Protestant denominations who have adjusted their views on the cinema:

> Film is a legitimate cultural medium to be used by Christians in the fulfillment
> of the cultural mandate. They must exercise responsible, Spirit-guided, and

enlightened discrimination in the use of the film arts, rejecting the message of those products which sanction sin and exercising responsible discrimination in the use of products from broadly Christian sources.

The church must educate its members in the discriminate use of the film arts, engage in constructive critique of the film arts with the help of specialists, and cooperate with others to produce Christian films, videos, and television. It also should warn its members against products which are contrary to the Christian way of life, promote products which meet the test of biblical principles, and help members to distinguish between good and evil in movies and television programs. (Christian Reformed Church 1966)

Other conservative Protestant denominations, however, did not adjust their policies on moviegoing until much later – 1985, for example, in the case of the Church of the Nazarene. As with the Christian Reformed Church, the original Nazarene position of cinematic abstinence was not intended as a boycott – a strategy to bring about change in the film industry by applying economic pressure. It was an expression of a desire for purity and holiness of life and thereby an attempt to keep from being seduced by the world's behaviors and values. Cinema-going was a waste of time and did not edify but only entertained. It distracted from higher pursuits, dulled spiritual sensitivities, and portrayed immoral behaviors in an attractive light. *As an institution*, cinema in and of itself was objectionable: you don't go to a trashcan to find good food.

But all of this would be complicated when the line between the cinema and the home began to dissolve in the 1980s. Recognizing the futility of singling out any one particular form of media such as the cinema as especially destructive, the Church of the Nazarene now added references to other media like literature, radio, television, and eventually personal computers and the internet. It still insisted that "the most rigid safeguards be observed to keep our homes from being secularized and worldly" and urged its members to "witness against whatever trivializes or blasphemes God, as well as such evils as violence, sensuality, pornography, profanity, and the occult, as portrayed by and through the commercial entertainment industry in its many forms and to endeavor to bring about the demise of enterprises known to be the purveyors of this kind of entertainment." But the denomination could now also find itself affirming "entertainment that endorses and encourages holy living and affirms scriptural values." It even encouraged its young people to "use their gifts in media and the arts to influence positively this pervasive part of culture" (Church of the Nazarene 2005: §34.1, 50).

What we see with the Christian Reformed Church and the Church of the Nazarene is indicative of a wider change in attitude on the part of many conservative Protestants from the 1970s through the 1980s – a change paralleled decades earlier among mainline Protestants – so that by the end of the twentieth century, their posture toward film had become more a matter of discernment and media literacy rather than abstinence, while still maintaining an activist stance against particularly objectionable films or broadcasts. Evidence of this transition is to be found also in the policy changes of evangelical periodicals during these two decades (Berckman 1980; Stevens 1989). A content analysis performed by Paul Stevens on 123 motion picture reviews from 1956 through 1985 in *Christianity Today*, for example, reveals an increased attention on the part of this leading evangelical magazine to motion pictures that were not explicitly religious. That in itself signals a change in attitude. Of course, as the magazine increasingly began reviewing films not endorsable by Protestant evangelicals, the reviews became increasingly mixed. But what Stevens' study reveals is a growing interest among evangelicals in film and a shift from a position represented by a 1956 article that presented the choice of whether or not to view a film as "whether I shall support Hollywood or the kingdom of God" to a position represented by a 1984 *Christianity Today* survey which found that clergy now attended the cinema more than their members (Stevens 1989:1).

Unwilling to leave concerns about onscreen violence to the conservative right, the NCC began to raise its voice once again, holding public hearings on the subject and distributing a fifty-page report in 1985 entitled "Violence and Sexual Violence in Film, Television, Cable and Home Video" (NCC 1985). The report appealed to research demonstrating an "undeniable" correlation between media violence and aggressive behavior, and stated, "The quality of life in our society is threatened by the amount, intensity and graphic persuasiveness" of violence and sexual violence on television. The report went on to recommend mandatory ratings for programs along with descriptions of violent content in the promotion of programs. It also suggested parental controls on cable installations and separate channels rather than channels that mix general programming with R- or X-rated films (*Time Magazine* 1985).

The NCC continued to educate, advocate, and collaborate around film in the years that followed, publishing another policy statement on "Violence in Electronic Media and Film" in 1993 (NCC 1993). The statement noted the complex roots of violence but asserted the powerful role that film and television play in over-representing violence in ways that desensitize viewers and habituate them to violence as an acceptable solution to problems while simultaneously increasing the public appetite for violent entertainment. The statement also highlighted the way violence is sexualized onscreen "by rendering it pleasurable and/or by depicting an erotic payoff for the protagonists who initiate the sexual violence." As a matter of policy, the NCC again affirmed free speech and objected to government censorship as a viable solution to the problem, but pledged to work with the film industry and the government "to find ways to respect free expression while abhorring and selectively limiting media violence, the moral equivalent of a harmful substance." The NCC also committed itself to ongoing assistance with education around critical viewing and film analysis and the cultivation within Christian communities and families of media literacy. Pressing for "corporate citizenship," the NCC's strategy for working with the media and film industries included:

(1) Ongoing dialogue with media management and professional media practitioners.
(2) Bringing together those who manage the media and the consumers who receive their products.

(3) Reinforcing a voluntary approach for protecting children from adult material, through the film industry rating board of the Motion Picture Association of America (MPAA).

(4) Publicizing advertisers of specific programs that depict significant values of the religious community.

(5) Encouraging investors, media management, and practicing media professionals to acknowledge their responsibility for ameliorating the climate of violence and for developing alternatives to gratuitous violence. (NCC 1993)

Protests and boycotts

With the end of censorship and the arrival of the new ratings system, Christians of all stripes increasingly found themselves resorting to other forms of influence where film was concerned. Given the loss of formal influence and control over the film industry enjoyed prior to 1960, Protestants turned to three other avenues of influence where they could still make a difference: (1) the production of their own films and the creation of their own production companies, (2) providing guidance around movie-viewing for fellow Christians, whether in the form of movie reviews, or a growing number of books, articles, journals, and websites that consider film from a variety of theological perspectives, written for both lay and scholarly audiences, and (3) activism in the form of organized protests, boycotts, or other means of economic and cultural pressure, especially in the case of controversial individual films.

Beginning with the third of these, a few examples taken from the post-Hays code era may illuminate typical Protestant concerns about film while also revealing some of the important differences among Protestants when it comes not only to film but to the larger question of the Church's relationship to culture: *The Last Temptation of Christ* (Martin Scorsese, 1988) and *Dogma* (Kevin Smith, 1999).

More than any other film to that point, Martin Scorsese's *The Last Temptation of Christ* in 1988 produced public debate and controversy around the treatment of the sacred on screen. Though the film was based not on the New Testament Gospels but on Nikos Kazantzakis' fictional exploration of "the eternal spiritual conflict" between the spirit and the flesh in his book by the same title, the portrayal of Jesus as human and as tempted sexually – especially in a dream sequence while hanging on the cross – was too much for many religious groups to tolerate. Not only did important differences surface between conservatives and liberals within Protestantism in response to Scorsese's picture, the film also revealed deep divides within American society and engendered conflict and even hatred between religious conservatives who protested the film and more liberal progressives, both religious and secular, who defended it (Riley 2003).

In 1983, Scorsese had reached an agreement with Paramount Studios to begin production of the film. Almost immediately upon the news of the deal becoming public, Christian activists began to organize against it. The controversy would continue to rage for the next five years leading up to its release in 1988 and thereafter.

The Moral Majority, headed by Jerry Falwell; Campus Crusade, led by Bill Bright; the Evangelical Sisterhood, a group of Protestant women; and other fundamentalist groups solicited letters from their constituencies against the film so that Paramount was receiving 5,000 letters a week by the end of the year asking that the film not be made (Riley 2003: 13). Paramount responded by convening a group of biblical scholars and theologians to advise on the film. Though the group noted the risks in producing the film, they concluded that the film "deserved to be made" (Baugh 1997: 51). Protests from religious activists only intensified and Paramount dropped the project less than a month before filming was to begin. MCA-Universal picked up the project in 1987 and shooting began while pressure continued to escalate from Catholics and Protestant evangelicals to shelve the project altogether.

When the film was finally released in 1988, the controversy that ensued was unlike anything the film industry had ever experienced. Protestant fundamentalists, led by people like Donald Wildmon of the American Family Association who had warned MCA-Universal that releasing the film would be committing "financial suicide" (Lyons 1997: 161), picketed in massive numbers both the studio and the film wherever it was shown. Virtually every major evangelical and fundamentalist leader made a statement against the film and urged their followers to work for its demise, with some of them warning that the film would set off waves of antisemitism (Lew Wasserman, head of MCA, was Jewish). The National Association of Evangelicals released a statement urging its members not to see the film (Riley 2003: 18). James Dobson, of Focus on the Family, described the film as "the most blasphemous evil attack on the Church and the cause of Christ in the history of entertainment" (Lyons 1997: 163) and warned that "God is not mocked" (Iannone 1996). Bill Bright, founder of Campus Crusade for Christ, claimed that "a handful people with great wealth and depraved minds are corrupting the world" (Lyons 1997: 163) and even went so far as to offer to buy the film from Universal so he could destroy all existing prints. Universal roundly rejected the offer in full-page newspaper ads claiming that First Amendment and other freedoms "were not for sale."

No treatment of *The Last Temptation of Christ* in this brief space can do justice to the staggering number of protests, letters, boycotts, petitions, and other forms of activism generated by conservative Protestants against the film. It should be noted, however, that mainline Protestants were not as agitated by the film, and sometimes spoke out in support of it. So, for example, Robert E. A. Lee, head of Lutheran Film Associates, which produced the successful *Martin Luther* film in 1953, commented that the film might stimulate healthy dialogue around the humanity of Christ (Riley 2003: 18). After viewing a pre-screening of the film for religious leaders (which conservatives refused to attend), Paul Moore, the Episcopal Bishop of New York, claimed the film was "artistically excellent and theologically sound," while William Fore, head of NCC's Communication Commission, described it as "a bit pompous" but added, "I think it's a shame that some Christians appear to be so unsure of their faith that they can't stand the thought of people seeing something different" (Harmetz 1988).

While protesting Protestants may have made more of a media impact on the film's reception, clearly not all Protestants were of the same mind about the value of the film, its potential threat to the Christian faith, or its affect on American culture. Similarly, *Dogma*, written and directed by Kevin Smith, a Roman Catholic, received both protest and support from Protestants when it was released in 1999, even if the protestors were more visible in the press. *Dogma* is the story of an abortion clinic worker who is also a disaffected Catholic and "the last scion" descended from the bloodline of Jesus. She is called upon by the "voice of God" in the form of an angel and a marginalized "thirteenth apostle" who drops naked from heaven (in the form of Chris Rock) to stop two banished angels from returning to heaven. The angels have found a loophole in Catholic dogma that will gain them forgiveness but, in exploiting the loophole, they will overturn the decree of God and thereby negate all existence. Aided by an ex-muse-turned-stripper and two rather unholy "prophets," the last scion rediscovers faith and not only rescues God (who was beaten up by some demons on the Jersey boardwalk during one of his skeeball excursions) and stops the angels, but ends up saving the world. God reappears at the end of the film (in the form of female rock singer Alanis Morisette) to set things right.

Not surprisingly, many Christians, both Catholic and Protestant, found the movie more than just a satire intended by its director as "a love letter to both faith and God almighty" (Kehr 1999), but offensive, defamatory, and blasphemous. The film goes after a multitude of cherished Christian beliefs while exposing both religious institutions and corporations to ridicule. The film was denounced by several Catholic and Protestant groups, bringing pressure on family-friendly Disney Corporation, whose Miramax Films subsidiary produced the film. The American Family Association, for example, said the film "proves that Disney does not take the cherished beliefs of Christians seriously, and that Hollywood enjoys nothing more than mocking Christianity" (Lansingh 1999a). Focus on the Family's Steven Isaac likewise rejected the film in its entirety: "If Kevin Smith hopes to provoke religious discussion he's sadly misguided. Families don't need the kind of 'discussions' likely to be prompted by *Dogma*" (Isaac n.d.).

When Disney began to balk at releasing the film, Harvey and Bob Weinstein, the heads of Miramax, worked out a deal to pay Disney $12 million for its share of the film, and then found other avenues of distribution, thereby eliminating Disney's role. Conservative Protestants declared victory in their ability to use their collective social and economic power in altering a major media business deal.

Yet *Dogma* was ultimately released and it did relatively well at the box office – precisely because of the controversy. Indeed, not all Protestants were upset at the film, with a number of Protestant film reviewers engaging Smith's questions and satire with seriousness. *Christianity Today*'s Steve Lansingh even headed his film review: "Kevin Smith's *Dogma* isn't just nonblasphemous, it is a presentation of Christianity to an unreached people group" (Lansingh 1999b).

Lansingh touches on an important interpretation in assessing Protestant responses to the film. By the end of the century when the film was released, almost 40 percent of Americans had no affiliation with organized religion, though as many as one in five of the total population had come to describe themselves as "spiritual, but not religious" (Fuller 2001). While this label meant different things to different people, in most cases it meant an openness to and interest in spiritual issues, spiritual growth, and spiritual practices combined with a lack of interest in, if not hostility toward, organized religion and its institutions. *Dogma* played directly into these sentiments in a way that was strikingly "Protestant," so to speak. Thus, while the usual cast of Catholic and Protestant evangelical protestors attacked the film for its blasphemy and ridicule of organized religion, a large number of Protestants for whom faith is important but institutions suspect embraced the film and discussed it widely in small groups, classrooms, over coffee, on web blogs, and even in churches.

It should also be noted that, if Protestants have at times organized themselves as an instrument of economic and cultural power in relationship to film, that organizing has not always been negative in the form of boycotts and protests, but also positive in the form of garnering support for a film and ensuring its success. Indeed, one could argue that, in the case of Mel Gibson's *The Passion of the Christ* (2004), even though Gibson, who produced, directed, and heavily financed the film, is a Roman Catholic, it was Protestants who gave the film its initial success and have continued to use the film in catechetical and evangelistic work. The film is a graphic, violent, and highly imaginative rendering of only the last twelve hours of the life of Jesus. Yet because it is designed to underscore the redeeming significance of Christ's suffering and death, evangelical Protestants immediately began to endorse it, despite concerns by the National Council of Churches, the US Conference of Catholic Bishops, and the Anti-Defamation League that the film contained antisemitism. As the president of the executive committee of the Southern Baptist Convention put it, "I don't know of anything since the Billy Graham crusades that has had the potential of touching so many lives. It's like the Lord somehow laid in our lap something that could be a great catalyst for spiritual awakening in this nation" (Goodstein 2004).

Evangelical support for the film was not automatic, however. *The Passion of the Christ* may well turn out to be a watershed moment in the history of the relationship of religion and film because of the sophisticated marketing processes Gibson employed that went well beyond creative use of tie-in merchandise and the internet. Gibson effectively bypassed the major studios and included personal invitations to pre-screenings for pastors and church leaders as well as other high-profile religious leaders as varied as the Pope and Billy Graham (Maresco 2004). Hundreds of Protestant churches bought blocks of tickets and promoted the film both within their congregations and in a variety of media outlets throughout their communities, especially emphasizing the film as a tool of evangelistic outreach (Goodstein 2004). In essence, Gibson discovered a huge pool of free marketing in the form of churches who were simultaneously marketing themselves – a strategy that has continued to be used by countless other distribution companies since, regardless of whether a film is explicitly religious or merely family-oriented.

Protestant filmmaking

Another of the primary ways that Protestants have interacted with the medium of film in the modern period is by making films themselves. Even those Protestants who have been highly critical of Hollywood culture or its values over the years have found in film a highly effective vehicle for their message, though one could argue that this utilitarian focus on message rather than medium (which some might claim is a characteristically Protestant approach) has too often had the consequence of diminishing the production values of these films and prevented Protestants from taking up more transformative approaches to culture or to filmmaking itself.

Any review of filmmaking by Protestants in the last half of the twentieth century must begin with Billy Graham, a Southern Baptist evangelist who has preached to more people around the world than any other person in history (Horstmann 2002). As far back as the late 1940s, Billy Graham had been making evangelistic movies for use in churches and other evangelistic venues. In 1951, Graham's evangelistic association created Worldwide Pictures as a vehicle for producing and distributing Christian films, and throughout the 1950s and 1960s the company made a string of films that typically portrayed the lives of sinful characters who subsequently become converted to Christianity, often in response to Graham's preaching, which is often edited into the films. In 1965, Worldwide Pictures produced *The Restless Ones*, a film that focused on the social problems experienced by teenagers, and in 1968 the film became the first Billy Graham picture to be shown in conventional movie theaters (Chattaway 2005). The films *Two a Penny* (1967), *For Pete's Sake* (1968), *His Land* (1970), and *Time to Run* (1972) followed, with a typical screening being followed by an evangelistic invitation from a trained worker standing at the front of the theater.

All in all, the Billy Graham Evangelistic Association (BGEA) and Worldwide Pictures produced close to fifty films in a variety of genres and with varying degrees of quality before the turn of the millennium, the most successful of those being *The Hiding Place* (1975), based on the autobiography of Corrie Ten Boom, whose family hid Jews during the Second World War, and *Joni* (1980), the real life story of Joni Eareckson whose automobile accident left her quadriplegic. Some of the Graham films continued to be shown in theaters, though increasingly the BGEA employed a strategy whereby the film would be given limited theatrical release and then be shown on nationwide television in place of the usual Billy Graham crusade, often with better evangelistic results than a televised crusade (Chattaway 2005).

In the late 1960s and early 1970s, and overlapping to some degree with the hippie movement of the time, the "Jesus movement" gained steam among a number of Protestants throughout the United States, especially teenagers and young adults (with some of its participants describing themselves as "Jesus Freaks"). Interest in the second coming of Christ intensified among conservative Protestants during this period (not unrelated to rising tensions in the Middle East), exemplified and instigated by a spate of books. Notable among the latter was Hal Lindsey's *Late Great Planet Earth* in 1970, which described the "rapture" of true Christians in the air to meet Christ prior to a period of tribulation on earth as imagined in the New Testament book of Revelation.

Not surprisingly, films also began to appear during this period that offered portrayals of end-time scenarios, most notably *A Thief in the Night* (1972), produced by Russell S. Doughten with the tagline "… and there will be no place to hide." The film's title comes from a description of Christ's return recorded in 1 Thessalonians 5, and the film tells the story of a young woman who wakes up one morning only to find that her husband and millions of others throughout the world have disappeared. They have been "raptured," leaving her and others similarly left behind to live through the last days of the planet under the control of the Antichrist. The frightening film was shown widely by Protestant groups at churches, rallies, and youth camps in the service of evangelistic efforts, the intent of which was clearly to scare the viewers toward conversion. The film was followed by three sequels: *A Distant Thunder* (1978), *Image of the Beast* (1980), and *The Prodigal Planet* (1983).

The "end-times" Christian film genre would resurface in 2000 with *Left Behind: The Movie*, a film adaptation of the highly successful *Left Behind* series of novels written by Tim LaHaye and Jerry B. Jenkins beginning in 1995. Here again, a conservative, dispensationalist interest in the Second Coming and a highly imaginative interpretation of biblical prophecy motivates the story of what happens when the true, secret church of Christ is removed from the planet. While the film may have had better production values, script, and acting than *A Thief in the Night* made three decades earlier, critics were generally disgusted with the film as overly propagandistic, with Desson Howe of the *Washington Post* describing it as "a blundering cringefest, thanks to unintentionally laughable dialogue, hackneyed writing and uninspired direction" (Howe 2001) and James Berardinelli of *Reelviews* calling it "Cheesy. Silly. Moronic. Dull. Plodding. Torturous." Two sequels appeared in 2002 (*Left Behind II: Tribulation Force*) and in 2005 (*Left Behind: World at War*), both being released directly to DVD and video.

While a number of other films generated by Protestants could be mentioned from the post-Hays code era, one additional film warrants special consideration. In 1979, the aforementioned Bill Bright, a fellow evangelist and friend of Billy Graham, produced the *Jesus* film, which may be the most watched film in the history of cinema. Bright founded Campus Crusade for Christ in 1951, which eventually became one of the largest interdenominational parachurch ministries in the world, committed "to helping take the gospel of Jesus Christ to all nations." Bright had long determined to make a film on the life of Christ with the potential of fulfilling that commission.

Bright, like some other evangelicals, was not opposed to the medium of film itself. In fact, he believed strongly in the power of film both to communicate and to bring alive the Christian Gospel, especially in countries where much of the population was illiterate. The Jesus project came about when Bright met John Heyman, a British producer who was also wanting to make a film about Jesus (Heyman had produced other notable films such as *Grease* and *A Passage to India*). As early as 1974, Heyman had begun work on making a film of the entire Bible, verse-by-verse, beginning with Genesis 1:1, and thus his production company was known as the "Genesis Project." The Genesis Project had already completed the first twenty-two chapters of Genesis and the first two chapters of Luke. But this venture was costly, so Heyman turned to Bill Bright for assistance, in hope that the religious community might be interested in supporting the work. The two came together around the "Jesus Project," as it was eventually called, the centerpiece of Heyman's larger work (the larger project was never finished because of the costs).

After polling hundreds of Protestant and Catholic thinkers on the subject, Heyman and Bright decided to focus on the single Gospel of Luke as the text for their new film about Jesus rather than attempting a harmonization of the four Gospels as in most movies on the life of Jesus. The project cast British Shakespearean actor Brian Deacon in the role of Jesus, and it was decided that nothing would be spoken by Jesus except what is found on his lips in the Gospel of Luke. Though Deacon was British – and white – most of the other actors in the movie were Yemenite Jews because "their facial features are thought to have changed little over the millennia," according to Paul Eshleman who was chosen by Bright to lead the Jesus project (Eshleman 2002). The film was released in 1979 at a final production cost estimated at around $6 million.

The team of people making the *Jesus* film decided that it had to meet five central criteria:

> (1) the film must be as archaeologically, historically and theologically accurate as humanly possible; (2) the presentation must be unbiased and acceptable to all as a true depiction of Christ's life; (3) the film story must appeal to all ages; (4) the script must be easily translatable into virtually any language on earth; and (5) the film must be of theater-viewing quality, and effective with both urban and rural audiences worldwide. (Jesus Film Project 2008)

Of course, the second of these criteria could not possibly be met, which begs the question of the "all" to whom or for whom the film is being made. The film's ending provides some answers to this question given that it is constituted by a seven-minute "altar call" segment in which a particular version of Protestant evangelical theology comes out explicitly, where the historicity of the virgin birth and bodily resurrection of Jesus are asserted, a substitutionary atonement proclaimed, and the viewer led through the "sinner's prayer."

Mainline Protestant denominations have tended not to utilize the film, whether because Campus Crusade tends to focus its work with theologically compatible partners or because mainline mission agencies have resisted using a film so obviously originating from North America and featuring a white Jesus. While some evangelicals have raised criticisms similar to those of mainline Christians about the film's lack of concern for local context, it would be no exaggeration to claim that most have tended to like the way the film works. Thomas Trask, General Superintendent of the Assemblies of God, praised the film for its "clear salvation message," while a former president of the Southern Baptist Convention described the film as "nonthreatening" and "nonintrusive" (Dart 2001: 28).

As a relatively low-budget evangelistic film, the *Jesus* film had only limited commercial success in the United States. Though one could argue that the film bombed at the box office, it took on a life of its own thereafter. As early as the spring of 1980, the ministry began dubbing the film's soundtrack into other languages to take the cinematic *Jesus* abroad. The film was telecast in Hindi to 21 million viewers in India. The first small team of Campus Crusade staffers, headed by Eshleman, took the Tagalog version to the Philippines. By the end of 1980, the film ministry had thirty-one language versions of *Jesus*, exceeding the record at that time of twenty-six translations of *Gone with the Wind*. At present, the project leadership claims that *Jesus* has received over 6 billion viewings (this includes multiple exposures per viewer) in over 200 countries of the world, in a thousand different languages. There are close to 3,000 "Jesus film teams" around the world in 108 countries, representing about 6,000 people. Something like 1,500 denominations and mission agencies around the world use the film (Jesus Film Project 2008).

Film education, guidance, and criticism

Though a loss of institutional power may have prevented Protestants from exercising a formal influence on Hollywood, Protestants would increasingly take it upon themselves to reflect on and engage film theologically in the latter half of the twentieth century through books, journals, movie reviews, newsletters, websites, and other educational resources. While often this engagement has consisted primarily of an evaluation of films on the basis of whether they reinforced conventional morality and respected Christian religious sensitivities (not that Protestants have agreed by any means on what these amounted to), increasingly Protestants have developed a deeper appreciation for film so that, like James Wall, longtime film critic and editor of the *Christian Century*, they have come to "an acceptance of film as film" (Berckman 1980: 298).

John Lyden describes the typical Protestant approach to film as dialectical, dialogical, or dualistic rather than synthetic or sacramental (which is more typically Catholic) insofar as the former "assumes an independence of religion and culture and seeks to bring them into dialogue in order to gain from that interchange" (Lyden 2003: 18). While there are certainly Protestants who stand as exceptions to Lyden's characterization, a survey of Protestant film reviews offered up in print or on websites confirms his basic point: the points of contact between Christianity and film often turn out to revolve around biblical parallels and overlapping or similar moral vision or theological message.

Even if Lyden is correct, however, there are still major differences among Protestants in how they have understood the aim of their interactions with film. So, for example, James Wall's reviews in the *Christian Century* reveal his appreciation for the deeper artistic and visional dimensions of a film that is markedly different from Protestant film reviews of an earlier generation and also from present reviews by other Protestants that tend to be more superficial or utilitarian. So, for example, the popular *hollywoodjesus.com* website, on the one hand, explores "pop culture from a spiritual point of view" and manages to find redeeming and dialogue-worthy elements in just about any film it reviews (not to mention lots and lots of Christ-figures) while Ted Baehr's *movieguide.org* website, on the other hand, rates films in descending order from "exemplary," "moral," and "wholesome" to those that require "caution" or "extreme caution," to those that are labeled "excessive" and "abhorrent."

Of course, the "Hollywood Jesus" web presence is not intended as a source of critical · film reviews but rather has a more evangelistic focus. As founder David Bruce puts it, "The idea behind the site was simple: to mine the movies for redemptive analogies, to find bridges in popular culture for the presentation of the gospel. The method, or a version of it, is tried and true: the apostle Paul used this cultural-engagement approach to reach those who had gathered on Mars Hill in Athens (see Acts 17:16–34)" (Bruce 2008). Likewise, Baehr's *Movie Guide* intends itself as "a ministry dedicated to redeeming the values of the mass media according to biblical principles, by influencing entertainment industry executives and helping families make wise media choices" (Baehr 2004). In both cases, Lyden's point is substantiated, but even beyond this, what one often sees in contemporary Protestant interactions with film is a more utilitarian focus on "message" and on the potential of a film either to open up or close off viewers to spirituality or to a Christian worldview.

Films are cultural texts. The relationship of religious communities to those texts – whether expressed through censorship, appreciation, boycott, protest, or even the growing use of film clips in Protestant worship, evangelism, and religious education – all embody profound theological commitments regarding the relationship of Christianity to culture. If a review of modern Protestant engagement with film demonstrates anything, it is that a rather profound divide characterizes Protestantism in this regard. Historically, Protestants have been of one mind neither when it comes to assessing films nor when it comes to determining what the Church's response should be to those films. While some Protestants have seen films like *The Last Temptation of Christ* or *Dogma* as an attack on and provocation to Christians, others have seen potential for public and ecclesial dialogue and discussion. The differences here turn largely on how one understands the role of the Church in society – whether, for example, the Church's task is to be that of a moral watchdog against infidels and blasphemers or whether, by contrast, the Church is to encourage free expression and liberty of conscience and speech, even if this offends and insults the cherished beliefs and ethical principles of Christians.

Bibliography

Baehr, T. (2004) *Movie Guide*. Online. Available HTTP: <www.movieguide.org> (accessed 7 May 2008).

Baugh, L. (1997) *Imaging the Divine: Jesus and Christ-Figures in Film*, Kansas City: Sheed and Ward.

Berardinelli, J. (2001) "Left Behind: A Film Review," *Reelviews*. Online. Available HTTP: <http://www.reelviews.net/movies/l/left_behind.html> (accessed 25 April 2008).

Berckman, E. (1980) "The Changing Attitudes of Protestant Churches to Movies and Television," *Encounter* 41: (3): 293–306.

Bruce, David (2008) "David Bruce: Webmaster, *HollywoodJesus.com*." Online. Available HTTP: <www.hollywoodjesus.com> (accessed 7 May 2008).

Chattaway, P. (2005) "Billy Graham Goes to the Movies," *Christianity Today* (23 August). Online. Available HTTP: <http://www.christianitytoday.com/movies/news/billygrahammovies.html> (accessed 25 April 2008).

Christian Reformed Church (1966) "Acts of Synod: Film Arts." Online. Available HTTP: <http://www.crcna.org/pages/positions_filmarts.cfm> (accessed 25 April 2008).

Church of the Nazarene (2005) *Manual – Church of the Nazarene 2005–2009*, Kansas City: Nazarene Publishing House.

Dart, J. (2001) "The Making of Jesus," *The Christian Century* (6–13 June): 26–31.

Eshleman, P. (2002) "The 'Jesus' Film: A Contribution to World Evangelism," *International Bulletin of Missionary Research* 26 (2): 68–70, 72.

Fuller, R. (2001) *Spiritual, but Not Religious: Understanding Unchurched America*, Oxford: Oxford University Press.

Goodstein, L. (2004) "Some Christians See 'Passion' as Evangelism Tool," *New York Times* (5 February).

Harmetz, A. (1988) "New Scorsese Film Shown to Religious Leaders," *New York Times* (15 July).

Horstmann, B. (2002) "Billy Graham: A Man with a Mission," *Cincinnati Post* (27 June).

Howe, D. (2001) "'Left Behind': Heaven Help Us," *Washington Post* (2 February).

Iannone, C. (1996) "*The Last Temptation* Reconsidered," *First Things* 60: 50–4.

Isaac, S. (n.d.) "Dogma." Online. Available HTTP: <http://www.pluggedinonline.com/movies/movies/a0000169.cfm> (accessed 25 April 2008).

Jesus Film Project (2008). Online. Available HTTP: <http://jesusfilm.org> (accessed 1 April 2008).

Johnston, R. (2000) *Reel Spirituality: Theology and Film in Dialogue*, Grand Rapids, MI: Baker Academic.

Kehr, D. (1999) "Deflator of the Faith? Director Begs to Differ," *New York Times* (1 August).

Lansingh, S. (1999a) "Film Forum: Eighteen James Bond Films Were Not Enough," *Christianity Today* (November). Online. Available HTTP: <hrrp://www.christianitytoday.com/ct/1999/novemberweb-only/24.0c.html> (accessed 25 April 2008).

—— (1999b) "Smile God Loves You!," *Christianity Today* 43 (13).

Lyden, J. (2003) *Film as Religion: Myths, Morals, and Rituals*, New York: New York University Press.

Lyons, C. (1997) *The New Censors: Movies and the Culture Wars*, Philadelphia: Temple University Press.

Maresco, P. (2004) "Mel Gibson's *The Passion of the Christ*: Market Segmentation, Mass Marketing and Promotion, and the Internet," *Journal of Religion and Popular Culture* 8.

May, J. (ed.) (1997) *New Image of Religious Film*, Kansas City: Sheed and Ward.

National Council of Churches (NCC) (1985) "Violence and Sexual Violence in Film, Television, Cable and Home Video," *Media & Values* 33.

—— (1993) "Violence in Electronic Media and Film." Online. Available HTTP: <http://www.ncccusa.org/about/comcompolicies.html#violence> (accessed 25 April 2008).

Riley, R. (2003) *Film, Faith, and Cultural Conflict: The Case of Martin Scorsese's The Last Temptation of Christ*, Westport, CT: Praeger Publishers.

Romanowski, W. (1995) "John Calvin Meets the Creature from the Black Lagoon," *Christian Scholar's Review* 25 (1): 47–62.

Schofield Clark, L. (2002) *Practicing Religion in the Age of Media: Explorations in Media, Religion, and Culture*, New York: Columbia University Press.

Stevens, P. (1989) "The Christian in the MGM Lion's Den: A Content Analysis of Changing Evangelical Attitudes toward Motion Pictures in *Christianity Today* Film Reviews from 1956 to 1985." MA Thesis, Virginia Beach: Regent University.

Time Magazine (1946) "Protesting Protestant: Have You Heard of the Reformation Mr. Crosby?" (21 January): 76.

—— (1985) "TV Protest: Church Alarm over Violence" (30 September): 72.

Trotter, F. T. (1969) "The Church Moves toward Film Discrimination," *Religion in Life* 38 (2): 264–76.

Wall, J. (1974a) "Church Clout at the Box Office," *Christianity Today* (16 January): 35–6.

—— (1974b) "A Cinema–Church Political Standoff," *Christianity Today* (20 February): 198–9.

—— (1974c) "Film Anarchy Threatens the Rating System," *Christianity Today* (30 October): 1003–4.

—— (1975) "A Matter of Taste," *Christianity Today* (30 April): 427–8.

Filmography

A Distant Thunder (1978, dir. D. Thompson)

Dogma (1999, dir. K. Smith)

For Pete's Sake (1968, dir. J. Collier)

The Hiding Place (1975, dir. J. Collier)

His Land (1970, dir. J. Collier)

Image of the Beast (1980, dir. D. Thompson)

Jesus (1979, dir. P. Sykes and J. Kirsch)

Joni (1980, dir. J. Collier)

The Last Temptation of Christ (1988, dir. M. Scorsese)
Left Behind: The Movie (2000, dir. V. Sarin)
Left Behind: World at War (2005, dir. C. Baxley)
Left Behind II: Tribulation Force (2002, dir. B. Corcoran)
Martin Luther (1953, dir. I. Pichel)
The Passion of the Christ (2004, dir. M. Gibson)
The Pawnbroker (1965, dir. S. Lumet)
The Prodigal Planet (1983, dir. D. Thompson)
The Restless Ones (1965, dir. D. Ross)
A Thief in the Night (1972, dir. D. Thompson)
Time to Run (1972, dir. J. Collier)
Two a Penny (1967, dir. J. Collier)

Notes

My thanks to Kathryn House, Xochitl Alvizo, and Holly Reed, who provided invaluable research assistance for this chapter.
1 For helpful overviews of various theological responses to film, see May 1997: 17–37; Johnston 2000: 41–58; and Lyden 2003: 18–27.

Part II

DEPICTIONS OF AND BY RELIGIOUS PRACTITIONERS IN FILMS

5
JUDAISM
Melanie J. Wright

Introduction: *Hester Street* as case study

Joan Micklin Silver's 1975 debut feature struggled, as most do, to negotiate the bottle-neck of distribution. The Hollywood majors deemed *Hester Street* (an adaptation of Abraham Cahan's 1896 story "Yekl, a Tale of the Ghetto") suitable only for the synagogue circuit (Antler 1995: 179). Their view was eminently reasonable – the film is shot in black and white, its dialogue is largely in Yiddish or accented English, with sometimes muffled sound and poorly synchronized subtitles. In a few scenes, a micro-phone dips into the frame. Above all, *Hester Street* tells a seemingly unremarkable yet decidedly niche story of Jewish immigrant life, with an emphasis on the confrontation between religious tradition and modernity: its protagonists are Jake and Gitl, a couple whose marriage disintegrates in the claustrophobic environment of a turn-of-the-century New York tenement.

Undeterred by the seeming lack of commercial appeal, Micklin Silver's husband took over the task of promotion. *Hester Street* found favor with critics and audiences. A positive reception at Cannes and European sales facilitated the first American screenings (Antler 1995: 179) ultimately establishing the careers of the director and Carol Kane, who received an Academy Award nomination for her performance as Gitl.

Why did the film succeed? For some audiences, ethnic nostalgia, which Kugelmass (1990) and Eisen (1998) identify as a significant driver of contemporary American Jewish behavior, may have been a factor. Largely assimilated viewers could mark their Jewish identity – even experience a kind of vicarious Judaism – by consuming *Hester Street*'s images of Orthodox observant culture. (At the end of the film, Jake is trapped by the secular, worldly Mamie, whilst traditionally minded Gitl marries the pious Mr. Bernstein, and opens a grocery store to fund his religious studies.) More specifically, the film takes its name from one of the most well-known thoroughfares in New York's Lower East Side, the district that plays a distinctive role in popular Jewish consciousness as the quintessential "Jewish place" in America, a neighborhood in which migrants from Europe gathered, later to emerge as "real" Americans. *Hester Street* was released in an age of heightened communal division in the Jewish community. In 1972, the first female Reform rabbi had been ordained, a move held by Orthodox authorities to be in violation of *halakhah* (religious law); and despite widespread rabbinical disapproval, more than one in four Jews married a non-Jew. Still, the film performed the collective memory of Jewish Americans, offering images of the Lower East Side as "a place of beginnings, of engaged senses, of passionate ideologies ... of life lived to its full" (Diner 2000: 5–6).

The film's popularity, and its Interfilm prize (awarded by a Protestant Christian jury at the Mannheim-Heidelberg festival), attest to an appeal extending beyond Jewish audiences. For some consumers, the promotional portraits of Silver and his wife Micklin Silver as figures who defied Hollywood conventions in order to tell a story that mattered personally to them, undoubtedly enhanced *Hester Street*'s charm. More specifically, the film offers a distinctively contemporary, universalizing account of immigrant life and its impact on traditional religious cultures (Diner 2000: 87–8; Wright 2005: 181). For example, it highlights the gendered character of migrant experience. Like Jake, many husbands emigrated first; their participation in the labor market encouraged their Americanization. Women followed later and acculturated more slowly because of their relative confinement to the domestic sphere. This asymmetrical experience compounded the pressures associated with overcrowding and poverty; *fin-de-siècle* concerns over family breakdowns amongst Jewish migrants prompted the formation of the National Desertion Bureau, which distributed financial assistance and tracked down absent fathers (Igra 2006: 601–10). Accordingly, *Hester Street*'s opening scenes are organized (narratively and visually) around Jake as he moves between tenement buildings, dance hall, and workshop. Gitl is a static, lesser figure. By the film's end, however, Gitl is trapped neither by poverty nor by the Judaism that Jake has rushed to shed. Religious observance is presented as a choice freely embraced, a vehicle for female empowerment. Gitl accepts Jake's *get* (religious divorce bill) only after negotiating a settlement large enough to establish a business; emboldened, *she* proposes marriage to Bernstein.

What the executives who rejected *Hester Street* did not comprehend is the extent to which works of "ethnic" cinema are as much about accentuating common values as they are about the distinctions between groups. In this case, the film's ending posits a world in which ethnic and religious values are emotionally significant but nevertheless subsumed by broader notions of liberation, economic advancement, and marriage relations grounded in love. In short, the story possesses broad appeal as an articulation of the American dream. As Rosenberg and Whitfield note:

> The image of the Jew in an American film is an image of America ... The specific textures of cinematic ethnicity are a measure of a society's openness, its collective aspirations, its social and cultural anxieties, its era and *Zeitgeist*, its reckoning with history. (2002: 1–2)

In this account of *Hester Street* both the potentially rich fruits of a study of Judaism and film and the challenges that face anyone undertaking such a task may be traced. Clearly, a simple catalogue of relevant screen images offers limited analytical purchase. The meanings or significance of filmic engagements with Judaism are not straightforwardly functions of their narrative content or visual style. To a consideration of the film "text" must be added an awareness of industrial questions and other matters. Just as Micklin Silver's adaptation of Cahan's novella – itself not an encyclopedia or ethnography of American Jewish life – reflects her location in 1970s discourses on civil rights and gender equality, so *any* representation embodies the position of its enunciation (Hall 1990: 222).

If these complexities might impact any attempt to talk about cinematic representation, further challenges are distinctive to this essay. Like other phenomena labeled as "religions" Judaism resists easy definition. Yet the invitation to think in such terms is implied by phrases like "Judaism and film" or "Judaism in film". An attempt will be made here to eschew the seductions of essentialist accounts of religion, which fail to articulate contemporary and historical Jewish religious diversity, whilst also resisting a postmodern tendency to construct "the Jew" as exemplar of the decentered, destabilized subject, a move that risks retreat into self-indulgent analysis and/or a fetishizing of Jews and their cultures, religious or otherwise (see further Johnston 2006). Also significant is Judaism's strong association with Jewish identity, traditionally acquired by birth (Orthodox Judaism regards any child born of a Jewish woman as Jewish) or sometimes by choice. Reflecting the inseparability of Judaism from the Jewish people, a convert/proselyte to Judaism also becomes a Jew (as in Ruth 1:16). But not all Jews are adherents of Judaism. Many people understand their Jewishness primarily in ethnic, cultural, or political terms. One might think here of Mike Leigh, director of *Secrets and Lies* (1996), *Vera Drake* (2004), and *Happy-Go-Lucky* (2008). Explicit Judaism is absent from his films, but their treatments of working-class experience arguably owe much to his upbringing in Socialist Zionist circles. Other people, whilst not denying their Jewish heritage, have little interest in a specifically Jewish identity, religious or otherwise.

The indeterminacy of the Judaism–Jewishness relationship has important implications for this essay. Many cineastes are familiar, for example, with the concept of "Jewish Hollywood." The idea that since the 1920s Jews have dominated Hollywood, constructing there an empire of their own (Gabler 1989), has been variously celebrated and decried. But whether Jewish participation in the American film industry is regarded positively (as a figure of immigrant capabilities or of the American dream) or negatively (as a manifestation of a desire to exert influence through control of a mass medium) such positions fail to attend to subjectivity, to consider the diversity and complexity of what being Jewish has meant or means to figures as unlike as Helen Lesnick, Marilyn Monroe, Molly Picon, and Rachel Weisz. Instead, they assume that "Jews … perennially act *as Jews*" (Carr 2001: 10). Such essentializing constructions erase the richness of relationships between Jewishness and Judaism. This essay will attempt to resist such elisions, instead regarding the shifting on- and offscreen place of religion in the configuration of Jewish identity as part of its subject matter.

Jews, Judaism, and early cinema

Judaism's engagement in the cinema stretches back over a century. A *Gesture Fight in Hester Street* – the title illustrates how, even then, the Lower East Side was a "Jewish place" in popular consciousness – released in 1903 by the American Mutoscope and Biograph Company, comprises a single shot and features the earliest surviving screen images of Jews. It is probably a filmed vaudeville sketch: two street peddlers argue and fight, until a policeman intervenes. *Gesture Fight* was intended as a comedy, the humor lying in the exaggerated gesturing and posturing that replaces the direct blows seen in "normal" fights. As such it depends on negative stereotypes of Jews, in which aspects of Judaism's material culture (hats, clothing, beards) and assumptions about Jewish character (an inability to fight openly and honestly; acquisitiveness; weakness or effeminacy) linked to prejudices about Judaism are implicated.

Whilst film technology and artistry quickly advanced, in many respects these first references to Judaism set the tone for features produced during and after the silent era. Focusing on American film, Zimerman (2002: 927) identifies three archetypes that dominated early screen representations of Jews and to varying degrees survived the rise of the Hollywood studios in the late 1920s. These are the *antisemitic* caricature of the greedy exploiter; the *old* Jew, traditional in appearance and manner, but clever enough to outwit his foes; and the *modern* Jew, who is industrious, brave, and capable of adapting to the realities of the New World. Judaism plays a role in each. Religious garments, *payess* (side-locks), and ritual objects commonly function as part of the canny old Jew's characterization, or as markers of a traditional Jewish culture that the modern must cast off as a precursor to social and economic success. In *The Jazz Singer* (Alan Crosland, 1927) religious practices (especially the observance of Yom Kippur, the Day of Atonement) and roles (specifically, that of *chazzan* or synagogue cantor) are left behind by Jakie Rabinowitz as he refashions himself as a popular entertainer, Jack Robin. Religion is also present in the cruder negative stereotypes; their features (acquisitiveness; dishonesty; inflexible judgementalism; vengefulness) have roots in Christian anti-Jewish prejudices and see mistaken characteristics of Judaism as somehow reflective of and formative for the character of "the Jew." Without compunction, Jakie's father beats him and then prepares immediately for his synagogue duties; he learns of the boy's penchant for jazz from Moisha Yudelsohn, who is tellingly described as "rigidly orthodox and a power in the affairs of the Ghetto."

Films with biblical themes featured significantly amongst the earliest, most widely consumed representations of observant Jews. Such features remain important because of their enduring popularity and because their images are, within the genre's conventions, presented as authoritative. Pre-1960, these images were generally cursory and disapproving, offering negative foils for a positively imaged Christianity. Thus *Intolerance* (1916) – which is often referenced by historians as an illustration of director D. W. Griffith's progressive politics – depicts ostentatious prayers by *tallit* (prayer shawl) and *tefillin* (phylactery) wearing Pharisees who thank God that they are better than other men, in a scene melding the New Testament (Matthew 6:5) and a distortion of *birkhot hashachar*, blessings traditionally recited by Jewish men each morning. The film presents itself as a credible guide to Judaism here, just as it does when inter-titles in a scene depicting the marriage at Cana (which, in an elaboration of John 2, Griffith's Pharisees despise) announce dependence on biblical scholarship and instruct viewers that the consumption of wine, and its offering to God, is "an important part" of Jewish religion. *Intolerance* is characteristically ready to narrate the Jew; in doing so it epitomizes a genre that downplays historical change and diversity within Judaism.

A brief discussion of *The Ten Commandments* (1923) and *The King of Kings* (1927) serves to amplify these points. In both films, director Cecil B. DeMille used Orthodox Jews as extras, believing that their "deep feeling of the significance of the Exodus" and their "appearance" would lend authenticity to the performance (Hayne 1960: 213). This rationale blends the discourses of "race" and theology in a manner that has continued into the twenty-first century, most recently resurfacing in 2004 when the Jewish identity of Maia Morgenstern, Mary Magdalene in Mel Gibson's *The Passion of the Christ*, was invoked in efforts to refute claims that the film was antisemitic. In retrospect, Jewish communal reactions to the 1920s films also appear as paradigmatic. Controversy surrounding the depiction of High Priest Caiaphas in *King of Kings* led to a long-term relationship between the Motion Picture Producers and Distributors Association and the Anti-Defamation League (ADL) of the B'nai Brith, reflecting a popular belief that screen images are persuasive influencers of public perceptions of Jews and Judaism (Ohad-Karny 2005; Wright 2005: 174–5).

Contemporaneous with Hollywood's rise was the development of another trans-national industry: Yiddish cinema. Before the Second World War, Yiddish was the language of 13 million Jews (Jacobs 2005: 3). Most Yiddish films engaged the worlds (actual or imaginary) of the *shtetl* ("little town" in Central-East Europe) or the New World immigrant ghetto – contexts in which Judaism was ubiquitous. Thus the now lost *Der Lamedvovnik* (*One of the Thirty-Six*, Jenryk Szaro, 1925) drew on a Talmudic-inspired legend to create its story of a *shtetl* attacked by Russians in the 1830s. At the film's climax, the village is saved by the self-sacrifice of one its most humble residents – unknown to his neighbors, he is one of the thirty-six righteous men whom legend has it exist in each generation, only to reveal themselves in time of acute crisis.

A more cautionary message is offered in *Der Vilner Shtot Khazn* (*The Vilna Cantor*, George Moskov and Max Nossek, 1940): its depiction of the trials that plague a cantor who abandons his responsibilities for a secular musical career may be regarded as a rejoinder to *The Jazz Singer* and argues, like numerous other *shund* or melodramatic "sin" films, that in the bid for success one should not forget one's Jewish identity and tradition. The focus on cantor-as-celebrity reflected a trend in the interwar period, when several performers found fame as recording artists. Exploiting this potential, numerous short films captured performances of liturgical music; New York cantor Moishe Oysher even starred in a feature based on his own life, *Dem Khazn's Zind* (*The Cantor's Son*, Sidney Goldin and Ilya Motyleff, 1937).

But if ever-present within Yiddish cinema, Judaism was not unchallenged there. Many Yiddishists were secularists and anti-clericalists, who sought to create a modern Jewish culture to rival the more liturgically based Hebrew one (Goldsmith 1998). Thus

Mordkhe's transformation, from disciple of the Kotzke rebbe to Polish militia man, in *Poylishe Velder* (*In Polish Woods*, Jonas Turkow, 1928), follows a narrative trajectory common in Yiddish films of the time (particularly those produced in Europe). The Polish censor showed the film to members of *Agudat Israel* (a traditionalist party of Orthodox Jews opposed to secularism and modernism) who protested its depiction of a youth's abandonment of Judaism and, more specifically, its images of physical intimacy between men and women (Goldman 1983: 27–8). In contrast, the search for a new cantor is the pretext for a much warmer American Yiddish film, *Khazan afn Probe* (*Cantor on Trial*, Sidney M. Goldin, 1931). But here, too, is a humorous reflection on both Jewish diversity in changing times and the impact of secular culture on New World Judaism: the candidates for the position are an Eastern European traditionalist, a modernizing German, and an American *chazzan*, who performs with "pep and jazz."

Unlike *Khazan*, but like *Poylishe Velder*, many Yiddish films drew on novels and plays steeped in religious culture, especially Hasidism, a mysticism-infused Judaism, dominant in Europe in the late eighteenth and nineteenth centuries. Like the satires performed at the festival of Purim, they juxtaposed dance and song with pious, symbolic scenes. The most well-known example is *Der Dibek* (*The Dybbuk*, Michal Waszynski, 1937), an adaptation of a play written by S. Ansky, who conducted ethnographic research in *shtetlach* in 1911–14. In *Der Dibek*, two friends, who are making their annual visit to their *tzaddik* (charismatic Hasidic leader), betroth their unborn children. Years later, the children meet when one, Khonnon, travels to the hometown of the other, Leah. Drawn irresistibly to Leah, Khonnon experiments with *kabbalah* (mysticism) in order to win her. He dies – historically, Judaism regarded *kabbalah* study as dangerous, suitable only for mature men – and his *dybbuk* (spirit) possesses Leah. Her family approach the *tzaddik* and request an exorcism, but shockingly, Leah prefers death, with Khonnon inside her, over a life alone. The film's handling of Hasidism is not unsympathetic; Leah and Khonnon first meet over a traditional *Shabbat* (Sabbath) meal. However, *shtetl* culture appears unfavorably in scenes highlighting divisions between rich and poor; and in *Der Dibek*'s closing moments, the figure of the wise but weary *tzaddik*, who lacks his predecessors' abilities to command the spirits of the dead, suggests an embattled, declining tradition – reflecting the ambivalent attitudes of assimilated Jews like Ansky and Waszynski.

Many factors, then, influence the changing fortunes of Judaism vis-à-vis the cinema. The ideas and intentions of filmmakers form one element of a complex whole, alongside regulatory, industrial, and artistic concerns. For example, the decline in openly antisemitic treatments of Judaism in the early 1930s is partly a function of changing technologies, and the shifts in narrative and visual idiom that accompanied them. Lacking both verbal soundtrack and developed conventions of continuity editing as means to anchor images and render them intelligible for viewers, very early films relied on strong visual formulae (cues in the form of costume, gesture, physiology) to suggest links between activity, character, and attitude (Ray 2001: 24). Caricatures of Judaism existed alongside similarly stock images of other religions. The advent of sound on film and other techniques saw these conventions weaken, but not disappear.

Judaism and Jewish–Christian relations in post-*Shoah* film

The *Shoah* (Holocaust) claimed the lives of 5 million Yiddish speakers and, with them, the viability of the Yiddish film industry, although some actors (like Molly Picon, "Yente" in *Fiddler on the Roof* [Norman Jewison, 1971]) continued in work. More generally, the devastation of European Jewry engendered a shift in screen images of Jews and Judaism. In *Gentleman's Agreement* (Elia Kazan, 1947), the protagonist, Phil (a Presbyterian journalist who poses as a Jew in order to investigate antisemitism), describes Judaism as just "a different kind of church"; in the wake of Nazism's abuse of "race," filmmakers overwhelmingly treated "Jewish" as a religious label rather than an ethnic one (Gilman 2006: 183). This, and other factors including the rise of multiculturalism, which meant that filmmakers no longer felt the need to shy away from portraying distinctively Jewish life; the popularity of openly Jewish writers, comedians, and popular musicians; and the general impetus toward self-examination triggered in the USA by events like the King and Kennedy assassinations, have also impacted screen cultures, resulting in more frequent – if not necessarily more serious – depictions of Jewish religious characters, practices, and ideas.

Several postwar biblical films are notable for their attempts to depict Jesus not against but within the context of first-century Judaism. *Jesus of Nazareth* (Franco Zeffirelli, 1977) was partly motivated by a desire to show Jesus as a faithful Jew, in keeping with new Catholic teachings on Judaism. Jesus' circumcision (a rite commemorating God's covenant with Abraham and his descendants) and *bar mitzvah* (attainment of religious majority) are depicted, as are Mary and Joseph's betrothal and marriage according to religious law (*halakhah*). Recitation of the *shema*, Judaism's oldest fixed daily prayer, punctuates the action. Nevertheless, Zeffirelli's wish to show Jesus' message as both continuation and fulfillment of Judaism leads to tensions, and the anachronistic projection of later rituals into the first century (the *bar mitzvah* scene, for example, owes much to ceremonies originating in medieval Germany) constructs Judaism as, at best, ahistorical; at worst, as a living fossil. Ambivalence persists in Jesus films to the present day. In *The Passion of the Christ* Jesus' mother and Mary Magdalene recite lines from the *seder* (liturgical meal commemorating Passover) but their purpose is to underscore Gibson's belief in Jesus' death as a liberating sacrifice that trumps the older one. Elsewhere, the film portrays ordinary Jews and their leaders in negative terms that flirt with anti-Judaism and antisemitism. Ultimately,

> Jesus biopics exhibit a discomfort with Jews and Judaism … What remains unresolved is not only the question of the role of Jews or Jewish leaders in Jesus' death, but what the answer to that question should mean for Christians and Jews today. (Reinhartz 2007: 255)

In contrast, the challenges – practical/demographic and philosophical/theological – that the *Shoah* continues to pose for *Judaism* are rarely reflected onscreen. *The Quarrel* (Eli Cohen, 1990) in which two survivors – one secular, the other Orthodox – debate issues of theodicy and survivor-guilt on Rosh Hashanah (New Year, the beginning of a period of self-reflection and repentance) is unusual. More commonly, rituals and imagery serve as cursory devices establishing a character's Jewish identity. In *Europa, Europa* (Agnieszka Holland, 1991) Solomon Perel's circumcised penis is the persistent reminder of his Jewishness, when he poses first as a communist, later as a fascist, in the quest for survival. *Schindler's List* (Steven Spielberg, 1993) opens with the inauguration of the Sabbath, signaled by the lighting of candles and recital of *kiddush* (blessing) over wine. Toward the film's end, the now freed laborers in Schindler's factory perform the same ritual. In these and numerous other *Shoah*-related films, such comparatively well-known images function as brief "Jewish moments" enacted by people of otherwise indeterminate origin and allegiance. (See comparatively Gershenson on post-Soviet Russian films, in which "Jew" is a similarly empty signifier [2008: 183].)

Whilst both the possibility and the morality of representing genocide are questioned by many, hundreds of *Shoah*-related films now exist (see Insdorf's filmography, 2003: 313–65). Moreover, only a minority of religious Jews today interprets Exodus 20:4 to prohibit *any* reproduction of human images. The general absence of Judaism from screen treatments of the *Shoah* therefore requires comment. It may be prompted by the need to appeal to a predominantly non-Jewish audience, or by a conviction that Jews are distinguished from non-Jews not by any significant differences – be these construed essentially or culturally – but simply because antisemites identify them as such: this is implied by Phil's easy ability to "pass" as a Jew in *Gentleman's Agreement*, and by the confusion that condemns the eponymous *Monsieur Klein* (Joseph Losey, 1976), a non-Jew, to the ranks of the deportees in Paris' Vel' d'Hiv. Alternatively, negative attitudes (actual or imputed) toward Judaism on the part of filmmakers and audiences may be a factor: perhaps an Orthodox observant character would not be expected by some to elicit readily the sympathies of a mass viewership?

Judaism's comparative absence contrasts with the prevalence of Christian imagery and ideology in many Holocaust films – examples here include Jesus Ortiz's and Sol Nazerman's cathartic suffering, complete with Christ-like *stigmata*, in *The Pawnbroker* (Sidney Lumet, 1964), and the quasi-baptismal passage through water that signals the Schindler-Jews' redemption in Spielberg's film. Whether or not this tendency reflects anything other than the extent to which the Christian metanarrative has been naturalized in Western culture (as Avisar 1987 suggests), it sometimes operates in tandem with the erasure or diminishing of Judaism. In *Obchod na Korze* (*The Shop on Main Street*, Ján Kadár and Elmar Klos, 1965) the elderly Mrs. Lautmann's obliviousness to unfolding events is typified by her determination to mark the Sabbath with candles, prayers, and a special meal, even as the exasperated "Aryan" Tono attempts to save her from deportation. And like Tono, Christian student Paul fails in his efforts to save Jews in *Les guichets du Louvre* (*Black Thursday*, Michel Mitrani, 1974); dialogue links the refusal of Yiddish-speaking Orthodox Jews to heed warnings about the impending tragedy to their determination to trust in the divine will.

If few films feature characters living Judaism-filled lives, fewer attend to the diversity of modern Jewish life. Unusually, *Left Luggage* (Jeroen Krabbé, 1998) juxtaposes a dysfunctional family headed by secular survivors with the religious Kalmans. They, too, are traumatized by their father's survivor-guilt. As a child, he saw his father and brother hanged in a concentration camp for refusing to curse the Torah. But the film suggests that religious practice, particularly Sabbath and festival observance, provides a positive sense of continuity and meaning amidst anomie and despair. Somewhat typically, the Kalmans' allegiance is to Hasidism, which features disproportionately in screen images of Judaism (on which, more later).

Aside from *Shoah*-related features, Judaism has been prominently represented in many genres since the 1970s, especially romantic comedies and films set in locations popularly perceived as quintessentially Jewish. Romance between Jew and Christian was a particularly common motif in the early cinema, where religious difference met the genre's requirement for some kind of obstacle that the couple must negotiate in order to secure happiness. Most frequently this "negotiation" entailed the abandonment of Judaism, or its thoroughgoing accommodation to non-Jewish norms. The pattern, operative in *The Jazz Singer*, persists as recently as *Suzie Gold* (Ric Cantor, 2003), in which Suzie finds life in London's mainstream Orthodox community superficial and brash. One suitor asks her for a date during *shiva*, the seven-day period of mourning following a funeral. Viewers are encouraged to join her in preferring a non-Jewish boy, Darren.

Recent films more obviously test or subvert older conventions. The differences that blight the "nervous romance" at the heart of *Annie Hall* (Woody Allen, 1977) are not religious, but when Alvy visits Annie's WASP family for a ham dinner, he appears – or suspects he appears – to her antisemitic grandmother as a bearded Hasid. Judaism's material expression looms large in the film's construction of difference. Alternative reworkings of Jewish–Christian romance are presented in the Argentinian feature *Sol de otogno* (*Autumn Sun*, Eduardo Mignogna, 1996) and *Keeping the Faith* (Edward Norton, 2000), which both suggest that Judaism is not an insurmountable obstacle to intimacy with a non-Jewish partner, even as they are also careful to move away from radically assimilationist positions. In *Sol*, Clara Goldstein needs someone to pose as her fiancé during the visit of her American brother. After placing a newspaper advertisement, she meets Raul, who is attractive but not the Jew that she and her brother require. Clara's attempts to teach him aspects of Jewish religion and culture gradually give way to an acceptance of Raul on his own terms and a genuine romance develops between the pair: the film's overall message challenges Judaism's preference for endogamy, by suggesting that relationships work only when both partners are able to retain their own identity and individuality. Like *The Jazz Singer*, *Keeping the Faith*'s protagonist is a Jake whose moment of decision comes on Yom Kippur. However, *Keeping the Faith*'s Jake is a Conservative rabbi, positively depicted as a loving son, friend (to his congregation and to non-Jews, especially Brian, a Catholic priest), and gifted preacher. Like *Sol*, the film privileges individual happiness and integrity over communal or familial expectations: after a secret romance, Jake eventually declares his love for the non-Jewish Anna. But the practical difficulties that might face a rabbi who marries a non-Jew are neatly sidelined in *Keeping the Faith*'s final scene, when Anna, making her own surprise announcement, tells Jake that she is already in the process of converting to Judaism.

Screen images of Hasidic Judaism

As noted, whilst *Suzie Gold* and *Keeping the Faith* image mainline Orthodox and Conservative Jewish communities respectively, a disproportionate and increasing number of films depict the most carefully observant or "ultra-Orthodox" forms of Judaism, especially Hasidism. The growth mirrors demographic and other trends. The overall Jewish population in Britain, USA, and Israel is stable or declining, but ultra-Orthodox numbers are increasing markedly (Paul 2007). At the same time, there has been a surge in the activities of groups that mediate Hasidic ideas and values (especially aspects of *kabbalah*) to Jews and non-Jews including celebrities like Demi Moore, Madonna, and Britney Spears. Heightened awareness of Hasidism is one factor impacting filmmakers, particularly in Israel, where such Jews figure prominently in the ranks of the Zionist project's most militant advocates – and in those of its harshest critics. Further afield, somewhat fantasized images of unified religious families and communities can possess strong emotional appeal in the context of current anxieties over Jewish intermarriage and continuity, or of more widely felt concerns over multiculturalism and the problematizing of identity in the context of postmodernism. Pragmatic factors, too, favor the onscreen depiction of ultra-Orthodoxy. In contrast to the more spiritualizing approaches of some contemporary Progressive Judaisms, a carefully observant lifestyle entails a host of distinctive, *visible* subcultural markers. In this respect the representation of ultra-Orthodox Judaism can be contextualized within a broader interest in ethnic and religious minority groups (including Amish, conservative Mennonites, and Plymouth Brethren, shown in *Witness* (Peter Weir, 1985), *Stellet Licht* (*Silent Light*, Carlos Reygadas, 2007), and *Son of Rambow* (Garth Jennings, 2007) respectively, whose lifestyles provide attractive resources for cinematic inscriptions of identity and difference.

The curiosity value of Hasidic culture may itself be a significant motivator of a film's action. Just as Phil's journalistic project provided a vehicle for comment on antisemitism in *Gentleman's Agreement*, so in *A Stranger Among Us* (Sidney Lumet, 1992) policewoman Emily's journey undercover in order to investigate a murder functions as a device for the mediation of aspects of Hasidic culture. *Stranger* explores the rhythms of a life centered on prayer and study, structured by regulations governing food preparation and sexual modesty. However, this milieu is ultimately a picturesque backdrop to Emily's professional and personal quests. By the film's end, her time with the Hasidim has enabled her both to identify the killer (a *baalat teshuva* or previously nonobservant woman who has adopted an Orthodox lifestyle – the film seemingly cannot countenance criminality amongst "real" Hasidim) and to swap her empty, cynical lifestyle for a more reflective one.

Not all images of Hasidic Jews are so positive. A group using *gematria* (converting Hebrew words into numbers, by assigning each letter a numerical value) to search for the divine Name (the pronunciation of which was largely proscribed in ancient Judaism, and was subsequently lost) is amongst the range of sinister figures encountered by mathematician Max Cohen in *∏* (Darren Aronofsky, 1998). The hero of *Ha-hesder* (*Time of Favor*, Joseph Cedar, 2000), Menachem, is a participant in the *Hesder Yeshiva* program (in which men combine religious studies with military service) but the film ultimately positions Judaism as a threat to Israel's security; one of Menachem's peers, fired by his rebbe's teachings, plots to bomb the Dome of the Rock. In contrast to *Hester Street*, where Gitl's self-realization is bound up with her active reassertion of traditional gender roles in the New World (her economic activity will support Bernstein's religious scholarship – the same pattern operates in *Kadosh* [*Sacred*, Amos Gitai, 2000]), carefully observant Judaism is also depicted negatively in a number of films emphasizing female experience. *A Price Above Rubies* (Boaz Yakin, 1998) follows a young woman, Sonia Horowitz, whose desires are thwarted by the strictures of life in a New York Hasidic community. Symbolizing his privileging of religious matters over personal ones, Sonia's husband Mendel insists that their first child be named in their rebbe's honor, ignoring Sonia's wish to name him after her dead brother. Soon bored by motherhood, Sonia joins the family business, but Mendel's brother, Sender, only permits this after she "accepts" being raped by him. Eventually, following more conflicts around Sonia's quest for autonomy, she begins an affair with a Puerto Rican, which Sender reveals to the family, leading to Sonia's divorce and ostracization. As in other features considered in this essay, Judaism per se is not *Rubies'* primary target. Most of the actual details of Orthodox life are absent; Sonia is an "everywoman", the ritual practices depicted function as a visible set of regulations that she must negotiate in her struggle for self-realization. But in making Hasidism the cipher for patriarchy, the film revives earlier archetypes. Judaism is part of that which Sonia, like the "modern" Jew of the silent film era, must shed in order to achieve her potential, whilst the depiction of Sender, a sexual predator who operates an untaxed store alongside a legitimate one, flirts with antisemitic caricatures of Jews as greedy exploiters.

Israeli films

If many films are simplistically nostalgic or retrogressive in their engagement with Judaism, since 1990 more challenging, complex treatments have also emerged. Moreover, as Desser and Friedman observe, on occasion "the lack of Judaism itself is a structuring absence" (1993: 9). In other words, Judaism *and its loss* can underpin the exploration of identities and identifications in the cinema.

Such issues are particularly apparent in Israel, where recent decades have seen a shift from "the politics of ideas" to "the politics of identity" (Loshitzky 2001: xi) and where cinema cannot avoid debates over such issues as Judaism's role in a multicultural, constitutionally secular democracy, relationships between Ashkenazim (Jews with European roots) and Mizrahim (those of Middle Eastern heritage), tensions between religious and secular Jews, and the Palestinian question. Israel's first permanent cinema opened in Jerusalem in 1908. Religious youths who protested the development were in turn castigated by their teacher, Rabbi Lipa, who argued that they "should have stayed at home all day, all night, all month, and all year, till their dying day; and cinema? … An abomination!" (Zimerman 2002: 912). Cinema was "abominable" for several reasons. Screen images of bodies and faces threatened traditional Jewish caution concerning the representation of the human form, whilst film theaters could serve as sites of inappropriate contact between the sexes. (Today, one Hasidic group suggests, "A date at the cinema ... sheds little light on anything, and only serves to bring the two to an emotional attachment before it is healthy for them to have one, for it interferes with the ability to make an objective decision" [Chabad.org, n.d.].) Above all, film could detract from the (male) Jew's highest calling, study of religious texts. But hostility was not the sole response. More typically, early Zionists sought to distinguish themselves from what they deemed the outmoded passivism of Orthodox Judaism and pressed film into the service of efforts to forge a new Jewish identity linked to aspirations for an independent national homeland.

Just as secular activists acknowledged Judaism's role in preserving Jewish identity in diaspora, but deemed it superfluous in a modern nation-state – dismissing aspects of Mizrahi Judaism in particular as mere "folk religion" or superstition – so Judaism provided many of the recurring myths and metaphors in Israeli film (see further Zanger 2003), but the plots of early features commonly eschewed explicit treatment of Judaism or criticized it. The revived Hebrew language predominated over Yiddish (Weitzner 2002: 187), and agriculture and self-defense were popular subjects. The image of Judaism in the satirical *Sallah Shabati* (Ephraim Kishon, 1964) is, in this respect, typical. When Sallah arrives in Israel from an Arab country, his deviation from Ashkenazi norms is inscribed in dress, language, and religious practice. Unlike the smartly dressed Western immigrants also shown arriving at Ben-Gurion airport, he kisses the runway and recites a blessing, met with an "Amen" from the members of his large, loosely defined family. *Sallah* satirizes many groups within Israeli society, including the Ashkenazi "establishment," who by turns seek to "exploit" or to "civilize" new arrivals. By the film's end, wisdom or good fortune (it remains unclear which) enables Sallah's family to move from a transit camp into better accommodation. But the airport scene, and a later one, in which Sallah takes a backgammon board to synagogue, perpetuate Ashkenazi/Orientalist constructions of Mizrahi Judaism as a showy, yet lightly worn garment.

More recent decades have seen a weakening confidence in Zionism's master narrative; events like the assassination of Prime Minister Yitzhak Rabin by Yigal Amir, a former *Hesder* student, in 1995 have laid bare the deep divisions within Israeli society. Onscreen, this is reflected in the construal of national identity in broader, more diverse terms (Avisar 2005). For leftwing filmmakers, tensions between Judaism and secular worldviews remain influential. Amos Gitai's *Kadosh* begins with a private moment: a Hasid wakes and begins morning prayers as his wife sleeps on. But *Kadosh* highlights the wider implications of such intimate events. Meir and Rivka have been married for ten years, but remain childless, and the couple's rebbe has ordered Meir to divorce and remarry so that he may fulfill the commandment to procreate (Genesis 1:28) and combat the rise of secularism. Despite Meir's (reciprocated) love for his wife, he eventually agrees to reject her. At the same time, Rivka's sister, Malka, is forbidden to marry the man she loves and is subjected to a violent arranged marriage. Reflecting Gitai's architectural interests, *Kadosh* privileges "the spaces and structures of orthodox life ... rituals, prayer and ... custom" over narrative progression (James 2000: 29). As in *Hester Street* and *Rubies*, sequences depicting the sisters in a small, bare apartment, painstakingly preparing food according to *kashrut* (dietary laws), suggest claustrophobia. The impasse of Meir and Rivka's sterility, and the conflicts it generates (eventually, Malka leaves the community; Rivka dies, broken-hearted), are figures for wider tensions in society. In *Kadosh* Judaism ultimately stands for that which constructs differences and divisions – in space and time, between and within people – giving the lie to the rhetoric of Israeli unity.

Ushpizin's (*Guests*, Giddi Dar, 2004) presentation of Judaism quite differently subverts the Zionist metanarrative. In a plot alluding to a mystical ritual in which seven "guests" from Judaism's past are symbolically invited into one's *sukkah* (shelter) during the festival of Sukkot, it juxtaposes two marginalized groups in Israeli society – criminals and ultra-Orthodox Jews. Moshe and Malli, a couple who are *baalei teshuva*, find themselves playing host to visitors from Moshe's criminal past. After attempting to rid themselves of the embarrassment, they eventually recognize the experience as a test of faith. Unusually, the lighthearted film was conceived partly as a bridge between secular (like Dar) and religious (like Breslover Hasidim Shuli and Michal Rand, who play Moshe and Malli) Israelis. Pre-release, the film was shown to a Hasidic audience and by agreement in Israel it is not exhibited on *Shabbat*. *Ushpizin* is, then, distinguished from most of the features discussed in this essay – not only because of its attention to Judaism as a total, lived culture, but also because its very creation rests on assumptions about film's ability to articulate a particular type of Judaism for a broad audience.

Judaism and postmodernism

Whilst debates concerning the relationships between Judaism and Jewish identity are particularly lively in Israel, films produced elsewhere may also treat Judaism in fresh, surprising ways. *A Family Affair* (Helen Lesnick, 2001) opens with images of a *huppah* (wedding canopy), a widely recognized signifier of Jewishness. Conventional expectations are, however, immediately undercut by the on-looking Rachel Rosen, who directly addresses the camera to reveal that, "I've known I was gay ever since I was DNA." The film's treatment of Rachel's story – from the moment she comes out, to her eventual marriage to Christine – perpetuates this initial juxtapositioning of Jewishness (articulated in religious terms as much as, or even more than, ethnic or cultural ones) and sexuality. Rachel's mother's grief on learning of her daughter's sexuality is represented by her sitting *shiva*, and her later activism for gay rights leads her to recast Passover as a "festival of freedom for all our GLBT loved ones." (Although it is played for comic effect, this innovation reflects a genuine tendency for new events and concerns to be subsumed within the festival's historic emphases of suffering and liberation.) Like Alvy in *Annie Hall*, Rachel is a Jewish New Yorker who falls in love with a WASP, and *Family Affair* references the construction of Jewishness in Allen's film. Echoing Alvy's experience with Annie's grandmother, Rachel, who fears Christine's plan to convert, and the desire for commitment that it represents, "sees" Christine's future as a Hasidic woman, surrounded by children as she prepares for *Shabbat*. At the same time, Rachel's own Judaism and the presence of an African-

American woman who is also a lesbian and a convert to Judaism, at the *Seder* table, disrupts popular associations between Judaism, Ashkenazi Jewish culture, and hetero-sexuality. (For additional, quite different explorations of Judaism and sexuality, see *Trembling Before G-d* [Sandi Simcha DuBowski, 2001], a documentary about gay and lesbian ultra-Orthodox Jews, and *Song of Songs* [Josh Appignanesi, 2006], a story about an incestuous relationship in north London's Orthodox Jewish community, which draws parallels between sadomasochism and the disciplining of the self by those who live according to *halakhah*.)

Further reworkings of traditional representations of Judaism are offered in *Lucky Number Slevin* (Paul McGuigan, 2006) and *The Big Lebowski* (Joel Coen, 1998). The former pits Shlomo, "a rabbi who would rather be a gangster and a gangster who would rather be a rabbi" (Abrams 2007: 65) against Slevin Kelevra (the surname means "bad dog" in Hebrew), also a Jew with few qualms about murdering his enemies. The film acknowledges and tests the assumptions and conventions that shape many screen engagements with Judaism. Thus in the course of a gangland power struggle, Shlomo's rival, "The Boss," decrees that his son, "Yitzchok the fairy," must die – Yitzchok's sexuality alludes to representations of Jewish males as weak and effeminate (a trope already present in *A Gesture Fight in Hester Street*), whilst his name and fate evoke *ha-akedah*. In similar vein, Walter Sobchak's Judaism is perhaps most readily inter-preted as one of a series of contradictions played for humor and shock value in *The Big Lebowski*. Sobchak, a disturbed Vietnam veteran, is a convert to Judaism who does not work, drive, or bowl on the Sabbath because, as he reminds his friend Jeff "the Dude" Lebowski, he's "Shomer fuckin' Shabbos!!" (someone who keeps the commandments relating to the Sabbath).

In marking the gap between the ideas of Judaism as narrated by Jews and/or by the wider non-Jewish world, and the actual appearance, attitudes. and activities of its adherents, these films are influenced by postmodernism. Pursuing postmodern ideas more deliberately, a few filmmakers have deliberately probed issues such as the enacting and embracing of Judaism and Jewish culture by non-Jews. This strategy is exemplified by *Dieu est grand, je suis toute petite* (*God is Great, I'm Not*, Pascale Bailly, 2001), a romantic comedy about a relationship between Michèle, a Parisian model who adopts Catholicism, Buddhism, and then Judaism in her search for meaning, and François, a secular Jew. *Dieu est grand* explores both the performance of Judaism by non-Jews (despite François's unease, Michèle fixes a *mezuzah* to his doorpost, attends Judaism classes, and begins to observe *Shabbat*) and by Jews who are largely removed from the symbols and traditions they enact for the entertainment and cultural enrichment of a predominantly non-Jewish public (at Michèle's request, François dons a *kippah* [skullcap], learns how to pray, and becomes *kosher*) – a European phenomenon that Gruber (2002) dubs "virtual Judaism."

In non-narrative film, similar trends are evident. For example, Rachel Garfield's photographic and video installations explore Jewishness in the broader framework of twenty-first-century identity which she invites viewers to consider not in fixed, essen-tializing terms but as "diasporic" – meaning here unstable, and subject to constant renegotiation in and through encounter with others. Her *So You Think You Can*

Tell? (2000) juxtaposes the stories of two women. One, who appears to be "black," describes her upbringing in a "white" English family, and explains how this has led her to embrace Judaism, in which she feels at home. The other, who appears to be "white" (we see only her mouth and nose) is a now nonobservant Orthodox Jew who has a "black" male partner and lives within the "black" community. Like the "disruptions" in *Family Affair*, the overall effect is "to throw into question our assumptions that *appearance* guarantees *identification*" (Amelia Jones, in Garfield 2005: 25). In issuing this challenge, Garfield's work reflects Hall's suggestion that representation in the cinema "is able to constitute us as new kinds of subjects, and thereby enable us to discover [new] places from which to speak" (1990: 236–7) – including new places from which to speak within and about Judaism.

Conclusions

Screen representations of Judaism arc, then, many and diverse, but they are united by several common impulses or tendencies. In almost all cases, the representation (in the sense of factual accuracy or verisimilitude) of Judaism is not the filmmaker's primary motivation. Instead, rituals and material culture, particularly ones which non-Jewish audiences are likely to recognize/perceive as Jewish, function as visual shorthands to establish the identity of a character or characters, to add exoticism to a plot's setting (perhaps to revive a tired genre), or to serve as an explicit/implicit comparator for another religious or ethnic culture.

Certainly, the past twenty years have seen the release of a significant number – perhaps a number unprecedented since the heyday of Yiddish cinema – of films that seek to address contemporary Jewish experience and identity, and Judaism's place within it. Amongst other things, this reflects the new possibilities for filmmaking signaled by the advent of digital technologies, and the opening up of new avenues of film distribution, including the development of Jewish Film Festivals, which showcase new work and occasionally fund production. But more generally, perhaps, Judaism's increasing presence in the cinema is indicative of its ongoing cultural or symbolic significance in many cultures (especially but not only in America, Europe, and Israel), a significance that persists in spite of the realities of actual Jewish religious practice and presence in a particular locale.

Finally, if Judaism often seems to be of comparatively little import to the film industry, this does not mean that film is of no consequence to Judaism. In *The Hebrew Hammer* (Jonathan Kesselman, 2004), the eponymous hero distributes videocassettes of movies popularly identified as ubiquitously Jewish – *Yentl* (Barbra Streisand, 1983) and *Fiddler on the Roof* (Norman Jewison, 1971) – to Jewish children whose identity is imperiled by their attraction to Christmas holiday celebrations. The scene's point is humorous, but its linking of cinema with Jewish continuity gestures toward bigger issues, ones that are implicit in the production and reception of many of the films this essay has discussed. Each of the images described here is a part of what Judaism "is" for many Jews and non-Jews alike. Whilst cinema remains – in a very serious sense – a vehicle of fantasy (one which allowed many early filmmakers to bury – and many later filmmakers to reimag[in]e – their Jewish "roots"), it also affords moments of Jewish religious community, intimacy, memory, and transcendence.

Bibliography

Abrams, N. (2007) "Heartless Violence and Hopeless Schmucks," *Jewish Quarterly* 205: 62–6.

Antler, J. (1995) *"Hester Street,"* in M. C. Carnes (ed.) *Past Imperfect: History According to the Movies*, London: Cassell: 178–81.

Avisar, I. (1987) "Christian Ideology and Jewish Genocide in American Holocaust Movies," in S. Pinsker (ed.) *Literature, the Arts and the Holocaust*, Greenwood, FL: Penkevill Publishing: 21–42.

—— (2005) "The National and the Popular in Israeli Cinema," *Shofar: An Interdisciplinary Journal of Jewish Studies* 24 (1): 125–43.

Carr, S. A. (2001) *Hollywood and Antisemitism: A Cultural History up to World War Two*, Cambridge: Cambridge University Press.

Chabad.org (n.d.) "Dating the Jewish Way." Online. Available HTTP: <http://www.chabad.org/library/article_cdo/aid/448427/jewish/Dating-the-Jewish-Way.htm> (accessed 17 April 2008).

Desser, D. and Friedman, L. D. (1993) *American-Jewish Filmmakers: Traditions and Trends*, Chicago: University of Illinois Press.

Diner, H. (2000) *Lower East Side Memories: A Jewish Place in America*, Princeton: Princeton University Press.

Eisen, A. M. (1998) *Rethinking Modern Judaism: Ritual, Commandment, Community*, Chicago: University of Chicago Press.

Gabler, N. (1989) *An Empire of Their Own: How the Jews Invented Hollywood*, New York: Crown.

Garfield, R. (2005) *You'd Think So, Wouldn't You?*, Hatfield: University of Hertfordshire (exhibition catalogue).

Gershenson, O. (2008) "Ambivalence and Identity in Russian Jewish Cinema," in Simon J. Bronner (ed.) *Jewishness: Expression, Identity, and Representation*, Oxford and New York: The Littman Library of Jewish Civilization: 175–94.

Gilman, S. L. (2006) *Multiculturalism and the Jews*, New York: Routledge.

Goldman, E. A. (1983) *Visions, Images and Dreams: Yiddish Films Past and Present*, Epping: Bowker.

Goldsmith, E. S. (1998) "Yiddishism and Judaism," in D. Kerler (ed.) *The Politics of Yiddish: Studies in Language, Literature and Society*. Walnut Creek, CA: Alta Mira Press: 11–22.

Gruber, R. E. (2002) *Virtually Jewish: Reinventing Jewish Culture in Europe*, Berkeley: University of California Press.

Hall, S. (1990) "Cultural Identity and Diaspora," in J. Rutherford (ed.) *Identity: Community, Culture, Difference*, London: Lawrence and Wishart: 222–37.

Hayne, D. (1960) *The Autobiography of Cecil B. DeMille*, London: W. H. Allen.

Igra, A. R. (2006) "Marriage as Welfare," *Women's History Review* 15 (4): 601–10.

Insdorf, A. (2003) *Indelible Shadows: Film and the Holocaust*, Cambridge: Cambridge University Press.

Jacobs, N. (2005) *Yiddish: A Linguistic Introduction*, Cambridge: Cambridge University Press.

James, N. (2000) "In a Harsh Light," *Sight and Sound* 10 (8): 28–30.

Johnston, R. D. (2006) "Joke-Work: The Construction of Jewish Postmodern Identity in Contemporary Theory and American Film," in V. Brook (ed.) *You Should See Yourself: Jewish Identity in Postmodern American Culture*, New Brunswick: Rutgers University Press: 207–29.

Kugelmass, J. (1990) "Green Bagels: An Essay on Food, Nostalgia, and the Carnivalesque," *YIVO Annual*: 57–80.

Loshitzky, Y. (2001) *Identity Politics on the Israeli Screen*, Austin: University of Texas Press.

Ohad-Karny, Y. (2005) "'Anticipating' Gibson's *The Passion of the Christ*: The Controversy of Cecil B. DeMille's *The King of Kings* [sic]," *Jewish History* 19 (2): 189–210.

Paul, J. (2007) "Three of Four Jewish Births in UK are Haredi," *The Jerusalem Post*, 1 August. Online. Available HTTP: <http://www.jpost.com/servlet/Satellite?cid=1185893692739&pagename=JPost%2FJPArticle%2FShowFull> (accessed 1 April 2008).

Ray, R. B. (2001) *How a Film Theory Got Lost and Other Mysteries in Cultural Studies*, Bloomington: Indiana University Press.

Reinhartz, A. (2007) *Jesus of Hollywood*, New York: Oxford University Press.

Rosenberg, J. (1996) "Jewish Experience on Film: An American Overview," in D. Singer (ed.) *Jewish Year Book 1996*, New York: The American Jewish Committee: 3–50.

Rosenberg, J. and Whitfield, S. J. (2002) "The Cinema of Jewish Experience: Introduction," *Prooftexts* 22 (1): 1–10.

Weitzner, J. (2002) "Yiddish in Israeli Cinema," *Prooftexts* 22 (1): 186–99.

Wright, M. J. (2005) "Lights! Camera! Antisemitism?: Jewish–Christian Relations and the Cinema," in E. Kessler and M. J. Wright (eds) *Themes in Jewish–Christian Relations*, Cambridge: Orchard Academic: 171–200.

Zanger, A. (2003) "*Hole in the Moon* or Zionism and the Binding (ha-ak'eda) Myth in Israeli Cinema," *Shofar: An Interdisciplinary Journal of Jewish Studies* 22 (1): 95–109.

Zimerman, M. (2002) "Jewish and Israeli Film Studies," in M. Goodman (ed.) *The Oxford Handbook of Jewish Studies*, Oxford: Oxford University Press: 911–42.

Filmography

Annie Hall (1977, dir. W. Allen)

The Big Lebowski (1998, dir. J. Coen)

Der Dibek (*The Dybbuk*) (1937, dir. M. Waszynski)

Dieu est grand, je suis toute petite (*God is Great, I'm Not*) (2001, dir. P. Bailly)

Europa, Europa (1991, dir. A. Holland)

A Family Affair (2001, dir. H. Lesnick)

Fiddler on the Roof (1971, dir. N. Jewison)

Gentleman's Agreement (1947, dir. E. Kazan)

A Gesture Fight in Hester Street (1903, American Mutoscope and Biograph Company)

Les guichets du Louvre (*Black Thursday*) (1974, dir. M. Mitrani)

Ha-hesder '(*Time of Favor*) (2000, dir. J. Cedar)

Happy-Go-Lucky (2008, dir. M. Leigh). ⟵

The Hebrew Hammer (2004, dir. J. Kesselman)

Hester Street (1975, dir. J. Micklin Silver)

Intolerance (1916, dir. D. Griffith)

The Jazz Singer (1927, dir. A. Crosland)

Jesus of Nazareth (1977, dir. F. Zeffirelli)

Kadosh (*Sacred*) (2000, dir. A. Gitai)

Keeping the Faith (2000, dir. E. Norton)

Khazan afn Probe (*Cantor on Trial*) (1931, dir. S. Goldin)

Dem Khazn's Zind (*The Cantor's Son*) (1937, dir. S. Goldin and I. Motyleff)

The King of Kings (1927, dir. C. DeMille)

Der Lamedvovnik (*One of the Thirty-Six*) (1925, dir. J. Szaro)

Left Luggage (1998, dir. J. Krabbé)

Lucky Number Slevin (2006, dir. P. McGuigan) ⟵

Monsieur Klein (1976, dir. J. Losey)

Obchod na Korze (*The Shop on Main Street*) (1965, dir. J. Kadár and E. Klos)

The Passion of the Christ (2004, dir. M. Gibson)

The Pawnbroker (1964, dir. S. Lumet)

// (1998, dir. D. Aronofsky)

Poylishe Velder (*In Polish Woods*) (1928, dir. J. Turkow)

A Price Above Rubies (1998, dir. B. Yakin)

The Quarrel (1990, dir. E. Cohen)

Sallah Shabati (1964, dir. E. Kishon)

Schindler's List (1993, dir. S. Spielberg)

Secrets and Lies (1996, dir. M. Leigh)

So You Think You Can Tell? (2000, dir. R. Garfield)

Sol de otogno (*Autumn Sun*) (1996, dir. E. Mignogna)
Son of Rambow (2007, dir. G. Jennings) ←
Song of Songs (2006, dir. J. Appignanesi)
Stellet Licht (*Silent Light*) (2007, dir. C. Reygadas)
A Stranger Among Us (1992, dir. S. Lumet) ←
Suzie Gold (2003, dir. R. Cantor)
The Ten Commandments (1923, dir. C. B. DeMille)
Trembling Before G-d (2001, dir. S. S. DuBowski)
Ushpizin (*Guests*) (2004, dir. G. Dar)
Vera Drake (2004, dir. M. Leigh)
Der Vilner Shtot Khazn (*The Vilna Cantor*) (1940, dir. G. Moskov and M. Nossek)
Witness (1985, dir. P. Weir)
Yentl (1983, dir. B. Streisand)

6

CHRISTIANITY

Craig Detweiler

The subtle and the spectacular

Where is God? How might the ineffable or even the Almighty be depicted onscreen? What efforts have filmmakers made to capture the Christian story? The biblical tradition celebrates both the transcendence of God and the immanence of Jesus. Some have pursued a *via negativa*, seeking to purge earthly desires. Others have embraced the abundance of images that surround us, embracing a *via positiva*. Filmmakers aspiring to capture Christian history onscreen have adopted both subtle and spectacular styles.

Many faith-fueled filmmakers trusted the Spirit to communicate through sparse means. The transcendental style identified by Paul Schrader strips cinema down to the barest essentials (Schrader 1972). It removes the manipulations of plot, acting, and musical score in an effort to pull audiences beyond their own egotism. This strand is found in the films of French Catholic Robert Bresson, Dutch Lutheran Carl Theodor Dreyer, and Russian Orthodox Andrei Tarkovsky. In contrast, Hollywood directors like Protestants Cecil B. DeMille and D. W. Griffith turned Bible stories into the most opulent productions possible. They employed special effects and a cast of thousands to bring audiences to their feet (and the box office). The abundant means of biblical blockbusters often emphasize spectacle over spirituality. Catholic directors like John Ford and Martin Scorsese merged their immanent, sacramental tradition with the many splendors afforded to filmmakers.

During the first century of cinema, over one hundred films chronicled the life and death of Jesus. Whether on a grand scale or as an intimate tragedy, the shifting depictions of Jesus mirror changes in both theology and technology. These diverse biopics reflect the particular issues of their era rather than the historical Jesus recorded in the Gospels of Matthew, Mark, Luke, and John (Reinhartz 2007). Along with biblical epics, Christianity has informed virtually every cinematic genre. Saints, nuns, and priests have been portrayed with reverence and ridicule in historical biopics. Christ-figures have arisen in westerns, science fiction, and horror films. Many of the more enduring dramas have asked troubling questions of theodicy, "How can a good God preside over a cruel and often unjust world?"

The finest directors have explored issues raised in their religious upbringing, often exorcising the demons of their childhood. A European art-house director like Ingmar

Bergman returned to Christian themes for his finest achievements. Filmmakers like Luis Buñuel and Roberto Rossellini rebelled against their religious upbringing with scathing satires and poignant, personal filmmaking. Those outside traditional bounds of faith, like Pier Paolo Pasolini, are often most adept at crafting genuinely inspiring stories. Christian theology continues to drive the poetic visions of Wim Wenders. Terrence Malick invites viewers to contemplate the glory of God's creation. Whether created out of devotion, revulsion, or exploration, cinematic depictions of Christianity have resulted in some of the most beloved film classics.

Go big, go biblical

When the movies "go big," they often go biblical. The grandest cinematic epics inevitably return to some form of what Christians embrace as "The Greatest Story Ever Told." From *The Ten Commandments* (e.g., 1923, 1956) to *The Passion of the Christ* (2004), biblical narratives have served as a dramatic opportunity for filmmakers who both espouse and despise Christianity. Sword-and-sandal epics like *Quo Vadis?* (e.g., 1912, 1925, 1951) and *Ben Hur* (e.g., 1907, 1925, 1959) have been remade and reimagined for successive generations of viewers with even grander special effects. Prolific filmmaker Cecil B. DeMille could not resist the temptation to restage *The Ten Commandments*. What began as a grand silent film in 1923 reached widescreen proportions in 1956. The parting of the Red Sea thrilled audiences in both incarnations. The enduring story of the Hebrews' exodus out of Egypt has even been retold as an animated musical (*The Prince of Egypt*, 1998).

Competing depictions of Jesus cropped up alongside the birth of cinema. In *The Passion Play* (1897), Marc Klaw and Abraham Erlanger documented the European church pageants that recreated the final week of Jesus' life. Their comparatively amateurish production was exceeded by *The Passion Play of Oberammergau* (1898). While ostensibly originating in Bavaria, this second theatrical version was actually filmed on a rooftop in New York City! Appreciative audiences did not seem deterred by this revelation, turning the twenty-three scenes comprising the silent film into a profitable sensation (Kinnard and Davis 1992). Other notable silent passion plays included the six-minute *Life of Christ* (1899) directed by Alice Guy and *The Life and Passion of Jesus Christ* (1902) from Pathé. The Kalem studio's *From the Manger to the Cross* (1912) was amongst America's first feature films and noted for its location shooting in Egypt and Palestine. It clings to a stagy, *tableau vivant* style.

Italian epics like *Quo Vadis?* (1912) inspired Hollywood pioneers like D. W. Griffith and Cecil B. DeMille to expand the length and scale of the Christ story – making it truly cinematic. The massive sets erected by Griffith for *Intolerance* (1916) nearly overshadowed the life of Jesus embedded amidst four converging storylines. Having already faced protestors' ire with *The Birth of a Nation* (1915), Griffith staged the crucifixion scene in *Intolerance* under the watchful eyes of a rabbi and an Episcopalian priest. His depiction of the Jewish community persecuting and crucifying Christ was eventually reshot with Roman soldiers serving as the prime instigators (Kinnard and Davis 1992: 27). The charges of antisemitism surrounding

Mel Gibson's staging of *The Passion of the Christ* have filmic precursors dating back to this time.

The grandest silent "Jesus film" is Cecil B. DeMille's *King of Kings* (1927). It opens with DeMille's patented blend of sex and salvation, as a scantily clad Mary Magdalene entertains a male audience. DeMille takes liberties with the biblical narrative, creating a love triangle between Mary, Judas, and Jesus. Yet, as the son of an Episcopalian lay minister, DeMille attempted to create an air of devotion on location (DeMille 1959). The first day of shooting included an ecumenical prayer service. Father Daniel Lord (coauthor of the Production Code) offered mass each morning the production shot on Catalina Island. The cinematic results have stood the test of time. H. B. Warner portrays Jesus with strength and confidence that stands in marked contrast to the doubt-filled Jesus depicted by Willem Dafoe in *The Last Temptation of Christ* (1988). The eerie special effects of *King of Kings* have held up over time as when the seven deadly sins exit Mary's body. DeMille continued to mine early Christian history for box office gold in *The Sign of the Cross* (1932). As the excessive Roman emperor Nero, Charles Laughton, and his consort Poppaea (Claudette Colbert,) provide a campy opportunity for DeMille to revel in sin while condemning its effects.

Borrowing from DeMille's formula, filmmakers continued to revel in the profane in order to attract viewers to sacred stories. The Bacchanalian rituals of ancient Rome were contrasted with the devoted Christian life. In some cases, studios conflated history for the sake of dramatic effect. The eruption of Vesuvius in AD 79 became concurrent with the crucifixion of Jesus in *The Last Days of Pompeii* (1935). In the Hollywood remake of *Quo Vadis* (1951), Peter Ustinov portrays a debauched Nero relishing the torture of countless Christian martyrs. A host of widescreen religious epics followed including *The Robe* (1953) and *Ben-Hur* (1959). They not only depicted the crowds following Jesus, but also attracted a mass following at the box office. Jesus became an almost otherworldly figure in the fifties, depicted with such reverence that only the back of his head could be revealed. These ambitious pictures reached their apotheosis in Nicholas Ray's *King of Kings* (1961) and George Stevens' *The Greatest Story Ever Told* (1966). The sincerity in both movies can be stifling as parades of Hollywood stars make distracting cameos. John Wayne's appearance as the Roman soldier stationed at the foot of the cross nearly killed the biblical epic.

As theology wrestled with "The death of God" movement, so filmmakers began their quest for the historical Jesus. Italian neo-realists stripped religious stories down to their bare essentials. While Hollywood went bigger, European cinema, rebuilding from the Second World War, went smaller. Christianity followed two divergent cinematic paths: religion as spectacle or as modest virtue. In *The Miracle* (1948), Roberto Rossellini lashed back against a Catholic Church that condemned his relationship (and child) with actress Ingrid Bergman. *The Miracle* arises when a poor woman sleeps with a bum she mistakes for St. Joseph. While she expects to give birth to the baby Jesus, the church and the village cast her out. The baby is born in a stable, rejected by the religious community. In his rejection of church dogma, Rossellini reclaimed the outsider status inherent in the nativity story.

Pier Paolo Pasolini's *The Gospel According to St. Matthew* (1966) is widely regarded as the most authentic and moving life of Christ on film. By casting nonprofessional actors and staging the life of Christ amidst a remote Italian village, Pasolini brought grit to the Gospels often lacking in more extravagant features. In *The Gospel According to St. Matthew*, Jesus is a man of the people, serving the poor, challenging religious and government authorities. As a gay man with Marxist leanings, Pasolini highlighted Jesus' solidarity with the masses, those outside the corridors of power. How does one seemingly beyond church borders create such a compelling portrait of Christ? Perhaps skepticism toward the biblical sources creates more resonant movies.

The foment arising from the 1960s resulted in vibrant reimaginations of the life of Christ. From Broadway musicals came *Jesus Christ Superstar* (1973) and *Godspell* (1973). Both use rock music to place Jesus' loyalties with hippies and flower children. While *Jesus Christ Superstar* retains a Middle Eastern setting, *Godspell* brings the Bible to New York City. Jesus becomes a holy fool, a clown, sporting a Superman logo and suspenders. These groovy time capsules made Christianity relevant to the turbulent era.

The demythologizing of Jesus occurring in academic circles led to several cinematic controversies. Christians protested the release of Monty Python's *Life of Brian* (1979), Jean-Luc Godard's *Hail Mary* (1985), and Martin Scorsese's *The Last Temptation of Christ* (1988). All three films generated more headlines than ticket sales. As a comedic satire, the *Life of Brian* demonstrated how cults are born out of disinformation. Many Christians failed to find the humor in the wacky chorus that accompanied the crucifixion: "Always Look on the Bright Side of Life." Iconoclastic director Jean-Luc Godard also courted controversy by updating the nativity story. His Mary works at a gas station that a taxi driver named Joseph frequents. Godard captures how troubling an Annunciation would be to any young couple. While frank language and ample nudity offended audiences, Godard's *Hail Mary* ultimately affirms the mystifying and inspiring aspects of the Immaculate Conception.

The charges of blasphemy reached a fever pitch with *The Last Temptation of Christ*. While director Martin Scorsese claimed he made the film as an act of devotion, some Christian leaders denounced it as an abomination. Protestors marched outside the offices of Universal Studios. Audiences failed to distinguish between the Gospel accounts of Jesus and Nikos Kazantzakis' novel (Riley 2003). The film depicts Jesus' temptation to eschew the cross for a life of domestic bliss as a dream. The courageous faith affirmed at the conclusion of the film was lost amidst the double-minded portrait of Jesus that preceded it.

Jesus of Montreal (1989) emerged as the mostly fully realized commentary upon the domestication of Jesus. It places the passion narrative within a Canadian theater troupe. A dwindling church eager to attract a crowd at Easter commissions a desperate actor to update the passion play. Daniel's private life begins to take on eerie parallels to Jesus' arrest and crucifixion. The underappreciated French film *He Who Must Die* (1956) may have inspired filmmaker Denys Arcand. Based upon a Nikos Kazantzakis novel, Jules Dassin's scathing satire *He Who Must Die* pointed out the Church's indifference to contemporary refugees. In both movies, the Christian community is too busy staging a passion play to notice the shocking parallels to the crucifixion in their midst. Artists outside the Church are often uniquely tuned in to hypocrisy.

In the next decade, few filmmakers dared to tread into the treacherous waters of Christ and cinema. Alternative versions of Jesus' life portrayed him as a black man combating racism and oppression. *The Color of the Cross* (2006) and *Son of Man* (2006) connected Jesus' persecution and death to the struggles of people of color. *Son of Man* placed the Gospel stories within a South African context. While generating acclaim at the Sundance Film Festival, the musical film never acquired wide distribution. Having made a series of foul-mouthed comedies starring Jay and Silent Bob, Kevin Smith seemed an unlikely candidate to create a religious film. Yet, *Dogma* (1999) arose as a committed Catholic filmmaker's sincere effort to address serious theological questions. *Dogma* unspools like a comic book catechism, offering outrageous depictions of fallen angels, desperate priests, and Rufus, the thirteenth (and forgotten) black disciple. Smith mocks the Catholic Church's attempts to take Christ off the cross and recast him as the buddy Jesus. But Smith's *Dogma* was greeted by death threats rather than applause.

The bloody Jesus depicted in Mel Gibson's *The Passion of the Christ* (2004) generated even more controversy. Charges of antisemitism appeared months before the movie's premiere. Gibson responded to the charges with defiance, creating huge anticipation for his privately financed act of devotion. With a script uttered in Aramaic, *The Passion* did not court mass audiences. Yet, this small movie, shot in the same Sicilian village as Pasolini's *Gospel According to St. Matthew*, became an international sensation. Love it or hate it, critics and the public rushed to see it. A cottage industry of commentary resulted (Plate 2004; Berenbaum and Landres 2004; Fredriksen 2006). One hundred years after the birth of cinema (and the first features rooted in passion plays), Mel Gibson managed to make the crucifixion of Jesus front-page news. Only in years to come, after the passion *around* the movie subsides, will we be able to judge whether it stands out as a work of profound beauty rooted in authentic faith or a catalogue of horrors unfit for human consumption (or a bit of both!).

Saints and sinners

Christianity spread through the fervent faith of Jesus' followers. The blood of countless martyrs fueled the nascent movement and provided an array of role models. The lives of Christian saints provided a dramatic arc for plenty of big-screen treatments. Amongst the most oft-filmed saints are France's Joan of Arc and Italy's St. Francis of Assisi. Carl Theodor Dreyer's *The Passion of Joan of Arc* (1928) places viewers inside Joan's trial. It uses close-ups to dramatic effect, turning the film into an extended encounter with a tortured, transfixed icon. Renée Falconetti entered so completely into the suffering and persecution of St. Joan that she never acted in another film. Ingrid Bergman portrayed *Joan of Arc* (1948) as a warrior leading an army. Yet, the gap between Bergman's private life and her cinematic role of saint turned moviegoers away from a highly admirable effort. Robert Bresson based *The Trial of Joan of Arc* (1962) upon court transcripts. As in all Bresson films, the static camera and the dry delivery by amateur actors puts the onus on audiences to supply the drama. Some will prefer the overwrought suffering of Dreyer's *Joan* to the austere version supplied by Bresson.

Robert Rossellini's *The Flowers of St. Francis* (1952) celebrates simplicity and finds the divine within nature. Rossellini cast real monks as Francis' followers. He equates sainthood with humor and a willingness to appear foolish. As the Franciscans spin on the ground, we're invited to experience religion as spontaneous joy rather than compulsion. "God's Jester," St. Francis, invites us to undertake a spiritual romp. Franco Zeffirelli's *Brother Sun, Sister Moon* (1972) portrayed St. Francis as a flower child. His vow of poverty and environmental sensitivities matched the counterculture movement of that era.

Amongst other saints filmed with quiet dignity are Bernadette Soubirous of Lourdes in *The Song of Bernadette* (1943), Vincent de Paul in *Monsieur Vincent* (1947) caring for the poor in medieval Europe, and the heroic stance of Thomas Becket (1964) against his friend King Henry II. Luis Buñuel offered a comic (but faith-affirming) exploration of temptation in *Simon of the Desert* (1965). More recent saint stories include biographies of St. Thérèse of Lisieux (1986), El Salvadoran martyr Oscar Romero (1989), Catholic worker Dorothy Day in *Entertaining Angels* (1996), and *Molokai: The Story of Father Damien* (1999). Saints make wondrous appearances to impressionable young people in smaller, independent films like Nancy Savoca's *Household Saints* (1993), Danny Boyle's Christmas story *Millions* (2004), and Julia Kwan's *Eve and the Fire Horse* (2005). While Protestants do not canonize their forebears, they have nevertheless celebrated Martin Luther (1953, 2003).

When Father Daniel Lord included a provision in the Hollywood Production Code (1930) that portraits of clergy must be positive, he paved the way for the beloved Father O'Malley in *Going My Way* (1944) and the singing nuns in *The Sound of Music* (1965). Bing Crosby and Julie Andrews put a warm, positive, and musical face upon ecclesiastical callings. In *Boys Town* (1938), Spencer Tracy portrays the real-life Father Flanagan with such conviction that the phrase, "He ain't heavy, he's my brother" crossed over into popular parlance. In *The Bells of St. Mary's* (1945), Irish Catholic director Leo McCarey includes a memorable scene of Sister Mary Benedict teaching a boy how to box. *On the Waterfront* (1954) showed audiences a priest who could also take a punch and keep on fighting on behalf of embattled longshoremen. *A Man Called Peter* (1955) follows the calling of Reverend Peter Marshall from his Scottish youth to his service as chaplain of the US Senate. The gentle humor found in *Sound of Music* and *The Singing Nun* (1966) gave way to the broader antics of *Nuns on the Run* (1990) and *Sister Act* (1992). The convent became a convenient place for criminals to hide (in drag). Energetic nuns doing song and dance routines result in easy laughs. Such films tread the line between ridicule and appreciation of religious orders, injecting playfulness into religious assumptions.

What about examples of faith found amongst the laity? Tales of ordinary Christians who displayed grace under pressure can be found in *The Inn of the Sixth Happiness* (1958), *Chariots of Fire* (1981), and *Hotel Rwanda* (2004). These underdog stories suggest that the principled stances of men and women can make a difference amidst trying circumstances. How much faith would we evince under similar settings?

Eventually, filmmakers challenged the Production Code's mandate to affirm Christian callings. The struggles of priests and nuns to keep their vows have created enduring drama from *The Nun's Story* (1959) to *Not of This World* (1999). Frustration and sensuality boil beneath the surface in *Black Narcissus* (1947). The Himalayan Mountains have a strange pull for the Anglican nuns fighting to forge a convent at a location that previously housed concubines. The evocative images and unnerving performances made *Black Narcissus* an erotic tragedy. The dark side of religious charlatanism surfaces in *Elmer Gantry* (1960). Rather than deterring such chicanery, Burt Lancaster's Academy Award-winning role seemed to embolden a cottage industry of televangelists in America. Perhaps the most chilling wolf in a clerical collar remains Preacher Harry Powell in *The Night of the Hunter* (1955). Director Charles Laughton contrasts the conniving plans of scripture-quoting Harry (Robert Mitchum) with the sheltering, shotgun-toting Christianity of Rachel Cooper (played by Lillian Gish). The evocative shadows in *Night of the Hunter* capture the eternal struggle between love and hate.

The complex relationship between Christianity and native peoples surfaced in a series of films about missionaries. The best-selling novel by James Michener received an overwrought, big-budget adaptation in *Hawaii* (1966). Max von Sydow portrays a humorless missionary willing to drag his beatific wife into tragedy to fulfill God's calling. This cautionary tale invites us to get our own house in order before we proceed to wreck others. Brazil becomes a battleground between Spain and Portugal in *The Mission* (1986). A Jesuit priest (Jeremy Irons) converts native peoples with the help of a repentant slave trader named Mendoza (Robert De Niro). Scenes of Mendoza's penitent ascent of a South American waterfall stand out as one of the most visceral realizations of Christian theology. His considerable burden is literally cut away, setting him free from a past that binds him. In *Black Robe* (1991), a Jesuit priest travels upriver to a mission in remote Quebec. Director Bruce Beresford resists the temptation to romanticize the Iroquois, Algonquin, and Huron and demonize the priests. This culture clash extracts a heavy price from all parties. Terrence Malick's *The New World* (2005) follows Englishman John Smith through the colonization of Jamestown. The natural beauty of Pocahontas embodies the unspoiled splendor of the Americas. Malick suggests the sense of loss that accompanies the Christianization of Pocahontas and her export to England. Mel Gibson challenges notions of the noble savage in *Apocalypto* (2006). The arrival of Christian missionaries brings the possibility of peace to a bloody Mayan culture.

Spanish director Luis Buñuel satirized church hypocrisy throughout his extravagant career. He sees such a gap between the teachings of Christ and the power hoarded within the church hierarchy that to follow Jesus seems an absurdity. His finest achievement remains *Nazarin* (1959). Father Nazario offers sanctuary for a murderous prostitute and her suicidal sister. He is accused of guilt by association. Buñuel contrasts the simple faith of a Mexican priest with a hypocritical Church. *Viridiana* (1961) follows the travails of a novice right before she becomes a nun. Seduced away by her uncle, Viridiana maintains her purity despite his deceit. Viridiana extends hospitality to beggars who take advantage of her compassion. Buñuel films an inverted Last Supper, suggesting that Viridiana's virtuous faith is wasted upon both an ineffectual Church and an indifferent people.

Other directors have also critiqued the Roman Catholic Church. The British production *Priest* (1994) dealt with the double life of a priest trying to conceal his homosexuality. Director Antonia Bird included explicit sex scenes in a film about the challenges of celibacy. Harvey Weinstein of Miramax attempted to stir up controversy by releasing *Priest* during the Christmas season, but it was met with indifference rather than outrage. The cruelty of Irish nuns informed the stark drama *The Magdalene Sisters* (2002). It portrayed a home for fallen women as a form of prison. A nineteenth-century Portuguese novel served as the source material for *The Crime of Father Amaro* (2002). It anticipated the scandals besetting the Catholic Church in the beginning of a new century. The story is updated to contemporary Mexico with one priest taking donations from a local drug lord, while another seduces an underage girl. While the priests cover up their scandalous behavior, the young girl pays the highest price. A host of documentaries chronicled the recent sexual-abuse scandals involving priests. *Deliver Us from Evil* (2006) interviews Father Oliver O'Grady, a pedophile priest who was shuttled across parishes in northern California for thirty years. *Twist of Faith* (2004) follows a brave victim as he confronts an abusive priest in Toledo, Ohio. Kirby Dick's empathetic documentary shows us one man's struggles to revive his marriage and his Christian faith.

Preachers and priests also wrestle with temptation in *The Apostle* (1997) and *The Third Miracle* (1999). While their resolve is tested, the strong performances by Ed Harris and Robert Duvall are ultimately faith affirming. Acknowledging their flaws and doubts made the drama and their characters even stronger. Perhaps these smaller, independent films represent a way forward for depictions of clergy. The lines between saints and sinners have blurred. But the most enduring films hold that tension together, never resorting to caricature or canonization. Even the most noble nuns and priests have flaws, but that need not disqualify their calling or their faith.

A consistent source of dramatic tension stems from a recurring theological conundrum. Many wonder how the Christian God's goodness and providence can be reconciled with pain, suffering, and death. In the broad comedy *Bruce Almighty* (2003), Jim Carrey shakes one too many fists at God. He is saddled with divine responsibility, sorting out a barrage of prayers. Questions of theodicy reside behind the anger of a former Episcopal priest in *Signs* (2002). When his wife is killed in a car accident, Reverend Graham Hess abandons his calling and his convictions. Director M. Night Shyamalan places a crisis of belief amidst an alien invasion. Graham's faith is restored when he comes to see that everything happens for a reason. A series of coincidences can be interpreted as divine provision for vanquishing the invading aliens. The tidy ending of *Signs* belies an ongoing tension: reconciling a loving God with a cruel world.

Christ-figures

How many films follow strangers with remarkable powers, arriving in a troubled community, being persecuted, but rising above circumstances? Is the cinematic Christ-figure a unique part of film history or just a tribute to universal dramatic elements?

The Christian story is so ingrained in Western culture that countless films can be seen as Christological in form and shape (Malone 1990). In *Shane* (1953), evil cattle rustlers terrorize a frontier community. A mercurial man of peace upsets the balance of power. His attempts to remain above the fray are rebuffed and he's drawn into a bloody confrontation. Shane is willing to die so that others may know peace. Clint Eastwood often incorporated Christian religious imagery for his heroic cowboys like *The Outlaw Josey Wales* (1976) and The Preacher in *Pale Rider* (1985). In *Josey Wales*, a community beset by Indians settles in a valley named Paradise. Josey must contend with a Judas-like rival named Fletcher. Having set up defense within a church, Josey and the town ultimately make peace with their Native American neighbors.

In *Whistle Down the Wind* (1961), three kids discover a bearded criminal hiding in a stable. Could the man be the second coming of Jesus? While the adults protest, only the innocence of children ensures a willing surrender. In *Cool Hand Luke* (1967), a defiant innocent is sent to prison on trumped-up charges. An evil warden warns him of their "Failure to communicate." Yet, Luke stands up to an unjust system, taking on the suffering for all prisoners. Even *E.T.: The Extra-Terrestrial* (1982) conforms to the Christ story. A non-violent alien descends to the earth, offering companionship and comfort to a lonely boy. Yet, the authorities cannot allow his visit to continue unabated. While E.T. aims to heal, the scientists submit him to study. Just when E.T.'s heartlight seems extinguished, he rises again, ascending to his home amongst the stars. Animator Brian Bird's first animated feature, *The Iron Giant* (1999), followed an outline reminiscent of Superman. A stranger from outer space arrives at a crucial juncture. The massive robot is misunderstood, perceived as a threat, rather than a prophetic warning. Yet the government marshals inordinate firepower to stamp out this nonviolent emissary. Will a nation on the verge of nuclear annihilation heed the Giant's call? Seemingly fallen and disarmed, the Iron Giant rises with an olive branch in his booster pack. The notion of a father sending his son on a dangerous mission to save our planet continues to captivate audiences.

Not all cinematic Christ-figures take on such grandiose forms. *The Count of Monte Cristo* (2002) numbers his days in prison. Given ample reasons to despair, he learns a different way of combating injustice. A priest in chains offers words of life that get him through the long journey to freedom. Amongst the quieter, more reflective stories of sacrifice for a community are *The Spitfire Grill* (1996) and *The Green Mile* (1999). Both are about innocents unjustly imprisoned. When Percy is released from prison, she attempts to restart her life at the Spitfire Grill in Gilead, Maine. But the townspeople judge Percy without knowing the depth of her struggle. As an outsider, Percy is both the recipient and conduit for grace, an unlikely Christ-figure. Stephen King's novel *The Green Mile* follows a gentle giant, John Coffey (J. C.!), who takes on others' pain. While he intends to heal others, his hulking presence is perceived as a threat. John Coffey is sent to the electric chair, walking the green mile (rather than the *via dolorosa*) for crimes he didn't commit.

Some dramas are more parabolic in shape. *The Shawshank Redemption* (1996) sprang from a Stephen King novella. Although wrongly convicted of his wife's murder, Andy Dufresne refuses to abandon hope. Andy plays beautiful music for his fellow inmates.

He is broken but unbowed, tricking the authorities, and chipping away at his freedom. Andy crawls through a river of human waste before he emerges victorious and washed clean. *Shawshank*'s broadly Christian themes of faith amidst injustice, freedom amidst imprisonment, and purity amidst refuse continue to resonate with moviegoers. A film like *Chocolat* (2000) contrasts the delicious freedoms offered by a chocolatier with the rigorous restraint practiced by a Christian count. It is set up as a power struggle for the soul of a community set against the backdrop of Lent. A young priest juggles the demands of Le Comte with the tasty art of Vianne. While Le Comte attempts to bury his desires, Vianne offers protection for an abused wife and a band of gypsies. Who is more Christ-like? Vianne, the friend of sinners, frees the village and the priest from the religious chains that bind them. *Smoke Signals* (1998) reimagines the parable of the loaves and fishes in a Native American setting. The loaves that Jesus multiplied are replaced by fry bread. Yet, the abundance that follows brings an equal amount of life to the reservation. These fresh takes challenge us to connect Christ's stories to our everyday lives. Can we recognize the sacred amidst the profane? Can we identify where Jesus' presence and loyalty resides?

Genre films

The gangster genre has tested the bounds of God's grace. Roman Catholic directors like Francis Ford Coppola and Martin Scorsese borrow from church teaching on penance and absolution to dramatic effect (Phillips 2004). The Catholic baptismal rite provides the framework for the defining sequence in *The Godfather* (1972). Coppola places Michael Corleone's affirmations of faith at his godson's baptism in opposition to the contract killings that consolidate his power. In a church setting, serving as godfather means renouncing evil and the power of Satan. According to *la cosa nostra*, the godfather does whatever is necessary to protect his mafia family and retain control of their illicit enterprises. *The Godfather* series became a study of Michael Corleone's soul, how the vows he broke at the baptismal font came back to haunt him.

Martin Scorsese's *oeuvre* explores men battling personal demons, attempting to resist their violent and self-destructive tendencies (Kelly 2003). Having studied for the priesthood prior to film school, Scorsese places his protagonists between the love of God and the lure of crime. *Mean Streets* (1973) opens with the sound of Scorsese's voice, "You don't make up for your sins in church; you do it in the streets." Local hoodlum Charlie (Harvey Keitel) places his hand over an open flame, both as a form of penance and as an approximation of where his choices may lead. Is his road to hell paved with poor choices? In *The Departed* (2006), Scorsese shows the brutal consequences that come from sweeping God from the stage. Crime boss Frank Costello insists, "A man makes his own way ... *non serviam*" right through a bloody conclusion. Scorsese and Coppola make cautionary tales for gangsters, thugs, and thieves like us.

Coppola and Scorsese inspired the next generation of gangster-obsessed, Catholic filmmakers. Quentin Tarantino filtered Scorsese's stylish visuals through a fractured, postmodern narrative in *Pulp Fiction* (1994). Two contract killers, Jules and Vinnie, adopt divergent responses to a close encounter with death. Jules attributes his second chance to divine intervention, while Vinnie refuses to attribute his safe passage to God. Jules becomes a scripture-quoting prophet dispensing rough justice. But the violence in *Pulp Fiction* was mild compared to the judgment exacted by *The Boondock Saints* (1999). It opens with the Lord's Prayer before embarking on a blue streak of profanity and stylized violence in the name of *veritas*, as fraternal twins Connor and Murphy McManus see themselves as God's shepherds ridding Boston of evil mafiosi. If the biblically informed gangster became an independent film cliché, then the serial killer as religious nut acquired equal ubiquity. The seven deadly sins of Catholic catechism took on disgusting form in *Se7en* (1995). The religious devotion of creepy killer John Doe became a convenient staple to explain all manner of antisocial behavior. Original sin was pushed to a frightening extreme.

Horror films remain a robust genre for combining Christianity and cinema (Cowan 2008). Powerful Christian symbols populate vampire films from *Nosferatu* (1922) through *Bram Stoker's Dracula* (1992). Horror provides a framework for a cosmic drama, as a cross-wielding vampire hunter like Van Helsing confronts a bloodthirsty immortal like Bela Lugosi in *Dracula* (1931). Having defied God and embraced the power of darkness, cinematic Draculas fear holy water and the piercing light. In *Dracula 2000*, the legendary count is even associated with Jesus' betrayer, Judas.

Perhaps the most chilling portrait of the devil and his minions remains Roman Polanski's *Rosemary's Baby* (1968). It places devil worshipers within an otherwise desirable New York apartment building. Rosemary becomes a surrogate for the most sinister plot possible, to give birth to the devil's son, the Antichrist. The devil possesses a teenage girl named Regan in *The Exorcist* (1973). Priests engage in a violent struggle for her soul, invoking all manner of ancient religious rites. While Regan may be released from Satan's grip, a wavering priest proves powerless compared to the devil's wiles. *Angel Heart* (1987), *The Devil's Advocate* (1997), and *The Ninth Gate* (1999) all involve deadly deals with the prince of darkness (and demonstrate how derivative the genre has become). *The Exorcism of Emily Rose* (2005) recreates a German court case. Evil is put on trial as a priest recounts the bold faith and confidence of Emily even amidst a battle for her immortal soul.

As a new millennium approached, the biblical book of Revelation informed a host of thrillers. Speculation regarding eschatology or the "end times" informs *The Omen* (1976). The Antichrist arrives as a young boy named Damien. While he may look innocent, the "666" tattooed on his head foreshadows his God-defiant power play. *The Seventh Sign* (1988) turns the Apocalypse of John into a ludicrous guilty pleasure. A pregnant Demi Moore fears that her child may be the Seventh Sign. *Fin-de-siècle* anxiety also drives *The Rapture* (1991). It satirizes southern California indifference toward religion, right until the Four Horsemen of the Apocalypse gallop toward us. *End of Days* (1999) applies Arnold Schwarzenegger's cinematic superhero powers to the end times. Satan roams the streets of New York in search of the woman who will bear his child just in time for the new millennium. Otherwise, he must wait another thousand years to make his power play. This big budget Hollywood treatment contrasted with the modest production values attached to films designed to frighten and convert their audiences. From *The Omega Code* (1999) to *Left Behind: The Movie*

(2000), faithful Christians have produced remarkably toothless films about speculative prophecy.

The most creative cinematic visions have reflected the positive side of Christian eschatology. After Armageddon and the day of judgment, Revelations closes with a new heaven and a new earth. John's apocalyptic vision anticipates streets paved with gold, rivers flowing with life, and trees with healing in their leaves. Fantasies like *The Lord of the Rings* trilogy (2001–3) offer visions of a verdant shire threatened by dark forces. Frodo Baggins wrestles with the lure of power, suggesting that resistance is possible only when accompanied by a fellowship of hobbits, elves, dwarves, wizards, and humans – beings who are diverse, and yet share faith, loyalty, courage, and friendship. Frodo's journey to Mordor involves epic fights with elephants, spiders, dragons, and orcs. Even the trees rise up to ensure their survival. Peter Jackson's Oscar-winning trilogy is rooted in author J. R. R. Tolkien's robust Christian faith. A small and lowly hobbit resists temptation, making room for a king to restore beauty to the shire.

While Mexican director Guillermo del Toro chronicles the horrors of his Catholic upbringing, the sacrificial actions at the heart of *Pan's Labyrinth* (2006) spring from the Christian story. A young girl in fascist Spain resists the oppressive actions of her new stepfather. Ofelia deepens her resolve through a series of tests administered by a fawn. Fairies and enchanted forests blend seamlessly with a frightening historical backdrop of Spain circa 1944. Ofelia's protection of her new brother costs her life, but ushers her into a golden kingdom where her father affirms her sacrifice. As digital effects become more affordable, filmmakers will continue to offer visions of another world, a better tomorrow, and a heavenly future.

Faith-fueled filmmakers

The tangled relationship between Christians and Hollywood has been stereotyped as Jewish moguls hiring Catholic directors to make movies for Protestant audiences. With notable exceptions like Cecil B. DeMille, most of the Christians making movies within the studio system were steeped in Catholicism. From the populism of Frank Capra and to the westerns of John Ford, Catholic filmmakers prospered in Hollywood.

As immigrants to America, Capra and Ford found their way into the nascent film industry. They cranked out a number of undistinguished early movies before honing their themes and style. Frank Capra's hope-filled films like *Mr. Deeds Comes to Town* (1936) and *Mr. Smith Goes to Washington* (1939) suggested that one man can make a difference. In Capra's America, a common, decent person can become a millionaire or a Congressman. *It's a Wonderful Life* (1946) brings an angel to Bedford Falls to convince George Bailey that his presence matters. Capra's Christmas classic restores audiences' faith in film every holiday season. John Ford's prolific career also affirmed a mythic America. He works out his salvation amidst western vistas. Whether dealing with a *Stagecoach* (1939) or an entire calvary unit in *Fort Apache* (1948), Ford populates his films with rugged men, following their ideals. A wistful longing for a peaceable kingdom hangs over the roughest outposts of Ford's westerns. In *My Darling Clementine* (1946), a frontier church provides a temporary respite from the ongoing battle to decide how the West will be won. *Three Godfathers* (1948) turns the Magi into outlaws on the run. The tough guys vow to bring an infant to safety, journeying through New Jerusalem, Arizona. Ford sprinkles Christmas carols like "Silent Night" throughout the action.

In *Afterimage*, Fr. Richard Blake noted how a Catholic imagination informed the classic films of Capra, Ford, Coppola, Scorsese, and even Alfred Hitchcock (Blake 2000). Their sacramental religious heritage crosses over into an attention to minute details within the frame. Their films are male dominated, not unlike their local parishes, with women often placed on an elevated plain much like the Virgin Mary. They focus upon God's presence in the world (an immanence), rather than an absence. Recent American filmmakers operating out of Catholic upbringings include Edward Burns (*Ash Wednesday*, 2002) and Abel Ferrara (*The Funeral*, 1996). Ferrara's graphic films often explore explicit theological concepts like penance (*Bad Lieutenant*, 1992) and blood sacrifice (*The Addiction*, 1995). Although he acknowledges the importance of his Catholic education and upbringing on the commentary to *The Killer* (1989), John Woo is rarely thought of as a religious filmmaker. Yet, Woo often explores the notion of good versus evil, opposites tied together by blood or destiny in *Hard-Boiled* (1992) and *Face/Off* (1997). While such themes can be traced to a Chinese notion of yin/yang, Woo's reliance upon candles and doves draws upon more Catholic imagery.

Given their suspicion toward icons, Protestant Christians have been less involved in big-screen image making. Protestants practice a word-based faith, rooted in *sola scriptura*, turning to the Bible as the final arbiter of faith. Protestants initially embraced the evangelistic possibilities presented by moving pictures. Pastors were encouraged to adopt the new technology for large-scale rallies or smaller screenings in church basements (Lindvall 2001). Just as the scandal surrounding Fatty Arbuckle sparked the creation of the Production Code, so Protestants eventually soured on the new medium. They became more cautious consumers than active producers of films. More conservative denominations rooted in pietistic or holiness traditions like Methodism and Wesleyans, came to avoid movies altogether.

Students educated at Christian colleges bristled against such prohibitions, eventually creating films that challenged their Protestant roots. Wheaton College graduate Wes Craven placed horror within a bucolic suburban setting in *Nightmare on Elm Street* (1984). Raised in a rigorous Dutch Calvinist tradition, Paul Schrader explored the total depravity plaguing his soul in *American Gigolo* (1980) and *Light Sleeper* (1992). In *Bull Durham* (1988), Ron Shelton offered "The Church of Baseball" as an alternative to his Christian upbringing. The iconoclastic tendencies of Terry Gilliam (*Brazil*, 1985) may have been forged in his grandfather's Lutheran church. *The Fisher King* (1991) may endure as the best fusion of Gilliam's fanciful visions with an enduring Christian legend.

Perhaps the most effective religious filmmaking combined Protestant words of screenwriter Paul Schrader with the Catholic imagery of director Martin Scorsese. Whether in the self-appointed vigilante justice of *Taxi Driver* (1976) or the self-destructive tendencies of *Raging Bull* (1980), Schrader and Scorsese mine the depths of human depravity. In *Taxi Driver*, Travis Bickle attempts to free a teen prostitute from her pimp. His violent past as a Vietnam vet comes to the surface in a bloody finale. But the violence is more reductive than redemptive. Scorsese and actor Robert De Niro went further down the self-destructive trail in *Raging Bull*. Boxer Jake LaMotta destroys his opponents in the ring, but cannot contain his animalist tendencies outside the arena. *Raging Bull* endures as a cautionary tale, a dark monument to a graceless life. Schrader and Scorsese reunited for *Bringing Out the Dead* (1999). The spirits haunting an ambulance driver are finally calmed in a closing shot rooted in Michelangelo's *Pietà*.

European directors also drew upon their austere Protestant roots to craft haunting meditations on the absence of God. Scandinavian filmmakers Carl Theodor Dreyer and Ingmar Bergman grew up in Lutheran homes. Dreyer stripped his films down to the barest of elements (Bordwell 1981). *Day of Wrath* (1943) points out the foolishness of witch hunts throughout history. Created during the Nazi occupation of Denmark, *Day of Wrath* challenges us all to be diligent in our resistance to evil. *Ordet* (*The Word*, 1955) explores the thin line between spiritual insight and madness. Johannes sees himself as the incarnation of the ancient Christ. In a miraculous finale, Dreyer affirms Johannes' madness, challenging us all to push past the rationalism that dismisses the supernatural to our own detriment. The religious film critics from www.artsandfaith. com even placed *Ordet* atop their list of the 100 Most Spiritually Significant Films. As the son of a Lutheran minister, Ingmar Bergman wrestled with Christian faith throughout his prolific and acclaimed career (Kalin 2003; Hubner 2007). Even as a young filmmaker, Bergman confronted death and the absence of God. A knight plays chess with Death in *The Seventh Seal* (1957). An old man looks back upon his choices in *Wild Strawberries* (1957). The absence of God hangs over Bergman's Spider Trilogy, especially for a widowed pastor in *Winter Light* (1962). Bergman's evocative films explore the questions that arose in the wake of the Second World War. Where was God amidst the horrors of the twentieth century? Does the Almighty remain hidden even now (Bandy and Monda 2003)?

The rich Scandinavian tradition started by Dreyer and furthered by Bergman has been continued in deeply religious films like *Babette's Feast* (1987) and *The Ox* (1991). They are anchored in small communities, struggling to survive, consistently restraining themselves. A gracious cook challenges the town to dine with gusto in *Babette's Feast*. They learn that Christian faith can also include aesthetics as well as ascetics. The *Dogme* 95 film movement initiated as a lark by Lars von Trier and Thomas Vinterberg revitalized Danish film (Stevenson 2003). Their playful "vow of chastity" called filmmakers back toward genuine human emotion (Hjort and Mackenzie 2008). In *Breaking the Waves* (1996), von Trier reawakened the tradition of suffering saints begun by Dreyer in *The Passion of Joan of Arc*. A childlike Bess (Emily Watson) gives audible voice to God's call on her life. She pursues a series of abusive sexual relationships as a way of resurrecting her husband from his paralysis. Shunned by her Christian community, Bess's sacrifices are affirmed by bells that chime from heaven itself. In *Adam's Apples* (2005), Anders Thomas Jensen turns the biblical story of Job into a black comedy. A Lutheran pastor houses all manner of people assigned to rehabilitation, including a violent neo-Nazi. Despite the skinhead's best efforts to undermine the pastor's faith, the minister refuses to renounce God. He manages to win over the skinhead by turning even the cheesy Bee Gees' song, "How Deep is your Love" into a lived reality.

Perhaps the most enduring form of Christianity onscreen adheres to what Paul Schrader defined as "the transcendental style." These austere films refrain from telegraphing emotions via established notions of acting, music, or plot. They draw viewers in, rather than projecting stories out. Audiences are invited into the drama, given room to discover themselves within the (in)action. French Catholic director Robert Bresson relies upon nonprofessional actors in *Diary of a Country Priest* (1951), *Pickpocket* (1959), and *Au hasard Balthazar* (1966) (Quandt 1998; Cunneen 2003). Bresson coaxes as blank an expression as possible from his "performers," forcing the audience to summon identification and sympathy from within themselves (Bresson 1997). The suffering of the country priest becomes an occasion for us to experience the notion that "all is grace" (Bazin 2004). While the pickpocket presents himself as a Nietzschean superman, he is consistently undone by his own longings and limitations. Only in prison does Michel discover the gift of grace embodied by Jeanne. *Balthazar* extends Bresson's ascetic aesthetic to its logical extreme. A donkey serves as the title character. The indignities thrust upon an innocent animal by his owners evoke compassion. When the donkey lies down with the sheep, we are all invited to lay down our agendas and egos.

Russian Orthodox director Andrei Tarkovsky drew upon a rich iconic tradition in *Andrei Rublev* (1969). The epic saga of Russian's greatest iconographer feels like it has been unearthed from the Middle Ages. Invasions by Tatar hordes are contrasted with the endurance of Byzantine Christianity. Are the Russian people so weak and fearful that they must be dominated (à la communism) or can they be freed to worship in spirit and truth (via Orthodoxy)? Andrei Rublev debates Theophanes the Greek in theological dialogues that echo Dostoyevsky's towering literature. Consequently, the forging of a massive bell for the local church takes on powerful resonance. How much suffering was required for Andrei Rublev or any artist exploring the sacred, to reach their lofty aspirations? Tarkovsky also applied his slow, languid, philosophical style to science fiction in *Solaris* (1972) and *Stalker* (1979) (Johnson and Petrie 1994; Bird 2008). Perhaps the most accurate and excruciating summary of his artistic vision concludes *Nostalghia* (1983). A Russian poet attempts to cross an empty pool bearing a lit candle. His efforts are vanquished when the wind repeatedly extinguishes the flame. Yet, each time, the writer returns to the beginning, relights the fire, daring to navigate the straits before him. Shot as an uninterrupted, almost nine-minute take, Tarkovsky's maddening scene exhibits unparalleled faith and determination in the actor and the audience (Tarkovsky 1989).

The thaw in communist countries informed the most spiritual films of Krzysztof Kieślowski and Wim Wenders. Kieślowski's monumental production of *Dekalog* (1989) located the ethical conundrums raised by the Ten Commandments within a Polish apartment complex. The loosely connected characters form a compelling patchwork of Europe on the cusp of freedom. Created for Polish television, each episode of *Dekalog* revolves around a single commandment. The first hour puts science to the test, invoking God's challenge to Israel, "Thou shalt put no other gods before me." A father has placed his faith in a measurable universe where laws of physics are immutable. His young son asks questions of Christian doctrine that the father cannot answer. When the son goes ice skating, the father's faith regarding predictability proves horribly misguided. The father takes his anger and grief to an Orthodox church. An icon of Poland's black virgin weeps with him. He receives consolation from the ultimate irony – a frozen block of holy water. Kieślowski extended his meditation upon our interconnectedness in his *Trois couleurs* trilogy. *Blue*, *White*, and *Red* are rooted in the colors of the French flag (Insdorf 2002). Can we attain liberty, justice, and equality? Kieślowski's humane, liminal filmmaking demonstrates how (Kickasola 2004).

Wim Wenders joined a wave of German filmmakers that emerged from the upheavals of the 1960s (Kolker and Beicken 1993). Over his accomplished career, Wenders adopted more overtly Christian themes. The evocative camera in *Wings of Desire* (1987) floats above Berlin with angels who watch over us. We enter their aural world, hearing the prayers and longings of the German people. The angels' stylish black and white existence ultimately pales in comparison to our color-filled world. The desire to be fully human overtakes the angels in the sequel *Faraway, So Close* (1993). They end up just as fallen as humanity. But audiences' rapturous responses to the angels renewed Wenders' faith. He told filmmaker Scott Derrickson, "It was seeing what the film did in other people, how the film affected them, that changed my mind. These figures that I created, my angel creatures, started to work on me and my spiritual life" (Derrickson 2002: 46). In *The End of Violence* (1997), Wenders offers a God's eye view of Los Angeles. Surveillance cameras are installed across the city as the promise of security. Only when a wealthy filmmaker is confronted by genuine violence, does he question the screen violence he created *sans* personal responsibility. Wenders locates wisdom within the Hispanic community. Their sacred approach to faith, life, and family offers a healing balm to a weary director. Wenders' subsequent films like *Million Dollar Hotel* (2000) and *Land of Plenty* (2004) reflected a greater interest in the subverting power structure created by Jesus' notion of the kingdom of God. Like a modest mustard seed, these outsider stories were largely overlooked by filmgoers.

The transcendental trails blazed by Bresson and Tarkovsky have been extended by the Dardenne Brothers. Working with nonprofessional actors in their native Belgium, Luc and Jean-Pierre Dardenne echo Bresson's spare approach. They adopt a documentary style to narrative film, following common people through their small, everyday dramas. The simplicity implied in titles like *Le promesse* (*The Promise*, 1996), *Le fils* (*The Son*, 2002), and *L'enfant* (*The Child*, 2005) demonstrate their minimalistic tendencies. Yet, by focusing on the basics of love, loss, and parenting, their humane filmmaking soars to universal heights.

A trio of Russian directors updates the transcendental style of their countryman Andrei Tarkovsky. Alexander Sokurov explores fundamental human relationships in *Mother and Son* (1997). A devoted son attends to his ailing mother. He bears witness to death and the immutability of the soul. In *The Return* (2003), Andrei Zvyagintsev follows two brothers who are suddenly confronted by a spectral father. A fishing trip becomes the ultimate test of faith. A seemingly crazed Russian monk inhabits *Ostrov* (*The Island*, 2006, dir. Pavel Lungin). Over time, his madness is revealed as genuine healing power. These spare films invite viewers to meditate upon their own families and faith. How much love is needed to navigate life? How much forgiveness is required to sustain a relationship? They slow the audience down, digging into the core issues. Where have we come from? Who will walk through life with us? Are we all prodigals, running either from or to our heavenly Father?

While critics continue to celebrate the transcendental style, mainstream audiences continue to resist it. A once vital art-house cinema led by Bergman and Fellini has been largely steamrolled by Hollywood blockbusters. American independent film has been largely critical of and even hostile toward Christianity. But a new breed of filmmakers employs abundant images for spiritual insights. The sacred themes floating through seemingly profane films from 1999 like *Magnolia, American Beauty,* and *The Matrix* suggest that old categories of transcendent and immanent are blurring (Detweiler and Taylor 2003). Harsh films like *Memento* (2000), *No Country for Old Men* (2007), and *There Will be Blood* (2007) can be read as timeless meditations on original sin. The miraculous moments infusing *Donnie Darko* (2001) portend a bright future for Christianity within cinema (Detweiler 2008). While painting, music, and dance slipped from their sacred roots into profane commercialism, a cinema born as a profitable enterprise may yet attain transcendent purposes (Schrader 1972). European directors, working in a post-Christendom context, have mined rich veins in ancient Christian themes and stories. Will a new generation of filmmakers embrace the austere, transcendental interests of the finest art-house directors?

Korean-American Lee Isaac Chung emerged as an unlikely inheritor of the transcendental tradition. Growing up as a first-generation immigrant in Alabama, Chung dropped a pre-med degree at Yale to major in film. Chung directs as a man on a literal mission, offering Rwandans an opportunity to tell their story. *Munyurangabo* (2007) was made with nonprofessional actors in the Rwandan language. It explores the horrors of the 1994 genocide, particularly through the cyclical sins of the past being visited upon the young. A teenage boy, Munyurangabo, plans to avenge his father's death. His friend, Sangwa, accompanies him. But life slows down at Sangwa's house in the country. And their revenge is diverted. In a moving shift, they stumble across a stranger who calls them to forgiveness. The national poet of Rwanda addresses the camera directly: we are all invited to slow down, take a deep breath, and remember our roots. In Chung's vision, we must treat each with dignity, recognizing the God-given beauty in everyone. Such simple, earnest pleas for reconciliation cut through the clutter for those who have eyes to see and ears to hear.

Bibliography

Bandy, M. and Monda. A. (2003) *The Hidden God: Film and Faith*, New York: The Museum of Modern Art.

Bazin, A. (2004) "*Le journal d'un curé de campagne* and the Stylistic of Robert Bresson," in *What is Cinema?* Vol. 1, Berkeley: University of California Press: 125–43.

Berenbaum, M. and Landres, S. (2004) *After the Passion is Gone: American Religious Consequences*, Lanham, MD: AltaMira Press.

Bird, R. (2008) *Andrei Tarkovsky: Elements of Cinema*, London: Reaktion.

Blake, R. (2000) *Afterimage: The Indelible Catholic Imagination of Six American Filmmakers*, Chicago: Loyola.

Bordwell, D. (1981) *The Films of Carl-Theodor Dreyer*, Berkeley: University of California Press.

Bresson, R. (1997) *Notes on the Cinematographer*, Los Angeles: Green Integer.

Cowan, D. (2008) *Sacred Terror: Religion and Horror on the Silver Screen*, Waco, TX: Baylor University Press.

Cunneen, J. (2003) *Robert Bresson: A Spiritual Style in Film*, New York: Continuum.

DeMille, Cecil B. (1959) *The Autobiography of Cecil B. DeMille*, Upper Saddle River, NJ: Prentice Hall.

Derrickson, S. (2002) "A Conversation with Wim Wenders," *Image: A Journal of the Arts and Religion* 35: 41–55.

Detweiler, C. (2008) *Into the Dark: Seeing the Sacred in the Top Films of the 21st Century*, Grand Rapids, MI: Baker Academic.

Detweiler, C. and Taylor, B. (2003) "Movies: Look Closer," in *A Matrix of Meanings: Finding God in Pop Culture*, Grand Rapids, MI: Baker Academic: 155–83.

Fredriksen, P. (2006) *On The Passion of the Christ: Exploring the Issues Raised by the Controversial Movie*, Berkeley: University of California Press.

Hjort, M. and Mackenzie, S. (2008) *Purity and Provocation: Dogme 95*, London: British Film Institute.

Hubner, L. (2007) *The Films of Ingmar Bergman: Illusions of Light and Darkness*, New York: Palgrave Macmillan.

Insdorf, A. (2002) *Double Lives, Second Chances*, New York: Miramax.

Johnson, V. and Petrie, G. (1994) *The Films of Andrei Tarkovsky: A Visual Fugue*, Bloomington: Indiana University Press.

Kalin, J. (2003) *The Films of Ingmar Bergman*, Cambridge: Cambridge University Press.

Kelly, M. (2003) *Martin Scorsese: A Journey*, Berkeley, CA: De Capo Press.

Kickasola, J. (2004) *The Films of Krzysztof Kieślowski: The Liminal Image*, New York: Continuum.

Kinnard, R. and Davis, T. (1992) *Divine Images: A History of Jesus on the Screen*, New York: Citadel Press.

Kolker, R. and Beicken, P. (1993) *The Films of Wim Wenders: Cinema as Vision and Desire*, Cambridge: Cambridge University Press.

Lindvall, T. (2001) *The Silents of God: Selected Issues and Documents in Silent American Film and Religion 1903–1925*, Lanham, MD: Scarecrow Press.

Malone, P. (1990) *Movie Christs and Antichrists*, New York: Crossroads.

Phillips, G. (2004) *Godfather: The Intimate Francis Ford Coppola*, Lexington, KY: University Press of Kentucky.

Plate, S. (2004) *Re-Viewing the Passion: Mel Gibson's Film and its Critics*, New York: Palgrave Macmillan.

Quandt, J. (1998) *Robert Bresson*, Toronto: Cinémathèque Ontario.

Reinhartz, A. (2007) *Jesus of Hollywood*, Oxford: Oxford University Press.

Riley, R. (2003) *Film, Faith, and Cultural Conflict: The Case of Martin Scorsese's The Last Temptation of Christ*, Westport, CT: Praeger.

Schrader, P. (1972) *Transcendental Style in Film*, Berkeley: Da Capo Press.

Stevenson, J. (2003) *Dogme Uncut: Lars von Trier, Thomas Vinterberg, and the Gang that Took on Hollywood*, Santa Monica, CA: Santa Monica Press.

Tarkovsky, A. (1989) *Sculpting in Time: The Great Russian Filmmaker Discusses His Art*, trans. K. Hunter-Blair, Austin: University of Texas Press.

Filmography

Adam's Apples (2005, dir. A. Jensen)
The Addiction (1995, dir. A. Ferrara)

American Beauty (1999, dir. S. Mendes)
American Gigolo (1980, dir. P. Schrader)
Andrei Rublev (1969, dir. A. Tarkovsky)
Angel Heart (1987, dir. A. Parker)
Apocalypto (2006, dir. M. Gibson)
The Apostle (1997, dir. R. Duvall)
Ash Wednesday (2002, dir. E. Burns)
Au hasard Balthazar (1966, dir. R. Bresson)
Babette's Feast (1987, dir. G. Axel)
Bad Lieutenant (1992, dir. A. Ferrara)
Becket (1964, dir. P. Glenville)
The Bells of St. Mary's (1945, dir. L. McCarey)
Ben Hur (1907, dir. S. Olcott)
Ben-Hur (1925, dir. F. Niblo)
Ben-Hur (1959, dir. W. Wyler)
The Birth of a Nation (1915, dir. D. Griffith)
Black Narcissus (1947, dir. M. Powell)
Black Robe (1991, dir. B. Beresford)
Blue (1993, dir. K. Kieślowski)
The Boondock Saints (1999, dir. T. Duffy)
Boys Town (1938, dir. N. Taurog)
Bram Stoker's Dracula (1992, dir. F. Coppola)
Brazil (1985, dir. T. Gilliam)
Breaking the Waves (1996, dir. L. von Trier)
Bringing Out the Dead (1999, dir. M. Scorsese)
Brother Sun, Sister Moon (1972, dir. F. Zeffirelli)
Bruce Almighty (2003, dir. T. Shadyac)
Bull Durham (1988, dir. R. Shelton)
Chariots of Fire (1981, dir. H. Hudson)
The Child (2005, dir. J. Dardenne)
Chocolat (2000, dir. L. Hallström)
The Color of the Cross (2006, dir. J. La Marre)
Cool Hand Luke (1967, dir. S. Rosenberg)
The Count of Monte Cristo (2002, dir. K. Reynolds)
The Crime of Father Amaro (2002, dir. C. Carrera)
Day of Wrath (1943, dir. C. Dreyer)
Dekalog (1989, dir. K. Kieślowski)
Deliver Us from Evil (2006, dir. A. Berg)
The Departed (2006, dir. M. Scorsese)
The Devil's Advocate (1997, dir. T. Hackford)
Diary of a Country Priest (1951, dir. R. Bresson)
Dogma (1999, dir. K. Smith)
Donnie Darko (2001, dir. R. Kelly)
Dracula (1931, dir. T. Browning)
Dracula 2000 (2000, dir. P. Lussier)
Elmer Gantry (1960, dir. R. Brooks)
End of Days (1999, dir. P. Hyams)
The End of Violence (1997, dir. W. Wenders)
Entertaining Angels: The Dorothy Day Story (1996, dir. M. Rhodes)
E.T.: The Extra-Terrestrial (1982, dir. S. Spielberg)
Eve and the Fire Horse (2005, dir. J. Kwan)
The Exorcism of Emily Rose (2005, dir. S. Derrickson)
The Exorcist (1973, dir. W. Friedkin)
Face/Off (1997, dir. J. Woo)

Faraway, So Close (1993, dir. W. Wenders)
The Fisher King (1991, dir. T. Gilliam)
The Flowers of St. Francis (1952, dir. R. Rossellini)
Fort Apache (1948, dir. J. Ford)
From the Manger to the Cross (1912, dir. S. Olcott)
The Funeral (1996, dir. A. Ferrara)
The Godfather (1972, dir. F. Coppola)
Godspell (1973, dir. D. Greene)
Going My Way (1944, dir. L. McCarey)
The Gospel According to St. Matthew (1964, dir. P. Pasolini)
The Greatest Story Ever Told (1966, dir. G. Stevens)
The Green Mile (1999, dir. F. Darabont)
Hail Mary (1985, dir. J. Godard)
Hard-Boiled (1992, dir. J. Woo)
Hawaii (1966, dir. G. Hill)
He Who Must Die (1956, dir. J. Dassin)
Hotel Rwanda (2004, dir. T. George)
Household Saints (1993, dir. N. Savoca)
The Inn of the Sixth Happiness (1958, dir. M. Robson)
Intolerance (1916, dir. D. Griffith)
The Iron Giant (1999, dir. B. Bird)
It's a Wonderful Life (1946, dir. F. Capra)
Jesus Christ Superstar (1973, dir. N. Jewison)
Jesus of Montreal (1989, dir. D. Arcand)
Joan of Arc (1948, dir. V. Fleming)
The Killer (1989, dir. J. Woo)
The King of Kings (1927, dir. C. DeMille)
King of Kings (1961, dir. N. Ray)
Land of Plenty (2004, dir. W. Wenders)
The Last Days of Pompeii (1935, dir. E. Schoedsack)
The Last Temptation of Christ (1988, dir. M. Scorsese)
Left Behind: The Movie (2000, dir. V. Sarin)
Life of Brian (1979, dir. T. Jones)
Life of Christ (1899, dir. A. Guy)
The Life and Passion of Jesus Christ (1902, dir. L. Noguet and F. Zecca)
Light Sleeper (1992, dir. P. Schrader)
The Lord of the Rings: The Fellowship of the Ring (2001, dir. P. Jackson)
Luther (2003, dir. E. Till)
The Magdalene Sisters (2002, dir. P. Mullan)
Magnolia (1999, dir. P. Anderson)
A Man Called Peter (1955, dir. H. Koster)
Martin Luther (1953, dir. I. Pichel)
The Matrix (1999, dir. L. Wachowski)
Mean Streets (1973, dir. M. Scorsese)
Memento (2000, dir. C. Nolan)
Million Dollar Hotel (2000, dir. W. Wenders)
Millions (2004, dir. D. Boyle)
The Miracle (1948, dir. R. Rossellini)
The Mission (1986, dir. R. Joffé)
Mr. Deeds Comes to Town (1936, dir. F. Capra)
Mr. Smith Goes to Washington (1939, dir. F. Capra)
Molokai: The Story of Father Damien (1999, dir. P. Cox)
Monsieur Vincent (1947, dir. M. Cloche)
Mother and Son (1997, dir. A. Sokurov)

Munyurangabo (2007, dir. L. Chung)
My Darling Clementine (1946, dir. J. Ford)
Nazarin (1959, dir. L. Buñuel)
The New World (2005, dir. T. Malick)
The Night of the Hunter (1955, dir. C. Laughton)
Nightmare on Elm Street (1984, dir. W. Craven)
The Ninth Gate (1999, dir. R. Polanski)
No Country for Old Men (2007, dir. J. and E. Coen)
Nosferatu (1922, dir. F. Murnau)
Nostalghia (1983, dir. A. Tarkovsky)
Not of This World (1999, dir. G. Piccioni)
Nuns on the Run (1990, dir. J. Lynn)
The Nun's Story (1959, dir. F. Zinnemann)
The Omega Code (1999, dir. R. Marcarelli)
The Omen (1976, dir. R. Donner)
On the Waterfront (1954, dir. E. Kazan)
Ordet (1955, dir. C. Dreyer)
Ostrov (2006, dir. P. Lungin)
The Outlaw Josie Wales (1976, dir. C. Eastwood)
The Ox (1991, dir. S. Nykvist)
Pale Rider (1985, dir. C. Eastwood)
Pan's Labyrinth (2006, dir. G. del Toro)
The Passion of the Christ (2004, dir. M. Gibson)
The Passion of Joan of Arc (1928, dir. C. Dreyer)
The Passion Play (1897, dir. M. Klaw and A. Erlanger)
The Passion Play of Oberammergau (1898, dir. H. Vincent)
Pickpocket (1959, dir. R. Bresson)
Priest (1994, dir. A. Bird)
The Prince of Egypt (1998, dir. B. Chapman and S. Hickner)
The Promise (1996, dir. J. Dardenne)
Pulp Fiction (1994, dir. Q. Tarantino)
Quo Vadis? (1912, dir. E. Guazzoni)
Quo Vadis? (1925, dir. G. D'Annunzio)
Quo Vadis (1951, dir. M. LeRoy)
Raging Bull (1980, dir. M. Scorsese)
The Rapture (1991, dir. M. Tolkin)
Red (1994, dir. K. Kieślowski)
The Return (2003, dir. A. Zvyagintsev)
The Robe (1953, dir. H. Koster)
Romero (1989, dir. J. Duigan)
Rosemary's Baby (1968, dir. R. Polanski)
Se7en (1995, dir. D. Fincher)
The Seventh Seal (1957, dir. I. Bergman)
The Seventh Sign (1988, dir. C. Shultz)
Shane (1953, dir. G. Stevens)
The Shawshank Redemption (1996, dir. F. Darabont)
The Sign of the Cross (1932, dir. C. DeMille)
Signs (2002, dir. M. Shyamalan)
Simon of the Desert (1965, dir. L. Buñuel)
The Singing Nun (1966, dir. H. Koster)
Sister Act (1992, dir. E. Ardolino)
Smoke Signals (1998, dir. C. Eyre)
Solaris (1972, dir. A. Tarkovsky)
The Son (2002, dir. J. Dardenne)

Son of Man (2006, dir. M. Domford-May)
The Song of Bernadette (1943, dir. H. King)
The Sound of Music (1965, dir. R. Wise)
The Spitfire Grill (1996, dir. L. Zlotoff)
Stagecoach (1939, dir. J. Ford)
Stalker (1979, dir. A. Tarkovsky)
Taxi Driver (1976, dir. M. Scorsese)
The Ten Commandments (1923, dir. C. DeMille)
The Ten Commandments (1956, dir. C. DeMille)
There Will be Blood (2007, dir. P. Anderson)
Thérèse (1986, dir, A. Cavalier)
The Third Miracle (1999, dir. A. Holland)
Three Godfathers (1948, dir. J. Ford)
The Trial of Joan of Arc (1962, dir. R. Bresson)
Twist of Faith (2004, dir. K. Dick)
Viridiana (1961, dir. L. Buñuel)
Whistle Down the Wind (1961, dir. B. Forbes)
White (1994, dir. K. Kieślowski)
Wild Strawberries (1957, dir. I. Bergman)
Wings of Desire (1987, dir. W. Wenders)
Winter Light (1962, dir. I. Bergman)

Further reading

Baugh, L. (1997) *Imaging the Divine: Jesus and Christ-Figures in Film*, Kansas City: Sheed & Ward.
Christianson, E. (2005), *Cinema Divinite: Religion, Theology and the Bible in Film*, London: SCM Press.
Humphries-Brooks, S. (2006) *Cinematic Savior: Hollywood's Making of the American Christ*, Westport, CT: Praeger Publishers.
Lang, J. (2007) *The Bible on the Big Screen: A Guide from the Silent Films to Today's Movies*, Grand Rapids, MI: Baker Books.
Lindvall, T. (2007), *Sanctuary Cinema: Origins of the Christian Film Industry*, New York: NYU Press.
Staley, J. (2007) *Jesus, the Gospels and Cinematic Imagination*, Louisville, KY: Westminster John Knox.
Stern, R. (1999) *Savior on the Silver Screen*, Mahwah, NJ: Paulist Press.
Tatum, W. (2004) *Jesus at the Movies: A Guide to the First Hundred Years*, Santa Rosa, CA: Polebridge Press.
Walsh, R. (2003) *Reading the Gospels in the Dark: Portrayals of Jesus in Film*, Philadelphia: Trinity Press International.

7

ISLAM

Amir Hussain

"They describe us," the other whispered solemnly. "That's all. They have the power of description, and we succumb to the pictures that they construct."

Rushdie (1988: 168)

Introduction

In March 2008, there was worldwide controversy over a short film called *Fitna* (Arabic for "discord"), released by Dutch politician Geert Wilders. In the Dutch newspaper *De Volkskrant*, Wilders wrote: "The film is not so much about Muslims as about the Koran and Islam. The Islamic ideology has as its utmost goal the destruction of what is most dear to us, our freedom" (Reuters 2008). Not surprisingly, the film was denounced in several Muslim countries, with counter films being made by the Arab European League as well as bloggers in the Muslim world. Unfortunately, there is nothing new in films, even those made by contemporary Dutch politicians, which denounce Islam and Muslim lives. Perhaps no other religion has been as misrepresented on film as Islam.

In the years before the terrorist attacks of 9/11, I would begin my courses on Islam with a standard historical introduction to the life of Muhammad and the beginnings of Islam (Peters 1994). I did this because my students – whether they were Muslim or not – often knew very little about Islam prior to taking my course. In the semester after 9/11, I found that this was no longer effective as the students came in with what they thought was a great deal of knowledge about Islam and the religious lives of Muslims. Unfortunately, most of their "knowledge" came from the popular media and was often at odds with the ways in which the majority of Muslims understand their own faith. As a result, I began to use a book that described how television news works (Postman and Powers 2008). I begin with this anecdote as it shows the power of the media in constructing our understandings of Muslims and Islam. In this chapter I discuss representations of Muslim lives and the religion of Islam on film.

The diversity of Islam

Islam is an Arabic word that means "submission" or "surrender." It also has connotations of "peace." So, Islam is sometimes translated as "peaceful submission" or "engaged surrender," viz., to the One God, the same God worshiped by Jews and Christians. Islam is the second largest religious tradition both in the world and in the West. In the world, there are over 1 billion Muslims. In North America and Europe, there are over 15 million Muslims, many more than this if we include Turkey as part of Europe. For countries such as Canada, France, and Britain, Islam is already the second largest religion behind Christianity. In the United States, depending on differing estimates, Islam may well be the second largest religion, and is certainly the third largest.

There is great diversity among these populations of Muslims due to the diversity of cultural and religious expressions of Islam. This is seldom recognized in media portrayals of Muslims, which tend to homologize all Muslims to an Arab (and usually terrorist) stereotype. In fact, most Muslims are not even Arab, and the nation with the largest Muslim population is Indonesia. There are also differences due to the individual conservatism or liberalism of Muslims. Again, this is not unique to Islam. There are many sorts of Christians, from fundamentalists to conservatives to liberals, and the same holds true of Muslims. There are moderate Muslim voices and radical Muslim voices, but once again, media portrayals seldom acknowledge anything but the perspective of the most reactionary. These portrayals also couple Islam and violence, and Islam and misogyny, so that the entire tradition is reduced to the dual tropes of violence and misogyny. One does not, for example, see filmic examples of Muslims patiently fasting during the month of Ramadan, or giving to charity, both required "pillars" for observant Muslims. Instead, one sees Muslims committing despicable acts of violence, while simultaneously abusing women.

Muslims also differ in the political systems that govern them. Some, such as those in Iran, live in a theocracy, where Islamic religious law or Shari'ah is the law of the land. Others, such as those in Pakistan or Libya, have been under a military dictatorship. Some, such as in Saudi Arabia, live under a monarchy. Others, such as those in Turkey or India, live under secular democracies. In the West, Muslims live as minorities in plural, democratic societies. This diversity, again, is seldom represented in film.

Islam has long existed in Western culture, first in Europe and later in North America. Prior to the Crusades, Muslims were relatively unknown by the European public. After the Crusades, with the making of enemy images on both sides, there was a great deal of polemic in European texts about Muslims. Norman Daniel has written the classic study of this time, his magisterial *Islam and the West: The Making of an Image* (1993). The ordinary European might come into contact with Muslims as merchants, traders, seafarers, or pirates. However, the educated classes read works of Islamic philosophy, as well as classics of Greek philosophy (such as Aristotle) translated into Arabic and then into Latin. Muslim physicians were among the best of their day, and Muslim scientists and mathematicians (in collaboration with non-Muslims) made great advances in the sciences. Nonetheless, such cultural interchanges did not remove the prejudices that continued to exist, largely due to military and political conflicts between Christians and Muslims from that time to our own.

Muslims first came to North America centuries ago, a fact of which most Americans remain unaware. There are reports by the Arab geographer al-Idrisi of Muslim sailors who reached America before Columbus. Several members of Columbus' crew are thought to have been Muslim (converted to Catholicism during the *reconquista*), as were other members of various Spanish expeditions into the New World. With the rise of the slave trade came more Muslims to North America. One estimate is that 20 percent of the slaves who were brought over from West Africa were Muslim. There are many extant slave narratives from the eighteenth and nineteenth centuries written by African Muslims, the earliest being *Some Memoirs of the Life of Job Ben Solomon*, written in 1734. Later, in the nineteenth and early twentieth centuries, Muslims were lured to the New World by economic opportunity, like other immigrant groups (Curtis 2007).

Muslims and the media

Viewers must be aware of the complexities of Muslim lives and avoid the easy trap of trying to simplify "Islam" as some sort of monolithic entity. When one shifts the focus to Muslims, it is easier to discuss variations in ethnicity, gender, sectarian differences, and so on. Given the misinformation about Islam and Muslims created by the media, it is often necessary to provide corrective information about Islam and Muslim lives. Since most people get their information about Islam and Muslim lives from television, it is important to begin with how television news works. In the introductory packet of readings for my Islam class, I include Edward R. Murrow's famous 1958 speech to the Radio and Television News Directors Association. Among the most prophetic lines, more important a half century after they were first spoken, are these:

> We are currently wealthy, fat, comfortable and complacent. We have currently a built-in allergy to unpleasant or disturbing information. Our mass media reflect this. But unless we get up off our fat surpluses and recognize that television in the main is being used to distract, delude, amuse and insulate us, then television and those who finance it, those who look at it and those who work at it, may see a totally different picture too late. (Murrow 1958)

One remedy to the power of the media illusions that Murrow predicted is media literacy. The literature in the field of religion and media is developing quickly (Hoover 1998; 2006; Hoover and Clark 2002; Badaracco 2005; Buddenbaum and Mason 2000; Giggie and Winston 2002). This work has shown both how religious groups use the media and how the media understand, misunderstand, and cover religion. Media portrayals of Muslims are a prime example of misrepresentation. These portrayals are discussed in many scholarly works (Karim 2003; Qureshi and Sells 2003; Said 1997). To take but one example, comedian Dave Chappelle actually is a Muslim, but this is never disclosed in his characters. The images of Muslims on television tend to be negative and violent, as they are most often terrorists or criminals (in shows such as *Sleeper Cell* or *24*). These portrayals do not, of course, reflect the realities of American Muslim life, where American Muslims are on average wealthier and better educated than non-Muslims. The situation is somewhat different in Canadian television than US television, with the Canadian Broadcasting Corporation's sitcom *Little Mosque on the Prairie*. In this show, one sees the poetry of ordinary Canadian Muslim lives enacted with humor on the small screen. This show has been quite popular in Canada. Unfortunately, an American television comedy with a major Muslim character, *Aliens in America*, was cancelled after its first season.

Negative portrayals of American Muslims on television must have some correlation with the ways in which actual American Muslims are perceived by those in the United States. The violent actions of a tiny minority of Muslim terrorists are amplified when they are virtually the only images available on television. One sees this, for example, in a poll by the Pew Forum on Religion and Public Life following the terrorist attacks in London in July 2005. In that survey 36 percent of US Americans felt that Islam was more likely to encourage violence in its followers (which was down from 44 percent in 2003), while those holding unfavorable opinions of Islam increased slightly (from 34 percent to 36 percent between 2003 and 2005) (Pew 2007). In 2006 the Council on American Islamic Relations (CAIR) recorded 1,972 civil rights complaints from US American Muslims, up almost 30 percent from 2005 and the most ever recorded by CAIR in its twelve-year history (CAIR 2006). Also in 2006, a poll by the *Washington Post* and ABC News showed that 46 percent of US Americans had negative views of Islam (up from 39 percent after the 9/11 attacks) (Deane and Fears 2006).

Muslims in American films

The situation just described for television portrayals of American Muslims is not markedly different from that in film. The classic study of Arabs in Hollywood films is *Reel Bad Arabs: How Hollywood Vilifies a People* (2001) by Jack Shaheen. Shaheen describes more than 900 films that portray Arabs. He describes Hollywood's portrayal of Arabs as the "systematic, pervasive and unapologetic degradation and dehumanization of a people" (Shaheen 2001: 1). As described by Shaheen, the early history of Hollywood images of Muslims showed a tendency to exoticize Islam and Muslims in films such as *The Sheikh* (1921) with Rudolph Valentino or *Lawrence of Arabia* (1962) with Peter O'Toole. Shaheen identifies six common tropes used in reference to Arabs: villains, sheikhs, maidens, Egyptians, Palestinians, and gratuitous slurs in cameos. In many of the movies he studied, beginning with *Imar the Servitor* (released by Majestic in 1914), Arabs are portrayed as villainous. A movie that Shaheen singles out in this regard is *Rules of Engagement* (2000). In the film, US Marines, led by Samuel L. Jackson, slaughter 83 men, women, and children in Yemen. The film was especially problematic for Shaheen, himself a veteran of the US Army, as it was supported by both the Department of Defense and the US Marine Corps. If filmic representations of Arabs are presented as anti-American, it becomes all too easy to justify the slaughter of actual Arabs.

The second trope that Shaheen identifies is the sheikh, an Arabic word that literally translates as "old man," and means a respected elder. However, from early Kinetoscope shorts like *Sheik Hadj Tahar Hadj Cherif* (1894) to the very first film shot in Los Angeles, *The Power of the Sultan* (1907), the Hollywood sheikh is lecherous and cruel. This is best exemplified in the 1921 film *The Sheikh*, where Rudolph

Valentino's title character, Sheikh Ahmed, boasts that "When an Arab sees a woman he wants, he takes her!" Arab women fare no better in the cinema. They are usually presented either as belly dancers, or as anonymous veiled women in black. In either case their humanity is stripped from them, and they are reduced to objects. What is also troubling for Shaheen is the gratuitous use of Arabs in film remakes. He points to *Father of the Bride II* (1995) as an example. The original film with Spencer Tracy and Elizabeth Taylor in 1950 had no Arab characters, and didn't vilify any group of people. In the sequel, Eugene Levy plays an Arab, Mr. Habib, who speaks a mix of Arabic, Farsi, and gibberish. In just a few short scenes, the Habib character is portrayed as coarse and vulgar, and as extorting money out of the main character. One wonders what audience reactions would be if the character portrayed was Jewish rather than Arab. There is a fifty-minute documentary film, also entitled *Reel Bad Arabs*, featuring Shaheen talking about his book. That film is quite useful, particularly the last two chapters, "Islamophobia" and "Getting Real," which effectively summarize Shaheen's arguments in eighteen minutes. As such, these last two chapters are ideal to view and discuss in a fifty-minute class.

These negative portrayals of Islam continue in animated films as well, with the Disney film *Aladdin* coming in for criticism from Muslim groups on its release in 1992. Of this film, Shaheen writes: "Disney animators anglicize the film's heroes, Aladdin, Princess Jasmine, and the Sultan. Conversely, they paint all the other Arabs as ruthless, uncivilized caricatures ... throughout, the action and dialogue imply that Arabs are abhorrent types, that Islam is a brutal religion" (Shaheen 2001: 51). The film opens with a lyric that contains these lines describing the setting of the film, a fictional Arab country, "Where they cut off your ear / if they don't like your face / it's barbaric, but hey, it's home." While the first two lines were removed when the film was released on video a year later, the final line remained. This led the *New York Times* to respond in an editorial, "To characterize an entire region with this sort of tongue-in-cheek bigotry, especially in a film aimed at children, borders on the barbaric" (Shaheen 2001: 51). In another scene, a street vendor threatens to chop off the hand of Princess Jasmine for taking an apple to feed a hungry child. This is a misrepresentation of Shari'ah law, as if all thieves summarily have their hands chopped off by the person they stole from, even if they were correcting an injustice by feeding the hungry.

Rubina Ramji has written an excellent article that expands the misrepresentation of Arabs to include Muslims. In the article Ramji notes that, after the 9/11 terrorist attacks, rentals of videos such as *True Lies* (1994), *Air Force One* (1997), and *The Siege* (1998), all of which feature Muslim terrorists, increased dramatically. In the case of *Air Force One*, whose plot revolves around Muslim terrorists hijacking the president's plane, rentals of the film were ten times higher in Canada than before the attacks (Ramji 2005: 12). Clearly, people were turning to films in light of current events. Given both the negative portrayals of Muslims in films and the movies' popularity post-9/11, it is important for people to understand the impact of these misrepresentations.

Ramji begins with a discussion of *Navy Seals* (1990), a film that fits into the "villains" category described by Shaheen. In this film, an elite American fighting force is dispatched to deal with Muslim terrorists who are attempting to attack American allies. In 1991's *Not Without My Daughter*, the threat becomes personalized against an American woman who is abused by her Iranian Muslim husband. Of course, the American woman is able to triumph over her Muslim enemies. Of the portrayal of Muslim women in film, Ramji concludes: "Since films are considered powerful conveyors of ideology and ethics, within these films, the cinematic representations of Islamic women show how they are situated in the mindset of American culture: they suffer at the hands of Islam, are made invisible by the fact that they are always covered and silenced. The inevitable link between Islam and oppression is reinforced through these films. In the rare instances that Muslim women step outside of their passive roles, they are either threatened or killed. They become, through their chadors and veils, the tragic depictions of bodily suffering and death within patriarchal Islam" (2005: 69).

There was a period when Muslims were occasionally portrayed positively in action films, because of the covert alliance between the US and the Afghan "freedom fighters" (mujahideen) during the Soviet incursion in Afghanistan in the 1980s. *Rambo III* (1988, dir. P. MacDonald), released almost a decade after the Soviet invasion of Afghanistan, is the third installment in the Rambo tetralogy. In this film, Rambo (the Vietnam War veteran played by Sylvester Stallone) goes to Afghanistan to rescue his mentor, who has been captured by the Soviets. In the course of the film he befriends and helps to train the Afghani mujahideen, who a decade later would become the Taliban. Here, in the last days of the Cold War, they are seen as noble heroes. The same sympathetic portrayal of the mujahideen is found in the James Bond film *The Living Daylights* (1987), although the comic portrayals of the Muslims are stereotypical and may do little to increase understanding of real Muslims.

Another modern film to offer positive portrayals of Muslims (although also guilty at times of romanticizing them) is Ridley Scott's *Kingdom of Heaven*, released in 2005. This film, which is set during the Crusades, received an award from the Council on American Islamic Relations for its portrayal of the Muslim leader Saladin.

Documentary films about Islam

Muslims have expressed their self-understanding in a number of documentary films, which give a much more accurate view of Islam, and demonstrate well its diversity. *Pilgrimage to Karbala* (2007) covers Iranian Shi'a pilgrims who travel by bus to the shrine of Imam Hussein in Karbala, Iraq. The film ends with an interview with a noted scholar of Shi'a Islam, Vali Nasr. One of the points that Nasr raises in the documentary is that many of the Iranians who make the pilgrimage would otherwise be considered "secular": one family of a rug merchant has a Western-style apartment complete with dog (an animal considered "unclean") and a mother who wears makeup and no hijab in front of strangers. Yet the son in the family desperately wants to make the pilgrimage. This problematizes the simple dichotomy between "secular" and "religious." The film is also obviously important in discussions of images of Shi'a Islam.

Another important topic is African-American Muslims, who make up at least 25 percent of American Muslims. A worthwhile introduction is a 1992 CBS news video titled *The Real Malcolm X: An Intimate Portrait of the Man* (produced by Brett Alexander). An important issue among American Muslims relates to the tensions that sometimes occur between African-American and immigrant Muslims. A wonderful film to illustrate this friction is Zareena Grewal's 2004 documentary, *By the Dawn's Early Light: Chris Jackson's Journey to Islam*. The film profiles Chris Jackson, the all-American point guard at Louisiana State University who changed his name to Mahmoud Abdul-Rauf when he converted to Islam. In 1996 Abdul-Rauf was suspended by his NBA team, the Denver Nuggets, for one game due to his refusal to stand for the national anthem due to his "Muslim conscience." This was seen as an important act of conscience by indigenous Muslims, but immigrant Muslims regarded it as an act of defiance that was somehow "un-American." The film ends with a discussion of Abdul-Rauf's work as a Muslim leader in his hometown of Gulfport, Mississippi.

A helpful documentary on women's roles in Islam is *Me and the Mosque*, directed by Zarqa Nawaz. The film is directly related to her own concerns as a Muslim woman, namely as to space available to her in the mosque. Nawaz has also made two short films, *BBQ Muslims* and *Death Threat*. In 2007 she was responsible for the Canadian Broadcasting Corporation's hit show *Little Mosque on the Prairie*.

Another documentary about women is *Football Under Cover* (2008), which tells the story of the Iranian women's national soccer team. The film details the events leading up to the first international women's match in Iran between the Iranian team and a German club team from Berlin. While the women are forced to wear headscarves, they present a very different portrayal of Iranian women than is usually seen.

Non-documentary films from Muslims, about Muslims

There are a number of films that present nuanced views of Muslim life. One such film, *My Son, the Fanatic* (1999, dir. U. Prasad), tells a father–son story set in England. The film is based on a story by the British Muslim writer Hanif Kureishi. The secularized father wants to assimilate to English culture; the son, who learns through racism and discrimination that his skin color and religion will never allow him to be considered "English," becomes much more religiously conservative. In light of the London bombings of 2005, the film becomes even more important.

An important filmmaker from the Muslim world was Youssef Chahine, who died in 2008. Born in Egypt, Chahine was a Christian who made over forty feature films. The films ranged from tragedies such as *Cairo Station* (1958) to love stories like *The Other* (1999), to autobiographical works such as *Alexandria . . . Why?* (1978). Writing Chahine's obituary in *Time* magazine, film critic Richard Corliss noted that: "at film festivals Chahine was for decades the prime, often the only, representative of an entire continent, Africa, and a world religion, Islam . . . He was both a nationalist and an internationalist, both an art-house auteur and a director of movies that were popular from Morocco to Indonesia" (Corliss 2008: 16).

Perhaps the best-known director in the Muslim world was Mustapha Akkad (1930–2005), who was killed in a terrorist bombing in Amman, Jordan. Akkad's most famous film was *The Message* (1976), which told the story of the revelations to Muhammad and the beginnings of Islam. In keeping with Muslim reservation about depicting the Prophet, there was no actor to portray him. Instead, the camera point of view was often used for Muhammad, and actors would speak to the camera as if they were speaking to Muhammad. Still, this proved to be controversial for some Muslims. The film, however, was one of the rare positive portrayals of Islam and Muslims, and featured actors such as Anthony Quinn and Irene Papas. Quinn would feature in Akkad's next film, *Lion of the Desert* (1981), where he played Omar Mukhtar, a Libyan leader of the resistance against Italian colonial rule. The film was shot on location in Libya, and financed by the Libyan dictator, Muammar Gaddafi. In spite of that, the film was an excellent historical epic, with strong performances by Quinn and Papas, as well as John Gielgud, Oliver Reed, and Rod Steiger.

One can use films from the Muslim world to illustrate the diversity of Muslim lives. While there are interesting movies from places such as Egypt, Pakistan, India, and Turkey, some of the best-known films from the Muslim world are from Iran. *Children of Heaven* (1997, dir. M. Majidi) tells the story of two children in postrevolutionary Iran, Ali and his sister Zahra. Due to their family's financial difficulties, the children have to share a pair of shoes. Majidi is renowned for his ability to tell stories of children, and this film is magical with respect to the youngsters' lives. At the time of this writing, with tensions existing between the United States and Iran, the film serves to put a human face on Iranians.

Egypt has long been the leader of cinema in the Arab world. An important contemporary film is the Egyptian blockbuster *The Yacoubian Building* (2006, dir. M. Hamed), based on the best-selling novel by Alaa Al-Aswany (originally published in Arabic in 2002). The film presents the building and its inhabitants as a microcosm of Egyptian society. While there is much repression and censorship in Egypt, the film is critical of the corruption in Egyptian society and within the Egyptian government.

In the age of file sharing, a good resource for films about Muslims is the Muslim Video Community located at the website http://tv.muxlim.com/. From the website one can download various films about Muslims from a broad range of categories.

One hopeful development is the number of new films that deal seriously with Islam. In 2008, Warner Brothers was set to release *Towelhead*, a film based on the autobiographical novel by Alicia Erian. One prominent Islamic advocacy group, the Council on American Islamic Relations, wanted the title changed because it was a common slur against Arabs. However, in the context of the film, which explores the life of an adolescent Arab-American girl, the title was well suited, challenging the prejudices faced by Arab-Americans. In this way, the insult is turned into a strength. Another 2008 release was *Traitor* starring Don Cheadle as US Special Operations Officer Samir Horn. Horn is a devout Muslim, who observed his father killed in a car bombing in Sudan. His mother moves him to Chicago, and the film picks him up thirty years later, arrested by the FBI for selling detonators to Muslim terrorists in Yemen. However, there is a tension between Horn and an FBI agent who works on his case, with the agent unsure if Horn is a terrorist or a patriot. The film is an excellent character study of a Muslim leading man.

There has been a clear and lengthy history of misrepresentation of Muslims and Islam in film. As noted above, however, one sees that changing, both in films made by Muslims, and in films made by non-Muslims. In Hollywood, this is perhaps due to both Muslim watchdog groups who draw attention to negative portrayals, and Muslims themselves being involved in the film business. In 2008, the Writers Guild of America hosted a workshop entitled "Rewriting the Divide: Hollywood and the Muslim World," allowing its members to talk with experts on Islam and the Muslim world. The workshop launched a new program, The Hollywood Engagement Initiative. In this way, more accurate information about Muslims is provided to screenwriters. One hopes that this translates into more accurate portrayals, for that is what is being asked for by Muslims; not to be represented only as villains, not to be represented only as heroes, but to be represented in the fullness of their humanity.

Bibliography

Badaracco, C. (ed.) (2005) *Quoting God: How Media Shape Ideas about Religion*, Waco, TX: Baylor University Press.

Buddenbaum, J. and Mason, D. (eds) (2000) *Readings on Religion as News*, Ames: Iowa State University Press.

Corliss, R. (2008) "Youssef Chahine," *Time*, 11 August: 16.

Council on American Islamic Relations (CAIR) (2006) "The Status of Muslim Civil Rights in the United States 2006: The Struggle for Equality." Online. Available HTTP: <http://www.cair.com/CivilRights/ CivilRightsReports/2006Report.aspx> (accessed 2 September 2008).

Curtis IV, E. (ed.) (2007) *The Columbia Sourcebook of Muslims in the United States*, New York: Columbia University Press.

Daniel, N. (1993) *Islam and the West: The Making of an Image*, Oxford: Oneworld.

Deane, C. and Fears, D. (2006) "Negative Perception of Islam Increasing," *Washington Post* (9 March). Online. Available HTTP: <http://www.washingtonpost.com/wp-dyn/content/article/2006/03/08/ AR2006030802221.html> (accessed 2 September 2008).

Giggie, J. and Winston, D. (eds) (2002) *Faith in the Market: Religion and the Rise of Urban Commercial Culture*, New Brunswick, NJ: Rutgers University Press.

Hoover, S. (1998) *Religion in the News: Faith and Journalism in American Public Discourse*, Thousand Oaks, CA: Sage.

—— (2006) *Religion in the Media Age*, London: Routledge.

Hoover, S. and Clark, L. (eds) (2002) *Practicing Religion in the Age of Media: Explorations in Media, Religion, and Culture*, New York: Columbia University Press.

Karim, K. (2003) *Islamic Peril: Media and Global Violence*, rev. ed., Montreal: Black Rose.

Murrow, E. R. (1958) "Speech to Radio and Television News Directors Association." Online. Available HTTP: <http://www.turnoffyourtv.com/commentary/hiddenagenda/murrow.html> (accessed 1 September 2008).

Peters, F. E. (1994) *Muhammad and the Origins of Islam*, Albany: SUNY Press.

Pew Forum on Religion and Public Life (2007) Online. Available HTTP: <http://people-press.org/ report/358/public-expresses-mixed-views-of-islam-mormonism> (accessed 2 September 2008).

Postman, N. and Powers, S. (2008) *How to Watch TV News*, rev. ed., New York: Penguin.

Qureshi, E. and Sells, M. (eds) (2003) *The New Crusades: Constructing the Muslim Enemy*, New York: Columbia University Press.

Ramji, R. (2005) "From *Navy Seals* to *The Siege*: Getting to Know the Muslim Terrorist, Hollywood Style," *Journal of Religion and Film* 9 (2) (October). Online. Available HTTP: <http://www.unomaha.edu/jrf/ Vol9No2/RamjiIslam.htm> (accessed 1 September 2008).

Reuters (2008) "Dutch Protest against Islam Critics Koran Film." Online. Available HTTP: <http://www. reuters.com/article/latestCrisis/idUSL22433652> (accessed 1 September 2008).

Rushdie, S. (1988) *The Satanic Verses*, London: Penguin.
Said, E. (1997) *Covering Islam: How the Media and the Experts Determine How We See the Rest of the World*, rev. ed., New York: Vintage.
Shaheen, J. (2001) *Reel Bad Arabs: How Hollywood Vilifies a People*, New York: Olive Branch.

Filmography

Air Force One (1997, dir. W. Peterson)
Aladdin (1992, dir. R. Clements and J. Musker)
Alexandria . . . Why? (1978, dir. Y. Chahine)
BBQ Muslims (1995, dir. Z. Nawaz)
By the Dawn's Early Light: Chris Jackson's Journey to Islam (2004, dir. Z. Grewal)
Cairo Station (1958, dir. Y. Chahine)
Children of Heaven (1997, dir. M. Majidi)
Death Threat (1998, dir. Z. Nawaz)
Father of the Bride II (1995, dir. C. Shyer)
Fitna (2008, dir. G. Wilders)
Football Under Cover (2008, dir. A. Najafi and D. Assmann)
Imar the Servitor (1914, Majestic)
In the Sultan's Power (1909, dir. F. Boggs)
Kingdom of Heaven (2005, dir. R. Scott)
Lawrence of Arabia (1962, dir. D. Lean)
Lion of the Desert (1981, dir. M. Akkad)
The Living Daylights (1987, dir. J. Glen)
Me and the Mosque (2005, dir. Z. Nawaz)
The Message (1976, dir. M. Akkad)
My Son, the Fanatic (1999, dir. U. Prasad)
Navy Seals (1990, dir. L. Teague)
Not Without My Daughter (1991, dir. B. Gilbert)
The Other (1999, dir. Y. Chahine)
Pilgrimage to Karbala (2007, dir. K. Sim)
Rambo III (1988, dir. P. MacDonald)
The Real Malcolm X: An Intimate Portrait of the Man (1992, prod. B. Alexander)
Reel Bad Arabs (2006, dir. S. Jhally)
Rules of Engagement (2000, dir. W. Friedkin)
The Sheikh (1921, dir. G. Melford)
The Siege (1998, dir. E. Zwick)
Towelhead (2008, dir. A. Ball)
Traitor (2008, dir. J. Nachmanoff)
True Lies (1994, dir. J. Cameron)
The Yacoubian Building (2006, dir. M. Hamed)

8

HINDUISM

Rachel Dwyer

It was the death of God. Or something very like it; for had not that outsize face, suspended over its devotees in the artificial cinematic night, shone like that of some supernal Entity that had its being at least halfway between the mortal and the divine? More than halfway, many would have argued, for Gibreel had spent the greater part of his unique career incarnating, with absolute conviction, the countless deities of the subcontinent in the popular genre movies known as "theologicals" … For over a decade and a half he had represented, to hundreds of millions of believers in that country in which, to this day, the human population outnumbers the divine by less than three to one, the most acceptable, and instantly recognizable, face of the supreme.

Rushdie (1988: 16–17)

Introduction: Indian cinema, Bollywood, Hinduism

Rushdie's invented genre of the "theological" passed largely ignored in *The Satanic Verses*, where he discusses religion and Indian cinema in an imaginative though nonhistorical way. Hollywood has barely updated colonial depictions of Hinduism as monstrous and barbaric, seen most recently in *Indiana Jones and the Temple of Doom* (1984, dir. S. Spielberg). Yet Indian cinema has engaged with religious beliefs and practices since its founding film, a mythological, *Raja Harischandra* (1913), and there are exciting developments continuing in the present day.

Indian cinema is known today in the west as "Bollywood," which in India is used to refer to the dominant form of Indian cinema, the Hindi cinema produced in Mumbai, formerly Bombay. This excludes the art-house cinema, whose most famous maker is Satyajit Ray, and other popular cinemas such as the Tamil and Telugu cinemas of South India. Hindi cinema is a national, popular, independent cinema, free from much state control, which has enormous domestic audiences (its popularity threatened only occasionally by Hollywood's global reach) as well as large overseas audiences.

Indian cinema has strong links with indigenous performative traditions, but much of it is the product of a new public culture that arose during the nineteenth century, whose hybridity is inherent to its very nature, as it brings together traditional Indian images with industrial technology. While new sources of the still image, notably chromolithography ("calendar art") and photography, were major influences on early cinema, the new urban theater was one of its most important antecedents, showing many features which we later find in Hindi films, notably the presentation of a series of "attractions," which interrupted the narrative. These attractions remain the distinctive feature of mainstream (commercial) Indian cinema, which is defined by its melodrama, glamor, song and dance, stars, and use of dramatic language, gesture, and visuality. However, there has also been a realist, middle-class cinema, appealing to educated audiences, as well as a whole slew of B-movies, which has also reached large audiences.

Hinduism is difficult to define, and here it is used in the loosest sense as a broad set of values, some shared, some not, which are held by the great majority (80 percent) of India's population as well as many outside India. India remains a deeply religious country, with the urban, educated population being more religious than the poor, less educated people in the villages (*Hindustan Times*, 24 March 2008). Religion (and secularism) in India, and the Hindu religion in particular, are very different from analogous phenomena in Western Europe and North America. Religion in India is very much part of the everyday, and the boundary between the everyday and the religious is porous or permeable. In Indian cinema religion is not just represented directly by divine presences or by religious communities, but also manifested in ways of creating an ideal world through the individual, the family, and society. The films do not just show literal representations of religions (mostly Hinduism, but also India's largest minority religion, Islam), and religious communities and beliefs, but are grounded in wider concerns of customs and society that can be said to be religious, however loosely. These concerns cross the boundaries of regional and religious communities so may be said to form pan-Indian views and beliefs which then reach beyond the artificial boundaries and limited imagination of the nation to the diaspora and to people of non-Indian origin in other parts of the world. One does not have to be a "believer" to be a Hindu; many members of other religions in India may not worship the Hindu gods, and are sincere in their belief in their own one God, but they are likely to acknowledge them and to have a notion of the Hindu world.

In India, secularism has a very different meaning from in the West, where it also varies, as Taylor (2004) and others have pointed out. In India, secularism means respecting all religions equally. In this sense, as Shyam Benegal argues, all Indian films are secular in that they do not exclude a choice of faith, although attention must be paid to the use of symbols. He mentions his film *Trikal*, in which the Roman Catholic family makes coconut offerings at a temple on certain days of the year. This needs no explanation in India. He also points out that Hindi cinema does not necessarily represent cultural spaces as regional cinema does (Benegal 2007).

In this essay, I use the term "Hindu imaginary," drawing on the concept of modern social imaginaries as posited by Charles Taylor (2004), to account for this broad view of Hinduism as part of history, culture, language, and even Indianness, as well as the inclusion of symbols and motifs. Taylor's account is suggestive as he uses it as a way of accounting for the different or multiple modernities we encounter in non-Western societies, a feature which Indian social scientist Ashis Nandy has repeatedly mentioned in the context of India and which we must approach carefully given the question of how Western some of modern India appears.

Film in India has been one of the key ways in which religion, and mythology in particular, has been mediated in India over the past century. Although new forms of media such as television are increasingly important, Indian cinema has mediated the imagination of the Indian nation across the subcontinent and in the diaspora. The consumption of Indian cinema through other media such as music, radio, television, and magazines has also affected religion, for example by popularizing rituals or even particular deities such as Santoshi Maa (see below).

This essay is primarily concerned with the filmmakers and their own images of Hinduism. I am not propounding auteur theory, nor do I try to suggest what the filmmakers intended as having any privileged meaning. I have interviewed them or read other interviews, biographies, and autobiographies to examine why they may have chosen certain themes and details within them or how they interpret their own films. Given that Indian society values religiosity highly, filmmakers often wish to be seen as being overtly religious at some times, whereas historically there have been times which may encourage other views such as secularism and religious tolerance. However great the religious feelings of individuals who have made these films, they are operating under constraints of the form, including narratives, images, and language, and by the commercial needs of producers and financiers. There are also political constraints, notably censorship which restricts the depiction of taboo practices and images of minorities. There is also the form of the film which does not require a happy ending but a moral resolution where good triumphs over evil, however sad it may be for the protagonists, in what is usually a Hindu worldview. In this chapter I question why individuals have chosen to make religious films or how their nonreligious films show a certain cultural depiction of religion and its role in the everyday. One does not have to be a believer to share in a wider worldview which may be shaped by Hinduism. I do not examine whether this is all a bogus morality and filmmakers are adopting such forms to appeal to the audiences; instead, I seek to explore how these practices influenced other filmmakers and how audiences received them.

Mythologicals and devotionals

There are three major genres in Indian cinema which are labeled as explicitly religious: the mythological, the devotional, and the Islamicate (or Muslim social). These genres show a clear religious presence, whether in terms of theology, ideology, or culture, which is readily identifiable by the industry and the audiences, as they have been throughout the century of Indian cinema. This essay focuses on the two which are relevant to depictions of Hinduism on screen, namely the mythological and the devotional.

The mythological film: the founding genre of Indian cinema

DeMille's much quoted remark that "God is box office," was certainly true of these and other films, whose attractions included great spectacle and often special effects for miracles as well as providing audiences with religious experiences. The first all-Indian feature film, D. G. Phalke's *Raja Harischandra* (1913), was a "mythological," a genre which is unique to India. The mythological has been given prominence in India as its founding genre and because of Phalke's eminence (and the survival of so much of his output).

The mythological genre is defined largely in terms of its narrative. The oldest versions of the stories are found in ancient Sanskrit texts such as the *Puranas*, which have been retold over the centuries. However, cinema has drawn more closely on India's two great epics, the *Mahabharata* and the *Ramayana*, the oldest versions of which are more than 2,000 years old. These are viewed as history, literature, and religion, not just as part of Hinduism but as part of Indian culture as a whole. Prior to the film era, these epics had already been conveyed by media such as theater, painting, music, and photography.

Phalke was a maker of chromolithographs (calendar art) as well as a photographer and so was familiar with the epics' iconic images (Pinney 2004). Geeta Kapur (2000) argues that the films use iconicity and illusionism to compensate for the descent of the gods into realism. This iconicity is reinforced by the manifestation of premodern ways of looking in the cinema, notably that of *darshan* ("seeing"). This term is used most often in the context of religious worship to refer to a two-way seeing between the god and the devotee. The narration invites *darshan* by its use of tableaux, a feature that has long been used in worship.

Another way the mythological distances itself from the everyday is by its use of the special effect. While the religious image is held to be efficacious in films as it is elsewhere, cinematic special effects of beams of vision and of light moving from eye to eye emphasize the very nature of the religious image.

Fewer than twenty of India's 1,000 plus silent films have survived to the present. Some of these are mythologicals, including several by Phalke, and Indo-German co-productions such as *Prem Sanyas / The Light of Asia* (1925), one of Himanshu Rai's collaborations with Emelka Studios in Munich. The film, on the Great Renunciation of Gautama, later the Buddha, was directed by Franz Osten, edited and processed in Germany and given English titles. It ran for only two weeks in India but ran in London for ten months (Shah 1950: 23).

Mythologicals as television soap operas

In the late 1980s, when the Indian government relaxed its restrictions on the depiction of religion on television, the mythological had a phenomenal success in the new form of religious soaps. The first major epic, Ramanand Sagar's *Ramayana*, was broadcast in January 1987 and ran for seventy-four episodes. It was soon followed by B. R. Chopra's *Mahabharata*, which had ninety-four episodes and broke all viewing statistics with its audience penetration.

Without wishing to enter debates over the comparisons of film and television and the interaction between the two, the striking difference that is relevant for the present analysis is that these television serials, although they drew on many film conventions (indeed Sagar and Chopra were both famous film directors for many decades), were received by their audiences in a very different way than cinema audiences had ever viewed the mythological film. Although mythologicals were and are often screened at particular festivals, there was no ongoing synchronicity compared to the television serials' national viewing at a particular time in the week. The viewing practices themselves were highly disparate, from the private or family viewing in domestic rather than public space, to the public screenings held in areas such as villages where televisions were unaffordable commodities. The creation of the viewing space as a sacred space was widely noted as religious ceremonies were performed around the television sets as if the deities themselves were present onscreen. In many ways, one may say that the television mythologicals, through the very nature of their medium and the popularity of the programs across social, and even religious, groups, succeeded in achieving what the film mythologicals had been trying to accomplish for eighty years with only a limited degree of success (Mankekar 2002).

The simultaneous viewing meant that audiences discussed the meanings of the epics again, creating new interpretative communities, and a simultaneous viewing of the national epics created a sense of a shared historical (more accurately, mythological) past at a time when the nation was undergoing some of the most rapid and dramatic changes in its history. However, the serials' conflations of existing beliefs about Hindu and India, history and myth, had enormous political implications, as did the screening of political and familial discussions sponsored by state television. Hindutva (Hindu nationalist) forces that were already on the rise had a canny assessment of media power, of which they made use (Rajagopal 2001).

The devotional film

The devotee, usually called a *sant*, is a person whose devotion makes them celebrated by a community of worshipers even though they are often drawn from the margins of society. The devotional films are often set outside Brahminical religion or question some aspects of it, and celebrate the introduction of vernacular languages into worship. Nearly every "regional" language of India has a strong tradition of *bhakti* or "loving devotion," and this means that even though these films were closely associated with the nationalist movement, they often present a much more regional nationalism than the mythological, which is often pan-Indian.

As well as the mythological, the devotional genre is also closely aligned with the historical in its presentation of historical figures rather than mythological, heroic, or divine characters (Mukhopadhyay 2004). By historical, I mean legendary or hagiographical figures as well as those from actual history. So while the life of the devotee may be hagiographical or the gods appear, a king or some other figure locates the film in historical rather than mythological time. The films all raise major social concerns which are set in the context of the rural, eternal, symbolic, and political. This kind of social questioning that was popular in Indian cinema from the 1930s to the 1950s, has largely moved outside the commercial cinema.

These films differ from the mythologicals as they show new visual relays of looks between the audience, the devotee, and the divine, allowing the audience to relate to the film very differently from the audience of the mythological film, which demands more awe on the part of the spectator who has to watch from something of a distance. Some of the appeal of *sant* films is the same as that of the mythologicals, in the familiar stories and in the manifestation of the divine in the everyday. The films draw on already popular songs, reinvigorate the traditions, make stories visible, and make devotion more accessible.

The *sant* film's rise in popularity in the 1930s was greater than that of the historical and mythological which had previously been more popular (Abbas 1963: 103). It is no coincidence that the devotional rose to such prominence during the 1930s when nationalism was one of the dominant public concerns in India, at a time when Gandhian nationalism was at its height. The Prabhat filmmakers (see below) had Gandhi in mind when making their films, as seen in the choice of name *Mahatma* for what was later retitled as *Dharmatma*, and in the kind of *bhakti* that these films depicted, which was clearly recognized by the audience.

Dadasaheb Phalke: art and technology in the mythological

Inspired by a "biblical" movie, D. G. "Dadasaheb" Phalke (1870–1944), "the father of Indian cinema," made the first entirely Indian film (*Raja Harischandra*, 1913), in which he established India's first filmic genre, the "mythological," creating an immediate connection between religion and cinema in India which persists to this day. Phalke dominates the history of early Indian cinema, not least because the major body of work from that period which survives is his, but also because of his writings in *Navyug* and Tilak's paper, *Kesari* (Phalke 1988/9), and his interview with the Indian Cinematograph Committee (ICC, 1927–8). Through recent research (Dharap 1985; Phalke 1988/9; Pinney 1997: 91–3; Rangoonwalla 1970; Rajadhyaksha 1993; Shoesmith 1988/9), we have much information about his training and background in the industrial arts of his time. The surviving parts of his films were assembled in 1956 for the Indian Motion Picture Producers Association.

Already a photographer, magician, and lithographer, Phalke decided to become involved in films after seeing *The Life of Christ* in 1910 (Dwyer 2009). He made some short films, then in 1912 went to London to buy filmmaking equipment and met the editor of the film magazine *Bioscope* and the British director Cecil Hepworth. His first film was very much a one-man effort, as Phalke told the ICC that he had to direct, write, photograph, print, and edit. Phalke used complex editing and was clearly a master of special effects, as his films are driven as much by spectacle as by narrative.

As Shoesmith (1988/9: 48) argues, this early cinema mixed art, capital, and politics. Phalke's writings and interviews show that he was interested in filmmaking as an act of nationalism. Phalke was closely associated with nationalist hero "Lokmanya" Tilak, who also realized that the British would censor the political unless it were presented under the guise of the religious. Phalke was a staunch supporter of the *swadeshi* movement (Phalke 1988/9: 55). This movement (lit. "belonging to one's own country") sought to ban the import of foreign manufactured goods to India and gathered momentum after the partition of Bengal in 1905.

Although Phalke was an orthodox Chitpavan Brahmin and a lifelong vegetarian, he traveled overseas three times when to do so was regarded as jeopardizing caste (though he underwent ceremonies of purification on his return). Familiar with religious stories from his family and from his upbringing in Tryambakeshwar, his writings indicate that he chose mythologicals as good subject matter to reach out to people, rather than as a form of devotion or with an intention to inspire his audiences to devotion. His films did have this affect on the audience, as Phalke's daughter, Mandakini, describes how she was worshiped by audiences after playing Krishna in Phalke's films (Watve 2004: 85). The films were also enjoyed by Europeans in India and non-Hindus such as the Parsi filmmakers J. B. H. Wadia and Ardeshir Irani.

Phalke's first film, *Raja Harischandra*, was premiered 3 May 1913 (Dharap 1985: 38). Phalke's first version of the film has disappeared but he remade the film in 1917, and 1,475 feet of this later version have survived (Rajadhyaksha and Willemen 1999: 243). This is a story transmitted from the ancient Vedic *Brahmanas*, through the *Mahabharata* and various *Puranas*. It was a staple of the Parsi Theatre, its most famous version being that performed by the Victoria Theatre Group, although Bharatendu wrote a version in Hindi, *Satya Harischandra* (1885). King Harischandra's noble sacrifices of everything he owns and his ultimate restoration to the throne had clear readings in the colonial situation.

Phalke's greatest success was *Lanka Dahan / Lanka Aflame* (1917), the story of Hanuman setting fire to Lanka with his tail; 501 feet of the latter have survived (in the NFAI, Pune) showing Sita in captivity and scenes with Hanuman and Ravana. This story from the *Ramayana* was a popular theme for chromolithography, even before Phalke, and Hanuman films have continued to be some of the most popular mythologicals. Other mythologicals of Phalke which have survived are *Shri Krishna Janma / The Birth of Shri Krishna* (1918), which shows well-known episodes from Krishna's childhood, including the sequence where Krishna rises from the River Yamuna on the demon snake Kaliya with the famous shot framed by his devotees. The final title-card reads, "May this humble offering be accepted by the Lord."

Prabhat Studios

Prabhat Film Company was founded in 1929 in Kolhapur, and then moved to Pune in 1933. It produced a number of mythologicals and famous socials, but was also well known for its devotional films in the 1930s and 1940s. Prabhat's most famous directors were V. Shantaram (1901–90), who made several mythologicals but only one devotional (*Dharmatma*, 1935) before switching entirely to social films, while Vishupant Govind Damle, a Brahmin, and Sheikh Syed Fattelal, a Muslim, made four films of which one was a mythological (*Gopal Krishna*, 1938) and three were devotionals (*Sant Tukaram*, 1936; *Sant Dnyaneshwar*, 1940; *Sant Sakhu*, 1941). Some filmmakers found that the communalism that was being mobilized by politicians in the 1930s made it hard for non-Hindus to make mythologicals, although several of the filmmakers (Wadia, Fattelal) and actors (Shahu Modak, Gohar) were non-Hindus.

Prabhat's devotionals, all in Marathi and some with Hindi versions, were concerned with Maharashtrian *sants*. Maharashtra's *sants* were mostly Vaishnava, often called the Varkari Panth (Pilgrim's Path), associated particularly with the cult of Vithoba at Pandharpur, one of the largest pilgrimage sites in India, which defines the geography of Maharashtra (Fuller 1992: 210–14). Vithoba is a form of Krishna, standing on a brick, with his consort Rukmini at his side. His cult focuses less on the erotic devotion of some of the Krishna cults and more on parental love toward the deity. Prabhat's films are superbly crafted, not only as religious films but in all elements of their making from narrative to music to visuals. Their mythologicals, devotionals, and social-reform films are crucial in the study of Maharashtrian and Indian nationalism, as they show a close connection with Ranade's reformism and Gandhi's quest for national unity.

One of the Prabhat directors, Rajaram Vankudre Shantaram (1901–90), better known as V. Shantaram, became one of India's most famous filmmakers, celebrated for his dramatic visual innovation. Son of a Jain father and a Hindu mother, he directed his first two talkies in 1931, both mythologicals. The first was a version of the story of Harischandra, *Ayodhyache Raja / Ayodhya Ka Raja*, while the second, *Maya Machhindra*, was set in the world of Nath yogis, where the great Machhindranath shows his disciple, Gorakhnath, that the world is *maya* (approximately "illusion"), which allows for many spectacles such as a beheading and restoration of the head. His third was *Amritmanthan* (1934), set in mythological times, with great spectacles such as the showing of the *amritmanthan* (the mythological story of the gods' churning of the ocean to extract nectar), where the special effects show a huge snake, Shesha, who appears to be using Mount Meru as the churning pole. All of Shantaram's mythological films are more about spectacle than piety. They do not inspire devotion as much as awe in the spectator with visual effects that are still breathtaking even today.

Vishupant Govind Damle (1892–1945) was a middle-class, educated Brahmin, who failed to become a school teacher, while Sheikh Fattelal (1893–1956), a painter, was from a Muslim family of masons who lived in Kolhapur. Friends from an early age, they both tried their hands at a variety of jobs before joining the Painter Brothers in Kolhapur. Their first mythological, *Karna* (1928, Maharashtra Film Company), based on the *Mahabharata*, was famed for its spectacular battle said to be inspired by their viewing of *Ben Hur* (1907), using every tonga (horse-drawn carriage) in Kolhapur alongside the Maharaja's elephants and horses (Watwe 1985: 6).

Sant Tukaram (1936, dir. Damle and Fattelal) was Prabhat's most famous and acclaimed film. Tukaram, Maharashtra's most loved poet and saint, was born in 1608 and vanished in 1650. He was a low-caste shudra, who lived in a village called Dehu, about 30 miles from Pune, on the banks of the River Indrayani. He wrote in colloquial Marathi using rich imagery of the everyday and his verses are used in the film. It is not surprising that Tukaram was taken up by nationalists such as Mahadev Govind Ranade (1842–1901), who sought to counteract reformist Hinduism in the nineteenth century that turned toward Brahminical texts. Damle and Fattelal empha-sized Tukaram's saintliness among the ordinary and everyday, with miracles depicted in the midst of strikingly realistic settings and performances, which make them seem part of life. Kapur (2000: 240–1) argues that the film allows the possibility of the audience forming part of the *satsang* or community of worshipers, not so much by the presence of the deity, but through the devotee himself. She draws attention to the shots of the god from over the shoulder to Tukaram and then in reverse from Tukaram so that the viewer adores both. The film has a timeless quality, seeming to be set in any Maharashtrian village and made with a great honesty and simplicity, or, as Shahani puts it, there is a "total and integrated conjunction of belief, social action, and the lack of deception, which gives it such dignity" (Shahani 1985: 202).

Actors as gods: NTR and the Telugu mythological film

The Telugu film industry has made many hugely successful mythologicals (Arudra 1984). It had a one-man mythological industry based around the actor Nandamuri Taraka Rama Rao (1923–96), better known as NTR, who acted in so many mytholog-icals (forty-two in total, of which twenty-three were stories from the *Mahabharata* and eight from the *Ramayana*) that it seems that these were the only roles he played and he became imbued with a godlike status himself. However, he also played emperors, kings, and folkloric heroes, making a film every six weeks on average. He was already a star when he took on his first divine role only in his thirtieth film, namely that of Krishna in *Maya bazaar* (1957, dir. K. V. Reddy). This became one of his more famous roles, along with Rama, which he played first in the *Sampoorna Ramanayanam* (1958, dir. K. Somu), made in Tamil then dubbed into Telugu. However, his biggest role was as Lord Venkateshwara of Tirupati in *Sri Venkateswara Mahatmyam* (1960, dir. P. Pulliah), where as an incarnation of the deity, he emerges from the idol and walks toward the audience. He played this role and other incarnations of Krishna/Vishnu in seventeen films. NTR was also a director and his extraordinary hit film *Daana Veera Shura Karna* (1977), where he played three roles (Karna, Duryodhana, and Krishna), is a tour de force.

As in Tamil Nadu, the Telugu film industry is very closely associated with politics. NTR's films were closely associated with Andhra linguistic nationalism (Vardhan 2007) as he was able to claim a Telugu identity embedded in a remote cultural-historical past. NTR founded the Telugu Desam Party in 1982 and was later Chief Minister of Andhra Pradesh.

Folk tales and horror films as mythologicals

One genre which produced some popular films was that of the new folk tale, whose story may have been made up for a film, featuring magic and popular religious belief rather than big mythologicals. From the 1940s to the 1960s, Telugu also had a popular genre of folklore films, which are perhaps regarded as localized mythologicals (Srinivas 2001). NTR was also a star of this genre, and indeed this genre helped make him a star, as Srinivas (2001) shows in his discussion of *Patala Bhairavi* (1951, dir. K. V. Reddy).

Gujarati films, which are mostly regarded as B-movies, include many local folk tales, in particular versions of the legend of Jesal and Toral, and stories of local gods and goddesses (Tripathi 1985).

Hindi cinema in the 1970s and 1980s saw some totally extraordinary horror films, often poor versions of Western films with very basic special effects and some concessions made to Indian religion such as brandishing an "Om" symbol rather than a cross. The great figures were the Ramsay Brothers, Tulsi and Shyam, whose films such as *Bandh darwaza* (1990) have become cult classics. One popular group among these films were "snake films" in which the hero and/or the heroine is a snake who takes on human form (Illuminated Lantern 2005; Hot Spot 2005). Snakes are not evil figures in Indian mythology but are auspicious and must be worshiped, especially on festivals such as Naag Panchami.

Jai Santoshi Maa

While the director of *Jai Santoshi Maa*, Vijay Sharma, is not a well-known figure, his film was the surprise hit of the year in 1975. This film is a generic mixture of the mythological, devotional, and the social in the manner of a *vratkatha* or story about a fast to propitiate a specific deity rather than a story from the Sanskrit repertoire (Lutgendorf 2003).

It is often said that Santoshi Maa was a new or local goddess who became popular as a result of the film, but there seem to be popular images of her from the 1960s by the well-known firm Sharma Picture Publications (Pinney 2004: 154-5). There are elements in the film which are not found in other stories about Santoshi Maa, such as her being the daughter of Ganesha, the naming of the goddess, and various plot devices.

Although the film is set in some vaguely north Indian village in roughly contemporary time, the cult of Santoshi Maa has become strong in the cities, in particular for lower-middle-class women, for whom this is a fairly easy *vrat* (fast), as it requires only the avoidance of sour foods and removes the need for intermediaries and large expenses. The story of the goddess is also appealing to women as it takes up the popular theme of *saas-bahu* (mother-in-law and daughter-in-law) which has become a staple of television soap operas.

Jai Santoshi Maa was the biggest hit of its type; however, it should be contextualized in a series of mother-goddess films based on *vratkathas* which became popular from the 1960s onwards. Many of these were about localized village mother goddesses, "Maa," or, further south, "Amma" figures. Most of these films had many special effects, mostly involving trident-hurling, but the *vratkatha*-type performances were more popular. Veena Das (1981) shows that *Jai Santoshi Maa* is a modern version of the goddess story, in which the goddess is not a form of *shakti* ("power") as she does not fight nor does she want anyone destroyed, but is a benevolent figure who only requires the suffering of a single devotee as her sacrifice. Satyavati is a *sati*-figure, a long-suffering and saintly woman, whose sacrifices and *vrats* force the goddess to intervene and fulfill personal desires. *Jai Santoshi Maa* may well be typical of a type of film which does not usually circulate on the main Bollywood circuits and belongs to a largely undocumented form of Indian cinema.

Although *Jai Santoshi Maa* predates VHS, the arrival of this technology in the 1980s and the decline of cinema-going may have encouraged the making of more specialized B-movies which could have only a video release, as exemplified by Peter Manuel's research (1993) on the impact of the cassette culture of the 1980s on music genres, when technology allowed the new medium to change the way music is marketed, consumed, etc. Similar changes might be expected with the mushrooming of cable and satellite television in the 1990s and then the relatively inexpensive VCD in recent years. Manuel notes that one of the major new genres created by this cassette culture was the explosion of devotional music as a major form (1993: 105–30).

Modern Hindu cinema

The gentrification of major and minor deities

Little has been written about the religious practices of new middle classes, who have emerged in India after economic liberalization (1991) to form one of India's dominant social groups and major media producers and consumers (Dwyer 2000). Rather than adopting the usual "Sanskritizing" practices described by M. N. Srinivas (1952), where upwardly mobile groups adopt elite practices to claim higher social status, the new middle classes have transformed deities and holy people who were formerly regarded as local or minor deities into national figures, even if they were previously associated with low-status groups. In other words, it seems the gods themselves are "gentrifying," as the gods of the poor and lower classes, of villagers and the lower castes are being adopted by middle classes, business elites, and diasporic Indians.

The gods who are gentrifying fastest are the mother goddesses, Mariamman or Amma in the south and Devi or Mata in the rest of the country, and this may be connected with the emergence of new deities such as Santoshi Maa (Younger 1980; Waghorne 2001; Nanda 2008). One film which shows gentrification very clearly is the *Jai Dakshineshwar Kaali Maa* (1996, dir. Shantilaal Soni), where we see not a new goddess but a new gentrified form of the goddess Kali. Although Kali performs her dance of destruction at the beginning of the film (a cameo by superstar Hema Malini), the film emphasizes loving devotion, especially in its maternal form, rejecting tantric and non-vegetarian forms of worship. Following the massive of *Jai Santoshi Maa* and other goddess mythologicals in the late seventies, many Gujarati films were made about Gujarati goddesses, such as *Jai Bahuchar Maa* (1980, dir. Ramkumar Bohra), the patron goddess of hijras (those who are neither exclusively male nor female).

The south Indian industry has had a different history of religious films. Although the mythological had declined in the Telugu film industry in the 1970s, the biggest hit of 1995 was a mother-goddess film, *Ammoru* (1995, dir. Kodi Ramakrishna). Kodi Ramakrishna has since made other goddess films including *Devi* (1999), about a snake goddess, *Devi Putrudu* (2000), about a goddess who helps avert calamities but is being sought as a source of power by evildoers, and *Devullu* (2001), in which an avenging goddess helps her devotee. None of these has had the success of *Ammoru*, which became something of a cult film as well as a major hit. It seems its success was largely due to its special effects (mainly "morphing") on which a British company, Digitalia, worked for two years. These are much more sophisticated than the flying tridents of traditional goddess movies (though there is one here too), showing instead the image of the village goddess turning into the Great Goddess in human form astride a tiger, then sending out fire and other forces from her body. This film was made on a large budget which was well spent on these special effects as well as other production qualities. However, the film also has a strong story, which is similar in some ways to *Jai Santoshi Maa*, in that it is about the conflict of a village woman, Bhawani, with her in-laws, in which she is helped by the mother goddess (Ammoru). The story again has the feeling of a *vratkatha* and there is much social drama as Bhawani's husband is a foreign-educated doctor who takes his wife's side against the rest of his family, but there is much in the way of the horror genre also as the in-laws are involved with tantric magic. The evil tantric Gorakh is related to them so Bhawani is not safe in the house. The goddess appears as a child servant in the house to help Bhawani in her fight but Gorakh manages to kill Bhawani's son and attacks her husband. The last scene of the film is breathtaking as Ammoru fights Gorakhnath in the temple with plenty of blood and gore. The film was dubbed into Tamil as *Amman*, where it was also a major box office success, but the Hindi version (*Maa ki shakti*) seems to have sunk without a trace.

Film stars as producers: Manoj Kumar and Shirdi Sai Baba

Another figure favored by the rising middle classes is a saint who has become popular nationally and in the diaspora and particularly with the Bombay film industry, Shirdi Sai Baba (1836-1918). A popular film about Sai Baba was produced by his devotee, the superstar Manoj Kumar, earlier famous for his roles as Bharat (the Sanskritic name for India), and actor in and director of many highly nationalistic films from the 1960s onwards, before becoming closely associated with Hindutva politics. *Shirdi ke Sai Baba* (1977, dir. Ashok Bhushan) is often regarded as one of the last great religious films made in India. Framed by a story of a sick boy (where Manoj Kumar himself appears as a devotee), reminding the family of Sai Baba's ability to heal, the film tells the life story of Sai Baba, showing him as a Muslim who calls himself a fakir and recites from the Quran, but also as a Hindu who recites from the *Bhagavad Gita*. Greedy, scheming Brahmins are mocked but others are shown to be good; untouchability is attacked; and people are reformed. The central performance of Dalvi is very strong and the film has a sincere feel, and the miracles are often moving, despite their technical simplicity and the tableau-style presentation of the scenes.

Many groups of organized Hindus which follow gurus and other leaders use privately circulated media, such as weekly blessings, DVDs, VHS tapes and CDS that are available at community centers/places of worship or through the internet. The Swaminarayan movement was quick to use these as part of structuring itself as a global movement (Dwyer 2004). Although the Swaminarayan temples show pictorial stories of Swaminarayan's life in narrative form and there is a television serial about the miracles of Swaminarayan, there seems to be only one film about his life, *Jai Shri Swaminarayan* (2006, prod. Saregama).

Hinduism in "nonreligious" genres

Hinduism shapes everyday life in India, reaching beyond its majority population (80 percent of more than 1 billion), as Hindu becomes the norm in a society where secularism means equal respect for all religions rather than a sharp division between Church (which does not exist in Hinduism) and state. Hinduism is also the religion of Nepal, and of much of India's diaspora who form minority populations in countries such as the UK and the USA. Hinduism is flourishing among the young and continues to shape ethical behavior. In Indian cinema, as in real life, naming a character normally ascribes a religion. Symbols that are clearly Hindu appear, as virtuous and wronged women are identified with goddesses and mythological figures such as Sita Savitri; avenging women with Kali; and wronged men with Karna. Films also depict widely held beliefs about reincarnation and the role of fate and destiny. The way that Hinduism continues to shape the imagination of many who work in the Indian film industry cannot be underestimated.

Satyajit Ray: art cinema

Alongside the commercial cinemas, India also has a major art-house or festival-circuit cinema, of whom Oscar-winning Satyajit Ray (1921–92) is by far the most famous. Although brought up as a Brahmo Samaji (a member of a nineteenth-century Bengali reformist sect that was heavily influenced by Christianity), Ray is always associated with a liberal humanism that is seen in most of his films. One of his most controversial films was his 1960 film, *Devi / The Goddess*. The film was based on Prabhat Kumar Mukherjee's short story of 1899, the idea of which was given to him by Nobel-prize winner Rabindranath Tagore.

Doyamoyee (Sharmila Tagore) is a young bride whose husband, Umaprasad, is studying English literature in Calcutta. Her father-in-law, Kalinkar Roy, dreams that she is the Devi and rushes to worship her. She rejects this but is unable to refuse her deification, especially when it seems she has performed a miracle by reviving a dead boy placed in her lap. People come from all over to see the Devi and her husband returns on hearing the news. Umaprasad and his father argue; the son thinks his father is mad, the father that his son is irreligious. Doyamoyee begins to believe in her powers, but when her beloved nephew falls sick, the family refuses medicine, claiming she will cure him, and he dies. Umaprasad tries to take Doyamoyee away but she feels that the goddess, shown by an image in the river, wants her to stay. Ray changed the end so that Doyamoyee doesn't commit suicide, though she is deranged. Ray says he was with Umaprasad at all times; as a Brahmo, he is clearly hostile to this kind of blind faith.

Mehboob Khan: from Islamicate films to the great Indian epic

One of India's greatest directors was undoubtedly Mehboob Khan (1906–64), who came to Bombay to work as an extra and founded a major studio (Reuben 1994).

Mehboob's early films were "Islamicate films" (Dwyer 2006: 97–131), including his *Humayun* (1945) which George (1994: 48–9) argues is very much about Muslim–Hindi unity, a key issue at the time of the film's making, mapped onto an ahistorical view of the Mughal emperor. Khan is best remembered for his social films, the most important of which is the great national epic, *Mother India* (1957).

Mother India was the first Indian film ever to receive an Oscar nomination as Best Foreign Film (1958). Showing all the strengths of a great Hindi film, it is still loved for its great music, visuals, and stars, but it is its depiction of the Indian woman who is willing to sacrifice anything for her sense of honor and to uphold the values of the nation for which it is most loved (Thomas 1989; Dwyer 2000: 129–37; Chatterjee 2002). The film's title has particular resonances in its reference to the goddess of Indian nationalism, Mother India. European ideas about the nation as a woman dovetailed with Indian ideas about the earth (Prithvi) as a goddess, whether wedded to the king, or as the "mother of the people" (Pinney 2004). Mehboob is said to have taken the story from Pearl Buck's novel, *The Good Earth*; he made an earlier version of this story in 1941 which he called *Aurat* or "Woman," but by changing the working title "This Land is Mine" into *Mother India*, he helped establish the epic and mythological resonances of the film. Even though Mehboob was a practicing Muslim, he understood the way in which mythology added to the depth of the film, helping to turn it into a national epic.

This film is about the life of a traditional Indian, or rather Hindu, woman, Radha, who can be identified with goddesses other than Mother India, namely the Sita-Savitri model of the ideal woman as well as her namesake, Radha, Krishna's beloved. Her husband is called Shyam, one of the names of Krishna. Radha's "good" son is called Ram, and her rebellious son, Birju (another name of Krishna). Even the moneylender identifies her with Lakshmi, the goddess of wealth, while the opening sequences of the film name her as Dharti Maa, Mother Earth. Radha is an ambivalent figure and can be dangerous, destroying those in contact with her, appearing more like Kali, the powerful goddess who punishes and destroys.

Mother India is an implicitly Hindu figure in independent India's "secular" mythology. There is no Islamic component of the new nation shown in the film, where the village is entirely Hindu, despite the number of prominent Muslims involved in this production, including the director, Mehboob, the heroine, Nargis, and the music director, Naushad Ali. Nargis' plea to the villagers to stay in their village and the use of a map of prepartition India imply a rejection of the ideology of Muslim separatism. One of the attractions of *Mother India* is that it eschews clearcut answers, allowing the audience to experience the pleasures of its ambiguities. These contradictions are made clear in the opening sequences which show Mehboob's production banner: while the image of communism, the hammer and sickle, appears on the screen, the voice-over intones his fatalistic motto: "No matter what evils your enemies wish for you, it is of no consequence. Only that can happen which is God's will."

Raj Kapoor: love and beauty

One of the other major filmmakers who first established himself in the 1940s, although his fame lasted over forty years, was Raj Kapoor (1924–88). His films were heavily influenced by Hollywood, with him even taking on a version of Chaplin's tramp, but he was one of the directors who established the Hindi film style with his use of music, song, dance, and melodrama. Although educated in Christian schools, he was said to be an orthodox Hindu, conservative in family matters but known for his affairs and enjoyment of the good life. His films began with an image of his father, the great Prithviraj Kapoor, worshiping Shiva, but his films had a less orthodox view of religion which was focused on love and beauty, with constant themes of fire, water, and purity, often with references to the River Ganges.

One theme in several of Raj Kapoor's films from *Aag* (1948) to *Satyam Shivam Sundaram (SSS)* (1978) was that people have an inner beauty, which is more important than the external appearance. In *Aag*, the hero is scarred by fire, whereas in *SSS*, it is the heroine. The latter ties in with Kapoor's obsession with water and purification, as a redemptive flood ends the film, whose heroine has spent much time in a waterfall, to allow maximum exposure of her flawless body. There are many overt references to the gods in *SSS*, as the heroine worships Shiva's *lingam* in the beginning to songs about Krishna and Radha, and these are entwined with the erotic as the traditions themselves support. Although, as the film's title ("Truth, auspiciousness, beauty") suggests, the major theme is religion, Raj Kapoor was also upfront about the erotic attractions of his films (Reuben 1995: 240–4). Kapoor's 1985 film, *Ram teri Ganga maili* (*Rama, Your Ganges is Polluted*), takes this all further as the eroticism and water links of Hindu mythology are brought ever closer (Dwyer 2000).

Raj Kapoor had a strong idea of ethics and morality in his films, valuing honesty and loyalty, seen more often among the poor than the rich. It would be hard to say if this is Hinduism or a generic morality. It would also be difficult to categorize his striking aesthetic of beauty, music, dance, and art, which come together in his famous dream sequence in *Awara* (1951), which is a mostly Hindu, though also partly Christian, blend of heaven and hell, with several songs, expressionist and stylized dance, and redemption offered by a beautiful woman.

Although there were said to be "Muslim" groups in the Hindi film industry (George 1994: 52), many of Raj Kapoor's closest associates in filmmaking were Muslims (Nargis, K. A. Abbas, Hasrat Jaipuri) as well as Hindu. Raj Kapoor's major work in the late 1940s and 1950s was particularly influenced by Nargis, who was from a mixed Hindu and Muslim background, having herself both a Hindu name (Tejeshwari Mohan) and a Muslim name (Fatima Abdul Rashid) as well as her stage names (Baby Rani, then Nargis).

Manmohan Desai: religious pluralism

Seen in his time as one of the most "commercial" of all Hindi filmmakers, Manmohan Desai (1936–94) is now appreciated as one of the great geniuses of the full-blown

Hindi film drama. Manmohan Desai made several films about families separated and reunited (almost constituting a separate genre called "lost and found"), one of his earliest films being about a partition separation. *Chalia* (1960) is one of the first films to use a Partition setting to express the ideal of communal harmony. When a Hindu husband rejects his wife who had been separated from him during the Partition and saved by a Muslim who helped her as she gave birth to their son, the imagery of Sita is invoked. The agent bringing the couple back together is not the kindly Pathan who looked after the mother and child, but Chalia, played by Raj Kapoor, who saves them from a burning effigy of Rama, seeming to step into the role of Hanuman, the devotee.

Desai's films often showed characters from different religions, his most famous being *Amar, Akbar, Anthony* (1977), which is now a byword in religious plurality. Three boys are separated from their parents on Independence Day, when their father leaves them at the foot of a statue of Mahatma Gandhi. Each is brought up by different parents, one a Hindu (Amar), one a Muslim (Akbar), and one a Christian (Anthony). The mother gets to know Akbar and Anthony but, as she was blinded in an accident, she does not realize they are her sons. The religious situation is kept simpler as the boys all fall for girls from their own communities. The Hindu's romance is sincere and reforming, whereas the Muslim man is an exhibitionist, though his beloved is a doctor, whom he woos by singing Sufi-style *qawwalis* ("Purdah re purdah") at an event where she wears a burqa, and by bringing eunuchs to shame her father into permitting the romance. The Christian is a drunk and a small-time crook but his girlfriend is virtuous although her father is a gangster.

The fact that the boys' real parents are Hindus and the Hindu son is a policeman reinforces the underlying Hinduness of all Indians, although there is much lip service to the religiosity of the Catholic priest and the sincere prayers of Akbar to Shirdi Sai Baba, whose devotees are shown clearly as both Hindus and Muslims. Akbar's prayers result in his blind mother's miraculous cure as two rays of light emanate from the eyes of the image. The token through which much of the family's recognition of each other occurs is an image of Santoshi Maa.

Miraculous intervention may also be associated with "Islamic" sources. For example, in *Coolie* (1983), Iqbal (whose girlfriend, Julie, is a Christian, and whose friend, Sunny, is a Hindu) is a Muslim who is proud of his coolie's badge number 786 (the numerological value of "*Bismillah al-Rahman al-Rahim* / In the name of God, the gracious and the merciful"). There are several "miracles" during the film, as memory is restored by falling prints of calligraphy from the Quran or, when during a song to God praying for her life, lightning surrounds Iqbal's mother to protect her. However, the most dramatic miracle is at the climax as Iqbal climbs the minaret at the tomb of Haji Ali. He survives the bullets shot at him by his enemy, Zafar (a Muslim), because he recites the *kalma* (the affirmation there is no God but God and Muhammad is His Prophet) and is draped in the *chador* (cover) of Haji Ali's tomb, which has verses from the Quran embroidered on it; he also writes "786" in his blood on the paint. The three bullets that are lodged in Iqbal's body are removed during an operation while prayers are said for him outside the operating theater by his Muslim parents. However, this is given a "secular" angle as each bullet is removed in between cuts to the coolies' prayers said in a temple, a church, and a Gurudwara. (Amitabh Bachchan suffered a near fatal injury on the set of one of his films and it was felt that it was divine intervention from the prayers of all faiths that brought him back to life.)

Images are shown to be efficacious when prayed to. In *Mard* (1985), the hero Raju, the eponymous *mard* ("The man"), Tangewala ("the tonga-driver") is played by superstar Amitabh Bachchan, who is always shown to be devoted to his mother, Durga (note the name), played as usual by Nirupa Roy, a former screen goddess. In this film, his mother's life is at risk, so he prays to the Devi, who grants his wish. Manmohan Desai was famous for his mixed genres and here he brings elements of the devotional into his film as the viewer is construed as a devotee of the Devi who can be brought into the request that the mother should live.

These three later films of Desai all starred Amitabh Bachchan, India's greatest superstar. Born a Kayasth, a caste of Hindus who are famous for their close association with courtly culture, Amitabh has received much negative press in recent years over his family's many pilgrimages which some have felt are a betrayal of secular values. Yet Amitabh's films have been successful in part because he has usually played characters who are religious or who turn their back on formal religion due to social injustices but who follow a morality which may lead them back to God before death. Amitabh has played many Muslim or quasi-Muslim roles, and even three-in-one in Desai's *Naseeb* (1981) where he is called Jaan Johnny Janardhan (Muslim, Christian, and Hindu respectively). These roles, which are all part of his star image, have contributed to making him a star who is secular in the sense of giving equal respect to all religions.

Yash Chopra: Hindu family values

Another of Amitabh Bachchan's favorite directors, Yash Chopra (1932–), has had a longer career than all the others, as, fifty years after he directed his first film, he is still reckoned the most powerful figure in Bollywood. Born an Arya Samaji, he is a great believer that religion requires a duty toward other people and that one should respect all religions; however, religion can also be one of the greatest sources of human conflict. He believes that God and Destiny have shaped his life, allowing his own hard work to be successful, and that his duty is to do his job well, working hard without hurting other people.

Yash Chopra says that many people have religious ceremonies around the films, partly to relieve stress, but also because the business is so uncertain with every film that one wants to do auspicious things; each film is an examination, and a filmmaker is only as good or as bad as his last film. He points out that people who don't believe in God still do good business and can make good films. However, he notes that in India a filmmaker cannot ignore the elements of Indian culture which are rooted in religion and family values. Whenever one feels weak, one decides to take shelter in something powerful, and worshiping God has that goal.

Yash Chopra's films set the style of the 1990s where Hindu family values triumphed at the box office, often in films which tied the diaspora and Indians together through the values of religiosity, consumerism, and the negotiation of duty and desire. As I have argued elsewhere (Dwyer 2006), these Hindu family values have often been mistaken for the ideology of Hindu nationalism which was politically successful during this period. However, the Hindi film industry has mostly remained secular for its own ideological reasons, but also because it is pragmatic and has an eye on the market and the censor.

Conclusion

Although there have been very few major religious films in the past few years, it is too soon to say that the genre will not be revived. The genre is thriving in the "B" and lower-grade circuits, as mentioned above with the gentrifying films. There is much talk of putting the religious epics on film with major names being mentioned in the press, but no film has yet materialized. Hindi film producers are well aware of the success of recent religious films such as *The Passion of the Christ* (2004, dir. Mel Gibson), which is now regularly screened in Christian areas of Indian cities at Easter, and there is no Hindu equivalent. Given the popularity of devotional songs available in other media (cassettes, CDs, radio, television), there is no reason that issues of morality, religion, and other spiritual questions may not reappear on film, in particular with the computer-generated images of recent years which could allow for spectacular miracles and historical reconstructions. It seems likely that one of the constraints is that India is acutely aware of its new global position as a rising superpower and that its dominant social group, the new middle class, want to portray themselves on the world stage as modern, rational world leaders. Their religious practices of worship for which they use new media (from online *pujas* to ringtones to viewing devotional materials) may feel more confined to the private than to the cinema, which has recently gained recognition in Europe and North America, as romantic, glamorous, and musical. However, emerging social groups often wish to pay attention to their history and cultural history, and it would not be surprising to see major films on these topics, which would in turn contribute to the revival of the A-grade religious film.

Bibliography

Abbas, K. A. (1963) "Changing Trends in Films," in B. K. Adarsh (ed.), *Film Industry of India Yearbook*, Bombay: n.p.

Arudra (1984) "Le cinéma telugu," in A. Vasudeva and P. Lenglet (eds) *Les cinémas indiens*, CinémAction 30, Paris: Éditions du Cerf: 114–19.

Benegal, S. (2007) Interview with author. 24 December 2007.

Chatterjee, G. (2002) *Mother India*, London: British Film Institute.

Das, V. (1981) "The Mythological Film and its Framework of Meaning: An Analysis of *Jai Santoshi Ma*," *Indian International Quarterly* 8 (1), special issue, ed. P. Krishen: 43–56.

Dharap, B. V. (1985) "Dadasaheb Phalke: Father of Indian Cinema," in T. M. Ramachandran (ed.) *70 Years of Indian Cinema (1913–1983)*, Bombay: Cinema India International: 33–48.

Dwyer, R. (2000) *All You Want is Money, All You Need is Love: Sex and Romance in Modern India*, London: Cassell.

—— (2004) "International Hinduism: The Swaminarayan Sect," in K. A. Jacobsen and P. Kumar (eds) *South Asians in the Diaspora: Histories and Religion Traditions*, Leiden and Boston: Brill: 180–99.

—— (2005) *100 Bollywood Films*, London: British Film Institute.

—— (2006) *Filming the Gods: Religion and Indian Cinema*, London and New York: Routledge.

—— (2008) *What do Hindus Believe?* London: Granta.

—— [2009] "Phalke, Dhundiraj Gon'nd [known as Dadasaheb Phalke] (1870–1944)," *Oxford Dictionary of National Biography*, Oxford: Oxford University Press <http://www.oxforddnb.com/view/article/96954>

Fuller, C. J. (1992) *The Camphor Flame: Popular Hinduism and Society in India*, Princeton: Princeton University Press.

George, T. J. S. (1994) *The Life and Times of Nargis*, New Delhi: Indus.

Hot Spot (2005) Online. Available at HTTP: <http://www.thehotspotonline.com/moviespot/bolly/reviews/d/DoodhKarz.htm> (acccesssed 16 March 2005).

Illuminated Lantern (2005) Online. Available at HTTP: <http://www.illuminatedlantern.com/cinema/features/snakes.html> (accessed 16 March 2005)

Kapur, G. (2000) *When was Modernism: Essays on Contemporary Cultural Practice in India*, New Delhi: Tulika.

Lutgendorf, P. (2003) "*Jai Santoshi Maa* revisited," in S. B. Plate (ed.) *Representing Religion in World Cinema: Filmmaking, Mythmaking, Culture Making*, New York: Palgrave Macmillan: 19–42.

Mankekar, P. (2002) "Epic Contests: Television and Religious Identity in India," in F. D. Ginsburg, L. Abu-Lughod, and B. Larkin (eds) *Media Worlds: Anthropology on New Terrain*, Berkeley: University of California Press: 134–51.

Manuel, P. (1993) *Cassette Culture: Popular Music and Technology in North India*, Chicago: University of Chicago Press.

Mukhopadhyay, U. (2004) "The Perception of the 'Medieval' in Indian Popular Films: 1920s–1960s." PhD Thesis, SOAS, University of London.

Nanda, M. (2008) "Rush Hour of the Gods – Religion Mixed with Politics and Science." Online. Available HTTP: <http://newhumanist.org.uk/1731> (accessed 24 April 2008).

Phalke, D. G. (1988/9) "Dossier: *Swadeshi* Moving Pictures," trans. N. S. Shahane, in B. Shoesmith and T. O'Regan (eds) *Asian Cinema*. Special issue of *Continuum: An Australian Journal of the Media* 2 (1): 51–73.

Pinney, C. (1997) *Camera Indica: The Social Life of Indian Photographs*, London: Reaktion Books.

—— (2004) *"Photos of the Gods": The Printed Image and Political Struggle in India*, London: Reaktion Books.

Rajadhyaksha, A. (1993) "The Phalke Era: Conflict of Traditional Form and Modern Technology," in T. Niranjana *et al.*, *Interrogating Modernity: Culture and Colonialism in India*, Calcutta: Seagull Books: 47–82.

Rajadhyaksha, A. and Willemen, P. (1999) *An Encyclopaedia of Indian Cinema*, 2nd ed., London: British Film Institute.

Rajagopal, A. (2001) *Politics after Television: Hindu Nationalism and the Reshaping of the Public in India*, Cambridge: Cambridge University Press.

Rangoonwalla, F. (ed.) (1970) *Phalke Centenary Souvenir*, Bombay: Phalke Centenary Celebration Committee.

Reuben, B. (1994) *Mehboob . . . India's DeMille: The First Biography*, New Delhi: Indus.

—— (1995) *Raj Kapoor: The Fabulous Showman*, New Delhi: Indus.

Rushdie, S. (1988) *The Satanic Verses*, London: Viking.

Shah, P. (1950) *The Indian Film*, Bombay: Motion Picture Society of India.

Shahani, K. (1985) "The Saint Poets of Prabhat," in T. M. Ramachandran (ed.) *70 Years of Indian Cinema (1913–1983)*, Bombay: Cinema India International: 197–202.

Shoesmith, B. (1988/9) "*Swadeshi* Cinema: The Writings of D. G. Phalke," in B. Shoesmith and T. O'Regan (eds) *Asian Cinema*. Special issue of *Continuum: An Australian Journal of the Media* 2 (1): 44–50.

Srinivas, M. N. (1952) *Religion and Society among the Coorgs of South India*, London: Oxford University Press.

Srinivas, S. V. (2001) "Telugu Folklore Films: The Case of Patala Bhairavi," *Deep Focus: A Film Quarterly* 9 (1): 45–50. Online. Available at HTTP: <www.sephis.org/pdf/srinivas2.pdf> (accessed 22 October 2004).

Taylor, C. (2004) *Modern Social Imaginaries*, Durham, NC: Duke University Press.

Thomas, R. (1989) "Sanctity and Scandal: The Mythologization of Mother India," *Quarterly Review of Film and Video* 11: 11–30.

Tripathi, B. (1985) "Gujarati Cinema," in T. M. Ramachandran (ed.) *70 Years of Indian Cinema (1913–1983)*, Bombay: Cinema India International: 340–8.

Vardhan, T. V. (2007) "After Godhood: The Political Career of NTR." Paper presented at Asian Cinema, Bangalore.

Waghorne, J. P. (2001) "The Gentrification of the Goddess," *International Journal of Hindu Studies* 5 (3) (December): 227–67.

Watwe, B. (1985) *V. Damle and S. Fattelal: A Monograph*, Pune: National Film Archive of India.

——. (2004) *Dadasaheb Phalke: The Father of Indian Cinema*, trans. S. A. Virkar, New Delhi: National Book Trust.

Younger, P. (1980) "A Temple Festival of Mariyamman," *Journal of the American Academy of Religion* 48 (4) (December): 493–517.

Filmography

Aag (1948, dir. R. Kapoor)
Amar, Akbar, Anthony (1977, dir. M. Desai)
Ammoru (1995, dir. K. Ramakrishna)
Amritmanthan (1934, dir. V. Shantaram)
Aurat (1941, dir. M. Khan)
Awara (1951, dir. R. Kapoor)
Ayodhyache raja / Ayodhya ka raja (1932, dir. V. Shantaram)
Bandh darwaza (1990, dir. S. and T. Ramsay)
Ben Hur (1907, dir. S. Olcott *et al.*)
Chalia (1960, dir. M. Desai)
Coolie (1983, dir. M. Desai)
Daana Veera Shura Karna (1977, dir. N. Rama Rao)
Deewaar (1975, dir. Y. Chopra)
Devi / The Goddess (1960, dir. S. Ray)
Devi Putrudu (2000, dir. K. Ramakrishna)
Devullu (2001, dir. K. Ramakrishna)
Dharmatma (1935, dir. V. Shantaram)
Gopal Krishna (1938, dir. V. Damle and S. Fattelal)
Humayun (1945, dir. M. Khan)
Indiana Jones and the Temple of Doom (1984, dir. S. Spielberg).
Jai Bahuchar Maa (1980, dir. R. Bohra)
Jai Dakshineshwar Kaali Maa (1996, dir. S. Soni)
Jai Santoshi Maa (1975, dir. V. Sharma)
Jai Shri Swaminarayan (2006, prod. Saregama)
Lanka dahan / Lanka Aflame (1917, dir. D. Phalke)
The Life of Christ (unidentified by Phalke; most probably *The Life and Passion of Christ* [1903], a British film of the Horitz Passion Play, or *La vie et la passion du Jésus Christ* [1905, dir. L. Nonguet and F. Zecce])
Mard (1985, dir. M. Desai)
Maya bazaar (1957, dir. K. Reddy)
Maya Machhindra (1932, dir. V. Shantaram)
Mother India (1957, dir. M. Khan)
Naseeb (1981, dir. M. Desai)
The Passion of the Christ (2004, dir. M. Gibson)
Patala Bhairavi (1951, dir. K. Reddy)
Prem Sanyas / The Light of Asia (1925, dir. F. Osten and H. Rai)
Raja Harischandra (1913, dir. D. Phalke)
Ram teri Ganga maili (1985, dir. R. Kapoor)
Sampoorna Ramanayanam (1958, dir. K. Somu)
Sant Dnyaneshwar (1940, dir. V. Damle and S. Fattelal)

Sant Sakhu (1941, dir. V. Damle and S. Fattelal)
Sant Tukaram (1936, dir. V. Damle and S. Fattelal)
Satyam Shivam Sundaram (1978, dir. R. Kapoor)
Shirdi ke Sai Baba (1977, dir. A. Bhushan)
Sholay (1975, dir. R. Sippy)
Shri Krishna Janma / The Birth of Shri Krishna (1918, dir. D. Phalke)
Sri Venkateswara Mahatmyam (1960, dir. P. Pulliah)
Trikal / Past, Present and Future (1985, dir. S. Benegal)

9

BUDDHISM

Francisca Cho

WHY FILM?

Is there a particular reason that the Buddhist religious tradition would have an affinity for film – that is, to find film a particularly conducive medium for telling its stories and illustrating its principles? Dzongsar Jamyang Khyentse (also known as Khyentse Norbu) has the distinction of being both an incarnate lama in the Tibetan Khyentse lineage and a feature filmmaker (*The Cup*, 2000; *Travellers and Magicians*, 2003). Understandably, he is frequently asked what these two identities have to do with each other. He tends to explain the matter quite simply by noting that Buddhism is the study of life and film a utensil for that study (Dzongsar 2008). Fair enough. Films can depict and make us think about the big questions in life – its meaning, its nature, and its purpose – pretty much the way that great literature can. In this sense, film is but a modern extension of the human penchant to tell stories as a way of making sense of ourselves and our lives.

But film's technological capacity to make the imagined, the fantastical, and the illusory *real* is unsurpassed. To be sure, all fictional literature shares this ability, in the way its characters and worlds can capture our imagination and become real to us. The Harry Potter phenomenon is a recent demonstration of the fact that even the most fantastical of literary worlds can come alive for us, and that their powers of enchantment cross the boundaries of age, education, and nationality. But film has the ability to do the imagining *for us*, outside of our own heads, through images and sounds projected onto a screen. Its sensory impressions are concrete rather than imagined. The bodies and environments projected onto a screen manifest as determinate images that can be experienced together, much in the manner that we experience social events in our everyday lives. To be sure, the collective experience of these projected bodies and landscapes does not mean that they are "seen" in the same way by each one of us, but that is no less true of the communal events that we undertake in actual life.

The advance that film represents in this respect is epitomized in the legendary story of the 1895 screening of Auguste and Louis Lumière's *Arrival of a Train at La Ciotat Station* in Paris, one of the first cinematic events in history. The startling realism of the image of a train traveling toward the audience caused a sensation. Although this response has been exaggerated in various tellings – some claimed that audience members screamed and ran to the back of the room – the event nevertheless marks the advent of the film age, with its unprecedented ability to create real sensory events. Continuing innovations via computer and special effects technologies augment film's capacity to conjure virtual worlds, from the most remote reaches of history to the most otherworldly of science fiction and fantasy realms. The virtual reality that film creates makes it natural and unsurprising that some viewers have a hard time distinguishing between life and cinematic illusion; between their favorite actors and the characters they play.

The unequalled power of film to create the illusion of "real life" makes film a natural medium for Buddhism. Film instantiates the Buddhist lesson that life itself is an illusory projection of our own minds, and it provides the means for exploring the features of this projection. In a press release for his feature film *Travellers and Magicians*, Khyentse Norbu invites us to consider the following:

> Let us imagine that we are born in a cinema and all we know is this screen in front of us. We do not recognize that we are looking at a film and that the events in the movie have no true existence. Everything we perceive on that screen – love, hatred, aggression, suspense, thrills – are in fact just the effect of a projection of light through film. But no one tells us this. We are sitting there watching, fixated on the film. If somebody tries to divert our attention, we say, "shut up!" We are so engrossed. Yet we are blind to the futility aspect of this projection. (Dzongsar 2004)

The title of these remarks, "Life as Cinema," makes Khyentse Norbu's analogical meaning quite explicit: Life itself is an illusion in that our constructions of reality are ultimately empty and insubstantial; our passions, desires, ambitions ultimately vainglorious. But two questions should be considered here: Does Khyentse Norbu mean to speak metaphorically – that is to say, is he *comparing* life to cinematic illusion – or is he saying that life and cinema are fundamentally no different? This is a philosophical and metaphysical question about the ultimate nature of "reality." To say that cinema is a metaphor for life makes an absolute distinction between "cinema" as a signifier and "life" as that which is signified by the metaphor. In this sense, cinema is an analogy for and characterization of life, but should not be confused with it. Although Khyentse Norbu's brief remarks do not venture into such philosophical dissections, the premise of this essay is that the weight of Buddhist tradition rejects the distinction between signifiers and signified, sanctioning the conclusion that cinematic illusion is ontologically no different from life itself.

The philosophical basis for such a conclusion will be examined in a moment. Presently, however, let us ask a follow-up question: If life and cinema are both illusory in the same way, why should we waste our time with movies when the point of Buddhist teachings is to wake ourselves up and liberate ourselves from illusion? This question is methodological, because it addresses the problem of *how* to attain Buddhist enlightenment, as well as the role of implements like icons, narratives, performances, and film. When we look to the history of Christianity, we see that religious representations are a double-edged sword. While Catholicism and Orthodox Christianity recognize the value of making the divine concrete through images, Christianity has been dogged by the question of whether icons engender devotion to God, or to the symbol itself. The potential for metaphysical confusion, in which the human and material is confused for the sacred, is an obvious concern. When we move to the realm of cinema, its religious value is even more ambiguous. Icons, both Buddhist and Christian, are encountered in religious contexts and subject to ritualistic means of control. Films, on the other hand, are the products of a commercial industry and subject to the vagaries of the market, as well as careerist directors. If icons are potentially dangerous, they are at least religiously serious. Films may aspire to spiritual significance, but they are ultimately the scions of the entertainment industry.

To deal with this methodological question in light of the philosophical assertion made above – that life and cinema are ontologically indistinguishable from each other – the rest of this section will sketch out a Buddhist semiotic theory. That is, we will construct a Buddhist view of the nature of the relationship between religious representations and the reality that they signify. Doing this automatically addresses the question of why we should bother with film, given its magnified ability to make the illusory seem real. The second section of the essay will go on to substantively survey examples of Buddhist film, organized into established traditions of Buddhist narrative and aesthetic themes.

A Buddhist semiotics

In the concluding gatha, or four-line poem, of the *Diamond Sutra*, the world of conditioned phenomena (samsara) is compared to ephemeral objects like dew, bubbles, and a lightning flash, as well as insubstantial clouds and flickering lamps. More to our purpose, life as we know it is also said to be like a dream, a "fault of vision," and a "mock show" (Conze 1958: 68). So in addition to being short-lived and fragile, the world that we experience and live within is ultimately a figment of our imagination. The comparison of life to a dream is a common Buddhist adage, as well as the vehicle of philosophical argument, as in Vasubandhu's *Vimsátika*. Faulty vision is another way of talking about the illusory nature of what we "see," with the point that what we take to be real is actually unreal, like the nonexistent hairs and flies perceived by those with an eye disease. The mock show denotes a magical illusion, or the conjurer's trick, whose intent is to deceive us.

Anything with the power to deceive also has the power to entertain us, however, and this is another double-edged sword. While dreaming, we experience actual sadness, terror, or joy, until we wake up and realize their cause does not exist in "reality." Many of us undoubtedly have had the experience of trying to go back to sleep when a happy dream was cut short by waking. Even knowing the "unreality" of the dream does not seem to diminish the pleasure of the experience. Vasubandhu uses the example of wet dreams to argue that even an illusory event can have persuasive and functional powers. With a magician's show, as with many films, we welcome and enjoy the fantastical spectacles it offers us, to the point of feeling wistful when it ends. Perhaps fundamental to the human condition, as the Buddha diagnosed it, is our willingness to be deceived by happy or flattering fantasies and our reluctance to accept "reality." All beings are deeply deluded, the Buddha taught, and awakening from delusion is fundamental to enlightenment.

It is at this point, however, that Buddhist semiotics takes a unique and unexpected turn. To speak of life as an illusion and to exhort people to wake up from their deluded state assumes the reality and possibility of awakening, understood as attainment of a truth beyond the samsaric realm of fantasy. Understood in this way, nirvana is a distinct and separate state from samsara. Mahayana sources, however, are rather vigorous about messing up this logic. They tell us that nirvana is not something *beyond* or *elsewhere*, outside of the tainted world of samsara. The Mādhyamika philosopher Nagarjuna avers, "There is not the slightest difference between cyclic existence [samsara] and nirvana. There is not the slightest difference between nirvana and cyclic existence" (Garfield 1995: 75). The Zen patriarch Huineng declares, "Good friends, enlightenment (*bodhi*) and intuitive wisdom (*prajñā*) are *from the outset* possessed by men of this world themselves" (emphasis added; Yampolsky 1978: 135). There is a profound semiotic significance to these standard and relentlessly repeated Mahayana assertions. To wit, the logic and necessity of a gap, or distance, between the realm of illusion and the realm of the "really real" of nirvana is refused.

In one sense, this spatial collapsing of the secular and the sacred is more rhetorical than historical. In the practice of Buddhism throughout its history, there has been very little confusion about the fact that monasteries and hermitages are the places of religious practice in contradistinction to the secular world outside of it. The rhetorical collapse of nirvana into samsara, however, has had significant historical consequences for the practice of Buddhism, particularly at the level of ritual and popular culture. The theoretical collapse between secular illusions and sacred reality is paralleled by a semiotic collapse of the distance between religious signifiers (such as film) and what they signify. When this distance, or the idea that there is a profound ontological difference between signifiers and the signified, is removed, the anxiety about metaphysical confusion is also neutralized. The result is a notable absence of the kind of anxiety that Christians have exhibited toward their own icons, and the free proliferation and use of religious objects.

Let us explore the idea of a semiotic collapse by seeing how it follows from the philosophical compression of nirvana and samsara. The Mahayana rejection of the gap between these two realms culminates in the Zen teaching that we are all already Buddhas by our very nature and that there is nothing for us to attain. One might say that this teaching completes the logic of Mahayana and renders the concept of "enlightenment" into an empty signifier: It does not indicate any place or "thing" distinct from what is ordinary and *not* enlightened. Another way of putting this is that "enlightenment" is a signifier of emptiness (súnyatā). "Emptiness" is the mother lode of Mahayana doctrine and its most direct term for the absolute. Different schools nuance the term in different ways, but it generally refers to the fundamental Buddhist teaching that all phenomena arise because of causes and conditions external to them.

For this reason, all things lack essence or "self-nature." Consequently, the meanings, labels, and values that we assign to an object or event are ultimately insubstantial conventions – our self-interested projections upon what is inherently empty. But being empty does not mean being nonexistent. Emptiness is better understood as the infinite openness and potentiality of things that are cramped and made small by our labels. This sense of fulsomeness moves Buddhist thought away from the negativity of anatman ("no self") doctrine, which focuses on what things *lack*, to emptiness as a constructive metaphysics: all things have emptiness as their ultimate nature. It is this absolute truth that we must seek.

But where is this emptiness to be found? "Emptiness" is itself an empty signifier because it does not point to anything distinct, but rather coincides with the totality of the forms we distinguish in ordinary life. Realization of emptiness means coming back to the phenomenal realm of samsara itself. We are brought back to the entertaining deceptions even as we are warned about them because it is not possible to realize emptiness anywhere else. The semiotic oddity of "emptiness" as "absolute truth" is its inability to signify anything discrete or special, instead reverting back to the illusory world that functions as its opposite term.

This has direct implications for religious practice, particularly the use of religious representations. In contrast to the monotheistic tendency to distinguish between the icon as copy and the divine as the original, the absolute of emptiness inheres only in phenomenal representations. The "original" emptiness and the phenomenal "copy" are two aspects of a single reality, one might say. This idea is made explicit by the Chinese Huayan school, which sees emptiness as the static principle (*li*) that is expressed and brought to life by dynamic phenomena (*shi*), whose apparent diversity and separateness actually interpenetrate each other in their inherent emptiness. The implication, then, is that the original is *in* the copy, or, to revert to Buddhist language, nirvana is none other than samsara; samsara is none other than nirvana. Consequently, Buddhist theory does not create the specter of (and anxiety about) the ontological confusion between two distinct realities.

We stated above that the power of phenomenal illusions to deceive and entertain us is a double-edged sword. But it is necessary to refine this idea in light of Buddhist semiotics. In Christian iconology, this double edge means the necessity of phenomenal representations with their ability to engage us, on the one hand, and the risk that we confuse the signifier for the signified, on the other. The dilemma in Buddhist practice, however, operates on an inverse logic: We have the inseparability of signifiers from the signified, on the one hand, and the human penchant to objectify emptiness as something *other than* and *separate from* phenomenal reality, on the other. This danger has led to a Buddhist version of iconophobia, which is easily mistaken for the Christian kind. Consider the Zen adage, "Don't mistake the finger pointing to the moon for the moon itself." This warning appears to be a caution against confusing signifiers and signifieds. But this reading is not coherent within the context of Buddhist metaphysics. Instead, the counsel is to refrain from diminishing emptiness, which is ubiquitous, into a single, arbitrary sign that is elevated above all others. Consider the words of the thirteenth-century Japanese Zen master Dōgen:

Men have flowed into the Way drawn by grasses and flowers, mountains and running water. They have received the lasting impression of the Buddha-seal by holding soil, rocks, and pebbles. Indeed, its vast and great signature is imprinted on all the things in nature, and even then remains in great abundance. (Waddell and Abe 2002: 16–17)

It is not only the pointing finger in the form of Buddhist scriptures and other overtly religious signs, but even rocks and trees that preach the profound and limitless Dharma. In the egalitarian world of emptiness, even insentient objects are equivalent to the historical Buddha in their Buddha-nature. The Zen anxiety about signs may be summarized as the fear that the discriminating aspect of all signs – that is, their bounded nature that leads us to distinguish "this" from "that," and "Buddha" from "not Buddha" – blinds us to the enlightening capacity of all things.

In spite of such anxiety, the inherent logic of Buddhist semiotics is to sanction and empower the use of religious representations. The worship of icons and relics, for example, has been central to both lay and monastic Buddhism throughout Asia, and instances of actual iconoclasm are generally unknown. To be sure, Chinese emperors have regularly ordered the destruction of icons in order to reclaim precious metals and the monastic lands on which they were housed. But this economic aggression is quite distinct from theologically driven iconoclasm.

One key area of Buddhist teachings that encourages overt "icon friendliness" arises from understandings of the nature of the Buddha himself. As the Pali sources attest, the historical Buddha Shakyamuni does not stand apart from the impermanent, dependently arising world of which he is a part. It is his body of teachings and the Buddha qualities that he perfected (dharmakaya: "dharma body") that are everlasting and important, not his mortal "form body" (rupakaya). The rupakaya is consistently disparaged in contrast to the dharmakaya, and yet, it is the indispensable vehicle that makes the Dharma known to the rest of us. Developments in Mahayana buddhology emphasize the idea that historical buddhas are illusions, in the sense of deliberate deceptions, that are created to liberate human beings. They are understood as "nirmanakayas," or the magical projections of bodhisattvas who act out of compassion. The connotation of "nirmana" as illusory manifestation is continuous with the earlier concept of manomayakaya, or the "mind-made bodies" that are projected by advanced yogis.

If the Buddha himself was a mere expedient illusion, then it is not so surprising that other illusions can stand in for the Buddha and do the same work. The worship of Buddha images in East Asia, for example, is chartered by the legend of King Udyana, who had an image of the Buddha fashioned from sandalwood while the Buddha was away. According to one of the Indian texts that tells this story, when the Buddha returned, the image got up and greeted the Buddha, who in turn responded, "In future ages you will perform Buddha-works on a grand scale" (quoted in Zurcher 1995: 5). As numerous scholars of Buddhism document, the belief that Buddha icons are actually alive and must be treated as such is pervasive in Buddhist popular practice. This may strike us as superstition or, at the very least, the result of an overactive imagination.

But inquiries into diverging cultural rationalities are irrelevant here. What is essential to note is that Buddhist semiotics does not demand constraint of such practice, aside from occasional reminders that the images are, after all, empty – which paradoxically is the very source of their power.

Buddhist films

Defining what qualifies as a Buddhist film is a tricky business. Khyentse Norbu's definition of Buddhism as "the study of life" is very general, allowing many serious and thoughtful films to qualify. He mentions, for example, Andrei Tarkovsky's *The Stalker* (1979), a Russian science fiction film that references no overt Buddhist language or imagery. There are, on the other hand, popular Hollywood films that play on Buddhist themes. *The Matrix* (1999) is a science fiction action film about how the life we experience is an illusory projection of mind – but with Hollywood-style good guys and bad guys. *Fight Club* (1999) and *Donnie Darko* (2001) also center on the lives that we project, fantasize, or dream. *Groundhog Day* (1993) is a humorous play on the idea of reincarnation. *I Heart Huckabees* (2004) is a quirky comedy featuring Lily Tomlin and Dustin Hoffman as "existential detectives" who preach a very Buddhist doctrine of interconnectedness, while battling their nemesis, a French existential detective who spouts nihilism.

Instead of loose constructions of the Buddhist film, however, the films discussed here are mostly of Asian provenance, from traditionally Buddhist cultures. The purpose of this is to see in what ways the trajectory of Buddhist tradition has led filmmakers to utilize the capacities of film. Khyentse Norbu, for example, is fond of comparing life to cinema, thus it is no surprise that his own filmmaking attends to the narrative nature of both. *The Cup* (2000) is a gentle and humorous depiction of young Tibetan Buddhist novices in India whose modern sensibilities are exhibited in their obsession with World Cup soccer, as well as their boarding-school-style antics. Much of the film is a meditation on change: the worldly ease of novices coming of age in India contrasts with the elderly and backward-looking abbot, who constantly prepares to return to Tibet. Depicting the very real phenomenon of how Tibetan Buddhism is changing is a reflection on time, history, and the way we construct their meaning. According to a story told within the film itself, a man is chased by a monster and when the man implores the latter to tell him what he should do, the monster replies that it is up to him – it is the man's dream, after all. Similar to the dreaming man, the story of what is happening to contemporary Tibetan Buddhism is constructed and open-ended in nature. Like classic Buddhist texts, *The Cup* self-reflexively creates symmetry between its religious message of the constructed nature of life stories, and the constructed nature of its own filmic medium.

Taking *The Cup* as exemplary, one key ingredient of the Buddhist film may be identified as storytelling. Storytelling, of course, is an aspect of all films, but the Buddhist film is self-aware (to varying degrees) of how telling stories is the way we construct "reality" and its significance. While part of the message is that we are the authors of our own worlds, there is also an attentiveness to the artistry of such constructions, and an appreciation of the fact that they are the only means we have of effecting religious progress. Let us trace some dominant ways in which this awareness is realized.

Journey narratives: Buddhas and pilgrims

The tale of the Buddha Shakyamuni and his journey to enlightenment is the founding story of Buddhist tradition. This story is augmented by Jatakas, or the 547 "birth stories" contained in the *Khuddaka-nikaya* of the Pali canon. These adaptations of Indian folk tales extend the Buddha's narrative journey by illustrating how he perfected virtues in his many former lives, which led to his final birth as the Buddha. Journeys are not the province of the Buddha alone. Buddhist literature is replete with the biographies of eminent monks, saints, and pilgrims. Thus one of the simplest forms of the Buddhist film is adaptations of classical narratives. Jatakas are popular moral fables that inspired artistic representations, in the form of relief carvings on stupas. It only stands to reason that film is used to extend this ancient storytelling tradition.

Bernardo Bertolucci's *Little Buddha* (1994) presents the only film effort to date that attempts a close reading of the canonical story of the Buddha. It is presented as a frame tale embedded in the story of an American boy who is identified by Tibetan monks as an incarnate lama, thus paralleling the journey of the Buddha with that of a contemporary family. The story of Angulimala is another well-known tale from the Pali canon. A ruthless murderer who has the habit of taking a finger trophy from each of his victims, Angulimala is converted by the Buddha but still must work off the fruits of his bad deeds. His story is used to demonstrate that even the worst of beings with the worst of karma can still be liberated. Angulimala's story was made into a film of the same name by Sutape Sunnirat (Thailand, 2003). Tibetan Buddhism is particularly prolific in the genre of saints' biographies, the most famous being the life of Milarepa, the late eleventh-century yogi of the Kagyu lineage. Milarepa's story is the subject of two films, Liliana Cavani's *Milarepa* (Italy, 1974) and Neten Chokling's *Milarepa: Magician, Murderer, Saint* (India, 2007). Moving to contemporary times, the present Dalai Lama's early life story is told by Martin Scorsese's *Kundun* (1997). The importance of religious biographies is certainly not unique to Buddhism, but Buddhist tradition is perhaps singular in the degree to which it understands that religion is a matter of telling stories of this kind: In the highly influential *Lotus Sutra*, the Buddha reveals that the classic story of his birth, enlightenment, career, and death as Shakyamuni Buddha was an illusory show expressly for the purpose of inspiring people to follow the Buddhist path.

Beyond Buddhas, monks, and saints, pilgrims are the more literal travelers in Buddhist narratives. Sudhana, the young pilgrim in the *Gandavyuha*, which is the last book of the immense *Avatamsaka Sutra*, establishes the paradigm. The *Avatamsaka Sutra* is one of the most influential texts in East Asian Buddhism, being the basis of the Chinese Huayan school (Korean: Hwaom; Japanese: Kegon). Its cosmic visions of infinite universes visible in even single pores on the skin of Buddhas and Bodhisattvas inspired the philosophy of the interpenetration of all phenomena mentioned above, and Sudhana's pilgrimage is an explicit affirmation of the idea that enlightening knowledge flows from all beings. Sudhana receives teachings from fifty-two serial "enlightening beings," most of whom are ordinary people, such as merchants, doctors, mathematicians, craftsmen, and even a prostitute. Jang Sunwoo's *Passage to Buddha* (Korea, 1993) adapts Sudhana's journey to modern-day Korea (see Cho 2003), taking advantage of the *Gandavyuha*'s message that all of the ordinary encounters of life are a part of one's spiritual journey.

It is no surprise that this notion of life as a spiritual journey is easily translatable across cultures as well as epochs. In Doris Dorrie's *Enlightenment Guaranteed* (Germany, 2000), two brothers travel to a Zen monastery in Japan as a way of dealing with their respective midlife crises. Almost immediately they get lost in Tokyo, forcing them to forfeit all of their belongings in the hotel they cannot relocate. This loss of possessions and bearings suggests a modern realization of Zen master Dogen's exhortation that one must first forget and lose the self in order to be enlightened by all things (Waddell and Abe 2002: 41). Finally making their way to the monastery far beyond the city, they stumble through the rigors of monastic life. The film juxtaposes a contemporary Western sense of spiritual journeying with the cultural spectacle of traditional Zen practice.

Another contemporary version of religious journeying comes to us in Ritu Sarin and Tenzing Sonam's *Dreaming Lhasa* (India, 2005). A Tibetan-American filmmaker, Karma, meets up with a former Tibetan monk, Dhondup, in Dharamsala, India. Both are on personal journeys: the filmmaker is fleeing a bad marriage in New York, and the ex-monk is fulfilling his mother's dying wish that he find a man from her past. This search ends up comprising three journeys – to Karma's heart, as she finds herself falling in love with the ex-monk, to Dhondup's self-identity, and to Tibetan religious-political history. "Lhasa," or the heart of Tibet, is the construct that creates both personal and historical meaning in these voyages.

In and out of hermitages: the dialectics of liberation

The ability to see the totality of our lives as being of religious significance is balanced in Buddhist tradition by the ideal of the explicitly religious life. In this vision, monasteries and hermitages form the loci of serious Buddhist practice. To enter them means leaving the burdens as well as the infatuations of the world behind. But the monastic ideal is plagued by ambiguity, especially in the Mahayana schools. If nirvana is none other than samsara, what need is there for separate religious places? Vimalakirti of the vitally influential *Vimalakirti Sutra* demonstrates the superiority of the layman's path by out-performing the best of the Buddha's monk-disciples, and the pilgrim Sudhana learns from ordinary beings, including the prostitute Vasumitra. The anti-monastic rhetoric of Mahayana Buddhism is best understood as part of a discursive dialectic that tacks back and forth between the necessity and extraneousness of the religious life. This dialectical structure is one particular and dominant version of how the story of the spiritual journey is told within Buddhist tradition.

The Buddhist-themed films of Korea are particularly focused on this dialectic. Im Kwontaek's *Mandala* (1981) and *Come, Come, Come Upward* (1989), Chung

Jiyoung's *Beyond the Mountain* (1991), Bae Yongkyun's *Why Has Bodhidharma Left for the East?* (1989), Joo Kyungjung's *Little Monk* (2003), and Kim Kiduk's *Spring, Summer, Fall, Winter . . . and Spring* (2004) all focus on monks and nuns who struggle with this inside/outside dilemma. The hermitage is a refuge from the world, but it cannot eradicate the longings and grievances carried within the heart. Child-monks who have been abandoned or deposited in the hermitage yearn to belong somewhere, to somebody; the adult monks who take refuge in the hermitage are still imprisoned by their mental afflictions. Korean directors look to the Buddhist hermitage as an estimable cultural legacy, but some, like Im Kwontaek, ponder monasticism's ability to address the social exigencies of the present. Classic Buddhist themes are made more pointed by modernized social sensibilities. The early twentieth-century monk-poet Manhae (Han Yongun, 1879–1944) captures the Buddhist dialectic in the following poem, entitled "Master's Sermon":

I heard the Master's sermon:
"Don't be bound to the chains of love and suffer.
Cut the ties and your mind will find joy."

That Master is quite the fool.
To be bound with ties of love is painful, but to cut them is more painful than
  death.
In the tight bind of love's ties lies its unbinding.
Thus great liberation lies in bondage.
My love, I feared that the ties that bind me to you might be weak, so I've
  doubled the strands of my love. (Cho 2005: 43)

As a modern Korean Buddhist, Manhae embraced politics, social engagement, and the full range of commitments that can be signified by his use of the term "love." Liberation lies in bondage, as Manhae says, and it is not surprising that most of the protagonists of these films end up leaving the hermitage. But such departure is only one half of the story. For Manhae, it is Buddhist training that brings out the religious value of secular activity, and this is the lesson that the movie monks struggle to learn.

Im Kwontaek's films are discussed sensitively by David James (2002), and I have discussed *Beyond the Mountain* and *Why Has Bodhidharma Left for the East?* in other articles (Cho 2003; 1999). Here I will focus on Kim Kiduk's *Spring, Summer, Fall, Winter . . . and Spring* as the most narratively balanced and unconflicted rendering of the Buddhist dialectic. The title itself gives indication of this equilibrium. The circularity of the seasons is a natural example of how opposing forces (heat and cold, decay and renewal) are all represented through time so that each may play its role. The film traces a full circle, from spring to spring, and each season correlates with a phase in the cycle of human life.

The setting is a small hermitage afloat in the middle of a mountain lake, occupied by an old monk and a young boy-monk. It is the spring of the boy's life – a time to sow seeds that will ripen in the future. The boy amuses himself by tying stones to small animals (a fish, a snake, a frog) and watching them struggle. The old monk discovers him and warns that the torment he is causing will be like a stone lodged in his heart for the rest of his life. Summer opens with the boy-monk now a fully ripened young man. The young woman who arrives at the hermitage to convalesce from an illness awakens his sensual desires and an affair ensues. Unable to stand her departure, the monk steals away to follow her, bearing a stone Buddha icon upon his back as he crosses over from the hermitage to the outside world. Fall sees the return of the monk, now a mature man in the prime of his afflictive passions: he has murdered his wife in a fit of jealous rage and seeks refuge from the law, as well as absolution at the hands of the old monk. He is retrieved and taken away by police detectives to pay his worldly penance. The season ends with the self-immolation of the old monk, who has completed his term of seasons. Winter entails another return of the departed monk, now in middle age. Having completed his tour of the outside world, he has returned to stay and steps into the matured role of his departed master. This transition is made clear when a young mother brings her infant son to deposit at the hermitage, under his care. But when the washing hole that the monk has chopped into the frozen lake causes her accidental death, the full weight of his spring karma is finally ripened: he has now precipitated the death of two women, paralleling the death of the fish and the snake in his spring phase. He imposes his own penance this time, dragging a millstone tied to his waist to the mountaintop for retreat and meditation. When spring arrives again, we see the infant boy now as a young boy (played by the same boy actor of the previous spring), amusing himself by worrying a turtle that has climbed up on the hermitage float.

There are multiple crossings into and away from the hermitage. Isolation cannot shield refugees from the worldly law of karma. But crossing into the outside world does not mean leaving the Buddhist one behind, as clearly signaled by the stone Buddha that the monk shoulders upon his departure, in pursuit of his carnal passions. The world outside the hermitage is the playing field where Buddhist law comes to fruition, and by virtue of that drama, hotheaded young men can return to the hermitage as mature monks. "Inside" and "outside" depend on and give rise to each other. Nalin Pan's *Samsara* (India, 2001) appears to reprise this dialectic, although I have not been able to obtain the film for viewing prior to this essay.

The dream tale: from the didactic to the aesthetic

The prevalence of the life-as-dream adage in Buddhism is illustrated by the dream-tale genre that has a long history in Asia (Cho 1996). Manifesting as a story within a story, the dream tale centers on a restless and ambitious protagonist, impatient to make his way in the world, and the dream that he dreams that awakens him to the futility of it all. The frame-tale structure has the effect of implicating the reader: if the protagonist of the story is effectively awakened to the illusory nature of his ambitions by a dream, the reader in turn is challenged to wake up to his own illusions by the power of the tale. The dream tale is the most explicitly self-reflexive in Buddhist storytelling.

Khyentse Norbu's *Travellers and Magicians* (2003) magnifies the effect by incorporating the "reader" into its story, thus adding another layer to the frame tale. Dondup is a young government employee in a small village in present-day Bhutan who dreams of going to America in search of excitement and fulfillment. On his hitchhiking journey to the capital in order to obtain a visa, he encounters a fellow traveler in a Buddhist monk who, to pass the time, tells Dondup the story of Tashi, a similarly restless young man who yearns for life outside his small village. Tashi's clever brother uses magic to make Tashi dream a dream of passion, intrigue, and murder that all go wrong. Tashi is cured of his desires upon waking, and Dondup too, within his frame, exhibits second thoughts about his dream of going to America.

Dondup, as the hearer of the dream tale, is equivalent to the reader, who is encased by the film into yet another narrative frame. The film, in turn, speaks to the throngs of youth in places like Bhutan who disparage their own culture and yearn for the imagined pleasures of the West. The dream tale is fundamentally didactic in unmasking the objects of human longing – they are illusory – but it is also aesthetic in encouraging appreciation of what is already in front of us. For Dondup, this comes via his growing attraction to the papermaker's daughter traveling with him. The achingly beautiful Bhutanese landscape captured by the film makes the same aesthetic point.

The (in)ability to appreciate what one already has is the theme of Kenji Mizoguchi's 1953 masterpiece film *Ugetsu*, which is based on a collection of Japanese ghost stories called *Ugetsu Monogatari* (*Tales of Moonlight and Rain*) by Ueda Akinari (1734–1809). A village potter in medieval Japan becomes consumed with greed as wartime economics allows his business to flourish. Selling his wares in town, Genjuro is seduced by a beautiful aristocratic woman who ultimately turns out to be a ghost. Realizing that his happiness with this glamorous woman in her palatial estate was nothing but an insubstantial reverie, the potter hurries home to the wife and child he has abandoned. He is initially greeted by an empty house, but a bit of remarkable camera work brings his dead wife Miyagi back to life for one night's reunion: The camera pans left from the cold hearth in the middle of the room and doubles back right to follow Genjuro (visible through the windows) running around the back of the house, calling for his wife. When the camera's point of view comes back to the hearth, it is suddenly glowing with a warm fire tended by Miyagi. It is only the next morning that Genjuro, waking to a house empty again, learns that his family perished in his absence. While he was out chasing ghosts, the precious and fragile happiness of his existing life was squandered.

The didactic message of the dream tale transcends cultural and temporal barriers. Art is driven to endless productivity by universal themes, but the idea that art and life are alike in their insubstantial yet engaging nature provides an added possibility for the art of film. Film, with its power to reproduce the sensory experience of life itself, can direct the audience's manner of seeing and encourage us to see deeply. The Buddha Maitreya informs Sudhana at the end of his pilgrimage:

> This is the nature of all things; all elements of existence are characterized by malleability and are controlled by the knowledge of the bodhisattvas; thus, they are by nature not fully real, but are like illusions, dreams, reflections. (Quoted in McMahan 2002: 128)

The *Gandavyuha* not only emphasizes the power of illusion to enlighten, it is also perhaps the best example of the Mahayana emphasis on seeing and vision as the superior path to enlightenment. As a primarily oral literature, the Pali canon founded its authority on the claim to transmit the actual words of the Buddha as *heard* by his followers. The Mahayana texts, being temporally removed from this oral transmission, stake their authority on *seeing* – a point emphasized by the extravaganza of fantastical visions that are the norm of Mahayana sutras. As David McMahan notes, this emphasis on vision was a pan-Indian movement that coincided with the emergence of writing in the final two centuries before the common era. "It is also noteworthy," he continues, "that visualization practices became more elaborate and important in both Buddhism and Hinduism at this time" (McMahan 2002: 99). Seeing and visualization are essential to Buddhist practice and film alike.

Japanese films often excel at this aesthetic task. The striking visual arrangements of Mizoguchi films, with their prolonged takes, or of Yasujiro Ozu's unmoving camera, even with the eye level of his seated actors, are frequently noted. Ozu's domestic dramas, such as *Late Spring* (1949) and *Tokyo Story* (1953), train the "life as dream" message on the family and the natural rhythms of life in which children grow and move away from their parents, both literally and emotionally. Ozu's quiet yet powerful dramatization of family life partakes of the medieval, Buddhist-derived aesthetic of "mono no aware," which expresses the quiet sadness and preciousness of our all-too-brief human attachments.

Hirokazu Kore-eda's *Maborosi* (1995) is particularly virtuous in its aesthetic gaze. Its manner of seeing, which I have described elsewhere (Cho 2008), extends the Noh drama aesthetics of "yugen," which like the Huayan notion of the total inter-penetration of all phenomena, offers us a glimmer of the profound and the deep in all things, if only we take the time to see. There is a suicide that anchors the events of this film, as well as the anguish of Yumiko, the young surviving wife. As William LaFleur notes, the film refuses to make the suicide intelligible – at least not in our usual discursive modes of meaning-making (LaFleur 2007). Instead, we are treated to sensually brilliant images of the sea, beaches, coastal landscapes, and the play of light and shadow that form the contours of our everyday world. Human actions are made an integral part of a vast nature that evokes Kant's notion of the Sublime, but unlike this Western aesthetic the Buddhist one alludes to no transcendent divinity. The deep and the profound are inseparable from the mundane things that we presume to already know. And so we must attend closely to what is before our eyes.

From Vietnam, Tran Anh Hung's *The Scent of Green Papaya* (1993) is a visually exquisite film, whose aesthetic attentiveness is reflected in the title and forms the chief attribute of the young servant girl, Mui, at the center of the story. Turning into a young woman, Mui attracts the attention of her master, a pianist, who sketches portraits of her that merge into images of the Buddha. Mui's uncomplaining servitude, and the depth of her quiet engagement with the sights, sounds, and smells of the world around her, contrasts sharply with the restless boredom and deep disquietude of her wealthy employers. The pianist breaks off his engagement to a pretty and well-connected fiancée to marry Mui.

Turning to American films, *Jacob's Ladder* (1990) by Adrian Lyne utilizes the Tibetan Buddhist concept of the bardo, or the liminal state between death and rebirth, to explore the psyche of an American soldier who dies in Vietnam. The sorrows and attachments of Jake's life – his divorce, the death of his young son, his attraction to a co-worker – create the karmic energy that sustains the illusion of life in the bardo phase. Jake's attachments are so strong that he does not realize that his life is over, but his recurring visions of monsters tell him that something is wrong. His chiropractor, Louis, is a Meister Eckhart-quoting guru who tells Jake that if he clings to life in fear of death, the devils come to tear him away; but if he accepts death, the devils are really angels helping him on his way. This bardo dream tale sounds the classic Buddhist lesson of detachment and the torments that arise when we are unable to let go of the self.

Finally, we should consider the possibility of Buddhist aesthetic values within Western films. Here the possibilities open up considerably because, like Kore-eda's *Maborosi*, a film does not need any reference to Buddhist teachings or institutions in order to be saturated with Buddhist ways of seeing. Rather than enumerate all possible contenders, I will focus on just one film in order to underscore some salient qualities. Ang Lee's *The Ice Storm* (1997) might be likened to Ozu's domestic drama. Set in the privileged suburb of New Canaan, Connecticut, during the Watergate scandal, the title is, like a haiku poem, both a reference to a natural event at the heart of the film and a description of human relationships, in this case, between husbands and wives, parents and children, and even adulterous couples. The Watergate hearings that constantly drone on the television set suggest an overall era of disillusionment, but the film never explains why the adulterers are cheating on their spouses and why adults cannot talk to their adolescent children. Psychological and sociological explanations, with their conceit of making sense of things, are avoided in favor of simply *looking*, which has the capacity to evoke moods of surprising strength. As in *Maborosi*, dispensing with stock explanatory mechanisms makes us more attentive to events.

The role of nature in *The Ice Storm* also exhibits parallels with *Maborosi*. The storm that intensifies throughout the night parallels the freeze of despair that advances as the grownups play a partner-swapping game at a party. But the ice storm does not function as a simple metaphor. One of the teenagers goes out into the frigid night to experience the storm, and its glacial beauty cannot be ignored – by him or by the audience. It is a rare moment in which someone is absorbed in a good way. But neither is nature to be romanticized: The boy is electrocuted by a live wire from a downed power line. The snaking and leaping electrical wire seems to be alive, and it is both menacing and beautiful. The boy's death is grievous to his community, naturally, but it is ambiguous what this stepping over into death is like for him. In *The Cup*, one of the novices asks the storytelling monk, "How does the story end?" "What is this obsession with endings?" the monk questions in turn. *The Ice Storm* ends rather haphazardly. Nothing is resolved; nothing is explained. We are simply asked to *look*.

Conclusion

Buddhist semiotics authorizes the use of religious signs because they are effective teaching devices that suffer no ontological deficiency relative to the absolute of emptiness that they are meant to signify. Some people may think the idea of a filmmaking lama is incongruous, but the medieval master Dōgen would not have trouble substituting celluloid projections for mountains and running water as a way of conveying the "lasting impression of the Buddha-seal." As a medium of self-reflexive storytelling, film can alert us to the ultimately illusory nature of our own stories, but it is also able to make us see in ways we are far too distracted from in "real" life. Buddhist seeing is marvelously realized by cinematic projections, and the art of film is substantively dignified by Buddhist perceptions.

Acknowledgements

I would like to thank Gaetano Maida of the International Buddhist Film Festival for sharing its filmography with me.

Bibliography

Cho, F. (1996) *Embracing Illusion: Truth and Fiction in* The Dream of the Nine Clouds, Albany: State University of New York Press.

—— (1999) "Imagining Nothing and Imaging Otherness in Buddhist Film," in D. Jaspers and S. B. Plate (eds), *Imag(in)ing Otherness: Filmic Visions of Living Together*, Atlanta: Scholar's Press: 169–96.

—— (2003) "The Art of Presence: Buddhism and Korean Films," in S. B. Plate (ed.) *Representing Religion in World Cinema: Filmmaking, Mythmaking, Culture Making*, New York: Palgrave Press: 107–20.

—— (trans.) (2005) *Everything Yearned For: Manhae's Poems of Love and Longing*, Boston: Wisdom Publications.

—— (2008) "Buddhism, Film, and Religious Knowing: Challenging the Literary Approach to Film," in G. Watkins (ed.) *Teaching Religion and Film*, Oxford: Oxford University Press: 117–28.

Conze, E. (trans.) (1958) *Buddhist Wisdom Books*, London: George Allen and Unwin.

Dzongsar, J. K. (2004) "Life as Cinema." Online. Available HTTP: <http://www.landmarktheatres.com/mn/travellersmagicians.html> (accessed 17 July 2008).

—— (2008). "Projecting the Dharma: Film and the Transmission of Buddhism to the West." Talk delivered at Yale University Law School, 25 January. Online. Available at HTTP: <http://www.siddharthasintent.org> (accessed 17 July 2008).

Garfield, J. (trans.) (1995). *The Fundamental Wisdom of the Middle Way: Nagarjuna's* Mulamadhyamakakarika, New York: Oxford University Press.

James, D. (2002) "Im Kwon-Taek: Korean National Cinema and Buddhism," in D. E. James and K. H. Kim (eds) *Im Kwon-Taek: The Making of a Korean National Cinema*, Detroit: Wayne State University Press: 47–83.

LaFleur, W. (2007) "Suicide Off the Edge of Explicability: Awe in Ozu and Kore-eda," in J. Mitchell and S. B. Plate (eds) *The Religion and Film Reader*, New York: Routledge: 153–63.

McMahan, D. (2002) *Metaphor and Visionary Imagery in Mahayana Buddhism*, London and New York: RoutledgeCurzon.

Waddell, N. and Abe, M. (trans.) (2002) *The Heart of Dōgen's Shobogenzo*, Albany: State University of New York Press.

Yampolsky, P. (trans.) (1978) *The Platform Sutra of the Sixth Patriarch*, New York: Columbia University Press.

Zurcher, E. (1995) "Buddhist Art in Medieval China: The Ecclesiastical View," in K. R. van Kooij and H. van der Veere (eds) *Function and Meaning in Buddhist Art*, Groningen: Egbert Forsten: 1–20.

Filmography

Angulimala (2003, dir. S. Sunnirat)
Beyond the Mountain (1991, dir. J. Chung)
Come, Come, Come Upward (1989, dir. K. Im)
The Cup (2000, dir. K. Dzongsar)
Donnie Darko (2001, dir. R. Kelly)
Dreaming Lhasa (2005, dir. R. Sarin and T. Sonam)
Enlightenment Guaranteed (2000, dir. D. Dorrie)
Fight Club (1999, dir. D. Fincher)
Groundhog Day (1993, dir. H. Ramis)
I Heart Huckabees (2004, dir. D. Russell)
The Ice Storm (1997, dir. A. Lee)
Jacob's Ladder (1990, dir. A. Lyne)
Kundun (1997, dir. M. Scorsese)
Late Spring (1949, dir. Y. Ozu)
Little Buddha (1994, dir. B. Bertolucci)
Little Monk (2003, dir. K. Joo)
Maborosi (1995, dir. H. Kore-eda)
Mandala (1981, dir. K. Im)
The Matrix (1999, dir. A. and L. Wachowski)
Milarepa (1974, dir. L. Cavani)
Milarepa: Magician, Murderer, Saint (2007, dir. N. Chokling)
Passage to Buddha (1993, dir. S. Jang)
Samsara (2001, dir. N. Pan)
The Scent of Green Papaya (1993, dir. A. Tran)
Spring, Summer, Fall, Winter . . . and Spring (K. Kim)
The Stalker (1979, dir. A. Tarkovsky)
Tokyo Story (1953, dir. Y. Ozu)
Travellers and Magicians (2003, dir. K. Dzongsar)
Ugetsu (1953, dir. K. Mizoguchi)
Why Has Bodhidharma Left for the East? (1989, dir. Y. Bae)

10
POSTCOLONIAL RELIGIOUS SYNCRETISM: FOCUS ON THE PHILIPPINES, PERU, AND MEXICO

Antonio D. Sison

Missionaries brought formal Christianity encoded in systematic theologies, churches, and institutions such as schools and hospitals. They assumed that traditional religions would die out as the gospel displaced animistic beliefs and practices. Today it is clear that old ways do not die out ... Christianity is an overlay, and the two coexist in uneasy tension.

Hiebert et al (1999: 13).

Introduction

The Philippines, my country of birth, possesses a unique postcolonial soulscape that, while determinately Asian, is more kindred with the spiritual geography of Latin America. This soulscape emanates from a shared history of four centuries of Spanish theocratic imperialism, which was characterized by the inextricable union of conquest and Christianization. Incontestably, geographical and cultural factors distinguish the colonization of the Philippines from the earlier, more sanguineous Spanish incursions in Mexico and Peru. Although we cannot go into an extensive description here, it is instructive to point out that the Aztecs and Incas had developed civilizations in complete separation from European culture, thus occasioning the forcible breaking down of the walls of isolation by the *conquistadores* with the goal of forging a connection between the New World and the Old World. Such an inordinate measure was hardly necessary in the case of the indigenous Filipinos who had encounters with Eurasian culture long before the arrival of the Spaniards (Phelan 1959).

The profound resonances between Mexican, Peruvian, and Filipino colonial experience may be appreciated by looking into the indigenous culture's reception of the Christianizing process. Roman Catholicism, the Spanish-imported religion, was successfully implanted by the Spanish missionaries who saw themselves as liberators ordained by God to wage spiritual battle against the devil's strong hold on the pagan peoples. The missionaries imposed Christianity as an entirely new religion and any resemblance they may have observed in the primal religions was believed to be a work of deception plotted by demonic principalities. This mindset primarily accounts for the iconoclastic zeal that characterized the Spanish missionary enterprise. This, however, did not result in the complete displacement of the indigenous religions by Roman Catholicism as the Spaniards had anticipated, but in a two-way mediation or fusion of these distinguishable religious identities. It is vital to remember that the cultures of the Aztecs, Incas, and native Filipinos shared a plasticity that allowed for the entry of the imported religion without the obliteration of the indigenous religion. Writing on the impact of Christianity on the Peruvian Andes, Harold Osborne notes that the Incas possessed the innate ability to integrate foreign elements into their core beliefs:

> For the Indian character is syncretic, receptive: integrating the new without ever discarding the old; prepared to conjoin the incongruous and marry the incompatible into a polycladous tradition multiradicate in the distant past. Pliant to new doctrines and cults, the Indian moulds them into new shapes of his own and no force can comply him to desquamate what he has once made his own. (Osborne 1952: 131)

A similar quality is attributed to the Aztecs of Mexico. Davíd Carrasco underscores the fact that the Spanish missionaries themselves had acknowledged the Aztecs' propensity for amalgamation:

> The Franciscan and Dominican priests, who spoke Nahuatl and observed the indigenous peoples adjusting painfully to the colonial order, realized that the Indians were not merely adopting Spanish Catholic practices. Rather they were mixing native and European beliefs together and sometimes disguising their continued worship of their spirits, deities, and ancestors in their devotion to Mary and other saints. (Carrasco 1990: 136–7)

In like manner, indigenous Filipinos received Spanish Catholicism but not without introducing local elements that made the imported religion acceptable to them. John Leddy Phelan emphasizes that in the hands of the Filipinos, the Iberian import had undergone an ingenious process of "Philippinization":

> As it happened, the Filipinos endowed certain aspects of the new religion with a ceremonial and emotional content, a special Filipino flavor which made

> Catholicism in the archipelago in some respects a unique expression of that universal religion. In this process of "Philippinizing" Catholicism the major role belonged to the Filipinos. They showed themselves remarkably selective in stressing and de-emphasizing certain features of Spanish Catholicism. (Phelan 1959: 72)

Spanish Catholicism, as such, found new roots in the New World and in Southeast Asia, but not in the original form within which it was delivered. For the colonized cultures, the religious syncretism would incarnate in multiform variants of Folk Catholicism or popular piety. The religious syncretism embodied in Folk Catholicism would remain even after the fall of the Spanish empire and would continue to characterize postcolonial religious practice in both Latin America and the Philippines.

In light of this religious-historical backdrop, it is not difficult to surmise that religious syncretism would find cultural validation in the respective cinemas of the Philippines, Peru, and Mexico. My project here is mainly hermeneutical. I wish to explore the ways in which specific films from the aforementioned countries represent religious syncretism within a contemporary postcolonial context. The feature films I have chosen as exemplars offer cinematic representations of religious syncretism as Folk Catholicism. My intent is not to homogenize cultural differences but to examine religious syncretism precisely within the cultural differences portrayed in the cinematic text. The film *Santa Santita* (2004) by noted Filipino filmmaker Laurice Guillen ushers us into the very marrow of Philippine Folk Catholicism where syncretistic practices form part of the quotidian. Claudia Llosa's *Madeinusa* (2006), on the other hand, has little direct connection with actual religious practice in Peru but offers a thought experiment that blends a surreal world of religious syncretism with unmistakable inflections of the historical. Santiago Parras' *Guadalupe* (2007) cues us to consider the Mexican Virgin of Guadalupe, the very image of which is a symbol *par excellence* of syncretistic Folk Catholicism. Aside from the richly textured imaging of religious syncretism in the three films and the postcolonial cultures they represent, I also considered their international accessibility: an indication that the films figure in current public discourse. All three titles are available on subtitled DVD format. It is important to emphasize that I give regardful attention to the films' stylistic strategies – *mise en scène*, cinematography, editing – in a committed effort to acknowledge the particularity of film as a cultural text. The Religion–Film dialogue has often been foxholed in the exploration of the thematic, literary bases of film as though film was a mere appendage to literature. The stylistic dimension, precisely what would trigger the hermeneutical impulse to examine film on its own terms, has fallen below the radar of a continuum of scholars engaged in the inter-discipline (Sison 2006). This essay puts emphasis on the interpretation of film *qua* film.

It is expedient that I clarify my use of the term "syncretism" as I am aware of the negative connotations attached to it in Christian theological understanding. Here, I graft onto the definition proposed by Robert J. Schreiter where the term may carry both positive and negative meaning:

I will continue to use syncretism to describe the formation of religious identity, always with the understanding that at times the new identity under examination will be in accord with, and even enrich, the religious tradition; and that at other times, it will not be in accord, and so must be rejected. (Schreiter 2004: 64)

Syncretism then represents the dialectical tension between the universality of the Christian faith and the particularity of the indigenous religious practices. Another qualification I wish to make concerns my use of the term "Folk Catholicism." Schreiter rightly points out that the politicized use of the word "folk" carries negative overtones that connote xenophobia and the glorification of peasant life (Schreiter 1985: 124). Here, Folk Catholicism has to do more with indicating a creative grass-roots reappropriation of Spanish colonial Catholicism, which continues to be lived out by the members of postcolonial Third World communities, the majority of whom form the lower rungs of the sociopolitical pyramid. In contrast to official Catholicism, Folk Catholicism is not expressed in a systematic, doctrinal theology that often proves too abstract and detached, but in religious feeling and popular communitarian practice. In this sense, my understanding dovetails with Benigno Beltran's description of Folk Catholicism as "the popular expression of the inarticulate, the unlettered, and the disenfranchised" (Beltran 1987: 4). What is represented in Folk Catholicism is an incarnational form of God-talk from humanity's underside – a "theology of the inarticulate."

Philippines: *Santa Santita*

Laurice Guillen belongs to the "third generation" of Filipino filmmakers whose works harvested critical acclaim in the 1980s and 1990s (Lacaba 2000). Previously known as an accomplished television and film actress, Guillen made her mark as a serious filmmaker with her fourth film *Salome* (1981), a fascinating study of gender hegemony where "truth" is portrayed as a slippery, heterogeneous reality in the storytelling mode of Akira Kurosawa's *Rashomon* (Japan, 1950). She had a string of commercial film projects through the 1990s and then took a hiatus in 1995. During this period of artistic hibernation, the Roman Catholic Guillen went through some serious soul-searching and became an ardent devotee of the Blessed Virgin Mary.

Guillen returned to active filmmaking in 2000 and, not surprisingly, her comeback vehicle was an unapologetically religious film, a family melodrama entitled *Tanging yaman* (*A Change of Heart*). By her own admission, Guillen considered *Tanging yaman* as a personal expression of her spiritual journey – "a way of sharing with my audience what God has done in our lives in all these years that I haven't been making movies." While an emotionally earnest film, not to mention a box office success, *Tanging Yaman* was not a masterpiece but simply the work of a master. Guillen's most artistically important film since *Salome* and the one that we pay close attention to is *Santa Santita* (also *Magdalena: The Unholy Saint*, 2004), which literally denotes "a saint who is just playing saint." Here, Guillen weds her artistic genius with her Catholic perspective and succeeds in creating a richly textured film that plumbs the depths of the Filipino postcolonial religious imagination.

Santa Santita follows the life of a young woman Malen who halfheartedly hawks religious articles within the vicinity of old Manila's Quiapo Church (also known as the Minor Basilica of the Black Nazarene). Her mother Chayong is a *magdarasal*, one of a number of self-ordained intercessors-for-pay who form part of the vibrant Folk Catholicism at the fringes of the church. Much to the chagrin of Chayong who believes her job to be a religious devotion, the pretty lolita beguiles customers into buying her wares and sees her job as an opportunity to socialize. Malen meets her match one day in the dashing hustler Mike, a rent-a-car driver who sidelines as a gigolo. She completely falls under his spell and Chayong strongly disapproves of her daughter's assumed promiscuity. After squabbling with her mother following an extended date with Mike, Malen storms out of the house and moves in with the young man. The distraught Chayong suddenly dies of a heart attack and, soon after, Malen takes over her ministry out of financial necessity if not faith. Chayong's old posse snipes at the greenhorn with murmurings of "blasphemy" until elated clients return to testify that their prayers were indeed answered through Malen's intercession. Malen fears that she has, in fact, become not just an intercessor like her mother, but a miracle worker.

The imaging of postcolonial religious practice as an admixture of Spanish colonial Catholicism and indigenous beliefs can be seen from the outset in *Santa Santita*'s *mise en scène*. The use of Quiapo Church as setting situates the story at the very heart of Manila's robust Folk Catholicism. In *verité* fashion, the camera presents us with pulsating images of popular piety flourishing around the church. Articles of devotion such as scapulars, crucifixes, and rosaries, which are meant for use in traditional Catholic ritual, are peddled by street vendors alongside a dizzying array of charms, amulets, and herbs that promise magical cures for just about anything that ails the body and spirit. In the Quiapo universe, the distinction between devotional objects sanctioned by official religion and magical charms derived from popular piety is blurred; they are not mutually exclusive. Catholic religious articles have niched seamlessly into the pre-Hispanic belief in the power of *anting-anting* or talismans. Indigenous Filipinos believed that wearing *anting-anting* close to one's person bestows invincibility and provides protection from evil. Residuum of this belief continues to thrive in postcolonial Folk Catholicism; thus, in *Santa Santita*, we see Malen dipping her scapulars in the basilica's holy water font and then hawking them as though they were *anting-anting*. She would boast to a fellow vendor that her wares were blessed with holy water twice, making them more effective in warding off evil. Interestingly, the incongruous blending of official ritual with vestiges of primal religion transpires within the premises of a Catholic basilica, raising questions about the degree of the church's tolerance for religious syncretism.

Another striking representation of Folk Catholicism in *Santa Santita* is the portrayal of the ministry of lay intercessors in Quiapo Church. The camera focuses on several "prayer-women" seated on portable stools by the church entrance, one of whom is Chayong who is listening earnestly to various prayer requests from her clientele. The indexical rooting of Quiapo's prayer-women points back to the role of the *babaylan* or shaman in precolonial Philippine society. The *babaylan* was a gifted individual who served as the community's spiritual leader and assumed the role of healer, exorcist, reconciler, and wisdom-figure. Believed to possess the ability to traverse in and out of the spirit world, the *babaylan* was the intercessor of community and individuals to the *engkantu* or spirits (de Mesa 2000). Intimations of the *babaylan* are evident in *Santa Santita*'s portrayal of the Quiapo intercessors. As previously mentioned, the intercessors in the film are a coterie of women, reprising the historical verity that the ministry of the *babaylan* was principally the domain of the feminine. The primacy of women as intercessors is reinforced in the film when the prayer-women are shown positioned at the church vestibule, connoting that they provide the faithful with the first line of pastoring even prior to the sacramental ministering of the ordained male priests of the institutional Church.

Conjointly, the correlation between the Quiapo prayer-women and the *babaylan* comes to sharper focus in the portrayal of Chayong and Malen as characters in the film. Besides discharging the role of a prayer-woman, Chayong conjures the *babaylan* when she is portrayed as an authoritative wisdom-figure dispensing pithy counsel to the lost sheep, who, in turn, receive her advice on the basis of faith. The character of Malen evinces the *babaylan* in the film's second half when she undergoes a trans-formative, mystical experience that would mark her conversion from sinner to saint. Hinted in the opening scene and fully revealed at a later dream sequence, we see a transfigured Malen dressed in a luminous white robe as she receives the gift of stigmata, the miraculous materialization of the crucifixion wounds of Christ, on her hands and feet. Akin to the *babaylan*, Malen gains privileged access to the spiritual realm, which gives her the behest to mediate between God and the community. The inauguration of Malen's miraculous healing crusade following her mystical experience only works to confirm her embodiment of the role of a contemporary *babaylan*. It is interesting to note that the representation of a unique supernatural event to launch the ministry of a *babaylan*-figure had been depicted in Philippine cinema earlier. Malen's beatific vision in *Santa Santita*, for instance, could well be an *hommage* to the acclaimed Filipino film *Himala* (*Miracle*, Ishamel Bernal, 1982) where a Marian visionary named Elsa receives the stigmata as an inaugural sign of her miracle crusade (Sison 2004).

Corollary to *Santa Santita*'s rendering of the theme of intercession is its foregrounding of the role of religious images of the saints as symbols of a latent mediation between humans and God. Pre-Hispanic Filipinos believed that *Bathala* or Creator-God delegated ordinary human affairs to a pantheon of spirit-beings after the completion of his act of creation. These spirits assumed the role of mediators for humanity. Upon the arrival of Spanish Catholicism, indigenous Filipinos began to equate the cult of the saints with the mediation of the spirits so that it effortlessly took root in the culture and flourished. Like the spirit-beings of the ancient world, the Catholic saints were believed to have the power to bestow blessings or to mete out punishment (De Mesa 2000). *Santa Santita* offers a vivid representation of this syncretistic belief in one peculiar scene – as Malen and Mike prepare to engage in sex at an early juncture in the film, their foreplay is suddenly interrupted when Malen rushes to the family altar and repositions her late mother's numerous religious statues so that their backs are turned against the bed. Compelled by guilt and the fear of chastisement, Malen makes sure that the saints do not "see" the sin she is about to commit. Only when each of the saints is turned the other way does she resume her activities with Mike in the tryst.

Finally, the veneration of the image of the Black Nazarene is a focal point in *Santa Santita*'s representation of syncretism as postcolonial Folk Catholicism. As mentioned earlier, the official name of Quiapo Church is the Minor Basilica of the Black Nazarene, in reference to the *Hesus Nazareno*, a statue of a cross-bearing, dark-skinned Christ brought to the Philippines by the Recollects around the sixteenth century (Beltran 1987: 116). The centerpiece ritual of Quiapo Church is a week-long celebration of the feast of the Black Nazarene, culminating in a massive gathering where the statue is borne in a procession that winds its way around the church environs. In what stands out as *Santa Santita*'s visual crescendo, we become virtual witnesses to a phenomenon not seen anywhere else in the world. We see wide-angle documentary footage of a multitude of men undulating like a singular organism as they move the *carroza* bearing the Black Nazarene in a hypnotic dance (Fig. 10.1). What finds cinematic representation here is the Filipinos' lopsided attachment and devotion to the victim-image of the suffering Christ at the expense of the liberating image of the resurrected Christ. Understood alongside the other widely venerated victim-images of Christ in Philippine Catholic ritual, namely the crucified Christ, and the *Santo Entierro* or the interred body of the Christ, the Black Nazarene becomes iconic of the mimetic appropriation of the passion of Christ in actual folk religious practice. I am referring to the morbid ritual of self-flagellation and crucifixion that is an annual Good Friday

Fig. 10.1 The documentary footage of the feast of the Black Nazarene in Manila's Quiapo Church serves as *Santa Santita*'s visual crescendo. The religious phenomenon is iconic of the way Spanish colonial ritual finds expression in Filipino Folk Catholicism. (*Santa Santita*, dir. Laurice Guillen, Unitel Pictures, 2004). Courtesy Tony I. Gloria and Tito Velasco, Unitel Pictures, Philippines.

devotion in Filipino popular piety, specifically among poor communities. Penitential self-mortification was a colonial import that was not accepted too easily by the native culture. Its fusion with the pre-Hispanic value known as *damay* or solidarity, however, caused the ritual to be viewed as empathy for and participation in the passion of Jesus Christ. Consequently, the religious syncretism found a secure place in Filipino popular piety notwithstanding its aberrance from present-day Church teaching:

> In popular religious movements, belief in the need to participate in Jesus' sufferings through pity and empathy is particularly stressed. The focus on the victim-Christ in folk Catholicism reinforces the desire to personally relate oneself to the Passion through ascetic practices. The practice of public flagellation is another instance where folk religious practices clash with official practice and with very little communication going on between the hierarchy and the penitents. (Beltran 1987: 115)

Though *Santa Santita* does not feature the practice of self-mortification as such, it portrays strong symbolic references to the practice in the depiction of the characters of Chayong and Malen. When Chayong is overcome by a paroxysm of emotion over Malen's rebellious ways, she is shown kneeling before her altar of saints with her arms outstretched in cruciform position, a foreboding of her tragic end. She is the weeping *mater dolorosa* crucified by the transgressions of a prodigal daughter. Malen, as discussed earlier, would bear the wounds of Christ when stigmata appear on her hands and feet in an eerie dream sequence. This is highlighted by close-up shots of thick drops of blood marking her path as she passes through an ethereal desert. When she awakens from the dream, Malen confesses that she could feel *de facto* the pain from the wounds. Although *Santa Santita* ends on a hopeful note, its key characters are made to be co-participants in the passion of Christ in an extended Good Friday, thus proving themselves to be true devotees of the cross-bearing Black Nazarene.

Echoing Phelan's argument that a "Philippinizing" process marked the reception of Spanish Catholicism in the Philippines, Filipino theologian José de Mesa asserts that "there is today a continuing discussion as to whether Filipinos had been truly Christianized, or whether Christianity had simply been Filipinized" (de Mesa 2000: 1). In the postcolonial Folk Catholicism of Laurice Guillen's *Santa Santita*, that question remains open-ended.

Peru: *Madeinusa*

Madeinusa, a wordplay of "Made in USA," is an existing proper name in Peru. It belongs to the same genus as "Johnfkenedi," "Marlonbrando," and other names that serve as coded paeans to the American dream. First-time filmmaker Claudia Llosa could not have chosen a more intriguing title for her inaugural film, which explores the abstruse religious rituals of a fictitious highland culture in Peru. International film festivals lauded Llosa's accomplished filmmaking; *Madeinusa* won the FIPRESCI Prize at the 2006 Rotterdam Film Festival and was nominated for the Grand Jury Prize at the 2006 Sundance Film Festival, among others. But hometown critics had a very different reception for the film; they were incensed that Llosa had painted an unreal representation of Peruvian culture as obtuse, barbaric, and so bewitched with the American dream that a child could be named Madeinusa. The film's diegesis, however, has to do with neither denigrating indigenous culture, nor glorifying the American dream. *Madeinusa* is an imagined world, a blurring of fact and fancy meant to evoke a visceral experience of religious syncretism. Llosa herself confirms this in the "extra material" of the film's DVD release. That said, *Madeinusa* stands out as the only film in this essay that portrays an imaginative construct of postcolonial Folk Catholicism where the realistic elements hang back as inflections, rather than accurate representations of their referents.

Madeinusa is a candidate to the annual "most beautiful virgin" pageant in Manayaycuna (Quechua for "the town no one can enter"), her remote hometown in the Peruvian Andes. The pageant ushers in the celebration of *El Tiempo Santo*, or "The Holy Time," which is based on the belief that God literally dies on Good Friday, hence would be unable to see humanity's sins until the morning of Easter. Madeinusa wins the pageant and is expected to undergo a bizarre rite of passage involving an incestuous encounter with her father. A geologist from Lima named Salvador makes an unannounced stopover at Manayaycuna en route to a mining outpost. Madeinusa is completely charmed by the gringo who has the European features of a Spanish mestizo. Unlike the xenophobic townsfolk, the young woman has a fascination for the foreign, established earlier when she is shown opening a box filled with baubles, makeup, and magazine clippings featuring blonde, Caucasian models. Madeinusa breaks away from the evening procession to seek out Salvador and they have a sexual encounter. Meantime, the entire town engages in pagan revelry. Having lived with an abusive father and a mean-spirited sister since her mother abandoned the family for the lure of the big city, Madeinusa convinces Salvador to take her to Lima so that she could search for her mother and start life anew. At the appointed time, she does not show up. The next day, her drunken father chokes in his sleep and, in an opaque turn, Madeinusa joins her sister in putting the blame on Salvador, crying out: "The gringo killed my father!" The film keeps us hanging about the fate of the gringo; in its abrupt ending, we see Madeinusa aboard a truck to Lima with a knowing smile on her face.

The postcolonial Folk Catholicism in *Madeinusa* revolves around the celebration of *El Tiempo Santo*, which exists neither in the Catholic Lenten tradition, nor in the actual ritual of the local Peruvian church. It is portrayed as a syncretistic folk reappropriation of two theological concepts – first, that Jesus Christ is God made flesh; second, that he died on the cross but was raised up on the third day. These basic theological elements are reconstituted in the distorted hermeneutics that if God as the human Christ dies on a Good Friday, then God cannot see the transgressions of the world until he resurrects on Easter Sunday. Further, the death of Jesus-God on the cross is not a once-for-all event but an annually recurring sacrifice. The equation would then have perverse consequences for the devotees; each year, from Good Friday until the break of Easter, they are given the rare opportunity to act upon their basest desires and commit sins with impunity.

Religious syncretism is vividly represented in the film's *mise en scène*. In the sequence portraying the Good Friday ritual, we see a life-size wooden statue of the crucified Christ, an otherwise customary image of Catholic iconography except for a unique attribute: its head and arms are movable. When the time comes for Jesus to die, the statue's head snaps to a final bow, and a couple of men proceed to pull out the nails from the statue's hands and lower its arms in preparation for burial. Consequently, the image of the crucified Christ has morphed into a *Santo Entierro* or "interred Christ," now lying on an illuminated glass coffin. Madeinusa, here dressed in brocaded velvet as Mary the Virgin Queen, approaches the coffin and, in a disquieting move, leans over to the *Santo Entierro* and plants a sensual kiss on its lips. She then ceremonially places a white blindfold over the eyes of the dead Christ. Iconic representations of the film's religious syncretism crystallize dramatically in this sequence. First, the manually postured, marionette-like Jesus is iconic of the way the townsfolk had taken hold of normative theological postulates and how they had conveniently reconfigured these postulates for their own purposes in the observance of *El Tiempo Santo*. The act of blindfolding the *Santo Entierro* is an eerie punctuation to this transgressive reappropriation; God officially cannot see the sins of the townsfolk until Easter. Second, the unholy kiss between the Virgin Mary and the *Santo Entierro* is iconic of the incestuous rite of passage that is expected to happen soon after. The *pietà* – the traditional depiction of a sorrowful Mary cradling the dead body of her son Jesus – loses its theological grounding as two practices in complete disharmony are made to consort with one another. Again, this syncretistic blending of Catholic traditional ritual and a bestial folk practice congeals within the frame of *El Tiempo Santo*.

Notwithstanding that *El Tiempo Santo* is a chimera, it does share some resonances with the character of syncretization that took place historically between Spanish Catholicism and the Inca religion of the Peruvian Andes in the sixteenth and seventeenth centuries where "Christian belief and cult, its meaning and intention often distorted out of all recognition, is incongruously welded in an ineluctable fusion with native practice" (Osborne 1952: 228). God the Father and Jesus Christ, for instance, were seen as two different gods in fellowship with each other; the latter often considered as the supreme deity. Another example was the identification of the Christian God with Inti, the Incan sun god. While Inti was identified with life and bountiful harvests, hence sharing congruent attributes with the Christian Creator-God, the syncretism went awry when further transfused with the belief that the sun god may be susceptible to sickness like humans, consequently causing outbreaks of disease in the community and water contamination during his state of illness.

Analogically, an assessment of the character of Madeinusa reveals that she herself is iconic of religious syncretism and all its contradictions. Although Madeinusa is fascinated with the foreign – her love for artifacts of Western culture, her view of Lima as an idealized elsewhere, and her attraction to the mestizo Salvador – she is still thoroughly a daughter of Manayaycuna and its superstitious, circumscribed culture. A review of *mise en scène* in a couple of pivotal scenes attests to this. During the coronation night of the "most beautiful virgin" pageant, Salvador surreptitiously takes a Polaroid shot of Madeinusa, which he later hands out to her as a present. Madeinusa loses no time in sewing a strip of velvet through the photograph so that she could wear it around her neck. Allusions to religious syncretism can be seen in two ways. First, the Polaroid of Madeinusa with the sewn-in strip of velvet conspicuously resembles a religious scapular. Madeinusa ascertains this when she wears the Polaroid-scapular underneath her blouse, the way religious scapulars are customarily worn, indicating that it is for her a badge of religious devotion. Second, the Polaroid photograph is an artifact of "foreign" technology yet the image it reproduces is that of Madeinusa as the muse of a cinctured religious ritual. These two points suggest that Madeinusa is an embodiment of two disparate worlds in constant tension. Yet, a closer consideration of the Polaroid-scapular signifies that in a profound sense, Madeinusa is first of all devoted to herself; she wears an icon of her own face close to her heart. She is able to maintain a sense of identity and agency despite the syncretistic two-way mediation. This is further evidenced in the sequence when Madeinusa takes the side of her native culture as she joins her sister in condemning Salvador and announces to all and sundry that the gringo was responsible for her father's death. Her reneging on their agreed exodus plan already represents a shift of personal boundaries; she does not allow the Spanish mestizo Salvador, a name which literally means "savior," to take her to Lima and save her. But at the same time Madeinusa does not, so to speak, put the genie back into the bottle; she takes the pragmatic option of journeying to Lima and pursuing her plans on her own. She does not represent a resolved "either/or," she finds a sense of self in the pendulous "both/and." For better or for worse, Madeinusa is a poetic synthesis of the humus of religious syncretism from which her character germinates.

Mexico: *Guadalupe*

A cursory search of "Guadalupe" on eBay will yield an astonishing bric-a-brac – medallions, posters, scented pillows, prayer cards, stickers, wall clocks, tote bags, earrings – bearing various renditions of the familiar Mexican Marian image. That said, the film *Guadalupe* forays into a subject matter that is well entrenched, not just in Mexican religious culture, but in popular Catholic devotions in general. With funding from the religious film outfit Dos Corazones and in consultation with the Higher Institute of Guadalupan Studies, Ecuadorian filmmaker Santiago Parras set out to create a film to coincide with the 475th anniversary of the Guadalupe apparition. The issue concerning source material for the story of Guadalupe is a contentious one as there are controverting schools of thought on the matter. One view credits the Guadalupe image to a deliberate indigenization of the Virgin Mary actualized by the colonial friars in an evangelistic strategy to convert the Nahuas; the other, a supernatural apparition (Brading 2001; Gruzinski 2001). The depiction of the Guadalupe Virgin in Mexican cinema mirrors these antithetical views. The controversial *Nuevo Mundo* (*New World*, Gabriel Retes, 1978) gives an account of a sixteenth-century Church-instigated plot to create an icon of the Virgin Mary that resembles a native Aztec woman. The film does not depict the Virgin of Guadalupe as such but references to the image are striking and unmistakable. On the other hand, *La Virgen de Guadalupe* (Alfredo Salazar, 1976), a film thoroughly wrapped in the accoutrements of devotional piety, amplifies the apparition account of

Guadalupe. Parras' *Guadalupe*, though a far more accomplished film than *La Virgen de Guadalupe*, follows a consonant trajectory. It depends on the *Nican Mopohua* (from the oral language Nahuatl meaning "Here it is Told"), the normative manuscript attributed to the mestizo chronicler Fernando de Alva Ixtilxóchitl, as a frame of reference for its Guadalupe narrative. Although it is informative to note Parras' source material, what is germane to our purposes is the question of how Mexican postcolonial Catholicism is portrayed in relation to the central trope of the Virgin of Guadalupe.

Guadalupe weaves together two parallel narratives, intercutting a modern-day story involving family and personal relationships, with a retelling of the *Nican Mopohua* apparition account. Jose Maria and his sister Mercedes are archeologists from Spain who, having won a research grant, embark on a study of the Guadalupe apparition. The apparition account relates the story of a Mexican native by the name of Juan Diego who is said to have seen a vision of the Virgin Mary in 1531, in his hometown near the hills of Tepeyac. In the vision, the Virgin Mary sends Diego on a mission to convince Bishop Juan de Zumarraga to build a temple for her on the hill. The bishop receives Diego but is slow to believe. He demands evidence that the apparition did occur and that the message truly originated from the Virgin Mary. Diego reports his dilemma to the Virgin and, in response, she instructs him to gather a bouquet of winter roses to show to the bishop. Obediently, the visionary seeks an audience with the bishop with the roses cradled on his *tilma* (cloak). When the *tilma* unfurls and the rose petals fall, the flabbergasted bishop beholds a luminous portrait of the Virgin mysteriously imprinted on the fabric. Jose and Mercedes are raring to investigate how much of this story is based on historiography, and how much of it is mythmaking. They take a trip to Tepeyac and examine the available artifacts firsthand. In the process, they are surprised to find that their own lives pivot around the Guadalupe investigation, which takes them to a sphere where they have to face their own personal demons.

It is well known that the image of the Virgin of Guadalupe is a syncretistic blending of Spanish colonial Catholicism and precolonial Aztec culture. That the origin of the Guadalupe image was attributed to a supernatural phenomenon and not to the work of human hands already infused it with an inclusive aura that laid down a bridge to both the colonizer and the colonized:

> The image was not European, despite a name taken from a particularly renowned Iberian devotion; it was neither the work of a Spaniard, nor of a native. A sign produced by a sign, it thus benefited from the assets of a "cultural transparency" that allowed it to be solidly tied to the Christian supernatural, the Church Tradition, and its native Mexican soil ... mixing representation and the divine mark onto a native mantle, the Blessed Virgin was as much a sacred object as it was an effigy ... The Tepeyac image was strangely close, in the piety of the people and the fancy penwork of the exegetes, to the native sphere of the *ixiptla*. (Gruzinski 2001: 130)

Ineluctably, the image of the Guadalupe Virgin as a leitmotiv in the film is the locus within which we explore the cinematic representation of postcolonial syncretism.

Several images of the Guadalupe Virgin appear at different junctures in the film, among them, footage of the original image enshrined in the Basilica of Guadalupe in Mexico. In *Guadalupe*, close-up shots of the original image spotlight the Virgin's dark skin and her decisively indigenous features. The imaging of the Virgin as an indigenous woman is a clear departure from the normative Iberian images of the Virgin Mary associated with the Spanish conquest. The fact that the Christian Virgin had appeared as a Nahuatl woman, *uno de ellos* (one of them), and had chosen to reveal her presence to a fellow Nahua, would have powerful reverberations for the indigenous culture. For the Nahua, the Spanish conquest meant that their deities had been toppled by the foreign gods and had deserted them; it was a sign of death. The irruption of the Guadalupe Virgin from the cruel context of the conquest thus meant the restoration of dignity and life:

> In the midst of death and destruction, a great sign of hope and liberation appears – Guadalupe, the mother of the awaited fifth sun, the new Quetzalcoatl. Holy Mary of Guadalupe, the maternal face of God, the beloved Mother of God, comes to console a suffering people. (Rodriguez and Fortier 2007: 17)

The import is consequential: the indigenous people are equal image-bearers of the divine; God's favor had come home to them in historical visibility. Yet the image is at one and the same time foreign and indigenous, signifying a utopian vision of a harmonious syncretism, the unity of a *mestizaje* culture that would become contemporary Mexico. The film dilates this in its *mise en scène*, specifically in the sequences that portray the apparition of the Guadalupe Virgin to Juan Diego. We see that the actress cast to portray the Virgin (Sandra Espil) has a contemporary mestiza look, with more distinct European features and with noticeably lighter skin as compared to the original effigy. The native Mexican housekeeper Juana would validate this when she spells out to the Spanish Mercedes and Jose Maria that the Virgin of Guadalupe has "your face and mine ... both of us."

It is worth noting that Tepeyac, apparition site of Guadalupe, is of itself indexical of religious syncretism. It was the former location of the temple of Tonantzin, one of the principal earth goddesses of the Aztec people. The association between the Christian divine mother and the Aztec earth goddess would then seem to be a natural, comprehensible one for the Nahua. Upon closer consideration, however, it was not a neat hand-in-glove correlation. While the Guadalupe Virgin did share with Tonantzin the identity of a generative "earth-Mother," she was also radically different from the Aztec goddess in that she was not a destroyer. Tonantzin was believed to possess a contradictory nature that was, at one and the same time, capable of creating and destroying life. In contrast, Guadalupe's role was clearly delineated as a protective mother who offers healing and comfort to her people (Rodriguez and Fortier 2007). The Guadalupe Virgin is not simply a Christianized incarnation of Tonantzin but a sign of transformation.

This finds representation when *Guadalupe* deals with the subject of human sacrifice, which was a rudimentary practice in Nahuatl ritual. In the first quarter of the film, we see Mercedes and Jose Maria visiting an ancient Mexican archeological site. Their guide notes that human sacrifices were continually offered on the site, qualifying that the ritual was understood as a way of bringing honor to the family of the sacrificed. When Mercedes queries about how long the practice of human sacrifice lasted, the guide responds that the practice went on until the people found another god to consecrate to. Through this sequence, we see fast intercuts of an archeo-astronomer located elsewhere, intently analyzing a computer-generated image of Guadalupe and matching it with the position of the stars on the day of the apparition. The juxtaposition of the two scenes suggests a cosmovision where the linkage between the anticipation of a new "god" and the Guadalupe apparition is established. A later scene reveals this connection in a fuller sense when Mercedes and Jose Maria listen to the housekeeper telling them her version of the Guadalupe story. Curiously, "Juana," the Mexican housekeeper's name, is the feminine version of "Juan," the first name of the Guadalupe visionary. We see a stained-glass version of the Guadalupe Virgin hanging on the wall as the animated Juana talks about the ritual of human sacrifice and how that was viewed by the Nahua as a way of ensuring the continuation of life. She then segues to the apparition story where the Guadalupe Virgin introduces a new covenant that renders human sacrifices superfluous; the Virgin offers the hearts of the faithful to "the one true God" without bloodshed. As such, the Guadalupe Virgin emerged as a life-giving sign of transformation and is credited for putting an end to the practice of human sacrifice.

As a comparative reference, one can look to another fairly recent Mexican film, *El crimen del Padre Amaro* (Carlos Carrera, 2002). In the film, the young priest Padre Amaro goes through a downward moral spiral – he transgresses the vow of celibacy, gets a girl pregnant, and arranges to have the child aborted. In a telling scene, he is shown standing before the statue of the Virgin of Guadalupe contemplating his moral options. Wishing to avert a scandal that could jeopardize his promising career, Padre Amaro then leads the girl to a dubious abortion clinic and she perishes during the procedure. As the distraught priest holds the girl's lifeless body, a close-up shot of the Guadalupe Virgin is juxtaposed to the scene. A "human sacrifice" is offered at the altar of Padre Amaro's egotism; he negates the power of the Virgin of Guadalupe as a life-giving sign. In an aporial way, *El crimen del Padre Amaro* authenticates *Guadalupe*'s proposition that the Virgin of Guadalupe is not just an image but a sign of transformation and the promotion of life.

Guadalupe further nuances the Guadalupe-Tonantzin correlation when Juana refers to the stained-glass image and points to the crescent moon at the Virgin's feet. The allusion to the moon would appear to support the idea that the Guadalupe Virgin is a direct extension of the Aztec goddess, who was believed to be a lunar deity. But Juana discounts this conjecture when she points to the stars surrounding the image, an indication that the Guadalupe Virgin represents a reality much bigger than herself. Juana would substantiate her interpretation by drawing attention to the Virgin's humble facial expression as evidenced by her lowered eyes. The point is that, unlike Tonantzin, the Guadalupe Virgin herself is not a goddess but a mediator between the Mexican people and God – "a divine signal from heaven … our ally to understand light." This is an important distinction as the image of a humbler, more human Guadalupe Virgin who is an "ally" works to underscore her proximity and solidarity with the Mexican quest for a fuller humanity. For the Mexican people, to "understand the light" means finding authentic identity and honor from within the crucible of a wounded colonial history; the Guadalupe Virgin reminds them of who they truly are as a people. Conversely, Guadalupe also stands as a subversive symbol that empowers Mexicans to seek liberation when the fuller humanity they seek is threatened. We see this rendered emblematically in the film's final sequence when the image of the Virgin of Guadalupe is emplaced alongside the Mexican flag. The allusion to patriotic fervor is confirmed by a voice-over narration explaining the subversive power of the Guadalupe Virgin at the 1810 dawning of Mexican independence when revolutionary leader Juan Hidalgo used the image as a rallying banner.

Guadalupe affirms that the image of the Tepeyac Virgin is a syncretism that brings two traditions in a place of dialogue and mutual valuation. In the dynamic relationship between the Catholic tradition and Aztec religious belief, inculturation takes the place of cultural displacement. As Carrasco imaginatively describes:

> In Guadalupe we see a curious and even furious syncretistic mixture. She is Indian and Spaniard. She is Earth Mother and a Holy Mother. She is a comforter and a revolutionary. She is the magnet for pilgrimages and she is a pilgrim herself, traveling in front of the rebel soldiers and entering every heart who needs her protection and comfort, as did the poor Indian Juan Diego in 1531. (Carrasco 1990: 138)

The Virgin of Guadalupe had given birth to a renewed Mexican identity. Juan Diego's mission had indeed been accomplished.

Guardian of popular memory

In the postcolonial Third World, film often plays the role of visual historiographer, codifying the collective subversive memories of the colonized culture lest they are erased by the systematic amnesia that customarily marks official versions of history. This critical role is akin to the sense by which Teshome Gabriel describes Third Cinema as "guardian of popular memory" where film serves to record and preserve "the testimony of existence and struggle" of the dispossessed culture, thus quickening a revisionist form of political awareness (Gabriel 1989: 63–4). In representing the detritus of primal religious practices incarnating in postcolonial Folk Catholicism, the films we have studied conjointly represent the colonial past as memories of native resistance. Though the Spanish conquest warranted its obliteration and death, the indigenous culture insists on survival and life. In Santa Santita, we feel its pulse within the very walls of a Philippine Catholic basilica, thriving in a rhythmic dance with official Catholic practices. We imagine its insidious shadow side in the mythopoetics of Madeinusa's El Tiempo Santo where it hijacks a normative Catholic ritual and infuses it with a completely alien meaning. And in Guadalupe, we behold its face in the image of the Virgin of Guadalupe, a fluid mirror of both Aztec and Catholic heritage, thus establishing an indigenous people as coequal bearers of *imago dei*. Cinematic images such as these are not neutral; they make visible the cultural memory that the indigenous societies were not merely swept away by the Spanish conquest but had, in some measure, endured. They serve to liberate the postcolonial imagination so that the subjugated culture can recast itself as a resilient survivor, not a mere passive victim, of the sentence of colonial history.

Bibliography

Beltran, B. (1987) *The Christology of the Inarticulate: An Inquiry into the Filipino Understanding of Jesus Christ*, Manila: Divine Word.

Brading, D. A. (2001) *Mexican Phoenix: Our Lady of Guadalupe, Image and Tradition across Five Centuries*, Cambridge: Cambridge University Press.

Carrasco, D. (1990) *Religions of Mesoamerica*, New York: HarperCollins.

Gabriel, T. (1989) "Third Cinema as Guardian of Popular Memory: Towards a Third Aesthetics," in J. Pines and P. Willemen (eds) *Questions of Third Cinema*, London: British Film Institute.

Gruzinski, S. (2001) *Images at War: Mexico from Columbus to Blade Runner (1492–2019)*, Durham, NC: Duke University Press.

Hiebert, P., Shaw, R. D., and Tiénou, T. (1999) *Understanding Folk Religion: A Christian Response to Popular Beliefs and Practices*, Grand Rapids, MI: Baker Books.

Lacaba, J. F. (ed.) (2000) *The Films of ASEAN*, Pasig: ASEAN Committee on Culture and Information.

Mesa, J. de (2000) "Primal Religion and Popular Religiosity," *East Asian Pastoral Review* 37 (1).

Osborne, H. (1952) *Indians of the Andes: Aymaras and Quechuas*, Cambridge, MA: Harvard University Press.

Phelan, J. L. (1959) *The Hispanization of the Philippines: Spanish Aims and Filipino Responses 1565–1700*, Madison: University of Wisconsin Press.

Rodriguez, J. and Fortier, T. (2007) *Cultural Memory: Resistance, Faith, and Identity*, Austin: University of Texas Press.

Schreiter, R. (1985) *Constructing Local Theologies*, Maryknoll, NY: Orbis Books.

—— (2004) *The New Catholicity: Theology between the Global and the Local*, Maryknoll, NY: Orbis Books.

Sison, A. (2004) "Himala: The Temptress, the Virgin, and the Elusive Miracle," *Cross Currents* 54 (1).

—— (2006) *Screening Schillebeeckx: Theology and Third Cinema in Dialogue*, New York: Palgrave Macmillan.

Filmography

El Crimen del Padre Amaro (2002, dir. C. Carrera)

Guadalupe (2007, dir. S. Parras)

Himala (1982, dir. I. Bernal)

Madeinusa (2006, dir. C. Llosa)

Nuevo Mundo (1978, dir. G. Retes)

Rashomon (1950, dir. A. Kurosawa)

Salome (1981, dir. L. Guillen)

Santa Santita (2004, dir. L. Guillen)

Tanging Yaman (2000, dir. L. Guillen)

La Virgen de Guadalupe (1976, dir. A. Salazar)

11

RELIGION IN JAPANESE FILM: FOCUS ON *ANIME*

Jolyon Baraka Thomas

Introduction

Audiences and directors of Japanese film play a significant role in the generation, adulteration, and maintenance of religious concepts, narratives, and ideologies. Religions in Japan have been using film to create propaganda at least since the early 1930s (Stalker 2008, 130–9), and superficially "secular" film has also served as a site for the perpetuation of religious characters and imagery throughout Japanese filmic history. Films have related Buddhist-influenced ghost stories and fables (such as Mizoguchi Kenji's 1953 film *Ugetsu* [*Tales of Moonlight and Rain*] or Shindō Kaneto's 1964 thriller *Onibaba* [*Demon Hag*]), folk beliefs (Akira Kurosawa's 1990 *Yume* [*Dreams*]), hagiographies of famous religious figures (Takita Yōjirō's 2001 *Onmyōji* [*Yin-yang Diviner*], the story of Abe no Seimei), satirical commentary on religion (Itami Jūzō's 1984 *Osōshiki* [*The Funeral*]), and documentary (Mori Tatsuya's 1998 film A, on the membership of Aum Shinrikyō).

Anime, or animated film, is a Japanese entertainment mainstay and primary cultural export with a demonstrable ability to attract and inspire audiences domestically and worldwide. A growing body of journalism has praised the global influence of the medium, and the successes of acclaimed directors such as Miyazaki Hayao (*Princess Mononoke* (1997), *Spirited Away* (2001)) and Kon Satoshi (*Paprika* (2006)) have mitigated conservative tendencies to disregard *anime* as frivolous or puerile. Recently, a handful of academic publications have approached *anime* as a legitimate subject of study (Napier 2005; Drazen 2003; MacWilliams 2008), but in the field of religion much work remains to be done on this influential genre.

Japanese film in general and *anime* in particular deserve scholarly attention in relationship to religion for several reasons. The willing suspension of disbelief inherent in the act of viewing film is just as easily characterized by the voluntary (if temporary) assumption of an attitude of belief, and this quality is enhanced in *anime* by the fact that audiences of both religious art and *anime* interpret illustrated images as reality. Films include religious themes and can also serve as sites for religious practice and ritual (Grimes 2002; Lutgendorf 2003); this is presumably evident in the ritual elements of *anime* culture such as fan conventions and costume play. Filmic lessons and the practice of viewing film influence worldviews and lifestyles (Plate 2003: 5), and the popularity of *anime* across demographics suggests that it has the potential to shape present and future views of religion in Japan. Furthermore, international *anime* fandom is a case study of local religious ideas being disseminated to a global audience; *anime* also incorporates – and therefore introduces local audiences to – foreign religious concepts.

A comprehensive study of religion in Japanese film (*anime*, in this case) will examine connections with local traditional religions and will also account for the existence of emergent religions in fan culture. Japanese religions such as Buddhism and Shinto are easily recognizable in film because of their historic longevity, and contemporary Japanese films make expedient use of concepts, vocabulary, and imagery from these traditions as well as from foreign religious traditions. However, religious themes in film may include satire and irreverence as much as veneration. Knowledge of Japanese attitudes toward religion helps to parse these phenomena.

Japanese attitudes toward religion

There are problems of definition and perception related to the word "religion" (*shūkyō*) in Japan. Statistically the majority of Japanese people deny any affiliation with religion or any claim to a specific faith (or will acknowledge a familial – but not a personal – connection with a particular denomination). Conversely, religions regularly report rather skewed statistics about their membership, meaning that the aggregate number of adherents as reported by religious institutions regularly exceeds the total population of Japan by a significant amount (Reader 1991: 5–7).

Petitions for "practical benefits" such as healing, academic success, or traffic safety comprise the fundamental orientations of Japanese religious practice (Reader and Tanabe 1998). When researchers examine regular participation in activities that are apparently "religious," it becomes clear that the majority of Japanese people take part in at least some of the following: annual visits to shrines, visits to temples and gravesites for memorial purposes, attendance at festivals derived from or associated with the worship of a particular deity, or payment of money for amulets, talismans, or ritual services at Shinto shrines or Buddhist temples. Pilgrimages to shrines and temples form a large part of domestic tourism (Reader 2005), and nearly always include some sort of evidently "religious" practice such as bowing, clapping, praying, and purchasing votive tablets (*ema*) or oracle lots (*omikuji*) in addition to sightseeing. Furthermore, although many Japanese claim not to be affiliated with any particular religion, a significant percentage of the population professes belief in *kami*, buddhas or bodhisattvas, or ancestral spirits (Yumiyama 1994).

The discrepancies between claims to affiliation, belief, and ritual practice can be explained by the fact that for many Japanese people "religion" implies allegiance – an attitude that has traditionally been marginal to Japanese religious practice and experience (Reader 1991: 13–14). Historically, Japanese people have participated in religion through ritual activity, narrative, and loose affiliations based on devotion to a particular deity or geographically determined and familial affiliations with a particular shrine or temple. Thus, ritual practices such as festivals or pilgrimage are more frequently deemed "culture," "tradition," or "habit" than "religion" in popular discourse.

However, despite contemporary Japanese claims to secularism, nostalgia for an earlier, more religious time forms an integral part of media depictions of popular pilgrimage routes and historic temple sites (Reader 2007). Interest in religious information can be seen in the popularity of television programs centered on divination and shamanic practices (Dorman 2007; Hamada 2006). The popularity of *seishin sekai* (spirit world) literature (roughly equivalent to "New Age" and other "spirituality" literature; see Shimazono 2004: 293–305; 2007a; 2007b) also attests to this. The diversification of religious thought into new media in the information age is manifest in internet-based worship practices (Fujiu 2007) and religions' use of electronic media to gain or retain adherents (Ishii 1996; 2004).

Overview of Japanese religious traditions

There is greater diversity in the Japanese religious world than indicated by most introductory texts on the subject. On the surface, the two seemingly monolithic traditions of Buddhism and Shinto dominate Japanese religious life and operate through an apparent division of labor that has led to the popular dictum "born Shinto, die Buddhist" (Reader 1991: 55–106). Yet these religions harbor a great deal of variety. For example, many Buddhist denominations exist (such as the Tendai, Shingon, Nichiren, Jōdo, Shin, Rinzai, and Sōtō schools), and within these denominations a number of factions have arisen. Similarly, there are several schools of Shinto, including some "new religions" like Tenrikyō. Even within the mainstream Shinto overseen by the Association of Shinto Shrines (Jinja Honchō) there are significant divisions regarding the place of particular deities within the Shinto pantheon that are predicated on divergent readings of the classics *Kojiki* and *Nihon shoki* and on differences in the origin stories and geography of particular shrines (Inoue N. 2003).

Conversely, the categories of "new religions" (*shinshūkyō*) and "new new religions" (*shin shinshūkyō*) obfuscate the continuities between these groups and Buddhism and Shinto. These categories can harbor religious elitism that equates historic longevity with legitimacy, and are only useful when contrasted with more carefully articulated terminology for "traditional" religions (such as "Temple Buddhism" or "Shrine Shinto") that point to salient differences in the groups' organizational structure. Additionally, the somewhat pejorative term *shinkō shūkyo* ("new fad religions") is often used in popular discourse to refer to groups that have developed relatively recently, as is the unmistakably derogatory term "cult." Christianity has had a tenuous history in Japan and Christians form a very small but somewhat influential minority in the country; other world religions (Islam, Judaism, Hinduism), while present, have minimal influence and visibility.

Shinto

Shinto is popularly conceptualized as the "indigenous" religion of Japan, but a large number of foreign elements have been incorporated into the tradition, including Daoism, geomancy, and Yin-Yang divination and theories of the Five Elements (*in'yō gogyō setsu*). Historically, Shinto shrines and Buddhist temples were closely related, sometimes being managed by the same priest (called a *shasō* or *bettō*); this conflation of Buddhism and Shinto based upon theories of (native) deities (*kami*) as manifestations of (foreign) buddhas and bodhisattvas continued until the Meiji government forced the separation of Buddhism from Shinto in the late 1860s. The Edo period (1600–1868) Nativist (*kokugaku*) push to elucidate the origins of Shinto and to establish a Shinto tradition in contradistinction to Buddhism and to Confucian thought resulted in the reconceptualization of Shinto as a unified religious system endemic to Japan, and provided the backdrop for the emergence of modern State Shinto in the late nineteenth century. Central to State Shinto thought is the notion of the emperor as the divine descendant of the sun deity Amaterasu and of Japan as a divine nation, concepts that partially contributed to Japanese militarism in the early twentieth century.

Japan's defeat in the Second World War led to the temporary suppression of Shinto by occupation forces, but the Association of Shinto Shrines was created in February 1946 to serve as an umbrella institution for most shrines in Japan and abroad today. Shrines serve as sites for the year-round cycle of festivals as well as for coming of age rituals, weddings, ritual purifications (*oharae*), and petitions for divine assistance. Many companies have their own shrines, and Shinto priests (*kannushi*) are regularly called upon for groundbreaking pacification rituals (*jichinsai*) for private homes and public buildings. Public debates about the constitutionality of the controversial Yasukuni Shrine (where millions of war dead are enshrined, some against their will or against the wills of their survivors) and the appropriateness of a female imperial heir keep Shinto in Japanese public consciousness. "Ancient Shinto" and "animism" have also surfaced as popular themes in recent years (Shimazono 2006: 227); these themes frequently appear in Japanese film.

Shinto and film

Deities in Shinto are known as *kami* and are often associated with natural phenomena. Anthropomorphic representations of *kami* are relatively rare in comparison to Buddhism, but many shrines house a *shintai*, an object that represents the *kami* (frequently a mirror). In *anime*, *kami* have featured in films such as Miyazaki Hayao's *Sen to Chihiro no kamikakushi* (*Spirited Away*) (see Yamanaka 2008). The protagonist interacts with several *kami* in the film, including two river deities whose natural habitats have been polluted or dammed by humans; this can be traced to traditional Shinto concepts of purity and pollution (Boyd and Nishimura 2004).

Sacred space is demarcated in Shinto with several symbols that often appear in film: the *shimenawa*, a hempen braided or twisted rope that is often adorned with zigzag paper streamers known as *shide*, the *torii* sacred arch, or a *himorogi* (a provisional worship space created with branches of green bamboo or *sakaki*). Shrine precincts, known as *keidai*, are generally filled with trees even in urban areas, perhaps one reason for popular conceptions of Shinto reverence for nature. Practices related to Shinto that may appear in film include purifications performed with *ōnusa* (ritual wands festooned with paper streamers), spirit possession (usually of a female medium), and intercessory incantations.

Buddhism

Buddhism was introduced to Japan around the late sixth century, and the religion was quickly aligned with the state. Buddhist institutions historically served bureaucratic (census-taking) and thaumaturgical functions (spells for the protection of the nation, for example) as well as soteriological ones. A great deal of traditional Japanese art and literature finds its origin in Buddhism, and as educational centers temples contributed significantly to Japan's relatively high literacy rate in the Edo period. Buddhism is thus highly respected as a repository of Japanese culture, and Buddhist temples are popular tourist destinations today.

However, because of their association with expensive mortuary and memorial rites, Buddhist denominations have been critiqued as avaricious and morbid. The lax interpretation of Buddhist precepts taken by most sects and their priests (most Japanese priests eat meat, marry, and have children) have also led to critiques of Buddhism as degenerate, and declining popular interest in Buddhist teachings has led some critics to decry the religion as moribund. Despite these critiques, the vast majority of people still rely on Buddhist institutions for funerals and memorial rites, and temples and priests provide ritual purification or petitions for divine intercession in worldly affairs (Covell 2005). Popular print and visual media related to Buddhism also abound (Shimazono 2006: 226; Tanabe 2004).

Japanese Buddhism in film

Temples are often represented as eerie in film because of their association with funerary and memorial rites. Satirical images of avaricious priests are common, but positive depictions of miracle-working priests such as the eponymous protagonist of the video series *Kujakuō* (e.g., the 1994 *Shin Kujakuō*) also occur. Buddhist statuary features quite prominently in film, and statues of Jizō (a bodhisattva known for liberating people from hells and for his protection of travelers and children) are particularly popular. In Miyazaki Hayao's *Tonari no Totoro* (*My Neighbor Totoro*, 1986), for example, the sisters Mei and Satsuki temporarily take shelter from a sudden rainstorm in a small *hokora* (shrine) and Satsuki offers a brief message of gratitude to this deity. Another popular image is of the Seven Gods of Good Fortune – a combination of Indian, Chinese, and local deities (Ebisu, Daikoku, Benzaiten, Hōtei, Bishamon, Fukurokuju, and Jurōjin) who ride in a ship filled with treasure; these deities appear in parodic form in the 1994 film *Heisei tanuki gassen ponpoko* (known in English simply as *Pom Poko*). Mountain-based ascetic practices (*shugendō*) may also appear in film. Buddhist images such as *mandala* also frequently appear.

New religions and Christianity

The guarantee of freedom of religion in the postwar period led to an explosion of new religious denominations. As mentioned above, new religions have generally derived from Buddhism and Shinto, so it is somewhat disingenuous to separate them from these older traditions. However, some of the new religions warrant this nomenclature because they exhibit a high level of eclecticism in doctrine and innovation in their organizational structures. Although they have been quite proactive in peace and educational movements, the popular image of new religions in general has been somewhat tainted by the aggressive proselytizing tactics taken by some groups, by the entry of some groups into politics (notably Sōka Gakkai and its association with the Kōmeitō [Clean Government Party]), and by the murder and terrorism perpetrated by the religion Aum Shinrikyō (the group that released sarin gas on the Tokyo subway system in 1995).

Christianity has never enjoyed broad popular support in Japan, although Christian groups have been significant players in humanitarian, welfare, and educational causes (Garon 1997). A large number of private schools and kindergartens are affiliated with Christian denominations, and between their influence and the exposure to Christianity through literature and Hollywood film, many Japanese people have some rudimentary familiarity with Christian tenets and beliefs. Many Japanese people participate in Christmas rituals such as gift giving, although rarely with any emphasis on Christian doctrine. Recent years have seen an explosion in the popularity of "chapel weddings," where couples exchange vows in Christian wedding ceremonies performed by freelance foreign ministers (who may not have sacerdotal credentials) in rental halls and hotels. It is difficult to gauge to what extent the aesthetic appeal of a chapel wedding or Christmas celebrations leads to increasing interest in Christian teachings per se, but Christians currently comprise only about 1 percent of the Japanese population.

Christianity and new religions in film

Popular critique of "cults" occasionally appears in film, as do satirical depictions of new religions as fronts for profiteering scam artists. In the 2006 film *Tekkon Kincrete*, for example, the local mob boss runs his seedy organization from the offices of the "Daiseishinkai" (Great Spirit Association). Christian images like crosses appear in films as well, although Christian imagery is rarely explicitly associated with Christian teachings and is often used more for its exotic appeal than to inculcate belief or evoke religious sentiment. As one example, the televised *anime* adaptation of the popular *manga D. Gray-man* is replete with Christian vocabulary and imagery, but it is used in a cavalier fashion and strays from traditional Christian doctrine. Reference to a singular, omnipotent deity (a concept generally foreign to Japan) also occurs with some frequency in *anime*.

Previous scholarship on *anime* and religion

The few studies of *anime* and religion conducted thus far have largely been of questionable quality for several interrelated reasons. The most obvious of these is the blurring of fandom with scholarship: many writers on *anime* in general have struggled to maintain sufficient critical distance from their subject of study, and scholars have often and necessarily relied on the (not unbiased) insider expertise of so-called *otaku* (geek) informants for their studies. Sociological studies have provided quantitative data on participation in *anime* culture, but have rarely offered qualitative presentations of whether and how participants perceive their *anime*-centric practices as religious. Within disciplines related to cultural studies (including literature and film studies), most examinations of religious thought in *anime* utilize structuralist literary critical methods that are predicated upon the search for "original" or ancient religious stories or themes; despite their emphasis on origins these studies are often ahistorical. Although these approaches may be helpful and indispensable to the study of *anime*, using them alone can result in oversimplification of the specifically religious elements of the film in question.

Non-Japanese fandom and scholarship

Audiences outside of East Asia have tended to be exposed to *anime* first and to *manga* (illustrated serial novels) secondarily, meaning that non-Japanese (particularly Western) audiences generally encounter redacted and simplified *anime* storylines more than the relatively complex *manga* from which most *anime* derive. There are problems of translation and interpretation as well: a vigorous Internet-based community revolving around the creation and exchange of "fansubs" (*anime* that are given subtitles by devoted fans) and "scanlations" (scanned *manga* that are given English text) exists, but the credentials of the translators and the quality of their translations are suspect. Some of the interpretation of nuances in stories is similarly dubious. North American publishers do release officially authorized subtitled or overdubbed versions of popular series, but they occasionally choose to redact scenes or terminology that are deemed unsuitable for their audiences.

Some Japanese critics suggest (speciously, in my opinion) that non-Japanese audiences are incapable of understanding the medium and its uniquely Japanese perspective on religion (e.g., Inoue S. 2004: 100). However, while non-Japanese audiences may not fully appreciate references to themes in Japanese religious literature, *anime* clearly retains international appeal and seems to incite apparently "religious" responses in international audiences (Napier 2006). The element of exoticism in some non-Japanese *anime* fan culture, however, should not be overlooked. Like the tropes of "Zen," "Shinto," and "animism" in commercials and other popular literature outside of Japan, fetishistic versions of allegedly indigenous, pristine Japanese religions sometimes appear in fan commentary and in scholarship (Schrader 2007, for example). Also, Judeo-Christian assumptions regarding religion influence interpretations of Buddhism and Shinto, and these traditions can become grossly oversimplified even in commentaries that are otherwise academically rigorous.

Literary criticism

Literary critical methods and textual analytical approaches are often relatively ahistorical, and thus their proclamations regarding the provenance of certain apparently religious themes may neglect to situate the doctrine or thought in question specifically at a point in history, leading to distorted representations of an allegedly original and reified religious concept or practice being perpetuated or reinvigorated in *anime* (e.g., Drazen 2003: 142–68; Pandey 2008). Few writers on religion in *anime* have sufficient knowledge of the Buddhist textual tradition to make significant pronouncements on the provenance of allegedly Buddhist themes in *anime*, and unfortunately Shinto is too frequently used as a catchall term for ostensibly indigenous (and therefore presumably unsullied) practices and beliefs. At their most egregious, studies that attempt to utilize Buddhism and Shinto as backgrounds for contemporary *anime* betray their authors' ignorance of the religious traditions in question.

Psychoanalytic tendencies

Literary critical approaches also emphasize psychoanalytic interpretations of allegedly religious tropes that may or may not have significant connection with the producer or audience in question. Susan J. Napier's (2005) categories of "apocalypse," "carnival," and "elegy," for example, may not resonate with the producers and consumers of *anime*, and without extensive ethnographic study the various perspectives of these important agents are elided if not omitted entirely. To her credit, Napier has done extensive ethnographic work among an international group of fans since, although this still begs the question of whether the aforementioned categories apply to Japan (see Napier 2006). Words like "spiritual" and "identity" are also frequently used without definition as placeholders for a range of concepts that may or may not have to do with religion, and thus serve as convenient rhetorical devices for academics to avoid the actual matters at stake (soteriology, existential crisis, psychosis, social malady; a quintessential example is Yamanaka 2008). The usage of vague categories such as "spiritual" to describe the experience of *anime* by an overly generalized, monolithic vision of the Japanese people does not allow for diversity in experience or interpretation.

Perceived and actual audiences

Unfortunately, most studies of *anime* and religion to date have neglected any serious consideration of how audiences might perceive the religiosity of the films, including the very high probability that audiences – particularly Japanese audiences – would ignore, downplay, or overlook references to "religion" due to problems of definition and perception of the word as described above. Thus, the zeal for tracing themes in *anime* back to the doctrines of Japanese religions like Buddhism and Shinto betrays a tendency to overlook the fact that producers and their audiences may only be passively aware of such doctrines. Audiences may likely deny any allegiance to these religions even if they do express casual or even fervent interest in these religions' teachings and practices.

Sociological and anthropological approaches

In contrast to literary critical and psychoanalytic approaches, anthropological and sociological analyses of religion and *anime* (with predominantly ethnographic and demographic orientations, respectively) tend toward synchronic "snapshot" depictions of their subject. These studies are obviously helpful in generating quantitative data, but have difficulty elucidating changes in religious thought over time. Additionally, sociological approaches to religion – especially in Japan – inherit a strongly Marxist bias that tends to treat religion as the byproduct of economic or political processes. The same bias gives perhaps too much credence to theories of secularization, which posit that religion is or will be the victim of processes like industrialization and urbanization – predictions that have not been borne out historically. Despite low claims to belief or affiliation, Japanese participation in religious activities remains strong, and the diversification of religion through new media channels is robust (Ishii 2004). Sociological studies of *anime* culture and religion thus struggle with the facts that: (1) religious doctrines and communities change; and (2) change does not necessarily demand or imply the demise of religion.

The secularization model assumed by the sociologists, while problematic, has positively contributed to understandings of how the production and consumption of religious thought has transferred from formal religious institutions to popular culture sites, and the role of media in religion has been addressed to an increasing degree (Ishii 1996; 2004). Sociological studies are also beginning to indicate that visual media such as *manga*, *anime*, and video games may be contributing to the preservation – not just adulteration – of religious information in the minds of young people (Hirafuji 2007). Additionally, sociologists have been helpful in recognizing how religious thought in *anime* has had recognizable influence on specific subcultures. Ōsawa Masachi, for example, indicated that the *manga* and *anime Kaze no Tani no Naushika* (*Naushika of the Valley of the Wind*) contributed to the religious thought of Aum Shinrikyō, the group responsible for the 1995 sarin gas attack on the Tokyo subway system (Ōsawa 1996: 93–7).

Religious studies

The academic study of religion simultaneously embraces synchronic and diachronic approaches to its subject and refuses to make religion a mere side effect of economic or political action. Studies of *anime* and religion conducted by people trained in this discipline remain the minority; this minority is also not above reproach. Masaki Akira's treatments of religious themes in Miyazaki Hayao's films (2001; 2002), for example, harbor serious methodological problems in their lack of chronological and thematic structure. Experts in Japanese religion have rarely deigned to study *anime* directly, and usually only refer to *manga* and *anime* obliquely (if at all). Some do so pejoratively (Gardner 2008).

There has been little research published on the presumably rich field of ritual studies in relationship to *anime*, despite the seemingly obvious ritual dimensions of *cosupure* (cosplay, an abbreviation of the words "costume play") activities among fan groups. With a very small number of exceptions (Thomas 2007; 2008) few people have addressed the possibility that *anime* and related genres of visual media might not only contain, but also might be (or function as), religion. Like films, religions rely upon audiences (formal adherents and the casually curious) for their dissemination and for their continued existence, and thus studies of the interactions between film and religion must address the fact that these audiences often overlap.

The history and stylistic characteristics of religious *anime*

I have partially dealt with the problem of treating audience responses to religious content in *anime* elsewhere (Thomas 2007). Here I set that particular issue aside in favor of a cursory overview of the religious context in which Japanese *anime* of the late twentieth and early twenty-first century has arisen. I also provide some analytic tools for analyzing the religiosity of *anime* vis-à-vis existing religious traditions, audience responses, and producer intentionality.

The usage of fiction and illustration to relate religious motifs has been common throughout Japanese religious history in various media. Examples include *emaki* (picture scrolls), *etoki* (picture-based sermons), *kibyōshi* (Edo-period illustrated novels), and *kamishibai* (oral performances of stories accompanied by picture cards successively slotted into a wooden frame). These various visual-verbal media have contributed to the spread of religious beliefs and practices, and have served as sites for satire and expropriation of religious themes from medieval times through the present (Kaminishi 2006: 193).

Medieval and early modern visual-verbal religious entertainment

The religious artwork and drama of premodern Japan served multiple functions simultaneously: it was entertaining, aesthetically pleasing, and soteriological. Pictures alone are not always worth a thousand words, and frequently these media were accompanied by captions, written explanations, or the performative element of a recited script. Itinerant preachers and nuns known as *etoki*, for example, utilized picture scrolls to supplement their storytelling for fundraising, proselytizing, and the generation of merit among their audiences (Ruch 2002; Kaminishi 2006). The juxtaposition of image and narrative helped to create a shared visual-verbal religious vocabulary among the laity, assisting in the dissemination of religious ideas. Illustrated miracle stories associated with a particular shrine or temple, for example, popularized belief in the efficacy of that location for providing a specific worldly benefit.

Edo-period *kibyōshi* also frequently included eerie tales of ghosts, satirical portraits of pompous preachers, and guidebooks to nominally religious destinations like pilgrimage sites that included sexual titillation and hilarity (Kern 2006:112, 97–8, 104). Buddhist-inspired moralistic storytales known as *sekkyōbushi* (sermon-ballads) of late Edo were also often accompanied by visual aids. This genre eventually gave rise to modern *kamishibai*, which formed a popular mode of visual-verbal entertainment in the early twentieth century and often included supernatural themes (Kata 2004: 3–9). These media gave way to modern *manga* and television in the postwar period, and some *kamishibai* illustrators moved to the production of *manga*, and – eventually – *anime* with similar themes (Schodt 1996: 177–82).

Manga *and* anime

Most studies of *anime* thus far have failed to look at the storylines of the *manga* upon which nearly 90 percent of *anime* are based (Berndt 2008: 297). This is problematic because audiences in Japan approach *anime* with background knowledge of the story that counterbalances the narrative redaction that inevitably takes place when *manga* storylines are transformed into *anime*. *Anime* have also inherited significant stylistic influence from *manga*, and thus understanding the relationship between these media (and between these media and religion) is crucial to understanding how *anime* might lend themselves to the treatment of religious themes or how they might act as sites for religious or ritual practice.

Manga are illustrated serial novels that are published in installments of around twenty pages in weekly or monthly magazines. These chapters are periodically compiled into hardback or paperback books and sold as single volumes, and a full set may run into several tens of volumes. Popular *manga* are often transformed into *anime*, and usually *anime* versions of *manga* storylines (especially those created for theater) are heavily redacted to fit the complexity of the story into a suitable time limit dictated by the attention span of an audience. A small number of *anime* that are not based upon *manga* are created directly for theater screenings, produced as serialized television programs, or made as direct-to-video works (called OVAs, "original video animation"). *Manga* are also turned into live action films, such as the immensely popular *Deathnote* (2006) and *Twentieth Century Boys* (2008). However, the transition to photography and film may diminish the inherent ability of illustration to represent the supernatural.

The power of illustration and *manga* and *anime* stylistic conventions

As modern iterations of religious illustrated fiction, *manga* are effective because they use cinematic techniques such as close-ups, panning, and the utilization of frames to situate static images on a diachronic narrative timeline. They use hyperbole, synecdoche, a combination of perspectives, and onomatopoeia to make a primarily visual experience an effectively multisensory one (Natsume 1997: 80–96). Scenes where images predominate allow artists to illustrate internal states and otherwise ineffable experiences, and iconic representation in *manga* heightens vicarious experience, conflating the personality of the viewer and the protagonist (McCloud 1993: 35–45). *Anime* inherits these techniques (such as scenes where the background disappears to draw attention to the protagonist's emotional state; see Drazen 2003: 21), resulting in a unique artistic form that is qualitatively different from European and North American animation (Poitras 2008: 62–3).

Illustrated images depict, but they also imagine and exaggerate. *Manga* and *anime* provide the illusion of juxtaposed static images as images in motion, making these media particularly appropriate for representing magic, miracles, apotheosis, enlightenment, or any other number of events or experiences related to religion. They also lend themselves to religious reception, since art and religion share a willingness to interpret illustrated images as reality (Gimello 2004). It is thus no surprise that religious groups would elect to utilize *anime* as a medium for proselytizing, nor is it surprising that lay directors would utilize religious imagery and concepts in their creations.

Types of religious *anime*

The development of contemporary religious thought happens not only in statements of belief or in cosmological or soteriological assertions, but also in satire, in the adulteration of traditional religious concepts for pecuniary or entertaining purposes, and in explorations of the meaning and end of divinity in the information age. The relationship between *anime* and religion is characterized by religions' use of *anime* for didactic purposes, by lay authors' and directors' use of religious themes for aesthetic purposes, by audiences' canonization of particular works (a "cult classic"), or in the adoption of those works for ritual purposes.

Broadly speaking, religious narratives can be arranged into two main types: aesthetic and didactic. Didactic products are those designed specifically to introduce audiences to religious information or information about religions, or to convert or instruct on religious doctrine. Aesthetic products, on the other hand, utilize religious vocabulary and imagery to promote affective responses ranging from casual diversion to strong conviction; sometimes these products incidentally give rise to religious sentiment or practice. Obviously there is some overlap between these types, and some products fully combine aesthetic and didactic elements, creating a third category that I label "emotive." Emotive products are characterized by heightened emotional response accompanied by refinements in intellectual, ethical, or moral orientations; they also sponsor canonization and ritual practices.

Within these three categories, I draw further subdivisions: aesthetic products include works that utilize religious vocabulary and imagery as well as occult products such as horror films; didactic products include proselytizing videos and similar institutional propaganda. Emotive products include personally inspiring works that effect changes in lifestyle or behavior, and products that eventually become canonized by formal religious groups or fan groups that are quasi-religious (groups that have not legally incorporated as religions but that venerate, canonize, or use a film in a liturgical fashion). These categories can be arranged on a continuum in terms of these responses, from boredom to ritual activity and belief – aesthetic usage of religion rarely invites fervent belief but may educe curiosity, and didactic products presumably aim to inculcate belief but may become sententious and therefore boring. In what follows, I offer a very brief case study of *anime* representative of each of these types; note that a crucial element of the categorization of a work as "emotive" has to do with observable audience responses to the material that can be deemed religious or ritualistic.

Aesthetic uses of religious concepts and themes

Religious traditions and stories provide a wealth of information about supernatural abilities and events, and thus form one of the most expedient narrative devices for equipping protagonists or antagonists with exceptional abilities (magic, superpowers) or overwhelming crises (apocalypse). *Anime* that use religious themes and concepts primarily for aesthetic purposes may also question the category of religion.

Serial Experiments: Lain

Serial Experiments: Lain is a serialized *anime* that was televised for several months in 1998 (see Napier 2007). The film traces religious themes through the story of the existential crisis and eventual apotheosis of a young girl, Iwakura Lain, who gradually discovers that she maintains an existence simultaneously in the "real" world and in the "Wired" – the communications network that blankets the near-future world in which Lain lives. Lain's wired avatar is autonomous and audacious where the embodied Lain is not. Fearful of this new brash version of herself at first, Lain learns to embrace and eventually to control it. The Wired Lain grows increasingly powerful, outperforming the most skillful hackers and breaking down the barriers between perceived reality and the Wired, which has merged with the collective subconscious. Lain performs miraculous displays such as appearing in the clouds above Tokyo, and her ability to control events within and outside of the Wired leads to her apotheosis – through the technology of the Wired she is nearly omniscient, nearly omnipotent, and nearly omnipresent.

Late in the narrative Lain confronts "God," actually a human computer programmer who built himself into the Wired as an omniscient presence. Lain's own apotheosis nears completion when she destroys this would-be deity. However, Lain retains anxieties about her ability to relate to other human beings, particularly her schoolmate Arisu. She decides that she will remove herself from reality in order to protect others from her nearly limitless power, resigned to a wandering existence as her consciousness floats in the nebulous realm of the Wired.

Films like *Lain* and *Kōkaku kidōtai* (*Ghost in the Shell*) question the category of religion through explorations of the possibility of apotheosis through technology. Films that incorporate the miraculous and the magical also make aesthetic usage of religious material, and some films also revamp older religious stories for new generations of audiences. A large number of *anime* include religious themes such as these without intentionally inculcating religious sentiment; films that attempt to educe such sentiment form a small but intriguing minority.

Didactic introductions to religious material

Like earlier religious didactic media, some *anime* aim to simultaneously entertain and instruct, although instruction takes precedence. Several groups (including Aum Shinrikyō and Shinrankai) have made such films, although animators who have worked on such projects complain about the tensions between doctrinal restrictions and artistic license (Okada 1997). Didactic *anime* thus run the risk of being perceived as pedantic, undermining their effectiveness as modes of entertainment.

Eien no hō

Eien no hō (*The Laws of Eternity*) is an *anime* created by Kōfuku no Kagaku, a group known internationally as the Institute for Research in Human Happiness (IRH) and more recently as "Happy Science." The movie debuted in Japan in 2006 under heavy media promotion, and utilized famous voice actors and high standards of production. In the story, Ryūta, Yūko, Roberto, and Patrick receive a mysterious message through a spirit medium from the spirit of Thomas Edison, build a "spirit phone" to contact the world of the spirits (*reikai*), and embark on an adventure through several dimensions. They tour through various heavens (where they meet Edison and Helen Keller, among others) and hells where Nietzsche and Hitler reside. The movie explains Kōfuku no Kagaku cosmology and moralizes as Ryūta and the others discover the "Truth" of the existence of the spirit world and reincarnation.

The movie includes Ryūta's heroic battles with the forces of evil, Yūko's unwavering devotion to Ryūta, and Roberto and Patrick as foils for the two. Patrick plays the role of the scientific skeptic who is gradually persuaded that the "spirit world" exists; Roberto's bumbling enthusiasm and attachment to success highlight his spiritual immaturity. Eventually the jealousy these two harbor for Ryūta and Yūko land them in hell. After Ryūta and Yūko heroically save their blundering companions, they travel to the ninth dimension and realize that they are "soulmates" who have been bonded throughout generations, from the lost continent of Atlantis to the present.

It is difficult to determine the extent to which films like *Eien no hō* have contributed to the popularity or growth in membership of Kōfuku no Kagaku domestically or abroad. Like other didactic films, *Eien no hō* borders on sententiousness; it may invite boredom or apathy as easily as curiosity or belief. The usage of the *anime* medium alone is not a guarantee of narrative success, nor will the creation of *anime* necessarily attract new adherents to a religion. Nevertheless, the superb technical execution of this film reflects the group's investment in the film and its message.

Emotive

The most powerful literature and drama generally fuse the didactic and aesthetic elements of storytelling. When these elements are combined particularly well, they can give rise to religious audience responses such as canonization, exegesis, ritual behavior, veneration of the author, director, or characters, and belief. These works may be incorporated into the liturgies or canons of established religious groups or may give rise to religious or quasi-religious groups of fans.

Emotive *anime* may prompt conversion experiences. For example, some fans of the OVA film series *Kujakuō* (the story of a Buddhist priest who performs exorcisms and battles the forces of evil) decided to take the tonsure in the Shingon denomination of Buddhism due to their admiration of its protagonist (Yumiyama *et. al.*, 2003: 16). Emotive *anime* may also serve as sites for repetitive and ritualized viewings (both in formally religious and casual settings) or as the basis for ritual activity such as costume play and reenactment. *Sailor Moon* fans, for example, have utilized Hikawa Jinja in Tokyo as a site for ritual practice related to the series (ISHII 1996: 205). Emotive *anime* also serve as lifestyle guides for individuals; many individuals have become more sensitive to environmental issues due to the influence of Miyazaki Hayao's films, for example (Thomas 2007: 85–7). These films may also be the impetus for people to deepen their knowledge of a particular religious tradition.

Neon Genesis Evangelion

Anno Hideaki's *Shinseiki ebuangerion* (*Neon Genesis Evangelion*) began serialization on Japanese television in 1995. *Evangelion's* obscure plot has invited extended exegetical practice revolving around viewings and reviewings and has given birth to a devoted fan culture of cosplay and esoterica (Napier 2007: 108; Tada 1998: 139). The series draws heavily on religious themes, most notably Judeo-Christian vocabulary and imagery (crosses, "angels," and Kabbalistic concepts). These themes seem to have been intentionally used more for their exotic flavor than for didactic purposes (Tada 1998: 147–8; Okada 1997: 212). Yet despite the director's intentions or motivations, *Evangelion* sponsored a boom in interest in literature on the Dead Sea Scrolls, Kabbalah, and Christianity (Tada 1998: 139), and the exegetical focus of the fan culture made the film a "cult classic."

Emotive films may not intentionally elicit religious responses, and certainly not all audience members will respond to films in the same way. However, observable behaviors that are normally associated with religion (such as conversion, exegesis, and ritual) do arise around these media, distinguishing this category from more casual relationships between *anime* and religion. Emotive *anime* are also the products from which it is most likely that formalized new religious groups will emerge.

Religious anime

The vast majority of religious *anime* uses religious vocabulary and imagery in a cavalier fashion for aesthetic purposes; religion is an expedient narrative device that provides characters with magical powers or stories with apocalyptic settings. Yet formal religions use the medium to share their messages with a broader audience, and occasionally lay artists and directors create *anime* that intentionally or unintentionally elicit religious responses. These relationships remain largely unexplored, and in conclusion I offer some suggestions for future research.

Areas for future research

Studies of *anime* in general have been plagued by a host of problems, including tendencies to ignore the *manga* from which most *anime* derive, to assume that *anime* are broadly representative of Japan or Japanese culture (ignoring the specific demographics toward which a particular *anime* is marketed), and to celebrate *anime* as uniquely Japanese (ignoring the very important role that Euroamerican cinema and animation have played in the development of the genre and its obvious global appeal). Scholars are increasingly aware of these problems but have not sufficiently addressed them (Berndt 2008), and examinations of *anime* and religion conducted in the future should correct for them.

Additionally, Japanese religions are not monolithic. Buddhism varies greatly according to denomination and time period, and the oft-repeated popular critique of Japanese Buddhism as moribund or degenerate (inaccurate as it may be) should be kept in mind when apparently Buddhist themes appear in *anime*. Scholars should carefully observe the usage of superficially Buddhist themes to determine if they are pejorative, adulatory, or merely incidental. "Shinto" is often idealized in *anime*, as well as in scholarship on *anime*, as the repository of an allegedly pristine indigenous culture. This attitude overlooks the obvious foreign elements of Shinto, its long association with Buddhism (Kuroda 1993), and its association with militarism and colonialism in the early twentieth century. Scholars interested in writing about Shinto in *anime* must recognize directors' (and their own) nostalgia for a reified Shinto that may not have ever existed.

New religions have been quite proactive in utilizing *anime* for their propaganda, and studies of how these groups have used the *anime* medium are overdue. However, scholars should be aware of the popular tendency to utilize "new fad religions" (*shinkō shūkyō*) and "cults" (Jp. *karuto* – the pejorative word would be translated as "sect" in some parts of Europe) as foils for "ordinary" religions or for secular society – this happens in journalism, in some scholarship, and also within some *anime*. Since the Aum Shinrikyō sarin gas attack, *anime* and *manga* bore the brunt of scholarly and journalistic critique regarding Aum's extremism, and negative attitudes toward these media persist as a result (Gardner 2008).

On the subject of new religions, *anime* can and do serve as sites of emergent religion, and this is one area that deserves closer academic examination. In order to determine how audiences may be responding to the content of certain *anime* religiously, scholars must engage in more in-depth ethnography and studies of fan culture, particularly the ritual aspects of filmmaking, film viewing, and peripheral activities such as cosplay. Ritual studies as they relate to *anime* are especially important because of the recursive processes at work between (religious) ritual and performance in traditional Japanese theater like *nō* and *kabuki*.

There is also much critical work to be done on the received scholarship on *anime* and religion. To date, there is not a single book-length manuscript on the subject in Japanese or in English of scholarly quality in print; of the various articles and books that exist on *anime* in general, few deal with religion with any rigor (the author's MA thesis is one exception; see Thomas 2008). Future research might investigate the proclivities and predilections of scholarship on *anime* and religion as a means of elucidating some of the problems the field should seek to overcome.

Students interested in doing research projects on a particular *anime* and religion (and the instructors who may oversee such projects) should carefully evaluate their ability to avoid apologetic or uncritical treatments of their subject matter. However, it is clear that insiders in the culture of *anime* fandom have greater access to the intricacies of that culture and especially to its protean characteristics. Finding the balance between scholarly critique and insider expertise is a mark of conscientious scholarship, and these stances do not have to be mutually exclusive. However, they demand methodological precautions.

Methodological concerns

Scholars must be careful with definitions and classifications. The researcher should ask him- or herself if the definitions he or she is using reflect obvious biases or – more perniciously – obfuscate less obvious prejudices. Furthermore, carefully delineated categories will serve as one defense against critics who dismiss studies of *anime* as frivolous or apologetic.

Scholars should also balance historical approaches with ethnographic ones. The creation and consumption of *anime* does not take place in a cultural vacuum, and understanding the history and cultural milieu of the director and audience will improve any analysis. Reading widely on Japan will bring nuance to an argument about *anime*, just as reading widely on religion will provide greater understanding of religion in Japan. Do note, however, that studies of Japanese religion have historically been dominated by an area studies approach (no doubt a reflection of the significance of Japanese-language mastery to the field) and that scholarship on Japanese religion rarely moves outside of Japanese geographic or cultural boundaries. This latter point can be seen as an opportunity for future transnational research.

Anime and the fan cultures surrounding them are replete with slang and with technical jargon, and understanding the vocabulary and narrative tropes that appear in *anime* requires extensive linguistic training "on the ground" in Japan. This does not mean that studies of *anime* in translation are impossible, but there is a wealth of material that is inaccessible without proficiency in Japanese. Future studies should – to the extent possible – be in dialogue not only with Euroamerican writings on *anime* and religion but also with Japanese writings on the subject. I also highly recommend that students read the *manga* from which an *anime* derives – there is almost certainly subtlety to the narrative that is lost in the process of modifying it for film.

We must also beware of academic prejudice against studies of popular culture and of corresponding apologetic attitudes on the part of scholars who choose to study it. While there is a growing amount of scholarship on Japanese visual culture, a great deal of it is still conciliatory, adulatory, or occasionally obstreperous in tone. Studying *anime* is neither as marginal as it once was (the popularity of the genre in Japan and abroad has convinced most critics of its cultural power), nor is it as iconoclastic as scholars might like to think (historical studies of popular literature and drama are quite common – if there is innovation in the study of religion and film it lies in the willingness to observe connections between religion and vernacular fiction in the present). Provocative scholarship on *anime* need not rely solely on the ostensibly transgressive act of studying popular culture seriously. There are far more interesting questions (of aesthetics, of intended versus actual audience, and of production) that can be addressed when taking *anime* as a topic, and of course many of these have to do with religion.

Concluding remarks

The study of religion and Japanese film is still largely unexplored territory, and the subject of *anime* and religion in particular demands academic attention. As suggested above, scholars who undertake such studies will necessarily tackle knotty methodological issues. However, the net result will be scholarship of greater quality that contributes to understandings of traditional Japanese religions in their contemporary forms, of Japanese attitudes toward religion and religiosity, and of emergent religions centered upon Japanese media.

Bibliography

Berndt, J. (2008) "Considering Manga Discourse: Location, Ambiguity, Historicity," in M. MacWilliams (ed.) *Japanese Visual Culture: Explorations in the World of Manga and Anime*, Armonk, NY: M. E. Sharpe.

Boyd, J. and Nishimura, T. (2004) "Shinto Perspectives in Miyazaki's Anime Film 'Spirited Away,'" *Journal of Religion and Film* 8 (2). Online. Available HTTP: <www.unomaha.edu/jrf/Vol8No2/boydShinto.htm> (accessed 25 January 2005).

Covell, S. (2005) *Japanese Temple Buddhism: Worldliness in a Religion of Renunciation*, Honolulu: University of Hawai'i Press.

Dorman, B. (2007) "Representing Ancestor Worship as 'Non-Religious': Hosoki Kazuko's Divination in the Post-Aum Era," *Nova Religio* 10 (3).

Dorman, B. and Reader, I. (2007) "Projections and Representations of Religion in Japanese Media," *Nova Religio* 10 (3).

Drazen, P. (2003) *Anime Explosion: The What? Why? and Wow! of Japanese Animation*, Berkeley: Stone Bridge Press.

Fujiu A. (2007) "Netto sanpai no kankangakugaku" [Tensions Regarding Online Worship], *AERA* (Asahi Shinbun Extra Report and Analysis), 20 (10.

Gardner, R. (2008) "Aum Shinrikyō and a Panic About Manga and Anime," in M. MacWilliams (ed.) *Japanese Visual Culture: Explorations in the World of Manga and Anime*, Armonk, NY: M. E. Sharpe.

Garon, S. (1997) *Molding Japanese Minds: The State in Everyday Life*, Princeton: Princeton University Press.

Gimello, R. (2004) "Icon and Incantation: The Goddess Zhunti and the Role of Images in the Occult Buddhism of China," in P. Granoff and K. Shinohara (eds) *Images in Asian Religions: Text and Contexts*, Vancouver: University of British Columbia Press.

Grimes, R. (2002) "Ritual and the Media," in S. Hoover and L. Schofield Clark (eds) *Practicing Religion in the Age of the Media: Explorations in Media, Religion, and Culture*, New York: Columbia University Press.

Hamada Nami (2006) "Uranai nippon doko e iku" [Where is fortunetelling Japan headed?], *AERA* (Asahi Shinbun Extra Report and Analysis), 19 (9).

Hirafuji K. (2007) "Rōru pureingu gemu no naka no shinwagaku" [Mythology in Role Playing Games], in Watanabe N. (ed.) *Shūkyō to gendai ga wakaru hon 2007* [The 2007 Guide to Religion and the Present], Tokyo: Heibonsha.

Inoue N. (2003) "The Modern Age: Shinto Confronts Modernity," in Inoue N. (ed.), M. Teeuwen and J. Breen (trans.) *Shinto: A Short History*, London: Routledge.

Inoue S. (2004) *Miyazaki Hayao: eizō to shiso no renkinjutsushi* [Miyazaki Hayao: Alchemist of Image and Thought], Tokyo: Shakai Hihyōsha.

Ishii K. (1996) "Jōhōka to shūkyō" [The Information Age and Religion], in Shimazono S. and Ishii K. (eds) *Shōhi sareru "shūkyō"* [Consumed "Religion"], Tokyo: Shunjusha.

—— (2004) "Denshi media no kanōsei to shūkyō no yukue" [The Possibilities of Electronic Media and the Direction of Religion], in Ikegami Y. *et al.* (eds) *Shūkyō no yukue* [The Direction of Religion], Tokyo: Iwanami Shoten.

Kaminishi I. (2006) *Explaining Pictures: Buddhist Propaganda and Etoki Storytelling in Japan*, Honolulu: University of Hawai'i Press.

Kata K. (2004) *Kamishibai Shōwa shi*, Tokyo: Iwanami Shoten.

Kern, A. (2006) *Manga from the Floating World: Comicbook Culture and the Kibyōshi of Edo Japan*, Cambridge, MA: Harvard University Press.

Kuroda T. (1993) "Shinto in the History of Japanese Religion," in P. Swanson et al. (eds) *Religion and Society in Modern Japan*, Fremont, CA: Asian Humanities Press.

Lunning, F. (ed.) (2006) *Mechademia*, vol. 1, Minneapolis: University of Minnesota Press.

Lutgendorf, P. (2003) "*Jai Santoshi Maa* Revisited: On Seeing a Hindu 'Mythological' Film," in S. B. Plate (ed.) *Representing Religion in World Cinema: Filmmaking, Mythmaking, Culture Making*, New York: Palgrave Macmillan.

McCloud, S. (1993) *Understanding Comics: The Invisible Art*, New York: Harper Perennial with Kitchen Sink Books.

MacWilliams, M. (ed.) (2008) *Japanese Visual Culture: Explorations in the World of Manga and Anime*, Armonk, NY: M. E. Sharpe.

Masaki A. (2001) *Hajimete no shūkyōgaku: "Kaze no tani no Naushika" wo yomi toku* [Beginning Religious Studies: Reading "Naushika of the Valley of the Wind"], Tokyo: Shunjusha.

—— (2002) *Obake to mori no shūkyōgaku: tonari no totoro to issho ni manabō* [The Religious Studies of the Spirit and the Forest: Let's Learn along with our Neighbor Totoro], Tokyo: Shunjusha.

Napier, S. (2005 [2001]) *Anime from Akira to Howl's Moving Castle*, New York: Palgrave.

—— (2006) "The World of Anime Fandom in America," in F. Lunning (ed.) *Mechademia*, vol. 1, Minneapolis: University of Minnesota Press.

—— (2007) "When the Machines Stop: Fantasy, Reality, and Terminal Identity in *Neon Genesis Evangelion* and *Serial Experiments: Lain*," in C. Bolton et al. (eds) *Robot Ghosts and Wired Dreams: Japanese Science Fiction from Origins to Anime*, Minneapolis: University of Minnesota Press.

Natsume F. (1997) *Manga wa naze omoshiroi no ka: sono hyōgen to bunpō* [Why is Manga Interesting? Its Expression and Grammar], Tokyo: NHK.

Okada T. (1997) "Firumu wa ikiteiru ka? Moto Oumu animeetaa no kokuhaku" [Is Film Living? Confessions of a Former Aum Animator], *Quick Japan* 3.

Ōsawa M. (1996) *Kyokō no jidai no hate: Oumu to sekai saishū sensō* [The End of the Age of Fiction: Aum and the Final World War], Tokyo: Chikuma Shinsho.

Pandey, R. (2008) "Medieval Genealogies of Manga and Anime Horror," in M. MacWilliams (ed.) *Japanese Visual Culture: Explorations in the World of Manga and Anime*, Armonk, NY: M. E. Sharpe.

Plate, S. B. (2003) "Introduction: Filmmaking, Mythmaking, Culture Making," in S. B. Plate (ed.) *Representing Religion in World Cinema: Filmmaking, Mythmaking, Culture Making*, New York: Palgrave Macmillan.

Poitras, G. (2008) "Contemporary Anime in Japanese Pop Culture," in M. MacWilliams (ed.) *Japanese Visual Culture: Explorations in the World of Manga and Anime*, Armonk, NY: M. E. Sharpe.

Reader, I. (1991) *Religion in Contemporary Japan*, Honolulu: University of Hawai'i Press.

—— (2005) *Making Pilgrimages: Meaning and Practice in Shikoku*, Honolulu: University of Hawai'i Press.

—— (2007) "Positively Promoting Pilgrimage: Media Representations of Pilgrimage in Japan," *Nova Religio* 10 (3).

Reader, I. and Tanabe, G. (1998) *Practically Religious: Worldly Benefits and the Common Religion of Japan*, Honolulu: University of Hawai'i Press.

Ruch, B. (2002) "Woman to Woman: Kumano bikuni Proselytizers in Medieval and Early Modern Japan," in B. Ruch (ed.) *Engendering Faith: Women and Buddhism in Premodern Japan*, Ann Arbor: University of Michigan.

Schodt, F. (1996) *Dreamland Japan: Writings on Modern Manga*, Berkeley, CA: Stone Bridge Press.

Schrader, P. (2007 [1972]) "Transcendental Style on Film," in J. Mitchell and S. B. Plate (eds) *The Religion and Film Reader*, London: Routledge.

Shimazono, S. (2004) *From Salvation to Spirituality: Popular Religious Movements in Modern Japan*, Melbourne: Trans Pacific Press.

—— (2006) "Contemporary Japanese Religions," in P. Swanson and C. Chilson (eds) *The Nanzan Guide to Japanese Religions*, Honolulu: University of Hawai'i Press.

—— (2007a) *Supirichuariti no kōryū: shinreisei bunka to sono shūhen* [The Rise of Spirituality: New Spirituality Culture and its Periphery], Tokyo: Iwanami Shoten.

—— (2007b [1996]) *Seishin sekai no yukue: shūkyō/kindai/reisei* [Whither the Spiritual World: Religion/ Modernity/Spirituality], Tokyo: Akiyama Shoten.

Stalker, N. (2008) *Prophet Motive: Deguchi Onisaburō, Oomoto, and the Rise of New Religions in Imperial Japan*, Honolulu: University of Hawai'i Press.

Tada I. (1998) "'Shinseiki ebuangerion' to Material children" ["neon Genesis Evangelion" and Material Children], in Yamaori T. and Nagata T. (eds.) *Nichibunken sōsho* 17.

Tanabe, G. (2004) "Popular Buddhist Orthodoxy in Contemporary Japan," in S. Covell and M. Rowe (eds) *Japanese Journal of Religious Studies* 31 (2).

Thomas, J. (2007) "*Shūkyō Asobi* and Miyazaki Hayao's *Anime*," *Nova Religio* 10 (3).

——(2008) "Religious *Manga* Culture: The Conflation of Religion and Entertainment in Contemporary Japan." MA thesis, University of Hawai'i at Mānoa.

Yamanaka H. (2008) "The Utopian 'Power to Live': The Significance of the Miyazaki Phenomenon," in M. MacWilliams (ed.) *Japanese Visual Culture: Explorations in the World of Manga and Anime*, Armonk, NY: M. E. Sharpe.

Yumiyama T. (1994) "Gendai Nihon no shūkyō" [Contemporary Japanese Religion], in Inoue N. (ed.) *Gendai Nihon no shūkyō shakaigaku* [The Sociology of Religion in Contemporary Japan], Tokyo: Sekai Shisōsha.

Yumiyama T. *et al.* (2003) "Anime ni miru shūkyōsei: osusume anime 'gekiron' zadankai" [The Religiosity Seen in *Anime*: The "Vehement" Roundtable Discussion of Recommended *Anime*], *Pippara* 472.

Filmography

A (1998, dir. Mori T.)

D. Gray-man (2006–8, dir. Nabeshima O.)

Deathnote (2006, dir. Kaneko S.)

Deathnote: The Last Name (2006, dir. Kaneko S.)

Eien no hō (*The Laws of Eternity*) (2006, dir. Imakake I.)

Heisei tanuki gassen ponpoko (*Pom Poko*) (1994, dir. Takahata I.)

Kaze no Tani no Naushika (*Naushika of the Valley of the Wind*) (1984, dir. Miyazaki H.)

Kōkaku kidōtai (*Ghost in the Shell*) (1995, dir. Oshii M.)

Mononoke hime (*Princess Mononoke*) (1997, dir. Miyazaki H.)

Onibaba (*Demon Hag*) (1964, dir. Shindō K.)

Onmyōji (*Yin-yang Diviner*) (2001, dir. Takita Y.)

Osōshiki (*The Funeral*) (1984, dir. Itami J.)

Papurika (*Paprika*) (2006, dir. Kon S.)

Sen to Chihiro no kamikakushi (*Spirited Away*) (2001, dir. Miyazaki H.)

Serial Experiments: Lain (1998, dir. Nakamura R.)

Shin Kujakuō (*True Kujakuō*) (1994, dir. Rintarō)

Shinseiki ebuangerion (*Neon Genesis Evangelion*) (1995–6, dir. Anno H.)

Tekkon kincrīto (*Tekkon Kincrete*) (2006, dir. M. Arias)

Tonari no Totoro (*My Neighbor Totoro*) (1986, dir. Miyazaki H.)

Twentieth Century Boys (forthcoming 2008, dir. Tsutsumi Y.)

Ugetsu (*Tales of Moonlight and Rain*) (1953, dir. Mizoguchi K.)

Yume (*Dreams*) (1990, dir. Akira K.)

12

NEW RELIGIOUS MOVEMENTS

Paul Thomas

At least part of the ATF motivation, even if it never rose to the surface of the discussion, was to enforce the morals of our society, to enforce the psyche of right thinking by retaliating against these odd people.

Henry S. Ruth, Independent Reviewer, US Treasury Report on Waco
(*Waco: The Rules of Engagement* 1997)

Ideological analysis and hegemony

My analysis of NRMs (new religious movements) in film is largely an ideological analysis, but this is not meant as an assertion that ideology is all one can find in these films. I accept John Lyden's cautionary note against "the assumption that popular films represent conservative ideology and little else" (Lyden 2003: 31). However, at this point I favor an ideological analysis of NRMs in film for several related reasons. First, though individual films have been examined, very little work has been done regarding the ideological content of NRMs in film as a whole. Second, though the so-called "cult wars" were largely fought in the 1970s and 1980s (Dawson 2006), the assumptions about NRMs (examined in detail below) that fueled the counter-cult movement are still prevalent in the popular imagination. Though it is not my intention in this chapter to refight the cult wars, I will demonstrate that the ideology espoused by the counter-cult movement still finds its expression in popular media.

To understand the multiple discourses that function in representations of NRMs in film, I apply a Gramscian analysis utilizing his theory of hegemony as elaborated by British cultural theorists like Stuart Hall. The application of Antonio Gramsci and the study of the hegemonic are not new in the study of popular culture, indeed, such work has been occurring since the early 1970s (Storey 2003). However, a consideration of how depictions of NRMs are used in a hegemonic system has yet to be presented. Though processes of negotiation are evident, and multiple readings can be discerned, depictions of NRMs in film are often hegemonic in that these alternative religious movements are depicted as undermining our most cherished Western values: individualism, family, and Christianity.

Focusing on the role of ideology and culture as it relates to social relations allowed Gramsci to illustrate how those things a culture regards as self-given cultural values are actually the result of a negotiation between dominant social groups and the general population. As a Marxist, Gramsci saw these social relations and cultural values as ones that ultimately support the interests of the dominant social group. Of particular interest here is the manner in which the hegemonic process actually disguises the constructed and negotiated nature of accepted cultural values. Gramsci reflects on "The 'spontaneous' consent given by the great masses of the population to the general direction imposed on social life by the dominant fundamental group; this consent is 'historically' caused by the prestige (and subsequent confidence) which the dominant group enjoys because of its position and function in the world of production" (Gramsci 1971).

Economic and political discourses cannot be separated from cultural values. It is through cultural values that political and economic structures are given a philosophical basis creating the illusion that such structures are self-evident and naturally given. Despite its importance, here I dwell less upon the world of production, but will, following Gramsci and others, pay heed to power relationships. I take as one of my fundamental assumptions that film represents various ways of knowing the world. John Storey tells us that in a hegemonic system one must consider those who have the "power to make their ways of knowing circulate discursively in the world, generate regimes of truth, which come to assume an authority over the ways in which we think and act; that is, provide us with 'subject positions' from which meanings can be made and actions carried out" (Storey 2003: 6).

Gramsci's nuanced analysis of the hegemonic demonstrates that the road to hegemony is rarely a wide and straight boulevard. Rather, hegemony advances through a series of negotiations with subjugated social groups. This works because the discourse is presented to subordinate actors in such a way that they are led to believe they participate in a universal moral expansion. The dominant social group seeks to promote a synchronicity between the dominant ideology and the interests of the subjugated. This serves to bring about, in Gramsci's words:

> not only a unison of economic and political aims, but also intellectual and moral unity, posing all the questions around which the struggle rages not on a corporate but on a "universal" plane, and thus creating the hegemony of a fundamental social group over a series of subordinate groups ... But the development and expansion of the particular groups are conceived of, and presented, as being the motor force of a universal expansion. (Gramsci 1971: 181)

Gramsci continues, saying "account [is] taken of the interests and the tendencies of the groups over which hegemony is to be exercised, and that a certain compromise equilibrium should be formed" (Gramsci 1971: 161). Such negotiations occur as a series of smaller discourses encompassed by the larger metanarrative collectively progressing toward a hegemonic goal. Storey points out that this compromise equilibrium serves to channel subversion into ideologically safe harbors (Storey 2003). To study culture is to recognize the practice and process of making shared meaning. It is in this manner that subordinated groups are allowed into the discourse and this helps to explain why, in the films I have examined, readings and voices that resist the dominant hegemonic position may still be identified.

New religious movements in film

A long history of scholarship resulted in definitions of NRMs that range from the simple to the highly complex.[1] It is not my purpose here to argue the merits and weaknesses of any particular typology.[2] Rather, I accept NRMs as having some combination of the following characteristics. Some NRMs are those movements, sometimes known as "cults," that may be described as innovative (in the sense that they are not clearly derived from and/or closely related to established religious traditions); exist in a relatively high degree of tension with society; are generally short-lived, small, with a high turnover rate; and are characterized by charismatic leadership. Other NRMs examined in this chapter are import religions, established religious traditions in new social contexts. Golden age movements draw their tenets from existing religious traditions or from an imagined golden age in world history; neo-Paganism and some forms of Wicca fall within this category. Finally, hybrid religious movements are syncretic movements that combine elements of an established tradition (Catholicism) and Shamanistic religious systems, such as Vodou and Santería in this chapter.

Cults, brainwashing, and deprogramming

The dominant hegemonic discourse about NRMs supports the casting of such movements in a negative light. Often NRMs are labeled as cults in the most pejorative sense of the term. Moreover, it is the cult leaders who receive the lion's share of hegemonic discourse, being depicted as sinister and manipulative masters of psychological persuasions popularly understood as "brainwashing." The purpose of such a narrative is to demonize such groups as anti-American and anti-Western. As James Richardson has noted, joining these groups seems, for many, to be a rejection of Western culture and values, "including religious, economic, and familial" (Richardson and Bromley 1980: 6; Richardson 1998: 217). If this is the case, then one would expect to find hegemony being exercised in those places in pop culture where discourse about NRMs is evident. The Jane Campion film *Holy Smoke* provides a good example of this discourse.

"I think they were on drugs": *Holy Smoke* (2000)
The film *Holy Smoke* (based on a book of the same name) tells the story of cult deprogrammer PJ Waters (Harvey Keitel) who is hired by the parents of Ruth Barron (Kate Winslet) to "deprogram" their daughter after her encounter with a guru in India. The initial Indian setting reminds viewers of the influence of the Far East on the formation of the 1960s counterculture and the variety of NRMs that arose in the same milieu.

From the outset the dominant hegemonic position is evident. Ruth Barron, a white, attractive, Western girl with a biblical name is set in the alien hustle and bustle of India. Ruth becomes curious about a specific group of religious practitioners and begins the process of joining this group. Eventually Ruth and her best friend Prudence visit Baba, the group's guru. Baba is a sinister-looking man with intense eyes who quickly casts his charismatic, mesmerizing spell over Ruth – the mere touch of his hand upon her forehead causes her to faint. While talking about this experience, Prudence delivers to the viewer the implied message in explicit form: "But oh, it was so scary … Some sort of freaky hypnotism happened. I think they were on drugs."

We learn much about the dominant hegemonic dialogue by critically examining popular notions of cult brainwashing and the "rescue" of individuals understood as "trapped" in such movements. The assertion that some hypnotic activity has occurred is designed to alert the viewer to the fact that only through coercive techniques would somebody like Ruth so completely turn away from her family and culture.

As Lorne Dawson points out, at the heart of brainwashing theory is a tension regarding the constitutional guarantee of religious freedom (Dawson 2003; Coleman 1985). When Americans began joining "cults," brainwashing theory provided a ready-made framework to explain why younger converts would seemingly reject parents and culture to join such groups (Dawson 2006). Families of converts approached the courts for help in forcibly removing their adult children from these groups. The only means of legally doing so was to demonstrate that converts did not join of their own volition – that coercive techniques were used to force converts to join and remain in place (Richardson 2003). Furthermore, they alleged the brainwashing techniques used by cult leaders damaged the mental health of the converts, thus creating the legal mechanism to place these adults under the legal protection of their parents (Dawson 2003).

Initially the courts were sympathetic to brainwashing claims. However, as more nuanced studies of brainwashing theories appeared, the scientific basis of brainwashing theory became suspect (Dawson 2003; 2006; Richardson 1998). As James Richardson and Eileen Barker have ably demonstrated, those who join new religious movements are seekers who struggle to take an active role in their spiritual journeys – they are not the unsuspecting "dupes" as proponents of brainwashing theory would have us believe (Barker 1984; Richardson 1998).

In the courts brainwashing theory has collapsed, but it lingers in popular culture. This explains why a film like Holy Smoke, released in 2000, still utilizes the discourse on brainwashing and the controlling, manipulative cult leader. Ruth's mother and father are convinced that the best course of action would be hiring an "exit counselor," otherwise known as a deprogrammer. The only way to get Ruth back, they are told, is to have her declared mentally incompetent. "These cults use coercive and deceptive methods," says Stan before presenting the deprogramming option to Ruth's mother Miriam.

The dialogue between PJ and Ruth is filled with hegemonic positions. The dominance of Judeo-Christian ethics is evident in PJ's ability to quote Bible verses, including his assertion to Ruth that the truth will set her free (John 8:32). The hegemonic position regarding NRMs is also evident when PJ shares with Ruth his experience with a cult leader in India that resulted in his sexual molestation. This, of course, draws upon all kinds of popular tropes regarding the deviant sexuality of religious leaders in NRMs. Such rumors continue to circulate in popular culture largely because they are perpetuated in both the counter-cult movement and media accounts of NRMs. Sexual impropriety was a concern raised by law-enforcement officials and the media concerning David Koresh and the Branch Davidians in 1993 and is found more recently in explanations justifying the 3 April 2008 raid of the Fundamentalist Church of Jesus Christ of Latter Day Saints community in Eldorado, Texas.[3]

Holy Smoke is interesting and complicated because the film contains the negotiated possibilities that Gramsci outlined. The final portion of *Holy Smoke* provides the clearest and strongest oppositional position when Ruth decides to turn the tables upon PJ and begins manipulating him. Here, we find that the hegemonic hero, the individualistic, Bible-verse-quoting deprogrammer falls into religious experiences not unlike those of Ruth in the early scenes of the film. The very things that PJ initially criticizes, explicitly and implicitly, are present in his own experiences, including an authoritative figure to whom he is totally devoted (Ruth), hypnotic music, perverse sexuality, and mirage-like visions, all of which culminate into his final plea to Ruth: "We'll see Baba, he can help us."

Oppositional though this may be, it ultimately fails to fully subvert the dominant hegemonic position. For, as Gramsci maintained, hegemony allows for negotiated positions while still moving its agenda forward. It is evident from the perspective of both the film and the book (written by Anna and Jane Campion) that many of the concepts that circulate about NRMs remain unchallenged in any serious manner. As Massimo Introvigne writes in his combined review of both the film and the book, the final bibliography of the book reads like a who's who list of cult deprogrammers, including works by Steve Hassan and Douglas Brooks. This hardly inspires confidence that the work of the director and the author are likely to contain insights from scholars of NRMs problematizing the issues of brainwashing and deprogramming (Introvigne n.d.).

Delivering that "Jonestown kindof feeling": *Believers* (2007)

Believers is a film evidently influenced by the Heaven's Gate and People's Temple suicides. In this film the "cult" in question, the Quanta Group, is preparing for the end of the world after a coming meteor shower. Composed of scientists, mathematicians, and philosophers, they are led by a charismatic leader known as The Teacher (Daniel Benzali).

By design, many stereotypical motifs that circulate in our culture about NRMs are found in this film. When members of the Quanta Group first appear and kidnap a pair of paramedics who were called to help an escaping cult member, the viewer learns extreme conformity is an aspect of this group. The members all wear the same drab uniforms that vaguely resemble doctors' scrubs, recalling the "uniforms" worn by the thirty-nine members of the Heaven's Gate group who committed suicide in Rancho Sante Fe, California, in 1997. The sensationalized Heaven's Gate suicides renewed debate concerning the role of suicide and violence in NRMs. *Believers* recalls those debates by presenting the Quanta Group in similar terms as the viewer watches cult members prepare for, and ultimately commit, suicide.

The hegemonic understanding of groups commonly termed as cults found its way into the creative efforts of Daniel Myrick, the director of *Believers*. In the DVD director's commentary Myrick admits to having a lifelong fascination with cults and purposefully uses this film as a vehicle for exploring why people "buy into them." Such a statement removes agency from members of NRMs who are active seekers. The statement that people "buy into cults" is a subtle assertion that cult members are somehow duped, as though buying a lemon from a savvy car salesman. Myrick's opinions are explicit in this regard. Speaking of popular preconceived notions about cults, he says, "Most of those preconceptions are right, they [cults] are usually kinda run by some charismatic figure that leads a bunch of impressionable people astray."

One of the problems with media (broadly conceived) depictions of NRMs is that they take extraordinary events relating to these groups as normative. This is particularly true concerning the topic of violence and NRMs. Acts of collective violence are actually rare in NRMs. From a small handful of examples (including Heaven's Gate and People's Temple) lifted from among thousands of NRMs, many universal assumptions have been perpetuated. For example, Daniel Myrick says of *Believers* that he was attempting to create a "Jonestown kindof feeling" while he was looking to cast an actor in the role of The Teacher who recalled a "Jim Jones charismatic kindof figure," thus revealing that events like that at Jonestown have become a conceptual framework for understanding NRMs. The problem is that such violent acts are hardly representative of these religious groups (Dawson 2006).

Neo-Paganism

In a very real sense neo-Paganism is an umbrella term used to describe a wide variety of religious practices. Broadly conceived, it may be said that neo-Paganism refers to a "broad range of nature-venerating religious traditions" (Partridge 2004: 269). It is a collection of diverse traditions, combining solitary practitioners with a sense of communal identity that includes well-known traditions like Wicca (discussed below), Druidry, and Heathenism.

Neo-Paganism traces its origins to the pre-Christian religious practices of Europe as well as indigenous religious traditions from across the world. As nature-venerating traditions, natural cycles feature prominently in ritual behavior. Body cycles, lunar cycles, and seasonal festivals "order the lives of most Pagans" (Partridge 2004: 270). Some neo-Pagans are pantheistic, venerating nature as divine. If some are reluctant to go that far, they at least view the divine and nature as intertwined and linked. Like the Wiccan traditions discussed below, neo-Pagans reject the Christian conception of a monotheistic, masculine God. Favoring balance in divinity and in nature, neo-Pagans view the masculine and the feminine as being of equal importance and venerate the Great Mother Goddess in her incarnations as Isis, Diana, and Astarte and the male principle in his manifestations as Bacchus, Pan, and Odin. Beyond these features, neo-Paganism is difficult to define largely owing to the fact that Paganism is a loose set of religious traditions that rely heavily on personal gnosis, eclecticism, innovation, and solitary practice (Cowan 2005).

Not doing "it": *The Wicker Man* (1973)

Depictions of NRMs in film are not always about maniacal cult leaders and Heaven's Gate-type mass suicides. An examination of the 1973 film *The Wicker Man* illustrates other areas of contention as well as providing a good example of the hegemonic process as it relates to neo-Paganism.

The Wicker Man follows Scottish police officer, Sgt. Neil Howie (Edward Woodward), who receives an anonymous tip regarding a missing girl (Rowan) on the island of Summerisle. While investigating the disappearance of Rowan, Sgt. Howie, a very devout Christian, becomes increasingly uncomfortable with the islanders who follow the Old Religion (something scholars label neo-Paganism). The girl's disappearance is revealed as a ruse planned by the inhabitants to lure Sgt. Howie to the island so that he could become a human sacrifice to the Pagan gods, thus ensuring a good crop of the island's famous apples in the coming season.

Before his burning in the great wicker man, however, Sgt. Howie has an opportunity to learn a great deal about the island's Pagan traditions, most of which shock him to his Christian core. For example, he is nearly overwhelmed with the overt sexuality of the island's inhabitants. The viewer is invited to understand this sexuality as part of the island's Pagan traditions meant to celebrate and encourage fertility. Propagandistic prohibitions against sex in the fields, something Sgt. Howie witnesses his first night on the island after dining at the Green Man Inn, are evident in the Bible (Leviticus 18:23).

The centrality of fertility flows through the entire film. During his first night at the Green Man Inn, Sgt. Howie (who does not believe in "it" before marriage) has a difficult time resisting the seductions of young Willow (Britt Ekland). Later in the film, Sgt. Howie is appalled regarding the lessons being taught to schoolchildren around a maypole and in a nearby classroom. When Sgt. Howie overhears a lecture on the maypole as a phallic symbol representing regenerative principles, he asks in a voice dripping with indignation if these children learn anything about Christianity. The things Sgt. Howie witnesses continue to challenge his moral vision. Pregnant women walk through orchards and naked young girls jump over fire. When Sgt. Howie expresses surprise that they would do this naked, Lord Summerisle (Christopher Lee) explains to him that it is much too dangerous to jump through fire with clothes on, and explains how the flames impart fertility to the women. Adopting the position of Sgt. Howie, what I would term the dominant hegemonic position, these images recall a long history of Christian accusations against non-Christians and their deviant sexual behavior, accusations that are still commonly leveled at NRMs.

Sgt. Howie's conversation with Lord Summerisle is the critical dialogue in the film. In this scene Sgt. Howie steps up as a defender of true religion against the false, or nonreligion, of Summerisle, while Lord Summerisle patiently explains that they are a deeply religious people.

HOWIE: Religious? With ruined churches, no ministers, no priests, and children dancing naked . . . You've got fake biology, fake religion. Sir, have these children never heard of Jesus?

LORD SUMMERISLE: Himself the son of a virgin, impregnated, I believe, by a ghost . . . It is most important that each new generation on Summerisle be made aware that here the old gods aren't dead.

HOWIE: And what of the true God?!

In his comments, Sgt. Howie reveals the dominant hegemonic position that the true and right religion is Christianity and other religious systems are either false, or not religion at all.

That the film is well researched does not mean the presentation is one of sympathy for the Pagan traditions of Summerisle. *The Wicker Man* has a sinister feel that builds toward the revealing of the wicker man, not to mention the fact that the reasons for luring Sgt. Howie to Summerisle are nefarious. Even allowing for instances of human sacrifice in ancient religions (though such claims are sometimes difficult to disentangle from propaganda), neo-Pagans are nearly unanimous in their disavowal of human sacrifice and violence in general. To find a living neo-Pagan community committing human sacrifice is unrealistic, but this depiction reenforces preexisting notions of NRM practitioners as subversive and dangerous. It is not surprising that a dominant hegemonic reading of *The Wicker Man* presents the inhabitants of Summerisle as sex-crazed, depraved killers.

The Wicker Man is one of those films about which viewers hotly contest the film's relationship to the religions being depicted. Some viewers accept this dominant-hegemonic reading. For example, the subject line of Neil Mackernan's post about *The Wicker Man* on Internet Movie Database.com (IMDB.com) reads "Chilling insight into ancient paganistic rituals" (5 January 1999). Likewise, Nergal-Is-Risen writes "An accidental tourist finds himself in Heathen Hell" (IMDB.com, 30 December 2004). Nergal even offers his or her own historical analysis, all the while buying into the dominant-hegemonic reading:

> WM [*Wicker Man*] represents the dark underbelly of the "Hippy" era; the stark clarification that tuning in, turning on, and dropping out of square society entailed buying into tenets and beliefs that, at heart, could carry with them unnamed dangers and terrors. WM showed that paganism at its raw, ragged-toothed centre was never cuddly nor chirpy. So many Hippies and New-Agers have selectively taken all the light frothy bits from the ancient religions of yore and forsaken the less digestible realities. (IMDB.com, 30 December 2004)

Some view the film as an empowering statement on behalf of neo-Pagan traditions and as a criticism of Sgt. Howie's "stick in the mud" Christianity, or, as Megan Weireter writes at notcoming.com, "the film resonates with a sadness that we as a species can't live up to the beauty of our rituals" (Weireter n.d.). Indeed, *The Wicker Man* is written and filmed in such a way that it easily invites this sort of reading, largely because, as Douglas E. Cowan points out, the theological debate between Sgt. Howie and Lord Summerisle remains unresolved, "allowing viewers to map onto the story their own experience and expectation of religious belief and practice" (2008: 229). As Melanie Wright states about Sgt. Howie, despite the fact that he is steadfast and dies the death of the Christian martyr, his rigidity, virginity, and intensity seem "out of step with modernity," especially in the social context of the late 1960s and early 1970s (Wright 2007: 87). Such a position is reflected in the comments of Debreard at IMDB.com:

> While some see it as "pro-christian" [sic], the film actually depicts Christianity just as harshly as paganism, if only because Sgt. Howie's dogmatic persistence in his beliefs are what actually make him, "the right kind of adult" to be sacrificed – every opportunity to break those rules is presented to him by the villagers, and he even wants to break away from his own narrow sexual mindset, but does not, which, in the end, is what gets him killed. (4 April 2006).

Wicca and Witchcraft

The very first episode (7 October 1998) of the popular television series *Charmed* was *Something Wicca This Way Comes*, and this illustrates the amount of attention Wicca received in 1990s popular culture. Numerous films have witchcraft as their topic, but very few intentionally take religion as a primary theme and few address the modern branch of witchcraft known as Wicca.

A variety of names are used to refer to Wicca, including "the Craft," Witchcraft, Wisecraft, and even "the Old Religion," hinting at the diversity in this conglomeration of religious practices largely rooted in Paganism (Partridge 2004). While recognizing that there is great diversity in Wicca, credit for the creation of modern Witchcraft often goes to Liverpool native Gerald Gardner (1884-1960) (Pearson 2002). A retired civil servant, Gardner claimed to be well versed in many occult and alternative traditions. The 1951 repeal of England's Witchcraft Act of 1735 made possible Gardner's publication of his influential works *Witchcraft Today* (1954) and *The Meaning of Witchcraft* (1959). In these texts Gardner outlines the basic contours of modern Witchcraft and creates a controversial history of Witchcraft that pushes the origins of modern Wicca to pre-Christian European Pagan traditions.

Currently, there are countless varieties of Wicca and Witchcraft (Gardnerian, Alexandrian, Dianic) identified by varying degrees of structural leadership and a stronger or weaker sense of personal gnosis. Moreover, modern Witchcraft shares many of the same characteristics outlined above regarding neo-Paganism (Cowan 2005). Rituals are performed to bring new members into the coven, to mark important natural events or to mark sacred time (such as the solstices), for rites of passage such as birth and marriage, and numerous other rituals performed for specific purposes like healing.

One of the characteristic features of Wicca is the use of magic (or "magick"). Magic is performed in a variety of ways, including the use of props like candles, knives, crystals, and mirrors, or performed through actions such as dancing and chanting, or a combination of both. Christopher Partridge describes two basic categories of Wicca magic: natural magic and high magic. Natural magic is materialistic in that it uses things like herbs, crystals, and candles in order to "harness what are believed to be natural forces in order to effect changes in the physical world, from healing sick minds and bodies to influencing the weather" (Partridge 2004: 295). High magic, on the other hand, takes as its goal the transformation of the self through contact with the Divine (Partridge 2004).

It is difficult to think of other groups as subject to hegemonic domination as the (either real or imagined) witch. Historically, purported witches have been subject to persecution and Inquisition. The most intense period of persecution, the so-called Burning Times (ca. 1550–1650), provides a source of solidarity and community among Wiccan practitioners – despite the impossibility of the commonly cited figure of 9 million witches executed and the fact that many of the victims (some estimate ca. 40,000 victims) were older, independent, widows or spinsters rather than what can be construed as practicing witches (Pearson 2002).

Like individuals who join NRMs, practitioners of Wicca also reject many of the most cherished values of Western culture. It is easy to understand how the witch would become a target of hegemony. As Partridge notes, Wicca rejects monotheism as patriarchal, instead elevating the figure of the Great Mother Goddess and a host of other minor gods and goddesses as manifestations of the Divine (Partridge 2004; Pearson 2002). In addition to rejecting some of the West's most cherished values, practitioners of Wicca also face the very real, very ancient, association of witchcraft with a variety of sins, the most important being uncontrolled sexuality and devil worship (Hanegraaff 2002). Having embraced a tradition that hegemonic Christianity has spent hundreds of years persecuting, practitioners of Wicca automatically place themselves outside mainstream Western values.

The Craft

One of the best known and most popular movies about witchcraft is *The Craft* (1996). *The Craft* goes to great lengths to demonstrate that practitioners of witchcraft are outsiders. The circle (rather than coven) of St. Benedict's Academy, Bonnie (Neve Campbell), Nancy (Fairuza Balk), Rochelle (Rachel True), and eventually Sarah (Robin Tunney), are clearly a group set apart – though arguably the prettiest and "coolest" outcasts in the history of cinema.

The striking beauty of the witches in *The Craft* seems to be at odds with other "outcast" films where the outcast protagonist has to rise above his or her stereotypical ugly duckling and awkward characteristics to find acceptance within the larger group. However, as Joanne Pearson has argued, the beautiful witch may best be understood within the context of a misogynistic discourse. "Witches in film are often used to signal the power of female sexuality, its terror, but also the desire which draws women to proclaim themselves witches and which attracts men to them" (Pearson 2002: 160).

This is a powerful hegemonic discourse that has a long history, forming, as Cowan notes (2008), an important part of the conceptual framework of the infamous witch-hunting manual *The Malleus Maleficarum*. Therefore, the beautiful witch, rather than the stereotypical crook-nosed green witch of *The Wizard of Oz* (1939) and *Hocus Pocus* (1993), has become the dominant image of the witch in film since the 1960s – ironically coinciding with the rise of modern feminism. Fear of the uncontrolled sexuality of women plays an important role in *The Craft*, especially considering the complicated relationship between Sarah and Chris that culminates in Chris's death.

One important element of the dominant hegemonic discourse about witches and magic in films like *The Craft* revolves around the topic of "unintended consequences." For neo-Pagans, this is the "Law of Threefold Return" in which one's actions are visited back upon one's self times three (Cowan 2008). For those reading the film outside a neo-Pagan framework, the message of unintended consequences functions like a flashing caution signal, warning the viewer that danger lies ahead – dabbling in occult arts, both good and bad, can lead to sticky and dangerous situations. Sarah, termed the "natural" and ostensibly "good" witch in *The Craft*, describes how, despite innocent intentions, her natural magical abilities often go awry. The things for which she wishes often work out in unintended ways. For example, she describes how wishing for rain once led to a water pipe bursting in her room or how wishing for quiet caused deafness for three days.

At one point the circle takes a field trip to the countryside to conduct an initiation ritual. Many Wiccans identify with the ritual sequences of this film because practitioners were used as consultants during production. Rather unlike other films dealing with witchcraft (*Hocus Pocus*, 1993), *The Craft* tries to honestly depict the mechanics of Wicca ritual. During this afternoon in the countryside, the four witches sit in a circle, knee to knee, chanting "earth, air, fire, water." In the next ritual move, the girls are depicted in pairs, each taking turns holding a dagger point against the throat of the other while saying, "It is better that you should rush upon this blade, than enter the circle with fear in your heart. How do you enter?" The respondent then replies "With perfect love and perfect trust" (this ritual sequence is very similar to the Gardnerian First Degree Initiation; see Cowan 2008). The ritual culminates on a picnic cloth upon which rests a pentacle and a tarot card. The girls prick their fingers and each allows a drop of blood to fall into a goblet of wine. Each girl makes a wish and then drinks. Sarah, who has a crush on Chris, a boy who already "played" her, wishes for his love.

After this ritual, the law of Karmic return starts taking over on a grander life or death scale. Chris, who had previously been spreading unseemly rumors about Sarah, finds himself inexplicably drawn to her. His infatuation with her grows to the point of sleeplessness when he finds himself outside Sarah's window at night. His debilitating obsession eventually becomes dangerous when he attempts to force himself upon Sarah. This ultimately leads to his death at the hands of Nancy who seeks revenge upon Chris for his man-handling ways.

The stakes get even higher later in the film when the circle engages in high magic, or calling upon the divine for personal transformation. The film ties this sequence to the invoking of the spirit, a ritual that Lirio, the owner of an occult book store, describes to Sarah as being very dangerous. The purpose of the ritual is to invoke Manon, ruler of the deep, and, from Nancy's perspective, is clearly intended to acquire power. Nancy cries:

> Serpent of old, ruler of deep ... show us your glory, show us your power, we pray of thee, we pray of thee, we invoke thee. O serpent one, hear our calls, hear our prayers. Ancient wise one, teach us thy ways, we summon and stir thee, lend us your powers, show us your glory. We invoke thee. Manon, fill me!

The ritual is evidently successful, for the next morning the viewer learns that Nancy can now walk on water. She says to Manon, "I can feel you in me; I am your daughter now." This image clearly sets her up in Christ-like terms, but as a perversion, an anti-Christ of sorts, because Nancy's actions from this point forward are presented as haughty and wicked. It is through the presentation of Nancy as a mocking imitation of Christ that one of the important functions (failures) of mainstream religion in these films rises to the surface. Keeping in mind that this film, and others discussed below, take place against a Christian (often Catholic) backdrop (the circle in *The Craft* all attend a Catholic school), then the presence of "culturally unfamiliar religions ... are often *invasive*, and their aspect of horrific metataxis challenges – either explicitly or implicitly – the ability of dominant traditions to function meaningfully" (Cowan 2008: 67). In the battle against chaos represented by "culturally unfamiliar religions" sometimes the established religious tradition proves ineffective and is actually subverted until such a time that order can be restored.

Bell, Book, and Candle

In this 1959 film Shep (James Stewart) is the object of the affections of a witch named Gil (Kim Novak). Many stereotypical elements appear, including the witch's familiar (the cat named Pyewacket), a cackling aunt, black capes and red dresses, and love potions. Shep, who publishes books on the supernatural, has a conversation with an author (Sidney) of books on witchcraft. Sidney states about witches, "They can't cry ... or blush, throw them in the water, they float."

Shep is the consummate rationalist, professing belief in providence rather than witchcraft. However, he begins to question his worldview when the truth about the love spell cast upon him by Gil becomes evident. Despite his lapse into doubt, the dominant hegemonic theme that witchcraft is unnatural and countercultural is upheld. The extraordinary nature of the witch community is revealed in a dialogue between Gil and her aunt Queenie (Elsa Lanchester). Gil asks Queenie if she ever wishes they were not witches, so that they could just "spend Christmas Eve in a little church somewhere, listening to carols instead of bongo drums." Gil expresses the desire to be an ordinary person, which is possible for her, but only if she falls in love. At the end of the film, falling in love with Shep reduces Gil to tears, a sure sign of her newly found humanity. When Shep asks Gil if she wants to stop crying, she responds that she does not think she can, "I'm only human." In this way the formerly cold, unloving, and unloved witch acquires a level of humanity that allows her to become an accepted part of society.

Practical Magic

Like *Bell, Book, and Candle*, witchcraft in *Practical Magic* (1998) is a family affair. Moreover, also like *Bell, Book, and Candle*, love is a roadblock for the witch. How many, one wonders, would agree that the expression of love is the ultimate signifier of an individual's humanity? In *Bell, Book and Candle*, Gil's inability to love is linked to her very nature as a witch. In *Practical Magic*, the inability for the main characters, Sally Owens (Sandra Bullock) and Gillian Owens (Nicole Kidman), to find and keep love is a direct result of a spell a family ancestor cast upon herself. The result for Owens family women is the death of the men with whom they fall in love. Like *The Craft*, the witches in *Practical Magic* are beautiful and romantic involvement with them is clearly dangerous. The focus of *Practical Magic*, as for *Bell, Book, and Candle*, is to find a way to overcome this handicap.

The theme of unintended consequences plays a significant role in the film *Practical Magic*. Gillian deals with her inability to find love by throwing herself into meaningless relationships, which eventually causes her to become involved with a shady character named Jimmy Angelov (Goran Visnjic). When Gillian and Sally unintentionally kill Jimmy, they bring him back to life with a spell. Though the spell works, the plan backfires and Jimmy comes back more dangerous than ever. Despite the fact that they banish Jimmy, his ghost takes possession of Gillian. His ultimate dispatch requires the work of a full coven, something for which Sally has to recruit incredulous women from the town.

Though the hegemonic claims are evident in this film, they are eventually subverted. For much of the film, the outcast status of the Owens sisters is emphasized, including children chanting "you are a witch" while throwing rocks, people and animals shying away from them, and even accusations of devil worship. Like *Bell, Book, and Candle*, there is a skeptical male protagonist, in this case Officer Gary Hallet (Aidan Quinn), who is investigating the death of Jimmy Angelov. Like Shep, Gary eventually becomes convinced of the reality of the witches' magic.

The biggest subversion of all occurs at the end of the film when the formerly hostile town matriarchs are enlisted to complete the coven needed to banish Jimmy Angelov. The women come together in a way that witch and non-witch do not in other films. They find something they have in common, femaleness, and in the context of the coven ritual that shared feminism is united in banishing the abusive Jimmy. There is a sudden realization that, through their common experiences as women, they are all more alike than different and, from that point onwards, the Owens family is an accepted part of the community. Here the film departs from the storyline of *Bell, Book, and Candle* because the witches do not have to leave witchcraft behind in order to join humanity.

Vodou and all that "mumbo jumbo": Afro-Caribbean religious traditions

The term "Afro-Caribbean religions" is used here to designate a collection of African-inspired religious traditions that formed in the Caribbean as a result of the European slave trade. The individual names will be familiar to most readers, from Cuban Santería to Haitian Vodou. These highly syncretistic religions developed as African slaves transplanted from their homeland forged a new sense of communal identity. Though placed here under the umbrella of Afro-Caribbean religions, I recognize that each individual tradition has its own distinct history and characteristics. However, as Margarite Fernández Olmos and Lizabeth Paravisini-Gebert have illustrated, Afro-Caribbean religions share a number of features, including (1) a combination of monotheism and polytheism characterized by a Supreme Being who emanates many other deities, (2) a cult of dead ancestors, (3) a supernatural power that can be made to invest objects, (4) animism, (5) rituals that allow for contact between the human and the spiritual world, (6) consecrated objects that serve as receptacles for the gods, (7) magic, (8) the use of music and rhythm to create an altered state of consciousness, and (9) spiritual possession (Olmos and Paravisini-Gebert 2003: 9–11).

Just as the hegemonic position in films about witchcraft expands to include misogynistic discourses, in films depicting Afro-Caribbean religions the hegemonic position expands into a discourse about race. The creation of the "alien other" finds clear expression in films depicting Afro-Caribbean religions for at least two reasons: (1) these traditions are largely practiced by people of African descent, which invites long-held racist discourses to emerge, and (2) Vodou and related traditions are syncretic religious traditions that feature elements of African religious practices, allowing for the expression of an Orientalist discourse about Africa as a dark, primitive continent.

"I don't call cuttin' up chickens a religion": *The Believers* (1987)

The dangerous black man makes his presence felt early in *The Believers*. In the opening scene, Lisa Jamison (Janet-Laine Green), wife of the film's protagonist, police psychologist Cal Jamison (Martin Sheen), is accidentally electrocuted by a short-circuited coffee pot while standing in a puddle of spilt milk. Here the futility of the established religious tradition to offer safety finds expression. During the electrocution, the camera pans across the cross around Lisa's neck before cutting from her agonized face to a mask worn by a Santería ecstatic. The Santería ritual that follows is dark and exotic as it depicts a white couple (with a dead child) watching while a goat is sacrificed to the upbeat and frenzied tempo of drums. These opening scenes create a visual link between these deaths, that of the white woman and the dead white child, to the rituals of the black man. The film then follows Cal as he uncovers a murderous Santería "cult" controlled by the black magic of the creepy and murderous Palo (Malick Bowens) who believes the ritual killing of children can confer great powers upon those willing to offer the sacrifice. Eventually Cal's own son Chris (Harley Cross) has to be rescued from the clutches of this evil group.

Through its depiction of Santería ritual, the film makes an unmistakable link between the primitive, the black, and Africa. The drumming that occurs in the park, in the outdoors and thus a "natural" setting, indicates the primitive nature of the practitioners, as though they are just stepping from the African jungles or savannah. The African roots of much of what Cal experiences over the course of the film (including headless and disemboweled birds, decapitated cats, lots of blood, candles, and broken pottery – all connected to mysterious rituals that have led to brutal killings) is confirmed by his anthropologist friends Kate (Elizabeth Wilson) and Dennis Maslow (Lee Richardson). It certainly is true that Afro-Caribbean religions like Santería and Vodou are syncretic and arise from the realities of the African diaspora, combining elements of African religious traditions with elements of Catholicism. However, the linking of the practices of Santería to its African roots does something more than acknowledge this fact. Here, this deliberate linkage serves to exoticize the practitioners and their rituals as well as presenting the Afro-Caribbean traditions as the dangerous primitive other.

Such an "out of Africa" presentation is problematic. As Ruth Mayer has correctly pointed out, the concept of "Africa" is a colonial construct, as "there is no such thing as an underlying cultural heritage that would pertain equally to Egypt and Nambia, Kenya and the Congo" (Mayer 2002: 1). To assert that things are "out of Africa" does a great disservice to the variety of cultures, each with its own history, that comprise the continent of Africa. Wherever they are found such ideas and images function as an Orientalist discourse designed to present the cultures of Africa, and its derivatives, as singular, primitive, strange, and dangerous – all for the purpose of legitimating the sorts of cultural imperialism we have examined thus far.

The danger that primitive Africa poses for white America is enhanced in *The Believers* in another way, for not far into the film the viewer learns the film's Santería group contains many upper-class white American devotees – including the anthropologists Dennis and Kate Maslow who have "gone native" in a rather dramatic fashion. There are different ways of reading this involvement. On one level, the control the whites exercise in this group recalls the control that white Europeans have exercised over people of African descent and their cultures for centuries. Here Santería and its culture function as little more than playthings to be consumed by the white upper class. A reading more in tune with the dangers represented by this alien religion requires viewing Santería as an intrusion into white culture, functioning as a fifth column, alerting the viewer to the ways in which the alien other can undermine society.

Like other films in the genre, the initial crisis, here the death of Lisa Jamison, creates a crisis of faith in the leading character. Cal becomes the damaged skeptic through the death of his wife, only to be hit between the eyes with the reality of religion when faced with events unexplainable in any other manner. This does not mean, however, that the reformed skeptic becomes accepting of any form of religion. In the hegemonic discourse analyzed thus far, the right religion is the one that supports hegemony. Thus, the film has characters who deride Santería and its practitioners. For example, Lt. Sean McTaggert (Robert Loggia) says of Santería, "I don't call cuttin' up chickens a religion." In this statement the viewer is presented with an ontological value judgment concerning the validity of Santería as a religion. Lying behind that statement is the perspective that requires minimizing the religion of the alien other as nonreligion, or false religion, reminiscent of comments made by Sgt. Howie to Lord Summerisle.

A similar dialogue occurs in *The Believers* between Cal, the defender of the rational, white, Western perspective, and Oscar Sezine (Raúl Dávila), an apologist for the practitioners of Santería. During this exchange Oscar's defense resembles that of Lord Summerisle in many ways:

> Oscar: My God, do you really think we are savages? That we'd be capable of killing children?
>
> Cal: You said in your book that human sacrifice was practiced at one time.
>
> Oscar: Name me one religion where atrocities have not been committed in the name of a God. Santería is a force for good! It is not a blood cult trading on innocent lives.
>
> Cal: What are you people so afraid of?
>
> Oscar: Of your ignorance, of your prejudice. You use it as a weapon against us.

Those with a more objective frame of reference might find themselves agreeing with Oscar. After all, as we have seen numerous times, the hegemonic discourse seeks to depict the different as dangerous and outside the norm. However, before we award this scene the grand prize for opposition to the dominant hegemonic code, we have to consider that the events of the film ultimately prove that Cal is right; the film's Santería practitioners are not only bloodthirsty killers, they go after our children, which happens to be among the media's favorite tropes for manufacturing consent against alternative religions.

Curse of the Voodoo

This 1965 film is notable for two reasons. First, it has very little to do with Vodou in actuality. Set in Africa, it deals with a curse placed upon large-game hunter Mike Stacey (Bryant Haliday) for killing a lion sacred to the Simbaza tribe. There are Vodou-esque elements, such as the use of a member of Mike's hunting party as a live Vodou doll used to torment Mike. Beyond this, the best this film can muster in terms of its depiction of Vodou is the association Vodou has with Africa. However, this is the point. In this film Vodou is taken wildly out of context as Vodou's connection to primitive Africa is stretched beyond the point of credibility.

As this film was created during the height of the civil rights struggle, it is not surprising that the racism in *Curse of the Voodoo* is far more obvious than the subtle varieties outlined above. Also, from the beginning this film confronts the viewer with an Orientalist discourse. Beginning with an extended scene of the Simbaza tribe dancing around a fire with a lone female in ecstatic dance, the camera lingers on her swaying pelvis and buttocks. Edward Said illustrated how sexual conquest and the (constructed) sexual and exotic nature of women in the Orient fit within the framework of cultural imperialism (Said 1978). Here it serves to exoticize those of alien cultures and provides an outlet for male fantasies regarding the sexually available primitive. If there is any uncertainty about the Orientalist attitude of this film, the narrative voice-over of the opening scenes leaves little doubt: "Africa, a country that for centuries was hidden from civilized man. Africa, where primitive tribes still practice evil religions which weave a dark web of death around all who sin against their gods." These ideas are reinforced through the comments of Major (Dennis Price), the safari guide, when he explains regarding the Simbaza, "They also practice a very potent black magic ... These people are further from civilization than stone age man." Even simple words like "these" or "they" function as racialized language, creating a binary opposition between us and "them," the alien other.

Satanism

It is difficult to think of a religious movement more diametrically opposed to the dominant Judeo-Christian hegemony than Satanism. Defining modern Satanism suffers from the same issues faced when defining neo-Paganism and Wicca. Groups that define themselves as Satanists come and go rather quickly and there is little real unity that ties Satanists of various stripes together. Satanism tends to be highly individualistic and there is no consensus regarding theological doctrine.

One of the difficulties writing about depictions of Satanism in film lies in the fact that there is a lot of confusion about what constitutes Satanism. On one level filmmakers follow a long tradition of Christian propaganda extending far back into the Middle Ages that conflates everything from the Pagan religions of old Europe to witchcraft in the latter Middle Ages as Satanic. Even today it is common to find this intentional confusion in films that mix Paganism and witchcraft with Satanism.

The Seventh Victim

There are a few films that depict the activities of intentional, self-consciously Satanic groups. Among the earliest is the 1943 Val Lewton film *The Seventh Victim*. Like many other films that depict Satanic groups (*Rosemary's Baby*, 1968; *The Omen*, 1976), *The Seventh Victim* is rooted in a Catholic context. Mary (Kim Hunter), a teen student at a Catholic school, travels to New York to find her missing sister Jacqueline (Jean Brooks), only to learn that Jacqueline is a member of a devil cult called the Palladists. As Mary slowly unravels the mystery of her missing sister, she learns that Jacqueline has been condemned to death by the group for betraying their confidence, an offense punishable by death.

This film is a good example of the importance historical context plays in both the creation and reception of these films. *The Seventh Victim* was filmed during a troubled period in world history. Already devastated by the Great War and well into the Second World War, the modernist ideal of constant progress toward the resolution of humanity's ills had collapsed. In some circles the ethical systems that did nothing to curb the inhumanity and brutality of world war and economic collapse came under scrutiny, resulting in existential relativism and angst.

In this film Jason (Erford Gage), a poet in love with Mary who is also investigating Jacqueline's disappearance, encounters this type of moral relativism with the Palladists. "The devil worshippers, the lovers of evil. It's a joke, a pathetic little joke. You're a poor, wretched group of people who have taken the wrong turning," Jason says, defending a Judeo-Christian hegemonic understanding of devil worship. In response to this comment, a Palladist states in fine existential fashion: "Wrong? Who knows what is wrong or right? If I prefer to believe in Satanic majesty and power, who can deny me? What proof can you bring that good is superior to evil?" What proof indeed, for the self-declared "good" had their chance while millions died in rat- and disease-infested trenches and millions more suffered through worldwide economic ruin in the 1930s.

The Satanism of *The Seventh Victim* represents a strongly countercultural ethic, one that maintains that the dominant ethical system has failed. As such, it actually foreshadows the arguments later made by Anton LaVey, the founder of the Church of Satan and the most recognizable voice in religious Satanism. Many misperceptions exist in popular culture regarding who religious Satanists are and what they believe. As with other alternative religious movements, misperceptions about Satanists are part of the dominant hegemonic system designed to denigrate and alienate these religious groups. In the case of Satanism, hegemonic maintenance is made that much easier because the history of Satan as the antithesis of Christianity spans millennia. Multiple discourses about Satanism have circulated in Western culture for hundreds of years, and are easily drawn upon and employed to reinforce popular misnomers.

The Satanism advocated by Anton LaVey (1930–97), finding expression in works such as *The Satanic Bible* (1969) and in his founding of the Church of Satan in 1966 (Year One, *Ano Satanas*), does not accept the literal, embodied reality of Satan (as opposed to Luciferean Satanists who do worship an embodied Satan). In the Church of Satan, Satan is a symbol of all things oppositional to Christianity, things that are thus glorified within the group. For LaVey, Satan was the symbol of personal freedom and individualism, including a Nietzschean individualism and the notion that the mighty and strong ought to naturally dominate the weak.

Anton LaVey's vision of the Satanic is vastly different from the hegemonic discourse that dominates the media about such groups, particularly as expressed in the mid- to late 1980s. In short, this period was rife with rumors of satanic cults engaged in nefarious deeds ranging from drug use, occult magic, rape, cannibalism, child molestation, abuse, and ritual sacrifice of humans and animals, to infiltrating our most cherished organizations and institutions "in order to subvert society, create chaos, and thus promote their beliefs in Satan worship" (Victor 1993: 4). The problem with this discourse is that it conformed to the characteristics of urban myth and acquired a life of its own as a rumor panic. As Jeffrey Victor points out, "None of these claims are supported by reliable evidence" (Victor 1993: 4).

The Satanists in *The Seventh Victim* hardly resemble the black-robed and hooded diabolical figures that many modern audiences may be expecting (*Satan's Playground*

2006, *Satan's Cheerleaders* 1977, *The Brotherhood of Satan* 1971). In fact, the Satanists in *The Seventh Victim*, and later in *Rosemary's Baby*, are interesting because they are so unexpectedly banal and similar to the "neighbor next door." DeWitt Bodeen, who helped write the screenplay, conducted research for *The Seventh Victim* by visiting a self-proclaimed satanic group in New York City. The things he witnessed hardly resemble the popular images of robed figures engaging in black magic and blood rituals. Rather, the Satanists were an older, rather ordinary, group of people who spent their time casting spells against Hitler – rather patriotic and well-meaning for a group one would expect to have sympathies for one of the most evil men in world history. What Bodeen witnessed found its way into *The Seventh Victim*, as the Palladists, a seemingly ordinary and older group who gather for things as mundane as cocktail parties. The Palladists of the screenplay, however, do not cast spells against murderers, but are murderers themselves – a clear case of how hegemonic discourse inverts reality in projecting evil onto the other.

Rosemary's Baby

The sociological characteristics of the Palladists are replicated in Roman Polanski's *Rosemary's Baby* (1968), though by this time the activities of devil-worshiping cults in film had become more sinister and cosmic in scope. Like Mary in *The Seventh Victim*, Rosemary Woodhouse (Mia Farrow) is a displaced Catholic in the big city. When Rosemary and her husband Guy (John Cassavetes) move into their new apartment, a building already associated with witches and devil worship, puzzling things begin to happen – things that culminate in Guy being inducted into a satanic cult and Rosemary becoming the mother of Satan's child. The vast network of Satanists who bring this plot to fruition are not marginal people or young kids playing with pentacles in the forest. The cult is mostly composed of kindly old people like Roman (Sidney Blackmer) and Minnie Castevet (Ruth Gordon) as well as respected professionals like Dr. Abraham Sapirstein (Ralph Bellamy). In some respects, the prospect that these Satanists came from unexpected social groups makes the idea that much more frightening. The Satanists in both *The Seventh Victim* and *Rosemary's Baby* are not easily identifiable and move in highly regarded, and trusted, social circles.

On a historical level, just as *The Seventh Victim* is understood better against the social context of the early twentieth century, *Rosemary's Baby* also should be viewed within the social context of the 1960s. We are well served by considering *Rosemary's Baby* against the backdrop of the 1960s sexual revolution and the struggle for reproductive rights (see Lucy Fischer who calls *Rosemary's Baby* "Gynecological Gothic," Fischer 1992: 4). Of particular importance in this regard is the introduction of the birth-control pill in 1960 and the national debate regarding abortion (banned, with some exceptions, in fifty states in 1965) that culminated in *Roe v. Wade* in 1973. As a woman who has a pregnancy forced upon her, Rosemary exercises no control over her body and the course of her pregnancy. Those who are forcing this pregnancy onto Rosemary are symbolic of the 1960s adversaries of reproductive control (often conservative Christians), thus adding nuance to their depiction as satanic and replicating a link often made in the past between midwifery and witchcraft (Fischer 1992).

Conclusions: "What of the true God?"

So, what of Sgt. Howie's true God? Though we have examined just a very small sample of films, it is evident his "true God" is present as part of a hegemonic system promoting a discourse about alternative religious traditions as antisocial and dangerous. Though I have argued for the presence of a dominant hegemonic discourse in these films, what is missing from this analysis are the agents of ideology – those with the power to circulate their ideology. Ideologies serve the powerful and "are expressions at the symbolic level of the fact of dominance. The ideologies of the powerful are central in the production and reinforcement of the status quo" (Bonilla-Silva 2003: 26). Lest the reader conclude that this journey into hegemony and ideology in film has been a dilettante's errand, remember those very real examples in which the hegemonic discourse regarding alternative religions and the political realities of power merged with disastrous results. When Sgt. Howie is placed in the Wicker Man, Lord Summerisle gifts him with the honor of a martyr's death. As the flames lick up the sides of the wicker structure, echoes of the inferno that engulfed the Branch Davidian compound in 1993 come to mind, and the martyrs therein, themselves very real victims of a hegemonic discourse.

Bibliography

Adamson, W. L. (1980) Hegemony and Revolution: A Study of Antonio Gramsci's Political and Cultural Theory, Berkeley: University of California Press.

Barker, E. (1984) The Making of a Moonie: Choice or Brainwashing?, Oxford: Basil Blackwell.

Bonilla-Silva, E. (2003) Racism Without Racists: Color-Blind Racism and the Persistence of Racial Inequality in the United States, New York and Oxford: Rowman and Littlefield.

Bromley, D. G. (2004) "Violence and New Religious Movements," in J. R. Lewis (ed.) The Oxford Handbook of New Religious Movements, Oxford: Oxford University Press.

Coleman, L. (1985) "New Religions and Deprogramming: Who's Brainwashing Whom?," in T. Robbins et al. (eds) Cults, Culture and the Law: Perspectives on New Religious Movements, Chico, CA: Scholars Press.

Cowan, D. E. (2005) Cyberhenge: Modern Pagans on the Internet, New York: Routledge.

—— (2008) Sacred Terror: Religion and Horror on the Silver Screen, Waco: Baylor University Press.

Dawson, L. L. (2003) Cults and New Religious Movements: A Reader, 2nd ed., Oxford: Blackwell.

—— (2006) Comprehending Cults: The Sociology of New Religious Movements, 2nd ed., Oxford: Oxford University Press.

Fischer, L. (1992) "Birth Traumas: Parturition and Horror in 'Rosemary's Baby,'" Cinema Journal 31 (3) (Spring): 3–18.

Gramsci, A. (1971) Selections from the Prison Notebooks of Antonio Gramsci, ed. and trans. Q. Hoare and G. Nowell Smith, New York: International Publishers.

Hanegraaff, W. J. (2002) "From the Devil's Gateway to the Goddess Within: The Image of the Witch in Neopaganism," in J. Pearson (ed.) Belief Beyond Boundaries: Wicca, Celtic Spirituality and the New Age, Aldershot: Ashgate.

Introvigne, M. (n.d.) "Deprogramming Kate Winslet: A Review of Holy Smoke by Anna and Jane Campion." Online. Available HTTP: <http://www.cesnur.org/testi/holysmoke.htm> (accessed 30 August 2008).

Johnson, B. (1963) "On Church and Sect," American Sociological Review 28: 539–49.

LaVey, A. S. (1976 [1969]) The Satanic Bible, New York: Avon.

Lyden, J. C. (2003) Film as Religion: Myths, Morals, and Rituals, New York and London: New York University Press.

Mayer, R. (2002) *Artificial Africas: Colonial Images in the Times of Globalization*, Hanover and London: Dartmouth.

Olmos, M. F. and Paravisini-Gebert, L. (2003) *Creole Religions of the Caribbean: An Introduction from Vodou and Santería to Obeah and Espiritismo*, New York: New York University Press.

Pearson, J. (ed.) (2002) *Belief Beyond Boundaries: Wicca, Celtic Spirituality and the New Age*, Aldershot: Ashgate.

Partridge, C. (ed.) (2004) *New Religions: A Guide*, Oxford: Oxford University Press.

Richardson, J. T. (1998) "A Critique of 'Brainwashing' Claims about New Religious Movements," in L. L. Dawson (ed.) *Cults in Context: Readings in the Study of New Religious Movements*, New Brunswick, NJ, and London: Transaction (2nd ed., 2003).

Richardson, J. T. and Bromley, D. G. (1980) *The Brainwashing/Deprogramming Controversy: Sociological, Psychological, Legal and Historical Perspectives*, Studies in Religion and Society, vol. 5, New York and Toronto: Edwin Mellen Press.

Said, E. (1978) *Orientalism*, New York: Vintage.

Stark, R. and Bainbridge, W. S. (1985) *The Future of Religion: Secularization, Revival and Cult Formation*, Berkeley: University of California Press.

Storey, J. (2003) *Cultural Studies and the Study of Popular Culture*, 2nd ed., Athens, GA: University of Georgia Press.

Troeltsch, E. (1931) *The Social Teachings of the Christian Churches*, vol. 1, New York: Macmillan.

Victor, J. S. (1993) *Satanic Panic: The Creation of a Contemporary Legend*, Chicago: Open Court.

Weber, M. (1930) *The Protestant Ethic and the Spirit of Capitalism*, trans. T. Parsons, London: Allen and Unwin.

Weireter, M. (n.d.) Review of *The Wicker Man*. Online. Available HTTP: <http://notcoming.com/reviews/thewickerman/> (accessed 30 August 2008).

Wilson, B. R. (1970) *Religious Sects: A Sociological Study*, London: Weidenfeld and Nicolson.

Wright, M. J. (2007) *Religion and Film: An Introduction*, London and New York: I. B. Tauris.

Yinger, J. M. (1970) *The Scientific Study of Religion*, New York: Macmillan.

Filmography

Believers (2007, dir. D. Myrick)
The Believers (1987, dir. J. Schlesinger)
Bell, Book, and Candle (1959, dir. R. Quine)
The Brotherhood of Satan (1971, dir. B. McEveety)
The Craft (1996, dir. A. Fleming)
Curse of the Voodoo (1965, dir. L. Shonteff)
Hocus Pocus (1993, dir. K. Ortega)
Holy Smoke (2000, dir. J. Campion)
The Omen (1976, dir. R. Donner)
Practical Magic (1998, dir. G. Dunne)
Rosemary's Baby (1968, dir. R. Polanski)
Satan's Cheerleaders (1977, dir. G. Clark)
Satan's Playground (2006, dir. D. Tomaselli)
The Seventh Victim (1943, dir. M. Robson)
Waco: The Rules of Engagement (1997, dir. W. Gazecki)
The Wicker Man (1973, dir. R. Hardy)
The Wizard of Oz (1939, dir. V. Fleming)

Notes

1 Ultimately derived from the work of Max Weber (1930) and Ernst Troeltsch (1931), many modern definitions of new religious movements rely heavily upon the typologies created by J. Milton Yinger (1970), Benton Johnson (1963), Bryan R. Wilson (1970), and elaborated upon by Rodney Stark and William Sims Bainbridge (1985).
2 For such a study see Dawson 2006: 14–38.
3 For deviant sexuality see Dawson 2006: 125–35.

Part III

ACADEMIC APPROACHES TO THE STUDY OF RELIGION AND FILM

13
FEMINISM
Gaye Williams Ortiz

Introduction

The first woman nominated for a Best Director Academy Award was Lina Wertmüller in 1977. The first American woman to be nominated for an Oscar for Best Director was Sophia Coppola in 2004 for *Lost in Translation*. In 2008, although the field for Best Original Screenplay boasted three women nominees, not one nomination for Best Director went to a woman.

The Guerrilla Girls, a group of feminist activists, for several years have drawn attention to the disparity in Academy Awards for women directors. A billboard they erected in 2002 in Hollywood made their point with an "anatomically correct Oscar" who is "white and male, just like the guys who win" (Guerrilla Girls 2002). Splashed across the billboard are these Academy Award facts:

> Best Director has never been awarded to a woman.
> 94% of the Writing awards have gone to men.
> Only 3% of the Acting awards have gone to people of color.

But it wasn't always this way. A delve into the vaults of filmmaking exposes a wealth of early female pioneers in the film industry. Ally Acker's 1993 book *Reel Women*, an amazing archeological excavation of those women, tells us that in the silent era of film women dominated the industry; Marc Wanamaker is quoted as saying, "more women worked in decision-making positions in film before 1920 than at any other time in history" (Acker 1993: xviii). Do we surmise, now almost a decade into the twenty-first century, that no measurable progress has been made by and for women in the film industry in the past century?

Feminism began as a struggle against inequalities perceived by women between the end of the nineteenth century and the postwar era. Decades later a critique of film grew out of the women's liberation movement, fueled particularly by the 1960s New Left in French politics and culture. Feminist critique moved on rapidly from the early years of "women's lib" to engage with and shape many aspects of film theory. It will help in understanding the wide-ranging nature of the feminist critique of film to highlight several issues identified as major trends in feminist film theory, and how they fare in the reassessment of feminist film theory four decades on. Within the context of contemporary academic study, where has feminist film criticism gone? Do theories from the 1970s, 1980s and 1990s maintain their relevance, or is some reevaluation necessary in the twenty-first century? Has the film industry changed – has feminism changed – requiring a change in feminist film theory? And finally, what is the significance of feminist film theory for the study of religion and film?

"Cine-feminists" go to the movies

Reading the early writings of 1970s feminist film theorists like E. A. Kaplan, Claire Johnston, Laura Mulvey, and Molly Haskell, one sees a concern with the roles and stereotypes imposed upon women in popular culture, and in particular, in the movies. These "cine-feminists" (so coined in Kaplan 1977: 393–406) questioned the myth of film and its relation to a system of values that informs culture in our society. Claire Johnston, who early on developed a critique of stereotypes using semiotic theory, observed that "myth transmits and transforms the ideology of sexism and renders it invisible ... and therefore natural" (Johnston 1977: 409).The pervasiveness of the victimization of women in society was one perceived element of Hollywood cinema that inspired feminist critics. *Alice Doesn't Live Here Anymore* and *A Woman Under the Influence* (both 1974), two films that were applauded in the early 1970s because the main characters provided strong roles for women, were roundly criticized in a 1975 article by Janet Maslin, who asks: "Must a film that simply centers on a female character be so loudly and perfunctorily hailed as a feminist tract?" (Maslin 1977: 44). With abuse and madness driving the narratives respectively, Johnston's observation that "within a sexist ideology and a male-dominated cinema, woman is presented as what she represents for man" (Johnston 1977: 410) seems applicable to these works of Scorsese and Cassavetes.

Early on, there was a difference in the approaches taken by American and British cine-feminists; Kaplan sums up this divergence by saying that the Americans were mainly writing pop sociology and lacked a disciplined or thoughtful approach to or concern with cinematic theory, while the British systematically developed theoretical and methodological foundations before commencing with criticism. And, it seems, these early feminist critics were not able to agree on the effectiveness of their efforts: Molly Haskell observes that in the early 1970s "the rhetoric of the women's movement, then peaking, was at its most romantically utopian, yet there were no signs of a corresponding influx of bold and defiantly up to date screen women" (Haskell 1987: vii). Indeed, Haskell suggests that in the mid-1970s, because there was a trickle of "feminist-inspired" films coming out of Hollywood, a real sea change was anticipated as an outcome of feminist action and philosophy: "Women would begin making mainstream films, entering the industry as decision-makers, starring in movies about the momentous changes in their lives. As stars, women would disengage themselves from the 'gaze' ... that ... had frozen women in postures that catered to male needs and anxieties" (Haskell 1987: 375). Instead, Haskell bemoans the abrupt disappearance about this time of women from the screen "as sex objects or anything else," which occurred because studio executives discovered the power of the youth market and all but abandoned filmmaking for adult audiences. Real progress in feminist influence on the film industry was stymied not by male chauvinist reaction to strident feminists, but by a much more pragmatic chase for the profit dollar.

However, according to Mary Ann Doane, it might have been a good thing that feminism at that time was not assimilated into the Hollywood mainstream: she claims that "what feminist film theory has to fear much more than the effects of marginalization is a certain orthodoxy and institutionalization" (Doane 1991: 6). Haskell criticizes the work of Mulvey and Johnston because she believes it was so narrowly focused on ideological and psychoanalytical critique that "they neglected the context in which the films they studied were made and seen, that tremendous audience diversity, that lack of consensus" (Haskell 1987: 383). Tania Modleski adds to Haskell's point by noting that the theoretical was set against the popular in these early days of feminist film critique and that "the critic is never wholly outside the culture she analyzes or completely resistant to its forces" (Modleski 1991: ix). According to Alison Butler, the feminist theorists of that decade narrowed their ambitions for film feminism to "the exercise of a feminine gaze, feminine desire and feminine narrative agency" (Butler 2002: 5). However, Smelik explains that the important theoretical shift for 1970s feminist critique was "from an understanding of cinema as reflecting reality, to a view of cinema as constructing a particular, ideological view of reality" so that the "always invisible" means of production creates the illusion of classical cinema (Smelik 1999). In their first attempts to analyze cinema from a feminist perspective, there was little agreement as to how its effects would be realized in any context apart from the academic.

Female as spectacle

Perhaps the most widely discussed theory arising from this time concerns woman as spectacle. The late 1970s saw the rise of psychoanalytically based film theory, and the language of that debate, with the centrality of castration and phallus, is evidence of this emphasis on the visual. According to Laura Mulvey, her seminal work on the male gaze (1975) was meant to apply to the popular mass-entertainment culture, in which mainstream film "coded the erotic into the language of the dominant patriarchal order" (Mulvey 1977: 414). Based on Freud's association of scopophilia (or pleasure in looking) with objectifying people by subjecting them to a controlling gaze, the voyeuristic visual pleasure is explained by the male gaze theory, which relies upon structuralism, semiotics, and psychoanalysis to examine the subtexts of films. Mulvey, in arguing that the voyeurism of classical cinema is a specifically male prerogative, highlights Alfred Hitchcock's way of imposing on the viewer an uneasy identification with the voyeur in his films (e.g., Psycho, Rear Window). She also explains the way in which fetishism, associated with stars such as Marlene Dietrich and Marilyn Monroe, combines with the male gaze to make cinema a patriarchal structure, unconsciously so because of the fascination with the "silver screen." Mary Ann Doane interrogates the helplessness to which women are doomed in Mulvey's theory of the gaze:

Even if it is admitted that the woman is frequently the object of the voyeuristic or fetishistic gaze in the cinema, what is there to prevent her from reversing the relation and appropriating the gaze for her own pleasure? Precisely the fact that the reversal itself remains locked within the same logic ... the very logic behind the structure of the gaze demands a sexual division. According to Christian Metz's analysis of voyeuristic desire the voyeur must maintain a distance between himself and the image ... this opposition between proximity and distance, control of the image and its loss ... locates the possibilities of spectatorship within the problematic of sexual difference. (Doane 1991: 21–2)

Any attempt to redefine woman apart from patriarchal control needs to go hand in hand with actually discovering what the "true" identity of woman is, what Anneke Smelik describes as "a theoretical contradiction of feminism." She identifies "two aspects of visual pleasure which are negotiated through sexual difference: the voyeuristic-scopophilic gaze and narcissistic identification," saying that both "depend for their meaning upon the controlling power of the male character as well as on the objectified representation of the female character" (Smelik 1999).

The concept of sexual difference dominated film debates from the mid-1970s into the 1980s, and as an example of approaches to the sexual subject and its relationship to cinema *The Sexual Subject*, the *Screen* 1992 reader on sexuality, features writings by, among others, Johnston, Jackie Stacey, Annette Kuhn, and Mulvey (reprising "Visual Pleasure and Narrative Cinema"). Mulvey expressed her hopes for a future alternative cinema that would subvert and discard traditional (patriarchal) film convention, which in turn would decline but would not be mourned ("with anything much more than sentimental regret") by women "whose image has continually been stolen and used" in a voyeuristic manner (Mulvey 1977: 428). By shunning traditional narrative and conventional filmmaking, feminists were urged to create a "counter cinema" that would allow them to engage in experimental film practice.

Female as spectator

When we look at the major trends in feminist film theory, the nature of female pleasure is addressed in the question, is there a cinematic aesthetic specific to women? Does female spectatorship imply that a female spectator has an intuitive, unquestioning emotional response to what she sees on the screen? It could be argued that because films are known to wash emotionally over the audience, who "feel" a film long before they analyze it, it is not a gender-related issue: we are all captives of the silver screen. But the implication that there can be a reaction in an essentialist manner, common to all women, assumes a uniformly passive experience through an implicit, patriarchally influenced assigning of qualities. Anti-essentialists argue that "there is no single trait or characteristic that is 'essentially' female, that by itself definitively captures the essence of womanhood" (Eller 2003: 14). However, there were female filmmakers such as Barbara Hammer who, with her films *Multiple Orgasm* (1976) and

Menses (1974), championed women's experience of their bodies in the early days of feminist filmmaking and whose work in that sense could be said to have promoted an essentialist view of women. Tania Modleski observes that the title of her 1991 book, *Feminism without Women*, could mean "the triumph either of a male feminist perspective that excludes women or of a feminist anti-essentialism so radical that every use of the term 'women' is allowed" (Modleski 1991: 14.). In her first chapter, "Postmortem on Postfeminism," she discusses how humanist notions of identity and the subject have, with the rise of poststructuralist gender studies, been disputed: "Since feminism has a great stake in the belief, first articulated by Simone de Beauvoir, that one is not born a woman, one becomes a woman … thinkers like Lacan and Foucault have provided the analytical tools by which we may begin the arduous task of unbecoming women" (Modleski 1991: 15). Associated with this concern is the issue of female subjectivity which, according to scholars such as Teresa de Lauretis, is tied to the narrative structure of film. Female characters in the narrative provoke a desire in female spectators to be like them, and can "seduce women into femininity with or without their consent" (Smelik 1999).

Kaja Silverman (1988) and Gill Branston (1995) have written about the gendering of voices in cinema through sound technology, and how the female voice lacks a legitimate signifying position of power. The psychoanalytic identification of a "lack" or symbolic castration plays a part here in how the female spectator experiences identity and desire.

A historical survey of representation

How the spectator negotiates her way into the film relates to the essentialism debate, but is also contextualized through historical concepts of sexuality which find their way into filmic scenarios. In this next section, I would like to further develop a survey of a century of female cinematic representation that I first undertook for an undergraduate course in feminist film theory, and which also appears in my chapter "Woman as Spectacle: Theological Perspectives on Women and Film" (in Deacy and Ortiz 2008). The decades of twentieth-century film history, during which cinema influenced and coincided with the "genesis of modern woman," feature a range of socially constructed trends in female representation: the sexless "doll-objects" seen prior to the First World War in the films of D. W. Griffith had little in common with the postwar vamp of Theda Bara. Flappers and working girls were popular in the films of the 1920s, and the Hollywood glamor machine cranked out films in the new genre of chorus girl movies. Marjorie Rosen says that "films of the 20s attempted to squash feminine self-determination" (Rosen 1973: 101); this is borne out by the basic chorus girl storyline, in which the ambitious girl with stars in her eyes is punished in her quest for success either by the loss of Mr. Right (which condemns her to spinsterhood) or by old age (which destroys her beauty). The Depression movies of the 1930s, showing women working by their wits in detective, spy, and gangster storylines, were also vehicles for the Blonde Bombshell era of Mae West and Jean Harlow. Another stereotype of this decade was the Femme Fatale, personified by Greta Garbo, whose characters combined fragility with toughness.

Janet Thumim (1992) suggests that a trend in the 1940s was women and sacrifice: in *Bells of St. Mary's*, *Brief Encounter* (both 1946), and *The Seventh Veil* (1945) female protagonists confronted moral problems in relation to contemporary social structures. For the first time film audiences were almost entirely female, and prominent in films of the 1940s was the career woman who reflected the change in culture. The post-Second World War reintegration of men into American society in the 1950s led to a decade of films that explored a variety of models of masculinity to the detriment of positive roles for women. Thumim says that where they appear, women motivate or impede the progress of the central male character; she points to *The Dam Busters* and *East of Eden* (both 1955), *Rebel without a Cause* and *The Searchers* (1956), where the male character is central and the dominant theme is the relation between masculinity and the nation and national unity. The interesting contrast in that decade between Marilyn Monroe (male fantasy figure) and Doris Day (wholesome virgin) held an even deeper significance, in that Monroe was playing a dumb blonde but Day's roles usually were women who were clever, independent, and ambitious – quite unlike the bulk of the roles for women in the 1950s. It is also worth noting the anti-female thrillers that underscored female helplessness made in the 1960s by Alfred Hitchcock, such as *The Birds* (1963), *Psycho* (1960), and *Marnie* (1964). Smelik reminds us, in the context of discussing women's guilt as the necessary pivot in classical narrative plots such as *Marnie* and *Psycho*, that Laura Mulvey said that "a story demands sadism" (Smelik 1999).

Another genre at its most popular in the postwar period, examined by Cheryl Exum in *Plotted, Shot and Painted* (1992), is the biblical epic. Exum focuses on representation and interpretation of sexual behavior, gender roles, and expectations found inscribed in the Bible, and asks whether women today, through portrayals of biblical women in popular culture, are still being given "the same gender messages" (Exum 1992: 8). Exum's readings of such films as *David and Bathsheba* (1951), *Samson and Delilah* (1949), and *The Story of Ruth* (1960) draw upon feminist film theorists (Mulvey, Kaplan, Kuhn, Stacey) as well as feminist biblical scholars (Alice Bach, Athalya Brenner, Phyllis Trible) in analyzing the way "unique combinations of the narrative and the visual ... produce a new narrative" (Exum 1992: 13). Exum's analysis of Delilah, for example, brings into play the work of Doane on femmes fatales, concluding that

> male self-esteem depends upon the image of the femme fatale. Men need the femme fatale and women will play her for the power she has over men. She is here to stay as long as gender relations remain fundamentally unchallenged. That may not be such a bad thing, if we can learn to recognize the figure for the construct it is and imagine new ways of seeing the trope (Exum 1992: 236).

Doane argues that the feminist critique must not lose its focus on "the enormous problems posed by a feminist aesthetics and by the concept of subjectivity as articulated with representation" (Doane 1991: 42). She is careful to point out the difference between an individual female character in a film and the sexual politics of the film.

In other words, representation is only one aspect of the feminist critique; there are larger issues that affect sexual difference, and until they are addressed we can expect the sexist constraints on the female character, such as the femme fatale, to remain as part of the visual vocabulary of film.

In the 1970s different roles for women emerged, in the sense of both a shift from women as relationship-centered to career-oriented (*Kramer vs. Kramer* [1979] and *The Turning Point* [1977]) and increased aggressiveness of women, as in *Norma Rae* (1979) and *Looking for Mr. Goodbar* (1977). Jane Fonda, in films such as *Klute* (1971) and *Coming Home* (1978), established herself as an actress who specialized in roles in which women began to question their sense of identity. Although the popularity of male "buddy" movies dominated the first part of the 1980s, Hollywood began to pay attention to women in the film industry who were popular actresses (such as Barbra Streisand). Two films, *Silkwood* (1983) which profiled a political heroine and *The Color Purple* (1985) with images of both lesbianism and the oppression of black women, came out of a Hollywood worried by Ronald Reagan's conservative policies (primarily by what effect they would have on the economic health of the studios). In the 1980s women began to achieve real power in the film industry as directors, writers, and producers but the latter part of the decade saw a backlash against feminism with the making of films such as *Working Girl* (1988) and *Fatal Attraction* (1987), which Quart and Auster describe as a well-made thriller that conveys the image of "the unmarried, professional woman as pathetic and mad and reaffirms the value of marriage and home as havens of warmth and stability and acts as a warning to women of the unnaturalness of living independent, solitary lives" (Quart and Auster 1991: 171).

In the early 1980s, issues of masculinity, the male body as spectacle, and gay politics broadened the critical film theory field. Molly Haskell observes that with the 1980s came a variety of themes that, through fragmentation and mobility, produced a diversity that acted as a safeguard against stereotype in women's roles. Within the context of lesbian film Chris Holmlund (2002) spots a subgenre arising in the 1980s of the "femme" movie, where films such as *Lianna* (1983), *Desert Hearts* (1985), and *Personal Best* (1982) invited mainstream audience reception through filmmaking that was non-voyeuristic by following the conventions of the women's film or "chick flick." The "woman's film" of the 1930s and 1940s tended to be a melodrama, with its roots in the nineteenth century, the genre offering stories in which women could both rebel and be submissive. Christine Gledhill, Mary Ann Doane, and Annette Kuhn have all written about the critical framework within which to best analyze the woman's film. Was the "chick flick" of the 1990s a natural evolution from the prewar melodrama? Some might suggest that female audiences negotiate their way through a film, knowing that they might be projecting their own desires and fantasies onto the screen, and simultaneously receiving affirmation in their own experiences of romance and relationships. Kathleen Rowe has analyzed the popularity of 1990s romantic comedies, such as *Green Card* (Peter Weir, 1990), *Pretty Woman* (Garry Marshall, 1990), and *Sleepless in Seattle* (Nora Ephron, 1993), and says that women were attracted to the image of a man in these films who is "liberated from machismo, sensitive to women's needs, attuned to the child or even the woman within" (Rowe

1995). The Tom Hanks-type of male romantic lead is contrasted by Rowe with Woody Allen, who uses his feminization to bolster his own authority, which is then invoked "to 'instruct' women about relationships, romance and femininity itself" (Rowe 1995: 187).

This period of filmmaking not only features roles in which men show their feminine side but even creates filmic situations in which men outdo women in romance. This blurring (or even appropriating) of feminine identity is also discussed by Kenneth MacKinnon (2002), who questions the traditional identification within film studies of male spectators with phallic, hard, active objectification, and the opposite identification of female spectators as passive, emotional, and empathic. He suggests that queer theory might be correct in its claim that masculinity is "not capable of being marked off from femininity so rigorously" (MacKinnon 2002: 10). MacKinnon refers to Laura Mulvey's "Afterthoughts" paper, in which she posits a fantasy of masculinity within the cinema that is enjoyed by the female spectator, thus implying that gendered identification is more fluid than admitted or proposed in previous arguments: as MacKinnon puts it, "it may be more fruitful to argue for a relationship between masculinity and femininity and the subject positions offered by certain genres than for a straightforward or direct relationship between gender and genre" (MacKinnon 2002: 16). Women may be making pleasure for themselves and playing with notions of identity as they consume chick flicks, and are competent in negotiating their own meanings and even accepting escapist cinema for what it is without engaging in critical analysis. In other words, instead of asking whether representations of women in chick flicks are "true," scholars might do better to ask what women who view these images do with them.

Crossing the gender divide in cinematic genres other than romantic comedy is something that Christine Gledhill addresses in an analysis of *Blade Runner* (Ridley Scott, 1982) (Gledhill 1995). The appeal of the vulnerability exposed beneath the rough surface of the male character Deckard, played by Harrison Ford, can be traced back to the nineteenth-century novel in which the figure of the Wounded Man is found. Its prevalence in women's writing and art, Gledhill suggests, is due to "its capacity to redress the power balance between the sexes – to force the male into the position of the woman" (Gledhill 1995: 87). The male character, who is wounded by patriarchy and thus able to better identify with the female character, offers a "gratifying spectacle" to the female spectator while "playing to a fantasy of similarity and rapprochement" (Gledhill 1995: 87). These theories, from men outdoing women in romantic and melodramatic roles to the redress of power through the physical weakness of the Wounded Man, contributed in the 1990s to the broadening out of the gender debate about representation, identity, and spectacle as the new millennium approached.

However, the issue of female lead characters, whose violent personas brought new focus to reception theory as applied to female audiences, was made prominent by the *Alien* films by Ridley Scott and James Cameron's *Terminator 2* (1991), only to be surpassed by the sensational effect of the gun-toting heroines in *Thelma and Louise* (Ridley Scott, 1991). Barbara Miller analyzes the cultural chaos ensuing from the film's empowerment of a female lead who "leaves her domestic sphere and enters the space at the margins of the social order" (Miller 2001: 204). Cultural discussions at the time focused on anxieties in social discourse regarding sexual difference and the widely divergent interpretations of the film's controversial ending: an act of defiance against the denial of freedom to and subjectivity of women or a nihilistic gesture and acknowledgment of powerlessness? A film to feed the fantasies of women who longed to buck the system or just another cinematic tale of the femme fatale who receives punishment for her transgressions against the status quo? The debate also drew upon notions of complicity with male fantasies and concerns about how the feminist cause is not helped by this kind of "fantasy-dominating realism" in depictions of women; in other words, we should ask to what extent fictional fantasies depicting transformative empowerment of housewives-turned-outlaws actually play to Hollywood clichéd stereotypes, titillating male viewers, rather than help real women find their political voices. Critics asked whether the audience (and particularly in this case, a female audience) could distinguish between maintaining feminist resistance and collaborating with oppressive, dominant elements in their readings of the film. Could women watching the film negotiate meaning while contradictory signals come from female characters who were capable of take-charge heroics yet were sexually vulnerable and attractive?

An appreciation of the cultural and political legacy of Thelma and Louise's transgressive behavior is more obvious for some than for others: Miller quotes Jon Katz, who comments that "the roar of women (and a few men) cheering in movie theaters all across the country was unforgettable" when the two women blew up the oil tanker, and that it "punctuated a defining moment in our shared popular and political culture" (Miller 2001: 205). The resonance of the Clarence Thomas Senate hearings in the early 1990s, with Anita Hill signifying women's resistance to the patriarchal status quo, and the subsequent mobilization of women in the political arena, are also mentioned as effects of the film's portrayal of female empowerment.

The postfeminist debate

In the 1990s there was another debate coming to the fore, which threw into question many assumptions about the future role of feminist theory and demanded a reassessment of the rationale behind feminism: that it had been a positive and indispensable social and political vehicle for women to advance on equal terms. Feminist film theorists began to look seriously at the burgeoning pluralism of women's cinema, especially film addressing women of color. The black feminist critic Gloria Hull observed in the 1990s that circumstances for her had changed since the 1970s: "Women's studies – though still vulnerable – and feminist scholarship have been institutionally recognized. There is now a generation for whom feminism is largely intellectual. There is no longer the same precise need for the consciousness we carried of being infiltrators and subversives" (in Juhasz 2001: 11). Alison Butler reflects upon the suggestion that since the mid-1980s feminist film theory has drifted away from its grassroots, and identifies factors including the decline of the women's movement; wider dissemination in the US of European theories of ideology, semiotics, and psychoanalysis, and the rise of new disciplines including Women's Studies and Film Studies (Butler 2002: 3). The pluralistic climate being developed in the aftermath of these occurrences gave rise to the term "postfeminism."

Sarah Projansky (2001) asks what kind of feminism is perpetuated in the concept of postfeminism, and whether the term assumes that feminism is now over. In her second chapter she offers five interrelated categories of postfeminist discourses, as seen in popular media. The first is (1) *linear postfeminism*, which is the representation of feminism's path from pre-feminism through to feminism and on to the end point of postfeminism as a historical trajectory. This construction ensures that feminism and postfeminism cannot exist simultaneously: "since postfeminism always supplants feminism, feminism logically no longer exists" (Projansky 2001: 67). Another category is (2) *backlash postfeminism*, which, as evident from the term, is an aggressive reaction to feminism. (3) *Equality and choice postfeminism* is a category that posits women's achievement of the goal of equal access to choice; since women no longer find the need to fight further, they have no need any longer for feminism. (4) *(Hetero) sex-positive postfeminism*, Projansky claims, emerged first in the 1990s and in defining feminism as antisex, puts itself forward as a more positive alternative. Lastly, (5) *men as feminists* embraces feminism for both men and women, although "not surprisingly men turn out to be better feminists than are women" (Projansky 2001: 68). This is an argument that feminism has been so spectacularly successful in reversing the effects of patriarchy that women are now in the position of oppressing men, who now need a social movement to liberate themselves. This range of postfeminisms features several common characteristics, in particular, "the assumption that feminism is no longer necessary" (Projansky 2001: 87).

Although also using a chronological approach, Patricia Mellencamp avoids the suggestion that feminism is at an end in her study of the five ages of film feminism (Mellencamp 1995). In the period from the early 1970s through the 1990s she observes that the first three ages – *intellectual feminism*, *irascible feminism*, and *experimental feminism* – emphasize sexual difference (Mellencamp 1995: 9) and are dominated by psychoanalytic theory and heterosexuality. The fourth age, *empirical feminism*, "moves from sexuality to history, from desire to thought, from sexual liberation to personal and collective freedom, and includes sound along with theories of vision" (Mellencamp 1995: 9). This is the period seeing a technological shift from silent to sound movies. Feminists begin in this age to question history (previously dominated by men) as well as the relationship of the sexual economy to the money economy. The dissonance that is created when empirical feminism uses and changes history makes women's experience legitimate. Whereas the faces and bodies of cinematic heroines had been standardized, "through casting, lighting, makeup, costume, and expression" (Mellencamp 1995: 219), avant-garde artists expanded the ways in which women are represented and helped to educate audiences about sexual and cultural difference. The fifth – *economical feminism* – emphasizes the money economy along with sexual economy, and is characterized by a reintegration of mind, body, and spirit that coincides with the merging of public realms with private thoughts and behaviors (Mellencamp 1995: 9). Mellencamp sees this latest period as very much a time of reintroduction of ethics into everyday material life. Sexual liberation has by now effected a shift from one story to many stories, from the male to the female point of view. Further, Mellencamp says that the economy is a story "that is just beginning for feminism" (Mellencamp 1995: 10). Using Virginia Woolf's writings as an example, Mellencamp points to the public sphere of men's work and the private, unpaid women's sphere as the norm in Woolf's time. Within the film world, economic history has been influenced and written from within both male-dominated market and Marxist premises; thus, for Mellencamp, positing a feminist economic history of cinema in this age of economical feminism is an exciting possibility.

Indicative of filmmaking in this age is the 1992 Sally Potter film *Orlando*, based on Virginia Woolf's novel, in which, Mellencamp claims, Potter explores the relation between the sexual and money economies. It is the story of the survival and liberation of a man who, only when he becomes a woman, can escape the "economic divide of public and private" that personified gender relations in Woolf's time (Mellencamp 1995: 281). Orlando, the young aristocrat who is the eponymous main character, receives a royal charter for property which is his to keep until he becomes a woman, at which point he loses his privileges and rights. Potter tells a tale across centuries of women and men as distinct economic, political, and sexual entities until the possibilities of postmodernity allow Orlando to find – and to free – herself. She becomes the writer (literally) of her own destiny. Sally Potter explains, "In order to come into the present, you have to give up the past, let go. It sounds simple but it's very hard to achieve in most of our lives. We're all driven by our histories" (Mellencamp 1995: 287). Mellencamp's desire, in this complex and deeply engaged study of film feminism, is to encourage feminists to take control of their own destinies and to write their own history.

Deirdre Pribram observes, "The relationship between history and so-called subjective processes is not a matter of grasping the truth in history as some objective entity, but in finding the truth of the experience. This ... has to do with women's own history and self-consciousness" (Pribram 1988: 184). The idea that feminist ideas can carry more weight in mainstream media, reaching a wider audience, increasing influence, and therefore provoking social change, has also convinced many feminist filmmakers, such as Michelle Citron (*Daughter Rite*, 1978), to try to work within the system today. However, the system has undergone tremendous change since the early days of feminist filmmaking: studios are still powerful but the independent film sector of the world market has provided opportunities for many filmmakers who stood no chance of commercial success or who refused to play studio politics. Some filmmakers now refuse to even accept the designation "feminist," preferring instead to broaden out identity politics and recognize many sources of empowerment in their work.

Reevaluating four decades of feminist film theory

In 2004 a volume of *Signs: Journal of Women in Culture and Society* was devoted to film feminism as "not only a changing conceptual apparatus but also as a pluralistic cultural praxis" (McHugh and Sobchack 2004: 1205). It drew in part upon the reflections of a number of feminist film scholars on the legacy of the "first wave" of feminist film theory, and also asked them to discuss whether it still existed as such or whether it had "been absorbed or diffused by broader and more global theories of media, culture and gender" (McHugh and Sobchack 2004: 1205). It also featured essays by film feminists whose established and recent work offers new perspectives on areas such as female spectatorship and identification. One obvious advance in film feminisms is the inclusivity or intersectionality (coined by Kimberlé Crenshaw) of gendered experience to include multiple layers of sex, class, age, race, and ethnicity. An often-voiced criticism of 1970s feminist film theory, especially psychoanalytic film theory, is that it privileged the perspective of the white, straight, middle-class woman who was at home in the Western cultural milieu. Recognition of the complexity of identity/identities challenges contemporary scholarship in visual theory and redefines the playing field for feminist film theory.

Another aspect of this reassessment comes from E. Ann Kaplan, whose work in the 1970s helped to establish feminist film theory, particularly in the area of oppressive social and political structures and stereotypes. In reviewing the shortcomings of that period of feminist film theory, she points not only to the privileging of the "white, Western woman" but also to the difficult and often imprecise nature of theory terminology and concepts, which came from Freud and psychoanalysis as well as Lacan and semiotics. Kaplan recalls a split between those who insisted on a close reading of these theories in order to develop accurate interpretations, and those (like herself) who felt the priority was to make the work accessible to students and consequently were charged with being somewhat reductionist. Kaplan acknowledges readily that today's post-9/11 world is a very different place than the Cold War-dominated one of the 1970s in which film feminism was originally developed. Her desire now is to encourage a multicultural film feminist scholarship that encompasses topics such as "trauma and ... the transmission of cultural differences between women" (Kaplan 2004: 1242). She issues a reminder that most women around the world still live in cultures that are heavily misogynistic and racist, as well as a warning that we downplay the need for psychoanalytic study of male dominance at our peril, for "the more the unconscious is allowed free reign, not studied, not acknowledged, the more it will control us without our 'knowing'" (Kaplan 2004: 1245).

Patrice Petro, in the essay, "Reflections on Feminist Study, Early and Late," observes that "the assumption that feminist film theory in the 1970s and 1980s was one dimensional and homogeneous plays into a simplistic notion of the past" and made for a too readily accepted notion that "... feminism always and inevitably amounts to the same thing" (Petro 2004: 1277). Petro argues that just because early feminist film theory was concerned primarily with discourse of a political and polemical nature, we should not assume that it is now irrelevant, especially when our attention is drawn instead to the growing interest in early cinema in feminist scholarship, making visible the invisible pioneers of the film industry from more than a century ago. But, as Petro points out, the recovery and retrieval of the feminist history of cinema cannot exclude as a topic of interest the contributions made by early cine-feminists.

But perhaps the most compelling essay in the *Signs* volume is "Looking at the Past from the Present: Rethinking Feminist Film Theory of the 1970s" by none other than

Laura Mulvey (2004). She poignantly begins her attempt to analyze the "then" of the 1970s, which defines her initial work in the field of feminist film theory, from the "now," from which she looks back over its development, by admitting the difficult nature of the task. It is difficult because she perceives a "fissure" in the continuity of history as regards the discipline of study, which she squarely puts down to a problem articulated thus: "the tradition of utopian aspiration, which marked my involvement with feminist theory and practice, foundered during the 1980s" (Mulvey 2004: 1287). She sees a loss of momentum in political feminist development, after the heady days of the "feminist challenge to patriarchal society," partly due to the tremendous changes that the world has undergone (an observation also made by E. A. Kaplan). The watershed events of the 1980s (already referred to by Kaplan in her essay but expanded upon by Mulvey to include the failure of leftist politics in postcolonial and developing countries) for Mulvey also mark a loss of privileging the problems of women and the priorities of film feminism.

Mulvey insists that since the 1980s feminism's cultural influence has "far outstripped any actual political movement" and has seen the expansion of involvement of women in the visual arts, enhanced by the innovation of new and accessible technologies. Paradoxically this innovation has also caused a "point of fissure" for cinema, because the celluloid medium has been superseded by digital technology. Mulvey, however, sees this situation as offering potential for a reassessment of cinema: "Itself facing an 'end of an era,' the cinema can thus provide a means for reflecting on history and its representation and for negotiating back across the divide" (Mulvey 2004: 1287). In her original essay, Mulvey applauded the technological innovations that allowed for the development of economic conditions in which both artisanal as well as capitalist cinema could exist. What is fascinating about her perspective on the change in her original "point of engagement" with feminist film theory – the voyeuristic gaze of the male spectator – is the observation that, along with the eroticized image of the female star, "then the concept depended, in the first instance, on certain material conditions of cinema exhibition: darkness, the projector beam lighting up on the screen, the procession of images that imposed their own rhythm on the spectator's attention" (Mulvey 2004: 1288–9). In other words, the cinematic spectacle held the spectator hostage, unable to escape from the effects of the images on the silver screen. The psychoanalytic theory, in essence, depended for Mulvey on the mechanistic conditions for transmitting the image in the darkened cinema. In contemporary modes of viewing, the equipment is often controlled by the viewer her/himself; for Mulvey, "as the spectator controls the unfolding of the cinematic image, so the drive of the narrative is weakened ... Not only does spectatorship find new forms, it can also allow space for reflection on time, on the presence of history preserved on film (whether as fiction or nonfiction), producing a 'pensive' spectator" (a term Mulvey credits to Raymond Bellour; Mulvey 2004: 1289). Originally, Mulvey insists, feminist theorists felt it very important to interrogate the relation between image and referent, "the celluloid image and its nonindexical carrier" (Mulvey 2004: 1291); however, the change in media – in particular the loss of the literalness of celluloid – gives her pause to reconsider the way in which we can question our assumptions about and ties to time and history.

The maturation of feminist film theory over four decades has come with the realization that criticism and theory are subject to history and context – film as cultural text, with its dominant, oppositional, and negotiated readings. The danger in neatly wrapping up history and experience in a postfeminist culture – as Sarah Projansky warns in her book *Watching Rape* (2001) – is the accompanying assumption that feminism is no longer necessary, feminist activism is no longer needed (is in fact, as discussed previously, the end point of a linear feminism). But as we can see demonstrated in the microcosm of the Oscars campaign of the Guerrilla Girls and in the larger arena of the 2008 election campaign, women continue to confront social, political, economic, and cultural issues of equality in "their complex relationships to work, family, sexuality and feminism in the contemporary moment" (Projansky 2001: 89).

Perhaps, in assessing the future path for feminist film theory, we should not only evaluate what has changed, but also identify what remains to be of concern for scholars in the field. The rise of gaming – video games and computer-generated virtual reality – has highlighted the fact that commodified images of women, especially degrading and victimizing representations, did not go away or even see much improvement after the consciousness-raising essays of critics like Maslin and Haskell. This field of study was greatly enhanced by the contribution of scholars such as Carol J. Clover, whose *Men, Women and Chainsaws* (1992) analyzed gender and the cinematic conventions of the horror film genre. If anything, the ability to inflict torture, injury, and death onto a female game character is all the more disturbing because the spectator is anything but passive. The objections made to Michael Powell's 1960 voyeuristic thriller *Peeping Tom* – that it used the camera to make the viewer complicit in the deranged attacks on innocent women victims – seem very dated now that the Nintendo Wii mimics physical motions as the gamer performs them: "the tool you have in the game is figuratively in your hand," and this major difference from previous forms of console hardware "enforces a sense of realism" that removes psychological boundaries (MacInnes 2007).

As regards women's presence in the film industry, some might think that the challenges that women once faced in terms of gaining access to industry jobs might have somewhat changed in nature; after all, there were record numbers of women working as directors, executive producers, producers, writers, cinematographers, and editors on the top 250 domestic grossing films in the late 1990s. However, according to Martha M. Lauzen's annual survey "The Celluloid Ceiling" (Lauzen 2007), 2007 saw a decline of 2 percent from 1998 in the number of women performing these jobs (comprising 15 percent of the total people employed in these positions in the US film industry). Lauzen found that, of these films that grossed over $9 billion, 94 percent had no female directors; 82 percent no female writers; 98 percent no female cinematographers. The genre women were most likely to work on in 2007 was romantic comedy, followed by romantic drama and documentary films; they were least likely to work on action-adventure, science fiction, and horror films. It seems that the anticipation with which feminist scholars such as Molly Haskell viewed the influence of feminist film theory on Hollywood in the 1980s – only to be dashed as filmmakers pursued the youth market – might be frustrated once again in the twenty-first century.

One observation we might make is that the world cinema market, while still subject to the charge of Hollywood hegemony, is much more diverse thanks to more affordable technologies and collaborative alliances amongst those who make, produce, fund, distribute, and exhibit films around the world. For example, there are more opportunities for postcolonial filmmaking, in terms of both attracting new audiences in other parts of the world and film practices that veer markedly away from the conventions and codes of Western/Hollywood filmmaking. Binnie Brook Martin says, "The cinema of which Deleuze and Trinh speak embraces the same filmic crevices that Hollywood cinema avoids. Postcolonial African cinema makes known the gaps and cracks in the visual/aural field, and the distribution of such African films to western cultures summons a new relationship between the western viewer and the nonwestern screen image" (Martin 2002: 192). These films present challenges to Western audiences, Martin says, who may presume to define or classify African women "on western humanist terms" (Martin 2002: 192): it is likely that they will either eroticize or make into a monolith the image of the African woman. Thus, going over the same ground that Western film feminists trod thirty years ago in an attempt to redefine woman as spectacle is an exercise in deconstructing the privileged cultural gaze. Patricia Mellencamp looks back at the 1970s and says that "feminist film theory opened academia's eyes to the inequity of white women – on screen and in audiences," but that since the 1990s an increasing body of work comes from women knowledgeable of feminist film theory: directors and producers who "see women through women's eyes, telling stories from women's point of view – women of all colors" (Mellencamp 1995: xi).

Conclusion

Tania Modleski writes that feminist criticism "is simultaneously performative and utopian, pointing toward the freer world it is in the process of inaugurating" (Modleski 1991: 48). Since the beginnings of feminist film criticism key questions have been asked: about the nature of spectatorship and the possibility of women's pleasure in watching films; about resistant audiences who negotiate their way through their own spectatorship and the cinematic text; about the gaze as influenced by psychoanalytic theory and the construction of woman as subject; about the construction of gender and the voice of the marginalized, such as queer and lesbian theory; about a postfeminist legacy that affirms the continued existence of feminism; about new technologies that alter and challenge considerations central to early theories of spectatorship; about Western notions of cultural domination and totalization that threaten to distort representation of postcolonial women in the wider discourse of world cinema; and about the diversity of feminisms that have developed since the privileged Western white feminism of the 1970s began to ask these questions. Few engaging in film feminist scholarship today can fail to take anything but a broad interdisciplinary view, due to the complexity of cinema, which Hilary Radner defines as "not a text, but an economic, cultural, social, and aesthetic institution that revolves around the production, distribution and reception of a given set of texts" (Radner 1998: 59). After four decades, the enthusiasm and engagement of theorists of film feminisms are proof enough that they are more than capable of pointing toward a freer world of academic thought and political possibility, but realistic enough in their maturity of vision to see the limitations of feminist theory alone in ensuring real change in the cinema of the twenty-first century.

The study of religion and film is enriched by the development of feminist film theory, because the feminist critique of religion and theology over the past forty years has followed much the same pattern of deconstruction and reconstruction. Feminist theology has alerted the faithful to the male authorship of sacred texts and dogma: Carol Christ, Rebecca Ann Parker, and Rita Nakashima Brock are contemporary scholars who have critiqued "malestream" religion and theology, following in the footsteps of earlier women such as Rosemary Radford Ruether and Mary Daly. The reassessment of the representation of women within sacred texts, and the concomitant recovery of the lives and writings of women within world religious traditions, parallel that process of critique and recovery within feminist film theory. The integration of women into the traditional male bastion of academia has led to an increase in the influence of women in setting the agenda of both film studies and theology and religious studies. And the flowering of feminisms that will determine the diversity of the future of the global community, enabled by the mobilization of cultures and increasing hybridity of identity, is perhaps the most important common characteristic for religion and film.

On the other (less optimistic) hand, the effect of feminism upon the status quo in leadership – whether it be in the church sanctuary or the studio boardroom – has yet to be manifested in the new century to any significant extent: Rita Brock observes that power in Christianity is structured as benevolent paternalism (Brock and Parker, 2001: 156). However, women who remain inside the systems of power in society and who work to transform its patriarchal limitations into equal opportunities should be heartened by the progress made in the past by their like-minded forebears. The vital interconnectedness and creative change so central to much of feminist thought in the twenty-first century grow out of relational ways of looking at the world: the global village is now a reality. The creative process in both religion and film that has been driving and inspiring the revolution in feminist thought will undoubtedly continue to be at work in changing the world, its stories, and its relationships.

Bibliography

Acker, A. (1993) *Reel Women*, New York: Continuum.
Branston, G. (1995) "... Viewer, I Listened to Him ... Voices, Masculinity, In the Line of Fire," in P. Kirkham and J. Thumim (eds) *Me Jane: Masculinity, Movies and Women*, New York: St. Martin's Press: 37–50.
Brock, R. N. and Parker, R. A. (2001) *Proverbs of Ashes*, Boston: Beacon Press.
Butler, A. (2002) *Women's Cinema*, New York: Wallflower Press.
Clover, C. J. (1992) *Men, Women and Chainsaws*, London: British Film Institute.

Deacy, C. and Ortiz, G. W. (2008) *Theology and Film: Challenging the Sacred/Secular Divide*, Oxford: Wiley-Blackwell.

Doane, M. A. (1991) *Femmes Fatales*, New York: Routledge.

Eller, C. (2003) *Am I a Woman?*, Boston: Beacon Press.

Exum, C. (1992) *Plotted, Shot and Painted*, Sheffield: Sheffield Academic Press.

Gledhill, C. (1995) "Women Reading Men," in P. Kirkham and J. Thumim, *Me Jane: Masculinity, Movies and Women*, New York: St. Martin's Press: 73–93.

Guerrilla Girls: Oscar Billboard (2002). Online. Available HTTP: <http://www.guerrillagirls.com/posters/oscarfinal.shtml> (accessed 21 February 2008)

Haskell, M. (1987) *From Reverence to Rape*, Chicago: University of Chicago Press.

Holmlund, C. (2002) *Impossible Bodies*, New York: Routledge.

Johnston, C. (1977) "Myths of Women in the Cinema," in K. Kay and G. Peary (eds) *Women and the Cinema*, New York: Dutton: 407–11.

Juhasz, A. (ed.) (2001) *Women of Vision*, Minneapolis: University of Minnesota Press.

Kaplan, E. A. (1977) "Interview with British Cine-Feminists," in K. Kay and G. Peary (eds) *Women and the Cinema*, New York: Dutton: 393–406.

—— (2004) "Global Feminisms and the State of Feminist Film Theory," *Signs: Journal of Women in Culture and Society* 30 (1): 1236–48.

Kay, K. and Peary, G. (eds) (1977) *Women and the Cinema*, New York: Dutton.

Kirkham, P. and Thumim, J. (eds) (1995) *Me Jane: Masculinity, Movies and Women*, New York: St. Martin's Press.

Lauzen, M. M. (2007) "The Celluloid Ceiling." Online. Available HTTP: <http://magazine.women-in-film.com/Home/POV/StatisticalResearch/Reports/tabid/96/ArticleID/110/CBModuleId/728/Default.aspx> (accessed 27 April 2008).

McCaughey, M. and King, N. (eds) (2001) *Reel Knockouts*, Austin: University of Texas Press.

McHugh, K. and Sobchack, V. (2004) "Recent Approaches to Film Feminisms," *Signs: Journal of Women in Culture and Society* 30 (1): 1205–7.

MacInnes, F. (2007) "It's Only a Wii Bit of Violence," *Escapist Magazine* (15 May). Online. Available HTTP: <http://www.escapistmagazine.com/articles/view/issues/issue_97/542-Its-Only-a-Wii-Bit-of-Violence> (accessed 26 April 2008).

MacKinnon, K. (2002) *Love, Tears, and the Male Spectator*, Cranbury, NJ: Associated University Presses.

Martin, B. B. (2002) "Sound and Visual Misprecision in Faces of Women: Visual Difference Redefined in Thought," in A. H. Karriker (ed.) *Film Studies: Women in Contemporary World Cinema*, New York: Peter Lang: 179–96.

Maslin, J. (1977 [1975]) "Hollywood Heroines Under the Influence: Alice Still Lives Here," in K. Kay and G. Peary (eds) *Women and the Cinema*, New York: Dutton: 44–9.

Mellencamp, P. (1995) *A Fine Romance*, Philadelphia: Temple.

Miller, B. (2001) "The Gun-in-the-Handbag, a Critical Controversy, and a Primal Scene," in M. McCaughey and N. King (eds) *Reel Knockouts*, Austin: University of Texas Press: 200–18.

Modleski, T. (1991) *Feminism without Women*, New York: Routledge.

Mulvey, L. (1975) "Visual Pleasure and Narrative Cinema," *Screen* 16 (3). Reprinted in K. Kay and G. Peary (eds) (1977) *Women and the Cinema*, New York: Dutton: 412–28.

—— (2004) "Looking at the Past from the Present: Rethinking Feminist Film Theory of the 1970s," *Signs: Journal of Women in Culture and Society* 30 (1): 1287–92.

Petro, P. (2004) "Reflections on Feminist Study, Early and Late," *Signs: Journal of Women in Culture and Society* 30 (1): 1272–7.

Pribram, D. (1988) *Female Spectators: Looking at Film and Television*, London: Verso.

Projansky, S. (2001) *Watching Rape: Film and Television in Postfeminist Culture*, New York: New York University Press.

Quart, L. and Auster, A. (1991) *American Film and Society since 1945*, London: Praeger.

Radner, H. (1998) Review of *Passionate Detachments*, *Film Quarterly* 52 (4) (October): 59.

Rosen, M. (1973) *Popcorn Venus*, New York: Coward, McCann & Geoghegan.

Rowe, K. (1995) "Melodrama and Men: Post-Classical Romantic Comedy", in P. Kirkham and J. Thumim (eds) *Me Jane: Masculinity, Movies and Women*, New York: St. Martin's Press: 184–93.

Silverman, K. (1988) *The Acoustic Mirror: The Female Voice in Psychoanalysis and Cinema*, Bloomington: Indiana University Press.

Smelik, A. (1999) "Feminist Film Theory," in P. Cook and M. Bernink (eds) *The Cinema Book*, 2nd ed., London: British Film Institute: 353–65. Online. Available at HTTP: <http:www.let.uu.nl/womens_studies/anneke/filmtheory.html> (accessed 14 April 2008).

Thumim, J. (1992) *Celluloid Sisters*, London: Macmillan.

Filmography

Alice Doesn't Live Here Anymore (1974, dir. M. Scorsese)
Alien (1979, dir. R. Scott)
Bells of St. Mary's (1946, dir. L. McCarey)
The Birds (1963, dir. A. Hitchcock)
Blade Runner (1982, dir. R. Scott)
Brief Encounter (1946, dir. D. Lean)
The Color Purple (1985, dir. S. Spielberg)
Coming Home (1978, dir. H. Ashby)
The Dam Busters (1955, dir. M. Anderson Sr.)
Daughter Rite (1978, dir. M. Citron)
David and Bathsheba (1951, dir. H. King)
Desert Hearts (1985, dir. D. Deitch)
East of Eden (1955, dir. E. Kazan)
Fatal Attraction (1987, dir. A. Lyne)
Green Card (1990, dir. P. Weir)
Klute (1971, dir. A. Pakula)
Kramer vs. Kramer (1979, dir. R. Benton)
Lianna (1983, dir. J. Sayles)
Looking for Mr. Goodbar (1977, dir. R. Brooks)
Marnie (1964, dir. A. Hitchcock)
Menses (1974, dir. B. Hammer)
Multiple Orgasm (1976, dir. B. Hammer)
Norma Rae (1979, dir. M. Ritt)
Orlando (1992, dir. S. Potter)
Peeping Tom (1960, dir. M. Powell)
Personal Best (1982, dir. R. Towne)
Pretty Woman (1990, dir. G. Marshall)
Psycho (1960, dir. A. Hitchcock)
Rear Window (1954, dir. A. Hitchcock)
Rebel without a Cause (1956, dir. N. Ray)
Samson and Delilah (1949, dir. C. DeMille)
The Searchers (1956, dir. J. Ford)
The Seventh Veil (1945, dir. C. Bennett)
Silkwood (1983, dir. M. Nichols)
Sleepless in Seattle (1993, dir. N. Ephron)
The Story of Ruth (1960, dir. H. Koster)
Terminator 2 (1991, dir. J. Cameron)
Thelma and Louise (1991, dir. R. Scott)
The Turning Point (1977, dir. H. Ross)
A Woman Under the Influence (1974, dir. J. Cassavetes)
Working Girl (1988, dir. M. Nichols)

14
AUDIENCE RECEPTION
Clive Marsh

Introduction

Paying attention to audience reception in religion/theology and film means doing justice to what happens to those who actually watch films. By "those who actually watch films" I mean real cinema-goers, or even real DVD-watchers, not film critics or academics. But doing justice to what film-watchers do with films raises a range of questions and issues which may prove intractable. Questions about audience reception go beyond theology's and religious studies' interest in film. There is even suspicion about religion scholars' and theologians' motives in being interested at all. And how do you find out what "ordinary cinema-goers" are actually making of, or doing with, films anyway? Asking them (in interviews or via questionnaires) may only produce the insights of particular types of film-watchers, not to mention the way in which the questioning process can always skew the responses. Even eavesdropping on viewers' responses on websites (e.g., the Internet Movie Database; Deacy 2005), only brings scholars into contact with those who write reviews and want to express in written form, for all the world to see, what they felt and thought. Turning to specific interests of theologians and religion scholars, are we studying the reception of religious films, of religious motifs within films, of themes and films conducive to theological or religious interpretation (though interpretation by whom?)? Are we exploring the religion-like experience which cinema-going practice can sometimes prove, or of the response to any films by the already religious viewer?

It is easy and true to say that full attention to audience reception involves all of this. Religion remains prominent as an explicit theme or an implicit complex of undercurrents, across the world of film. This pertains whether we are speaking of film with a Western origin, and with serious or seemingly light-hearted intent (say, Scorsese's *Kundun* [1997] or Anderson's *There Will Be Blood* [2007] as opposed to Shadyac's *Bruce Almighty* [2003] and *Evan Almighty* [2007] though even the latter are not simply light-hearted), or work from elsewhere in world cinema (e.g., Rivas' *The Color of Olives* [2006]). There could, then, be entire studies devoted to the reception of such films in different locations and amongst different groups of viewers. Such inquiry would be a mammoth task. It would need to be a critical, interdisciplinary exercise. It would need to investigate how religion is "carried" culturally in different cultures, what religious and nonreligious viewers do with films with *religious* content, and would perhaps give an indication of whether the cinema-going public includes a greater or lesser proportion of religious people than in the general population.

Aside from the logistics (especially the feasibility, and the finding of funding) for such vast studies, it is worth asking whether this approach would actually get at the questions of most interest both within and beyond the theology/religion and film world. For the issues raised by attention to audience response are not at their sharpest or most socially and politically pertinent when the already-religious watch religious films. Attention to audience reception is at its most significant when it is asked what film-watchers, whether religious or not, are doing with *any* films that they watch. Study of audience reception examines what this means for contemporary patterns of meaning-making and of the function of so-called "leisure activities" or "entertainment" vis-à-vis consumption of the arts and popular culture in contemporary society.

In this chapter, therefore, I explore how films are being "used" (consumed) by viewers, and how they "fit" within the worldviews and lifestyles of cinema-goers. This is of religious interest, because religious people may be no different in their consumption of the media and the arts than the non- or a-religious. My context is Western. I live and work in the UK. I operate in academic and ecclesial contexts professionally, though I inhabit a broader social cultural space when I watch films at the cinema, and a narrower domestic space (the living room, usually within a nuclear family) when I watch films on DVD. It is the academic context, of course, which presses me critically to examine what goes on in all the other contexts and to move beyond my own experience. But I resist the notion that such parochialism is problematic for the academic study of film reception. Limited it may be, but all audience reception is concrete and particular. This brief study cannot do everything. It rises above the limitations of my own specific context insofar as it looks at studies that do exist and uses them in relation to theology/religion and film discussion. This chapter complements that of Kent Brintnall in this collection (Chapter 16) by focusing largely on *conscious* interaction of film-viewers with the films that they watch. Whether the approaches of the two chapters, and the methodologies implicit within them, can be considered complementary, or whether they are in tension or conflict, must be left for readers to judge.

A framework for understanding audience response

What are people doing when they watch films? That question is larger than the question of what people *think* they are doing when they watch films, but this chapter probes the potential gap between declared and actual "use" of film without reference to psychoanalytical accounts of what may be going on. In other words, it is crucial to ask questions of actual film-watchers about the social habits and practices which surround their watching of film as well as what they receive from the content of films and the experience of film-watching itself. As the empirical evidence shows (e.g. Hoover 2006; Haines Lyon and Marsh 2007), a process of inquiry and reflection may be needed to enable a viewer to perceive and highlight the significance of choices made and insights gained. Furthermore, suspicion about what academic inquirers might be doing in asking probing questions is never far away. But the focal point of audience response work is ultimately what viewers themselves are happy to accept is "really going on" when they watch films, whether or not this may have been their initial thought. Audience reception work is thus the branch of theology/religion and film discussion which makes use of sociological and social-psychological approaches to religion and media and responds to a cultural studies approach in film and media studies. It does its work with full awareness of a variety of theories of religion and of how worldviews are being constructed by contemporary Western citizens.

At its simplest an audience reception agenda is asking whether, and if so how, the practice of film-watching fits into people's patterns of meaning-making. By "meaning-making" I mean in the most general sense a clarification of personal identity (e.g., gender, sexuality, ethnicity, though also political, national, religious) and the gaining of an understanding of one's social location, of a purpose in life and a determining of a life-stance or worldview and ethical outlook. As Haines Lyon and I have observed: "People's structuring of their lives, and the shaping of their life-practices (e.g. how they earn and spend money, how they use natural resources, how they conduct their personal relationships, how they spend their leisure time, whether and how they value family ties) are all informed, and worked out, in conversation with the texts and practices of popular culture ... Meaning-making is thus best understood as a set of practices in and through which, consciously and unconsciously, human beings 'make sense' of themselves and their world" (Haines Lyon and Marsh 2007: 115). I have also noted elsewhere how, in order to enable such meaning-making to occur, film invites affective responses on the part of the viewer, promotes attentiveness, gives pleasure, stimulates the imagination, and provides a communal context in which the viewing can occur (Marsh 2007a: 69–71). In all of these respects, film-watching is admittedly not a unique medium or art form. As Stewart Hoover's research has convincingly shown, the way Western citizens consume media is as a "package" (Hoover 2006: 266). People may therefore have a particular interest in films, or have developed a particular liking for (even a habit of) cinema-going. But they may equally be avid TV-watchers, listeners to the radio, or MP3 users. The likeliest scenario, however, is that film-watchers, TV-viewers, and MP3-listeners all use multiple forms of media in and through which to undertake their meaning-making. No sharp distinction need be drawn between film-watching and other use of media culture or the arts, however differently these forms of culture and art may be accessed and used.

What is it, though, that people "do" with film or media within this process of meaning-making? Here, it is necessary to consult the work of media specialists in order to create a framework within which to understand how a religious or theological use of film may be taking shape. Janet Staiger makes use of Cecilia von Feilitzen's work in suggesting that there are four basic "causal relations" which occur in the way that the individual and the media interrelate (Staiger 2005: 18–19). These are: an education model, a reinforcement thesis, a mediation model, and a power relation. All of these can be adapted to open up examination of how film is being used in the task of meaning-making.

Education model

The education model suggests that when people use media, or interact with art, they are receiving something they did not have before. They are being informed about something. The implication here is that viewers are "empty vessels" waiting to be filled. The "knowledge transfer" occurring here is clearly one-way: from medium to receiver. In the case of theology/religion and film, then, two scenarios are possible. In films which are explicitly religious, or contain religious elements, viewers are being informed about a specific religious tradition or about themes with which religions deal. More generally, films can be deemed to offer "universal values" or "spiritual themes" which unite all religions and which operate as a putative undercurrent of all attempts to make meaning and shape meaningful human behavior. This has been the approach of much theology/religion and film writing, for example that of Hurley and May (Mitchell and Plate 2007: 327–36). Even though arising from a specifically Christian context, the attempt has often been made to show how a universal theology of some kind is implicit in what films evoke in viewers.

Leaving aside the important question of whether education is the appropriate term to use for such a one-way model of knowledge transfer (education is at its best much more interactive), a major question has to be posed about the appropriateness of this basic model in theology/religion and film discussion. Viewers who are not religious may well be educated about religion through film. But this is a byproduct of other, more basic, motives for film-watching (e.g., entertainment or escape). Religious cinema-goers do not go to the cinema for their basic religious education. That occurs through participation in a religious community. If the possibility exists that film-watching supports more general participation in some universal theology or philosophy, then this would require considerable substantiation. This is especially the case given the sheer variety of films that can be watched, and the place of film-watching within the broader media package which Hoover has identified. Furthermore, the notion of education of this kind being in effect a subliminal shaping of film-watchers into a universal worldview would begin to sound more like the second causal relation to be discussed.

Reinforcement thesis

The reinforcement thesis maintains that the media preserve the existing social order. Whatever consumers of media may think they are doing they are in fact being constantly reminded of a dominant view of the world, as promulgated explicitly or implicitly within the media being consumed. In the case of film, then, it could be argued that something like "the Judeo-Christian tradition" can be identified within or behind the majority of films watched by Western cinema-goers. There is, then, a theological traditionalism operating within the world of film. Even being able to pinpoint many exceptions merely proves the rule: Judaism and Christianity remain the norm despite the religious pluralism of the West and despite the questioning of whether religion has at all a positive function in society, especially in Western Europe.

As Staiger notes, there are conservative and liberal versions of this thesis (Staiger 2005: 18). In terms of film reception, the conservative version would be represented in the assertion, for example, of "family values." Whether an accurate reading of Jewish or Christian approaches to the family or social living is being presented here, it is easily assumed that "family films" are tapping into a bedrock of cultural tradition with which Judaism and Christianity would feel comfortable. By contrast, a liberal version of this thesis would see films proving an obstacle to creative critical thinking about culture or religion. In this case, one might also expect to see a distinction opening up between "popular movies" and "art-house cinema." The former would perpetuate a conservative version of Judeo-Christianity, not wholly recognizable as either specific religious tradition, though with something identifiable from each. The latter would be more demanding viewing (e.g. Bergman) and ask hard questions explicitly, without being completely negative, of the way that religious tradition has shaped, and continues to shape, culture.

The reinforcement thesis is in many ways an argument for the education thesis in a more hidden, even insidious, form. It assumes that culture and values have already been shaped by religion – two religions in particular (Judaism and Christianity). But that this is so is less explicit than in the education model. However, when applied to film it does highlight the extent to which film is a modern medium. Those influenced by Judaism and Christianity have undoubtedly called the shots for much of the history of Western film. The Disney Studios have begun to address a wider world of religion and spirituality, in a way which also picks up religious traditions older than Christianity (e.g., *Pocahontas* [1995] and Native American spirituality). But this relatively recent phenomenon, as well as being commercially driven, merely takes the reinforcement thesis in a new direction. In terms of religious and cultural development in the United States, despite the lack of explicit support for any particular religious tradition, Judaism and Christianity have been influential – Protestant Christianity in particular. The secular union of states has never been without plenty of religion. In a new phase of secularity, however, "what the audiences want" is arguably a range of films which support a spiritual approach to life, are conducive to religious interpretation, and yet do not permit a single religion to dominate. This is the contemporary background, then, which causes Christians in favor of family values to express concern about films (for the values espoused are not "simply Christian") and secular liberals to bemoan films for being too conservative (i.e., religious at all). Meanwhile, if audiences are happy, then this rendering of the reinforcement thesis shows that what films do in their reflection of a culture's basic convictions and values is give people what they want (and audiences lap it up).

Two critical asides are, however, needed before I offer an assessment of what both of these first two models of audience reception imply. First, is there such a thing as "the Judeo-Christian tradition"? Historians and theologians alike question whether assumptions about an essential uniform thread running through Western culture can quite so easily be found, and can so easily correlate these two distinct religious traditions. Even when converted into the phrase "the three Abrahamic faiths," as if, when Islam is added, a clear shared religious, spiritual, ethical strand in human culture becomes evident, it is questionable whether essential uniformity can be so easily assumed or concluded. Second, is such a clear theological/philosophical strand what even mainstream movies, let alone art-house films, are actually purveying? Leaving aside the further question whether mainstream movies can be said to be "purveying" anything in such a uniform fashion, Jewett and Lawrence suggest that movies communicate more of a great American monomyth, related to the quest for perfection, than any such religion-related single strand of meaning (Jewett and Lawrence 1988; cf. Jewett 1993: 91). What is "reinforced" by regular film-watching may therefore not be good news for interpreters of audience reception interested in religion and theology.

These first two models for understanding what might be happening to film audiences, however, pay little attention to what audiences might *consciously* be doing in and with their film-watching. Things may well be happening to audiences without their being very aware of it, and psychoanalytical approaches to film reception may take what those things are to a deep psychological level, but there is still the point, as Graeme Turner notes, that audiences may not be "dupes" (Turner 2002: 4). We turn then to two further ways of understanding how films work which acknowledge a more active role for the film-viewer.

Mediation model

The mediation model relates to the work of social scientists on "rituals ... mood regulation and 'uses and gratification' theory" (Staiger 2005: 18). In other words, when audiences interact with media of various kinds, much is going on at many levels in human experience. Powers of imagination, memory, and perception are also drawn upon in addition to cognition and affect. Audiences need not, of course, even here be fully aware of what happens to them. They may remain "empty vessels waiting to be filled." It just so happens that how they are filled and what they are filled with is not simply an idea, a belief, or a value, but possibly a feeling, a memory, and a bodily sensation too. Exploration of how embodied experience, emotions, and cognition interrelate therefore features as part of any inquiry into this model. Mention of ritual is, however, highly significant. This suggests an active choice on the part of a media user to participate in a particular practice and enjoy an experience which contributes to the structuring of his/her life.

It is scarcely surprising, then, that in the context of theology/religion and film discussion much has been made of the religion-like practice of cinema-going or attention paid to the function of film within active choices about meaning-making (e.g., Herrmann 2003; 2007; Marsh 2004). Such claims may be no more than observations about sociological similarity. To adduce a religious significance or draw conclusions about theological meaning may be to read too much into what is going on. But noting of the parallels at least invites interdisciplinary attention to be paid to social practices in and through which meaning-making happens which goes beyond the cognitive. Interactive, participatory cinema-going is now happening at more than showings of *The Rocky Horror Picture Show* (1975) (Turner 1999: 114–15; Jones 2008). Furthermore, ritual practices in which people choose to participate for multiple reasons, and with complex results, are worthy of attention on more than sociological or even psychological terms alone. It can be shown that whatever audiences *declare* they are doing when they watch films is significant. But if it can also be shown that what happens to them goes beyond their declared intention but that they are happy to accept that what happens coheres with what they intend, then this is important on many levels (Haines Lyon and Marsh 2007).

It is here where much of the most fruitful research in audience reception work, both in media and film studies and in the theology/religion aspect of such inquiry, is beginning to take place. To put it at its starkest: religious, nonreligious, and anti-religious people all go to the cinema. Even if they all go "to be entertained," what happens to all of them is complicated. Does their film-watching have much impact on religious people's beliefs and lifestyles, or do they assume that their religious views and spirituality are shaped elsewhere? If there is any impact, how does this interaction happen? What kind of experience are the nonreligious and anti-religious expecting? How does meaning-making happen independently of a religious framework? How do forms of entertainment and powerful aesthetic and affective experiences, both of which film-watching can provide, inform meaning-making processes? Given that people – religious and not – choose activities which accentuate such experiences, what is being sought? Whether much religious activity has been displaced in Western culture to a whole range of such activities as sport, travel, spiritual retreats, video games, fitness drives, music, film, art, and so on is a moot point and would take us well beyond the scope of this chapter. But that film-watching and cinema-going can appear at all under the heading of the "mediation model" of media reception is highly significant. A viewer's active "use" of film becomes the focal point of interest in theology/religion and film debate. Such use occurs in the midst of the two forms of consumption which exist – "defensive consumption" and "stimulating consumption" (Scitovsky 1992). "Defensive consumption" denotes use which fends off need or want: the things we *have* to buy or do. "Stimulating consumption" indicates a form of consumption which seeks pleasure and moves beyond the merely necessary. At its best, it enhances life. It therefore becomes crucial to explore, at a time of evident decline in support of organized religion, how the stimulating consumption of the arts and popular culture enables people to engage in religion-like practices and the inevitable human task of making meaning (Taylor 2008). This is where the mediation model of media reception and the theological/religious "use" of film intersect, as attention is paid to actual audience response.

Power relation

Finally, reference must be made to the power relation which exists in the reception of media. This model acknowledges the capacity of media to captivate the receiver. In the case of film, viewers, despite having the power to resist, may simply be mesmerized by the experience of watching a film. This fourth model could be taken positively insofar as the viewer is clear that what is happening in the cinema is illusory (in the sense that the people, objects, and landscapes being projected are not "really there").

The viewer is choosing to be "taken out of herself" and readily uses her imagination in order to enter another world (suspending disbelief). The sheer power of media can, however, mean that the balance of the power relation may more easily tip in favor of the medium over the receiver. When construed negatively, then, the power relation could be seen as an extended form of the reinforcement thesis. It is not surprising that the attention given to mass media by the Frankfurt School emphasized so heavily the media's capacity to overpower the viewer.

Appreciating the power relation positively, by contrast, means respecting that the viewer knows what is going on and is "using" the media for a clear purpose within the development of a worldview or life-stance. This is admittedly a very optimistic approach to what it is possible for viewers to do. It is also possible for this to spill over into *abuse* of media. The charge that contributors to theology/religion and film discussion have often wanted films to mean what interpreters want them to mean, or that what cinema-goers are doing is what religious interpreters would like to think is happening, is never far away. That said, this positive aspect of the power relation serves as a reminder that what any receiver of media/viewer of film is doing is undertaking a critical, hermeneutical exercise. (What is this film saying? Do I agree with it? Why/why not? How does it square up with what I know of my basic worldview?) Much of the questioning which makes up this critical exercise is rarely made explicit. In educational circles the process of critical reflection is actively encouraged. In religious communities it may not be. Whilst it is quite wrong to assume, as religion's critics often do, that religious groups inevitably stifle critical inquiry, it is equally wrong to suppose that religious communities consciously foster it. Be that as it may, in public life, the interplay of media consumption, education, and worldview-fashioning is socially, philosophically, and politically crucial. It is thus also the nub of audience reception work. For the cultivation of critical, hermeneutical reflection in a way which serves individuals and society and which respects religion, and yet is not bound to discussion within religious contexts alone, is decisive for more than those who are engaged in theology/religion and film debates. For those who are, however, detailed, informed audience reception work is important. Whether the meaning-making which occurs in public life in the context of media consumption can be counted as "religious" can only be adjudicated once the practices of meaning-making are examined. The point of such an ascription, and what would be meant by it, then becomes part of the critical, evaluative work undertaken around the process of examining an audience's reception of a work of art or of popular culture.

Checking the empirical evidence: an extended case study

Audience reception in theology/religion and film work thus locates itself in the realm of viewers' conscious efforts to "use" film in their enjoyment of it, and in the process of consciousness-raising about how films function within the complex field of meaning-making. Because meaning-making within culture draws on many different practices and resources, the place of religion and theology is problematized. Though religion may appear easy to define, the necessity of appeal to (a) supernatural being may be disputed, in favor of a more phenomenological or functionalist definition (Marsh 2007b: 34–9; Lynch 2007a). But however defined, the way in which use of media and the arts features as part of explicit religious practice, or of meaning-making practices which are religion-like, is difficult to dispute. Hoover can even conclude that "media and religion have come together in fundamental ways. They occupy the same spaces, serve many of the same purposes, and invigorate the same practices in late modernity. Today, it is probably better to think of them as related than to think of them as separate" (Hoover 2006: 9; cf. also Ornella 2007). Exactly the same can be said of the arts or popular culture (see e.g., Marsh 2006; Romanowski 2007; Taylor 2008). Whether film is considered as popular culture/media or art, if Hoover is right, as I believe he is, then it participates in that same space as religion.

But theory is all very well. How does the practice bear this out? If audience reception is to be explored with respect to a mediation model or in terms of a power relation, then how does this play out? And is there evidence that it is really so, or does it remain the hope of scholars of religion (in the West, Christian theologians especially) that theology remains alive and well in the cinema, when its public role is negligible because of the decline of support for organized Christianity?

In this section I shall draw on empirical film studies research to explore what cinema-goers themselves think is going on when they watch a film. It has been recognized for some time in film studies and in interdisciplinary work related to film that theoretical speculation about actual audience response has to be backed up with evidence of what viewers themselves say, believe, and do. It has also been acknowledged that there is not yet enough hard data to work with. The gathering of such data continues apace, for different purposes (e.g., in theology and religious studies: Deacy 2005; Haines Lyon and Marsh 2007; Herrmann 2007; Axelson 2008; Haines Lyon 2008; though see Barker 2003 and contributors to the online journal *Particip@tions* for entry into a wider world). But however much delving goes on into "the film-watching experience," and whatever disciplines are used (psychology, sociology, philosophy, anthropology, religious studies, theology, cultural and media studies) to analyze the phenomenon, there is no escaping the need to gather such data.

Martin Barker has been at the forefront of such empirical study (e.g., Barker and Austin 2000; Barker *et al.* 2001, and as co-editor with Sue Turnbull of *Particip@tions*). The global research project into the reception of the third film in *The Lord of the Rings* trilogy, *The Return of the King* (2003), a project which Barker directed, becomes a good test case of what empirical research into audiences can produce. Inevitably, it could be claimed that choosing such an example to explore in an essay of theology/religion and film is to choose a conducive film text. It should, though, be stressed that the research was not undertaken from any particular philosophical, and certainly not any theological, slant. Data produced which is of interest to religion scholars and theologians has thus been produced incidentally. In addition to identifying and analyzing such material, it will also be important to see how the many perspectives from which the global research has been studied by Barker and Mathijs' team suggest a framework within which all similar processing of audience responses might occur.

The Barker and Mathijs study (2008) produces seven points of importance for the concerns of this chapter. First, there is the concept of "involved reception." In Vorderer's words, this is: "the attitude of reception in which the recipients are so cognitively and emotionally involved in the fictive events … that they are no longer aware of the reception itself, but 'live' in what they are perceiving" (cited in Mikos et al. 2008: 114). This spells out what being "wrapped up in a film" entails, when viewers speak of "experiencing" rather than merely "watching" a film (Turnbull 2008b: 186–7). Audience reception work entails detailed analysis of this phenomenon.

Second, it is necessary to delineate the many dimensions to this "involved reception." Film-watching (or film-experiencing) is an embodied experience. There is a visceral element to it. It is affective. In work that chimes in with that undertaken by many other film studies scholars (e.g., Plantinga and Smith 1999), *The Lord of the Rings* project shows how multilayered the film-watching process is, and how complex is the analysis needed to understand it. "Affect" could be identified with "emotion." Turnbull distinguishes affect from emotion on the grounds that the latter comes later. Identifying emotions is already to begin to reflect on what is happening to oneself as a viewer affectively. Indeed, "'emotion' precedes 'feeling', with the latter being a kind of cognitive appraisal of the former" (Turnbull 2008b: 185). Whether such detailed distinctions are ultimately tenable will remain a matter of debate within psychology. But at least the embodied and the emotional, though connected, can be distinguished. In addition, film-watching is an aesthetic experience demanding responses to often stunning aural and visual stimuli, and evoking pleasure and inviting evaluation of what is seen and heard. All of these dimensions of audience response are also connected to cognitive processing. Audiences do not simply "think." But they do think in the process of experiencing and feeling film, and especially *after* having had the experience of watching. Film-watching is thus a "whole person" experience. As *The Lord of the Rings* studies show, viewers do considerable emotional and aesthetic work in watching the trilogy (Klinger 2008: 75–6; Turnbull 2008b: 184–5).

Third, attention must be paid to the difference between "ordinary" and what we may call "specialist" film-watchers. These are not the categories which the Barker and Mathijs studies use. There, the preference is for "vernacular" and "engaged" viewers, the latter meaning enthusiasts who watched *The Return of the King* many times. My point is not to quibble with terms, but to note the many ways in which "specialist knowledge," skill in viewing and commitment to a narrative, takes shape. If there is such a thing as an "ordinary viewer" (or "ordinary reader") of any film/text, then it is someone who participates in an act of viewing or reading for fun, interest, diversion, escape, or pleasure. The act of viewing or reading is not undertaken explicitly for any broader purpose or with any deep psychological, philosophical, or theological intent. That said, regular film-watchers have developed skills of watching merely through the repetition of the social practice of cinema-going or film-watching. These skills are aesthetic ("how to read a film") and ethical (being aware of what is real and what is not, and as to how to process what they see and hear). They involve intertextuality – not just seeing allusions to other films, but noting links which may assist interpretation – and often complex cognitive processing. But such skills are often left hidden and, for those for whom film-watching is clearly a leisure activity, left unarticulated and underdeveloped. The lines between "ordinary" and "specialist" (or "skilled") viewer are thus real, but often difficult to draw.

Noting a possible distinction between the ordinary and the specialist viewer leads to a fourth observation: the way in which viewers' expectations are already shaped both by the way they are prepared (through marketing) for their viewing and by their prior convictions and commitments (Biltereyst *et al.* 2008; Luthar 2008). Barker and Mathijs' "engaged" viewers are those who know the trilogy (of both books and films) well. In other words, the "specialist" viewers are those who are familiar with a narrative. In a clear sense, *The Lord of the Rings* narrative is one they live with, or even "within." The "engaged" ("skilled" or "specialist") viewers are thus not only skilled in film-watching. They are knowledgeable about the narrative/s which the trilogy seeks to present and will thus be interested to some degree as to whether they are "true to the books" (Turnbull 2008a; Mikos *et al.* 2008). But they are committed viewers also in the sense that they want to use narratives in their personal development and in the life-choices they make about values and ethical commitments. The evidence for this is clear (Barker 2008: 155, 160, 165, 167, 171, 174–5).

This observation is not, however, a feature of film-watching which makes *The Lord of the Rings* viewers different in kind from other viewers. The case study merely accentuates what is always going on. Viewers live their lives against a background of some "narrative" or other, or a combination of narratives, whether or not it/they relate/s explicitly to what is being portrayed onscreen. A major hermeneutical question which then arises is the degree to which viewers are aware of the narratives they live by. Are viewers, in other words, conscious of the processing which is constantly going on with respect to the practice of consuming any work of art or popular culture in the context of daily living? This crucial point will be returned to in the final section.

A fifth key thread running through the studies of *The Return of the King*'s reception is the question of what constitutes the "text" that people were "reading" when watching the film. The use of terms may indicate a prioritizing of literary approaches to film, though this is understandable when a film is an adaptation of a book. But examination of audience response highlights the extent to which film reception is different from the process of reading a written text. Furthermore, the multiple aspects of viewing a film open up awareness of broader contextual factors which influence the interpretative process. Hence, studies of the preparation of viewers which occurs through the marketing of the *Lord of the Rings* trilogy (Biltereyst *et al.* 2008), public discussion of the films' appearance (Luthar 2008), and the considerable impact of DVD versions of the film (Egan and Barker 2008) accentuate the fluidity of the "text" being interpreted.

This leads, sixth, to the question on whether there are any checks on the range of interpretations possible of a film. Are viewers free to make of a film what they want? In discussing *The Return of the King*, Luthar can still speak of "the meaning" of the film, even whilst emphasizing the contextual factors surrounding its reception in Slovenia, the focus of her study, and the "multiple determinations" which influence meaning-making. Mikos presses the interplay between (film as) text and reader much more in his examination of the reception of a text as a "cultural practice" (Mikos 2008). There is clearly evidence of viewers' active "use" of *The Lord of the Rings* narrative/s in an intentional way (Biltereyst and Van Bauwel 2008: 202–3). Viewers choose to make meaning *for themselves* with this narrative. Furthermore, whilst some see this as a very individual undertaking (Klinger 2008: 74; Turnbull 2008b: 187), others are conscious of the viewing communities within which they are located. Whether these are real or virtual communities (actual audiences, "fan communities," or "communities of the imagination"), viewers can be conscious of being members of, in the words of one film-watcher, "a community of believers" (cited in Mikos *et al.* 2008: 126).

Whether conscious of the claims of the text behind the film, or of the communities of which they are a part, this dimension of the viewing experience indicates that there are constraints in the interpretative process. There are some controls which limit the range of possible meanings a viewer may ascribe to a film. But this range may be very wide indeed. Of equal, if not greater, importance is the *use* to which such meanings are put. Here, the question of legitimacy (can *The Return of the King* mean what this person wants it to mean?) also dovetails with that of identity and ethics (for what is a viewer using *The Return of the King* in terms of their discovery/expression of who they are and how they are choosing to behave?).

Finally, an observation must be made about the communities to which viewers might see themselves belonging as they are watching *The Lord of the Rings*. Narratives are carried by communities. *The Lord of the Rings*, as already noted, produces real or virtual communities of supporters ("communities of believers") who live "by" or "within" the narrative. Study of such a phenomenon would need to draw on fan studies. How and why do such fans behave as they do? What is entailed in such fandom? Even if the link between such use of *The Lord of the Rings* trilogy and religious belief is explicable in sociological or social-psychological terms, it is of huge interest to scholars of religion. For meaningful and purposeful participation in the narrative and communities which relate to *The Lord of the Rings* phenomenon are an example of how commitment to a particular narrative takes shape. It matters whom you trust, and with whom you associate. It matters which communities you belong to and how you gain access to a narrative or set of narratives within which to live. It is crucial to see how the process of interpretation of "the text" occurs, who undertakes such interpretation, and what role any reader or viewer can play in the interpretative process.

These seven points, distilled from the discussion of the reception of *The Return of the King*, offer a useful list of key issues which arise from attention to audience reception pertinent to the concerns of theology and religion. They can be summarized thus:

- Film-watching is a complex, involved phenomenon.
- It is embodied, affective, aesthetic, and demands active cognitive processing on the part of the viewer.
- Ordinary viewers can be distinguished from skilled viewers but the distinction is not always clear, for regular film-watching itself enables skills of viewing to develop.
- All viewers bring baggage to their viewing, be that knowledge of "the book behind the film" or a set of ethical, political, philosophical, or religious commitments in

relation to which a film is watched. The viewing experience draws on and demands interaction on the viewer's part with these "narratives that they live by."

- "The text" of a film is bigger than what is on screen, or what is viewed in a single viewing.
- Films cannot simply mean what viewers want them to mean, but interaction between viewers' worldviews and value systems means that meaning is interactive and discursive.
- Viewers are members of multiple communities of meaning (which relate to the narratives by which they live and the value systems they support), and these may include fan communities relating to the films they watch.

It is now necessary to draw on the framework of media reception spelled out in the previous section and the more specific film-related issues identified here with respect to the concerns of religion scholars and theologians. If all this is indeed happening to audiences, then so what? Are audiences being introduced explicitly or subliminally to a theology, religious outlook, or spirituality through film (via some form of "education" or "reinforcement" model of media reception)? Are they having religious experiences? If so, is that only with some films, in some contexts? Or is any religious or theological "take" on what is happening to and for film audiences only possible because of what viewers are *already* like, and the baggage they already carry with them *to* the cinema? This would suggest that audience reception presupposes a "mediation model," but that this only works for the already-religious. It is to these crucial questions that we turn in the next section.

Assessing the gains for religion, theology, and film

Religious people can turn any text or life experience into a theological resource. They are hermeneutically trained to do so. If the whole of life is lived with respect to God/ the Divine, then it is inevitable that any cultural product – a film, for example – can be interpreted through a theological lens. Indeed it must be so. This does not make all films "religious films." It is simply the way that religious/theological hermeneutics happens. A religious film-viewer therefore operates within an interpretative world which is informed by a specific narrative, set of narratives, or range of social (religious) practices. These all come into play as life is lived and the arts and popular culture are consumed.

Alongside the "religious viewer" stands "the religious film." A film which is explicitly *about* religion, or takes a religious theme as its main focal point, would obviously be of interest to scholars in the field of theology/religion and film. The two strands of inquiry could even be put together: what do religious people do with religious films? If these scenarios were the sole ways in which theology/religion and film were seen to be in relationship, however, then the field of study would be very limited indeed. That the field of study is broader, and much more interesting, than this is why this whole volume exists. This section must therefore clarify the further ways in which audience reception of film informs theology and religion, beyond these most obvious ones, and what can be deduced from this.

Deacy's study of what reviewers have been posting on the Internet Movie Database in response to films watched is a good attempt to broaden the base of what needs to be studied between the extremes of "religious viewer" and "religious film" (Deacy 2005). Deacy explores the IMDb to discover what actual viewers are saying about a range of particular films, not all of which can be labeled "religious." His is therefore a bold and imaginative attempt to get behind and beyond the critics and the academics to discover how so-called "real" or "ordinary" film-watchers are reacting and responding to film. Admittedly, it could be claimed that the responses in which Deacy becomes especially interested derive from already-religious viewers, regardless of the films being watched. Furthermore, it cannot even be known whether or not this is the case. So there is no firm confirmation that Deacy's work actually takes us beyond the realm of "religious viewers" interpreting films through the filter of the lenses already shaped by their prior religious commitments.

When considered alongside the results of Barker and Mathijs' study, however, Deacy's work is cast in a fresh light. Deacy works from a perspective of the scholarly study of religion. Barker and Mathijs had no such interests. This is not to say that they had none, merely that their interests lay elsewhere. Common to each study, however, is the fact that moviegoers engage in sufficient numbers with the practice of film-watching in a way which indicates how they use film for meaning-making purposes. The religion-likeness of the use of the film is sometimes very explicit. As was noted with respect to the Barker and Mathijs studies, the Tolkien narrative functions authoritatively for viewers (in book and film form, a "second Bible"; Barker 2008: 171). It creates communities of followers/users. The viewers actively engage with the text in clarifying their life-choices and values and they participate in the *experience* of watching the films (sometimes repeatedly) both for enjoyment and for purposes of personal development. All of these features, I suggest, indicate the religion-likeness of the reception of the film. To conclude, as Barker does, that "the films attract a distinctive following who love them as a form of nonreligious spirituality" (Barker 2008: 175) is somewhat limiting. It does not appear to me legitimate to conclude that followers automatically adopt a nonreligious stance. It would be more accurate to say that the films function as a form of spirituality which some will see as religious and some not, but that the practice of reception is sociologically (phenomenologically and functionally) akin to a religion. Neither Deacy's nor Barker and Mathijs' study can show whether the religion-likeness of the use is explicit for the already-religious, or whether it is more general. But that the religion-like use occurs at all is clear.

These findings have been confirmed in studies undertaken in the UK by Charlotte Haines Lyon (Marsh 2007c; Haines Lyon and Marsh 2007; Haines Lyon 2008) and more extensively in Germany by Jörg Herrmann (2007) and amongst young people in the US by Jack Gabig (2007). Haines Lyon's work shows that whatever motivations audiences have for going to the cinema, the way in which films are used in viewers' lives often extends well beyond the initial intention and the experience of watching. Haines Lyon found four main areas which are especially prominent in regular cinemagoers' enjoyment of film: education, inspiration, values and morality, and "what if?" scenarios (Haines Lyon and Marsh 2007: 118–20). Film-watchers can, then, expect to be educated, about all sorts of things. This is both a risk and a value of the cinema. Poetic license taken with historical data or ambiguity about the past can mislead. This highlights how responsible filmmakers have to be about their subject matter, religion included. But education can be a clear, expected byproduct of regular film-watching. "Inspiration" means that films can actually spur cinema-goers into action. *The Day After Tomorrow* (2004) inspired environmental concern and action. The extent to which films encourage viewers to think about "values and morality" also became evident in Haines Lyon's research. This coheres with findings from the Barker and Mathijs studies. Even if people do go to the cinema to "escape" or "be entertained," the escape is not always a form of world-avoidance or world-denial. It can be the creation of space for reflection in the midst of a "good night out" or whilst being entertained. "What if?" scenarios are perhaps amongst one of the most important features of film-watching. The horror genre may be the most obvious case of film's capacity to enable viewers to go on an imaginative journey in the safety of the cinema. But it is merely an extreme case of what often happens for the viewer, be the theme of a film human relationships, environmental catastrophe, natural disaster, or adventure. As an example of "stimulating consumption," films actively encourage viewers to work imaginatively through a range of scenarios in life. In the way they respond, meaning is made, through discovery or construction of the value systems and ethical outlooks viewers choose to inhabit. Significantly, however, the explicit role of film in doing this for a viewer is often hidden and left undeveloped. As Haines Lyon discovered, it was *the research project itself* which both helped viewers discern how they were using film, and encouraged them to do more with what they watched (Haines Lyon and Marsh 2007: 121–2; Marsh 2007c: 154–5).

Herrmann's study appears in a series of studies in pastoral theology. In many respects it undertakes on the German scene what Hoover's work did for North America: it analyzes in detail the way in which media and religion now interweave. In the case of Herrmann, the use of film plays a more prominent role than for Hoover. On the basis of a number of extensive interviews with people in their twenties and thirties, Herrmann is able to identify what he calls the "religious dimensions" to his research subjects' use of film. These are: the provision of role models; engagement with significant themes pertinent to understanding self and world; handling life issues; searching for authenticity; enhanced aesthetic experience; encounter with transcendence; and ethical reflection (Herrmann 2007: 279–88).

In the case of both Haines Lyon and Herrmann, of course, it could be argued that these are cases of religion-orientated scholars finding what they want in the evidence, even formulating questions and constructing interviews to enable the "right" answers to be given. Such a response would, however, be disrespectful of the integrity of the researchers and indicate a reluctance to accept the increasing evidence of the ways that religion, theology, and spirituality continue to take shape within and to influence culture. Contrary to proponents of theories of secularization, though Christianity may be numerically on the wane in the West, "religion" is a hot topic. Suspicion of religion and of religions exists in the West, as if religiosity is an unwelcome lingering trace of medieval practice in a post-Enlightenment age. Nevertheless, it is vital to note that what religions have traditionally been addressing, and what may at its most general be termed "spirituality," is still alive and well and mutating into a variety of social practices, including film-watching and media consumption.

How then is the "religion-likeness" of the practice of film-watching to be summarized? What insights does attention to audience reception of film produce for the study of theology and religion in the contemporary world? Haines Lyon and Herrmann have offered summaries of their own. In adding a different kind of summary I wish simply to draw together some insights which can inform where theology and religious studies need to go from here, in the light of what audiences (whether explicitly religious or not, and whether or not we can even know) are evidently doing with their film-watching.

Theology/religious studies must be interested in where meaning-making is happening

Both theology and religious studies cannot make do with studying simply the explicit resources of religious traditions. They must do this (historically and with respect to contemporary religious practice and use of traditions). But they must also pay attention to where religious materials appear (e.g., in films) and how that material is being processed in society. In addition, both disciplines must pay heed to where religion's subject matter is poached within contemporary culture. For example, the scale on which contemporary films address the topic of "redemption" cannot but be of interest to theologians and scholars of religion (Marsh 2007b: 94–5).

Religious and nonreligious viewers are not different from each other in kind

Whether or not people believe in God may not be the most pressing question for scholars interested in audience reception. Attention to audience reception shows that many other prominent factors must first be addressed, for example regularity of attendance, context of watching, film literacy, attention to emotions, place of film-watching within reception of other arts and media, awareness of ethical/ethnic/political background, purpose of viewing (Bird 2003; Klinger 2006). Explicitly religious motifs and resources are inevitably bound up within the task of processing film-watching for those who are religious. But the social and psychological dimensions of the practice of media consumption are the same for religious and nonreligious viewers. This means that the broad space beyond attention paid to religious films and religious viewers is where audience reception research will prove most fruitful, for theologians, religion scholars, and all other analysts of media and culture alike.

Theology and religion, and audience reception of film, all require attention to be given to multiple intelligences

Theology has been permitted to become much too cognitive. This is strange given how closely it relates to the practice of religion. Religion touches the heart as well as the mind. It is sensual, making powerful use of visual imagery, drama, movement, gesture, and the physicality of symbols (e.g., water, bread). Film does not do all of this in quite the same way, for it uses the illusions of photography and CGI. But it evokes a range of responses in viewers which demands that attention be paid to many kinds of intelligence (e.g., aesthetic, emotional, ethical, social). This can bring the practice of film-watching close to religion, and invites consideration of how film reception feeds spirituality, with which theology and religion are inevitably closely linked.

As a discursive discipline, theology must adapt itself to a dialogical understanding of audience reception of film

Scholars of religion and theologians must especially note this with respect to the dialogical understandings of media/arts consumption, as opposed to the more "transmission" based models. In other words, the mediation model of understanding media reception is worthy of closest attention however significant the education and reinforcement models can prove to be. For if it is so that film-watchers are active users of film (and other media and arts) as they discover or make meaning, then this is a challenge to too linear an understanding of how religion and theology work. If a mediation model is to be respected in a complex, pluralistic culture, then religion and theology need to take care on two fronts. First, the definition of what counts as authoritative media in religion is open to scrutiny. Believers do not simply read scriptures or engage in authorized practices. Their faith and beliefs are shaped via multiple routes. Second, even the way in which authoritative sources and resources are accessed ("mediated") occurs in diverse ways. Bibles are not simply written texts with a single meaning. They are heavily interpreted and widely marketed texts about which films (and TV and radio programs) are made.

Conclusion

Attention to audience reception in theology/religion and film therefore does two things. It urges scholars of religion and theologians to attend to how meanings are discovered and made in contemporary society. Believers are watching films as part of their meaning-making and this has consequences. Second, it encourages all interpreters of contemporary culture to note where religion fits in explicitly and implicitly in the ways that meaning is made. Whether or not a concern for Truth or truths remains viable, and whether or not the question demands a theological reference or response, lies beyond the scope of this essay. But that human beings still make meaning is beyond dispute. How they are doing that today in the West requires all who are interested in the question to attend to what people are doing with films.

Bibliography

Axelson, T. (2008) "Movies and Meaning: Studying Audience, Fiction Film and Existential Matters," *Particip@tions* 5 (1) (May). Online. Available HTTP: <http://www.participations.org/Volume%205/Issue%201%20-%20special/5_01_axelson.htm> (accessed 14 July 2008).

Barker, M. (2003) "Review of K. Schroeder *et al. Researching Audiences," Particip@tions* 1 (1) (November). Online. Available HTTP: <http://www.participations.org/volume%201/issue%201/1_01_schroder_review.htm> (accessed 14 July 2008).

—— (2008) "The Functions of Fantasy: A Comparison of Audiences for *The Lord of the Rings* in Twelve Countries," in M. Barker and E. Mathijs (eds) *The Lord of the Rings: Tolkien's World Audiences*, New York: Peter Lang: 149–80.

Barker, M., Arthurs, J., and Harindranath, R. (2001) *The Crash Controversy: Film Censorship and Audience Reception*, London: Wallflower Press.

Barker, M. with Austin, T. (2000) *From Antz to Titanic: Reinventing Film Analysis*, London and Sterling, VA: Pluto Press.

Barker, M. and Mathijs, E. (eds) (2008) *The Lord of the Rings: Tolkien's World Audiences*, New York: Peter Lang.

Biltereyst, D., Mathijs, E., and Meers, P. (2008) "An Avalanche of Attention: The Prefiguration and Reception of *The Lord of the Rings*," in M. Barker and E. Mathijs (eds) *The Lord of the Rings: Tolkien's World Audiences*, New York: Peter Lang: 37–57.

Biltereyst, D. and Van Bauwel, S. (2008) "The Fantasy of Reading: Moments of Reception of *The Lord of the Rings: The Return of the King*," in M. Barker and E. Mathijs (eds) *The Lord of the Rings: Tolkien's World Audiences*, New York: Peter Lang: 198–205.

Bird, S. (2003) *The Audience in Everyday Life: Living in a Media World*, New York and London: Routledge.

Carroll, N. (1998) *A Philosophy of Mass Art*, Oxford: Clarendon Press.

—— (1999) "Film, Emotion, Genre," in C. Plantinga and G. M. Smith (eds) *Passionate Views: Film, Cognition, and Emotion*, Baltimore and London: Johns Hopkins University Press: 21–47. Reprinted in N. Carroll (2003) *Engaging the Moving Image*, New Haven, CT, and London: Yale University Press: 59–87.

Deacy, C. (2005) *Faith in Film*, Basingstoke, UK and Burlington, VT: Ashgate.

Egan, K. and Barker, M. (2008) "The Books, the DVDs, the Extras, and their Lovers," in M. Barker and E. Mathijs (eds) *The Lord of the Rings: Tolkien's World Audiences*, New York: Peter Lang: 83–102.

Gabig, J. (2007) *Youth, Religion and Film: An Ethnographic Study*, Haverhill: YTC Press.

Haines Lyon, C. (2008) "*Kill Bill 2*: A Film Worthy of Meaning Making?," *Particip@tions* 5 (1) (May). Online. Available HTTP: <http://www.participations.org/Volume%205/Issue%201%20-%20special/5_01_haineslyon.htm> (Accessed 7 May 2008).

Haines Lyon, C. and Marsh, C. (2007) "Film's Role in Contemporary Meaning-Making: A Theological Challenge to Cultural Studies," in S. Knauss and A. D. Ornella (eds) *Reconfigurations: Interdisciplinary Perspectives on Religion in a Post-Secular Society*, Vienna and Münster: LIT Verlag: 113–25.

Herrmann, J. (2003) "From Popular to Arthouse: An Analysis of Love and Nature as Religious Motifs in Recent Cinema," in J. Mitchell and S. Marriage (eds) *Mediating Religion: Conversations in Media, Religion and Culture*, London and New York: T&T Clark: 189–99.

—— (2007) *Medienerfahrung und Religion: Eine empirisch-qualitative Studie zur Medienreligion*, Göttingen: Vandenhoeck & Ruprecht.

Hoover, S. M. (2006) *Religion in the Media Age*, London and New York: Routledge.

Jewett, R. (1993) *Saint Paul at the Movies: The Apostle's Dialogue with American Culture*, Louisville, KY: Westminster John Knox Press.

Jewett, R. and Lawrence, J. S. (1988) *The American Monomyth*, 2nd ed., Lanham, MD: University Press of America.

Johnston, R. K. (ed.) (2007) *Reframing Theology and Film: New Focus for an Emerging Discipline*, Grand Rapids, MI: Baker Academic.

Jones, A. (2008) "How the Fans Stole the Show," *Independent*, 31 July.

Klinger, B. (2006) *Beyond the Multiplex: Cinema, New Technologies and the Home*, Berkeley, Los Angeles, and London: University of California Press.

—— (2008) "What Do Female Fans Want?: Blockbusters, *The Return of the King*, and US Audiences," in M. Barker and E. Mathijs (eds) *The Lord of the Rings: Tolkien's World Audiences*, New York: Peter Lang: 69–82.

Knauss, S. and Ornella, A. D. (eds) (2007) *Reconfigurations: Interdisciplinary Perspectives on Religion in a Post-Secular Society*, Vienna and Münster: LIT Verlag.

Luthar, B. (2008) "Promotional Frame Makers and the Meaning of the Text," in M. Barker and E. Mathijs (eds) *The Lord of the Rings: Tolkien's World Audiences*, New York: Peter Lang: 59–68

Lynch, G. (2007a) "What is this 'Religion' in the Study of Religion and Popular Culture?," in G. Lynch (ed.) *Between Sacred and Profane: Researching Religion and Popular Culture*, London and New York: I. B. Tauris: 125–42.

—— (2007b) "Film and the Subjective Turn: How the Sociology of Religion Can Contribute to Theological Readings of Film," in R. K. Johnston (ed.) *Reframing Theology and Film: New Focus for an Emerging Discipline*, Grand Rapids, MI: Baker Academic: 109–25.

Marsh, C. (2004) *Cinema and Sentiment: Film's Challenge to Theology*, Milton Keynes and Waynesboro, GA: Authentic Media.

—— (2006) "'High Theology'/'Popular Theology'?: The Arts, Popular Culture and the Contemporary Theological Task," *Expository Times* 117: 447–51.

—— (2007a) "Theology and the Practice of Meaning-Making," *Expository Times* 119: 67–73.

—— (2007b) *Theology Goes to the Movies: An Introduction to Critical Christian Thinking*, London and New York: Routledge.

—— (2007c) "On Dealing with what Films Actually do to People: The Practice and Theory of Film Watching in Theology/Religion and Film Discussion," in R. K. Johnston (ed.) *Reframing Theology and Film: New Focus for an Emerging Discipline*, Grand Rapids, MI: Baker Academic: 145–61.

Mikos, L. (2008) "Understanding Text as Cultural Practice and as Dynamic Process of Making," in M. Barker and E. Mathijs (eds) *The Lord of the Rings: Tolkien's World Audiences*, New York: Peter Lang: 207–12.

Mikos, L., Eichner, S., Prommer, E., and Wedel, M. (2008) "Involvement in *The Lord of the Rings*: Audience Strategies and Orientations," in M. Barker and E. Mathijs (eds) *The Lord of the Rings: Tolkien's World Audiences*, New York: Peter Lang: 111–29.

Mitchell, J. and Plate, S. B. (eds) (2007) *The Religion and Film Reader*, New York and London: Routledge.

Ornella, A. D. (2007) "Networked – Subjectivity Revisited," in S. Knauss and A. D. Ornella (eds) *Reconfigurations: Interdisciplinary Perspectives on Religion in a Post-Secular Society*, Vienna and Münster: LIT Verlag: 217–31.

Plantinga, C. and Smith, G. M. (eds) (1999) *Passionate Views: Film, Cognition, and Emotion*, Baltimore and London: Johns Hopkins University Press.

Romanowski, W. D. (2007) *Eyes Wide Open: Looking for God in Popular Culture*, rev. ed., Grand Rapids, MI: Brazos Press.

Scitovsky, V. (1992) *The Joyless Economy: The Psychology of Human Satisfaction*, rev. ed., Oxford: Oxford University Press.

Staiger, J. (2005) *Media Reception Studies*, New York and London: New York University Press.

Taylor, B. (2008) *Entertainment Theology: New-Edge Spirituality in a Digital Democracy*, Grand Rapids, MI: Baker Academic.

Turnbull, S. (2008a) "Understanding Disappointment: The Australian Book Lovers and Adaptation," in M. Barker and E. Mathijs (eds) *The Lord of the Rings: Tolkien's World Audiences*, New York: Peter Lang: 103–9.

—— (2008b) "Beyond Words?: *The Return of the King* and the Pleasures of the Text," in M. Barker and E. Mathijs (eds) *The Lord of the Rings: Tolkien's World Audiences*, New York: Peter Lang: 181–9.

Turner, G. (1999) *Film as Social Practice*, 3rd ed., London and New York: Routledge.

—— (ed.) (2002) *The Film Cultures Reader*, London and New York: Routledge.

Filmography

Bruce Almighty (2003, dir. T. Shadyac)
The Color of Olives (2006, dir. C. Rivas)
The Day After Tomorrow (2004, dir. R. Emmerich)
Evan Almighty (2007, dir. T. Shadyac)
Kundun (1997, dir. M. Scorsese)

The Lord of the Rings: The Fellowship of the Ring (2001, dir. P. Jackson)
The Lord of the Rings: The Two Towers (2002, dir. P. Jackson)
The Lord of the Rings: The Return of the King (2003, dir. P. Jackson)
Pocahontas (1995, dir. M. Gabriel and E. Goldberg)
The Rocky Horror Picture Show (1975, dir. J. Sharman)
There Will Be Blood (2007, dir. P. Anderson)

15
CULTURAL THEORY
AND CULTURAL
STUDIES
Gordon Lynch

Introduction

To date, most of the academic literature on religion and film has been produced by writers working in the fields of theology, biblical studies, and religious studies. Forged in the secularized academic ethos of the 1960s and 1970s, in which a common assumption was that religion was a diminishing social force not worthy of serious attention, film studies and cultural studies have typically shown very little interest in religion. In practice this has meant that the study of religion and film has often been influenced by the kinds of questions and methods of study that biblical scholars, theologians, and scholars of religion find interesting or useful. One of the strengths of this literature has been that its contributors usually have a much greater religious literacy than their academic peers in cultural studies or film studies, and are able to comment with greater insight and authority on religious traditions, communities, and practices (see, e.g., Part II in this *Companion*). One of the disadvantages, however, is that this literature has at times proceeded with little more than a shallow engagement with questions, theories, and methods used in other approaches to the study of film.

One of the effects of this academic history of the study of religion and film is that a specific set of interests and questions has tended to influence this literature. With some exceptions, films have typically been studied as theological or religious texts, even when they contain no overt reference to religious traditions, stories, or characters (Nolan 2003).[1] One rationale for this approach is that films can be seen as examples of contemporary myth, dramas that play out the religious, moral, and existential concerns of a given society, or that they consciously or unconsciously rework religious ideas or symbols such as the messianic hero (Martin and Ostwalt 1995; Lyden 2003). From such a perspective, grounded in religious studies, it makes sense to treat films as examples of texts that convey religious symbolism and significance. Another rationale, underlying theological approaches, is that films can be seen as just another kind of (narrative) theological text which deals with religious and existential questions (e.g., what is redemption? how can we understand the nature of good and evil? what does it mean to live a good life and die a good death?). As such, they can be subjected to theological reflection and critique like any other kind of text that explores questions of the nature and meaning of life (see, e.g., Deacy 2001; Deacy and Ortiz 2007; Marsh and Ortiz 1997; Marsh 2007a).

Whilst these interests and motivations have a valid place in academic work in this field, they also pose certain risks. At its most extreme, studying films as religious or theological texts can lead to a highly reductive view of film as simply a device for delivering religious ideas or dealing with theological themes. As a consequence, attention to the distinctive features of film as a medium or cultural institution can be lost. I have heard of one occasion on which a scholar taking part in a conference panel discussion of a specific film declared at the start of his paper that he hadn't actually seen the film, but felt able to comment on its ideas because he had read the novel on which it was based. Such disinterest in the issues raised by the particular medium of film is problematic. As Melanie Wright (Wright 2007: 22), an important advocate of cultural studies approaches to religion and film, puts it, if such an interest in theological ideas dominates over an interest in the medium of film, "could it be that ... *film* is not really being studied at all?"

More recently, it has certainly been the case that theologians and religious scholars have aspired to develop interpretations of films that are more informed by theories and debates in film studies or other approaches to textual and narrative analysis (see Christianson 2007; Deacy and Ortiz 2007; Howell 2007; Johnston 2000; 2007, for good examples of this). But this work is still heavily influenced by an interest in films as theological or religious texts. An emphasis on film as text is also evident in the work of biblical scholars who have been interested in what can be learned about the cultural representation of biblical characters and narratives through studying film (Exum 1996), or in the possibilities of film as a hermeneutical resource for interpreting biblical texts (Kreitzer 2002). In this chapter I will argue that cultural theory and cultural studies offer important approaches and resources that could broaden the field of religion and film in interesting new ways as well as leading to the more rigorous analysis of film in the context of social, cultural, economic, and political processes. In developing this argument, I will begin by providing a brief overview of cultural theory and cultural studies, before going on to develop a framework for approaching the study of religion and film in terms of the "circuit of culture." At the end of the chapter, though, I will turn this discussion round, and ask what cultural theory and cultural studies approaches to film might have to learn from the study of religion. If the study of religion and film is a genuinely multidisciplinary endeavor, this means not abandoning our disciplinary backgrounds but recognizing how the questions and methods of each might lead to a richer, complex, and more rigorous approach to our shared field of study.

What are cultural theory and cultural studies?

What, then, do we mean by "cultural theory" and "cultural studies," and how have they informed the study of film? A number of very good introductions have already been written about the place of cultural theory and cultural studies in analyzing film or popular culture more generally (see, e.g., Edgar and Sedgwick 2002; Hayward 2006; Storey 2006; Strinati 1995; Tinkcom and Villarejo 2001: 1–29; Turner 2000; 2002; 2003). The account of cultural theory and cultural studies presented in this chapter is only intended as an initial overview, and readers wanting to engage in more depth with cultural theory and cultural studies approaches should also refer to these longer introductory texts.

"Cultural theory" and "cultural studies" are not single approaches to academic study, but both terms refer to a range of ideas and approaches relating to analyzing culture. Whilst in principle "cultural theory" can include theoretical insights about culture that have been developed through empirical fieldwork, in practice the term "cultural theory" tends to be used to refer to wider theories of knowledge, language, power, psychology, gender/sexuality, and society which have been applied to the analysis of culture. Key theories used in this way have been Marxism, psychoanalysis (including Freudian, Jungian, and Lacanian theories), feminism, structuralism and poststructuralism, postmodernism, and, more recently, postcolonial and queer theory. A distinction can be drawn between the use of such *cultural theories* in film studies and early forms of *film theory*. From the opening decades of the twentieth century, film theory sought to identify the distinctive qualities and possibilities of film as a new art form alongside more established forms of the visual and literary arts. Some film theorists drew on the Western, romantic tradition of the inspired, individual artist to argue that a select group of film directors could be treated as serious "auteurs," whilst others sought to categorize and analyze film genres or make sense of the visual "language" through which film constructs particular meanings and effects. Questions of aesthetics were also important in film theory (how does one judge what is a good film?), as were debates about the relationship between the visual images of film and the social and physical "realities" which they depicted (illustrated in the difference between Eisenstein's formalist approach and the cinematic realism advocated by Bazin). Early forms of film theory thus approached the study of film as a distinctive art form, seeking to explain how it worked, or could work, as an artistic medium, and developing ways of making aesthetic distinctions between good and bad film. Whilst film theory did not ignore the commercial interests and systems through which films were produced, its emphasis was more on how films might still function as valid art despite these commercial constraints, rather than thinking more widely about the implications of the cultural production and uses of film. By contrast, when studied through the lens of cultural theory, film is not treated as a discrete form of artistic practice to be judged on its own terms, but as another form of culture which should be analyzed in the context of wider social structures, and wider cultural processes of power, ideology, oppression, and mystification.

A common assumption underpinning the use of such cultural theories is that theory plays an important role in enabling us to see beyond what is usually taken for granted in everyday social and cultural life. Theory is understood as a vital resource either in helping to uncover hidden structures that can have a damaging effect on human life, or in making us more aware of the traditions and habits of thought that lead us to interpret the world and live our lives in particular ways. The promise of cultural theory is that it might generate insights that could lead to more authentic, imaginative, and liberating forms of human culture, or help us to see the world in more complex ways in which we do not compress human experience into limiting categories or conventions. In the context of the study of film, cultural theory has been used to challenge the idea that film is simply a source of innocent pleasure. For example, Theodor Adorno (1991), inspired by Marxist thought, argued that the Hollywood "star-system" was just another way in which the capitalist culture industry presented the general public with illusory and unimportant choices. By giving cinema-goers a sense of choice in relation to which stars they wanted to watch or idolize, he argued that the culture industry acts to conceal their lack of choice in far more important questions about the political, social, and economic framework of their lives. Similarly, Laura Mulvey (1995 [1975]), in another much-cited theoretical critique, argued that narrative films typically seek to present their stories and characters for a "male gaze," constituted around male desires, and that identification with film can serve as a powerful tool by which women learn to subject themselves to this gaze. Whilst some forms of cultural theory – particularly poststructuralism and postmodernism – have challenged the idea that the scholar can claim any privilege or expertise in discerning the true structures of culture and society, cultural theories are still widely used and debated as a resource for the analysis and critique of individual films and the wider institution of the film industry.

The term "cultural studies" is generally used to refer to an academic tradition in the analysis of culture which has drawn on both cultural theory and on empirical studies of cultural objects, spaces, practices, and lifestyles. In some senses, the field of cultural studies resists definition. In his influential article, "What is Cultural Studies Anyway?," Richard Johnson (1986/7) wrote that "a codification of methods or knowledges (instituting them, for example, in formal curricula or in courses on 'methodology') runs against some of the main features of cultural studies as a tradition: its openness and theoretical versatility, its reflexive even self-conscious mood, and especially, the importance of critique … From this point of view cultural studies is a process, a kind of alchemy for producing useful knowledge; codify it and you might halt its reactions" (Johnson 1986/7: 38). In other words, cultural studies could be seen less as a tightly defined academic discipline, and more as an intellectual project that seeks to explore the relationship between culture, social relations, power, and the capacity of individuals and groups to define and meet their needs.

"Cultural studies" first took institutional form in the Centre for Contemporary Cultural Studies (CCCS), which was created at the University of Birmingham in 1964. The CCCS developed out of a growing academic interest in the study of contexts of everyday life, fueled by a sense of the rapidly changing nature of postwar society, but also became closely allied with the attempts of the New Left to develop leftwing, post-communist, social analysis. Whereas previous academic engagement with popular culture had typically adopted a theoretical and highly polemical critique of it as debased, manipulative, and vacuous, the Birmingham school of cultural studies sought to investigate the relationship between culture and social change without these negative presumptions (Lynch 2005: 1–19). Indeed, the CCCS developed an alternative theoretical account of popular culture, seeing it as a site of struggle between attempts to transmit dominant ideologies, and attempts to resist this and to create alternative cultures. The contribution of the Birmingham school to the formation of cultural studies as a discipline was not, however, simply in its theoretical account of cultural struggle, but in the way in which it developed this analysis in relation to original empirical studies. During the 1970s, under its second director, Stuart Hall, the CCCS increasingly turned its attention to a series of empirical studies of working-class youth cultures, including reggae, mod, and punk scenes which led to the development of particular theories of subculture (Hall and Jefferson 1976; Hebdige 1979; Bennett and Kahn-Harris 2004). Whilst this early phase of research paid particular interest to issues of power, youth, and social class, subsequent empirical work undertaken through the CCCS sought to explore other sites of adult culture such as television audiences (Morley 1980) and to reflect more on the cultural politics surrounding gender (McRobbie 1990) and race (Centre for Contemporary Cultural Studies 1982).

Defining the relationship between cultural theory and cultural studies is a complex task. Since the early work of the CCCS, cultural studies has become a global academic phenomenon, and the theoretical, political, and methodological emphases of cultural studies have varied as it has developed in different periods of time and in different geographical contexts (Grossberg 1993; Hall 1999). Some scholars working in cultural studies have drawn on cultural theory to develop analyses of cultural texts without engaging in any empirical study of the actual processes of production and consumption of those texts (e.g., McRobbie's 1978 analysis of magazines for teenage girls). Such approaches to cultural studies, which draw on cultural theory rather than using empirical research methods, have been particularly common in North America, where cultural studies often found an institutional home in university departments of literature in which textual analysis was a more common form of research than empirical methods such as ethnography. At the same time, other scholars would argue that cultural studies should not rely simply on theoretical analysis, but should engage in the study of real-world settings through empirical research methods such as individual and group interviews, archival work, surveys, and participant observation. Such empirically inclined approaches to cultural studies do not reject the use of cultural theory altogether. Indeed, it would be extremely unusual for a scholar working in contemporary cultural studies not to make use of cultural theory at some point to make sense of their work. For example, Jackie Stacey's (1994) influential examination of women's spectatorship of Hollywood films of the 1940s and 1950s is informed both by feminist theory and by a commitment to understand women's experience of film-watching through empirical research (in Stacey's case, by asking women to write about their experiences). Whilst cultural theory is widely used in cultural studies, it is important however to be aware of the different ways in which it is used, and in particular whether scholars adopt purely theoretical approaches to their work or relate theory in some way to empirical research.

This tension between purely theoretical and empirically informed approaches to the study of culture might seem rather abstract, but it reflects fundamentally different understandings of the nature of academic work which can find expression in strongly felt disagreements. A good example of this is the intense debate that developed in the 1980s around what became known as *Screen* theory. During that period, the film journal *Screen* became associated with a form of film analysis that was heavily influenced by the neo-Marxist theory of Louis Althusser and the psychoanalytic theory of film developed by Christian Metz (Turner 2003: 85–9). This cultural theory-influenced approach to film analysis adopted Althusser's concept of "interpellation" – the idea that social institutions "hail" or position their participants into particular ways of seeing the world – to argue that the enjoyment of mainstream, commercial films fixed audiences into ideological positions that support the dominant cultural and economic status quo. This view placed a strong emphasis on the power of cultural texts like film to shape their audiences' views, and on the ability of scholars guided by particular forms of cultural theory to "read" these films in a more insightful, critical, and liberating way. Such an account of the ways in which films influence audiences was strongly contested by other, empirically inclined, cultural studies scholars. Their counter-argument was that *Screen* theory failed to take account of the ways in which audiences exert power and imagination in the ways in which they interpret and make use of cultural texts, something that had been explored through empirical studies of subcultures and media audiences (Brooker and Jermyn 2003).[2]

Underlying the *Screen* debate about the relative power of texts and audiences is a more fundamental epistemological split that has run through the history of Western thought. Since the early days of classical Greek philosophy, there has been an unresolved tension between Plato's belief that the appearances of the natural world can be misleading and that a sure knowledge of the world is possible only through reference to abstract ideas, and Aristotle's belief that knowledge of the world is best obtained through empirical observation. This tension finds itself replicated in contemporary forms of cultural analysis which either emphasize the importance of theory and ideas for providing us with real insight about our existence or which have a basic regard for the empirical study of social and cultural worlds. Both sides of this split in cultural studies can be highly critical of the other. Some scholars who adopt purely theoretical approaches sometimes see their empirically inclined counterparts as having a naïve faith in field-research, arguing that such research is over-reliant on the stories and perceptions of research participants who are unable to reflect adequately on the psychological, social, and cultural structures that really affect their lives. Scholars more sympathetic to empirical approaches can sometimes be critical of the disregard for real-life settings shown by theoretical approaches to cultural analysis which can perpetuate inaccurate ideas about real social lives and generate a form of scholarship which, whilst claiming to be committed to social change, is in fact self-referential and disengaged from the realities of social, economic, and political life. Far from being abstract or esoteric disputes, the battle-lines here are drawn over basic issues such as how we might best gain knowledge of our social and cultural worlds, what degree of respect we should give to ordinary people's ability to comment insightfully about the social and cultural contexts of their lives, and what it means for academic scholarship to contribute toward constructive social transformation.

When drawing on cultural theory and cultural studies, scholars working in the area of religion and film should be aware of these background tensions and reflect on how they want to locate their own work in relation to these fundamental questions. My own view is that scholarship on contemporary religion must take empirical research seriously if it is to generate insightful and useful understandings of the ways in which religion, culture, and society are intertwined. Whilst there are significant challenges in designing, conducting, and presenting such research in critical and nuanced ways, and empirical studies need to be theoretically informed, scholarship which offers purely theoretical accounts of contemporary religion are in danger of offering inadequate, and at times straightforwardly wrong, accounts of the world in which we live. The approach to using cultural theory and cultural studies in studying religion and film that I will set out in the remainder of the chapter reflects this basic stance on my part, and readers will see that my own sympathies lie more with empirically inclined approaches to cultural studies.

Studying religion and film through the circuit of culture

What, then, might the study of religion and film have to learn from ideas and methods that have developed in cultural theory and cultural studies? As I suggested at the start of this chapter, one of the promises of turning to cultural theory and cultural studies in the study of religion and film is that it might help a shift away from a narrow focus on film as text. One way in which this might be achieved is through the use of the idea of the "circuit of culture."

The model of the circuit of culture was first proposed by Richard Johnson (1986/7), who had been an active member of the Birmingham Centre for Contemporary Cultural Studies in the 1970s and 1980s. Johnson argued that a more systematic and rigorous approach to cultural analysis needed to work on the basis of a model of how cultural systems operate. Without such an appreciation, Johnson argued, it could be harder for scholars to see connections between their various research projects, or to appreciate what specific moment in cycles of culture they were focusing on. He therefore proposed a holistic approach to studying cultural systems which would be interested in the contexts, structures, and processes of cultural *production*, the *texts and artifacts* produced, the ways in which these texts and artifacts were *read or used by people* in real-life settings, and how these processes of cultural production and consumption related to *wider social structures and relations*. By conceiving of these elements as being part of circuits of culture, Johnson also hoped to focus attention on how systems of production, cultural products, the consumption of cultural products, and wider social structures were bound together in a dynamic field of relationships. For example, as a more recent study of men's magazines based on Johnson's circuit of culture showed (Jackson *et al.* 2001), magazine editors and production companies were heavily influenced in their choices about what to include in their publications by their perceptions of what was appealing and marketable to their readers. Patterns of consumption could therefore influence the process of production, rather than just being a response to whatever producers choose to provide. With the emergence of new media, the relationships between media producers and audiences become even more closely intertwined, with, for example, film review websites containing content commissioned by the website from established reviewers, as well as informal reviews sent in by members of the public.

One of the most influential developments of the circuit of culture was presented in a key textbook on cultural studies co-written by Paul du Gay, Stuart Hall, Linda Janes, Hugh Mackay, and Keith Negus (1997), which used the circuit of culture approach to analyze the production and consumption of the Sony Walkman. The book presented a revised model of the circuit of culture, which broke it down more specifically into processes of *production*, issues of *representation* in relation to cultural objects and texts,[3] the ways in which cultural products relate to the *formation of social identities*, the ways in which cultural texts and objects are *used and consumed*, and the structures which *regulate* how cultural products are produced, distributed, and used (Du Gay *et al.* 1997: 3–4). It is this revised model that I shall make use of in this chapter.

It is not difficult to see how the circuit of culture encourages us to raise questions that go beyond analyzing film content as text. Attention to processes of *production* raises questions about the commercial and editorial mechanisms through which films are funded and produced, and what effects this has on the budget, content, and casting of films that get made. This may also involve analyzing the significance of different kinds of economic integration in the film industry, for example the emergence of corporations owning a range of different media producers and outlets, including newspapers, websites, and TV channels which carry reviews, advertising, or other marketing offers for their own films ("horizontal integration") and of corporations who finance films as well as owning film-production companies, distribution networks, and cinema chains ("vertical integration") (see Wood 2007). Exploring the processes of film production can also involve analyzing the significance of technology for film production, the ways in which distribution processes influence what films get seen and where they get seen, and the implications for film production of informal and professional relationships between specific funders, production-company executives, directors, producers, writers, actors, cinematographers, set designers, casting agents, camera crews, and sound and lighting technicians (see, e.g., Lovell and Sergi 2005). It may also require thinking about how the design, marketing, and production of particular films is tied in with other products such as computer games, toys, themed fast-food products, comic books, novels, or soundtrack CDs, or the meanings leant to a film by particular strategies of advertising or marketing (e.g., carrying an advertisement for the film *The Passion of the Christ* on the hood of the car of a NASCAR competitor). Thinking about editorial and marketing decision-making within film production can also help to shift the focus from thinking about film as a text that has been designed to convey particular meanings to thinking about film as a commercial product whose elements may have been designed specifically to appeal to particular audience demographics or national and global markets.

Exploring the relationship between film and the *formation of social identities* involves thinking both about the nature and significance of film-viewers' identification with particular filmic events, stories, or characters, and also the ways in which watching certain types of film may be associated with certain kinds of social identities. Think, for example, about the different possible connotations for someone's social identity of enjoying teen-market horror movies, art-house films, cult films with a particular fan-base, or pornographic films distributed only through licensed sex shops. Even the ways in which people discuss films (e.g., with reference to film stars or film directors) can be a subtle social marker of taste and class (Bourdieu 1987). *Regulatory* structures also play a crucial role in the production and consumption of film, and merit careful attention. Such structures can include government policy to encourage or influence the filmmaking process (e.g., through subsidies or tax-breaks for filmmakers, creating regional networks to support filmmaking, or processes for state censorship of film content), other regulatory structures relating to film certification, or less formal kinds of regulation such as expectations from funders about what degree of financial return they expect from their investment in particular films.

The study of the audience *consumption* of film has developed in the context of a wider literature on media audiences (Gripsrud 2000). Key issues that have been explored here include media effects (e.g., does watching violent films make people more disposed to violence?), the ways in which films are read according to the particular desires, needs, and interests of their audiences, the significance of fan cultures as distinctive forms of film consumption, and the significance of class, gender, ethnicity, nationality, and sexuality in shaping the ways that audiences read film. Exploring the ways in which audiences consume film raises issues about how people interpret what they see onscreen, the grounds on which they enjoy or dislike film, the significance of film watching for their wider lives, and the importance of the context in which they get to watch films. These processes of film watching will be influenced by the particular biographical circumstances of a person's life, and the histories of the groups of which they are a part. It will also be shaped by the real-world settings in which they take place. For example, does a person have to negotiate what films they watch with other significant people in their lives? Are there types of film which other people deem appropriate or inappropriate for them to see? Does their economic or social position put constraints on the range or number of films they are able to see? Similarly the context in which people watch film, for example, whilst out on a date, on a church outing, or at home whilst doing the ironing, will also have an effect on the viewer's emotional experience of the film and the quality of their attention to it. The ways in which gender, age, family status, sexuality, social class, and religious affiliation are bound up with structures of social power in different societies will also shape people's access to, and experience of, watching film.

By focusing on these questions of production, social identity, consumption, and regulation, the text of the film is placed in a much broader historical, cultural, social, political, and economic framework. Thinking about film in terms of the circuit of culture moves us away from the idea of films as static texts, and toward understanding film within dynamic social and cultural processes whose meaning and significance depend on the point in the circuit of culture from which one views it.

How might the model of the circuit of culture form an agenda for the study of religion and film? There are a number of interesting areas to explore in relation to film production. For example, how do perceptions about the marketability of films with particular religious content shape the production process of film in different parts of the world, for example filmmakers' awareness of the potential market for products depicting spiritual warfare for Pentecostal audiences in West Africa (Meyer 2003)? Under what social and economic conditions does it become possible or desirable to produce films for specific religious audiences (e.g., the rise of films produced with Christian audiences in mind by major production companies like Walden Media or New Line)? What are the implications of using alternative distribution networks managed by religious groups for the ways in which films are viewed and for the formation of religious subcultures (e.g., the distribution of the film *Left Behind: Tribulation Force* directly for viewing in churches when it was rejected for mainstream cinema distribution)? What might be the significance of new technologies (e.g., the cheap distribution of film through HD/DVD-quality internet downloads) for the capacity of religious-interest groups to be able to produce and distribute films outside the structures of the major film corporations? And in what ways do religious commitments or identities influence, or not influence, the film-production process, for example the significance of Hindu–Muslim collaboration in the production of films based around Hindu myth for Indian audiences (Dwyer 2006)?

In thinking about the formation of social identities, we might ask how religious identities are bound up with the different kinds of identification that people develop in relation to particular films, and how such identities might frame the way in which viewers experience film. Why was it, for example, that many Christian viewers of *The Passion of the Christ* were able to perceive the graphic torture of Christ in the film as moving and constructive when they would have felt very differently about watching similar forms of violence in the context of a horror film (Mitchell and Plate 2007)? Similarly we could ask what role watching, or not watching, particular films or film genres plays in the formation of different kinds of religious identity, or the ways in which secular identities shape the way in which religious material may be treated by film producers and audiences. This might also involve thinking about how people's approach to film defines a particular identity for themselves within their broader religious tradition, for example through their response to controversial films (see, e.g., Wagner 2003 on different Christian responses to the Harry Potter films). In the context of regulation, we might ask about the role that religious groups have played in relation to formalized systems of film certification or censorship (e.g., Ortiz 2003), the ways in which religious groups maintain informal or tacit forms of film censorship amongst their members (e.g., through sermons, peer pressure, or niche media such as religious film review articles or websites), or the ways in which religious content in film may be encouraged or discouraged by different forms of state involvement and market regulation. As a backdrop to all these questions, it is also possible to reflect on the role of broader media structures through which different interest groups present and contest positions on both individual films and wider issues relating to religion and the film industry (see, e.g., Wagner 2003; Silk 2004).

The study of audience consumption in relation to religion and film is still largely undeveloped, despite a growing acknowledgment of the value of such work (see Lyden

2003; Marsh 2004; Nolan 2003; Lynch 2007b). There are, however, other recent studies in the wider literature on religion and popular culture which provide good examples of audience reception research. At the forefront of such work have been a range of audience studies conducted through the Center for Media, Religion and Culture at the University of Colorado, Boulder (see, e.g. Hoover, *et al.* 2003; Hoover 2006; Schofield Clark 2005). Other valuable audience reception work has also been conducted in Frykholm's (2004) study amongst readers of the *Left Behind* novels and Neal's (2006) study of readers of Evangelical romance fiction. Where audience reception work on religion and film has been undertaken so far (Deacy 2005; Marsh 2007b), it has arguably been too closely wedded to a theological agenda of exploring the ways in which audiences make use of film as an implicit theological resource for making sense of their lives. Clive Marsh (2007b), for example, has used a question-naire-based study of cinema-goers' reflections on specific films to argue that the process of watching films is a meaning-making activity, and as such is loaded with theological significance.

But greater care needs to be taken with regard to the notion of "meaning-making" in this context. In one sense, the act of watching film, like any form of cultural activity, generates meaning for its audiences, but this meaning is not necessarily (or indeed usually) at the level of existential meanings or theological understandings about the meaning of life. As the anthropologist Clifford Geertz (1973: 5) has argued, the human person is "an animal suspended in webs of significance that he [sic] himself has spun" and these webs of meaning constitute human culture. But as Geertz also argued, through his seminal work on the "thick description" of culture, such meanings can function at the level of mundane, everyday activities such as the act of winking. Theological interpretations of meaning-making aspects of culture are still often influenced by Paul Tillich's (1959) idea that, at heart, human culture is constructed around basic religious and existential issues of "ultimate concern." But if scholars in the study of religion and film attend only to evidence of how audiences use film to negotiate such issues of ultimate concern, they risk missing and undervaluing the far more mundane meanings that films may have for their audiences. If we are to develop more general accounts of how film may function as a source of religious and existential meaning for people in cultural settings in which fewer people engage directly with traditional, institutional forms of religion, then we need to be equally attentive to the ways in which films do not function in this way if we are to have a nuanced sense of the real significance of film watching in people's lives. Cultural studies approaches to religion and film would also encourage us to explore a wider range of issues in the audience consumption of film beyond the possible functions of film as a source of religious and existential meaning. For instance, what role does religious belief and commitment play in the kinds of films that people watch and the nature of their viewing experience? Do fan cultures in relation to particular films operate in religion-like ways (e.g., Jindra 2000), and is it possible to identify fan cultures with specifically religious identities and interests? And what might we learn from the ways in which people with different secular or religious commitments interpret and respond to religious content in film? Exploring these questions effectively would also entail building up a richer picture of the place that film watching holds in the wider context of people's lives – something that would require more detailed ethnographic engagement with people's social worlds than has currently been achieved in the religion and film literature.

Another fruitful area to explore in terms of audiences' consumption of film is in the nature of the film-viewing experience itself. The cognitive, emotional, and aesthetic experience of watching film has attracted considerable scholarly attention, not least from those concerned about the potential of film to seduce its audiences into ideologically suspect views of the world. Writers in the field of religion and film have also started to pay attention to the immediate experience of film watching. Clive Marsh (2004), for example, has argued that it constitutes a worship-like experience in which people are drawn into an emotional and aesthetic engagement with meaningful narratives, echoing Margaret Miles' (1996) earlier account of film watching as a significant context for engaging with visions of the good life and Greg Watkins' (1999) suggestion of the ethical and religious potential of the visual practice of seeing film. Connections have also been drawn between film watching and religious practices of seeing the sacred, such as Christian practices of viewing images of saints (Sanders 2002) or the Hindu practice of *darshan* (Dwyer 2006). Such studies are very promising in terms of moving interest in religion and film away from a focus on religious symbols and ideas embedded in film texts, toward greater attention to religious practices of seeing and hearing. Cultural theory and cultural studies might contribute to such studies by providing theoretical frameworks for analyzing how social, cultural, and power relations cut across these sacred practices, and for exploring the ways in which, for example, viewing film stars may or may not be analogous to religious interaction with sacred figures (see, e.g., Dyer 1998; Nolan 2003).

Thinking about religion and film in terms of the circuit of culture encourages us to go beyond seeing the religious dimensions of film purely in terms of the content of film texts. It invites us to explore how lived forms of religion (and indeed lived forms of secular identity) interact with different stages of the cycle of film production, distribution, and consumption. It draws attention to the ways in which religion intersects with film not simply in terms of religious myth, symbols, narratives, or ideas, but in terms of the motivations, practices, and resources of social, political, and religious institutions and networks. It encourages us to think about religion not simply as a resource through which to think about life-issues, but as a social form that is bound up with other social, economic, and political processes, and through which run particular kinds of power relations. In the spirit of the project of cultural studies, it asks us to reflect on what bearing these processes may have on people's ability to live in open and imaginative ways in the context of tolerant, fair, peaceful, and reflexive societies. These questions not only are of interest to those wanting to develop a social and cultural analysis of the relationships between religion, culture, and society from a social scientific or cultural studies perspective, but also raise the possibility of theological engagements with film that are not concerned simply with the content of film texts, such as a theological analysis of the nature of desire in the act of watching film or of our ethical responsibilities in relation to visual and material culture (see, e.g., Pattison 2007). Thinking about religion and film through the framework of the circuit of culture also raises questions about the nature of religion and film scholarship itself as a form of cultural activity bound up within its own circuits of culture. It encourages greater reflexivity amongst religion and film scholars to think about the cultural processes in which their own work is embedded, the assumptions and motivations that guide their work, as well as the intended and actual consequences of their work (see Beaudoin 2007 for a fuller discussion of the nature of such reflexivity).

Studying religion and film in terms of the circuit of culture is still, at present, a relatively unexplored approach. Whilst some writers have examined different stages of the circuit of culture in the religion and film literature (e.g., Deacy 2005; Dwyer 2006; Marsh 2007b; Wright 2007), I am not aware at present of a case study in this literature which provides a detailed, rigorous, and systematic analysis of an individual film across all the stages of the circuit. This is perhaps unsurprising, as it would demand a degree of time and multidisciplinary expertise that would be beyond the resources of most individual scholars (and certainly most people writing short projects on religion and film as part of undergraduate and postgraduate courses). To develop such detailed case studies, it is likely that we would need projects involving scholars from a range of disciplinary backgrounds, and such collaborative ventures may be a valuable part of religion and popular culture research in the future (Morgan 2007). There would also be value in developing a comparative analysis of different stages of the circuit of culture in different national contexts. For example, what might we learn from the different roles that religion plays in relation to film-production processes in North America, Western Europe, West Africa, Iran, and India?

Conclusion

In this chapter, I have argued that scholarship on religion and film has been too fixated on studying film as a text conveying myth, religious symbolism, or theological ideas, and that there would be value in broadening this field to examine how religion intersects with different aspects of the production, distribution, and consumption of film in real-world settings. In one sense, the preoccupation with film as text in current scholarship in this field is not surprising. Most writers currently working on religion and film have initially trained in theology, biblical studies, or religious studies, and have often come to the study of film out of their own personal enjoyment of film. The kinds of questions about the social, economic, and cultural processes in the production and consumption of film that have been raised in this chapter are not obvious or indeed a precondition for enjoying film, and it is perhaps not surprising that scholars who have come to study film out of their own personal enjoyment of it have not always thought of these questions as worth pursuing. In challenging the dominant textual approach to the study of religion and film, I do not intend to deny its value in helping us to explore theological issues or to examine the ways in which religious and existential questions are explored through contemporary media. Indeed using film as a framework for developing normative discussions about meaning and value represents a distinctive and valuable contribution that theology and religious studies can make to the wider range of approaches of studying film. Rather, I am arguing that attention to cultural theory and cultural studies may open up a much wider range of scholarship in the study of religion and film, which might also inspire new forms of theological engagement with film.

I hope it is clear from this chapter that cultural theory and cultural studies have much to contribute to the study of religion and film. But this should not simply be a one-way process. The failure of cultural theory and cultural studies to address issues of religion and the sacred means that they cannot be assumed to provide sufficiently nuanced tools for analyzing contemporary forms of religion. This begs the question as to whether religion and the sacred have distinctive social and cultural properties that mark them out in certain ways from nonreligious forms of culture (Orsi 2006; Lynch 2007a). This is, of course, a contentious point and there is a strong movement in contemporary religious studies to treat religion in the same way as any other form of culture (see, e.g., Fitzgerald 2000). But there is still value in an ongoing discussion as to whether cultural approaches to the study of religion and film need to take account of distinctive religious phenomena which secularized approaches to cultural studies have failed to recognize. A good example of this is the religious practices of seeing and hearing that we noted earlier, such as the Hindu practice of *darshan*. Is there, as David Morgan (2005) suggests, a "sacred gaze" – distinctive ways of seeing that are grounded in particular religious traditions, communities, and practices? If so, how might such a sacred gaze find expression in the ways in which particular audiences experience film? Such sensitivity to the potential distinctiveness of some religious forms of cultural practice and experience is almost entirely lacking in the mainstream of cultural studies and cultural theory.

Whilst the concepts and methods of cultural studies discussed in this chapter offer an important resource for broadening the study of religion and film, we cannot therefore assume that they offer an entirely adequate framework for studying religious phenomena. An important resource for such cultural analysis is an emerging body of literature, informed by prior concepts and debates in anthropology, cultural studies, and media studies, but which filters and reworks these concepts and debates through careful analysis of lived forms of religion and the sacred. Examples of this include Birgit Meyer's (2006) work on the role of power and aesthetics in the cultural mediation of the sacred (including via the medium of film), and a recent major volume on key concepts in the cultural study of religion edited by David Morgan (2008). We have reached an exciting point in the cultural study of religion where we can move beyond simply importing concepts and methods developed by scholars who have had little or no interest in religion to developing critical approaches which make constructive use of earlier traditions of cultural studies whilst also developing new approaches for making sense of religion and the sacred. The cultural study of religion and film therefore not only has the potential to broaden this field from a study of the film text to the study of film as a social and cultural phenomenon, but might also be one way in which questions of religion and the sacred begin to be addressed more adequately within the field of film studies and cultural studies as well.

Bibliography

Adorno, T. (1991) *The Culture Industry: Selected Essays on Mass Culture*, London: Routledge.

Beaudoin, T. (2007) "Popular Culture Scholarship as a Spiritual Exercise: Thinking Ethically With(out) Christianity," in G. Lynch (ed.) *Between Sacred and Profane: Researching Religion and Popular Culture*, London: I. B. Tauris: 94–110.

Bennett, A. and Kahn-Harris, K. (eds) (2004) *After Subculture: Critical Studies in Contemporary Youth Culture*, Basingstoke: Palgrave Macmillan.

Bourdieu, P. (1987) *Distinction: A Social Critique of the Judgment of Taste*, Cambridge, MA: Harvard University Press.

Brooker, W. and Jermyn, D. (eds) (2003) *The Audience Studies Reader*, London: Routledge.

Centre for Contemporary Cultural Studies (CCCS) (1982) *The Empire Strikes Back: Race and Racism in '70s Britain*, London: Routledge.

Christianson, E. (2007) "Why Film Noir is Good for the Mind," in J. Mitchell and S. B. Plate (eds) *The Religion and Film Reader*, London: Routledge: 353–7.

Deacy, C. (2001) *Screen Christologies: Redemption and the Medium of Film*, Cardiff: University of Wales Press.

—— (2005) *Faith in Film*, Aldershot: Ashgate.

Deacy, C. and Ortiz, G. (2007) *Theology and Film: Challenging the Sacred/Secular Divide*, Oxford: Blackwell.

Du Gay, P., Hall, S., Janes, L., Mackay, H., and Negus, K. (1997) *Doing Cultural Studies: The Story of the Sony Walkman*, Milton Keynes: Open University Press.

Dwyer, R. (2006) *Filming the Gods: Religion and Indian Cinema*, London: Routledge.

Dyer, R. (1998) *Stars*, 2nd ed., London: British Film Institute.

Edgar, A. and Sedgwick, P. (eds) (2002) *Cultural Theory: The Key Concepts*, London: Routledge.

Exum, C. (1996) *Plotted, Shot and Painted: Cultural Representations of Biblical Women*, JSOT supplement series, 215, Sheffield: Sheffield Academic Press.

Fitzgerald, T. (2000) *The Ideology of Religious Studies*, New York: Oxford University Press.

Frykholm, A. (2004) *Rapture Culture: Left Behind in Evangelical America*, New York: Oxford University Press.

Geertz, C. (1973) *The Interpretation of Cultures*, New York: Basic Books.

Gripsrud, J. (2000) "Film audiences," in J. Hill and P. Church Gibson (eds) *Film Studies: Critical Approaches*, Oxford: Oxford University Press: 200–9.

Grossberg, L. (1993) "Formations of Cultural Studies: An American in Birmingham," in V. Blundell, J. Shepherd. and I. Taylor (eds) *Relocating Cultural Studies: Developments in Theory and Research*, London: Routledge: 21–66.

Hall, S. (1999) "Cultural Studies and its Theoretical Legacies," in S. During (ed.) *The Cultural Studies Reader*, London: Routledge: 97–111.

Hall, S. and Jefferson, T. (1976) *Resistance through Rituals: Youth Subcultures in Post-War Britain*, Birmingham: University of Birmingham Press.

Hayward, S. (ed.) (2006) *Cinema Studies: The Key Concepts*, London: Routledge.

Hebdige, D. (1979) *Subculture: The Meaning of Style*, London: Routledge.

Hoover, S. (2006) *Religion in the Media Age*, London: Routledge.

Hoover, S., Schofield Clark, L., and Alters, D. (2003) *Media, Home and Family*, London: Routledge.

Howell, S. (2007) "Screening the Temptation: Interpretation and Indeterminacy in Cinematic Transformations of a Gospel Story," *Journal of Religion and Film* 11 (2). Online. Available HTTP: <http://www.unomaha.edu/jrf/vol11no2/HowellTempt.htm>.

Jackson, P., Stevenson, M., and Brooks, K. (2001) *Making Sense of Men's Magazines*, Cambridge: Polity.

Jindra, M. (2000) "It's about Faith in our Future: 'Star Trek' Fandom as Cultural Religion," in B. Forbes and J. Mahan (eds) *Religion and Popular Culture in America*, Berkeley: University of California Press: 159–73.

Johnson, R. (1986/7) "What is Cultural Studies Anyway?," *Social Text* 16: 38–80.

Johnston, R. (2000) *Reel Spirituality: Theology and Film in Dialogue*, Grand Rapids, MI: Baker Academic.

—— (ed.) (2007) *Reframing Theology and Film: New Focus for an Emerging Discipline*, Grand Rapids, MI: Baker Academic.

Kreitzer, L. (2002) *Gospel Images in Fiction and Film: On Reversing the Hermeneutical Flow*, Sheffield: Sheffield Academic Press.

Lovell, A. and Sergi, G. (2005) *Making Films in Contemporary Hollywood*, London: Hodder Arnold.

Lyden, J. (2003) *Film as Religion: Myths, Morals and Rituals*, New York: New York University Press.

Lynch, G. (2005) *Understanding Theology and Popular Culture*, Oxford: Blackwell.

—— (2007a) "What is this 'Religion' in the Study of Religion and Popular Culture?," in G. Lynch (ed.) *Between Sacred and Profane: Researching Religion and Popular Culture*, London: I. B. Tauris: 125–42.

—— (2007b) "Some Concluding Reflections," in G. Lynch (ed.) *Between Sacred and Profane: Researching Religion and Popular Culture*, London: I. B. Tauris: 157–63.

McRobbie, A. (1978) *Jackie: An Ideology of Adolescent Feminity*, Occasional paper for the Centre for Contemporary Cultural Studies, Birmingham: University of Birmingham Press.

—— (1990) *Feminism and Youth Culture*, Basingstoke: Palgrave Macmillan.

Marsh, C. (2004) *Cinema and Sentiment: Film's Challenge to Theology*, Milton Keynes: Paternoster.

—— (2007a) *Theology Goes to the Movies: An Introduction to Critical Christian Thinking*, London: Routledge.

—— (2007b) "On Dealing with What Films Actually Do to People: The Practice and Theory of Film Watching in Theology/Religion and Film Discussion," in R. Johnston (ed.) *Reframing Theology and Film: New Focus for an Emerging Discipline*, Grand Rapids, MI: Baker Academic: 145–61.

Marsh, C. and Ortiz, G. (eds) (1997) *Explorations in Theology and Film: Movies and Meaning*, Oxford: Blackwell.

Martin, J. and Ostwalt, C. (eds) (1995) *Screening the Sacred: Religion, Myth and Ideology in Contemporary Film*, Boulder, CO: Westview Press.

Meyer, B. (2003) "Pentecostalism, Prosperity and Popular Cinema in Ghana," *Culture and Religion* 3 (1): 67–87.

—— (2006) "Religious Sensations: Why Media, Power and Aesthetics Matter in the Study of Religion." Inaugural lecture delivered at the Free University of Amsterdam, 6 October 2006. Online. Available HTTP: <http://www.fsw.vu.nl/images_upload/5625947C-A436-57E7-522C1BB606595F3F.doc>.

Miles, M. (1996) *Seeing and Believing: Religion and Values in the Movies*, Berkeley: University of California Press.

Mitchell, J. and Plate, S. B. (2007) "Viewing and Writing on 'The Passion of the Christ,'" in J. Mitchell and S. B. Plate (eds) *The Religion and Film Reader*, London: Routledge: 343–7.

Morgan, D. (2005) *The Sacred Gaze: Religious Visual Culture in Theory and Practice*, Berkeley: University of California Press.

—— (2007) "Studying Religion and Popular Culture: Prospects, Presuppositions, Procedures," in G. Lynch (ed.) *Between Sacred and Profane: Researching Religion and Popular Culture*, London: I. B. Tauris: 21–33.

—— (2008) *Keywords in Religion, Media and Culture*, London: Routledge.

Morley, D. (1980) *The "Nationwide" Audience: Structure and Decoding*, London: British Film Institute.

Mulvey, L. (1995 [1975]) "Visual Pleasure and Narrative Cinema," *Screen* 16 (3): 6–18.

Neal, L. (2006) *Romancing God: Evangelical Women and Inspirational Fiction*, Chapel Hill: University of North Carolina Press.

Nolan, S. (2003) "Towards a New Religious Film Criticism: Using Film to Understand Religious Identity Rather than Locate Cinematic Analogue," in J. Mitchell and S. Marriage (eds) *Mediating Religion: Conversations in Media, Religion and Culture*, London: T&T Clark: 169–78.

Orsi, R. (2006) *Between Heaven and Earth: The Religious Worlds People Make and the Scholars Who Study Them*, Princeton: Princeton University Press.

Ortiz, G. (2003) "The Catholic Church and its Attitude to Film as an Arbiter of Cultural Meaning," in J. Mitchell and S. Marriage (eds) *Mediating Religion: Conversations in Media, Religion and Culture*, London: T&T Clark: 179–88.

Pattison, S. (2007) *Seeing Things: Deepening Relations with Visual Artefacts*, London: SCM Press.

Sanders, T. (2002) *Celluloid Saints: Images of Sanctity in Film*, Macon, GA: Mercer University Press.

Schofield Clark, L. (2005) *From Angels to Aliens: Teenagers, the Media and the Supernatural*, New York: Oxford University Press.

Silk, M. (2004) "Gibson's Passion: A Case of Media Manipulation?" *Journal of Religion and Film* 8 (1). Online. Available HTTP: <http://www.unomaha.edu/jrf/2004Symposium/Silk.htm>.

Stacey, J. (1994) *Star Gazing: Hollywood Cinema and Female Spectatorship*, London: Routledge.
Storey, J. (2006) *Cultural Theory and Popular Culture*, 4th ed., Harlow: Prentice-Hall.
Strinati, D. (1995) *An Introduction to Theories of Popular Culture*, London: Routledge.
Tillich, P. (1959) *Theology of Culture*, New York: HarperCollins.
Tinkcom, M. and Villarejo, A. (eds) (2001) *Keyframes: Popular Cinema and Cultural Studies*, London: Routledge.
Turner, G. (2000) "Cultural Studies and Film," in J. Hill and P. Church Gibson (eds) *Film Studies: Critical Approaches*, Oxford: Oxford University Press: 193–9.
—— (2002) *The Film Cultures Reader*, London: Routledge.
—— (2003) *British Cultural Studies: An Introduction*, London: Routledge.
Wagner, R. (2003) "Bewitching the Box Office: Harry Potter and Religious Controversy," *Journal of Religion and Film* 7 (2). Online. Available HTTP: <http://www.unomaha.edu/jrf/Vol7No2/bewitching.htm>.
Watkins, G. (1999) "Seeing and Being Seen: Distinctively Filmic and Religious Elements in Film," *Journal of Religion and Film* 3 (2). Online. Available HTTP: <http://www.unomaha.edu/jrf/watkins.htm>.
Wood, M. (2007) *Contemporary European Cinema*, London: Hodder Arnold.
Wright, M. (2007) *Religion and Film: An Introduction*, London: I. B. Tauris.

Filmography

Left Behind: Tribulation Force (2002, dir. B. Corcoran)
The Passion of the Christ (2004, dir. M. Gibson)

Notes

1 This is true of virtually all of the articles posted to date at the online *Journal of Religion and Film*. Exceptions to this textual approach include Lyden's (2003) discussion of film in terms of ritual, and Marsh's (2004) concept of cinema-going as a worship-like experience. Such alternative ways of conceiving of film in terms of wider social and religious practices have not yet been subjected to substantial empirical investigation.

2 Whilst the notion of the passive audience is generally rejected in cultural studies, the nature and extent of audiences' agency in resisting dominant ideologies that are encoded into cultural texts and objects is still contested (see Brooker and Jermyn 2003: 91–3 for a good summary of this debate).

3 Whilst questions of representation in film are an important element of analysis in the circuit of culture, I do not address these in this chapter as the textual bias of the religion and film literature has already produced a good deal of work on issues of the representation of religious characters and stories. I would argue that, whilst issues of representation should not be ignored in future film and religion research, it is more important to focus on issues of production, distribution, identification, and consumption if we are to get a genuinely richer picture of film as a social and cultural phenomenon.

16

PSYCHOANALYSIS

Kent Brintnall

Introduction

In "The Dissolution of the Oedipus Complex," Sigmund Freud summarizes the key features of the complex, its relation to castration anxiety and the gender-specific ways that male and female children negotiate it. When discussing the male child, Freud writes:

> The Oedipus complex offered the child two possibilities of satisfaction ...
> He could put himself in his father's place ... and have intercourse with his
> mother ...; or he might want to take the place of his mother and be loved by
> his father .... His acceptance of the possibility of castration ... made an end
> of both possible ways of obtaining satisfaction from the Oedipus complex.
> For both of them entailed the loss of his penis – the masculine one as a
> resulting punishment and the feminine one as a precondition .... A conflict
> is bound to arise between his narcissistic interest in that part of his body
> and the libidinal cathexis of his parental objects. In this conflict the first of
> these forces normally triumphs: the child's ego turns away from the Oedipus
> complex. (Freud 1924: 176)

This passage charts the difficult terrain of desire and identification the male child must traverse. To identify with the father and desire the mother is to risk castration as a punishing blow; to identify with the mother and desire the father is to risk castration as an enabling gesture. The male child is able to move beyond the Oedipus complex (only) because of his love of the penis and the pleasures it affords. Investment in the penis, which is stronger than his attachment to either parent as love-object, causes him to identify with the father as a fellow penis-bearer; it also compels him to stop desiring the mother. Freud goes on to explain that the critical choice between penis and parents causes the child to sublimate all sexual desire, until a proper substitute for the mother can be found and desire is reignited at puberty (Freud 1924: 176–7).

According to Freud, psychosexual development is grounded in the body and its pleasures. Before concluding that Freud's text necessarily endorses biological determinism, however, I suggest attending more closely to the dance between desire and identification it describes. This passage identifies two possible satisfactions within the Oedipus complex: one with a heterosexual object and one with a homosexual object. Although Freud describes the heterosexual outcome as the one that "normally triumphs," this should be read as "typically" rather than "automatically." Moreover, the resolution of the Oedipus complex and entry into "normal" heterosexuality centers on an investment in the penis and an introjection of "the authority of the father" which "forms the nucleus of the super-ego" (Freud 1924: 176). As Freud discusses elsewhere (Freud 1914: 96), this allows the male child to retain a portion of his erotic fascination with the father – desire for the father is translated into identification with a normative ego ideal, forever blurring the line between desire and identification, at least as far as masculine subjectivity is concerned. Heterosexual identity and homoerotic desire are bound up together in the Freudian account. With respect to the naturalness of the heterosexual outcome, both heterosexual and natural should be read as surrounded by quotation marks. According to Freud, heterosexuality is haunted by homoerotic desire and is only one among many possible developmental outcomes, an outcome privileged rhetorically for cultural reasons left unarticulated in Freud's text.

By reading Freud closely – and, in many ways, against himself – we begin to see how the ideal of heterosexual masculinity instantiates itself within a patriarchal cultural order and what it must disavow in order to do so. Psychoanalytic texts, on my reading, are most valuable when they help us see more clearly the complex structures of identity, desire, sexuality, and subjectivity operating in cultural discourses. Whether or not Freud's account of the Oedipus complex and its resolution is true or empirically verifiable, it provides a useful heuristic for thinking about the kinds of desires and identities that are represented – and repressed – in the texts, images, and practices that comprise a given cultural order. For example, films of the action genre are heavily invested in main characters that stand as paragons of masculine strength and invulnerability. At the same time, these ideal masculine subjects almost always have fractured relationships with their father-figures and the films' plots typically feature the restoration of this relationship. What questions might we ask about this juxtaposition of normative masculinity and longing for the lost father after considering this passage from Freud?

This essay intends to orient the reader to the role of psychoanalytic theory in the study of film and religion. Both film and religion foster certain kinds of desire, solicit particular identifications, present certain fantasies regarding the nature of reality, and seek to establish certain subjectivities. Whether or not psychoanalytic accounts are "true," they are hermeneutically valuable for examining how religion and film utilize desire and identification to present fantasies of subjectivity to their respective audiences.

I begin with a quoted passage from Freud to remind the reader that an engagement with psychoanalysis should, ideally, always begin with a careful reading of primary texts. Summaries of Freud, for example, frequently depict the Oedipal triangle as consisting solely of desire for the mother and conflict with the father; this is a distortion of Freud's actual argument and it diminishes the value of his work as an interpretive tool. Unfortunately, given the vastness and variety of the literature, this essay can provide neither a comprehensive overview nor a close reading of Freud, his major (re)interpreter Jacques Lacan, or the dozens of theorists who have modified, defended, and criticized the work at the heart of the psychoanalytic canon. Similarly, given the breadth and depth of psychoanalytic film theory, this essay cannot begin to summarize all of the work that might be considered important. To compensate for the requisite generality and selectivity of the exposition, I provide a list of suggested reading at the conclusion of the essay. This essay should be read as an invitation to explore psychoanalytic film theory in more detail. If it manages to foster a sympathetic curiosity in the reader, I will consider my effort successful.

I begin with a particular interpretive gloss on this passage from Freud to show that there are many ways to read psychoanalytic texts. Psychoanalysis has legitimately come under fire for the ways it privileges the masculine subject, attempts to render heterosexual desire normative, and understands itself as a science. "Dissolution" is guilty of all these failings. In my interaction with psychoanalytic materials, I strive to show how their arguments and analyses mirror the masculinist and heterosexist assumptions they frequently support. In other words, I read psychoanalytic materials critically and diagnostically, considering them as symptomatic of a larger patriarchal logic. Rather than rejecting them out of hand, I examine psychoanalytic accounts of identity and desire to see what light they shed on the operation of cultural discourses of gender, sexuality, and subjectivity.

In this essay, I provide an overview of the psychoanalytic concepts that have proved most important to film theory, a highly selective set of examples of psychoanalytic film theory, an overview of how psychoanalytic film theory has already been received in religion and film scholarship, and a very brief case study intended to demonstrate the possible value of psychoanalytic approaches for the study of film and religion.

Psychoanalytic theory: Freud and Lacan

Taking desire as one of the lodestars for our consideration of psychoanalysis, I begin this section with a discussion of the distinction between need and desire. Every human being has basic needs for survival – for example food. The human infant receives food from a care-giver; for both Freud and Lacan, this is imagined primarily as the child suckling the mother's breast. Provision of food, however accomplished, does more than meet a need for nutrition. While being fed, the infant smells the care-giver's breath, hears the care-giver's voice, tastes the milk, and feels the warmth of the care-giver's skin. Fulfillment of the need is accompanied by a range of pleasures. At some point, however, the need for food is met in a different way. The child is taught to hold a bottle, eat with a spoon, prepare meals. Although the need is still met, the child's maturation – or, more specifically, enculturation – entails the loss of certain pleasures. While the child may never again try to suck the mother's breast, there is a powerful psychic connection to the pleasures it afforded. Desire for the pleasures that accompanied fulfillment of the need, according to Freud, does not disappear. It continues to operate in psychic life, even if it is not available to conscious awareness.

The unconscious is the key concept in psychoanalytic theory. Contrary to centuries of philosophical speculation, Freud argued that the psyche and consciousness were not symmetrical; the former was more extensive than the latter and contains a range of conflicting desires, needs, and wants not accessible to the latter. In his early articulations, Freud described the psyche as comprising the unconscious, the preconscious, and the conscious – hypothesizing that some sort of censoring mechanism prevented unconscious desires from entering conscious awareness in undisguised form. To understand the relation between these structures, Freud studied dreams, jokes, verbal slips, obsessional behaviors, and hysterical symptoms. Each of these phenomena were disguises worn by the latent, or hidden, contents of the unconscious as they became manifest, or apparent, to consciousness. In his later work, Freud presented a new topography of the psyche, one comprising the id, the ego, and the super-ego. The id was the realm of instinctual desire; the super-ego was the filtering mechanism; the ego was the individual's sense of "self," constructed through a constant struggle between id and super-ego. Although the id of this latter description shared many features of and is often identified with the unconscious, Freud was clear that all three had conscious and unconscious dimensions. Freud's insight about the unconscious led film theorists to distinguish between the manifest and latent content of the work, to look "behind" the images and narrative to find other meanings. Recall my earlier observation about the action film and its representation of masculinity. What desires and wishes might the longing for the father be pointing to that the manifest content of the film does not – or cannot – acknowledge?

For Freud, proof of his theoretical explorations was to be found in his therapeutic success in eliminating or reducing neurotic, obsessional, and hysterical behaviors. By correctly identifying, in conjunction with the patient, the latent source of manifest symptoms, the psychic energy of the latent conflict could be discharged and the manifest symptoms would disappear. Contrary to Freud's insistence that psychoanalysis is a science, any particular interpretation of unconscious structures and contents, such as the Oedipus complex, could never be conclusively proven, but could only be made to seem more and more plausible as it led to further therapeutic success. This reveals why psychoanalysis would be attractive to those seeking to analyze how a culture's signifying systems – such as literature, film, and religion – make their meaning and shape the individual's sense of identity and desire: psychoanalysis is fundamentally an interpretive endeavor. Similarly, the validity of psychoanalytic interpretations of cultural phenomena is established by whether they provide critical insight into, and leverage against, the system of ideas, desires, and fantasies that comprise a particular cultural order.

For French psychoanalyst Jacques Lacan, practicing therapists – in their attempts to systematize, simplify, and codify psychoanalytic theory – failed to recognize the radicality of Freud's "discovery" of the unconscious. Lacan read Freud through the structural linguistics of Ferdinand de Saussure, after the "linguistic turn" that reformulated numerous disciplines at the beginning of the twentieth century. Lacan's seminars are filled with subtle jokes based on rhyming, punning, and word-play that are often quite challenging to capture in translation. His texts are notoriously difficult to comprehend and interpret, but their linguistic complexity relates directly to his understanding of the unconscious. For Lacan, the unconscious is structured like a language, but it is the most foreign and incomprehensible of languages. In his seminars, Lacan attempts to mirror the style of the unconscious, forcing his audience to perform the interpretive task of the therapeutic encounter.

While the Freudian unconscious is linked primarily with his notion of repression, the Lacanian unconscious is linked primarily with his notion of the Other. The unconscious is the language spoken by the Other: it is the site from which the Other solicits desire and establishes meaning. Taking seriously the Saussurian insights that a language system always precedes the individual language user and exceeds the individual language user's control, Lacan argues that language provides an apt metaphor for understanding Freud's notion of the unconscious. The unconscious is a source of symbols, ideas, images, meanings, and relations in and through which we find our identity, but over which we never have absolute control. A given culture's understandings of gender, sexuality, race, embodiment, family – to name just a few coordinates of identity – preexists any single individual. The person's self-understanding must be mapped on the coordinates of these languages issuing from elsewhere – an elsewhere that, in its entirety, is always mysterious, ungraspable, and overwhelming. The self, then, is structured by the unconscious, which is best understood, according to Lacan, as the discourse of the Other.

The mirror stage is central to Lacan's conception of self and Other (Lacan 1949). According to Lacan, the infant does not comprehend its body as a single entity – rather, feet and hands simply appear; touching, tasting, and manipulating these objects produces pleasure and satisfaction. Similarly, the infant is not always clear about the precise boundaries of her or his own body. When feeding at the mother's breast, the child experiences a sense of unity with the mother's body. At some point, however, the infant spies him- or herself in a mirror: in this reflected image, the infant acquires a bodily *imago*, a sense of both unity and boundedness – these hands and feet belong to "me"; that breast does not. As Lacan points out, this sense of wholeness is built on a misrecognition: it does not come from the body itself, but rather from the body's reflection, the body at a distance, the body in representation. Moreover, this sense of unity is culturally mediated by a set of concepts regarding bodily integrity. Or, as Lacan will express it elsewhere when writing on the function of the gaze (1973), our sense of ourselves as a unified, coherent whole is mediated by vision, but it requires the look of the Other to secure and guarantee it: I recognize myself in the mirror not solely, or even primarily, because I see myself there, but because my sense of a unified self is guaranteed by the gaze of my mother who is holding me in front of the mirror. Thus, the sense of "self" is the source of a double-alienation – first, it comes from a reflection in a mirror; second, it is guaranteed by the gaze of an Other. Given its privileging of the visual register, Lacan's mirror stage has been a lodestar in psychoanalytic film theory. The film is understood like a mirror that provides an image that the viewing subject accepts as a reflection; the film is also spoken by an Other, a discourse outside the viewing subject's control.

Lacan's understanding of the unconscious also leads him to develop a triadic understanding of psychic life. In the realm of the Imaginary, typified by the experience of the mirror stage, the fantasy of identity is characterized by unity, linked primarily to the body, and secured by the dyadic relation between ego and ego-image, between mother and child. Even in this order, however, the child – both male and female – becomes acutely aware of lack. First, the child is the object of the mother's desire; this marks the mother as lacking something. Therefore, the child attempts to become that which will answer the mother's desire, but soon realizes that she or he is incapable of answering and fulfilling that desire. In Lacanian thought, the phallus is the privileged signifier for that which answers the lack that generates desire. Through the experience of circulating desire, both the male and female child come to realize that the mother does not possess the phallus and they strive to become the phallus for her. When the child passes into the Symbolic order, the order of cultural signification, they become aware of how the privileged signifier and lack are tracked onto sexual difference. In the Symbolic order, the relationship becomes triadic – father, mother, child – and fantasies of identity and desire are related primarily to signification. Here, the father prohibits the child's desire for the mother as well as the child's striving to become the phallus for the mother, thus highlighting the child's castrated status. The female child learns that the phallus signifies her status as the object of desire – that is, she *is* the phallus; the male child learns that the phallus signifies his status as the agent of desire – that is, he *has* the phallus (Lacan 1958). For both male and female child, however, the phallus is not an object, not a body part, but rather the signifier of a position within a cultural order of sexual difference, identity, and desire.

Contrary to Freud's treatment of the penis as a body part, Lacan treats the phallus as a signifier of desire and lack, insisting on the non-identity of phallus and penis. In other words, Lacan describes a set of meanings within a cultural system, rather than the relation between bodies and identity. The Lacanian Symbolic, then, potentially opens up the possibility of critiquing the cultural order and its organization of desire, unlike the Freudian account that is grounded in the specifics of biology. This does not mean, however, that the body is absent from Lacanian psychoanalysis. The third Lacanian order is the order of the Real, or that which is completely inassimilable to signification. The Real is the realm of trauma, anxiety, and corporeality that exists outside the Imaginary and the Symbolic. Like the unconscious, the Real influences and shapes the Imaginary and Symbolic, but can never be comprehended within the terms of those orders. This shows the influence of Saussurian linguistics: the Real is similar to the referent that exists outside of language, but which can never be completely known independent of a signifying system.

For both Freud and Lacan, the Oedipus complex and castration anxiety are privileged schemas for understanding how identity and desire are shaped and experienced. On the Freudian account, both the male and female child have an initial belief that all human beings possess a penis. At some point, usually after seeing the genitals of the opposite sex, the male child realizes that woman is castrated and that he could possibly be castrated; the female child realizes that she is already castrated, that her clitoris is an "inadequate" penis. As noted above, the male child's anxiety over being castrated helps him negotiate the conflicting desires of the Oedipus complex in the direction of heterosexual masculinity. The female child's course through the Oedipus complex is much more complicated and is resolved through the proper incorporation of a sense of inferiority in light of the discovery of genital difference. While Freud's account of the female child's "penis envy" has been criticized by feminists since its original articulation – Karen Horney, for example, argued that the clinical evidence showed that male patients were much more likely to be envious of women's fecundity than female patients were likely to be envious of men's penis-possession (1932) – it is important to note that he describes penis envy as both a desire to possess the organ and a desire to possess the cultural power that the organ signifies. In other words, at the precise moment that Freud declares biology is destiny, he also unwittingly acknowledges that biological destiny requires a cultural order to secure its meaning. On this reading, penis envy is not the worship of the penis, but rather an awareness of the privileges that penis-possession secures within a particular cultural order. Castration anxiety, then, should be understood as grounded not primarily in narcissistic investment in the penis, but rather in the uncertainty that power will always be organized phallically. Similarly, Freud's insistence that well-adjusted females understand that their position is one of passivity and inferiority should be understood not as a descriptive conclusion, but a defensive and normative command grounded in castration anxiety.

For Lacan, castration is a ubiquitous element of the subject's experience. Insofar as the unconscious is the discourse of the Other, insofar as the self's *imago* is based on a misrecognition, the subject – male or female – is always already castrated, always already split, always already fractured. In the Imaginary order, both the male and female child are aware of their lack and incompletion. It is only in the Symbolic order, the order of cultural signification, that the male and female child begin to understand that their relation to lack is significantly different. Lacan's explicit recognition of the importance of signification potentially opens the door to reconfiguring cultural understandings of gender differences by reconceptualizing the relation between power and lack. At the same time, insofar as Lacan insists on the intractability of Symbolic structures, his system is even less usable than the Freudian analysis that – perhaps unwittingly – creates a fissure between biology and culture.

Just as castration anxiety and the Oedipus complex are central to the work of Freud and Lacan, they are also central to psychoanalytic film theory. Literally hundreds of essays and monographs have been written tracing how certain films and certain directors narrate and visualize the negotiation of Oedipal desires and fears. While some of this work is pedantic and derivative, and some of it is far-fetched and implausible, the most insightful work seeks to show how film works as a cultural discourse in relation to the masculinist and heterosexist presumptions that the Oedipus complex and castration anxiety seek to mark as real, true, normal, and natural. Relying on psychoanalysis' mapping of a form of the patriarchal imagination, psychoanalytic film theory exposes how film works to sustain or disrupt certain fantasies of gender and sexual subjectivity.

Psychoanalytic film theory

Christian Metz and cinematic pleasure

Returning to the lodestar of desire, I begin this brief excursus into psychoanalytic film theory with Christian Metz's 1977 study, *The Imaginary Signifier*. Given his interest in the pleasures afforded by cinema, Metz famously observed that in order to study film, the analyst must hate it – or, at least, the analyst could not love it in the same way that the viewer loved it. To be caught up in the libidinal economy of cinema was to be unable to maintain the appropriate critical distance. It was in relation to this question of pleasure that Metz thought psychoanalysis could contribute to the understanding of cinema, for psychoanalysis was an account of the relation between desire and subjectivity.

In *The Imaginary Signifier*, Metz discusses how films are like and unlike dreams. He notes that the film's images, unlike dreams, are immediately known by the viewer to be false. All film viewers are fully aware that the film is the play of shadow and light on a two-dimensional screen. And yet the vast majority of film viewers become genuinely invested in cinematic stories and authentically experience joy, lust, sorrow, and terror in reaction to the images on the screen. This observation led Metz to link the practice of cinema-going to the practice of the fetishist. According to Freud, the fetish was an object – like a patent-leather shoe or a red feather boa – that allayed castration anxiety by grafting a fantastic penis on the woman's body (1927). The fetish covers the lack of castration and operates through the process of disavowal. Unlike repression that removes an unpleasant truth from conscious awareness, disavowal both acknowledges and denies the unpleasant truth at the same time. According to Metz, disavowal enables the cinema-goer to take a certain kind of pleasure in the screened image: by denying the unreality of the image and experiencing its reality effects. This disavowal is mediated primarily through the positioning of the camera and the spectacle of the image – the film's technical and formal brilliance is a fetish that covers over the absent object that the film promises but cannot deliver.

The camera, on Metz's account, gives the spectator godlike access to the cinematic world. Its omnipresence and mobility overcome the unreality of the image. Moreover, because the viewer does not see her- or himself reflected on the screen, the camera's look provides a point of identification. Relating cinematic identification to Lacan's mirror stage, Metz observes that the viewer is not reflected in the image and is thus compelled to identify with the perceptual presence of the camera as the site that reflects the viewer's perceptual activity. This active, voyeuristic pleasure compensates for the viewer's necessary passivity in relation to the film's discourse. The subjective experience associated with the power of this look is the source of the viewer's libidinal investment in cinema.

Jean-Louis Baudry and the cinematic apparatus

Metz's study built on prior work by Jean-Louis Baudry. Baudry also concluded that cinema generates a viewing subjectivity that is transcendent, coherent, and unified, but added it is particularly effective in establishing this fantastic experience of subjectivity due to the conditions under which film is viewed (1970). In the theater, the viewer watches the film in a darkened space, relatively immobile and quiet, while images and sounds are projected from a location that the viewer does not see. Given the similarity to dreaming, Baudry argued that cinema causes the viewer to regress to a childlike state and thus renders the viewer particularly susceptible to its manipulations. In addition to allusions to the dream-state and mother–child fusion, Baudry also likened the experience to that described by Plato's analogy of the cave and argued that cinema has no true beginning, but that it answers a deep and abiding need in the psyche for a particular fantastic construction of subjectivity (1975). The cinematic apparatus, in other words, is only the most recent instantiation of a larger and longer desire for an experience of subjective unity and coherence. How Baudry's observations must be amended in an age when people watch movies in their homes, on their computers, in airplanes, and on cell phones is a question that falls outside the scope of this essay.

Laura Mulvey and the cinematic gaze

In "Visual Pleasure and Narrative Cinema" (1975), British filmmaker and theorist Laura Mulvey argued that the pleasures available through the cinematic apparatus as well as the coherent subjectivity generated by it are gendered. Mulvey's essay has a unique and remarkable place within film theory. On the one hand, it is among the most frequently anthologized and cited essays in film studies. On the other hand, virtually no one, not even the most ardent feminist psychoanalytic film theorist, would endorse Mulvey's conclusions in their entirety. Mulvey's essay is important not because it represents current thinking in the field, but because it was an absolutely field-changing piece of work. After Mulvey, it is simply impossible to think about the formal devices of cinema without also thinking about their gendered and sexual meaning.

As her title suggests, Mulvey, like Metz, was interested in the pleasures available in narrative cinema and how these pleasures were related to the look or the gaze as it is constructed within the film. Mulvey noted that the look was divided along gender lines: male characters look; female characters are looked at – or, men *possess* the gaze, while women *bear* it. While there are numerous films from the period about which Mulvey was writing, and even more since, that challenge the universality of this distinction, many films are (still) organized along these lines. Think, for example, of the oft-repeated scene where a female character, usually one who has been an "ugly duckling," enters a room. As she descends the stairs, time stops; the camera shows the man's stunned face; it then moves to occupy his position so that the viewer is now looking at the woman. The camera pans the woman's body revealing every beautiful and breathtaking detail of her physiognomy, coiffure, makeup, and costume. As Mulvey observes, the woman is a spectacle who stops the narrative, while the man's actions and desires control the movement of both the camera and the story. In such a visual and narrative economy, the only pleasures available, according to Mulvey, are those of the male viewer.

The woman, however, is never solely a source of pleasure. As Freud observed, the woman's body always carries with it the specter of castration. Mulvey noted that the anxiety generated by the woman's body is handled in at least two ways in classical Hollywood cinema. On the one hand, the woman can be reduced to a fetishistic spectacle, a pure object of beauty: Mulvey's example was Josef von Sternberg's treatment of Marlene Dietrich. On the other hand, the woman can be overcome by the power of the voyeuristic gaze, caught in a narrative of punishment and abuse: Mulvey's example was Alfred Hitchcock's treatment of his heroines. Although Mulvey's introduction of castration might be read as an excessive reading typical of psychoanalytic film theory, her film analysis serves to confirm the Freudian hypothesis. It is beyond question that mainstream cinema is fascinated with beautiful women; it is also true that mainstream cinema frequently circumscribes their narrative power or somehow punishes, undercuts, or destroys them. How do we explain the ubiquity of these phenomena? Freud's notion of castration anxiety provides an explanation. Moreover, once we have used psychoanalysis to understand the (masculine) pleasures cinema offers, we can rely on this insight to decode and disrupt both cinematic pleasure and psychoanalytic discourse. Just as Metz claimed that the analyst must hate cinema, Mulvey argued that we must work to destroy the pleasure of cinema and find alternatives that do not depend on the objectification and eradication of women.

Theories of spectatorship after Mulvey

Although Mulvey's essay was a watershed event in the study of how film makes meaning, it was almost immediately challenged. The first set of challenges came from other feminists who asked whether Mulvey's argument left any room for female pleasure in relation to cinema. Although Mulvey contended that women only experienced pleasure "transsexually" or from the site of masculine subjectivity (1981), other feminists gave various accounts of how women could find pleasure in cinema (cf. Kaplan 2000). An additional set of qualifications came from authors who analyzed "looking relations" in cinema. What happens, for example, when a woman looks? Linda Williams examined classical horror narratives and found that when the woman investigates she is frequently punished and that her active looking connects her to the monster (1984). Mary Ann Doane examined films in which a woman's look is featured, and contended that this look is often ridiculed and must be abandoned if the woman wants to regain her status as desirable object (1982).

Other theorists asked whether men could bear the look. Although Mulvey rejected this possibility, Steve Neale examined the strategies for presenting the male body as an erotic object (1983). When the male body is on display, it is often in action, rather than a pure spectacle, and it is frequently subjected to violence. In other words, the display of the male body almost always has some narrative excuse in addition to its mere beauty and allure; its status as erotic object is disavowed. Lesbian and gay theorists began to ask questions about the identity of the looker in Mulvey's scheme. After all, gay men have frequently enjoyed watching films with beautiful female characters, but how does this relate to the "male" pleasure Mulvey describes? And how does a "lesbian gaze" fit into Mulvey's account? Does a beautiful female body generate pleasure only for a male viewer? And why is gender the only difference inscribed by the look? Can we think of racial, class, body-size, and national differences as organized by cinema's looking relations? Do we need to think more particularly about style? Can the look be subverted or ironized by performance?

The most significant challenge to Mulvey, and the torrent of "spectator" theory that came in her wake, however, is the question of the viewer. The viewer is the flesh-and-blood entity sitting in the darkened theater; the spectator is the fantastic identity the cinematic artifact generates. As the unconscious is the central concept of psychoanalytic theory, the spectator is the central concept of psychoanalytic film theory. These concepts are related: the spectator is not a person, but rather a site of identity generated through the interaction of the film and the viewer's unconscious fantasies, desires, and wishes. The cinematic text activates the spectator.

Psychoanalysis provides an account of how this activation works. What happens when the viewer and the spectator are not identical? For example, what happens when a female viewer watches a Dietrich film? Does she become a masculine spectator, or does she retain her identity as a female viewer, or is there some combination? The action film also provides a useful example. Arguably, the spectator of the action film is supposed to admire the strength and power of the hero's muscular form: the action hero is a site of identification, but not desire. Some viewers, however, might also admire the beauty and erotic allure of the hero's muscular form. Is this viewer reading against the grain, reading something into the film? Or, are there multiple spectatorial positions, each activated by the film's images, with very different meanings? Moreover, given that the film itself can trigger both identification and desire, how do we assess an audience member's report of the pleasure they obtain from a film? If a heterosexual male viewer states that he "couldn't take his eyes off Tobey Maguire while watching *Spider-Man*," to what do we credit the fascination? Is it merely a reaction to the film's technical brilliance, an identification with Spider-Man's moral virtue and physical prowess, a desire for Maguire's lithe and graceful muscular body, or some mixture of all three? And given societal opprobrium against homoerotic desire, how much can we trust a viewer who denies any such interest in the male body? Although a cultural studies' focus on audience reception provides an important supplement – and sometimes corrective – to psychoanalytic film theory's interest in the text and its spectator, understanding audience response to a film fully may require attention to both the viewer and the spectator.

Louis Althusser and ideological analysis

Psychoanalytic film theory is primarily concerned with the identity of the spectator activated by the film's formal and narrative features. Different theorists emphasize different elements of the film's meaning-making system and disagree about what kind of spectator is activated by a particular film or genre. The majority of theorists committed to this interpretive approach, however, are interested primarily in thinking through how desire and identification generate certain fantasies of subjectivity and the kind of ideological work these fantasies perform in a given cultural order.

The notion of ideology operating in spectator theory is borrowed from the French Marxist Louis Althusser. In his essay "Ideology and Ideological State Apparatuses" (1970), Althusser joined Marxist and Lacanian insights and extended ideological analysis beyond class conflict and false consciousness. For Althusser, ideology "represents the imaginary relationship of individuals to their real conditions of existence" (1970: 109). In this definition, we see the influence of the psychoanalytic commitment to the unconscious. We can also see why such a definition might be useful to the study of film and religion, both of which are, *inter alia*, systems of representation. Althusser went on to argue that the imaginary relation is maintained by the subject positions – for example student, child, criminal, worker – produced by a given cultural order. The rituals, practices, images, and texts of the social system "interpellate" – or hail, call forth, summon – certain subjects, and only certain subjects. To participate in the cultural system, one must recognize oneself in its call. For example, in contemporary American society, one must recognize oneself as male or female. Perhaps one can recognize oneself as a female who needs to become male, but to try to persist as some third category or outside gender renders one culturally unintelligible. Films – as well as religious discourses – provide scripts for subject positions. Cinema hails spectators with particular identities, desires, and fantasies. Insofar as these subject positions relate to systems of power that might work to the disadvantage of women, lesbians and gay men, and people of color – to name only a few – the Althusserian ideological critic hopes to point out precisely how they are activated, how the construction of identity is a fantasy and how that fantasy might be undone or replaced.

Psychoanalytic film theory in the study of religion and film

Psychoanalytic film theory does not have a strong presence in the literature comprising the academic study of religion and film. This is somewhat surprising given that the period in which religion and film scholarship came into being is roughly coincident with the period during which psychoanalysis held the strongest sway in film studies. The earliest monographs in religion and film, however, were motivated primarily by concerns about secularization. These works turned to film as a means of making God-talk relevant again, with a particular interest in reaching religiously disaffected youth. By the time the religious study of film came into its own, and truly began to be methodologically self-conscious, the field of film studies had shifted away from psycho-analytic approaches. In other words, when psychoanalysis was in ascendence in film studies, religion and film scholarship was not yet in conversation with the discipline; by the time the study of religion and film began to be a genuinely interdisciplinary endeavor, psychoanalytic film theory was no longer the first among equals in film theory.

One of the most thoroughgoing, self-conscious, and persuasive monographs in religion and film relying, in part, on psychoanalytic theory is Erin Runions' *How Hysterical: Identification and Resistance in the Bible and Film* (2003). Each of the book's chapters compares a film and a biblical passage to ask what forms of identity, desire, and subjectivity are being fostered by the texts under consideration. For example, Runions compares a passage from Ezekiel with the film *Boys Don't Cry* (1999, dir. K. Pierce) to examine questions of gender identity, gender ambiguity, and violence. Although Runions' work stands alone as the only book-length study of religion and film to utilize psychoanalysis, it is also an exemplary work for what psychoanalysis can bring to the table in helping to chart how both film and religion work as scripts of identity and as sites of resistance.

Two essays from George Aichele and Richard Walsh's *Screening Scripture* also rely heavily on psychoanalytic texts and film theory. Julie Kelso provides a clear and cogent summary of feminist theories of the gaze in her discussion of the David and Bathsheba story, in both its cinematic and textual versions, and the kinds of desires and identifications to which it gives rise (2002). In the same volume, Roland Boer considers *Total Recall* (1990, dir. P. Verhoeven) and the writings of the Apostle Paul alongside psychoanalytic texts on psychosis. Boer argues, persuasively and intriguingly, that Paul is a psychotic author and Christianity is a psychotic discourse (2002).

Steve Nolan has also insisted on the importance of psychoanalytic film theory for the study of religion and film. In his published work, however, Nolan relies on spectator theory to examine liturgy, rather than examining film itself (1998b; 2001). In a review article from 1998, Nolan criticized religion and film scholars for failing to engage "with theories of ideology, semiotics, psychoanalysis, and gender" and called for "a more sustained interaction with film theory" (Nolan 1998a: 11).

Several works written after Nolan's review heeded his call – in part. Melanie Wright echoes Nolan's insistence that religion and film scholars consider more fully film studies discourses, but she focuses on audience reception studies rather than approaches that concentrate on the text and the spectator (2007: 25–7). This interest in the viewer over the spectator has been echoed in a number of recent works (Deacy 2005; Lyden 2003; Marsh 2004). These works are primarily interested in straightforward accounts of what audiences actually do, rather than speculative accounts of what spectators might be doing. As Clive Marsh notes, however, viewers may not always understand what they are doing when watching movies, and may need the help of the researcher to formulate their experience with precision (2007: 152). In fact, this is an assumption that (implicitly) grounds much religion and film scholarship. Insofar as scholars argue that filmgoing is a ritual activity, or a religious experience, or has transcendental significance, this will strike many viewers as absurd, counterintuitive, or wrong. Both those who research viewers and those who research spectators bring theoretical tools to bear when describing the experience and interpreting the relevant data. The theoretical disagreement between cultural studies and psychoanalysis will not be settled by letting the audience, rather than the interpreter, speak, because in both situations the scholar-as-interpreter is a necessary interlocutor.

Another critique of psychoanalytic approaches is implicitly contained in worries about ideological criticism. Mitch Avila contends that ideology – "like 'phlogiston' and 'ether'" – is "an orphaned concept" (2007: 220). Because "we" have abandoned ideology as a concept, "there is no use for the practice of ideology critique" (Avila

2007: 220). Avila's conception of ideology is simply too narrow – hewing to a particular understanding of Marxism and its supposed demise. Moreover, I would strongly object to the view that ideological critique is no longer necessary. As I write this essay, newspapers are reporting on human rights abuses in China, US military involvement in Iraq, rising gas and food prices, and the advisability of same-sex marriage. It seems that ideological critique is as necessary as it ever was, and that it might need to focus on mass-media images and religious discourses. Although John Lyden has equally strong concerns about ideological criticism, as he worries that it "may represent a Trojan horse out of which could pour an army of hostile soldiers who are just as happy to reduce religion to ideology as to view film in this way," he also acknowledges that it is "an essential tool for understanding certain aspects of" religion and film, and even engages in ideological critique in the genre analyses that comprise the second half of his book (2003: 32). The fundamental disagreement here, it seems to me, is about the purpose and function, not simply of religion and film scholarship, but of the academic study of religion generally. How suspicious should we be of how religion, as a cultural discourse, shapes meaning, identity, desire, and subjectivity? As a queer feminist, I have strong reservations about religious and cinematic discourses and the fantasies of subjectivity they promulgate. Psychoanalytic theory provides insight into how these fantasies operate and how they might be disrupted.

Case study: *The Passion of the Christ*

In a study of audience reactions to Mel Gibson's *The Passion of the Christ* (2004, dir. M. Gibson), a team of researchers reported that "men were almost uniformly more likely to report concerns about the [film's] violence than women, regardless of religious or political leaning" (Woods *et al.* 2004: 176). This is a somewhat surprising finding that runs counter to traditional assumptions about how men and women respond to cinematic violence. Because my research focuses on representations of the suffering male body and fantasies of masculine identity, I am interested in why male viewers reacted in this way. In private correspondence with the authors of the study, I learned that their surveys did not gather narrative responses. This piece of audience research, then, could not provide an answer to my question.

Assume, however, that the authors had gathered narrative responses. What might they look like? "The violence was too intense, too bloody, too graphic." "I felt uncomfortable, nauseous, afraid." "I found it difficult to connect the violence to my understanding of God." "The violence was boring, repetitive." "The violence seemed too unreal." "The violence seemed too real." In other words, like Marsh and others have observed, audiences are not always able to provide researchers with clear, explicit answers to the questions that interest them. These responses would not fully answer why men had reservations about the violence or why men more than women had reservations. After all, why does intense violence – or repetitive violence, or realistic violence – create reservations in the first place?

In *Male Subjectivity at the Margins* (1992), Kaja Silverman argues that masculine identity depends on a fantastic conception of power, unity, and wholeness that is supported by a vast array of cultural discourses. At the same time, fantasies of masochism – of male suffering – give lie to the dominant fiction of masculine plenitude and expose the situation of lack that haunts masculine identity. Elsewhere I have argued that *The Passion of the Christ* participates in this masochistic disruption of masculinist fantasies, while at the same time recuperating this disruption with its resurrection scene (Brintnall 2006). Given male viewers' reservations about the violence in the film, I might need to modify my conclusions about the effectiveness of the resurrection scene to assuage the spectator. Relying on Silverman's analysis, we might conclude that the violence in this film is more disturbing to male than female viewers precisely because it poses a greater challenge to fantasies of masculine identity. Watching a male body being beaten, flayed, and pierced, watching a male body submit to overwhelming brutal violence – that is, watching a male character become a bloody spectacle rather than remain a narrative agent – may simply be more traumatizing to the identity of the masculine spectator.

On the one hand, this example shows that audience reception studies and psychoanalytic theory might not be oppositional approaches. Consideration of both "actual" and "fantastic" responses to cinematic signification may be necessary to understand how films function. On the other hand, this example shows that ideological critique is necessarily part of the study of religion and film. To watch *The Passion of the Christ* and conclude that it is not attempting to say something about gender, violence, bodies, suffering, power, and desire is to have failed to attend carefully to the film. Understanding more precisely how desire, identity, and subjectivity are supported, echoed, challenged, or critiqued by religious and cinematic discourses will help us to understand the operation of a cultural order more fully.

Conclusion

From the opening Freudian quotation to the closing consideration of Gibson's *Passion*, I have focused on issues of desire, identity, and subjectivity. Religious discourses have shown a keen interest in shaping the desires and identity of their adherents, often promising the possibility of transformation to something "better." Similarly, cinematic discourses offer a fantasy space where the audience can take up new forms of experience. The varying subjectivities they offer may foster community, humility, or compassion; they might encourage violence, hatred, and exclusion. Psychoanalytic theory provides a map for how desire and identity structure subjectivity; psychoanalytic film theory shows how these maps interact with the formal and narrative organization of cinematic signification. Understanding how these systems generate fantasies of subjectivity – whether we call it ideological interpellation or spiritual formation – seems important to the future of religion and film scholarship.

Bibliography

Althusser, L. (1970) "Ideology and Ideological State Apparatuses (Notes towards an Investigation)," in *Lenin and Philosophy*, New York: Monthly Review.

Avila, M. (2007) "From Film Emotion to Normative Criticism," in R. Johnston (ed.) *Reframing Theology and Film: New Focus for an Emerging Discipline*, Grand Rapids, MI: Baker Academic.

Baudry, J.-L. (1970) "Ideological Effects of the Basic Cinematographic Apparatus," in P. Rosen (ed.) *Narrative, Apparatus, Ideology: A Film Theory Reader*, New York: Columbia University Press.

—— (1975) "The Apparatus: Metapsychological Approaches to the Impression of Reality in Cinema," in P. Rosen (ed.) *Narrative, Apparatus, Ideology: A Film Theory Reader*, New York: Columbia University Press.

Boer, R. (2002) "Non-Sense: *Total Recall*, Paul, and the Possibility of Psychosis," in G. Aichele and R. Walsh (eds) *Screening Scripture: Intertextual Connections between Scripture and Film*, Harrisburg, PA: Trinity Press International.

Brintnall, K. (2006) "Mel Gibson's *The Passion of the Christ* and the Politics of Resurrection," *English Language Notes* 44: 235–40.

Deacy, C. (2005) *Faith in Film: Religious Themes in Contemporary Cinema*, Burlington, VT: Ashgate.

Doane, M. (1982) "Film and the Masquerade: Theorising the Female Spectator," in E. Kaplan (ed.) *Feminism and Film*, Oxford: Oxford University Press.

Freud, S. (1914) "On Narcissism: An Introduction," in J. Strachey (ed.) *The Standard Edition of the Complete Psychological Works of Sigmund Freud*, vol. XIV, London: Hogarth Press.

—— (1924) "The Dissolution of the Oedipus Complex," in J. Strachey (ed.) *The Standard Edition of the Complete Psychological Works of Sigmund Freud*, vol. XIX, London: Hogarth Press.

—— (1927) "Fetishism," in J. Strachey (ed.) *The Standard Edition of the Complete Psychological Works of Sigmund Freud*, vol. XXI, London: Hogarth Press.

Horney, K. (1932) "The Dread of Woman: Observations on a Specific Difference in the Dread Felt by Men and by Women Respectively for the Opposite Sex," in H. Kelman (ed.) *Feminine Psychology*, London: Norton.

Kaplan, E. (ed.) (2000) *Feminism and Film*, Oxford: Oxford University Press.

Kelso, J. (2002) "Gazing at Impotence in Henry King's *David and Bathsheba*," in G. Aichele and R. Walsh (eds) *Screening Scripture: Intertextual Connections between Scripture and Film*, Harrisburg, PA: Trinity Press International.

Lacan, J. (1949) "The Mirror Stage as Formative of the I Function," in B. Fink (ed.) *Écrits: The First Complete Edition in English*, London: Norton.

—— (1958) "The Signification of the Phallus," in B. Fink (ed.) *Écrits: The First Complete Edition in English*, London: Norton.

—— (1973) *The Four Fundamental Concepts of Psychoanalysis*, London: Norton.

Lyden, J. (2003) *Film as Religion: Myths, Morals, and Rituals*, New York: New York University Press.

Marsh, C. (2004) *Cinema and Sentiment: Film's Challenge to Theology*, Waynesboro, GA: Paternoster.

—— (2007) "On Dealing with What Films Actually Do to People: The Practice and Theory of Film Watching in Theology/Religion and Film Discussion," in R. Johnston (ed.) *Reframing Theology and Film: New Focus for an Emerging Discipline*, Grand Rapids, MI: Baker Academic.

Metz, C. (1977) *The Imaginary Signifier: Psychoanalysis and Cinema*, Bloomington: Indiana University Press.

Mulvey, L. (1975) "Visual Pleasure and Narrative Cinema," in *Visual and Other Pleasures*, Bloomington: Indiana University Press.

—— (1981) "Afterthoughts on 'Visual Pleasure and Narrative Cinema' inspired by King Vidor's *Duel in the Sun* (1946)," in *Visual and Other Pleasures*, Bloomington: Indiana University Press.

Neale, S. (1983) "Masculinity as Spectacle," in *The Sexual Subject: A Screen Reader in Sexuality*, London: Routledge.

Nolan, S. (1998a) "The Books of the Films: Trends in Religious Film-Analysis," *Literature & Theology* 12: 1–15.

—— (1998b) "Worshipping (Wo)men, Liturgical Representation and Feminist Film Theory: An *Alien/s* Identification?," *Bulletin of the John Rylands University Library of Manchester* 80: 195–213.

—— (2001) "Representing Realities: Theorizing Reality in Liturgy and Film," *Worship* 75: 149–72.

Runions, E. (2003) *How Hysterical: Identification and Resistance in the Bible and Film*, New York: Palgrave Macmillan.

Silverman, K. (1992) *Male Subjectivity at the Margins*, London: Routledge.

Williams, L. (1984) "When the Woman Looks," in M. Doane, P. Mellencamp, and L. Williams (eds) *Re-Vision: Essays in Feminist Film Criticism*, Los Angeles, CA: University Publications of America.

Woods, R., Jindra, M. C., and Baker, J. D. (2004) "The Audience Responds to *The Passion of the Christ*," in S. Brent Plate (ed.) *Re-Viewing* The Passion: *Mel Gibson's Film and its Critics*, New York: Palgrave Macmillan.

Wright, M. (2007) *Religion and Film: An Introduction*, New York: I. B. Tauris.

Filmography

Boys Don't Cry (1999, dir. K. Pierce)
The Passion of the Christ (2004, dir. M. Gibson)
Spider-Man (2002, dir. S. Raimi)
Total Recall (1990, dir. P. Verhoeven)

Further reading

Creed, B. (2000) "Film and Psychoanalysis," in J. Hill and P. Church Gibson (eds) *Film Studies: Critical Approaches*, Oxford: Oxford University Press. (Short, lucid introduction to psychoanalytic film theory.)

De Lauretis, T. (1994) *The Practice of Love: Lesbian Sexuality and Perverse Desire*, Bloomington: Indiana University Press. (Early, influential work of lesbian film theory.)

Evans, D. (1996) *An Introductory Dictionary of Lacanian Psychoanalysis*, London: Routledge. (Cogent guide to the meaning and development of Lacanian terminology.)

Farmer, B. (2000) *Spectacular Passions: Cinema, Fantasy, Gay Male Spectatorships*, London: Duke University Press. (Recent, lucid work of gay film theory; provides thorough overview of relevant theoretical background.)

Freud, S. (1900) *The Interpretation of Dreams*, in J. Strachey (ed.) *The Standard Edition of the Complete Psychological Works of Sigmund Freud*, vols V–VI, London: Hogarth Press. (Chapters 6 and 7 have been especially influential in film studies.)

—— (1905) *Three Essays on the Theory of Sexuality*, in J. Strachey (ed.) *The Standard Edition of the Complete Psychological Works of Sigmund Freud*, vol. VII, London: Hogarth Press. (Freud's earliest, and most influential, articulation of psychosexual development.)

—— (1923) *The Ego and the Id*, in J. Strachey (ed.) *The Standard Edition of the Complete Psychological Works of Sigmund Freud*, vol. XIX, London: Hogarth Press. (Classic text discussing the id, ego and super-ego.)

—— (1925) "Some Psychical Consequences of the Anatomical Distinction between the Sexes," in J. Strachey (ed.) *The Standard Edition of the Complete Psychological Works of Sigmund Freud*, vol. XIX, London: Hogarth Press. (Concise summary of the male and female child's response to castration anxiety and the Oedipus complex.)

Grosz, E. (1990) *Jacques Lacan: A Feminist Introduction*, London: Routledge. (Lucid, comprehensive introduction to Lacan and his feminist interpreters, defenders, and critics.)

Lacan, J. (1953) "The Function and Field of Speech and Language in Psychoanalysis," in B. Fink (ed.) *Écrits: The First Complete Edition in English*, London: Norton. (Also known as the "Rome discourse," the essay in which Lacan demonstrated his unique character and perspective as a psychoanalyst, influenced by structural linguistics.)

—— (1975) *On Feminine Sexuality – The Limit of Love and Knowledge*, London: Norton. (Book XX of Lacan's seminars; a notoriously difficult, but incredibly influential, account of gender identity and its relation to lack.)

—— (1981) *The Psychoses*, London: Norton. (Book III of Lacan's seminars; very useful in understanding the Symbolic, the role of the Father in establishing a coherent subject, and the function of the phallus.)

Laplanche, J. and Pontalis, J. B. (1967) *The Language of Psychoanalysis*, London: Norton. (A classic reference guide to the meaning and development of Freudian terminology.)

Silverman, K. (1988) *The Acoustic Mirror: The Female Voice in Psychoanalysis in Cinema*, Bloomington: Indiana University Press. (Parallels Mulvey's gendered account of the gaze by attending to the voice in cinema; Chapter 1 is a masterful close reading of Freud and Lacan on castration and lack.)

—— (1992) "The Lacanian Phallus," *differences: A Journal of Feminist Cultural Studies* 4: 84–115. (A very helpful essay for understanding the various ways Lacan uses "phallus" and how his understanding of the phallus might be appropriated by feminist theory.)

Stam, R. (1992) *New Vocabularies in Film Semiotics: Structuralism, Post-structuralism and Beyond*, London: Routledge. (Advanced introduction to contemporary theory and film studies; Part IV discusses psychoanalysis.)

17

THEOLOGICAL APPROACHES

Robert K. Johnston

Films, like most art, are often most interesting to the theological enterprise when they are being least theological.

Jasper (1997: 246)

Introduction

Almost from the beginning of cinema a century ago, there have been those interested in understanding film theologically. The New England Congregational minister Herbert Jump was one of the first, offering a theological rationale for movies in his pamphlet "The Religious Possibilities of the Motion Picture" (1911). Jump likened the Church's use of movies to Jesus' use of parables, focusing in particular on the dramatic story of the Good Samaritan found in Luke 10:30–7. It, like the motion picture, was "a dramatic story of contemporary experience, exciting in character and thus interesting even to the morally sluggish, picturing negative elements such as crime, accident, ignorance, sin, and thus commending itself as true to life, but in the end showing the defeat and expulsion of these negative elements by positive qualities, virtuous souls, God-like traits" (Jump 1911: 56). Writing as a contemporary of Jump but using more generic religious language, Vachel Lindsay also believed cinema to be an important medium for religious ideas and spiritual sentiment. In "The Art of the Moving Picture" (1915), she argued that by offering a universal language through its picture-writing – its hieroglyphic images – silent movies could in the hands of a "prophet-wizard" become "a higher form of vision-seeing" (see Loughlin 2005: 302).

Not all, of course, have agreed that such amusements are supportive of faith and/or helpful for society. In the 1930s and 1940s, religious publishing houses, like Zondervan, produced books and pamphlets decrying the theater as harmful, if not sinful. Some of these books were shrill. In *Movies and Morals* (1947), Herbert Miles labeled cinema "the organ of the devil, the idol of sinners, the sink of infamy, the stumbling block to human progress, the moral cancer of civilization, the Number One Enemy of Jesus Christ" (Miles 1947: 20). Others were more moderate, like Paul Rees' *Movies and the Conscientious Christian* (3rd edition, 1940), which went through several editions. Given the greed of the industry and the tarnished morals of movie stars, given the philistine nature of audiences which must be pandered to for reasons of profit as well as the general environment of the theater that tends to drag one down, and given the fact that movies tend to show the unreal and misleading, weakening the morals of individuals, family, and society, Rees advised that though he would not judge those who sometimes went to the theater, there were "better ways of getting our recreation than by the 'chewing gum relaxation' of the movies" (Rees 1940: 23).

Although the fundamentalistic and pietistic reasonings of these early preachers have now often been replaced by the arguments of the academy, and though the writers' political ideology now leans as often to the left as to the right, some of the same critique and/or caution can be heard today. In his incisive and helpful overview, *Understanding Theology and Popular Culture* (2005), Gordon Lynch centers his analysis on theology and film, given that this sub-discipline is more developed at present than that of dialogue with other popular culture expressions. Appreciative of the writings of Theodor Adorno (who argued that with capitalism there has been through popular culture an "aestheticization" of everyday life, a false sense of happiness provided for the masses), Lynch concludes his study by emphasizing the "on-going need for the theological and cultural criticism of the everyday and for imaginative and constructive interventions in contemporary culture." He writes, "Whilst I do not fully share Adorno's pessimism about the nature of contemporary culture, I find his analysis more compelling than those who adopt a more celebrative approach to popular culture" (Lynch 2005: 193). Lynch also considers Neil Postman's influential book, *Amusing Ourselves to Death* (1985), which reinforces the notion that we have become a society of cultural dupes. While criticizing Postman for rendering the spectator as merely passive, Lynch concludes that though we can be resisting spectators, we are also easily seduced by representations that reinforce prevailing political and cultural ideologies and preserve negative stereotypes.

That the pleasurable can be dehumanizing and morally dangerous is but one of the themes in Lynch's book. Such reservations, however, can be said to characterize the writings in theology and film of both Michael Medved, a faithful Jew and conservative cultural commentator (*Hollywood vs. America*, 1992), and Margaret Miles, a leading historian of the Christian Church and cultural progressive (*Seeing and Believing: Religion and Values in the Movies*, 1996). The writings of both of these theological critics have been widely influential in the field, but both also have their limitations. Medved's analysis of Hollywood's "attack on religion" seems ideologically driven and is not always supported by the data. Moreover, the last decade of Hollywood movies has shown his conclusions regarding Hollywood's near univocal hostility to spirituality and religion in cinema to need significant modification. Miles is no doubt right in her belief that Hollywood has continued to shape our culture's attitudes toward race, gender, class, and sexual orientation through its patterns, stereotypes, and symbol markers, but she ignores the fact that Hollywood is also shaped by them. Moreover, her sharply focused lens sometimes causes her to adopt idiosyncratic and unconvincing readings of her film examples. Theory, at times, trumps artifact.

Although theology and film criticism has existed for almost a hundred years, it was not until the late 1960s and early 1970s that what might be labeled an incipient discipline was formed. Due in large part to the influence of the "artistic" films of such European directors as Bergman, Fellini, Buñuel, and Antonioni, several religious publishing houses came out with exploratory ventures in the field: Cooper and Skrade (1970); Drew (1974); Hurley (1970); Jones (1967); Kahle and Lee (1971); Konzelman (1971); McClain (1970); Summers (1969); and Wall (1971). But with most readers being unable to actually see the movies that were discussed (there were no videos or DVDs!), few bought the books, and this publishing experiment went on hold, awaiting new technology.

It was in 1979 that George Atkinson opened the first video rental store, making possible the viewing and re-viewing of previously released movies. Thus, a new critical discipline came to life. Somewhat predictably, many theological critics initially turned to religiously themed movies such as *A Man for All Seasons* (1966), *The Mission* (1986), and *Babette's Feast* (1987). Such dialogue continues today on these and other such movies (e.g., *The Passion of the Christ* [2004], and *The Chronicles of Narnia* series [2005, 2008]). Mel Gibson's movie, in particular, has spawned a virtual library of critical responses: see Plate (2004); Fredriksen (2006); Beal and Linafelt (2006); Corley and Webb (2004); Landres and Berenbaum (2004); and Cunningham (2004).

Other critics have mined film for the presence of the Bible, whether as a prop, in a direct quotation, or as a biblical allusion to characters or story (e.g., in *Pulp Fiction* [1994], or in *Magnolia* [1999]). Adele Reinhartz's *Scripture on the Silver Screen* (2003) is one such scholarly aid to biblical literacy, as is George Aichele and Richard Walsh's edited work, *Screening Scripture: Intertextual Connections between Scripture and Film* (2002). Both observe how film can reawaken and reinterpret scripture. Still others have focused on movies about Jesus or which contain Christ-figures. Peter Malone's *Movie Christs and Antichrists* (1990) and Lloyd Baugh's *Imaging the Divine: Jesus and Christ-Figures in Film* (1997) are two of the best. But despite such helpful work on the overtly religious aspects of film, David Jasper (quoted in the epigraph to this chapter) is also right: a movie is usually more interesting theologically if it is less explicitly religious. For this reason, it is to more "secular" movies that the discipline has increasingly turned its attention.

Two theological typologies of culture

Now after three decades of more concerted scholarship, the field of theology and film has begun to take shape. But given the wide range within Christianity of possible theological understandings of culture, there is still great variety in the field. Some see this diversity as a continuing weakness within the discipline (Eichenberger 1997). But the interchange of conflicting viewpoints has also sparked new insight. Seeking to understand the kaleidoscope of perspectives that have presented themselves within the field, critics have turned in particular to the typologies of Paul Tillich and H. Richard Niebuhr, two of the most influential twentieth-century Christian theologians of culture. Both have provided theological mappings of possible Christian perspectives on culture that have proven helpful in describing the emerging discipline of theology and film, whether descriptively or prescriptively.

In Clive Marsh and Gaye Ortiz's book, *Explorations in Theology and Film* (1997), Marsh, a Methodist clergyman, makes use of the writings of both Niebuhr and Tillich. Niebuhr's classic typology of the five ways Christ and culture have interrelated are reworked and reduced to three (Niebuhr 1951). Niebuhr's "Christ Against Culture" becomes Marsh's first category – stark opposition. Here, there is no real possibility of interdisciplinary dialogue. At the other end of the spectrum, Niebuhr's "Christ of Culture," which submerges Christian theology into culture, also loses the possibility of real interchange. It is the third approach which Marsh affirms (a synthesis of Niebuhr's "Christ and Culture in Paradox," "Christ Above Culture," and "Christ the Transformer of Culture"), one that recognizes that film can have a constructive role to play in theology, yet recognizes as well the need for theology to interact with it critically. That is, theology and film must be seen as "in dialog: existing in a critical, dialectical relationship" (Marsh 1997: 27). Marsh also amends Tillich. Tillich's theology of correlation which brought together cultural questions with Christian answers was, thinks Marsh, (1) not sufficiently grounded in the arts themselves, (2) too univocal in its reading of culture, and (3) too highbrow in its taste (cf., Tillich 1951: 59–66). Moreover, the dialogue was not sufficiently multidirectional. Nevertheless, Marsh finds Tillich helpful in working out theology's relevance and public dimensions. He recognizes that film can enable theology both to do justice to the emotional and aesthetic dimensions of life and to connect with common life. He concludes by labeling his theology a "revised Tillichian theology of culture," one that seeks "'theology by negotiation' rather than correlation."

Writing in the same year as Marsh (1997), John May, a Roman Catholic literature professor, also turns to Paul Tillich for help in describing the emerging field (cf., Tillich 1969). Building on an earlier essay he wrote (May 1982) where he noted parallels with the already established discipline of religion and literature, a discipline where Tillich's influence has been substantial, May applies to film Tillich's three approaches to a theology of culture. Following Tillich, "heteronomy" considers film the handmaiden of faith; "autonomy" insists that film should be judged only by its own norms; and "theonomy" sees both theology and film to be grounded in Ultimate Reality. While May's essay in 1982 had remained largely a theoretical, albeit influential, exercise, by 1997 there was a sufficiently large body of critical literature in the field for May to now ground his theory empirically, turning to practitioners in the field itself as he fleshed out his paradigms. Moreover, while retaining Tillich's insights, May broadened his categories to five: (1) "Religious discrimination" (closely related to "heteronomy") seeks to judge film, in particular its morals, by a Christian discrimen. (2) "Religious visibility" as a theoretical approach limits the field of films to be considered to those with identifiable religious elements. (3) "Religious dialogue," typical of American Protestant churches in the early 1970s, seeks a conversation between the two disciplines, though in its initial form it remained implicitly defensive. (4) More ecumenically inclusive is "religious humanism" (which has close affinities to Tillich's notion of "theonomy"), where practitioners search for a harmony between basic human attitudes resident in film and Christian values. (5) Lastly, "religious aesthetics" (Tillich's "autonomy") recognized the priority of film as story and image, the finite particular calling up sacred meaning from its inner depths.

My own contribution in describing the field is also inductive in design, rooted in the work of practitioners in the field (Johnston 2000). Rather than being grounded in Tillich's theology of culture as was May's, my typology has more affinity with Niebuhr's. The five approaches I identify are: "Avoidance," "Caution," "Dialogue," "Appropriation," and "Divine Encounter." Viewed historically, "avoidance" was more typical of critics in the 1920s, "caution" in the 1940s, "dialogue" in the 1960s, "appropriation" in the 1980s, and "divine encounter" is becoming more prominent now as we have entered the new millennium. Of course, all five approaches have been present throughout the hundred years in which moving pictures have existed, but writings have tended to cluster around certain approaches depending on the historical epoch.

All five approaches to cinema have theological warrant, finding both ecclesial expression and biblical analogue. Fundamentalist, Pentecostal, and some Baptist churches, for example, typically teach avoidance; other Baptists and conservative Evangelicals express caution; Reformed churches and more progressive Evangelicals often encourage dialogue; Roman Catholics, appropriation; and liberal Protestants, divine encounter. Similarly, I John might be read as counseling "avoidance"; Paul's epistles, "caution"; Proverbs, as "appropriating" at times the wisdom of those outside Israel; and Paul on Mars Hill (Acts 17), as praising the Athenians for their "divine encounters." Those theologians who concentrate on the ethical (avoidance and caution) usually begin the conversation by moving from theology to film. This word-oriented perspective is most typically Protestant. Those theologians focusing on the aesthetic begin with the film text itself, and discover theology within it. This sacramental approach is more typically Roman Catholic.

A diversity of understandings of "theology"

While affirming the value of such initial mappings, I believe it also useful to turn to a second way of describing the diversity of viewpoints within the field, for models both reveal and mask. In what follows below, we will survey the field again, asking how "theology" itself is being understood.

In his book *Theologia* (1983), Edward Farley explores the history of the concept "theology," finding the term "fundamentally ambiguous" (Farley 1983: 29–48). By this Farley does not simply mean that theologians debate the nature and method of "theology," but that "the term (itself) refers to things of entirely different *genres*" (italics his). There were, states Farley, two fundamentally distinct premodern senses of the term. Does it refer to an individual cognition of God and things related to God, that is, is it a personal quality, a form of wisdom, attending to faith? Or, is it a self-conscious, scholarly enterprise or understanding which issues in a body of teaching? One description is of a "habitus," a habit of the human soul; the other sees theology as a "discipline," usually occurring in a pedagogical setting. Such a distinction between first-order "wisdom" (what we might today label as "spirituality") and second-order "knowledge" is not unique to theology. It follows in the tradition of Western philosophy, where Aristotle's term for knowledge, *episteme*, could mean both true knowledge and an organized body of knowledge based on deliberate inquiry.

In the patristic and early medieval period prior to the rise of the medieval university, theology centered on the first of these genres; it meant "the true, mystical knowledge of the one God" which issued forth in wisdom. The period from the origin of universities in the twelfth century up to the Enlightenment and the rise of the modern university understood theology in its second sense, as "a cognitive enterprise using appropriate methods and issuing in a body of teaching," that is, a discipline. In the modern period, from the seventeenth century to the present, "theology" has undergone still further transformation. From a unitary discipline, it has become an aggregate of specialties – Bible, history, systematics, etc. And adding still a third genre to the mix, "theology" has come to be understood as "training for ministerial activity" based in these various specialties. From "sapiential habitus" to "a body of knowledge," theology has come to mean "practical know-how." Here is the work of the twentieth-century seminary.

What has this to do with the discipline of theology and film? Jolyon Mitchell, in his insightful chapter on theology and film for David Ford's *The Modern Theologians* (2005), ends by saying, "Seeing with the help of film can be encouraged ... through communal worship, caring practices and reflective education" (Mitchell 2005: 755). Here is expressed the same three distinct, yet overlapping, foci for theology that Farley identifies. The diversity of genres for the term "theology" finds its analogue in the diversity of interests among theology and film scholars. Some would concentrate on theology as a discipline – on the use of film as an aid for theological reflection. Others would focus their attention on practical know-how pertinent to ministry – on film's ecclesial and missional potential. And still others would have us concentrate on a first-order knowledge of God – on film as revelatory. The concerns of "theology and film" can, thus, be understood as threefold in nature – reflection, faithful practice, and contemplation.

Using film for theological reflection

When Joel Martin and Conrad Ostwalt published their book *Screening the Sacred* in 1995, there were few books in the field of religion and film. They desired to explore the relationship between these two cultural forms and to systematize an approach to their study. Theology, as they presented it, was one of three ways that the field theorized, myth and ideology being the other two. Calling for an eclecticism in approach, they suggested that the film itself should determine which methodology might best be used. Theological criticism, as they understood it, studied "cathedrals" built by cinema. It looked for traditional theological concepts within cinema such as redemption, hope, and grace, in order to understand a film's intent. When such concepts were present, critics might put a film into conversation with similar themes found within religion. Here, they believed, was an appropriate method for studying films like *Places in the Heart* (1984) and *The Fisher King* (1991), *Platoon* (1986), and *Pale Rider* (1985).

Not all who practice theological criticism will agree with Martin and Ostwalt concerning the need to remain merely descriptive and not normative. Among those who would challenge them most strongly is Brian Godawa, the screenwriter of *To End*

All Wars (2001). In his book *Hollywood Worldviews: Watching Films with Wisdom and Discernment* (2002), Godawa offers "the confession of a screenwriter: how we storytellers try to influence you the audience with our worldviews." His goal for the book, he states, is "to aid the viewer's ability to discern the ideas being communicated." Movies with existential, postmodern, or neo-Darwinian perspectives, for example, need to be exposed for what they are. We must watch movies with our "eyes wide open" (Godawa 2002: 20, 11, 177; see also Romanowski 2001). Godawa seeks theological engagement with film, but his reduction of narrative to plot and his word-oriented, highly Reformed theology sometimes cause him to miss a movie's power and meaning (e.g., his commentary on *Grand Canyon* [1991] which highlights existential "meaninglessness" rather than "wonder" [Godawa 2002: 62]); cf., Romanowski's discussion of *Titanic* [1997] in Romanowski 2001: 162–71, which he considers as simply a Hollywood melodrama based in the American dream rather than also being a movie about the gift of salvation given by Jack to Rose).

It is neither extreme – mere description or controlling dogma – that best characterizes the discipline, however. Both lose the intended dialectic in the conversation between theology and film. Better the theological dialogue that characterizes the contributors to Clive Marsh and Gaye Ortiz's *Explorations in Theology and Film* (1997). In his introductory essay in that book, Marsh outlines a dialogical method that allows film to contribute with its own integrity to Christian theology, while also bringing its own agenda to the interchange. There must be a critical, dialectical relationship. What follows in the book are essays on *Shane* (1953) as a drama of salvation, *Edward Scissorhands* (1990) as offering Christological insight, the redeeming violence of Martin Scorsese's films, the spirituality of *Shirley Valentine* (1989), and intertextual studies of *The Piano* (1993) and Mark's Gospel, as well as *Groundhog Day* (1993) and Galatians. Here is incarnational theology, one grounded in the film text, yet rooted in a clear theological identity, and one expecting mutual critique and reformulation.

A second book-length example of film's critical use for theological reflection is Gerard Loughlin's methodologically complex *Alien Sex: The Body and Desire in Cinema and Theology* (2004). Calling his "cinematic theology" an "ecclesiacinema," he explores the possibility of doing "theology in and through film, and through writing on film" by offering a series of jump cuts between film texts, theology, scripture and philosophy, arguing for the theological and ethical importance of dispossessive desire with regard to our sexuality (Loughlin 2004: xx). Among other of his provocative conclusions, Loughlin believes the doctrine of creation is best understood not as static and past, but always in a state of yearning. Christopher Deacy's *Screen Christologies* (2001) explores *film noir* as expressive of the Christian idea of redemption, particularly through the *noir* protagonists who in their realism and brokenness reflect Christ (e.g., Travis Bickle in Scorsese's *Taxi Driver* [1976]). Unique to Deacy is a second focus as well – the audience's "theological" response. This approach takes on added importance in his second volume, *Faith in Film* (2005). Having gone to the movies to see someone else's life, we often come away with something more, an *apologia* for our own lives. This is the perspective of Clive Marsh, as well, in his highly influential *Cinema and Sentiment: Film's Challenge to Theology* (2004).

While the most common form of dialogue between theology and film might be that which is thematically based, another large group of writings is the intertextual studies between Bible and film that biblical scholars have entered into. Larry Kreitzer has been a pioneer, arguing in four volumes that in the dialogue between literature/ film and scripture, one should "reverse the hermeneutical flow," letting literature and film be the interpretive lens by which to better understand scripture (e.g., *The New Testament in Fiction and Film: On Reversing the Hermeneutical Flow* [1993]).

Perhaps the best known of any of the Bible and film studies is the work of Robert Jewett, whose *Saint Paul at the Movies* (1993) and *Saint Paul Returns to the Movies* (1999) bring film and biblical texts into conversation by means of an interpretive arch that is rooted at one end in the writings and world of Paul and at the other end in our contemporary culture as reflected in the movies. His goal in correlating biblical texts with film is not merely to illustrate truths already known, but to illumine new understandings, as he does in his discussion of Romans 2 and *Grand Canyon* (1991). While film and text are perhaps more equal partners in the conversation than with Kreitzer, Jewett's interest is also ultimately in biblical illumination. He asks, "Could it be that certain movies afford deeper access to the hidden heart of Paul's theology than mainstream theologians like myself have been able to penetrate?" (Jewett 1999: 20). For Jewett, the question is largely a rhetorical one, contemporary film's portrayal of shame (and not just individual guilt) having helped to break open his understanding of the biblical text during his writing of one of the major twentieth-century commentaries on Romans (Jewett 2007). My own *Useless Beauty: Ecclesiastes through the Lens of Contemporary Film* (2004) has a similar goal to that of Jewett, though this time directed at one of the most enigmatic books of the Old Testament. But though the primary purpose remains biblical theology, there is also an attempt to make the conversation even more fully bidirectional, the movies helping to interpret this Old Testament sage, but Ecclesiastes also illumining films like *American Beauty* (1999) and *Magnolia* (1999).

A third example of the use of film for theological reflection that has occurred over the past decade has been the trio of books that have made use of the Apostles' Creed as a dialogue partner with film: David Cunningham's *Reading is Believing: The Christian Faith through Literature and Film* (2002), Bryan Stone's *Faith and Film: Theological Themes at the Cinema* (2000), and John May's *Nourishing Faith through Fiction: Reflections of the Apostles' Creed in Literature and Film* (2001). Cunningham's is representative, and perhaps the most theologically substantive of the three. He begins his book with two questions: Why use story? And why the Creeds? Story is valuable to the theologian, he thinks, for it involves the reader by focusing on the everyday. Moreover, story acknowledges the humanity of others, evoking our sympathy. Finally, it relates belief to actions. Of course the use of story in theology is also fitting for Christianity's basis is also in story. As to the use of the Creeds, Christianity, if it is to mean anything, must have a recognizable shape. The Apostles' Creed, being biblically based, historically attested, and commonly used, provides us such a mooring. Cunningham states that in his book, he is not trying to be missional (creeds aren't). Rather he is providing readers a resource for study and conversation. Recognizing that his is only one reading of many that are possible, one influenced by his background in theology and ethics, Cunningham does not shy away from letting his concerns come to the forefront in discussing the various literary and film stories. Here is a way to make theology come to life, to explain why beliefs are important, and to show what difference beliefs might have for the Christian life.

In his interdisciplinary dialogue, Cunningham's emphasis is clearly on the discipline of theology – he is, after all, an Episcopalian theologian. Roy M. Anker, on the other hand, writes his theological reflections as a professor of English who regularly teaches courses in film at Calvin College. Not surprisingly, in *Catching Light* (2004) his focus is on film's "story," not on theology per se. Using the metaphor of light to suggest how divine Light might show forth from the screen of a darkened room, Anker offers close and illumining "textual readings" of a dozen classic films. The headings of three of his book's sections are adapted from writer and theologian Frederick Buechner's little book on Christian religious understanding, *Telling the Truth: The Gospel as Tragedy, Comedy, and Fairy-Tale* (1977): (1) "Darkness Visible," or the lack of light (e.g., *The Godfather* saga [1972, 1974, 1990] and *Chinatown* [1974]); (2) "Light Shines in the Darkness" (e.g., *Tender Mercies* [1983], *Places in the Heart* [1984]); and (3) "Fables of Light" – where young and old alike long for divine help, given human circumstances (e.g., *Star Wars* [1977], *Superman* [1978]). To these Anker adds a fourth section ("Found"), stories in which more or less normal people are struck by unexpected light (e.g., *Grand Canyon* [1991], *American Beauty* [1999]). What is particularly noteworthy in Anker's volume is the increased importance given to image and sound as he unpacks these film stories. Film narrative need not be reduced to word alone, even by an English professor.

Providing practical know-how pertinent to ministry

Engaging the theological themes of movie stories is one means of being theological. Reflecting practically on how film might be used within the life and witness of the Church is a second. As Jolyon Mitchell and Brent Plate remind us in their helpful *The Religion and Film Reader* (2007): "From its earliest days film was used for many religious purposes, including as an aid to teaching, a memorable way of presenting familiar stories, a tool for proselytism, a focal point for moral censure, a catalyst for expressing pastoral concerns, and a way simply of attracting a crowd" (Mitchell and Plate 2007: 10). There are multiple reasons for this practical interest; Mitchell and Plate are correct. But key, surely, is the fact that "film education situates itself on the side of the viewer, of the public" (Hoekstra 1997: 183).

A representative essay which focuses film's theological interest more practically is Anthony Clarke's "Gaining Fresh Insights: Film and Theological Reflection in a Pastoral Setting" (2005). Clarke provides guidance for the use of movies in the Church by reflecting on the hermeneutical circle (what has been labeled "the pastoral cycle" in practical theology). When we engage in reflection on a movie, whether as part of a home group or as part of the sermon, we need to first experience the film. We can then explore what we have seen and how it connects with our lives, let it provoke our theological reflection, and then respond, suggesting how we might live out the consequences of the dialogue in which we have been engaged. In using film in a church context in this way, the goal should not be, according to Clarke, to illustrate Gospel truth or to allegorize a film's meaning, but rather to bring our "reading" of a movie side by side with our reading of scripture or other theological texts in order to see what might emerge.

Having set out their methodology in the first section of *Flickering Images*, Clarke and his co-editor Paul Fiddes (2005) turn to examples of theological reflection of particular films (e.g., *Big Fish* [2003], *Sliding Doors* [1998], *The Terminator* series [1984, 1991, 2003], *Schindler's List* [1993], *Pleasantville* [1998]) and end their book with a study guide of eleven movies created by Larry Kreitzer and John Weaver which is meant to serve as a resource for creative Bible studies and small group discussions. Theirs is but one of a number of volumes that seek to resource the Church by providing study guides for use within and beyond the Church's borders: see Sara Vaux's *Finding Meaning at the Movies* (1999), Catherine Barsotti and Robert Johnston's *Finding God in the Movies* (2004), Richard Burridge's *Faith Odyssey* (2003), and Edward McNulty's *Films and Faith* (1999) as well as his more recent *Faith and Film* (2007). Important as well is the growing number of websites that offer ministry-directed study guides. David Bruce's www. hollywoodjesus.com, Mark Moring's CT at the Movies (www.christiantoday.com), Jeffrey Overstreet's www.LookingCloser.org, and www.damaris.org/olr/films.html are some of the best. The basic premise of these volumes and internet sites might best be summarized by Clarke and Fiddes: "there is much value in watching and reflecting on secular films, so that, by entering into dialogue with the world of film, we may be able to gain fresh insights into our own faith" (2005: 231). Or in the words of Barsotti and Johnston, the goal here is to have "the movie's *reel faith* … strengthen real faith" (2004: 16).

In their ongoing series of books, *Lights, Camera … Faith!: A Movie Lover's Guide to Scripture* (2001, 2002, 2003, 2006), Peter Malone and Rose Pacatte have integrated their reflections on film into the liturgical life of the Church, placing them in dialogue with the Gospel lectionary texts for each week. Geared to the three-year cycle of the Church's lectionary, the first three books in the series suggest films for the weekly lectionary texts and provide film synopses, commentary, Gospel dialogue, key scenes, questions, points for reflection and conversation, and even a prayer. The sheer magnitude of the project (well over 200 conversations between biblical text and film text) makes it significant, but so too its execution. The authors believe Hollywood to be a splendid resource for the pulpit, not just a threat to morality. Written as a guide, the book demands engagement and action on the part of its readers if they are to discover how a conversation between film and biblical text might relate to the practice of faith. If the first three volumes were intended to enrich the worship life of the parish, Malone and Pacatte's latest volume seeks to enrich catechetical ministry through a set of film conversations with the Ten Commandments. And more are to come (a volume on the Beatitudes and the Seven Deadly Sins is next). Malone, the theologian, and Pacatte, the media church educator, seek to show that theology is both modern and relevant, helping those in the Church know what it means concretely to live out a life of faith.

Finding God in the movies

As with art more generally, the potential of film to mediate the Transcendent has long been affirmed. Many who write in the area of theology and film begin their reflections with narratives of such accounts. For Greg Garrett, it was during his initial viewing of *Pulp Fiction* (1994) that he felt himself to be "in the presence of something holy ... God got involved" (Garrett 2007: xiii). For Jeff Overstreet, it was *The Story of the Weeping Camel* (2003) that proved revelatory for him. As he watched on the screen the mystery of a musician's song heal a camel's heart, allowing its infant offspring to suckle for the first time, Overstreet says he encountered glory (Overstreet 2007: 16–40).

For me, it was while watching the movie *Becket* (1964) that I heard God calling me to the active Christian ministry, just as the same movie was responsible for Father Gregory Elmer hearing his call to the more contemplative monastic life (Johnston 2000 [2006]: 37–9). For Craig Detweiler, that transcendent moment came while he was a teenager watching the ending of Martin Scorsese's *Raging Bull* (1980) (Detweiler 2008). The movie critic Roger Ebert relates his "spiritual experiences" came while watching *Do the Right Thing* (1989), *Cries and Whispers* (1972), and *Ikiru* (1952) (Ebert 2000).

Movies which call up such transcendent experiences need not even be of particularly high quality. The wind/Spirit (Hebrew, *ruach*) blows where it wills! Two of the readers of Overstreet's web-based reviews, for example, related to him how it was *Herbie the Love Bug* (2005) and *Runaway Bride* (1999) that ushered them into God's presence. Though this may be, it is also the case that certain movies seem more able to carry the weight of glory than others, for example *Field of Dreams* (1989), *American Beauty* (1999), *Magnolia* (1999), *Breaking the Waves* (1996), *Babette's Feast* (1987). As we seek a fuller "theological" understanding of film, we must turn from our emphases on "information" and on "formation" to also attend to the viewer's experience of "revelation."

Those interested in exploring film's experiential dimensions have often written in a style of personal memoir, believing that their experiences with and reflections on film can help readers in their spiritual journeys. Three of the best of these are Gareth Higgins *How Movies Helped Save My Soul* (2003), Jeffrey Overstreet's *Through a Screen Darkly* (2007), and Craig Detweiler's *Into the Dark* (2008). Higgins, a twenty-eight-year-old product of the Christian charismatic movement with a PhD, whose present work focuses on peacemaking in Northern Ireland, writes the book in the hopes his filmology will be "a small contribution to the understanding of film, an appeal for its location in the pantheon of life-enhancing art, and a defense of the idea that in a God-breathed universe, there can be no sacred–secular division." He admits he can only speak about movies in terms of his own life experience, but each chapter of informal reflection on multiple films opens out onto a more general theological reflection triggered by the movies, in the hope that readers too will "invest the time to create the space for God to make you human again" (Higgins 2003: xix, 255).

In *Through a Screen Darkly*, Overstreet, a theology and film columnist on the web and the creator of *Christianity Today*'s Film Forum, reminisces on movies that have been theologically important in his life in order to help those within a Christian culture expand their theological vision and enlarge their wisdom. Responding to criticism he has received on his reviews from evangelical readers, Overstreet shares stories of his own changing relationships with selected movies and the events that transformed him, along with his conversations with moviegoers and filmmakers. His writing is somewhat more didactic than Higgins as he often addresses his critics, those who question, for example, his response to film's sex, violence, profanity, and criticism of the Church. But, like Higgins, he challenges his readers to learn to "look closer" (the name of his website). Alluding to the intention of C. S. Lewis' Narnia tales, he finds in cinema "a road that leads farther up, farther in, to greater majesty and more transforming truth" (Overstreet 2007: 21).

The most intentionally theological, and perhaps the best of the three, is Craig Detweiler's *Into the Dark* (2008). Believing the Internet Movie Database (IMDb) to "offer an unparalleled, highly democratic portrait of films that have moved the human spirit," he chooses for consideration in his study of general revelation those movies which were produced since the year 2000 that appear as part of a freeze frame of IMDb's Top 250 Films captured on 1 January 2007. His receptor-oriented study uses the populist sentiments of IMDb users to explore "how the same God who spoke through dreams and visions in the Bible is still communicating through our celluloid dreams – the movies." According to Detweiler, the Spirit of God who spoke through unexpected sources in biblical times (the ruthless Chaldeans, the non-Israelite Agur, poems dedicated to Zeus) also inspires actors, screenwriters, and directors today. A Hollywood filmmaker with an eye for the visual, as well as a scholar trained as a theologian, Detweiler has written a book of theology for and about "general audiences," an exploration of how "God speaks through people, places, and experiences *outside of Scripture*, specifically, within the feature-film-going experience."

It is not these Protestant forays into the presence of God in film, however, that can be said to characterize the field. Rather, the focus on film's sacramental possibilities to mediate the presence of God has particularly been the purview of Catholic critics. In the writings of Andrew Greeley, John May, Richard Blake, and Thomas Martin, the focus has been not simply on a film's morality or on its religious content and themes. These writers have instead turned to consider the observer-critic's experience of the Divine. Leaning heavily on the work of David Tracy in his book *The Analogical Imagination* (1982), Greeley argues that with film studies, it is not ideas alone, but a sacramental sense of awe and wonder that should be seen as significant. For him, film is unique in its ability to create epiphanies because of its "inherent power to affect the imagination." He writes, "the pure, raw power of the film to capture the person who watches it, both by its vividness and by the tremendous power of the camera to concentrate and change perspectives, is a sacramental potential that is hard for other art forms to match" (Greeley 1988: 250). In *God in the Movies* (2000), written with Albert Bergesen, Greeley and Bergesen develop this thesis by considering some of the movies that have proven revelatory to them – *All That Jazz* (1979), *Fearless* (1993), *Babette's Feast* (1987), *Breaking the Waves* (1996), *Pale Rider* (1985), *Ghost* (1990), *Dogma* (1999).

While central in their thinking and writing, a focus on film's transcendental possibilities has not been limited to Catholic scholars as we have seen. Worthy of mention, as well, is the provocative book by the Protestant David Dark, *Everyday Apocalypse* (2002). Dark finds in the Coen brothers' movies, and in such films as *The Truman Show* (1998) and *The Matrix* (1999), apocalyptic visions that open out unto epiphany. A biblical analogue, for him, is the story of Nathan the prophet whose story to David provides David a transcendent perspective, an apocalyptic moment which proves transformative. The Presbyterian pastor Ed McNulty, in addition to his movie study guides written for the Church, has also published two volumes entitled *Praying the Movies* (2001; 2003). In his film discussions, he looks for "that elusive moment ... an 'Aha!' moment, when the spirit awakens us to something special in the film ... making us aware that we are on holy ground" (McNulty 2003: 13).

But surely the leading Protestant influence on the field has come from the filmmaker Paul Schrader. In his master's thesis which was published as *Transcendental Style in Film: Ozu, Bresson, Dreyer* (1972), Schrader argues that in the sparse, abstracted work of these three classic movie directors, one can discover a "common expression of the Transcendent in motion pictures" (Schrader 1972: 10). This universal style has both an ascetic aesthetic – long takes and slow camera movement, silence, detached acting and editing – and a narrative arc that moves from the mundane through a time of crisis to a final stasis where the transcendent is revealed. In his own filmmaking, Schrader has attempted to enflesh this universal style, for example in the endings of *Raging Bull* (1980), where Jake mocks his former false sense of importance by reciting the "I could have been a contender" speech from *On the Waterfront* (1954); of *American Gigolo* (1980), where Julian accepts the unconditional goodness of Michelle, achieving in the process spiritual grace; and of *The Last Temptation of Christ* (1988), where stasis is achieved with Jesus at peace on the cross, his final smile proving revelatory. Though the response to these movies has perhaps been mixed, the testimony of Craig Detweiler to the transformative power of *Raging Bull* in his own life speaks to the possibilities of Schrader's transcendental style (particularly when matched with Martin Scorsese's visual style). So too, does Peter Fraser's *Images of the Passion: The Sacramental Mode in Film* (1998). Using Schrader's turn toward formalism as his critical model, Fraser looks at a series of fifteen movies where the spiritual breaks through the physical and material, redeeming it in the process. As with Schrader, film technique is crucial for Fraser (lighting, non-diegetic musical cues, cinematic gesture, symbolic composition), helping to evoke a divine intrusion metaphorically. And again, a frozen moment, a stasis, breaks through the surface narrative, creating a transformation of both character and plot which allows the viewer to be "brought into a sacramental experience with the living God" (Fraser 1998: 11).

Finally, a sacramental presence has also been explored by Gerard Loughlin in two insightful articles. In the first, he asks "whether film can attain to the power of religious parable, to the austerity of the great icons, and itself become the occasion of hierophany" (Loughlin 2005: 302). In the second, he finds in Tarkovsky an answer, noting how the Russian Orthodox filmmaker used a "carefully crafted vocabulary of natural motifs [rain, fire, water, wind, and snow] and meditative camera movements (slow zooms and lengthy panning and dolly shots)" to enable "a form of transcendent 'vision-seeing'" (Loughlin 2007: 289). Tarkovsky's *Andrei Rublev* (1969) and *The Mirror* (1975) are not so much metaphors conveying spiritual truth as they are icons – images which stand only for themselves, allowing the invisible to be glimpsed in the visible.

Conclusion

Given the infancy of the discipline, initial critical work has not been without its recognized limitations, as even those in the field have recognized. (1) Selections of movies have too often been dominated by personal taste, resulting, for example, in insufficient attention being given to world cinema, as Gaye Ortiz has helpfully pointed out (Ortiz 2007). Jolyon Mitchell and S. Brent Plate's *The Religion and Film Reader* (2007) offers an important corrective in this regard, with half of the large book being devoted to a consideration of African and Middle Eastern, Asian and Australasian, European, and South and North American perspectives. But much more needs to be done, as the oftentimes limited theological treatment within many of the anthologized sources attest. It is also the case that personal preference has caused the same small catalogue of movies to be discussed too often (though it is significant from a receptor-oriented perspective that the "same" movies appear time and time again as inviting theological engagement). Could it be that some movies invite a theological gaze? As the discipline continues, the *oeuvre* of films considered will need to increase. But it is also the case that reflection needs to be focused on why it is that certain movies invite our theological gaze.

(2) The conversation between theology and film has also oftentimes been too narrow, other critical partners (e.g., sociology, religious history, critical theory) being overlooked. But, again, changes are afoot as Gordon Lynch's *Understanding Theology and Popular Culture* (2005) and Terry Lindvall's *Sanctuary Cinema* (2007) attest. Again, (3) it has been observed that the film as "text" has too often been the critic's sole focus rather than the experience of the "viewer" of that text also entering in. But books like Clive Marsh's *Cinema and Sentiment* (2004), as well as the works of many others writing of film's sacramental potential, belie such criticism.

(4) Fourth, much of the writing in theology and film (whether thematic, pedagogical, or experiential) has been directed at popular audiences, with the result that too little sustained theological analysis or foundation has yet been carried out. But Christopher Deacy's work on *Screen Christologies* (2001), Gerard Loughlin's focus on the body in Christian theology and film in his book *Alien Sex* (2004), and Craig Detweiler's focus on general revelation in *Into the Dark* (2008) suggest that, again, self-correction is at work. (5) It is the case, though, that given the Church's history of heavy-handed criticism of the arts, and film in particular, many currently working in the field have shied away from engaging in normative criticism. But as John Lyden suggests, theology and film might helpfully be considered a form of interreligious dialogue, a dialogue that "occurs *between religions,* and so presupposes that those involved in it have a stake in how it comes out." He writes, "It is then essentially a theological task, on each side,

as normative claims about truth are made by each participant." With film viewed "as religion," informed judgment should be the goal (Lyden 2007: 210).

Some like Steve Nolan and Melanie Wright have charged the discipline with both a lack of interest in critical theory and too heavy a reliance on literary models of criticism (see Wright 2007 and Nolan 2005). While the latter criticism was perhaps true in the first decades of the discipline, there have been significant advances in how film is understood, as this chapter attests. (One might look in particular at the work of Roy M. Anker and Craig Detweiler, where word, image, and music are all given a critical place.) With regard to the use of film theory, theology and film critics need to draw from the academy for its critical models as well as from filmmakers. In seeking to understand that "thick viewing" of film which is foundational to theology and film reflection and underlying of any authentic transcendent experience, there are critical models available to the theology and film scholar also from the side of theology. I have, for example, found the fourfold method of interpretation used by Christian medieval scholars in their biblical exegesis – one that moves in faith, love, and hope through a literal interpretation of a text to the spiritual – to be highly suggestive (see Johnston 2007b). It is the case that many who go to the movies not only view the film, but often end up discovering themselves present in it, engaged in such a way that their lives are impacted and their faith quickened. Here is multifaceted response not dissimilar to that which medieval biblical scholars used in their work and Dante adapted for his.

Critical self-correction is a continuing process in any discipline, but in one as young as theology and film, it is perhaps even more pronounced. There are changes presently going on that are "re-framing" the field. This is as it should be. The next decade will evidence continuing advance.

Bibliography

Aichele, G. and Walsh, R. (eds) (2002) Screening Scripture: Intertextual Connections between Scripture and Film, Harrisburg, PA: Trinity Press International.

Anker, R. M. (2004) Catching Light: Looking for God in the Movies, Grand Rapids, MI: Eerdmans.

Barsotti, C. M. and Johnston, R. K. (2004) Finding God in the Movies: 33 Films of Reel Faith, Grand Rapids, MI: Baker Books.

Baugh, L. (1997) Imaging the Divine: Jesus and Christ-Figures in Film, Kansas City: Sheed & Ward.

Beal, T. K. and Linafelt, T. (eds) (2006) Mel Gibson's Bible: Religion, Popular Culture, and The Passion of the Christ, Chicago: University of Chicago Press.

Bergesen, A. J. and Greeley, A. M. (2000) God in the Movies, New Brunswick, NJ: Transaction.

Blake, R. (2000) Afterimage, Chicago: Loyola Press.

Buechner, F. (1977) Telling the Truth: The Gospel as Tragedy, Comedy, and Fairy-Tale, San Francisco, CA: Harper.

Burridge, R. A. (2003) Faith Odyssey: A Journey through Life, Grand Rapids, MI: Eerdmans.

Clarke, A. (2005) "Gaining Fresh Insights: Film and Theological Reflection in a Pastoral Setting," in A. J. Clarke and P. S. Fiddes (eds) Flickering Images: Theology and Film in Dialogue, Oxford: Regents Park College.

Clarke, A. J. and Fiddes, P. S. (eds) (2005) Flickering Images: Theology and Film in Dialogue, Oxford: Regents Park College.

Cooper, J. C. and Skrade, C. (eds) (1970) Celluloid and Symbols, Philadelphia: Fortress.

Corley, K. E. and Webb, R. L. (eds) (2004) *Jesus and Mel Gibson's The Passion of the Christ: The Film, the Gospels and the Claims of History*, New York: Continuum.

Cunningham, D. S. (2002) *Reading is Believing: The Christian Faith through Literature and Film*, Grand Rapids, MI: Brazos Press.

Cunningham, P. (ed.) (2004) *Pondering the Passion: What's at Stake for Christians and Jews?*, Lanham, MD: Rowman and Littlefield.

Dark, D. (2002) *Everyday Apocalypse: The Sacred Revealed in Radiohead, The Simpsons, and Other Pop Culture Icons*, Grand Rapids, MI: Brazos Press.

Deacy, C. (2001) *Screen Christologies: Redemption and the Medium of Film*, Cardiff: University of Wales Press.

—— (2005) *Faith in Film: Religious Themes in Contemporary Cinema*, Burlington, VT: Ashgate.

Detweiler, C. (2008) *Into the Dark: Seeing the Sacred in the Top Films of the 21st Century*, Grand Rapids, MI: Baker Academic.

Drew, D. J. (1974) *Images of Man: A Critique of the Contemporary Cinema*, Downers Grove, IL: InterVarsity.

Ebert, R. (2000) "Preface," in A. J. Bergesen and A. M. Greeley, *God in the Movies*, New Brunswick, NJ: Transaction: vii–ix.

Eichenberger, A. (1997) "Approaches to Film Criticism," in J. R. May (ed.) *New Image of Religious Film*, Kansas City: Sheed & Ward: 3–16.

Farley, E. (1983) *Theologia: The Fragmentation and Unity of Theological Education*, Philadelphia: Fortress.

Fraser, P. (1998) *Images of the Passion: The Sacramental Mode in Film*, Westport, CT: Praeger.

Fredriksen, P. (ed.) (2006) *On The Passion of the Christ: Exploring the Issues Raised by the Controversial Movie*, Berkeley: University of California Press.

Garrett, G. (2007) *The Gospel according to Hollywood*, Louisville, KY: Westminster John Knox Press.

Godawa, B. (2002) *Hollywood Worldviews: Watching Films with Wisdom and Discernment*, Downers Grove, IL: InterVarsity Press.

Greeley, A. (1988) *God in Popular Culture*, Chicago: Thomas More.

Higgins, G. (2003) *How Movies Helped Save My Soul: Finding Spiritual Fingerprints in Culturally Significant Films*, Lake Mary, FL: Relevant Books.

Hoekstra, H. (1997) "Film Education in a Christian Perspective: Some Contemporary Approaches," in J. R. May (ed.) *New Images of Religious Film*, Kansas City: Sheed & Ward: 181–96.

Hurley, N. P. (1970) *Theology through Film*, New York: Harper & Row.

Jasper, D. (1997) "On Systematizing the Unsystematic: A Response," in C. Marsh and G. Ortiz (eds) *Explorations in Theology and Film: Movies and Meaning*, Oxford: Blackwell: 235–44.

Jewett, R. (1993) *Saint Paul at the Movies: The Apostle's Dialogue with American Culture*, Louisville, KY: Westminster John Knox Press.

—— (1999) *Saint Paul Returns to the Movies: Triumph over Shame*, Grand Rapids, MI: Eerdmans.

—— (2007) *Romans: A Commentary* (Hermeneia), Minneapolis, MN: Fortress.

Johnston, R. K. (2000) *Reel Spirituality: Theology and Film in Dialogue*, Grand Rapids, MI: Baker Academic. (2nd ed., 2006).

—— (2004) *Useless Beauty: Ecclesiastes through the Lens of Contemporary Film*, Grand Rapids, MI: Baker Academic.

—— (ed.) (2007a) *Reframing Theology and Film: New Focus for an Emerging Discipline*, Grand Rapids, MI: Baker Academic.

—— (2007b) "Transformative Viewing: Penetrating the Story's Surface," in R. K. Johnston (ed.) *Reframing Theology and Film: New Focus for an Emerging Discipline*, Grand Rapids, MI: Baker Academic.

Jones, G. W. (1967) *Sunday Night at the Movies*, Richmond: John Knox.

Jump, H. (1911) "The Religious Possibilities of the Motion Picture," in T. Lindvall, *The Silents of God: Selected Issues and Documents in Silent American Film and Religion 1908–1925*, Lanham, MD: Scarecrow Press: 54–77.

Kahle, R. and Lee, R. E. (1971) *Popcorn and Parable*, Minneapolis, MN: Augsburg.

Konzelman, R. G. (1971) *Marquee Ministry: The Movie Theater as Church and Community Forum*, New York: Harper & Row.

Kreitzer, L. J. (1993) *The New Testament in Fiction and Film: On Reversing the Hermeneutical Flow*, Sheffield: JSOT Press.

Landres, S. and Berenbaum, M. (eds) (2004) *After The Passion is Gone: American Religious Consequences*, Walnut Creek, CA: Altamira.

Lindvall, T. (2001) *The Silents of God: Selected Issues and Documents in Silent American Film and Religion 1908-1925*, Lanham, MD: Scarecrow Press.

—— (2007) *Sanctuary Cinema: Origins of the Christian Film Industry*, New York: New York University Press.

Loughlin, G. (2004) *Alien Sex: The Body and Desire in Cinema and Theology*, Oxford: Blackwell.

—— (2005) "Spirituality and Film," in P. Sheldrake (ed.) *The New SCM Dictionary of Christian Spirituality*, London: SCM Press: 302–3.

—— (2007) "Within the Image: Film as Icon," in R. K. Johnston, (ed.) *Reframing Theology and Film: New Focus for an Emerging Discipline*, Grand Rapids, MI: Baker Academic: 287–303.

Lyden, J. C. (2007) "Theology and Film: Interreligious Dialogue and Theology," in R. K. Johnston (ed.) *Reframing Theology and Film: New Focus for an Emerging Discipline*, Grand Rapids, MI: Baker Academic: 205–18.

Lynch, G. (2005) *Understanding Theology and Popular Culture*, Oxford: Blackwell.

McClain, C. (1970) *Morals and the Movies*, Kansas City: Beacon Hill.

McNulty, E. (1999) *Films and Faith: Forty Discussion Guides*, Topeka, KS: Viaticum.

—— (2001) *Praying the Movies: Daily Meditations from Classic Films*, Louisville, KY: Geneva.

—— (2003) *Praying the Movies II: More Daily Meditations from Classic Films*, Louisville, KY: Westminster John Knox Press.

—— (2007) *Faith and Film: A Guidebook for Leaders*, Louisville, KY: Westminster John Knox Press.

Malone, P. (1990) *Movie Christs and Antichrists*, New York: Crossroad.

Malone, P. with Pacatte, R. (2001) *Lights, Camera . . . Faith!: A Movie Lover's Guide to Scripture, A Movie Lectionary – Cycle A*, Boston: Pauline Books & Media.

—— (2002) *Lights, Camera . . . Faith!: A Movie Lover's Guide to Scripture, A Movie Lectionary – Cycle B*, Boston: Pauline Books & Media.

—— (2003) *Lights, Camera . . . Faith!: A Movie Lover's Guide to Scripture, A Movie Lectionary – Cycle C*, Boston: Pauline Books & Media.

—— (2006) *Lights, Camera . . . Faith!: A Movie Lover's Guide to Scripture – The Ten Commandments*, Boston: Pauline Books & Media.

Marsh, C. (1997) "Film and Theologies of Culture," in C. Marsh and G. Ortiz (eds) *Explorations in Theology and Film: Movies and Meaning*, Oxford: Blackwell.

—— (2004) *Cinema and Sentiment: Film's Challenge to Theology*, Bletchley, Milton Keynes: Paternoster.

Marsh, C. and Ortiz, G. (eds) (1997) *Explorations in Theology and Film: Movies and Meaning*, Oxford: Blackwell.

Martin, J. W. and Ostwalt, C. E., Jr. (eds) (1995) *Screening the Sacred: Religion, Myth, and Ideology in Popular American Film*, Boulder, CO: Westview.

Martin, T. M. (1981) *Images and the Imageless: A Study in Religious Consciousness and Film*, Lewisburg: Bucknell University Press.

May, J. R. (1982) "Visual Story and the Religious Interpretation of Film," in J. R. May and M. Bird (eds) *Religion in Film*, Knoxville: University of Tennessee Press: 23–43.

—— (1997) "Contemporary Theories Regarding the Interpretation of Religious Film," in J. R. May (ed.) *New Image of Religious Film*, Kansas City: Sheed & Ward: 17–37.

—— (2001) *Nourishing Faith through Fiction: Reflections of the Apostles' Creed in Literature and Film*, Franklin, WI: Sheed & Ward.

Medved, M. (1992) *Hollywood vs. America: Popular Culture and the War on Traditional Values*, New York: HarperCollins.

Miles, H. (1947) *Movies and Morals*, Grand Rapids, MI: Zondervan.

Miles, M. (1996) *Seeing and Believing: Religion and Values in the Movies*, Boston: Beacon.

Mitchell, J. (2005) "Theology and Film," in D. F. Ford with R. Muers (eds) *The Modern Theologians: An Introduction to Christian Theology since 1918*, 3rd ed., Oxford: Blackwell: 736–59.

Mitchell, J. and Plate, S. B. (eds) (2007) *The Religion and Film Reader*, New York: Routledge.

Niebuhr, H. R. (1951) *Christ and Culture*, New York: Harper & Row.

Nolan, S. (2005) "Understanding Films: Reading in the Gaps," in A. J. Clarke and P. S. Fiddes (eds) *Flickering Images: Theology and Film in Dialogue*, Oxford: Regents Park College: 25–48.

Ortiz, G. (2007) "World Cinema: Opportunities for Dialogue with Religion and Theology," in R. K. Johnston (ed.) *Reframing Theology and Film: New Focus for an Emerging Discipline*, Grand Rapids, MI: Baker Academic: 73–87.

Overstreet, J. (2007) *Through a Screen Darkly: Looking Closer at Beauty, Truth and Goodness in the Movies*, Ventura, CA: Regal.

Plate, S. B. (ed.) (2004) *Re-Viewing The Passion: Mel Gibson's Film and its Critics*, New York: Palgrave Macmillan.

Postman, N. (1985) *Amusing Ourselves to Death: Public Discourse in the Age of Show Business*, New York: Penguin.

Rees, P. (1940) *Movies and the Conscientious Christian*, 3rd ed., Grand Rapids, MI: Zondervan.

Reinhartz, A. (2003) *Scripture on the Silver Screen*, Louisville, KY: Westminster John Knox Press.

Romanowski, W. D. (2001) *Eyes Wide Open: Looking for God in Popular Culture*, Grand Rapids, MI: Brazos (revised and expanded ed. 2007).

Schrader, P. (1972) *Transcendental Style in Film: Ozu, Bresson, Dreyer*, Berkeley: University of California Press.

Stone, B. P. (2000) *Faith and Film: Theological Themes at the Cinema*, St. Louis, MO: Chalice Press.

Summers, S. (1969) *Secular Films and the Church's Ministry*, New York: Seabury.

Tillich, P. (1951) *Systematic Theology*, vol. 1, Chicago: University of Chicago Press.

—— (1969) *What is Religion?*, ed. J. Adams, New York: Harper & Row.

Tracy, D. (1982) *The Analogical Imagination*, New York: Crossroad.

Vaux, S. A. (1999) *Finding Meaning at the Movies*, Nashville, TN: Abingdon.

Wall, J. M. (1971) *Church and Cinema: A Way of Viewing Film*, Grand Rapids, MI: Eerdmans.

Wright, M. (2007) *Religion and Film: An Introduction*, London: I. B. Tauris.

Filmography

All That Jazz (1979, dir. B. Fosse)
American Beauty (1999. dir. S. Mendes)
American Gigolo (1980, dir. P. Schrader)
Andrei Rublev (1969, dir. A. Tarkovsky)
Babette's Feast (1987, dir. G. Axel)
Becket (1964, dir. P. Glenville)
Big Fish (2003, dir. T. Burton)
Breaking the Waves (1996, dir. L. von Trier)
Chinatown (1974, dir. R. Polanski)
The Chronicles of Narnia: The Lion, the Witch and the Wardrobe (2005, dir. A. Adamson)
The Chronicles of Narnia: Prince Caspian (2008, dir. A. Adamson)
Cries and Whispers (1972, dir. I. Bergman)
Do the Right Thing (1989, dir. S. Lee)
Dogma (1999, dir. K. Smith)
Edward Scissorhands (1990, dir. T. Burton)
Fearless (1993, dir. P. Weir)
Field of Dreams (1989, dir. R. Robinson)
The Fisher King (1991, dir. T. Gilliam)
Ghost (1990, dir. J. Zucker)
The Godfather (1972, dir. F. Coppola)
The Godfather: Part II (1974, dir. F. Coppola)
The Godfather: Part III (1990, dir. F. Coppola)
Grand Canyon (1991, dir. L. Kasdan)
Groundhog Day (1993, dir. H. Ramis)
Herbie Fully Loaded (2005, dir. A. Robinson)
Ikiru (1952, dir. A. Kurosawa)
The Last Temptation of Christ (1988, dir. M. Scorsese)

Magnolia (1999, dir. P. Anderson)
A Man for All Seasons (1966, dir. F. Zinnemann)
The Matrix (1999, dir. A. and L. Wachowski)
The Mirror (1975, dir. A. Tarkovsky)
The Mission (1986, dir. R. Joffé)
On the Waterfront (1954, dir. E. Kazan)
Pale Rider (1985, dir. C. Eastwood)
The Passion of the Christ (2004, dir. M. Gibson)
The Piano (1993, dir. J. Campion)
Places in the Heart (1984, dir. R. Benton)
Platoon (1986, dir. O. Stone)
Pleasantville (1998, dir. G. Ross)
Pulp Fiction (1994, dir. Q. Tarantino)
Raging Bull (1980, dir. M. Scorsese)
Runaway Bride (1999, dir. G. Marshall)
Schindler's List (1993, dir. S. Spielberg)
Shane (1953, dir. G. Stevens)
Shirley Valentine (1989, dir. L. Gilbert)
Sliding Doors (1998, dir. P. Howitt)
Star Wars (1977, dir. G. Lucas)
The Story of the Weeping Camel (2003, dir. B. Davaa and L. Falorni)
Superman (1978, dir. R. Donner)
Taxi Driver (1976, dir. M. Scorsese)
Tender Mercies (1983, dir. B. Beresford)
The Terminator (1984, dir. J. Cameron)
Terminator 2: Judgment Day (1991, dir. J. Cameron))
Terminator 3: Rise of the Machines (2003, dir. J. Mostow)
Titanic (1997, dir. J. Cameron)
The Truman Show (1998, dir. P. Weir)

Part IV

CATEGORIES APPLICABLE TO RELIGION AND FILM STUDIES

18
NARRATIVE
Roy M. Anker

Introduction

The vast majority of films ever made have narratives at their core. The taste for stories of one kind or another – and there seem to be almost infinite kinds of stories – constitutes a central human appetite. People in general, all around the world and in every culture, like and rely on stories for reasons ranging from personal pleasure and identity formulation to cultural mapping and negotiation. Questions about the nature of narrative appeal and its psychological and cultural functions remain matters of sometimes fierce theoretical debate, pitting Marxists against Lacanians against feminists, *ad infinitum*. However, no matter what sort of theoretical prism one brings to moviegoing, it is clear that, in cinema at least, almost all stories rely on what is called "unified narrative," a term derived from classical Greek philosopher Aristotle, who contended that stories have a three-part structure: beginnings, middles, and ends that proceed both chronologically and causally. Indeed, that is the preeminent structure of most stories, cinematic or otherwise: a single character, a protagonist, somewhere finds herself (beginning) confronted by variously complicating difficulties, usually involving an antagonist of some sort, whether the sea or a villain (middle), that only resolve (denouement) by the finish of the story (end), providing what is usually called closure. That holds true for both comedy and tragedy, though with the prevailing demand that movies end happily the latter are rarer (the most notable American exception, perhaps, is *The Godfather, Part III* [1990]). Some film theorists postulate four phases or acts to a film; others hold out for six. Regardless, the controlling concerns in cinematic storytelling are with chronological sense and plausibility, even in the improbable worlds of science fiction and fantasy or, for that matter, in tales told backwards, as in cult favorite *Memento* (2000). If done well, the story entices viewer appetites for knowing: "To understand a film's story is to grasp what happens and where, why, and when it happens," says David Bordwell in his classic text on *Narration in the Fiction Film* (Bordwell 1985: 34). Stories that bog down, digress, zigzag, leave gaps, or clumsily repeat other films exasperate viewer expectations and pleasure. In fact, one of the chief markers of experimental or art-house films – namely, their willingness to diverge from conventional narrative – often results in a heavy toll in box office.

That is not to say that within modes of classic storytelling there is not room for divergent kinds of plots, though their boundaries do not stray or stretch very far from the causative model described above. Two common variations on tightly unified plotting are the more loosely constructed epic, for example, Homer's *The Odyssey* (see Carroll 2008), and what has come to be called the "network narrative." Both typically consist of an array of sub-narratives that sometimes have but slight connection to one another. In *The Odyssey*, for example, events are tied together by a transfixing single character and a central concern or quest. For Odysseus, this is reaching home and family in Ithaca after years fighting the Trojan War; however, one seemingly random event after another befalls Odysseus, and these seem to have little narrative reason or linkage other than perhaps to display different facets of the hero's character. The journey itself amounts to one unforeseeable incident after another – the Cyclops, the Sirens, the Lotus Eaters, and so on – while the narrative periodically switches to Ithaca to glimpse how Odysseus' son and wife fend off greedy suitors who wish to capitalize on the presumed death of the long-missing Odysseus. Compared to tightly unified narratives, the epic seems to lack narrative cohesion and expedition. Insofar as the reader can tell, Odysseus' wandering is somehow dimly connected to a spat among the gods over the measure of his virtue, for he and his faithful crew have done in the eyes of some deities great wrong. The narrative appetite for "What next?" and closure remain, to be sure, but they operate at a different pitch to fasten on questions of possible connectedness in events rather than quite so much on causality and event. That holds as well in another popular form, a cousin of sorts to the epic, the "network narrative," which typically features not one central story or character but multiple plots, usually depicting an array of diverse people tenuously associated with several central characters. Robert Altman's *Short Cuts* (1993) explores the way people do (or do not) connect, and Woody Allen's best film, *Crimes and Misdemeanors* (1989), a tale of murder and guilt, frames the issues of possible human connectedness and responsibility as a vexing theological riddle.

Neither age nor frequency has dimmed the popular appeal of any of these forms. Contemporary audiences show considerable appetite for countless amalgams of multi-stranded episodic tales in their love for serial storytelling in a variety of formats. What cohesion there is threads through the challenges that create the primary narrative interest of each episode. Here the appeal for viewers is not only the question of what might happen next to whom but how the apparently random and disconnected might (or might not) come together to what effect. In sum, tastes for chronology and causality establish a fabric of plausibility that obtains even in the most far-fetched plots.

The challenge to telling religious stories

Not surprisingly, then, given viewer preferences for sensible veracity, both visual and logical, for a fabric of "this-worldly" plausibility – what we might call "the palpable real" – filmmakers who wish their stories to convey the supernatural face a daunting challenge. As a medium whose hallmark achievement is the replication of what at least seems objectively real, film might seem ill-suited to convey religious or spiritual reality, which eludes adequate expression or objectification. Philosophy and theology

332

talk about the ineffable, music and literature about the inexpressible, and the visual arts, film included, wrestle with making the invisible perceivable. The challenge may loom largest for cinema, given its implicit bent for the "palpable real." In a question asked in the first pages of one of the first substantive approaches to religion and film, Michael Bird wonders "how does the artist render visible that which is inherently invisible?" (Bird 1982: 4). Bird distinguishes between the cinematic display of the extraordinary divine (theophany) and the emergence through the ordinary, the "everyday real," of some variety of divine presence (hierophany) (Bird 1982: 3, 8). Critic and filmmaker Paul Schrader first laid out this scheme in his groundbreaking *Transcendental Style in Film* and added another category: "the human experience of transcendence," meaning one's own encounter with some aspect of the divine as evident, for example, in impressionistic painting and psychological novels of religious conversion (Schrader 1972: 6).

Whatever capacities cinema has to capture any of these dimensions of experience face further challenges in the tendency of modern audiences to privilege a strictly logical physical world. This is further compounded by the pervasive theological claim that the divine lies beyond human comprehension and representation. Islam and parts of Protestant Christianity have in fact been aniconic, resisting any effort to capture or picture the divine either visually or aurally in material form, a process that for them inexorably reduces and contains the supernatural in the natural. Given this suspicion of material representation and the elusiveness of the divine in general, the challenge for the filmmakers is to find appropriate cinematic means to convey whatever it is that they wish to dramatize about the divine, an entity whose nature, agency, and magnitude, most religions assert, are mysterious, immaterial, and markedly beyond human comprehension. Representing the divine itself is a perilous business; but no less difficult, given the bias of the medium, is the task of representing the subjective realities of individual consciousness, the contours of what Bordwell labels "subjective stories" (Bordwell 2006: 80–2). The same applies to the inward apprehension of the divine as applies to the external manifestation of the divine; it cannot be fully seen or shown. Historians and psychologists of religion have for a century tried to parse and display the processes and variables of personal religious experience (Otto 1958; Fuller 2006). A marked challenge follows: how might filmmakers convey some portion of divine reality in material terms, an artistic and aesthetic Everest on which religions, musicians, poets, and a host of others have perennially striven?

The surprise is, though, that much of the great classic work in cinema in the West has done just that. Admittedly, this focus on the religious has in the history of cinema, proportionally speaking, gotten but scant attention, and when it has, the result has often been maudlin, contrived, dogmatic, or sensationalistic. On the other hand, the question of how to dramatize a numinous reality has spurred a disproportionate number of cinema's great masters: Bergman, Bresson, Dreyer, Tarkovsky, Goddard, and Kieślowski. Nor does this pattern show any signs of waning if one considers some of the work of celebrated contemporary filmmakers Lars von Trier, P. T. Anderson, Steven Spielberg, Majid Majidhi, Carlos Reygadas, Wim Wenders, Jean-Pierre and Luc Dardenne, and Terrence Malick, to name but a few. They and others have deployed a wide range of narrative and stylistic structures, often strikingly innovative, to evoke some sense of a pressing religious reality within human affairs. Indeed, this very challenge seems to have stretched the expressive range of the medium as it strives for the means to display the mysteries of divine presence in human affairs. What follows catalogues the methods and capabilities of different sorts of narrative structures different filmmakers have deployed to display some sort and measure of divine reality. The list is tentative, very much a first step in charting a diverse and far-ranging territory, and it, needless to say, invites additions, revision, and refinement. Presently we seem to have a great lumping together of diverse films under a generic heading called "religious," a term that in itself has more than enough difficulties. The following discussion, then, tries to parse what swirls indistinctly under the nebulous heading of religious film, trying to tease out for a descriptive taxonomy, however tentative, narrative strands from within a tangled skein of movies. The essay will also wonder about what sorts of narratives assert what dimensions of divine presence. Indeed, it seems often that certain structures evolve naturally from the sort of story being told or mystery probed. Different narrative modes focus on different religious domains and possibilities. Perhaps each form in itself contains its own distinctive metaphysical proposition about the nature of the divine and its means of disclosure. In the simplest terms, perhaps form does contain metaphysic. These range from quiet manifestation in individual lives, such as in *Tender Mercies* (1983), to parables and fables of redemption in *Star Wars* (1977), to meditative probings of the nature of nature in *The Thin Red Line* (1998), and to the wild eruption of divine presence in the strange liminal world of *Magnolia* (1999).

Realism and its varieties

Realism, the predominant narrative mode in cinema, is a slippery term. Within the history of cinema, and the larger culture, it has numerous referents, ranging from a philosophical posture to a particular film style. Here we give it in a generic, common-sense denotation, both philosophic and stylistic, to suggest that regardless of story type, whether sci-fi or spy thriller, and setting, whether Middle Earth or 1950s Washington, stories have to look and feel plausible and "real," matters that not only have to do with narrative causality but also questions of lighting, production design, editing, sound design, music, acting, narration, and so on. This mode of storytelling demands the creation of a recognizable human world, regardless of era or setting, that proceeds sensibly and plausibly according to "real" parameters of motivation, behavior, and possibility, very much of the kind that Bordwell repeatedly insists dominates Hollywood filmmaking, even among the new crop of filmmakers who came to the fore in the 1970s (Bordwell 2006). As is typically the case, visual and narrative believability bestow credibility on the tale, allowing audiences to engage the story cognitively and emotionally. Three sorts of religious genres seem to thrive within cinematic realism.

Holy history

One cinematic tradition where cinematic realism seems ideally suited is the "telling" of holy history, meaning stories taken from sacred sources such as the Bible, Roman Catholicism's "lives of the saints," and Protestantism's "heroes of the faith." In this genre, the signal realism of movie storytelling has proven a great boon. In short, realism has given vivid and often compelling narrative immediacy to historically distant religious figures. In this, the British tradition of spectacle filmmaking has excelled, producing films of rich historical pageantry on the lives of martyrs to ravenous kinds of evil, usually kings and tyrants. These include *Becket* (1964), the story of the twelfth-century archbishop who fatally opposed one-time close friend King Henry II, and *A Man for All Seasons* (1966), which details the events that led King Henry VIII to order the execution of Sir Thomas More when the latter remained faithful to the Roman Catholic Church. Franco Zeffirelli lushly treated St. Francis of Assisi in his *Brother Sun, Sister Moon* (1972). The latest iteration of the genre is the recent treatment in *Amazing Grace* (2006) of early nineteenth-century anti-slavery crusader William Wilberforce. The careful historical realism of these films made remote, seemingly arcane lives of religious belief, and even the notion of belief, not only plausible but fetching. They are impressively set and told, albeit with some embellishment for "dramatic purposes," as the customary disclaimers of complete historical accuracy confess.

The same can be said for the international genre of biblical epic, especially of the numerous lives of Jesus Christ (Baugh 1997; Reinhartz 2007). These included Nicholas Ray's *King of Kings* (1961) and George Stevens' *The Greatest Story Ever Told* (1965), as well as Pier Paolo Pasolini's *The Gospel According to St. Matthew* (1964), a film as stark and fierce as mainstream films were lush and dignified (and often ponderous). An Italian communist, Pasolini set his revolutionary Jesus in a dire landscape among barely civilized people. One appeal of all these films was the opportunity to glimpse the historical realities of Jesus' setting and experience, an aspect emphasized in advertising for many of the films, even though the films were, as Adele Reinhartz has argued, very much constructed through the prism of one's own cultural setting and stresses (Reinhartz 2007: 4–5, 10). The fullest treatment of Jesus in the era was Franco Zeffirelli's richly detailed six-hour television miniseries *Jesus of Nazareth* (1977). The emphasis on realism, especially on the cost of Jesus' physical suffering, has nowhere been more prominent than in Mel Gibson's very graphic and controversial *The Passion of the Christ* (2004).

The appeal of these films lies in a complex of factors. The most obvious is their sense of eyewitness proximity to heroic historic figures and events which in varying degrees all manifest, quite literally, aspects of the character of the divine, except, of course, in the case of Jesus whose claim was divinity itself wherein we glimpse God straight-on, so to speak. That appeal arises from appetites for awe and inspiration, the longing to be struck firsthand by the majesty of the divine. The demand for grandeur and awe explains to some extent the push toward cinematic spectacle in setting and sets. These elements alone can evoke the gravity and drama of historic beliefs and action, a strategy that recalls in some measure the eighteenth-century aesthetic theory

335

that sublime settings give rise to sublime moral action. Also playing in the mix are, at least for some viewers, devotional impulses, meaning an effort to comprehend better so as to revere more deeply the mystery of divine presence.

These historically based films of saints and heroes work best to display the moral consequences of the inner sensibleness and integrity of belief. By and large, though, they do not explore, except perhaps by implication, the usually complex interiority of belief, meaning its rationale, either intellectually or psycho-emotionally, within the life of belief. Distance from that "subjective story" seems quite natural insofar as cinema seems most adept and comfortable rendering the externality of the visual world – behavior displayed in history – and it is primarily by dramatization of action that audiences glimpse what they do of interior realities.

Mundane realism

Some of the same pleasures that inform "holy history" characterize the stories of conventional linear realism that transpire within the mundane, the "everyday real," as Michael Bird has called it (Bird 1982: 9). Narratively, as is typical of movie realism, the usual "what will happen" lies at the center, though that now mixes with the question of how these films show whatever religious freight they carry, embedded as they are in the mundane grit of the ordinary. These stories begin and end, for the most part, within the distinct confines of profane "this-worldly" reality where plausibility and causality prevail; and at least in the best of the genre, the toll of evil is not minced. The narratives unfold in direct, sequential fashion, typically offering a history of a central character's movement toward religious affirmation and perhaps the consequences of that. Whatever religious progress the protagonist does achieve seems reasonable and plausible within the character's psycho-spiritual history and the events of the film, and, further, the viewer understands, though sometimes only after careful reflection on the film, why the character turns in a given direction. These stories of everyday reality most often tend to be tales of offense, guilt, and grace, or a path from lostness to meaning, patterns that are readily understandable to most audiences. Perhaps the most striking example of this sort of personal religious history, following one soul from predatoriness through conversion to martyrdom, is David Puttnam's *The Mission* (1986), though the film is, through its use of Ennio Morricone's music, a rather loose kind of realism, for the score allows insight into souls themselves.

This sort of thing happens as well with Mac Sledge in *Tender Mercies* (1983), Matthew Poncelot in *Dead Man Walking* (1995), Sonny Dewey in *The Apostle* (1997), and Anna in *Private Confessions* (1996). What most often proceeds is a plausible, understandable grace whose agency is generally clear, though it is often rendered in subtle cinematic terms. Almost everything that transpires in the film takes place within a crisp and limited diegetic world, save perhaps for the sometimes pivotal use of music for expressing interior realities. Most of these films, though, use non-diegetic music sparingly or not at all.

So scrupulous are these films in depicting the social, physical, and personal worlds that their stories seem like phenomenological meditations on the sensible means by which individual people progress toward an apprehension of divine presence. What sort of divine presence manifests itself appears in the interplay of event, interchange, and consciousness of the separate characters and usually through the mediation of another person. Aspects of story and setting may assume symbolic meaning, but this arises always from within the narrative confines of the story. And, paradoxically perhaps, it is this emphasis on the palpable real that makes religious movement credible when it does take place. Perhaps the foremost example of that is the unsettling raw physicality of Jean-Luc Godard's hotly controversial *Hail Mary* (1985), a contemporary reframing of the Virgin Birth. It is Godard's insistence upon so very fully and graphically embedding this "miracle" in the intractable flesh that imparts a strange plausibility to its spiritual claims of supernatural presence. Here, and in these other films, there are no conspicuous *deus ex machina* appearances of an otherworldly divine (no annunciating angels in Godard, for example), at least not in direct empirical display. All is minutely observed for audiences – they indeed see it all – though the camera limits access to thought, except for what can be derived from script, acting, lighting, and so on. While the camera is omnipresent, it is not omniscient. The task here, quite literally, is to make the invisible, the "subjective story," with its spiritual contours and history, interior thought and feeling, into the visible, the interior perceivable, insofar as the bounds of cinematic realism allow. What most often results is a plausible, sensible, understandable grace manifest in conduct and attitude and whose agency is transparent, and the characters, and audience, generally know they've come upon it. Few films, in fact, toe that line narrowly, and sometimes with good reason.

A masterful example is *Tender Mercies*, a tale of an ex-country music star, for which screenwriter Horton Foote and star Robert Duvall won Oscars. The script is very spare, containing very few confessional speeches to provide access to any character's thoughts or feelings. Instead director Bruce Beresford, in his first American film, uses the flat and empty Texas landscape to emphasize Mac Sledge's aloneness and finitude as an alcoholic and violent lost pilgrim wanderer. He woos and weds a young war widow Rosalee (Tess Harper) who in the outback supports herself and her young son with a small motel and a few gas pumps. Her tough-love tender mercy, straight from her southern evangelical Christianity, hauls Sledge out of his self-loathing to resume music-writing and performance, join the church, and affirm the reality, even amid wrenching tragedy, of a transcendent "pure, sweet love," a line Sledge sings from the song "The Wings of a Dove." What access we have in this redemption story to the interior or "spiritual" life of the largely silent Sledge comes in musical voice-over, namely Sledge's own songs that play as he goes about his daily life. They offer as much of a window to his soul and psyche as the viewer gets. Other than that, the point of view in the film stays firmly within the empirical diegetic lives of the characters, meaning what is observable by the camera. The only departure from this comes at the film's close as Sledge and his stepson throw a football while enclosed by the arms of the small hotel, a visual trope that suggests both Rosalee's love and divine love. As Rosalee from a distance quietly watches, it is clear that these orphaned males in her life have found a home with one another, with her, and within divine care. And here the realism finally breaks. With a sort of Bressonian flourish, a raucous country love ballad rises, not heard before or from within the story itself, providing a kind of benedictory coda over this long closing sequence.

While it seems disruptive in the assiduous realism of *Tender Mercies*, the use of non-diegetic music works effectively within the lush realism of *The Mission*, which won the Palme d'Or at Cannes in 1986. The film's only departure from its insistent realism, and this departure is persistent, comes with its wonderfully successful score by Ennio Morricone. It does occur diegetically from within the film's action as Father Gabriel plays on his recorder a delicate and playful air as a means of enticing indigenous people to give him and his message a hearing. However, that same tune resonates non-diegetically before and after in various settings and accompaniments to express the exultant texture of interior religious apprehension, most especially in the case of Rodrigo Mendoza, the Paulista mercenary and slave trader, as he finds forgiveness by the people on whom he had preyed. The music overlays the realism of the narrative telling, providing an additional domain that interpolates the action of the film while it happens, and supplying the viewer with another frame of reference with which to feel and understand subjectivity and motivation. It is, then, as in the close to *Tender Mercies*, a musical correlative for an otherwise hidden interior state.

A strict realism also shapes Tim Robbins' masterful *Dead Man Walking* (1995), though he crucially departs from it to supply an alternative calculus for assessing the question of the morality of the death penalty. For virtually its whole length, *Dead Man Walking* undertakes a painstakingly realistic account of Helen Prejean as she counsels her first death-row inmate during his wait for a fast-approaching execution. That relationship culminates in Matthew Poncelot (Sean Penn) in the last minutes of his life confessing and repenting of crimes he has denied. The persistence of Prejean's agapic love for him finally defeats his vehement macho bravado as he acknowledges divine forgiveness: "who would have thought I'd have to die to find love." As a kind of thief on the cross, saved in the last breaths of life, audiences no doubt come to sympathize with Poncelot in wishing he might live. However, Robbins upsets this sympathy, and likely opposition to the death penalty, when in the execution sequence he injects extra-diegetic shots of the brutal rape and double homicide, a sequence that culminates with the faces of the young murdered couple looming over the body of the dead convict. The sequence as a whole suggests a satisfying kind of equivalence, a tit for tat, in the mutuality of death. The insistent realism throughout prepares for the subtle, critical insertion of these shots to problematize the gist of the primary narrative. Realism prevails, save when it serves filmmakers' purposes for making certain kinds of points, typically at crucial moments of the story.

Minimalist realism

In their pretty rigorous cinematic realism, both Beresford and Robbins follow the spare realism of the great French writer-director Robert Bresson (1901–99). It is Bresson who fashioned in his slim body of work the "peculiar realism" that gave rise to what writer-director-critic Paul Schrader named, in the title of his 1972 book, *Transcendental Style in Film* (Schrader 1972: 72). Bresson eschewed established cinematic practice, instead fashioning a subversive style that brings audiences cognitively, experientially, to encounter, purely and directly, the Transcendent itself, or such is Schrader's interpretation of Bresson's narrative style. The words most often used to describe Bresson's cinematic style are severe and austere, though sparse may in fact be more apt. In short, Bresson withheld from his viewers the usual conventions and satisfactions of film viewing, in effect stripping down reality to its barest narrative level, until the last frames when he laid it on thick to deliver something he deemed far more substantial – a revelatory religious moment in which in great mystery God shows up.

The clearest glimpse into Bresson's notion of realism comes in his approach to acting and camera. In classic pictures like *The Diary of a Country Priest* (1951), *The Pickpocket* (1959), and *Au hasard Balthazar* (1966), Bresson typically used nonprofessional actors to efface personality and emotion from his films. In addition, his actors played their roles flat with uninflected readings and immobile faces. And usually Bresson shot them at middle distance, foregoing close-ups and other cinematic ploys that cultivate emotional intimacy. And last, he chose mundane faces in order to emphasize the unexceptional and the ordinary. Bresson also avoided film music and the visually picturesque, flattening both screen and story. In *Balthazar*, for example, he used a single 50mm lens. His hope was to detach audiences from emotional engagement so certain other narrative "recognitions" might happen, such as seeing the soul instead of personality, sensing not plot but divine presence, and finally, grasping the iconic beauty of grace when it comes clear in the film's close.

Typically Bresson flipped this mode around for his conclusions, saving all the medium's usual "lushness" for his dramatic conclusions. In his last frames he leapt from minimalism to dramatic musical, and visual plenty, relatively speaking, in order to confront the viewer with, in Schrader's words, "the Wholly Other he would normally avoid." Events and images request the viewers' "participation and approval ... [The ending] is a 'miracle' which must be accepted or rejected" (Schrader 1972: 81). These last frames of a visual icon challenge the viewer to embrace a new perception of the world: in *The Trial of Joan of Arc* (1962), the last shot shows the empty, smoke-shrouded stake on which Joan burned, an echo, for sure, of the empty tomb. In Bresson's most famous film, the 1959 *Pickpocket*, an alienated Dostoyevskian hero, solitary and sealed off, and imprisoned for his crimes, finally acknowledges the need for human linkage, and Bresson accompanied this with a burst of music and the hero's confession that "It has taken me so long to come to you." So enamored is Schrader of this Bressonian flourish in the denouement of *The Pickpocket* that he has adapted it twice for use in his own films, *American Gigolo* (1980) and *Light Sleeper* (1992). Bresson wished in these closing tableaux to present existential choice, suggesting to the viewer that the world is not flat, hollow, and impersonal but full of the richness presented in those last frames. In closing, Bresson breaks from his own storytelling to present with sudden, even shocking clarity the richness of the realm of grace that has, unbeknownst to characters and audience, operated mysteriously throughout the story. Viewers are left to grapple with the existential residue of the characters' lives, and that is put within a clear frame of transcendent reference. With his narrative style, Bresson pushes viewers psycho-spiritually into the gap where the divine presence shows in ways that are not necessarily clear even to characters in the film. Bresson displays, in effect, the nature of the divine and how the divine does its redemptive work. That fixed closing image constitutes an iconic, revelatory moment that can only be displayed but not verbalized. In an otherwise opaque world, these denouements show the moment of grace, here made palpable, lambent, and trenchant. This final disclosure, replete with close-ups, emotion, and music, overwhelms and envelops (Anker 2007: 126–30).

The footprints of Bresson abound in contemporary religious film, though few try to hew to the sparseness of his narratives. There is Schrader, of course, and there is also Lars von Trier and the dogme movement. Von Trier's *Breaking the Waves* (1996) uses a raw documentary narrative style, stripping the lushness out of character and landscape to end with a Bresson-like flourish in approval of the desolate main character's sacrifice. The brothers Jean-Pierre and Luc Dardenne have developed their own neo-Bressonian camera style, acting style, and narrative structure, and the results, in such films as *The Son* (2002) and *L'enfant* (2005), are critically acclaimed internationally.

Parabolic

Fast on the heels of these varieties of realism is what I'll refer to as parable, which for the most part looks and feels like realism, its stories tracking through a fully realistic world. It does, however, by its end, very clearly resonate in domains of allusion and metaphor that have slowly welled up from within the film itself in the course of its telling. For the most part, films in this mode seem as linear and literal as those of realism, transpiring fully within mundane everyday life – save, that is, for two elements that transpose the story to another dimension of meaning. The first of these lies in the starkly simple circumstances and events of the story itself, so stark that, in hindsight at least, they readily assume that metaphoric heft, becoming plainly symbolic, nearly archetypal resonances that grab audiences by stealth, so to speak: a handsome young banker, wrongly convicted of murdering his wife, descends into a penitentiary hell, which eventually makes him repent of sins he did not know he had committed (*The Shawshank Redemption* [1994]); an arrogant yuppie gigolo sees his world turn on him (*American Gigolo* [1980]); and a fugitive damsel named Grace takes refuge in a mountain hamlet inauspiciously named *Dogville* (2003).

Despite this apparent surplus of meaning in the terms of the narrative, the stories seem conventional enough till the very end, in what is the second dimension of parable, in which their rudimentary dramatic dynamics transform into full-blown parable. The frame of reference suddenly shifts from the material, causally bound, very predictable real world to the utter strangeness of an altogether surprising, grace-like reality. In the surprise of the climax, the implicit religious meaning of all that has gone before becomes fully clear. Usually these narrative metaphors show what, in the Christian tradition at least, grace looks and feels like – "the kingdom of God is like this." The dramatic wallop of that denouement can exult audiences, as in the case of *The Shawshank Redemption*, one of the most popular films ever made. For Andy DuFresne, the banker falsely accused of murdering his wife, freedom and new life come only after recognizing his own deep coldness of heart, the instigating agent for her death, and then, in the escape itself, swimming a literal and also deeply symbolic sewer of feces. Thereafter, the convict banker is forthwith washed clean in rain and lightning, a fearsome baptism full of water and light. In Schrader's *American Gigolo*, the forsaken prince, now forsaking life itself, is made whole by the sacrifice of one who forsakes wealth and privilege to rescue him. In von Trier's *Dogville* (2003), the character named Grace, long-suffering servant and exile, is rejected and reviled by all only to have Grace finally condemn them all, reprobate and fully deserving of execution.

Here the religious freight emerges by indirection, obliquely, telling the truth slant, lest, as Emily Dickinson says, the brilliance of truth blind. And ultimately, the enormous surprise and elation viewers experience in the finales convey the substantive contours of grace and, even more so, its essential preposterousness, though neither characters nor viewers may leap to recognizing it as grace as such. It is in these sorts of tales, though, that the well-worn theological abstraction finds freshness, clarity, and pertinence. The assumption, then, is that the divine is best apprehended through metaphor because the divine nature is too radical, bright, and surely ungraspable. The best humankind can manage, like Moses on the mountain wishing to see God's face, is to see by metaphor, to glimpse the hem of the garment, so to speak. The cinematic structure in these sorts of film clearly borrows from Bresson's notions of climactic disclosure, but they prove at once more conventionally realistic in structure, style, and in making clear their parabolic freight.

Fable

At the furthest remove from realism is fable, perhaps the West's most popular movie form, a territory somewhere between parable and fairy-tale where realism is doused with the fantastic, or the other way around. In these films, human longing and the divine are let loose, so to speak, and then anything can, and usually does, happen. The fantastic and implausible become real, and throughout there is ready help from beyond for all kinds of human misfortune. Worlds float, the dead rise, evil is vanquished, the lost are found, and small green creatures bear the wisdom of the ages. Obvious examples are found in some of the most popular films of all time: *Superman* (1978), the *Star Wars* saga (1977–2005), and *E.T.* (1982). Nor does the power of the form go away, as demonstrated by the recent success of *The Matrix* series (1999–2003), *The Lord of the Rings* (2001–3), and now emerging, the film adaptations of C. S. Lewis' *Chronicles of Narnia*, first *The Lion, the Witch and the Wardrobe* (2005) and then *Prince Caspian* (2008). The perennial struggle between good and evil goes diametrical, magical, and metaphysical. This is not a world without serious peril; what look like children's stories are often very harrowing. Finally, though, into a densely evil world breaks Light. It may take a long time to arrive (usually three films), but rescue happens, and in the end comes unimaginable joy, as if from Heaven itself. Much of this parallels the fable-making undertaken by some contemporary avant-garde novels, as detailed in Robert Scholes' 1967 book, *The Fabulators*: simple plot design that pits the hero against towering odds; heavy but delightful didacticism; and a calculated loss of realism in a world of fantasy whose primary concerns are ideas and ideals. In short, while these tales may begin in a constricted empirical world with its surfeit of tragic reality, they quickly move toward an unimaginable realm of supernatural power that heals the woebegone world in which the central characters suffer. It too is full of imaginative play and great surprise, usually exalting unlikely or mysterious heroes into savior figures.

Once again the divine is refracted through an imaginative prism, showing up usually in sources of wisdom who clearly function as proxies for divine wisdom in the struggle with titanic forces: Yoda, Gandalf, Jor-el, Aslan, E.T., the Oracle, etc. The young go through long processes of apprenticeship to learn the ways of the Force or the Matrix: Neo, Luke Skywalker, Kal-el, Frodo, and Elliott. These are tales of hope that the world might work as humankind in its lostness yearns that it might. And because it is a realm of hope, the divine does not usually show up firsthand, lest it be as a lion, but God's proxies are all about in the form of wizards, Jedi Masters, and lost aliens. And, of course, there is the Force, the Matrix, the Ring, or some mysterious trans-human power, either good or bad, that shapes and directs human experience, for better or worse.

Meditative

Philosopher of film Stanley Cavell uses the term "meditative" to describe the narrative style of the singular contemporary American filmmaker Terrence Malick, though other filmmakers also fit well into this category (Cavell 1979: xiv–xvii). As David Davies has neatly surveyed, Cavell and others wish to understand Malick through the lens of modern philosophy, seeing his work as consistently dramatizing and exploring the deep mystery inhering in the "nature of being itself," the age-old philosophical riddle emphasized anew in the twentieth century by German philosopher Martin Heidegger (Davies 2008). The name is apt, for Malick's last three films – *Days of Heaven* (1978), *The Thin Red Line* (1998), and *The New World* (2005) – consist of repeated, sustained meditative or contemplative "looking" at aspects of the natural world. In *Days of Heaven*, Malick locates these gazes with the points of view of several of his characters and also, at critical times, with the more or less objective realistic camera of an implied narrator who differs from the voice-over supplied by the story's titular narrator, teenager Linda (Linda Manz). The camera locates multiple-story perspectives with its five principal characters; and beyond those, there functions an organizing, seemingly omniscient point of view that observes them and the natural physical world that they inhabit. Like all of Malick's films, *Days of Heaven* contains enormous, in the words of Seymour Chatman, "semantic complexity" in the identi-fication of narrators and point of view beyond the obvious, distinct perspectives displayed in the film text (Chatman 1990: 76). In *Days of Heaven*, all of these points of view at times gaze at, and seem to revel in, the picturesque Texas plains – indeed, days of heaven – especially in stark contrast to the film's beginning in the dire grittiness of mere survival among the laboring poor in industrializing Chicago. It is this external narrator, however, who seems to supply the irresolvable dilemma in the film, namely the simultaneous existence in human experience of great beauty, in nature and in human relationships, and also of an indiscriminate predatory evil that dwells, again, both in nature and in people. Moreover, the question of who is preying on whom drives the narrative. The insistent looking of the camera, though, at the beauty and the horror, effectively displays the philosophical and religious poles contending in the film. In this finally grim tale, Darwin seems to win, for nature and people alike seem prone to mere physical survival that destroys heedlessly what gets in their path. It is finally, as one pair of critics summarize, a "stunning and evocative portrait of the beauty and fragility of earthly existence" (Furstenau and MacAvoy 2007: 181).

That is not the case, however, in Malick's "second career." After *Days of Heaven*, Malick simply left filmmaking, and he did not make another film for twenty years. That absence ended with his film version of James Jones' novel of the Second World War battle for Guadalcanal, *The Thin Red Line*, which surely ranks as one of the most unusual war films ever made. Malick reframes the debate in *Days of Heaven*, again providing long contemplative shots of nature and also the indigenous people who live in it. Through most of these, the primary narrator, Private Witt (James Caviezel), ponders in ruminative voice-over the nature of nature, existence generally, the meaning of death, and the possibility of immortality. Among the array of philosophical positions critics have ascribed to Witt, and Malick, the most cogent seems a religiously charged Transcendentalism wherein the narrator, even amid the terror, horror, and death of war, all vividly displayed, sees in nature a divine presence "smiling" at the beleaguered, wondering human creature. In this instance Malick deploys, in the words of one critic, "the beauty and power of the image as a carrier of meaning," even of, we might add, a metaphysical sort (Mottram 2007: 15). And finally, perhaps, the film rests on visual argument, as the film's last words from the deceased Private Witt invite viewers to "Look out through my eyes" to see "All things shining." Witt's voice-over musings play over the visual scheme of the film, whose content in turn gives them warrant. Cinematic effect and affect reciprocate. Humankind can ravage one another all the while, but still, strangely, seeing the world aright, in its luminous splendor, all things shine, even into death.

Malick is not entirely alone among filmmakers in conjuring the distinctive meditative means inherent in cinema, although no others push it as far or as insistently as he does. The great Russian filmmaker Andrei Tarkovsky (1932–86) uses this mode, especially in his autobiographical film *The Mirror* where his camera simply watches and rewatches certain scenes such as the wind blowing the trees of a nearby wood. Within that film, at least, this device emphasizes not only cinematic self-consciousness but viewer contemplation amid the wonder of perception and the beguiling pressure of the picturesque. In Sam Mendes' *American Beauty* (1999) a secondary character, boy-next-door Ricky Fitts (Wes Bentley), carries a video camera filming virtually everything he sees because he does not want to miss its beauty. "For Ricky, love suffuses the world ... and that reality fosters in him a posture of radical wonder, awe, and gratitude for the splendor of it all ... what counts most in human life is pure, astonished amazement at the fact that anything at all should exist and, greater still, that anything and everything should display such beauty" (Anker 2005: 357). Mendes' mix of images and words becomes, in fact, the very posture the film's troubled main character and narrator comes to embrace in the last sequence of the film.

A similar style suffuses Krzysztof Kieślowski's *Three Colors: Blue* (1993), the first in a trilogy of films based on the meanings of the colors of the French flag. Here, just as Malick uses an irresistible visual beauty, Kieślowski deploys music that haunts and hounds and ultimately revives a soul willfully dead after the accidental death of her daughter and famous composer husband. Only late in the film does the audience come to understand what the music bids her to do, which is to love again all of life. The regular mysterious, enveloping returns of the music and other related events prod her, and viewers, to contemplate what life calls all to do. Here, as in Malick's *The Thin Red Line*, hints of another reality erupt in extraordinary, even surreal visions of transfixing transcendent presence. Out of nowhere, a radical Presence breaks into human affairs to manifest a reconciling Love that supersedes and transfigures very tragic human reality. The blindness of the characters, and even more so the blindness of the audience, at which that fringe material has been sniping, comes clear as Light smashes in.

In a long essay on *The Thin Red Line*, critics Leo Bersani and Ulysee Dutoit argue that this sort of meditative cinema may in fact answer questions that language cannot: "the film's verbal questions are responded to visually," going so far as to suggest that "the film enacts the image's superior inclusiveness over the word" (Bersani and Dutoit 2004: 143). This is carried through Witt's "look" of bedazzlement, "a mode of registering the world," and it is a look that Malick encourages "*us* to collaborate with" insofar as the film's arresting images of beauty expose "an (unspoken) intentionality directed at us," inducting viewers into wonder and praise (144, 164). "The immense yet beneficent demand being made upon us is that ... we imitate that receptivity ... when we leave the film and return again to the world outside it" (164). Ultimately, the authors see Malick's film as an antidote to the *jouissance* that breeds war, but what they exactly mean by Malick as fostering a sense of "Allness" remains elusive, even though they deem this the highest capacity of art. Whatever their conclusions about the nature of Malick's religious pondering in *The Thin Red Line*, Bersani and Dutoit do suggest that meditative filmmakers such as Malik and Kieślowski might well induct viewers into a mode of perception, mysterious and supra-verbal, that in fact trumps language in their capacity to respond to the world's most vexing riddles.

Mosaic narrative

This essay identifies the mosaic narrative as a variety of network narrative, though thus far the two terms have been used pretty much interchangeably. The term "network narrative" denotes films with complex plots involving many characters who are to a greater or lesser degree somehow linked together. A host of prominent filmmakers, religious and otherwise, have memorably deployed this narrative scheme to great effect in such award-winning films as, to name only the most recent, *Crash* (2004), *Babel* (2006), *No Country for Old Men* (2007), and a host of others. David Bordwell focused attention to the frequency and prominence of this narrative shape in his 2006 study of classic Hollywood film, *The Way Hollywood Tells It: Story and Style in Modern Movies*. These sorts of plots typically feature numerous diverse characters who variously link together, seemingly as a result of "contingency" or chance, in improbably complex plots "woven out of ill-fated romances, cross-class comparisons, intermingled causal lines, and contrasts between dramatic crises and mundane routine" (Bordwell 2006: 96). Two years later Bordwell elaborated at length in *Poetics of Cinema* (2008), even supplying a list, dating to 1945, of over 200 films, American and international, roughly 150 of these coming along since 1990 (245–50, 191). By no means new or uncommon, the network narrative is in fact a well-established and malleable classic form, finding early embodiment in *Grand Hotel* (1932) and *Stagecoach* (1939) and then informing 1970s formulaic disaster thrillers *The Poseidon Adventure* (1972) and *The Towering Inferno* (1974), to name a few.

The network narrative is, in short, a much-used, popular, and profitable scheme for storytelling. Typically, plot configurations in network stories dwell primarily on two, three, or four dissociated lives with still others circling about in less prominent but still important ways. Some random element, whether a boat ride, traffic accident, or a burning building, bring them, at the very least, into physical proximity and, more than likely, degrees of relationship that range from incidental to intimate. In a serious exploration of the potential of the form, the celebrated American director Robert Altman in *Nashville* (1975) and then again in *Short Cuts* (1993) brought together great arrays of people only to show, in a sort of wry pessimism, the difficulty and randomness of human connection. Indeed, if the term "network" implies the establishment of at least some measure of human connection, Altman's films perhaps deserve the label of anti-network, for what relationships do exist at the beginning of his films seem to come apart in their unfolding. What network there is has emerged randomly and passes as quickly as it came. If we look for some sort of overarching design in the patterns of social life, we face disappointment, for no design or meaning of any sort exists. Quentin Tarantino's cult classic *Pulp Fiction* (1994) uses the form simply to add unpredictability and suspense. Woody Allen's best film, *Crimes and Misdemeanors* (1989), deftly manages a network plot, but the pervasive irony of the film goes to show that, if anything, the wicked prosper and the good, few though they may be, prove the real losers in ill-luck and despair.

Unlike Altman and Tarantino, a great many filmmakers have used the network narrative to probe events in individual and social life for traces of divine purpose and presence, asking if what seems random is in fact not. These filmmakers raise the possibility of design or a pattern within a seeming welter of coincidence, and for these the term "mosaic" seems apt since mosaics, even the most abstract, indeed contain design of some measure. Oddly perhaps, many of these films rank as the most innovative and thoughtful of our time in their portraiture of people in dire circumstances who sometimes come upon new linkages that supply them with new measures of love and hope. These filmmakers question (1) whether individual and social histories might have behind them a superintending guidance of some kind that fortuitously arranges events and connections for human flourishing; (2) the intent and nature of that guidance; and (3) to what extent people, either characters or audiences, might be capable of perceiving this sort of divine intention amid their lives. Very often the filmmakers themselves seem to posit their stories as wonderments, as scholar Joe

Kickasola has suggested (2008): tentative speculations whether indeed there "just might" be Someone or some thing out there beyond human ken who shepherds diverse lives toward new and profound embrace of the goodness of human life, especially in its relational dimensions. So strange, wondrous, benign, and rich does life seem to be at times (even though at other times not) that any other conclusion than a supernatural one seems impossible. In these stories, events seem determined to bring people together in some variety of configuration that prods audiences to wonder whether that all might not be, thanks to some measure of divine guidance, random, capricious, arbitrary, and meaningless as human life usually seems. At the end of such tales, audiences seem apt to wonder if indeed some active providence might steer lives toward the embrace of human interdependence and love.

Certainly, the most significant filmmaker to explore these suspicions is the late Polish filmmaker Krzysztof Kieślowski (1941–96), whose work with co-screenwriter and friend Krzysztof Piesiewicz was finally becoming well known in the West at his untimely death after cardiac surgery. Kieślowski's early fiction films show a thirst for exploring anew and freshly perennial religious questions. Kieślowski's first full plunge into the network narrative came in his investigation of connections in random lives in *Decalogue* (1989–90), a ten-part series on the Ten Commandments that he and Piesiewicz undertook for Polish television. All the one-hour stories take place in a large housing complex in Warsaw in the grim years before the fall of the Iron Curtain; and while each episode focuses on different characters, these same appear in other installments, even though that is as incidental as sharing an elevator. Through all looms a mysterious young man who simply watches both the tragedy and hope that flourishes in this tangled world. The effect is to ingratiate the suspicion that Something more and beyond is afoot in and through these lives at least as observer if not also as judge and benefactor. Kieślowski resolutely leaves the identity and status of the fellow unresolved, apparently satisfied with leaving audiences with a tantalizing hint of what might be.

Kieślowski pushes these concerns through the brief length of his remaining career in his *Three Colors* trilogy, each episode based thematically on one of the symbolic colors of the French flag (1993–4). In each film, he tracks how plentiful uncanny events, both tragic and fortuitous, shape the narratives, thrusting characters into relationship through events of which they had no inkling and for which they had no appetite. All of this works because within the story itself the vast preponderance takes place within a thoroughly empirical world, a strategy that, according to literary critic Wendy Faris, characterizes "magical realism." The very realism of so much of the story serves to make whatever wondrous intrusion occurs – what Faris calls the "irreducible" – all the more credible. Thus, says Faris, when "the irreducible" does come along in the text it is taken as rather ordinary because those "irreducible elements are well assimilated into the realistic textual environment, rarely causing any comment by narrators or characters, who model such an acceptance for the readers" (Faris 2004: 3, 8). These films together suggest that not only do strange events occur that thrust random people into relationship with one another but that whatever Force propels this alignment is benign in seeking to foster an embrace of the goodness of human connection and love. Moreover, as in *Decalogue*, Kieślowski cycles these primary characters from one film through others, culminating with the display of all in the surprising ending in the finale of the trilogy in *Three Colors: Red* (1994). This sort of closure is meant, according to Faris, to induce wonder at "how all the things of this world are linked" (Faris 2004: 10).

One of the great surprises in recent cinema is how frequently the mosaic tales show in the works of prominent North American filmmakers. Director Lawrence Kasdan's *Grand Canyon* (1991) is a sprawling tale he co-wrote with wife Meg. Set in a mildly dystopic contemporary Los Angeles of traffic, drive-by shootings, and earthquake, the film pointedly questions whether human life and meaning amount to anything more than random Darwinian survival of the fittest. Or might life and meaning, as events in the film suggest, derive from some unseen power of which we catch glimpses in unforeseeable timely interventions and linkages? By its end, the film seems to insist, as one of the film's nine consequential characters puts it, the story's many interventions and meetings are in fact "miracles" that we miss because we do not expect them. These many new linkages among the assorted characters display a God that orchestrates human life toward trust and intimacy with others. To some extent writer-director Paul Haggis' *Crash* (2005), winner of the Academy Award for Best Picture, seems a harder-edged remake of *Grand Canyon*. Of greater note for its stunning stylistic virtuosity is Paul Thomas Anderson's *Magnolia* (1999), a whirling apocalyptic tale of a wild array of different people amid dire relational fracture in a spiritually benighted Los Angeles. From his frame prologue to its replay at the end, and throughout his wildly inventive three hours of storytelling, Anderson pushes hard the notion that through what seems coincidence and chance, a mysterious supernatural presence pushes his characters – eleven in all, and all connected in some manner to a dying television magnate – toward self-recognition and reconciliation. The same thematic drives the complex relational networks of the celebrated Mexican screenwriter Guillermo Arriaga and director Alejandro González Iñárritu in *Amores perros* (2000), *21 Grams* (2003), and *Babel* (2006), all pushing, and variously "answering," the question of how and why people link, or do not link, together and under whose aegis.

The work of these major filmmakers suggests that all willingly consider the possibility that behind the apparent sad randomness of human life lies a mostly hidden transcendent Other that labors, in spite of the world's darkness and confusion, to foster human flourishing in relational care and intimacy, which is the end for which the divine works. Unlike Altman, these filmmakers glimpse, with wonder and perhaps gratitude, mosaics of associations that bespeak transcendent intention. It seems wise, then, to distinguish network tales, meaning the work of Altman *et al.*, from mosaic tales. In the visual arts historically, mosaics have gathered individual pieces to create meaningful figures or patterns, however minimal or abstract, so little as splashes of color that sufficed to suggest that there is a maker behind them. In any case, in mosaics, a multitude of disparate pieces arrayed together at least intimate intention and design. In this sense the mosaic narrative may stand starkly opposed to the Altmanesque network narrative, creating a distinct category of its own, or it may be best understood as a variety of network narrative.

Conclusion

In short, a multitude of narrative modes thrive and proliferate, and many of these have proven amply capable of carrying remarkable religious freight. The most conspicuous "religious" films have been historical dramas that seek to capture the vision and mettle of historical figures ranging from Sir Thomas More in *A Man for All Seasons* to Mel Gibson's *The Passion of the Christ*. These films have for the most part relied on the conventions and expectations of cinematic realism. Others have labored to stretch the means of realism to display, as in the films of Robert Bresson, the revelation of the divine itself. And a host of other realist filmmakers have followed suit in trying to delve into the nature and means of divine reality in such notable realist films as *Dead Man Walking, Tender Mercies,* and *The Mission*. Other filmmakers, making ostensibly secular films, have imbued their stories with a parabolic significance, as in *The Shawshank Redemption*, that places the tale in a wholly different frame of religious reference. The same informs the host of fantasy films, from the *Star Wars* saga to *The Chronicles of Narnia*, that dramatize amid their alternative worlds central religious stories and themes of Western Christianity. The popular "network" tale often links disparate people in such a way as to suggest providential design in the seeming randomness of events.

All of these varied cinematic efforts, and a multitude of others from around the world, can perhaps best be understood as part of an effort at "the redemption of reality," to adapt a term from film theorist Siegfried Kracauer. In the controversial "Epilogue" to his 1960 *Theory of Film*, Kracauer locates in film the potential to reinvigorate a material world diminished by the reductionism of modern science. For Kracauer the physical world has become "abstract," meaning impersonal and devoid of meaning (Kracauer 1997: 292). The necessarily close attention of cinema to the physical world, Kracauer suggests, can provide an antidote of sorts by provoking an "aesthetic apprehension" of materiality, an "experience of things in their concreteness" that restores lost "poignancy and preciousness" (Kracauer 1997: 298, 296). What Kracauer claims for the cinematic image applies as well to narrative, though of this he was skeptical for various reasons (if Kracauer had lived longer to see what we have, he might have come to deem the powers of narrative more highly). Indeed, stories that freshen worn formulas and overturn genre conventions can again imbue the world with wonder and mystery, at times narrating manifold unforeseeable varieties of redemption.

Bibliography

Anker, R. (2000) "Lights, Camera, Jesus," *Christianity Today* (22 May): 58–63.
—— (2005) *Catching Light: Looking for God in the Movies*, Grand Rapids, MI: Eerdmans.
—— (2007) "'Like Shining from Shook Foil': Art, Film, and the Sacred," in D. J. Treier, M. Husbands, and R. Lundin (eds) *The Beauty of God: Theology and the Arts*, Downers Grove, IL: InterVarsity Press.
Baugh, L. (1997) *Imaging the Divine: Jesus and Christ-figures in Film*, Kansas City: Sheed & Ward.
Bazin, A. (1997) *Bazin at Work: Major Essays and Review from the Forties and Fifties*, ed. Alain Pierre and Bert Cardullo, New York: Routledge.
Bersani, L. and Dutoit, U. (2004) *Forms of Being: Cinema, Aesthetics, Subjectivity*, London: British Film Institute.

Bird, M. (1982) "Film as Hierophany," in J. R. May and M. Bird (eds) *Religion in Film*, Knoxville: University of Tennessee Press.

Blake, R. (2002) "From Peepshow to Prayer: Toward a Spirituality of the Movies," *Journal of Religion and Film* 6 (2).

Bordwell, D. (1985) *Narration in the Fiction Film*, Madison: University of Wisconsin Press.

—— (2006) *The Way Hollywood Tells It: Story and Style in Modern Movies*, Berkeley: University of California Press.

—— (2008) *Poetics of Cinema*, New York: Routledge.

Carroll, N. (2008) "Narrative Closure," in P. Livingston and C. Plantinga (eds) *The Routledge Companion to Philosophy and Film*, London: Routledge.

Cavell, S. (1979) *The World Viewed*, enlarged ed., Cambridge, MA: Harvard University Press.

Chatman, S. (1990) *Coming to Terms: The Rhetoric of Narrative in Fiction and Film*, Ithaca, NY: Cornell University Press

Davies, D. (2008) "Terrence Malick," in P. Livingston and C. Plantinga (eds) *The Routledge Companion to Philosophy and Film*, London: Routledge.

Faris, W. (2004) *Ordinary Enchantments: Magical Realism and the Remystification of Narrative*, Nashville, TN: Vanderbilt University Press.

Fuller, R. (2006) *Wonder: From Emotion to Spirituality*, Chapel Hill: University of North Carolina Press.

Furstenau, M. and MacAvoy, L. (2007) "Terrence Malick's Heideggerian Cinema: War and the Question of Being in *The Thin Red Line*," in H. Patterson (ed.) *The Cinema of Terrence Malick: Poetic Visions of America*, 2nd ed., London: Wallflower Press: 179–91.

Kickasola, J. (2008) "Multi-Valence and the Contemporary Cinema." Paper presented at the Society of Cinema and Media Studies Annual Conference, Philadelphia, 7 March.

Kracauer, S. (1997) *Theory of Film: The Redemption of Physical Reality*, trans. M. B. Hansen, Princeton: Princeton University Press.

Mottram, R. (2007) "All Things Shining: The Struggle for Wholeness, Redemption, and Transcendence in the Films of Terrence Malick," in H. Patterson (ed.) *The Cinema of Terrence Malick: Poetic Visions of America*, 2nd ed., London: Wallflower Press: 14–26.

Otto, R. (1958) *The Idea of the Holy*, 2nd ed., London: Oxford University Press.

Reinhartz, A. (2007) *Jesus of Hollywood*, Oxford: Oxford University Press.

Scholes, R. (1967) *The Fabulators*, Oxford: Oxford University Press.

Schrader, P. (1972) *Transcendental Style in Film: Ozu, Bresson, Dreyer*, Berkeley: University of California Press.

Filmography

Amazing Grace (2006, dir. M. Apted)

American Beauty (1999, dir. S. Mendes)

American Gigolo (1980, dir. P. Schrader)

Amores perros (2000, dir. A. Iñárritu)

The Apostle (1997, dir. R. Duvall)

Au hasard Balthazar (1966, dir. R. Bresson)

Babel (2006, dir. A. Iñárritu)

Becket (1964, dir. P. Glenville)

Breaking the Waves (1996, dir. L. von Trier)

Brother Sun, Sister Moon (1972, dir. F. Zeffirelli)

The Chronicles of Narnia: The Lion, the Witch and the Wardrobe (2005, dir. A. Adamson)

The Chronicles of Narnia: Prince Caspian (2008, dir. A. Adamson)

Crash (2005, dir. P. Haggis)

Crimes and Misdemeanors (1989, dir. W. Allen)

Days of Heaven (1978, dir. T. Malick)

Dead Man Walking (1995, dir. T. Robbins)

Decalogue (1989–90, dir. K. Kieślowski)

The Diary of a Country Priest (1951, dir. R. Bresson)

Dogville (2003, dir. L. von Trier)
L'enfant (2005, dir. J.-P. and L. Dardenne)
E.T.: The Extra-Terrestrial (1982, dir. S. Spielberg)
The Godfather, Part III (1990, dir. F. Coppola)
The Gospel According to St. Matthew (1964, dir. P. Pasolini)
Grand Canyon (1991, dir. L. Kasdan)
Grand Hotel (1932, dir. E. Goulding)
The Greatest Story Ever Told (1965, dir. G. Stevens)
Hail Mary (1985, dir. J. Godard)
Jesus of Nazareth (1977, dir. F. Zeffirelli)
King of Kings (1961, dir. N. Ray)
Light Sleeper (1992, dir. P. Schrader)
The Lord of the Rings (2001–3, dir. P. Jackson)
Magnolia (1999, dir. P. Anderson)
A Man for All Seasons (1966, dir. F. Zinnemann)
The Matrix (1999, dir. A. and L. Wachowski)
Memento (2000, dir. C. Nolan)
The Mirror (1975, dir. A. Tarkovsky)
The Mission (1986, dir. R. Joffé)
Nashville (1975, dir. R. Altman)
The New World (2005, dir. T. Malick)
No Country for Old Men (2007, dir. E. and J. Coen)
The Passion of the Christ (2004, dir. M. Gibson)
The Pickpocket (1959, dir. R. Bresson)
The Poseidon Adventure (1972, dir. R. Neame, and remake, 2006, dir. W. Petersen)
Private Confessions (1996, dir. L. Ullmann)
Pulp Fiction (1994, dir. Q. Tarantino)
The Shawshank Redemption (1994, dir. F. Darabont)
Short Cuts (1993, dir. R. Altman)
The Son (2002, dir. J.-P. and L. Dardenne)
Stagecoach (1939, dir. J. Ford)
Star Wars (1977, dir. G. Lucas)
Superman (1978, dir. R. Donner)
Tender Mercies (1983, dir. B. Beresford)
The Thin Red Line (1998, dir. T. Malick)
Three Colors: Blue (1993, dir. K. Kieślowski)
Three Colors: Red (1994, dir. K. Kieślowski)
Three Colors: White (1994, dir. K. Kieślowski)
The Towering Inferno (1974, dir. J. Guillermin and I. Allen)
The Trial of Joan of Arc (1962, dir. R. Bresson)
21 Grams (2003, dir. A. Iñárritu).

19
REDEMPTION
Christopher Deacy

Christian concepts of redemption

In order to establish whether there is any scope for juxtaposing, conflating and/or developing critical links between redemption and film, it is clear that much hinges on the question of definition. Religious traditions often speak of how, in their unique and diverse ways, by means of various doctrines, prayers, rites, meditations, and rituals, there is scope for human individuals and communities to be redeemed from the structures of this world and its attendant problems of evil, suffering, and meaninglessness. As Vergilius Ferm's *Encyclopedia of Religion* puts it, redemption takes place when humankind "is already enmeshed in evil or spiritual ruin and needs to be extricated or delivered" (Ferm 1976: 639). In the case of Christianity, the traditional belief, as presented in the New Testament, is that, as a consequence of the Resurrection, the believer will be resurrected and judged at the end of history, and depending on whether or not he or she has been redeemed through Christ's atoning death on the Cross, will accordingly spend the afterlife in a heavenly, or paradisal, environment. According to Hebrews 9:15, Christ "is the mediator of a new covenant, so that those who are called may receive the promised eternal inheritance, since a death has occurred which redeems them from the[ir] transgressions." The redemptive work of Christ is thus a victory of good over evil, with the Cross "effecting an actual transformation of the consequences of evil into good" (Wheeler-Robinson 1943: xxii). In terms of the negative realities from which Christ redeems, Hebrews 2:3 suggests it is from divine wrath, while according to Galatians 4:8 and Colossians 1:13 it is from some kind of bondage to demonic powers, if not, indeed, the Devil. However it is conceived, the New Testament speaks of redemption as comprising God's work to facilitate the restoration of humankind to union and communion with God, as outlined in 2 Corinthians 3:18 – "And we all, with unveiled face, beholding the glory of the Lord, are being changed into his likeness from one degree of glory to another" – as well as healing and renewing the cosmos itself, as in the case of Romans 8:21 which speaks of "creation" being "set free from its bondage to decay" and obtaining "the glorious liberty of the children of God."

On such a reading, it is difficult to see how such a qualitatively theological process, entailing as it does deliverance from Original Sin – and the concomitant moral and spiritual transformation on the part of the believer – and the elevation of creation to its prelapsarian state, is sufficiently malleable to become detached from the remit of faith and belief and to be applied to the "secular" medium of film. Would this not be to obscure and distort such a heavily value-laden term in which there is no obvious scope for redemption to operate outside of God's jurisdiction and which involves the restoration of the torn fabric of personal relationships between God and a fallen and depraved human race? Even if one were to identify film as a site of redemptive activity, it is hard to see how this could correspond with the emphasis in traditional Christian belief and practice on the shedding of the blood of Christ for one's sins and the concomitant "efficacy of God's love available without limit to all in need" (Reed 2004: 234). As Esther Reed rightly points out, "redemption" may well be a term that is used in everyday discourse, as in the case of supermarkets and book shops where it is possible to "redeem" points on a customer loyalty card or book voucher against the value of a product, but the language is very distinct from that of its basis in theological discourse where it has connotations with the ideas of release (see Luke 2:38), ransom (Mark 10:45), and the payment of a price to set free (or "redeem") a prisoner or slave (1 Peter 1:18–21) (see Reed 2004: 226–7).

In the Old Testament, indeed, the term "redemption" is used 132 times, principally in the context of money payments for the recovery of property (Leviticus 25:25f.), for the firstborn (Numbers 3:44–51), and from slavery (Exodus 21:7–8). In the New Testament, Christ's blood is the medium, or price, of redemption. In Ephesians 1:7, we learn that the forgiveness of sin is paid for by "redemption through his blood" – a perspective also taken by St. Augustine in the early fifth century. In his *Confessions*, Augustine offers the following petition to God: "You know how weak I am and how inadequate is my knowledge: teach me and heal my frailty. Your only Son … has redeemed me with his blood. Save me from the scorn of my enemies, for the price of my redemption is always in my thoughts" (Augustine 1961: 251–2). Although Augustine does not specify to whom the price of redemption is to be paid, traditionally it has been supposed that it is to be paid to the Devil, with Augustine taking the line that the Cross constituted a mousetrap, baited with the blood of Christ (see Richardson 1986: 101). This "ransom" model of redemption held force in Christianity until the twelfth century, when Anselm proposed his "satisfaction" model of redemption-atonement, according to which God sent his Son to earth to assume full humanity and thereby render satisfaction on behalf of humanity by his innocent death on the Cross. The "debt" of honour was thus "paid for man by God incarnate as man," such that "God's violated honour" was "repaired" (Richardson 1986: 102), and God could therefore forgive humankind its sins without needing to resort to punishing the entire human race.

A revised version of this doctrine emerged during the Reformation, when Calvin and Luther developed the penal substitution theory. According to this model, in offering himself as our substitute, the sinless Christ is deemed by God to be a sinner and thus in need of punishment, and so was punished on humanity's behalf, to the effect that we are substitutionally redeemed in faith. In Luther's words, Christ was to be of all men the greatest robber, murderer, thief, profaner, blasphemer, and so on ... who bears in his own body all the sins of men – not in that he committed them, but in that he took upon his own body the things committed by us, to make satisfaction with them with his own blood. (Quoted in Richardson 1986: 104)

While an atonement theory of redemption has a widespread usage in the history of the Christian Church, it is very far from readily amenable to contemporary discourse in theology and film, posing as it does inscrutable problems in contemporary moral philosophy and theology. In the Victorian era, it may have been largely thought a moral duty to preach humanitarian values and to aspire to bring about "the progress and improvement of human society" (Altholz 1988: 156), yet according to the New Testament all humanity is wholly depraved and corrupt, to the point that God requires the sacrifice of an innocent human being for his satisfaction – and the redemption of the human race – to be accomplished. Insofar as Christ is Redeemer by virtue of bearing the sins of Adam on behalf of humanity, and paying our penalty by standing in our place under divine judgment, the difficulty is that one thereby acquires a vested interest in the vicarious nature of Christ's death. While the Redeemer himself is condemned, the human race alone secures the good for which the payment was made. In short, as Paul Badham points out, "It has been asked in what sense the death of an innocent person can take away the guilt of sinners, whose conscience should be still further troubled by the notion of an innocent suffering in their place" (Badham and Badham 1984: 58). It may have been acceptable to Origen in the second century that "man" had, through Adam's sin, sold his soul to the Devil, and that God had repurchased "man" for himself by paying to the Devil the ransom of Christ's life, but, in Richardson's words, such a theory "seems incredibly crude to us" (Richardson 1986: 99) today. Reed similarly writes that the "unpalatable association of redemption with 'the blood of Christ' and 'sacrifice' brings blushes of embarrassment to the cheeks of many believers – not least because of the supposed idealization of victimhood, victory through violent death, and traditional associations with the satisfaction of male honor" (Reed 2004: 227). Even the understanding of redemption as entailing the renewal of the cosmos, as identified in Romans 8:21 and Revelation 21:5, in which "the whole earth will be healed, restored, and transfigured, sounds faintly absurd to the average person struggling to make a living and reading in a newspaper about the latest natural disaster" (Reed 2004: 228).

Applying "redemption" to film

In such terms, there is no obvious bridge between such an ostensibly archaic theological doctrine as redemption and the medium of film, which comprises, in Johnston's words, "our Western culture's major storytelling and myth-producing medium" (Johnston 2007: 16). What scope is there for filmmakers to grapple with such distinctively, and problematically, theological discourse? It may be that films are able to tell religious stories, and there may be a market for religious epics and Jesus films, as the commercial success of Mel Gibson's *The Passion of the Christ* (2004) proved when it sailed past the $200 million mark at the American box office in just two weeks in March 2004 (see Deacy 2005: 8). But, is an equivalent process taking place? It may be the case for Paul Schrader, in his landmark publication *Transcendental Style in Film*, that even films made in the realist style are able to evoke a sense of transcendence by pointing a viewer beyond the austerity and barrenness of the everyday world toward a higher, transcendent reality (see Deacy and Ortiz 2008: 43) – even to the point that the "holy" can be captured on celluloid and that "for an hour or two the viewer can become that suffering, saintly, person on the screen" (Schrader 1972: 14). However, the fact that theologians may be interested in what Robert Pope refers to as the experience "of viewing a film, of being drawn into its narrative and of somehow participating in the journey undertaken by the characters on the screen" (Pope 2007: 56) does not amount to a redemptive experience or phenomenon per se. A film may be able to cultivate moral and spiritual growth or transformation on the part of its audience, but how analogous is this to deliverance in theological terms from Original Sin? A film may be able to inspire transcendence, but, as Pope correctly notes, it is questionable as to whether this really amounts to a divine encounter or simply an overcoming, or transcendence, of human limitations. In his words, "It may enable people to feel that there is something beyond the confines of the self as we empathize with, and almost live the life of, the character portrayed on the screen," but this is not the same thing as "an encounter with the 'wholly other,'" since "Transcendence here is achieved not through contemplating higher things, not through encountering God, but through imagining that the bounds of human capability can be crossed" (Pope 2007: 65).

At the same time, however, the boundary between the human and the divine is inevitably going to be a permeable one. Redemption in Christianity is not just a story about God but about God's relationship with humanity (see Marsh 2007a: 106), and, in Marsh's words, what makes Jesus' story a redemptive story is that it is "inhabited in the act of following by those who are so impressed that they want to imitate the actions of Jesus" (Marsh 2007a: 107). For many theologians, indeed, the focus in accounts of redemption is not simply on the sacrificial role performed by Christ for the sins of humanity but on the role of the recipients of Christ's redemptive act. As I have written elsewhere, redemption may be inextricably bound up with the person of Christ, but those whose lives have been variously touched and transformed by Christ's redemptive work, and who have subsequently sought to model their lives after him, are categorized, in effect, as Christ-figures (Deacy 2001: 70). As St. Paul wrote in his first epistle to the Christian community at Corinth, the challenge is for all Christians to become followers, or models, of Christ, in line with his own behavior – "Be imitators of me, as I am of Christ" (1 Corinthians 11:1). For H. A. Williams, similarly, "Christians find in Christ nailed to the cross the universal symbol of [human] power-lessness," whose presence "establishes our personal identity" (Williams 1972: 175), and who thus epitomizes the redemptive journey that all humans have the capacity to undergo.

The seeds of a new line of thinking can be found in Enlightenment discourse, during which, as Paul Fiddes puts it, "there was a widespread suspicion of any notion that help was available from beyond the human mind" (Fiddes 1989: 10). Rather, what was ultimately needed if redemption was to be operative was a change in human beings themselves as opposed to the appeasing of divine or supernatural agencies. None of this is to say that God and Christ did not play a pivotal part in the redemptive process. But, in the Enlightenment period, there was a general movement toward understanding the manner in which each individual human being has the capacity to undergo redemption within themselves, with Jesus the primal historical paradigm of such a process. Without disputing that "interest in what God intends for the created order, and how humanity and the whole of creation are to be 'made right', have been consistently important throughout Christian history," Marsh is certainly correct when he writes that "Concern for the manner of redemption and for the plight of the sinning individual might admittedly be claimed to be an especially post-Reformation preoccupation" (Marsh 2007a: 93). For a number of Protestants after the Reformation (with the notable exception of Lutherans and Calvinists for whom the orbit of redemption lies entirely within God's hands), including Methodists and Quakers, what particularly mattered was the character of each individual human person in the redemptive journey. Redemption is thus something that each person can attain on his or her own, in terms of the way one emulates or imitates Jesus' praxis, or moral example, as in the case of Kant, for whom the moral individual must bear the responsibility of his or her own actions (see Deacy 2001: 73). On such a reading, there is no reason why even in films which do not explicitly focus on the influence of God or the sacrifice of Christ in the course of their narratives, a film character might not in some sense be said to comprise a functional equivalent of Christ, who, as I have argued elsewhere, "performs the Christ-like role of undertaking a process of redemption from sin, guilt and alienation, the benefits of which may be passed on and imparted to other human beings" (Deacy 2001: 76).

There are certainly dangers with such an approach. As Marsh sees it, there is a risk for Christians that instead of seeing God as "the centre and focus" of their religion, it is "the impact of the presence and action of God on religious people which takes precedence," to the point, indeed, that God "slips off the scene" (Marsh 2007a: 94). In any theology–film conversation, it is thus pivotal that what Marsh calls "the human interest angle" (Marsh 2007a: 94) is not allowed to dominate. However, the fact that there is, in theological terms, a universal dimension to redemption – the entire human race is believed to be in thrall to sin and Christ's redemption thus has potential consequences for everyone – makes it difficult to delimit the boundaries of redemption to Christian discourse alone. As Dietrich Bonhoeffer argued in the 1930s and 1940s, the distinction between the sacred and the secular, the "Church" and the "world" is effectively an artificial and outmoded one since the forging of just such a distinction denies the *unity* of God and the world as achieved through the incarnation. In reconciling himself to the world, God began the process of reconciling, and redeeming, the world to himself, to the point that, as I have argued elsewhere, "There is, for Bonhoeffer, no God apart from the world, no supernatural apart from the natural, and no sacred apart from the profane" (Deacy 2007: 245). It need not follow, therefore, that a film has to presuppose the Christian faith in order to be of theological significance. Since theologians themselves must necessarily live both in the Church and in the world, any separation between the two "distorts both the task of Christianity's self-understanding and self-presentation, and the task of theological construction itself" (Marsh and Ortiz 1997: 254). Writing in the 1960s, Amos Wilder went even further: "If we are to have any transcendence today, even Christian, it must be found in and through the secular ... If we are to find Grace it is to be found in the world and not overhead" (quoted in Cox 1966: 228).

In line with Bonhoeffer's message that authentic Christianity was concerned not with rituals and metaphysical teachings "but to be a man," and that it "is not some religious act which makes a Christian what he is, but participation in the suffering of God in the life of the world" (Bonhoeffer 1963: 123), then there is, of necessity, a sense in which redemption need not be antithetical to the "secular" medium of film. For Bonhoeffer, indeed, at the heart of the Christian message is the obligation to be a person for other persons, and that "As Christ bears our burdens, so ought we to bear the burdens of our fellow-men" (Bonhoeffer 1959: 80). Whether or not one is immersed in the Christian tradition, Marsh is right in his affirmation that "Redemption addresses a basic assumption about human being: there is some aspect of humanity, and of every individual, that needs 'redeeming', and without which we are 'trapped'" (Marsh 2007a: 93). Films can thus engender serious reflection on what it means to be rescued or redeemed from sin, suffering, and alienation in a manner that corresponds to the basic tenet of redemption in Christianity that the "rediscovery of life and life's purpose – to love and to live in peace with God and all people – is not something that it is possible to do unaided" (Marsh 2007a: 104). There may be differences between Christian redemption and cinematic redemption, in that redemption vis-à-vis film tends to be focused on the role of human beings rather than of God, but, as Lyden acknowledges, "though less than ultimate from a Christian point of view, it is not intrinsically bad to have self-confidence and courage or to believe that humans can truly love each other" (Lyden 2007: 217).

Accordingly, whether one subscribes to Original Sin or not, Greg Garrett is right in his affirmation that "there seems little question that in this broken world, evil is real and humans are sinful, that even though we may wish to do good we are capable of doing great harm, that it is easier to be bad than to be good" (Garrett 2007: 72). At the same time, filmmakers are interested in exploring issues of hope, fulfillment, conversion, and, indeed, redemption. Theological purists may be dismissive of any attempt at forging a precise correlation between Christian and cinematic forms of redemption, but, in Marsh's words, redemption is "a preoccupation of many Western films" (Marsh 2007a: 94). Indeed, according to the American theologian David Kelsey:

> as an assiduous reader of reviews of fiction, plays and movies, I have been impressed by the frequency with which reviewers comment on the presence or absence of a "redemptive" note or theme in the work under review or debate whether there might be such a note. Sometimes the presence of a redemptive note seems to count in favor of the work and its absence to count

against it. Although I am often unable to tell just what the reviewer means by "redemption" or "redemptive," it is clear that the words are used in the context of certain practices that help make up Western cultural life. (Quoted in Marsh 2007a: 94)

Films as redemptive texts

Such findings match my own experience of reading film reviews, which was, in turn, the impetus behind my decision to pursue doctoral work in this area. Back in the mid-1990s, I was drawn to film reviews which commonly cited redemptive terminology. The *Radio Times* review of *Taxi Driver* (Martin Scorsese, 1976), when it was first screened on terrestrial television in the UK in August 1995, identified the protagonist, Travis Bickle (Robert De Niro), "as the Vietnam vet spiralling into one of Scorsese's most frightening circles of hell, as he seeks a twisted redemption by saving the soul of a child prostitute" (*Radio Times* 1995: 45–6). A number of other films, from *The Fisher King* (Terry Gilliam, 1991) to *Spy Game* (Tony Scott, 2001), have also traded in the vocabulary of redemption, with an internet review of the latter, by James Berardinelli, saying of Nathan Muir, the character played by Robert Redford – a CIA operative on the verge of retirement – that "His career may have been founded on treating human beings like disposable commodities, but, in the end, he sacrifices everything for a shot at redemption" (Berardinelli 2001).

Greg Garrett also points to a number of cinematic works which address the theme of redemption in his 2007 publication *The Gospel according to Hollywood*. Referring to Hitchcock's classic spy thriller *North by Northwest* (1959), for example, Garrett writes that "Roger Thornhill's redemption comes from risking himself for another – which allows him to fill that hollow spot inside himself" (Garrett 2007: 96). Garrett also identifies *Pulp Fiction* (Quentin Tarantino, 1994) as "One of the great stories of redemption in recent American film," paying particular attention in this regard to the character of the hit man, Jules Winnfield (Samuel L. Jackson), who may not on the surface be an obvious candidate for theological exploration, "caught up as he is in typically American patter about television and fast food" (Garrett 2007: 86). Garrett attests, however, that "[a]lthough his sins are outsize and dramatic" – in view of his status as someone who kills for a living – "Jules nonetheless stands in for us and for our own fallen natures. All of us need to change; the contrasts in Jules's story just make that need a little more obvious" (Garrett 2007: 86).

This may be a far cry from what Augustine, Anselm, and Luther had in mind when they employed the language of redemption. But, it is at the very least territory that the theologian can ill afford to dismiss. No matter how far removed the vocabulary used in film reviews may be from that of traditional Christian discourse, the discussion of Bonhoeffer has established that there is, ultimately, no clear line of demarcation between the sacred and the secular, and Christians and theologians themselves cannot be immune from cultural contexts in which the vocabulary of redemption is commonly adduced. This is not to say that the theologian will or should necessarily applaud the theology that he or she may encounter in such contexts, but irrespective of the quality of the theological "resources" that are out there, it does say something vital about the way in which ordinary people – both "religious" and "secular" – are *actually* appropriating theological doctrines and beliefs.

Robert Jewett typifies the skepticism felt by some theologians when biblical language is being requisitioned in a "secular" context. Writing with specific reference to the prison-escape drama *The Shawshank Redemption* (Frank Darabont, 1994), Jewett, writing in 1999, is concerned that a "new form of salvation is clearly being offered in this film, one that replaces the intervention of Yahweh at the Exodus and of Christ on the Cross," in which "Salvation now comes through the little rock hammer in the hands of an intelligent and determined person who refuses to give up hope in his own capacity to achieve freedom against all the odds" (Jewett 1999: 181). In this and a number of other films from the 1990s, Jewett feels that what we have here is "the unexamined results of a process of secular derivation that remains critical of biblical religion while continuing to use its redemptive language" (Jewett 1999: 181).

In response to Jewett, however, it might be countered that, as Aichele and Walsh put it, readings from outside biblical scholarship "have offered rich insights into biblical texts" (Walsh and Aichele 2002: vii). Everyone reads a text – whether cinematic or scriptural – from their own unique cultural and ideological vantage points and it is questionable as to whether anyone could thus be said to have "privileged access" (Walsh and Aichele 2002: vii) to authoritative interpretation. If Aichele and Walsh are thus right, and there "is no proper or correct *exegesis* of any text," only *eisegeses* – that is, the reading *into* a text on the part of the reader – then it is difficult to affirm the existence of an absolute, preeminent and definitive interpretation of redemption, in relation to which all other readings fall short. Instead of privileging the biblical understanding of redemption, in the manner of Jewett, there is, rather, scope for going down the path proposed by Walsh and Aichele, for whom there is greater mileage in bringing films and biblical texts "into a genuine exchange that will open up illuminating connections between them" (Walsh and Aichele 2002: ix). In such terms, there must be a sense in which traditional theological accounts of redemption and their modern secular counterparts in film will facilitate a two-way dialogical conversation whereby both can learn from – and be challenged and changed by – one another. As Gordon Lynch affirms by way of his "revised correlational" approach to the theology-film field, there needs to be "a complex conversation between the questions and insights of both religious tradition and popular culture," one that allows, moreover, "for the possibility that both religious tradition and popular culture can be usefully challenged and transformed through this process" (Lynch 2005: 105).

Accordingly, once one has become acquainted with redemption in Christianity, this is invariably going to "color" one's apprehension of, say, *The Shawshank Redemption*'s treatment of this theme, as has happened in the case of Jewett's critique – he just does not think that the film, which seems "uncomfortably similar to the escapist trends in current American society," adequately matches up to "the original story of Christ suffering on behalf of prisoners, the ill, the outsiders, the lame, the halt, and the blind" (Jewett 1999: 175). Watching *The Shawshank Redemption*, it may be that the "redemption" on offer in this film contains marked differences from the way theologians have historically treated this topic. Jewett, indeed, is concerned that whereas in the film "redemption" "is essentially the hope for happy endings" (Jewett 1999: 164), in St. Paul's understanding in Romans those who are redeemed are not necessarily completely freed from physical forms of adversity and oppression in the manner of *Shawshank*'s Andy (Tim Robbins) and Red (Morgan Freeman) who are literally released from prison, and he cites in this regard Romans 8:24-5 which presupposes, in its talk of "in this hope we were saved," a situation of ongoing vulnerability for those who have been redeemed. On this reading, there is more to "redemption" than mere change of circumstance – "The slaves and former slaves who made up the bulk of the Roman Churches could not entirely overcome exploitation by their masters and patrons" (Jewett 1999: 164). Similarly, Adele Reinhartz concedes that "the hope that Andy and Red share is not the eschatological hope to which Paul refers in 1 Corinthians 13" but is, rather, "a more mundane, this-worldly, and limited hope" (Reinhartz 2003: 138) that is not grounded in the traditional heaven of theological discourse but has as its apotheosis an earthly paradise in Zihuatanejo on the Mexican coast.

However, the reverse of this is also true. Just as theological understandings of redemption affect the way the film is interpreted (as in Jewett's case), so the film has the capacity to change the way in which theologians understand the traditional usage of redemption. Compared to what redemption traditionally refers to, *The Shawshank Redemption*'s representation of redemption as comprising a "new world of sun, beach, and water" (Reinhartz 2003: 141) may well be construed as somewhat incomplete and partial, but, as Reinhartz puts it,

> it nevertheless has a broader role and application than the anticipation of the good life on a Pacific beach. The very ability to hope, to nurture a dream, to envisage a life after Shawshank allows Andy to endure prison and to retain a sense of his own worth and individuality in an institutional setting that aims to erode its prisoners' innate personhood. (Reinhartz 2003: 138)

It is also, as I have suggested elsewhere, a new life in another world that is as dichotomous from the protagonists' former life on earth, when they were dehumanized and institutionalized inmates in a corrupt prison, as heaven is from earth in traditional Christian interpretation (see Deacy and Ortiz 2008: 198).

Dialogue between filmic and theological concepts of redemption

The fact that the film does not bear witness to what St. Paul meant by redemption does not therefore mean to say that any "redemption" on display in the film is theologically worthless. The film may not exhort the sinful and depraved human individual to believe in the victorious gospel of Christ's death for their transgressions and in Christ's subsequent resurrection from the dead, but, as Kelsey sees it, any "extra-Christian" uses of the term "redemption," as in the case of the medium of film, "doubtless shape" the way in which they are used "in the context of the common life of Christian faith communities, and vice versa" (quoted in Marsh 2007a: 95). There is, therefore, an interweaving – a two-way dialogue and exchange – between Christian and non-Christian interpretations. As Marsh puts it, "Exploration of such public, cultural usage will ... prove crucial to theological understanding of what it means to be human" (Marsh 2007a: 95).

All of this may be an anathema to traditional theological discourse, but many theologians are already taking on board the empirical reality that the reason, for example, that students are interested in studying theology at university is not because they are necessarily interested in learning about Original Sin and substitutionary atonement per se, but because they have encountered the use of such theological terminology as "redemption" in popular culture and they wish to see what theology in turn has to say about this. As Marsh puts it, the students of theology today "are those who sit in lecture- and seminar-rooms across the world and may not have begun to examine the differences between salvation, liberation and atonement, but *are* interested in tackling them and have seen *The Shawshank Redemption*" (Marsh 2007a: 4). This may not be a good thing from the point of view of all theologians, but if one puts "together a religious concern for redemption and cinema's interest in portraying stretching human stories," then, as Marsh sees it, "a powerful combination results" (Marsh 2007a: 94). Garrett similarly attests, from a missiological point of view, that the reason "movies often tell stories of redemption, the Shawshank variety and otherwise" is because "dramatically, stories do seem to work best when characters are required to change," and despite the "nonreligious" nature of the "conversion experiences" that take place in such films "they all shed light on the action that takes place when a person experiences a life-changing relationship with God" (Garrett 2007: 84). This may be taking things too far – nonreligious, indeed nontheistic, audience members may resent being told that in encountering a "conversion experience" in a film, they are witnessing a quintessentially religious event – but there is scope for finding correlations, rather than contradictions, between theology and film "in any context where encounter with issues, challenging of the mind, personal psychological and social development, and establishing a direction in life are taking place" (Marsh 2007b: 152). Should the theologian simply pretend that this is not happening? The type of hope or redemption that is on display may differ from traditional accounts of redemption in Christianity, but, as Lyden affirms, "it is a hope nonetheless, and its religious character should be recognized" (Lyden 2007: 217).

If the net result of such exchanges between cinematic and theological accounts of redemption is that theologians are encouraged to revisit the exclusivity of redemption in Christianity, then this has much positive value. On close inspection, indeed, it is not self-evident that "redemption" in Christianity is such a homogeneous process that it has no role to play outside the teaching and doctrines of the Christian tradition. While acknowledging that the doctrine of redemption has an intrinsically Christian foundation, it is conspicuous from an historical perspective that the manner in which such a doctrinally specific concept has been interpreted over the centuries betrays a considerable diversity of expression. As Richardson puts it, although in the first five centuries of the Christian Church many "individuals attempted to think out the mode" in which redemption was to be understood, "the Church as a whole embraced no theory" (Richardson 1986: 95). In his words, "The New Testament, the Creeds and the Chalcedonian Definition all insist upon the great principle that God in Christ has redeemed man, but there is nowhere in them a hint of theory" (Richardson 1986: 96). Moreover, in the specific case of Origen in the second century, it is significant that although the Redemption wrought by Christ is integral to his Christology and theology, scholars "have often found Origen's thoughts on the redemption complex to the point of being mutually irreconcilable, and have been hard put to it to discover a unifying theme in them" (Kelly 1958: 186). Accordingly, Kelly is right that "while the conviction of redemption through Christ has always been the motive force of Christian faith ... it is useless to look for any systematic treatment of the doctrine" (Kelly 1958: 163) in early Christian theology. Even when, as he points out, it is "true that the Apostolic Fathers make numerous references to Christ's work," it is nonetheless the case that they are simply "rehearsing the clichés of catechetical instruction, so that what they say smacks more of affirmation than explanation" (Kelly 1958: 163). Hence, notwithstanding Gustav Scholem's consideration that redemption is "certainly one of the fundamental subjects with which the historian of religion has to deal" (Scholem 1970: 8), it is clear that, to paraphrase David Wells with respect to the term "salvation," "like a lady of the night," the concept "wanders through the pages of contemporary print making casual alliances almost at random" (Wells 1978: 9). Even though, as R. J. Zwi Werblowsky affirms, "writers on messianic, millenarian, nativistic and revival movements as well as students of mysticism, Gnosticism and prophetic types of religion have produced typologies galore of redemption," it remains the case that "many of these typologies do not go beyond" a mere "labelling of the variety of phenomena" (Werblowsky 1970: 247) involved.

There are, for example, numerous ways of interpreting redemption in terms of the destiny of the individual, such as in terms of its elevation from the present to a higher state of existence, its dissolution into some form of cosmic consciousness, or even its transcending of it (Scholem 1970: 9). In the Hebrew Bible, in marked contrast, redemption is a decisive experience of a distinctly social, national, and corporate nature, whereby it is the prevalence of the tribe or clan – and, in due course, the Israelite nation – that ultimately matters. It is also ambiguous in the New Testament as to whether it is the entire human race that will be redeemed by Christ's atoning death, in the manner of Romans 5:18 which affirms that "just as one man's trespass led to condemnation for all men, so one man's act of righteousness leads to acquittal and life for all men," or whether redemption is the privilege only of those who have been elected or "predestined" to salvation, as is suggested by Romans 8:29.

Furthermore, although redemption in Christianity refers to what happened on the Cross 2,000 years ago, it is also bound up with what will happen in the future, beyond death, in another cosmic dimension, and so refers to the future consummation of all things, in the form of the Second Coming, or Parousia. In this light, we can, in the present, thus see no more than only "the beginning of what redemption means" (Morris 1983: 122). Although we can account in large part for the expectation of the Parousia in terms of contemporary historical circumstances – whereby the first generations of Christians were being subject to persecutions and so were hardly living in a redeemed state, such that eschatological beliefs came to be projected into the future – it is clear that there are what Scholem calls "very diverse experiences" (Scholem 1970: 8) and "infinite variations" of what we mean when we use the language of redemption, many of which are "mutually exclusive" (Scholem 1970: 9) to one another. While this diversity is to be expected of a religious tradition which has developed over the course of two millennia, the roots of which can be traced back even further to Greek and Jewish thought, it does suggest that redemption is not such a unified and coherent concept that its sphere of activity may be definitively ascertained.

Escapism, idealism, and hope

In a similar manner, with respect to film, it is clear that there are a variety of ways in which any given film or genre of film may be perceived as redolent in redemptive significance. Each filmic "text" operates on many different levels, to the point, indeed, that even though the ostensible reason for going to see a movie may be one of recreational or escapist intent, Marsh is right there will also be those people who "go for purposes of education or intellectual stimulation" (Marsh 2007b: 148), such that "the de facto function of what occurs is much more complex" (Marsh 2007b: 150). Just as redemption in Christianity is far more heterogeneous than an initial reading might suggest, so in the case of film redemption may be found to be a far more fluid and complex phenomenon than might at first appear to be the case.

This is not the view I have always adopted in the past. In *Screen Christologies*, I argued that escapist film was an inadequate site of redemptive activity in that such films are capable merely of facilitating a momentary and hollow transformation from the problems of human existence, and that *film noir*, in contrast, "may be seen to engage in a highly focused and theologically constructive fashion with the estranged, disaffected, despairing and fragmentary quality of human existence" (Deacy 2001: 37) from which redemption is sought. Accordingly, on this reading, since *noir* corresponds to the Christian understanding of humanity as spiritually dead and in slavery to sin that St. Paul writes about in Romans 6:20, then the fact that "*films noirs* bear witness to ... the Christian understanding of sin and alienation ... raises the possibility that *film noir*, too, is a vehicle capable of engendering an experience of *hope* and a sense of *integration* out of the all-encompassing chaos, disorder and despair" (Deacy 2001: 52). The argument being adduced, here, is that since there can be no redemption without suffering, then films of an overtly escapist sensibility, with their penchant for happy endings, simply lack the depth that makes redemption such a complex process, and so that *noir*, with its social and psychological realism and authentic character development, is a much more theologically fecund sphere of activity. However, this is not to say that escapism is entirely removed from the orbit of redemption. It may be the case that, as Lyden puts it, the "neat" endings supplied by many films "belie the messy character of real life, which does not always satisfy us in the same way," to the point that many popular films "often give us an ideal world filled with unrealistic hopes that are magically fulfilled by the time we leave the theater" (Lyden 2007: 216). But,

Lyden is also correct that this absence, of realism is itself what imbues such films with a religious character, "since they portray an ideal world that we can juxtapose with the real world, and that we can aspire to achieve" (Lyden 2007: 216). In other words, they can "provide a model of how reality might be, and a portrait of something we can strive toward" (Lyden 2007: 217).

Similar ideas have been put forward by the theologian of liberation, Leonardo Boff, according to whom "fantasy is not mere fancifulness or a mechanism for escaping from conflict-ridden reality," but "the key to explaining authentic creativity" (Boff 2004: 285). Escapism can thus serve a positive function, with Boff finding in fantasy "the richest source of human creativity," which translates in theological terms as "the image of the creator God in human beings" and "the soil in which humanity's capacity for invention and innovation flourishes" (Boff 2004: 285). If the vision of escapist films can, as it were, "rub off on reality" (Lyden 2003: 201) and engender in audiences the hope that, for all its problems, this world is not beyond redemption, then there is no reason why such films cannot play an important theological role, offering as they do constructive models of human negotiation and interaction. In contrast to *film noir* which, it could be said, presents the world as it presently is – enmeshed in evil, suffering, and despair – escapist films can thus be said to play an important redemptive role in that they have the capacity to inject into this world a degree of hope and aspiration as to how life could, and should, be. Redemption in traditional Christian discourse may be focused on Original Sin and the depravity of the human race, but this is not to say that redemption in Christianity does not also possess a much more escapist- and fantasy-oriented dimension, in a manner that corresponds with the "happy ending" predilection of many movies. As Lyden sees it, there is a very real sense in which "the Bible provides a rather neat and happy ending in the resurrection of Jesus Christ and the hope for his second coming," and where suffering "does not have the last word" (Lyden 2007: 217). The affirmation of life and capacity for being amenable to the possibilities of growth and change that are intrinsic to so many escapist films is thus very much in keeping with the spirit of the Christian story of redemption, even to the point that it may be possible to discern in such films the shape of our own redemptive journeys.

It need not therefore be the case that only downbeat, pessimistic, and cynical perspectives of the world, as evinced in *film noir*, have the capacity to be theologically, and redemptively, meaningful. Despite my having written in the past that "Although 'going to the movies' is normally deemed an escapist experience, the more remarkable films are those that invite the audience to *confront* rather than to escape reality" (Deacy 2005: 38), I agree with Pope that it is not appropriate to draw "too great a distinction between hope which emerges amid despondency" – as in the case of *film noir* – "and the hope which may be kindled through a more optimistic context or even in fantasy" (Pope 2007: 163). He continues that

> if all film can do is portray the grit, violence, cynicism and unpleasantness of the real world, then it is difficult to see how this will effect the transformative experience of which Deacy writes. All it would do is confirm in the minds of

the viewers that this world is not a particularly pleasant, or "wonderful", place in which to live. (Pope 2007: 164)

Pope is referring, here, to my argument that although the *noir* world is "intrinsically fatalistic and hopeless," it is nevertheless the case that "audiences can come to experience the antithesis of a helpless and impotent response to such films, upon engaging with their fatalistic and oppressive images and narratives" (Deacy 2001: 58). As with the spirit of the Old Testament Book of Ecclesiastes, I have argued that *film noir* "does not proffer the idealistic hope that present existence can materially or outwardly improve, or that a better, more coherent world is even attainable" – and that it is all the better for that, since any redemption we can speak of "emanates from one's ability to *confront* and come to terms with the intrinsically volatile and fragmentary nature of human existence, rather than in the form of an escape from it" (Deacy 2001: 64). This, I have suggested, is the only way in which one is in a position to face up to the challenges of human existence, in which "the guilty often go unpunished, and come to feel no contrition for, their actions" (Deacy 2001: 68). Pope's concern here, though, is that any hope or redemption that emerges in this situation "would tend to take on the characteristics of mere endurance until such a time as the forces of oppression are destroyed," to the point that what we have is not redemption but a mere "opiate" (Pope 2007: 164). While both traditional Christianity and *film noir* are both obsessed, therefore, with sin, the problem with restricting the scope of cinematic redemption to *film noir* is that, in Pope's eyes, there is a concomitant assumption that "the violent and unpleasant forces" which typify the *noir* universe "are too great to combat" (Pope 2007: 164). For Pope, there needs to be a greater "hardening of resolve to transform a situation," whereas a dependence on *noir* (and the spirit of Ecclesiastes) will lead only to an acquiescence that present existence will not materially or outwardly improve – and this, says Pope, is "to remain blinded by sin" (Pope 2007: 164).

While Pope's argument is a judicious one, it does, however, raise the same question that applies to Jewett's reading of *The Shawshank Redemption* – namely, whether there needs to be a physical or material change in circumstances in order for redemption to have been accomplished. For Jewett, it is the very physicality of the "redemption" (or, rather, escape) that is actualized in Darabont's film that diminishes a theological reading, contrary as it is to what Paul teaches in Romans concerning the more inner and spiritual nature of what it means to be redeemed. Pope, on the other hand, is concerned that the absence of social or material change in *noir* is insufficiently empowering or transformative, and that a greater effort is required to challenge the status quo in order for such films to be categorized as redemptive. Where we would both agree, though, is in seeing "virtually any film" as being a potential "catalyst for change" (Pope 2007: 165), and thus as redemptive. Pope rightly feels that my concentration on *noir* is too restrictive, and that the conversation partners should be extended to include any film "which sparks the ontological characteristics in the imagination to image different future possibilities" (Pope 2007: 165).

Scholars will continue to debate, of course, whether this squares up to the traditional Christian understanding of redemption from Original Sin, and as to whether there is a sufficiently central role in the redemptive schema for Jesus Christ as the paradigm or model of any redemptive activity that takes place in the individual. But, at the same time, for redemption in Christianity to be meaningful, then, as Paul Fiddes puts it, it "must touch every moment of every life" (Fiddes 2000: 190). If there is no line of demarcation between the sacred and the secular, then it is difficult for the theologian to completely separate out the redemption wrought by Christ on the Cross from the way in which "secular" film characters are confronting their human inadequacies and weaknesses and undergoing a process of spiritual and moral transformation which is, if not strictly analogous to, then at least not inconsistent with, Christian tradition.

Indeed, it is the intrinsically flawed, fallible, and human nature of many of the film characters discussed in this chapter (from *Pulp Fiction*'s Jules to *Shawshank*'s Red) that enables one to forge a connection with the Antiochene Christological model of the early Church which held that only a tainted and sinful individual could be in a position to speak to, and address the needs of, a flawed and sinful humanity. Just as Christ had to take on the sins of humankind for the redemption of the human race to be accomplished – as typified by Ambrose of Milan's understanding in the fourth century that "He condemned sin in order to nail our sins to the cross" so that "the Eternal God who spared not His own Son, but made Him to be sin for us, acquitted us" (quoted in Turner 1952: 107) – so films where the activities of criminals are "at the centre of the narrative" and whose actions are "brutally, vividly and even sympathetically portrayed" (Christianson 2005: 112) can be of prodigious redemptive significance, bearing witness as they do to the eternal struggle between guilt and innocence, salvation and damnation. This is not to say that films necessarily have all the right answers. As Marsh points out, there is too often a tendency by filmmakers to focus on what people need to be rescued from – such as guilt or suffering – rather than on what people are redeemed for or into (Marsh 2007a: 105). But, this is not to say that, in line with Lynch's revised correlational model, and Aichele and Walsh's call for a genuine exchange between the Bible and film that will open up illuminating connections between them both, that either the theologian or the filmmaker has privileged or exclusive access to the remit of redemption. Rather, when it comes to exploring the manner and extent to which redemption may be understood in cinematic and theological discourse, it is clear that both theology and film can shed important light on the other. Redemption may be difficult to capture on celluloid, and perhaps, even, to paraphrase Marsh, "harder to conceptualize theologically" (Marsh 2007a: 106) – but the resources are certainly there and it may not be entirely wide of the mark to construe film as a potentially fertile site of redemptive significance in contemporary culture.

Bibliography

Altholz, J. (1988), "The Warfare of Conscience with Theology," in G. Parsons (ed.) *Religion in Victorian Britain*, vol. 4: *Interpretations*, Manchester: Manchester University Press: 150–69.

Augustine, St. (1961) *Confessions*, Harmondsworth: Penguin.

Badham, P. and Badham, L. (1984) *Immortality or Extinction?* London: SPCK.

Berardinelli, J. (2001) Review of *Spy Game*, in James Berardinelli's Reelviews. Online. Available HTTP: <http:www.reelviews.net/movies/s/spy_game.html>

Boff, L. (2004) "Liberating Grace," in G. E. Thiessen (ed.), *Theological Aesthetics: A Reader*, London: SCM: 284–5.

Bonhoeffer, D. (1959) *The Cost of Discipleship*, London: SCM.

—— (1963) *Letters and Papers from Prison*, London: Fontana.

Christianson, E. (2005) "An Ethic You Can't Refuse?: Assessing *The Godfather* Trilogy," in W. Telford, E. Christianson, and P. Francis (eds), *Cinéma Divinité: Readings in Film and Theology*, London: SCM: 110–23.

Cox, H. (1966) *The Secular City*, New York: Macmillan.

Deacy, C. (2001) *Screen Christologies: Redemption and the Medium of Film*, Cardiff: University of Wales Press.

—— (2005) *Faith in Film: Religious Themes in Contemporary Cinema*, Aldershot: Ashgate.

—— (2007) "From Bultmann to Burton, Demythologizing the *Big Fish*: The Contribution of Modern Christian Theologians to the Theology-Film Conversation," in R. K. Johnston (ed.) *Re-Viewing Theology and Film: Moving the Discipline Forward*, Grand Rapids, MI: Baker Academic: 238–60.

Deacy, C. and Ortiz, G. (2008) *Theology and Film: Challenging the Sacred/Secular Divide*, Oxford: Blackwell.

Ferm, V. (ed.) (1976) *An Encyclopedia of Religion*, Westport, CT: Greenwood Press.

Fiddes, P. S. (1989) *Past Event and Present Salvation: The Christian Idea of Atonement*, London: Darton Longman & Todd.

—— (2000) *The Promised End: Eschatology in Theology and Literature*, Oxford: Blackwell.

Floyd, W. W. (2005) "Dietrich Bonhoeffer," in D. Ford with R. Muers (eds), *The Modern Theologians*, 3rd ed., Oxford: Blackwell: 43–61.

Garrett, G. (2007) *The Gospel According to Hollywood*, London and Louisville, KY: Westminster John Knox Press.

Jewett, R. (1999) *Saint Paul Returns to the Movies: Triumph over Shame*, Cambridge: Eerdmans.

Johnston, R. K. (2007) "Introduction: Reframing the Discussion," in R. K. Johnston (ed.) *Reframing Theology and Film: New Focus for an Emerging Discipline*, Grand Rapids, MI: Baker Academic: 15–26.

Kelly, J. N. D. (1958) *Early Christian Doctrines*, London: Adam & Charles Black.

Lyden, J. C. (2003) *Film as Religion: Myths, Morals and Rituals*, New York: New York University Press.

—— (2007) "Theology and Film: Interreligious Dialogue and Theology," in R. K. Johnston (ed.) *Re-Viewing Theology and Film: Moving the Discipline Forward*, Grand Rapids, MI: Baker Academic: 205–18.

Lynch, G. (2005) *Understanding Theology and Popular Culture*, Oxford: Blackwell.

Marsh, C. (2007a) *Theology Goes to the Movies: An Introduction to Critical Christian Thinking*, London: Routledge.

—— (2007b) "On Dealing with what Films Actually Do to People: The Practice and Theory of Film Watching in Theology/Religion and Film Discussion," in R. K. Johnston (ed.), *Re-Viewing Theology and Film: Moving the Discipline Forward*, Grand Rapids, MI: Baker Academic: 145–61.

Marsh, C. and Ortiz, G. (1997) "Theology beyond the Modern and the Postmodern: A Future Agenda for Theology and Film," in C. Marsh and G. Ortiz (eds) *Explorations in Theology and Film: Movies and Meaning*, Oxford: Blackwell: 245–55.

Morris, L. (1983) *The Atonement: Its Meaning and Significance*, Leicester: Inter-Varsity Press.

Pope, R. (2007) *Salvation in Celluloid: Theology, Imagination and Film*, London: T&T Clark.

Radio Times (1995) Review of *Taxi Driver* (26 August–1 September): 45–6.

Reed, E. (2004) "Redemption," in G. Jones (ed.) *The Blackwell Companion to Modern Theology*, Oxford: Blackwell: 227–42.

Reinhartz, A. (2003) *Scripture on the Silver Screen*, Louisville, KY: Westminster John Knox Press.

Richardson, A. (1986) *Creeds in the Making*, London: SCM.

Scholem, G. (1970) "Opening Address," in R. J. Zwi Werblowsky and C. Jouco Bleeker (eds), *Types of Redemption: Contributions to the Theme of the Study-Conference Held at Jerusalem, 14th to 19th July 1968*, Leiden: E. J. Brill: 5–12.

Schrader, P. (1972) *Transcendental Style in Film: Ozu, Bresson, Dreyer*, Berkeley: University of California Press.

Turner, H. E. W. (1952) *The Patristic Doctrine of Redemption: A Study of the Development of Doctrine during the First Five Centuries*, London: A. R. Mowbray.

Walsh, R. and Aichele, G. (2002) "Introduction: Scripture as Precursor," in G. Aichele and R. Walsh (eds), *Screening Scripture: Intertextual Connections Between Scripture and Film*, Harrisburg, PA: Trinity Press International: vii–xvi.

Wells, D. F. (1978) *The Search for Salvation*, Leicester: Inter-Varsity Press.

Werblowsky, R. J. Zwi (1970) "Types of Redemption: A Summary," in R. J. Zwi Werblowsky and C. Jouco Bleeker (eds), *Types of Redemption: Contributions to the Theme of the Study-Conference Held at Jerusalem, 14th to 19th July 1968*, Leiden: E. J. Brill: 243–7.

Wheeler-Robinson, H. (1943) *Redemption and Revelation in the Actuality of History*, London: Nisbet.

Williams, H. A. (1972) *True Resurrection*, London: Mitchell Beazley.

Filmography

The Fisher King (1991, dir. T. Gilliam)
North by Northwest (1959, dir. A. Hitchcock)
The Passion of the Christ (2004, dir. M. Gibson)
Pulp Fiction (1994, dir. Q. Tarantino)
The Shawshank Redemption (1994, dir. F. Darabont)
Spy Game (2001, dir. T. Scott)
Taxi Driver (1976, dir. M. Scorsese)

20
APOCALYPTIC

Conrad Ostwalt

Introduction

Apocalyptic themes have long been a part of the popular culture of the West and Near East and have informed literature, music, art, and other cultural forms. So it should be of no surprise that apocalyptic images and messages should find their ways into films as well. In fact, in many ways, film is the best medium for presenting the fantastic visions and imagery that often accompany the apocalyptic genre. Auditory effects and visual graphics available to contemporary filmmakers bring the bizarre and surreal to life in realistic presentation. Such realism gives apocalyptic presentations an impact through film that is potentially more powerful than literary or other visual presentations of the same or similar themes.

Apokalypsis (the revelation, the unveiling); this begins St. John's famous text that ends the canonical Bible. It is this book more than any other that defines the understanding of apocalyptic themes and categories as a genre of literature that is carried over to other areas of culture and other media. Apocalyptic literature evolved in the Jewish and Christian literature during the years 200 BCE to 200 CE and finds its most well-known expressions in the biblical books of Daniel, Ezekiel, and John's Revelation. As a genre in the Jewish and Christian traditions, apocalyptic work can be distinguished by several features. Apocalyptic works are characterized by dreams, visions, and symbols that unveil the events associated with the end of the world. The consummation of history is accompanied by battles between good and evil, ushers in God's kingdom, and results in the destruction or punishment of the evil and the elevation of the good to righteousness. Underpinning this dualistic cataclysm is the assertion and promise of God's ultimate and final sovereignty, and it is divine intervention into the apocalyptic drama that allows the end of history to be meaningful. A vision of the end of the world without a sovereign reality beyond the world results in nihilism, and this is the outcome the apocalyptic drama wishes to avoid. In fact, most apocalyptic literature arises out of precarious situations, political, existential, or psychological, and combats the tendency toward a nihilistic solution or conclusion.

A quick survey of the above themes readily suggests that many contemporary films contain one or more of the characteristics of the apocalyptic genre. For example, westerns and science fiction films are often dualistic and draw out the boundaries between good and evil; psychological dramas might include visions; mysteries might rely on symbols; disaster movies might even rely on a plot that includes the end of the world or at least the possibility of it. However, inclusion of or reliance upon one or multiples of these characteristics does not make a movie apocalyptic in the traditional sense. The essential element that technically makes a drama an apocalyptic one is that the dualism, the visions, the symbols, and even the end are controlled by a divine power, not by fate, by human intervention, or by accident but by design – the end is controlled by divine prerogative that thwarts the nihilistic and fatalistic visions. As such, traditional apocalyptic scenarios are deeply rooted in a vision of divine justice and define eschatology as a just consummation of history and a just inauguration of a new age. Technically, many of the films that employ end-of-the-world scenarios and even apocalyptic language are not apocalyptic because they lack this element of divine sovereignty and justice. For example, *Armageddon* (1998), a film titled after the famous battle from Revelation, uses apocalyptic imagery and language and the plot is based on the possibility of an end-of-the-world cataclysm as a huge asteroid hurtles toward earth on a collision course. Nevertheless, using the traditional understanding of apocalypse, *Armageddon* would not be an apocalyptic movie because events are not controlled by divine agency and the end does not usher in a new, just age of God's kingdom.

In like yet opposite fashion, many contemporary films incorporate visions of an afterlife and even base the afterlife on an imposition of divine justice. While these films are otherworldly and justice-centered, they are not apocalyptic because they are not rooted in an end-of-the-world scenario that includes the inauguration of the Kingdom of God. The dualistic organization of the universe continues, life on earth continues, and the focus is on an afterlife and its implications, not on a new order and consummation. As Christopher Deacy makes clear in his work on eschatology and film, such films abound in popular culture (Deacy 2008: 183–4). Deacy points out that films like *What Dreams May Come* (1998), *Defending Your Life* (1991), and even *Ghost* (1990), are rich with theological themes concerning life after death and justice and often perpetuate a dualistic vision of cosmic justice. Nevertheless, such films are not apocalyptic for the consummation theme is missing along with visions and other characteristics associated with the apocalyptic genre.

One of the purposes of this essay is to help distinguish those contemporary films that are traditionally apocalyptic (those including the crucial characteristics of God's Sovereignty and kingdom, justice, and consummation of history) from those films that might include the plot of world-ending catastrophe but not the promise of divine resolution, or from those films that might promise divine justice or other apocalyptic characteristics but do not include the consummation of history. In addition, I hope to highlight that popular culture and contemporary scholarship on eschatology and film sometimes fail to distinguish films that are true to the apocalyptic formula from films that borrow from and revise the formula, even if in subtle ways. As a method of engaging these issues, I will highlight four predominant trends in scholarship or popular appropriation of contemporary films with end-of-the-world themes and then provide examples of the last approach, which I find to be the most helpful in guiding observers through the critical assessment of these films.

Trends in contemporary scholarship and criticism on apocalypticism and film

The variety of criticism and the multiplicity of scholarship on religion and film have witnessed tremendous growth during the past decade and a half. And the existence of films that have been considered apocalyptic has multiplied as well. It is my intent here not to be comprehensive in a survey of critical approaches or even of films that might be identified as apocalyptic. Rather, I hope to summarize and identify trends and, in so doing, to provide a framework for dealing with religion and film issues either in the classroom or in further scholarship. For the purposes of this framework, I find four basic trends in the study of religion and apocalyptic films. These trends are not mutually exclusive and often overlap, but looking at the treatment of apocalyptic films from these perspectives is helpful as a study aid if nothing else. (1) First, some criticism categorizes films as apocalyptic simply because the films contain eschato-logical or "end-of-the-world" themes. (2) Second, an extension of the first approach is to categorize films as apocalyptic even if they ignore the revelatory content or divine agency aspect of the apocalyptic genre. I will suggest in the fourth approach that films without revelatory or divine causation should only be considered apocalyptic if one accepts a contemporary and secular redefinition of the apocalyptic tradition. (3) Third, one academic tendency in the scholarship of such films is to classify and categorize. Once again, these attempts take us well beyond the traditional understanding of apocalyptic. (4) Fourth, I will make a case for understanding apocalyptic categories in film studies from two perspectives: (a) the traditional apocalyptic film arising from and based upon the traditional Jewish–Christian genre; (b) the secular apocalyptic film.

"End-of-the-world" themes classified as apocalyptic

One of the most prominent trends in contemporary criticism of apocalyptic films is a thoroughly uncritical classifying of films based on themes rather than forms or genres. Some film criticism seeks, finds, and highlights apocalyptic themes in films and immediately classifies these films as apocalyptic. Most often, such criticism focuses on the end-of-time scenario as the main or even sole prerequisite for apocalyptic stories. In fact, the end of time in these approaches does not even have to be realized but merely threatened. It has become part of our popular nomenclature to identify any horrific scenario that threatens humanity as apocalyptic, so much so that we talk about apocalyptic scenarios with nuclear arms, diseases, war, and the like. And while all such scenarios are tragic and frightening, they rarely rise to the level of apocalyptic because they deal with only the end of civilization or the threat of such an end while other aspects of the apocalyptic genre are entirely missing.

One might liken this critical tendency to the all-too-familiar search for Christ-figures in literature and film. Literary criticism was long plagued by the tendency to equate any sacrificial character in fiction to the sacrificial Christ. Thus, critics searched for and found Christ-figures everywhere and dubbed story after story as a "Christ story" or "Christ film." This tendency in literary criticism and film criticism is reductionistic, and one can find the same tendency in criticism directed at so-called apocalyptic films. Just because a film has a sacrificial character this does not necessarily make that character a Christ-figure, and just because a film has an end-of-the-world scenario this does not make that film an apocalyptic film. Such reductionism does not fully appreciate the intricacies of the apocalyptic tradition and is not helpful for theology, religious studies, or cultural criticism. It is at this point that religious studies and theology can serve to inform the popular appropriation of the apocalyptic label.

An example of this reductionism is the 1998 film *Armageddon* (Ostwalt 2003: 172–5). In this film, earth is threatened by destruction from an approaching asteroid of huge proportions. When it becomes clear that unless something is done, the asteroid will impact the earth and destroy life, a multinational group assembles and launches a mission to destroy the asteroid by planting a nuclear bomb in the interior of the asteroid itself. An unlikely hero leads the mission, he sacrifices his life to save earth, the asteroid is destroyed, and earth is saved. While the plot is predictable, it is interesting to note that the potential destruction is enough to include apocalyptic references, biblical language is invoked, and religious celebrations break out around the world when the disaster is averted. While the film has very little if anything to do with God or a theological concept of apocalypse, biblical and religious allusions abound. While fate produces the threat, and science and human heroism win the day, the filmmakers cannot escape a religious overlay. While the film is not apocalyptic given traditional definitions, the threat of world destruction is enough to invest it with apocalyptic allusions in popular culture.

Armageddon's title is lifted directly from the book of Revelation (16:14–16). Armageddon is referenced as the site of the final battle between good and evil that ushers in the apocalyptic age, leads to the ultimate and decisive defeat of evil by a sovereign God, and paves the way for the establishment of God's kingdom. Theologically, the reference to Armageddon is rich and suggests all of the above in the apocalyptic drama. Yet, as the film progresses, the viewer finds quickly that there is really very little connection to this biblical reference. Even if one accepts a very generic definition of Armageddon as a final and decisive battle, it stretches the imagination to think of blowing up an approaching asteroid as a battle rather than a technological challenge. There is no struggle with evil, no dark forces, no ultimate victory of goodness (although there is self-sacrifice), no kingdom of God, and not even an end of the world since the heroes in the film save earth. The title suggests apocalyptic battles and destruction and the plot implies the end of days, but in the end, the viewer is treated only to melodramatic heroism. Yet, this film, because it deals with a potential end-of-the-world scenario, is generally classified or understood as an apocalyptic film (e.g., "Disaster" 2007; Bendle 2005). This reductionism results from assuming apocalyptic content because of the title and end-of-the-world scenario, not from form or actual content.

Lack of divine agency

The second tendency grows out of the first popular tendency but reverses the reductionism. Instead of finding any apocalyptic theme and referring to the film as apocalyptic, the second tendency ignores one crucial apocalyptic theme and calls films apocalyptic anyway. The crucial theme I am referring to is reference to divine revelation and causation. The very term *apokalypsis* means revelation or unveiling, and in the tradition that gave apocalyptic its genesis and form, the revelation is a divine unveiling of the reality of God's complete and utter sovereignty. Eschatology is one aspect of this, but the crucial requirement is a divine revelation of God's ultimate control of all things including time, space, and justice. Some commentators ignore this characteristic of the tradition or choose to discount it and refer to films that might deal with other apocalyptic themes (justice, end of time, good versus evil, etc.) as apocalyptic even in the absence of divine revelation.

Perhaps ignoring this aspect of the apocalyptic drama is a development from a long secularizing trend in Western culture and is to be expected. However, if one is to treat the tradition honestly, one should at least acknowledge that films without divine revelation are a secularized or desacralized version of the apocalyptic drama and differ significantly from the traditional apocalyptic drama in this aspect. Thus, films without reference or the need of divine revelation and sovereignty are at best "secular apocalypses" and depart from traditional apocalypses in significant ways. I will, in fact, argue that such a genre exists in contemporary films dealing with end-of-the-world scenarios in the fourth and final trend in criticism of contemporary apocalyptic films.

The desacralization of the apocalypse (ignoring divine imperative) is not localized to film in our culture or studies. Popular culture tends to equate the concept of apocalyptic with anything that includes unimaginable or at least hard to imagine suffering. War zones are considered apocalyptic; often postmodern scenarios are described as apocalyptic; political revolutions are viewed as apocalyptic in their desire to abolish and create new worlds; destroyed natural landscapes are viewed as apocalyptic crisis; and perhaps science, technology, and science fiction promise at times to provide a new earth if not a new heaven. In a recent issue of the *Journal of the American Academy of Religion*, Robert Geraci published an article entitled, "Apocalyptic AI: Religion and the Promise of Artificial Intelligence." Geraci provides in this article an examination of the genre he calls "Apocalyptic AI" in which scientists and roboticists write idealistic literature based on the promises of science and artificial intelligence. Geraci argues that some of the hopes and characteristics of Jewish and Christian apocalyptic literature (namely the desire for a new heaven and "purified bodies" that grows out of alienation) are given scientific validity in Apocalyptic AI. The scientific hope is that individual consciousness can be combined with machine technology to create immortality. In Apocalyptic AI, evolution replaces God, and technology promises to provide the coming of a newly conceptualized kingdom and immortality (Geraci 2008: 138–40, 159). Extrapolating from Geraci's work, one might consider that expelling the supernatural from the apocalypse is a natural extension of secularization, and indeed, that seems to be the case in other areas of life as well.

The films *The Matrix* (1999) and *Contact* (1997) provide good examples as to how the supernatural is ignored in films that might be considered apocalyptic. In *Contact*, humankind is faced with its first encounter with alien intelligence, and while some characters in the movie view this encounter with scientific curiosity if not spiritual awe, others respond with political fear of annihilation by an alien civilization. The demonization of the alien brings the apocalyptic drama into the open. Yet, in this drama, science reigns supreme and seems reasonable while religion is portrayed as simplistic if not dangerous. *Contact* removes the apocalypse from the realm of religion and places it squarely within the domain of science as the way of knowledge best suited to handle the apocalyptic threat. *Contact* substitutes aliens for "the Other" (God) and science for religion, a complete secularization of the threat of humanity's annihilation (Ostwalt 2000: 2-3). In *The Matrix* a different dynamic takes place but once again illustrates the removal of the supernatural from the apocalyptic drama. In *The Matrix*, a post-apocalyptic world is masked by an alternative and virtual reality constructed by computers and machines. The hero of the story, Neo, learns of the illusion and comes to "unveil" or "reveal" the virtual world to others (Bendle 2005: 13). In *The Matrix*, the revelatory element of the unveiling is retained, but the one who receives the revelation and unveils the truth is not the supernatural but the human hero, Neo. Divine sovereignty in this film is replaced by calculating machines and illusion, while the hero takes on messianic, but human, characteristics – God has been replaced by the machine and humans.

Classification approaches

A third, significant tendency in dealing with so-called apocalyptic films classifies by dividing and subdividing films into categories under the broad rubric of apocalyptic. Both formal studies and informal criticisms have been dedicated to this system of classification in the attempt to be more inclusive of films that might fit the broad category of apocalyptic. Once again, such an attempt, while helpful for organization purposes, often ignores the theological or religious elements of the apocalyptic drama in favor of ease of identification. We see this tendency first in the uncritical attempt to classify the apocalyptic vision in contemporary films, usually by labeling "apocalyptic" all that is dark or otherworldly and threatening. The internet, for example, has websites dedicated to so-called apocalyptic or doomsday films such as *Dawn of the Dead* (2004) and *Planet of the Apes* (1968) (e.g., "Disaster" 2007; "Apocalyptic Movies" n.d.; "Doomsday Film" n.d.). The cultural tendency to see such movies as part of the apocalyptic genre is dependent on the acceptance of an uncritical classification system. Almost anything that has dark, supernatural components or end-of-the-world implications is included as apocalyptic even if it is perhaps more rightly categorized as a subgenre of science fiction or horror.

One can find a variety of attempts to categorize. Some divide the apocalyptic drama between apocalyptic (process or means of the end of civilization) and post-apocalyptic (setting following the end of civilization as we know it). Others include virtually any doomsday film or disaster film where doom is ultimately averted. This broadens the categorization to include science fiction, horror, war, and even environmental films into the apocalyptic category. Such broad categorization of the apocalypse includes zombie films and alien films and makes no attempt to differentiate between such genres and a more traditional apocalyptic story except perhaps for differentiating who or what the agents of terror or redemption happen to be. One blog even created an "apocalypse scale" grading the level of threat to humanity or earth. While the scale is quite good in categorizing contemporary assumptions about threat to human existence, it nonetheless ignores the critical assumptions of the apocalyptic genre. The scale, from 0 to 7, ranges from "Regional catastrophe," to "Human die-back," "Civilization extinction," "Human extinction – engineered or natural," "Biosphere extinction," "Planetary extinction," and "Planetary elimination" ("Disaster" 2007). The scale, posted by "Disaster," is helpful in creating a level of disaster in the movies, but the scale does not depend on divine agency or even imply divine agency. This takes us back to tendency number two, the secular trend toward removing any notion of divine revelation from our vocabulary about the apocalypse. This makes sense to the extent that apocalyptic notions have been trivialized in popular culture. While helpful, perhaps, in classifying disaster movies, the scale is not very helpful from a theological perspective or a critical religious studies perspective because it trivializes or even ignores the importance or substance and complexity of the traditional apocalyptic worldview, that is, the sacred worldview of divine sovereignty.

A more critical attempt to classify and categorize can be found in some formal studies on apocalyptic films and can be very helpful in coming to grips with the essentials of apocalyptic works. In general, when classification is based on critical analysis with reference to either theology or religious studies, the categorization helps to differentiate the film that is traditionally apocalyptic from those that depart from the genre. Reference to two books will suffice in illustrating this point. Charles Mitchell's *A Guide to Apocalyptic Cinema* (2001) demonstrates the complexity of trying to produce a classification system for the genre. For starters, his definition of apocalyptic films is reduced to a plot that includes a threat to human extinction. He then classifies apocalyptic films by the origin of those threats. The categories, based on this assumption, are religious and supernatural (traditional approach), celestial collision, solar disruption, nuclear war, disease, alien intrusion, or scientific causation. A second book, John Martens' *The End of the World: The Apocalyptic Imagination in Film and Television* (2003), uses categories such as traditional apocalypses, alien apocalypses, post-apocalyptic dystopias, and technological apocalypses. He therefore distinguishes between the traditional religious apocalypse and other types, and he uses theological analysis even when dealing with the nontraditional categories. In both classification schemes, the multiplicity of categories can become confusing.

The point I would make about this third approach to understanding apocalyptic films is that numerous categories can be established with or without reference to the traditional standards of the genre. This can be helpful but it can also be uncritical and confusing. So while all three approaches outlined here have been helpful in ways that have brought the study of religion and film into the consciousness of popular culture, none is without its difficulties. In what follows, I will try to address these difficulties by suggesting another type of classification that avoids the problems of overly complex or broad categorization (third approach), the tendency to hunt for and identify themes that seem to be apocalyptic but might not necessarily make for an apocalyptic film (first approach), and the tendency to ignore the secularization of the apocalypse (second approach).

Typology: two types of apocalyptic

A fourth approach, which I suggest elsewhere and reiterate here, might be seen as yet another classification system. However, I posit only two types or categories. The reason for suggesting there are two types of apocalyptic films in popular movies is not simply to classify but rather to point out a fundamental worldview difference between the traditional apocalyptic view and what might be considered a secularized view of end-of-the-world imaginative works. In articles and books, I have tried to demonstrate that popular culture has developed an apocalyptic imagination that while based on traditional Jewish and Christian models has departed in significant ways from the traditional genre. In particular, while contemporary movies with an eschatological focus incorporate some of the "image and symbolism from the Jewish and Christian apocalyptic dramas, most are not apocalyptic per se in the sense that Jewish and Christian apocalypses 'unveil' or 'reveal' God's sovereignty" (Ostwalt 2003: 170).

For the purpose of studying apocalyptic films, I suggest limiting the classification of films as apocalyptic to those that fall into one of two groups: (1) films are apocalyptic if they follow or respond to the traditional form/pattern of the religious apocalyptic genre (Jewish and Christian apocalyptic texts); (2) films are apocalyptic in another sense if most of the traditional form is retained but without the sacred content or reference to sacred agency (thus the traditional apocalyptic form is secularized). Given this categorization, the film *Left Behind* (2000) would be a traditional apocalypse while the movie *The Matrix* would be a secular apocalypse. The rest of the essay defines the two types of apocalyptic films in contemporary movies and provides some examples to illustrate the types.

The traditional apocalyptic film is religious in content and is based on the Jewish and Christian genre with all its characteristics. The traditional apocalyptic story maintains several characteristics that were mentioned earlier: such works are characterized by dreams, visions, and symbols that unveil the events associated with the end of the world. This revelation is supernatural and demonstrates to humankind the sovereignty of a divine being. The consummation of history is accompanied by battles between good and evil, ushers in God's kingdom, and results in the destruction or punishment of evil and the elevation of the good to righteousness. Sovereign justice is a major component of the drama. Underpinning this dualistic cataclysm is the assertion and promise of God's ultimate and final sovereignty, and it is divine intervention into the apocalyptic drama that allows the end of history to be meaningful and just. A vision of the end of the world without a sovereign reality beyond the world results in nihilism or perhaps a world ruled by chance, and this is the outcome the apocalyptic drama wishes to avoid. In fact, most apocalyptic literature arises out of precarious situations and infuses those situations with meaning based on the idea of a sovereign protector of the righteous. It should be noted that while films that are traditional apocalyptic films maintain these characteristics, they are not necessarily biblical in a literal sense. For example, the traditional apocalyptic film might depict the events of Revelation or other traditional apocalyptic texts yet fictionalize these events in ways to make them understandable or relevant. *The Seventh Sign* (1988) and *The Rapture* (1991) provide good examples of this.

The secular apocalypse differs from the traditional in several key respects. What follows is based on my work on this topic elsewhere (Ostwalt 2003: 170–2; 2000: 2). First, the secular apocalypse often borrows images and themes or symbols from the traditional apocalypse, but the notion of a supernatural "unveiling" of supernatural sovereignty is missing. Second, secular apocalyptic dramas often contemporize evil through the genre of science fiction so that the sources of potential destruction are ones familiar to contemporary audiences. Nuclear weapons, global warming, viruses, and aliens not only function as the evil enemy of humankind but also replace God as the causative factor of destruction. Whereas in the traditional apocalypse, God destroys evil in the process of consummation, in the secular apocalypse it is often the "evil" that threatens to destroy the world. The identification of evil as "natural" rather than "supernatural," the absence of a supernatural struggle, and the revised role of evil mark major departures from the traditional apocalypse. Third, in the secular apocalypse, the end of civilization and humanity is avoided or at least the attempt to avoid complete destruction often dominates the plot. A hero arises to save the world or a portion of it. Again, in the traditional apocalypse, the end is unavoidable and, in fact, welcomed by the righteous community and initiated by the heroic divinity. The secular apocalyptic represents a complete reversal of the traditional apocalyptic drama's fatalistic acceptance of the end by supernatural causation. Finally, and this is implied previously, the secular apocalypse is also a humanistic or anthropocentric apocalypse. God has been replaced by human effort – often in the cause of the events bringing about the end and generally in the attempts to avoid the end.

In this classification, the emphasis is not so much on what causes the end or how destruction takes place but rather on the desacralization of the apocalyptic drama in the secular version: the traditional apocalypse retains an "unveiling" of divine agency while the secular apocalypse replaces that with an "uncovering" of human ascendency and heroism. With this distinction made, we can view and analyze films about the end with theological sensitivity and critical acuity for the relationship between religion and contemporary films. Perhaps more than anything, the distinctions made here between these two tendencies in apocalyptic films tell us more about our sense of ourselves and place in history.

The traditional apocalypse in film

The traditional apocalypse comes in different varieties but they share a certain form and content. Film is perhaps the medium perfectly suited for dealing with a topic like apocalyptic stories, with its multimedia character and combination of sensory elements. Film can bring the apocalyptic drama to life with stunning visual effects and effective aural stimuli to give the drama impact. Some of these traditional apocalypses are designed to thrill and entertain as films from the science fiction and horror genres are. Others are designed for this as well as to carry an explicit theological message, usually an evangelical Christian eschatological vision. Following are examples of quite different films that fit the general description of traditional apocalypse.

The Seventh Sign represents a traditional apocalyptic movie in its attempt to combine Jewish and Christian apocalyptic imagery and folk tradition (such as the legend of the wandering Jew) in a creative telling of events surrounding the potential end of the world (Ostwalt 1995: 59–60). The film, despite ending with human effort thwarting the divine plan to end the world, maintains many of the traditional characteristics of the apocalyptic genre: there are signs, references to apocalyptic texts like Joel and the book of Revelation, realization of prophetic events from apocalyptic texts, a strong dualism, supernatural agency, and a messianic deliverer, to name a few. And even though the end is averted, this occurs through an application of supernatural procla-mations – the supernatural element in the film is present from beginning to end and allows the film to retain its traditional apocalyptic character.

The Rapture also takes its title from the Christian apocalyptic tradition and, like *The Seventh Sign*, retains its connection to the tradition. The "rapture" is a concept associated in general with dispensationalism, developed by John Nelson Darby (1800–82). According to Darby, there are a series of "dispensations" or "ages" that mark God's relation to history. These ages will culminate with the advent of God's kingdom and the "millennium" when Christ will rule for a thousand years on earth. According to some dispensationalist views, faithful Christians will be "raptured" or removed from earth prior to the period of the "Tribulation" (Ahlstrom 1972: 808–12). Dispensationalism generally develops 1 Thessalonians 4:17 and is popular among many evangelical Christians while remaining controversial among biblical scholars (e.g., Rossing 2005; Thigpen 2001). The event of the rapture is portrayed in the film *Left Behind*, the movie based on the best-selling novel by the same name. In *Left Behind*, when the rapture occurs, people disappear instantaneously and chaos occurs as events cascade toward the end of time as foretold in Revelation. In the film *The Rapture*, the term once again invokes the apocalyptic premise of the Christian tradition, but this time the term might also carry a more general sense of religious and spiritual ecstasy that results from or leads to insanity. This film does not portray the apocalypse but rather the consequences of obsessively embracing the traditional apocalyptic worldview.

The opening scene of *The Rapture* scans a nondescript, colorless office cubicle space where the protagonist (Sharon) sits and answers the phone until her shift is over. Her boring, meaningless job is balanced by a swinging lifestyle as she and a male friend go bar cruising looking for sexual encounters with other couples. Sharon is obviously searching for some meaning in her life and, in a vulnerable state, she overhears a religious discussion among her co-workers and is visited by missionaries, who witness to her that she must be saved because they live in the last days. During one of her sexual encounters, she becomes enamored with a tattoo on the back of a female partner. She learns that the tattoo pictures a dream about a pearl, and she confronts her co-workers about the dream. Sharon begins to put all her experiences and her life frustration together, and she starts to find God and some spiritual meaning to overcome the emptiness in her life. Sharon's search leads her to a group of visionaries who listen to the apocalyptic prophecies of a young boy. The rest of the film follows Sharon's life as she marries, has a child, and becomes increasingly obsessed with her otherworldly apocalyptic faith. When her husband is killed, she is comforted by her faith in the Second Coming and rapture, and convinces her daughter that she will be reunited with her father. Sharon falls further into her apocalyptic obsession, and she and her daughter go to the desert to await the Second Coming and reunification with her husband. As they wait and increasingly fall into despair, Sharon kills her daughter so she can be reunited with her father. The film ends with a series of apocalyptic visions including trumpets, the horsemen of the apocalypse, and other apocalyptic images and visions. The film ends ironically when Sharon refuses her visions and is refused entry into heaven. The film suggests the danger of an obsessive personality fixating on the book of Revelation. A profoundly disturbing film that portrays a perverse picture of apocalyptically oriented Christianity, *The Rapture* attempts to portray the apocalyptic worldview and the ultimate consequences of embracing such a worldview. But the film is a traditional apocalypse in that the worldview of its protagonist is based on the Christian apocalyptic genre. This film, while staying true to the genre, points out the failure of an uncritical, otherworldly, and apocalyptic worldview.

Since the late 1990s, a series of films have emerged based partly on Dispensationalist Evangelical views of eschatology and apocalypticism. Films like *The Omega Code* (1999), *Megiddo: The Omega Code 2* (2001), and the *Left Behind* (2000, 2005) movies attempt to dramatize biblical apocalyptic texts by placing them in contemporary contexts, a strategy to make the particular eschatological vision relevant to a modern audience. The filmmakers of this genre admit to creative license but also claim to remain true to the biblical texts (Nelson 2001: 353). In addition, there is a sense in which these films are produced as a way of communicating the Christian message, a particular version of the Christian message, but the Christian message all the same (Nelson 2001: 314). Such films as *Left Behind* have tapped into the power of film to dramatize the apocalypse in contemporary fashion.

Left Behind: World at War (2005) is the third in the series of movies based on the *Left Behind* novels. The stories, originally written by Tim LaHaye and Jerry Jenkins, are based on the concept in popular apocalyptic scenarios that true Christians will be raptured from the earth before the events leading to the end of the world. These events are based on a particular way of reading biblical apocalyptic texts and include tribulations for those left behind after the rapture, the rise to power of the Antichrist, and the ultimate battle between good and evil, Armageddon. The *Left Behind* movies provide a contemporary interpretation of Revelation and other apocalyptic texts to create riveting dramas. I categorize them as traditional apocalyptic movies, not because they are biblical since they take liberties in providing the biblical texts with contemporary settings, but because they include the various characteristics discussed earlier of the traditional apocalyptic genre, including the apocalypse unfolding as part of a divine plan with supernatural causes and effects. As with *The Omega Code* and *Left Behind*, this film uses the apocalyptic drama to espouse evangelical values and teachings.

Left Behind: World at War opens with a reference to the rapture that has already occurred and has dramatically changed the world. In the months following that event, one man has risen to power and has established the Global Community. Nicolae Carpathia has led the world to "peace," convincing one country at a time to give up its sovereignty in the effort to create a world community. The President of the United

States becomes one of many who is taken in by Carpathia's charisma and idealism. By the time this movie opens, the Global Community has created a hellish world for Christians, where the Church is outlawed and underground. In this world, the Bible is considered hate literature and Christians are considered terrorists. Carpathia has developed biological weapons and is secretly using the agents to poison Bibles and, thereby, Christians. Meanwhile, Carpathia also plans to attack the United States with weapons he has collected in the name of peace. Carpathia embodies evil in this drama and is none other than the Antichrist mentioned in Revelation.

After being born again, the President, now an agent of God, is determined to thwart Carpathia. The battle between good and evil approaches as the two confront one another and the President is able to call an air strike on Carpathia's command center. While Carpathia is not killed, his plans are delayed and the implication is that God's power will ultimately prevail over evil. The film ends with Carpathia emerging unscathed from the flames of his destroyed headquarters, and even though the Global Community is in shambles, one gets the feeling that a final confrontation is but a short time away. *Left Behind: World at War* does not end with the final battle, but it sets the stage, and many who know this particular version of the apocalyptic drama recognize the consummation that is to come, based as it is on the sacred worldview of the Bible and biblical stories. But what happens if this sacred worldview of the Bible fails to resonate with viewers? For them, what is "left behind" is the secular apocalypse.

The secular apocalypse in film

The secular apocalypse in film also comes in a variety of forms and is often the subject of attempts at categorization. Secular apocalypses generally differ from traditional ones in the exclusion of the supernatural as a means of agency for the end of time. With no divine agency to rely upon, stories about the end of time turn to a variety of means to the end: aliens, disease, chance, natural disasters, and the like. What normally occurs in these disaster films is that humankind replaces God in the apocalyptic drama in that humanity becomes responsible either for the destruction of the earth or the salvation of it or both. This anthropocentric element is the key feature of the secular apocalyptic drama, yet most critical attempts at categorization focus on the origin of the threat or on the setting after destruction. Here, I am more concerned with the commonality of human control than the diversity of agents leading to disaster. Many films have followed this pattern. For example, two recent films from 2007, *I Am Legend* and *Sunshine*, illustrate the secular apocalypse. *I Am Legend* makes disease the agent of the apocalyptic drama – humanity is threatened, if not destroyed, by a mutated virus that was created by a scientist to cure cancer. In the spirit of *12 Monkeys* (1995), *I Am Legend* works on the premise that humankind itself might bring about the apocalypse, or something akin to it, by attempting to play God and by usurping the role of divine prerogative. In *Sunshine*, the apocalypse is promised by a natural cause – a dying sun; however, human action prevents apocalyptic consummation. Another example, *Waterworld* (1995), also views human agency as key to apocalyptic threats to the world as an uncontrolled greenhouse effect changes life on earth and threatens the very continuation of life. However, in all these cases, human and technological ingenuity provide the key to avoiding apocalypse. In the secular apocalypse, it is human beings and not divine will that controls the end.

Sunshine

The sun, Sol, worshiped by many through the ages, makes life as we know it possible. We are perhaps connected to it in ways that we do not fully appreciate. My scientist friend once told me the story of a student who had existential terrors after learning from class about the life cycle of stars and, in particular, that the sun would eventually die. Even though the event would not affect the student, the mere conceptualization of human extinction brought on the angst. The death of the sun and the extinction of life on earth is the focus of the film *Sunshine*. The setting is 2057 and the sun of earth's solar system is dying. Earth is locked in deep winter and the extinction of all life is a certainty with the death of the sun. But there is a plan. A group of astronauts and scientists travel on a mission to save the sun by delivering a nuclear bomb to the sun that will, theoretically, reinvigorate the sun and prevent or delay its death. In general, the movie is unconvincing, the plot predictable but muddled with numerous plot twists, and the scientific basis supporting the plot is not believable. Nevertheless, visually the movie is a treat, filmed with spectacular contrasts of light and color, scale and perspective. But despite the film's failures and successes, for the purposes of this treatment of apocalyptic films, the movie illustrates the basics of the secular apocalypse better than most.

The end of the world seems certain in this film, but the supernatural element is missing either as agent of the end or as solution to survival. Instead, the end is coming about as a consequence of the natural evolution of the solar system. However, human ingenuity, heroism, and technological promise take on the challenge of the unthinkable, creating a mock big bang and a new star. In other words, this secular apocalypse puts science and humanity in the role of creator, thus completely replacing the divine in the order of the universe. Here humanity attempts to thwart the apocalypse by bringing a new creation into order; humanity has replaced the gods, and this story represents a complete secularization of divine sovereignty when it comes to time, space, creation, and apocalypse. The movie takes the viewer ever closer to the source of life as the star ship *Icarus 2* approaches the sun, just as science promises to take us ever closer to the origin of life by unveiling an understanding of the Big Bang. This apocalyptic drama is based on the death of that which gives life and the attempt to create again the source of life.

The formula for the secular apocalypse is followed faithfully, and the heroes of the *Icarus 2* mission save humanity through technology and self-sacrifice. The heroes become divine creators by harnessing the power to create and destroy in the surreal reaches of deep space. They observe the increasingly intense light of the sun and are profoundly affected by it, either receiving some enlightenment or revelation of a higher reality, or falling into insanity. Perhaps the enlightenment itself leads to insanity, as seems to have been the case for the original *Icarus* mission. The *Icarus 2* crew discovers that the original *Icarus* crew failed to deliver its payload and they also discover evidence that the original crew sabotaged its own mission. The Captain from the original *Icarus* mission (Captain Pinbacker) sabotaged the first mission, somehow survived the years in space, makes his way onto the *Icarus 2*, and is intent on thwarting *Icarus 2* precisely, it seems, because he believes the mission to save the sun goes against the divine will for the world to end. Pinbacker believes that God wants the world destroyed. Since Pinbacker is insane, his idea that God wants to bring the world to an end is an insane idea. In the end, Pinbacker fails, the *Icarus 2* mission succeeds (although all the crew die), and the secular apocalypse creates a new world, a new sun. And if one wants to push the secular apocalypse in this film to its logical conclusion, human will wins out over divine will. The sun rises because of human will, and a new heaven and new earth rise with it.

Waterworld

Instead of a dying sun that threatens to freeze the world and ultimately engulf it, *Waterworld* portrays a world in which global warming leads to melted polar icecaps, rising sea levels, and the loss of dry land – a world where dry land is but a mythic memory. In this film, a portion of humanity has survived the modern-day flood and has adapted to life on water, the new world. This new world vision is post-apocalyptic since the disaster has already destroyed most of the earth. *Waterworld* illustrates the secular apocalypse well because it is human activity that has led to the destruction of the world, but it is also human will that continues on in spite of the end of the world. In this inundated world of the future, the new earth represents a place and time of trial and tribulation brought on by human activity. But what drives the story is not so much survival in the new world but rather searching for and finding paradise beyond the world of water – a new heaven, dry land. Throughout the movie, it is not clear whether dry land exists or whether its existence is mythic. Yet, when dry land is found, humans are clearly at home in this new heaven and earth, the remnant of what human beings had nearly destroyed.

As a secular apocalypse, *Waterworld* portrays the apocalyptic scenario in nonsacred terms and in ways clearly understood by contemporary society. The destruction of the world is not a divinely caused event, nor is deliverance to paradise. The apocalypse occurs as a direct result of human activity; the apocalypse is self-destruction. But the deliverance from self-destruction also seems to lie with humanity. In this case, a little girl, Enola, leads the way to a rediscovery of dry land, paradise, and a new start (Ostwalt 2003: 177–80). The secular apocalypse raises humanity to the level of God by allowing humanity to initiate the apocalypse, makes paradise (a new heaven) a rediscovery of "earth" rather than an otherworldly heaven, and gives humanity the primary role in bringing about paradise. All the elements of the sacred, traditional apocalypse are humanized and secularized in the secular apocalypse.

Conclusion

The end of time and space, the end of the earth, the end of humanity – these are all prevalent themes in contemporary, popular movies. Often in criticism, both formal and informal, these themes have been used to classify a movie as apocalyptic. There is a need to provide some critical guidelines for understanding the complexity of many of the films that deal with these themes. I have tried to outline some of the ways critics have attempted to deal with the ever increasing number of films that, while crossing genres, have in common some of the characteristics popular culture has come to know as apocalyptic. In this chapter, I suggest a way of simplifying the growing complexity of categories in dealing with apocalyptic films by suggesting that most of these films can be understood as either a traditional apocalypse or a secular apocalypse. Not only does this provide a classification system, but more importantly, this classification system allows us some understanding of how our contemporary secular worldview differs from an ancient sacred worldview.

By recognizing the contrasts between ancient and modern worldviews as well as contrasts between how traditional religionists and contemporary secularists perceive the end of the world, we can avoid the pitfalls of uncritical approaches to watching films that are categorized as apocalyptic. Critical understandings of both worldviews and approaches allow traditional and secular values to provide correctives to excesses of either worldview in isolation. Traditional worldviews might devalue the environment or the world by a focus on a heavenly kingdom while secular worldviews might overvalue human effort and science. But if we allow traditional and secular worldviews to enter into dialogue, we can more clearly see what we value and how we can preserve what we value. By understanding the difference between the traditional apocalypse and the secular apocalypse, we can also understand what we fear, whether supernatural or natural, and in what we have faith, be it God or technology. Perhaps the movies can help us in this quest.

Bibliography

Ahlstrom, S. (1972) *A Religious History of the American People*, New Haven, CT: Yale University Press.

"Apocalyptic Movies" (n.d.) Online. Available HTTP: <http://blog.apoclaypse.org/apocalyptic-movies/> (accessed April 2008).

Bendle, M. (2005) "The Apocalyptic Imagination and Popular Culture," *Journal of Popular Culture* (Fall). Online. Available HTTP: <http://www.usask.ca/relst/jrpc/art11-apocalypticimagination.html> 1–16 (accessed April 2008).

Deacy, C. (2008) "Heaven, Hell, and the Sweet Hereafter: Theological Perspectives on Eschatology and Film," in C. Deacy and G. Ortiz (eds) *Theology and Film: Challenging the Sacred/Secular Divide*, Malden, MA: Blackwell.

"Disaster" (2007) "Apocalypse in 7 Not-so-easy Steps." Online. Available HTTP: <http://www.futurist-movies.com/blog/index.php/2007/01/24> (accessed April 2008).

"Doomsday Film" (n.d.) Online. Available HTTP: <http://en.wikipedia.org/wiki/Doomsday_film> (accessed April 2008).

Geraci, R. (2008) "Apocalyptic AI: Religion and the Promise of Artificial Intelligence," *Journal of the American Academy of Religion* (March): 138–66.

Martens, J. (2003) *The End of the World: The Apocalyptic Imagination in Film and Television*, Winnipeg: Shillingford.

Mitchell, C. (2001) *A Guide to Apocalyptic Cinema*, Westport, CT: Greenwood Press.

"Movies/Scenes Representing Apocalyptic Themes." Online. Available HTTP: <http://www.textweek.com/movies/apocalyptic.htm> (accessed April 2008).

Nelson, J. (2001) "God Is On Line One," *Gentlemen's Quarterly* (March): 310–15, 352–3.

Ostwalt, C. (1995) "Hollywood and Armageddon: Apocalyptic Themes in Recent Cinematic Presentation," in J. Martin and C. Ostwalt (eds) *Screening the Sacred: Religion, Myth, and Ideology in Popular American Film*, Boulder, CO: Westview: 55–63.

—— (2000) "Armageddon at the Millennial Dawn," *Journal of Religion and Film*. Online. Available at HTTP: <http://www.unomaha.edu/jrf/armagedd.htm> 1–6.

—— (2003) *Secular Steeples: Popular Culture and the Religious Imagination*, Harrisburg, PA: Trinity Press.

Rossing, B. (2005) *The Rapture Exposed: The Message of Hope in the Book of Revelation*, New York: Basic Books.

Thigpen, P. (2001) *The Rapture Trap: A Catholic Response to End Times Fever*, West Chester, PA: Ascension Press.

Filmography

Armageddon (1998, dir. M. Bay)
Contact (1997, dir. R. Zemeckis)
Dawn of the Dead (2004, dir. Z. Snyder)
Defending Your Life (1991, dir. A. Brooks)
Ghost (1990, dir. J. Zucker)
I Am Legend (2007, dir. F. Lawrence)
Left Behind (2000, dir. V. Sarin)
Left Behind: World at War (2005, dir. C. Baxley)
The Matrix (1999, dir. A. and L. Wachowski)
Megiddo: The Omega Code 2 (2001, dir. B. Trenchard-Smith)
The Omega Code (1999, dir. R. Marcarelli)
Planet of the Apes (1968, dir. F. Schaffner)
The Rapture (1991, dir. M. Tolkin)
The Seventh Sign (1988, dir. C. Schultz)
Sunshine (2007, dir. D. Boyle)
12 Monkeys (1995, dir. T. Gilliam)
Waterworld (1995, dir. K. Reynolds)
What Dreams May Come (1998, dir. V. Ward)

21

HEROES AND SUPERHEROES

Robert Jewett and John Lawrence

Hero worship exists forever, and everywhere ... it extends from divine adoration down to the lowest practical regions of life.

Carlyle (1907: 281–2)

Introduction

To sustain their faiths, world religions often celebrate stories of heroic testing, expecting that sympathetic audiences will emulate heroic acts. Compared to the early appearance of motion pictures, none of the older forms of religious art emerged with such cheerful expectations for transforming effects. Thomas Edison forecast in 1907 that moving images would conquer significant evils: "It will wipe out narrow-minded prejudices which are founded on ignorance, it will create a feeling of sympathy and a desire to help down-trodden peoples of the earth, and it will give new ideals to be followed" and would lead to "the moral advance of the great masses of people" (Edison 2001: 39–40).

Edison was not alone in promoting film as spiritually transforming technology. The screen image stimulated ministers and laypersons of several US Protestant denominations to capture cinema's uniquely persuasive imagery for tasks of instruction and inspiration. Reverend Herbert Jump declared: "Joseph and Esther and Moses and Paul and Jesus are better known to the theater-goers today than they ever were before, thanks to Mr. Edison's invention. Ere long we shall give our Sunday School scholars the same advantages in biblical instruction that are now offered to the patron of the nearest 'Pastime' or 'Bijou'" (Jump 2001: 70). The enthusiastic world responses of religious audiences to Mel Gibson's enormous box office success *The Passion of the Christ* (2004) indicate that such hopes are still alive.

These fervent prophecies raise tantalizing questions. Has film art given impetus to a wider and deeper awareness of historic heroism? And how might heroic imagery on the screen enable heroic behavior in the viewer's life? A full century of film history offers a fascinating window for such questions. Here we pursue answers through these steps: (1) defining types of religious heroism; (2) describing technology's influence on heroic portrayals; (3) analyzing some significant films; (4) estimating film's success in achieving moral changes envisioned by early advocates of film; (5) placing filmed heroism within frames of debate about idolatry (worshiping false gods) and iconoclasm (the rejection of those false gods). In this we will focus on films that demonstrate most clearly the reworking of the myth of the hero along distinctively American lines.

We hope to persuade our readers that heroic films can convey insights that form conduct. Yet we are cautious about the overall influence of film. Applying Marshall McLuhan's notion "the medium is the message," we note that corporations often market their religiously themed entertainments as celebrations of the film industry's technology, budgets, shooting locations, and stars. Moreover, Hollywood filmmakers often give pious garb to reigning versions of American civil religion. Such expressions of national pride and commercial purpose, we suggest, are the idolatries of filmed religious heroism that help explain why cinema has sometimes aroused theological scorn or church-organized iconoclasms. We nonetheless maintain that film's apparent power to touch human hearts ensures continuing optimism, even among the critically sophisticated, about film's ability to prompt religiously insightful behavior.

Types of religious heroism

Within motion pictures' dramatic frames, protagonists typically express ethical goals and virtues esteemed by audience members. In acting out those values, they sacrifice themselves to advance the welfare of others. For those tempted to interpret religion broadly as the effort to establish life goals and norms for conduct, it follows that virtually every dramatic film depicts religious heroism. Film scholar Melanie J. Wright sensibly remarks that it is hard "to conceive of a narrative film devoid of *any* trace of the religious impulses that underpin the cultural construction of feelings, institutions, relationships" (Wright 2007: 7; italics in original). Yet, to affirm that every dramatic film contains the religious-heroic invites the hazard of overlooking some distinctive subjects explored within historic faith traditions; it also discourages selecting a coherent group of films. Therefore we limit our treatment to a few titles of continuing significance that deal with familiar religions.

Religious films reveal a variety of heroic types. Those that we here call initiatory heroines and heroes of a faith tradition are historically celebrated founders, disciples, missionaries, saints, spiritual innovators, martyrs, and crusaders. Those we designate ordinary heroines and heroes of faithfulness are uncanonized, unsung figures exemplary in their commitment; some carry the names of historically recorded individuals while many are fictional. The protagonists of superheroic fantasy are marked by extraordinary capabilities for moral discernment and physical strength. They precisely control extra-human powers to punish evildoers while protecting the innocent. These categories are not mutually exclusive, because initiatory heroes and heroines are often rendered through a mythic styling borrowed from the superheroic narratives. And the superhero films often use a dual identity theme in which an ordinary life, like that of Clark Kent, is despised by the unknowing. As we discuss a few leading examples from each category, we will also mention some perspectives suited to clarifying their religious significance. Affecting every category of heroic portrayal has been film technology itself, which is crucial to offering an experience that engages mind and emotion.

Cinematic technology and heroic portrayal

Early developments in photography popularized realistic, fine-grained imagery. Later in the century flexible, celluloid film stock permitted moving frames to capture and to replay motion. Close-focusing and telephoto lenses permitted camera artists to present the actor's face in isolation and thus to intensify emotional expression. Early in the twentieth century, composite imagery, color, and stereophonic sound enriched the cinematic experience. By the century's closing decades, computer-generated images could produce synthetic characters and objects that achieved onscreen physical parity with ordinary things and people. This evolution for narratives of religious heroism can be illustrated by several innovative productions.

From the Manger to the Cross (1912), an early film adhering to words from the New Testament Gospels, was a breakthrough for the representation of Jesus. No longer bound by the limitations of mere painting or statuary, Jesus (Robert Henderson-Bland) could be shown moving about Palestine, recruiting disciples, performing miracles, and speaking to crowds. Reflecting both film's limits and scripture's elevated cultural status in that era, the "voice" of the screen-silent Jesus consisted of inter-title New Testament verses accompanied by chapter and verse citation (Figs 21.1, 21.2). Earlier film's inability to capture motion smoothly meant that Jesus performs a slow

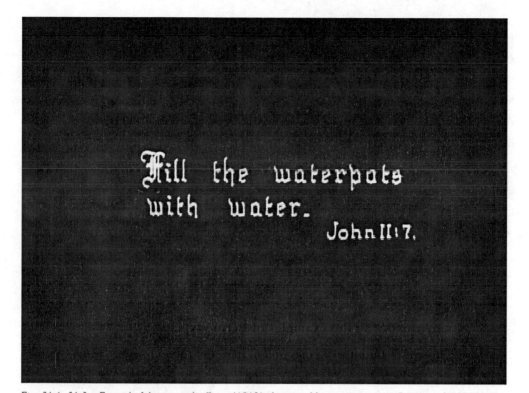

Figs 21.1, 21.2 *From the Manger to the Cross* (1912) alternated between screens of verse and rather static images of actors. The inter-title quotes John 2:7 just before we see Jesus standing beside the pots. Courtesy Kalem Company.

pantomime that grants the Gospel texts an onscreen authority roughly equal to that of Jesus himself, whose silent gestures illustrate its words. This impression is confirmed by a *New York Times* article titled "Jesus in Moving Pictures," which reported religious controversy associated with the British screening of the film. Against those who decried "the suitability of such a sacred theme for cinematograph purposes," defenders contended "that it was no more irreverent than the use of sacred subjects in art and was likely to bring home to people the beauty of the Bible's teachings" (1912: C3).

A mere ten years later, another biblical story, Cecil B. DeMille's *The Ten Commandments* (1923), displayed film's ability to present a fuller sensory experience of miraculous heroic action. The sets and costumes were opulently crafted and the crowd scenes convincingly staged. The *New York Times* review "Remarkable Spectacle" exulted that "it is probable that no more wonderful spectacle has ever been put before the public in shadow-form" (1923: 8). Telling the story of the Israelites' liberation by Moses and their wandering toward Mt. Sinai, DeMille enhanced the heroic aspects with surprising special effects and a music track. The Red Sea parted for the Israelites at the command of Moses, and then engulfed the attacking pursuers; Yahweh's words on the tablets at Mt. Sinai were inscribed with fiery tendrils accompanied by smoke and orchestral sounds. Moses (Theodore Roberts), speechless except through the scriptural and faux-scriptural inter-titles, was a towering, muscular white-haired and bearded man who physically dominated his scenes. Retrospectively, we can see that this Moses presaged that future Bible characters would be more than conveyers of prophetic wisdom.

That potential was fulfilled in films such as DeMille's 1956 remake of *The Ten Commandments* and in the faith-themed *Star Wars: Episode IV – A New Hope* (1977). Both films received Special Effects Oscars, and in each film the powers of heroic action were amplified by advancing technologies of illusion. Memorable scenes of *The Ten Commandments* occur when Moses (Charlton Heston) commands his shepherd's staff to become a serpent that swallows the rival serpents of the pharaoh Rameses (Yul Brynner). Moses' threatening confrontations with the pharaoh also bring a vaporous green plague that crawls along the streets of Egypt, spreading death and killing Rameses' own son. More remarkable advances for magical representation come in *Star Wars*, with Luke Skywalker (Mark Hamill) featured in stunning aerial fight scenes and in battles with humming light sabers. In the wake of *Star Wars*' world success, realistically rendered miraculous powers for superheroes in human bodies became routine in large-budget films.

Film examples of heroic types

Initiatory heroes and heroines of the faith

While all religions have founders, disciples, martyrs, and saints, not all have been depicted in notable films. For example, St. Paul, St. Augustine, and Martin Luther are major influences on Christianity, yet they remain absent from the most acclaimed and widely seen films. The institutions of Islam have exerted discipline to prevent the representation of Muhammad. The depiction of Jesus was banned in British films from 1912 until after the Second World War, and a special license was required for the exhibition of DeMille's 1927 *King of Kings* (Telford 1997: 130). Thereafter dozens of Jesus films were created, giving rise to entire books that describe differing approaches to his heroic character. There have been fifty-three films on Joan of Arc (Spoto 2007: 30) and thirty-three on Moses (International Movie Data Base 2008). A small sample of other historically significant figures in widely seen films includes Gautama Buddha, St. Thomas More, St. Bernadette of Lourdes, and Archbishop Oscar Romero.

How should films that advertise their historical authenticity be approached? Given the circumstance that religions seek to ground their authority in the facts of their tradition, this issue is important. A film plausibly recreating crucial moments of history among key figures would provide a lively complement to documents and physical monuments. It would become the celluloid-theatrical counterpart of visiting a sacred place or standing in the presence of a founder's authentic relic. Thus thoughtful viewers will examine correlations between represented images and historical sources. They may also feel an intellectual challenge when a film so emphatically presents its scientific credentials, as did the Cecil B. DeMille studio in its *Ten Commandments* of 1956. Collaborating with Paramount Pictures, the University of Southern California published Henry Noerdlinger's *Moses and Egypt* to coincide with the premiere of the film. The university's press release endorsed it thus: "With the Bible as the controlling source for events depicted on the screen ... DeMille at the very inception of the work set the standard of absolute authenticity in every detail insofar as was humanly possible" ("Moses and Egypt" 1956: 2). The book is packed with footnotes, references to consultations with museum curators and other marks of diligence concerning the film's architecture, art, and costumes. While visual accuracy – frequently called "surface realism" – is valuable in recreating some aspects of the environment, it does not diminish the tendency to render great deeds in a way that is permeated by ideological or mythic themes. These framing elements can create misleading impressions of factual history insofar as it would normally be understood through standard written sources and commentaries. When we look in detail at the Moses of *The Ten Commandments*, we notice significant qualifications to "the standard of absolute authenticity" latent in the publisher's phrase "insofar as was humanly possible."

Consistent with the Torah, the filmed Moses is presented as a shepherd, a liberator of Israelites, a prophetic judge of their failings during the forty years of wandering, and an agent of Yahweh's commandments at Mt. Sinai. But prior to these events, the film presents Moses as an imperial warrior, master builder of cities, favored successor to pharaoh's throne, and the object of intense lust by pharaoh's daughter, Nefretiri. Once having left Egypt, he is presented as love object for Jethro's flirtatious daughters and an exceptionally keen goat trader. Noerdlinger's account of the script honestly admits the silence of the Bible regarding the period of Moses' life from birth until mature adulthood. He modestly quotes Martin Buber who wrote that in dealing with sagas and legends related to Moses, "There can be no certainty of arriving ... at 'what really happened'" (Noerdlinger 1956: 14). Nonetheless, Noerdlinger offers historical grounding for DeMille's Moses of the missing years by drawing upon the ancient historians Flavius Josephus, Eusebius of Caesarea, and Philo Judaeus, all of whom lived many centuries after the periods suggested in the biblical narrative.

The decisive support for the film's heroic premises is Josephus' report that Moses led a military expedition to conquer Ethiopia and took as his bride a Princess Tharbis (Esther Brown) in exchange for her city's surrender and mercy to its conquered inhabitants (Noerdlinger 1956: 71). As this episode is refracted by DeMille, Moses appears as military conqueror returning with Ethiopians who have come to pay tribute to the pharaoh Sethi (Cedric Hardwicke). The princess is in the group. Yet, rather than being portrayed as Moses' wife, she is a lithe woman scantily dressed in the manner of a Las Vegas showgirl – exuding a steamy erotic attachment to Moses that he ignores. In this way, stereotypes of Africans as primitive and exotic are reinforced, and the controversial possibility of displaying an interracial marriage is sidestepped. Moses' booty-bride of war becomes an occasion to illustrate his powers to resist sexual entreaty and to strengthen his monogamous tendency (likely exceptional at the time, given that Exodus 21:10 and Deuteronomy 21:15–17 prescribe rules for polygamy).

Lying behind the DeMille construction of Moses – and this is true for many other religious films – is a mythic alchemy through which ancient cultural materials are transmuted to match a contemporary paradigm of American mythic tastes: a set of expectations that we call the American monomyth. In the violent, male version of this recurring story pattern, a lone hero is summoned by destiny to a mission of redeeming innocents suffering depredations by evil powers. The hero marks himself as morally fit by renouncing sexual and material temptations, thereby enabling him to rescue the community whose institutions are too weak to protect it from predators. This mythic pattern is common in the cowboy western novels and films, in super-heroic films, and in television figures such as Kirk and Spock of *Star Trek*. The biblical Moses story, which begins with some initial congruence with this American paradigm, is further tailored to match until he is much more familiar and comforting to a popular audience.

In *The Ten Commandments*, adult sexuality was removed by showing Moses rejecting the seductive approaches of Tharbis, Princess Nefretiri (Anne Baxter), and all of Jethro's daughters except Sephora (Yvonne De Carlo), who becomes his wife. Even after marriage, Moses seems to become sexually monastic, an unbiblical twist. In a conversation with Nefretiri, his wife Sephora complains that "Moses has forgotten both of us. I lost him when he found his God." In a final touch that conforms the film's ending to those of serialized heroes who disappear to return in another episode, Moses abandons the entire community, including his own family. Sephora volunteers to remain with him, but he says, "I am called by the Lord, Sephora. I go alone." He does not say where. She replies, as a dutiful wife, with praise, "You are God's torch that lights the way to freedom," confirming his lonely departure from the community whose redemption conforms to the central concept of the American civil religion.

In dealing with the source of evil, DeMille's *Ten Commandments* resorts to melodra-matic stereotyping of an enemy within. The sin of the Golden Calf episode is shifted onto Dathan (Edward G. Robinson), a member of the tribe that has collaborated with the Egyptians. While Exodus 32 suggests a collective failing in the idolatry, the film emphasizes Dathan's leadership in organizing the calf's construction. His evil is supported by a sheepish willingness of followers, which matches the American mythic model of the innocent but stupid public, easily misled by the evil few, and perpetually waiting for the lone hero to bring salvation by miraculous means.

Within American monomythic conventions, Moses is transformed into a super-heroic redeemer figure. When he returns from Sinai, his face shines, and the awestruck Sephora comments, "There is a great light that shines from your face, Moses. Perhaps some day I shall come to understand it." And Aaron (John Carradine) says, "He is more than human." Joshua (John Derek) adds, "The light of God shines from you, Moses." It is also Moses, rather than God, who wants Israel to be saved. The Moses of the film complains several times that God does not perform, whereas in the biblical text, it is God who first declares his compassion for the Israelites. The biblical Yahweh calls Moses to a task that he does not want to accept. DeMille's Moses even becomes the redeemer of the pharaoh Rameses, who at film's end declares belief in the universal God.

These efforts at mythic shaping should be understood as an effort to script Moses as an advocate of liberty as Americans understand it. DeMille himself makes a forceful onscreen appearance at the film's beginning to state that "this man alone" paved the road to "freedom." He says, "We have an unusual subject. The story of the birth of freedom – the story of Moses … The theme of this film is whether man ought to be ruled by God's law, or by the whims of a dictator like Rameses. Are men the property of the state, or are they free souls under God? This same battle continues throughout the world today. Our intention was not to create the story, but to be worthy of the divinely inspired story." The film thus presents Moses as an American superhero. When he says, "There is no freedom without the law," Moses has obviously been drafted for the conflict between Western capitalism and Soviet communism, a major diplomatic and military concern when the film was created.

The text-critical and cultural methods employed here would be equally appropriate in analyzing A Man for All Seasons (1966), in which Sir Thomas More (Paul Scofield) is rendered as a champion of liberty of conscience – despite the fact that the More of history "defended the right of the Church Courts to try men and women for heresy, and the duty of the State to burn relapsed heretics" (Guy 2000: 16). This omission highlights the problematic suggested by Albert Schweitzer's remark that "each successive epoch of theology found its own thoughts in Jesus; that was, indeed, the only way in which it could make him live" (Schweitzer 2001: 6). In a similar spirit, More's attacks on William Tyndale's Bible translations and Tyndale's resultant death at the stake disappear from A Man for All Seasons. More's freedom of conscience was for him and those who shared his Catholic faith, but not for Protestants like Tyndale.

When turning to films such as Carl Dreyer's The Passion of Joan of Arc (1928), historical issues recede because scholarly credentials are not presented on behalf of elaborate narrative fictions. However, The Passion omits her career as a charismatic political leader and warrior and limits its treatment to her imprisonment, trial, and execution by English sympathizers in France. Using inter-titles with words taken from the records of interrogations by the Chamber of Deputies at the University of Paris, the film's documentary authenticity seems sufficiently grounded to withstand severe skepticism. Although Dreyer compresses months of interrogatory dialogues, the script is nonetheless derived from transcriptions and the context of extreme hostility remains. The film shows the tortured face of a courageous Joan (Renée Falconetti) juxtaposed to the hateful, leering faces of her accusers. As Richard Alleva describes Dreyer's depiction, "Hair cropped, big eyed, lips parched, fly-tormented, Joan is like a child who has fallen into the hands of pedantic molesters. And yet she retains her insuperable strength: she has seen angels and heard the voice of God" (2005: 19). Despite St. Joan's civic honors in France, Dreyer's film reaches beyond mere national chauvinism because his Joan resonates with chronic struggles between all institutions of religious authority and individual conscience. The Passion of Joan of Arc is also a reminder that saints are usually regarded as troublemakers, a circumstance thematized in The Song of Bernadette (1943). Because Bernadette Soubirous lived in the nineteenth century and church records of her examinations seem intact, the film credibly conveys the fact that Bernadette (Jennifer Jones) was initially regarded as an embarrassment to the Church. Her persistent belief in her vision of "the Lady" (a Virgin Mary figure) at Lourdes came to be regarded as sincere by the initially skeptical. Her heroism onscreen consists not of healing miracles or manipulation of others, but of radiant sincerity and selflessness.

How have the screen heroines and heroes affected their audiences? There is doubtless some inspiration for conduct and intellectual stimulation of interest in the past. Yet one can also recognize that *The Ten Commandments* seems captive to American civil religion and heroic styles. The narrow accuracy of *The Passion of Joan of Arc*, filled with torture and suffering, may inspire little more than awe at a charismatic leader and anger toward her long-deceased tormenters. *The Song of Bernadette*, in Theresa Sanders' opinion, is rendered as a battle between religion and science, a false dichotomy that invites a forced choice between faith and reason (Sanders 2002: 196). And contrary to the possibilities for transcendent inspiration, there is a contrary tendency to turn religious heroes and heroines into narcissistic projections of one's own culture. The ancient Greek poet Xenophanes articulated this tendency. One of his fragments discusses a hypothetical discourse about divinity among horses, cows, and lions: if they "had hands … and produced works of art as men do, horses would draw the figures of gods like horses and cows like cows, and they would make their bodies just as the form which they each have themselves" (Freeman 1962: 22).

Ordinary heroes and heroines

At a second tier in historical significance are uncanonized, unbeatified characters who are exemplary in their faithfulness to particular religious ideals. Sometimes they are real, as with Sister Helen Prejean (Susan Sarandon) of *Dead Man Walking* (1995), or Alvin Straight (Richard Farnsworth) of *The Straight Story* (1999), but they are often fictional persons such as Babette Hersant (Stéphane Audran) of *Babette's Feast* (1987). Such films portray tasks of moral reconciliation among people alienated from one another or tempted to act vengefully. Movements toward reconciliation often require painful courage, especially if hatreds have festered for years. Unlike the calls to found a religion or to be a martyr, reconciliation does not require a historically significant moment or a dramatically large cause.

One film that dramatized these ordinary conflicts as an opportunity for significant religious achievement is *The Straight Story* (1999), based on the life of the real Alvin Straight of Laurens, Iowa. In the film's setting, Alvin is presented as a retired seventy-three-year-old security guard who lives with a daughter, Rose (Sissy Spacek), whose mental limitations have led to the loss of her children. Alvin has poor vision, bad hips, and many regrets related to killings he carried out as a sniper in the Second World War. An alcoholic, he suspects his own responsibility for the death of his daughter's child in a fire. Alvin wants to visit his alienated brother in Wisconsin who has had a stroke. Because Alvin is legally blind and can't drive a car, he rigs a riding lawn mower to pull a trailer for the 325-mile journey. We gradually learn that he is on a pilgrimage for personal atonement. He meets people along the way and shares such life wisdom as he has, but he makes no pretensions about being a healer of other people's souls. He carries the memory of many failures, some of which he acknowledges to a sympathetic priest who finds him camping in the parish cemetery, but it is clear that he cannot tell "the straight story" of his life. After many encounters and delays, he finally reaches his brother's home. They laconically acknowledge one another and are reconciled to the

degree conveyed by their mutual presence. His courage to take the journey of reconciliation becomes a story of pride reduced, self-knowledge increased, and the exercise
of willpower to rectify an old wrong.

These are the ordinary virtues that people must also summon in quelling their
impulses for vengeance, an important theme in *Dead Man Walking* (1995). Sister
Helen Prejean's personal story related to her work against the death penalty exposes a
public-policy issue with religious dimensions. Prejean's prison ministry "conscripted"
her, as she put it in her book, when a bishop assigned her the task of counseling a
death-row prisoner. After this experience, and then watching his execution, she began
a campaign against capital punishment, which led to the publication of her eponymous
best-selling book in 1993. A strikingly revelatory aspect of *Dead Man* is Sister Helen's
own moral education as she encounters the thicket of moral issues involved in capital
punishment. She lacks any infallible moral instincts that would allow her to make
quick decisions about the good and evil characters in her landscape. She hesitates
to take her first assignment, a condemned rapist-murderer Matthew Poncelet (Sean
Penn), because she cannot imagine how to carry out her mission. When she meets
Poncelet, she senses his self-destructive rage and self-pity; yet she is partly conned by
his plea that he is innocent of murder and thus offers some assistance to his last-minute
appeals. By the time she has witnessed his execution, she has seen through his scams.
She has not converted him, but at least she elicited his choked apology to the parents
of the victims in the rape-murder. This element of redemption is not a point of closure
for either the book or the movie, in that both also strive to create a panoramic view
of those unwillingly linked to one another at executions: the condemned and their
families, the families of the victims, and the officials whose job it is to administer
death.

Sister Helen learned from her first execution not only the pain of the condemned
and his family but also the anger of the victims' parents. So she began to meet
with these families, uncomfortably at first, but eventually establishing a continuing
relationship of counseling with them as well. She also begins to meet with support
groups for victims' families; she encounters prison officials in distress over their work,
some of whom find themselves pressured and sleepless. Just as Sister Helen strove to
avoid stereotyping or excluding anyone's concerns, the film avoids presenting the
condemned as an innocent victim of circumstances. Neither the book nor the film
has any simple "solution" to the issue of the death penalty. What they both show
is the commitment of a determined woman to find a humane alternative to capital
punishment.

On the role of the Church in Sister Helen's story, there is one additional noteworthy
difference from popular stereotypes. She does her work within the framework of an
institution that offers support for her conception of ministry. But there are prickly
moments when Sister Helen feels that some of her superiors share the very public
attitudes against which she is fighting. As with other adversaries against whom she
wages her gentle war, she pleads and persuades rather than stereotyping others or
sidestepping the issue. In providing this realistic picture of the Church, *Dead Man
Walking* goes against decades of the American monomythic tradition that depicts

congregations as collections of timid fools who lack the stomach for violent retaliation. Instead of being frustrated by an imperfect institution, she is partially enabled by it.

Babette's Feast approaches the theme of alienation through a concept of grace – the bestowal of an unearned gift that imparts to the recipient a sense of self-worth, enabling a warm acceptance of others. Set in Jutland, the film centers upon the diminished life of two sisters who have turned away from romance and career to serve their father and his legacy as a pastor to a small sect. The members of the religious community clustered around the church lead a joyless life until Babette enters the village as a refugee. Recommended by a former suitor for one of the sisters, she becomes their servant. Babette carries out these duties faithfully while concealing the fact that she was once a famous chef and that she has suffered grievous family losses. The transforming moments come when a lottery ticket purchased in Paris wins an extraordinary prize. Instead of using it to flee her grim circumstances, she sets about to give her adoptive community a magnificent feast and to transcend her own losses.

Babette's hosts become suspicious and divisive as her culinary cargo begins to arrive, but she patiently coaxes them to allow the sumptuous meal she plans. The bickering members of the congregation appear at the appointed time, but are resolved to resist the temptations of extravagant fare. Yet they are coaxed to seat themselves and begin to eat and drink. The crotchety ones begin to overcome long-felt grudges, and an older, washed-up general among them begins to savor life again. As the mediator of grace, Babette has not scolded or demanded. She has lovingly given something her community needed, creating within them a new perspective more accepting of one another. Babette's caring form of heroism, which is also a kind of healing for her as well, is very accessible for audiences. Each person can easily imagine recognizing the needs that are characteristically ignored. The film is really a parable about small acts that could make a great difference to the spiritual lives of others.

In a more explicitly religious story with early historical setting, *The Robe* (1953) narrates several episodes of ordinary heroism. The inspiration comes from a Gospel verse describing the Roman soldiers who crucified Jesus after dividing his personal articles. They consider tearing his robe into equal pieces: "Let us not rend it, but cast lots for it, whose it shall be" (John 19:24). The robe is won by the libertine centurion Marcellus Gallio (Richard Burton), who immediately loses it in the storm following the crucifixion. His nightmares about having killed an innocent man are initially attributed to the robe's evil magic.

Searching for the robe and his Greek slave Demetrius (Victor Mature) who escaped with it, Gallio encounters the Christian community at Cana and learns to his surprise that they are aware of his role in the crucifixion but have forgiven him. When a Roman battalion attacks the Christians, Marcellus duels with its commander to protect them; when Marcellus wins, he refuses to kill his adversary but asks him to leave peacefully. By this courageous and compassionate act, he solidifies an identity with the beleaguered Christians and decides to follow Jesus. He refuses the task of spying on Christians in Rome, and rescues his former slave Demetrius from torture in a Roman prison, although remarkably without killing anyone. Marcellus lives out the apparent contradiction of being a Christian Roman soldier who is brave yet nonviolent, loyal to Rome and to Jesus. Marcellus believes there is no contradiction, but the Emperor Caligula disagrees; he accuses him of treason, and insists he renounce Christ to show his loyalty to Rome. Marcellus takes a defiant stance during his trial while arguing for the compatibility of Jesus and the Empire. His fiancée Diana (Jean Simmons), repelled by the rule of Caligula (Jay Robinson), allies herself with Marcellus and, with him, faces martyrdom in the Colosseum.

At the time of its release, this film carried blatant advertising for its innovative Cinemascope and stereophonic sound. Spectacular vistas and huge faces on the screen led some critics to believe that technology dwarfed the story (Crowther 1953: 119). Like other biblical spectacles of the era, *The Robe* contained traces of Cold War polemic, demonizing Roman values as totalitarian (Winkler 1997). For example, after hearing Marcellus' anguished account of the crucifixion, Emperor Tiberius (Ernest Thesiger) proclaims: "man's desire to be free ... the greatest madness of them all."

Despite the triumphal fanfare and political allegory of its times, *The Robe* can be seen as a contribution to its viewers' historical imagination. How could a minority faith, an object of persecution, become the official religion of the Roman Empire by the time of Constantine? The heroism of this film lies in a centurion's costly sense of accountability and repentance for his act. It is also manifest in the courage of the slave Demetrius and in the sharing and forgiving spirit of the Christians in Cana. It is by such ordinary acts of moral conscience and faithful living that viewers gain sustenance from this kind of film. Nonetheless, the film perpetuates the American monomyth in its simplistic conclusion that Christianity and empire can exist harmoniously, effectively ignoring the pacifist witness of early Christians against militarism and empire.

Superheroines and superheroes

Superman is the oldest of the superheroes to have evolved toward a new religious screen identity. Like many licensed characters in popular culture, Superman's iconic values have changed significantly over time. Born in the 1930s as a steel-muscled brawler on comic-book pages, he eventually acquired a religious aura that some have found inspiring. Anton Karl Kozlovic has worked out twenty Jesus–Superman narrative parallels and eight Christic personality traits for the Superman films of 1978 and 1980 (Kozlovic 2002: par. 1). In the spirit of such recognitions, Ken Schenck uses religious language of "the call" to cast Superman as cultural messiah: "If reality is measured by the effect something has on the world, then Superman is real. He has inspired and impacted countless lives and continues to do so. He calls us to follow his example and fight for truth and justice in the world" (Schenck 2005: 44). Filmmakers who see in religious resonance for viewers like Schenck an important marketing tool bluntly cast their Christ analogues. In *Superman: The Movie* (1978), for example, Jor-El (Marlon Brando) articulates a kind of trinitarian theology in saying to his infant son before his launch from planet Krypton, "You will make my strength your own, see my life through your eyes, as your life will be seen through mine. The son becomes the father and the father becomes the son." Later in the film, when Superman returns to the Fortress of Solitude to regain his bearings,

Jor-El lifts from the Gospel of John to characterize humanity and Superman's unique redemptive role for them. "They can be a great people, Kal-El. They wish to be. They only lack the light to show the way. For this reason above all – their capacity for good – I have sent them you. My only son." The resonance of these words is clearly scriptural.

Superman II (1980) enhanced the Christological mythos by explicitly working out the requirement for permanent renunciation of intimate partnership, and, with it, the disclosure of his secret identity as savior. The narrative takes Superman (Christopher Reeve) and Lois Lane (Margot Kidder) to Niagara Falls on a honeymoon story assignment. When his identity is accidentally disclosed to Lois, Superman cannot resist flying with her to the Fortress of Solitude, where he gives up his powers in order to become a mortal so that they can make love. The horrifying consequences of succumbing to sexual temptation are immediate. When the romantic pair pauses at a truck stop for a meal, Clark is bullied by a trucker who savagely beats him, even causing him to bleed. Intimacy has drained away Superman's strength to save the world from three escaped Kryptonians who have terrorized the planet in his absence and compelled the humiliating surrender of the US president. Only a return to the Fortress and stern counseling from his mother Lara about his destiny make him realize the consequences of his selfish happiness with Lois. "You no longer can serve humanity if you invest your time and emotion in one of them at the expense of the rest. Surely this is not how you repay their gratitude, Kal-El. Could you really abandon the weak and the needy merely to fulfill some selfish dream?" Superman rushes back to a world ruled by the evil trio from Krypton and defeats them. Then he deep kisses Lois in a way that erases her memory of Clark as Superman. His regeneration after permanent rejection of intimacy and family is the American monomythic version of resurrection. It also echoes those scriptural admonitions of Jesus that promise family divisions as the kingdom of God is realized (Matthew 10:34–6; Luke 12: 49–53). This view of Superman as the celibate self-sacrificial savior of the world is reinforced in the more recent *Superman Returns* (2006). In the latter, when Lois Lane (Kate Bosworth) insists that the world does not need a savior anymore, Superman (Brandon Routh) replies, "Everyday I hear them crying for one." Superman chooses to sacrifice his own personal happiness for the greater good.

Other important films have taken up the challenge of using superheroes to inspire religious sentiments. The first *Star Wars* film is perhaps the most important single film for establishing the idea that a fantasy film could arouse widespread religious response. Confessional communities have formed and serious, admiring religious commentaries on *Star Wars* theology have appeared (Bowen and Wagner 2006; Porter 2006). Interviewed some two decades after the initial film, George Lucas explained his vision of the religious elements:

> I see *Star Wars* as taking all the issues that religion represents and trying to distill them down into a more modern and easily accessible construct – that there is a greater mystery out there ... I put the Force into the movie in order to try to awaken a certain kind of spirituality in young people – more a belief in God than a belief in any particular religious system ... I think it's important to have a belief system and to have faith. ("Of Myth and Men" 1999)

Lucas saw himself reviving some wholesome spiritual values and he chose to do so in a story that bestows superpowers upon both protagonists and villains. The theme of Force-assisted violence, directed by a higher power, threads through *Star Wars* from the moment in the initial film when Luke turns off his targeting computer to destroy the Death Star and on to the final battle between Anakin (Hayden Christensen) and Obi-Wan (Ewan McGregor) in *Revenge of the Sith* (2005). In the novelization of *Revenge* that George Lucas himself edited, Matthew Stover writes of Obi-Wan that "He was only a vessel, emptied of self. The Force, shaped by his skill and guided by his clarity of mind, fought through him" (Stover 2005: 285). Celebrating Obi-Wan's transcendence of rationality and his surrender to the violence that the Force directs him to perform, Stover–Lucas write that during his battle with General Grievous "he had no need for a plan, no use for tactics. He had the Force" (Stover 2005: 122). There are other elements, of course, that fans in *Star Wars* respond to, such as loyalty, willingness to sacrifice, the bivalent complexity of Anakin/Darth Vader, and the implied critique of American militarism. But the idea of the Force and the weapons that it directs provides the premise for the weapons merchandising and video games that allow fans to reenact the struggles of the saga.

Whether directly emulating the success of *Star Wars* or responding to other imperatives, the theme of divinely inspired warfare also helped build other world mythic franchises for *The Matrix* trilogy and *The Lord of the Rings* film trilogy. The latter is especially suitable for the discussion of superheroism because J. R. R. Tolkien wrote that

> *The Lord of the Rings* is of course a fundamentally religious and Catholic work; unconsciously so at first, but consciously in the revision. That is why I have not put in, or have cut out, practically all references to anything like "religion," to cults or practices, in the imaginary world. For the religious element is absorbed into the story and the symbolism. (Tolkien 2000: Letter No. 142 to Robert Murray)

Comparing the films to Tolkien's trilogy allows one to understand the changes to his religious vision introduced by filmmaker Peter Jackson. We see accommodations to multimedia merchandising, wherein the film is an expensive property that must serve a worldwide marketing program that includes violently themed video games. The reshaping process converts heroism to superheroism, thus inverting several key religious values in Tolkien. The film's dramatization of the novel is a considerable achievement in its own right, recognized by the Academy Awards. For that very reason, its alterations are especially instructive about where superheroism takes us.

The Lord of the Rings trilogy narrates a collective project – the destruction of a seductive but awful ring that carries the power to dominate others. Forming the Fellowship of the Ring is an acknowledgment of individual weaknesses that can only be overcome by solidarity. Within the Fellowship, heroes are consultative and deferential to others. The trip to destroy the ring at Mount Doom is so daunting that Frodo and Sam are often lost and starving, yet trudge on in hope. Several times in both film and novel, the values of mercy/pity are highlighted and the refusal to destroy others is ultimately shown to be wise because even the despised figure of Gollum (Andy Serkis) ultimately plays a role in the ring's destruction (although the film does not highlight this point so emphatically as does the book).

In these aspects, the film exhibits fidelity to the novel. Nonetheless, merchandising opportunities for superheroic products dictated radical role changes for principal characters. The Frodo of the novel, a relatively mature hobbit of fifty-one, was apparently chosen as the agent of the ring's destruction because of his wisdom. The film's Frodo (Elijah Wood) is presented as a barely pubescent waif, who is easily frightened and sometimes faints. The film logic is apparent in that Frodo's timidity contrasts with other protagonists who ride the elevator to superheroism. We agree with Victoria Gaydosik's observations that the literary Arwen presents aspects of the Psyche archetype: "beauty, obedience, and patience marred by curiosity" (Gaydosik 2005: 218) as opposed to the film Arwen (Liv Tyler), who is one of those "pumped-up, butt-kicking fearless heroines who are masters of machinery, weapons, battle tactics, physical hardship, and emotional adversity, but can also nurture a child and experience romantic attachment" (Gaydosik 2005: 216). Arwen's superheroine alterations coalesce in the incident where Frodo is rescued from the Nazgûl, where she first taunts Aragorn (Viggo Mortensen) that she can do it: "I am the faster rider. I will take him." There Arwen commands lightning, scaring off the wraiths before she scoops up the comatose Frodo-child. In another scene, Arwen again dominates manly Aragorn, stealing up on him and placing a sword at his throat, taunting him with, "What's this? A ranger caught off his guard?"

In his turn, Aragorn too is scaled up from his literary persona, where he is merely an effective but equal member of the Fellowship, steadily and modestly consulting and deferring to others. As a film presence he commands, even bristles with aggression to establish his dominance. For example, one desperate task in fighting Saruman's forces is to recruit the Dead Men of Dunharrow. These quasi-living soldiers were condemned to remain in Middle Earth after breaking a vow of alliance to King Isuldur. In the novel Aragorn's group travels the Paths of the Dead and comes to a cave where they sense a rustling presence. Aragorn shouts: "Oathbreakers, why have ye come?" A faint voice replies: "To fulfill our oath and have peace." Aragorn replies, "The hour is come at last" and promises that "I will hold the oath fulfilled" and declares himself heir (Tolkien 1994: 772–3). It is a friendly meeting without coercion or threats. In the film, the King of the Dead refuses to let Aragorn's company pass and threatens to kill them, striking directly at Aragorn, who retaliates with Anduril, his sword, whose point he thrusts toward the king's neck. Having established his physical authority, Aragorn declares himself Isuldur's heir, "Fight for me! And I will hold your oath fulfilled!" and again extends his own fabled sword. "What say you?" The king capitulates and joins their military enterprise. The usual lament about literary-film adaptations is that so much is lost, but in this case a spare and amiable exchange escalates into several lines of dialogue highlighted by several shots of snarling intimidation. The values of the cinematic Ring, in other words, trump friendly accommodation. Although she does not analyze this scene, Janet Brennan Croft has established that the film depicts

Aragorn as a repackaging of the American monomyth. The innocent community of Hobbits, threatened by evil outsiders, is rescued by the superheroic few (Croft 2005). The Tolkienian sense that evil is in all humans, betrayed by a craving for a ring of power over others, is diminished. Consistent with this sanitation, the film inserts long battle scenes while deleting Tolkien's "The Scouring of the Shire," in which many of the Hobbits are revealed as collaboraters with Saruman's cruel regime while Frodo and companions were absent on their mission.

A similar observation can be made concerning Mel Gibson's depiction of Jesus in *The Passion of the Christ*. With a narrative shaped to the contours of medieval Catholic piety, it contains unhistorical elements of gratuitous violence such as a black raven that plucks out the eyes of the crucified thief who fails to repent and the depiction of Jesus' grimly retributive visage in the resurrection scenes (Bartchy 2005). This conforms to superheroic films directed by Clint Eastwood and others, with protagonists savagely beaten before returning to take vengeance. In this instance, the villains are Jews with "stereotypical hooked noses and ugly visages" while the Jesus played by James Caviezel is "a 'hunk' complete with a finely-sculptured Roman nose" (Bartchy 2005: 318) who conforms to the image of a typical American superhero.

How should one respond to the religious superheroines and heroes along with their embedded mythic conventions? At one end of the spectrum, we have the worshipful responses of scholars like Ken Schenck who treat them as a source of inspiration. In addition to the exegeses and appreciative commentaries on the *Star Wars* and *Star Trek* series, some scholars focus their devotion upon individual superheroes. It seems plausible that the realm of superheroic fantasy tends to discourage behavior according to religious ideals. Rather than sending a call to personal responsibility, such fantasies lead audiences to follow leaders who act as vigilantes to rid the world of evil. It should not be surprising that this message occasionally comes from some superheroes themselves.

There is perhaps no better example of this than *Superman IV: The Quest for Peace* (1987), a film that veers away from the Jesus overlays of *Superman* (1978) and *Superman Returns* (2006), where Superman was cast as "the only son" sent to earth "to show the light." In *Superman IV*, Superman (Christopher Reeve) becomes irritated with the ineffectiveness of the United Nations in supervising the elimination of nuclear weapons. To eliminate the danger permanently, he confronts the UN's General Assembly and announces that "I am no longer a visitor. The Earth is my home too. We cannot live in fear. I cannot watch you stumble into the madness of nuclear destruction. So I have come to a decision … to do what your governments have been unable to do … I will rid our planet of all nuclear weapons." He quickly seizes the world's supply of nuclear weapons – even those of the United States – and hurls them into the sun. He does not know that Lex Luthor (Gene Hackman) has contrived to create a new nemesis, Nuclear Man (Mark Pillow), out of the explosion. Subsequently Superman himself is almost destroyed by this new enemy. Chastened by this failure in unilateral crusading, he returns to the UN for an apology. "Once more we have survived the threat of war. And once more we've found a fragile peace. I thought I could give you all the gift of freedom from war. But I was wrong. It is not mine to give."

The superhero of the American monomyth does not free us from violence, but perpetuates it even as he claims to be a force for "peace" in his own use of rationalized violence. Films that rehearse this myth have reworked traditional religious ideas of the hero according to a new mythic pattern, one that echoes the ideology of American exceptionalism and the idea that we have a mission to create peace through a heroic "just war" on behalf of "freedom" against the forces of evil in the world. In this way, we can see how contemporary media religious images both represent and support American political discourse through their use of religious ideas that have been remade as distinctively American.

Bibliography

Alleva, R. (2005) "Corruption and Transcendence: The Films of Carl Dreyer," *Commonweal* 132 (6): 19.

Bartchy, S. (2005) "Where is the History in Mel Gibson's *The Passion of the Christ?*" *Pastoral Psychology* 53 (4): 313–28.

Bowen, J. L. and Wagner, R. (2006) "'Hokey Religions and Ancient Weapons': The Force of Spirituality," in M. Kapell and J. S. Lawrence (eds) *Finding the Force of the Star Wars Franchise: Fans, Merchandise, and Critics*, New York: Peter Lang: 75–94.

Carlyle, T. (1907) *On Heroes, Hero Worship, and the Heroic in History*, ed. J. C. Adams, Boston: Houghton Mifflin.

Croft, J. B. (2005) "Jackson's Aragorn and the American Superhero Monomyth." Paper presented at the Popular Culture and American Culture Associations conference, San Diego, CA.

Crowther, B. (1953) "Now Cinemascope! A Look at 'The Robe' and the New System in Which it is Put On," *New York Times* (27 September): 119.

Edison, T. (2001 [1907]) "A Brief Editorial from a Great Inventor," in T. Lindvall, *The Silents of God: Selected Issues and Documents in Silent American Film and Religion 1908–1925*, Metuchen, NJ: Scarecrow Press: 39–40.

Freeman, K. (1962) *Ancilla to the Pre-Socratic Philosophers: A Complete Translation of the Fragments in Diels, Fragmente der Vorsokratiker*. Cambridge, MA: Harvard University Press.

Gaydosik, V. (2005) "'Crimes against the Book?' The Transformation of Tolkien's Arwen from Page to Screen and the Abandonment of the Psyche Archetype," in J. B. Croft, (ed.) *Tolkien on Film: Essays on Peter Jackson's The Lord of the Rings*, Altadena, CA: Mythopoeic Press: 215–30.

Guy, J. (2000) "The Search for the Historical Thomas Moore," *History Review* (March): 15–20.

International Movie Data Base (2008) Moses Filmography. Online. Available HTTP: <http://www.imdb.com/character/ch0006190/> (accessed 25 April 2008).

"Jesus in Moving Pictures" (1912) *New York Times* (27 October): C3.

Jump, H. (2001 [1911]) "The Religious Possibilities of the Motion Picture," in T. Lindvall *The Silents of God: Selected Issues and Documents in Silent American Film and Religion 1908–1925*, Metuchen, NJ: Scarecrow Press: 54–78.

Kozlovic, A. K. (2002) "Superman as Christ-Figure: The American Pop Culture Movie Messiah,"*Journal of Religion and Film* 6 (1). Online. Available HTTP: <http://www.unomaha.edu/jrf/superman.htm> (accessed 2 May 2008).

"Moses and Egypt by Henry S. Noerdlinger" (1956) University of Southern California Press Release, Pacific Film Cinefiles Archive document at University of California-Berkeley.

Noerdlinger, H. S. (1956) *Moses and Egypt: The Documentation to the Motion Picture* The Ten Commandments, Los Angeles: University of Southern California Press.

"Of Myth and Men." (1999) *Time* (26 April). Online. Available HTTP: <http: www.time.com/time/magazine/article/0,9171,990820-1,00.html> (accessed 30 March 2008).

Porter, J. E. (2006) "'I am a Jedi': *Star Wars* Fandom, Religious Belief, and the 2001 Census," in M. Kapell and J. S. Lawrence (eds) *Finding the Force of the Star Wars Franchise: Fans, Merchandise, and Critics*, New York: Peter Lang: 95–114.

Porter, J. E. and McLaren, D. L. (1999) *Star Trek and Sacred Ground: Explorations of Star Trek, Religion, and American Culture*, Albany, NY: SUNY Press.

"Remarkable Spectacle" (1923) New York Times (22 December): 8.

Sanders, T. (2002) *Celluloid Saints: Images of Sanctity in Film*, Macon, GA: Mercer University Press.

Schenck, K. (2005) "Superman: A Popular Cultural Messiah," in B. J. Oropeza (ed.) *The Gospel According to Superheroes: Religion and Popular Culture*, New York: Peter Lang: 33–48.

Schweitzer, A. (2001) *The Quest of the Historical Jesus*, ed. J. Bowden, Minneapolis, MN: Augsburg Fortress.

Spoto, D. (2007) *Joan: The Mysterious Life of the Heretic Who Became a Saint*, San Francisco, CA: HarperCollins.

Stover, M. (2005) *Star Wars, Episode III – Revenge of the Sith*, New York: Del Rey.

Telford, W. R. (1997) "The Depiction of Jesus," in C. Marsh and G. Ortiz (eds) *Explorations in Theology and Film*, Oxford: Blackwell: 115–40.

"*Ten Commandments, The*" (1923) (review) *New York Times* (22 December): 8.

Tolkien, J. R. R. (1994) *The Lord of the Rings*, 2nd ed., Boston: Houghton Mifflin.

—— (2000) *Letters of J. R. R. Tolkien*, ed. H. Carpenter and C. Tolkien, Boston: Houghton Mifflin.

Winkler, M. M. (1997) "The Roman Empire in American Cinema after 1945," *Classical Journal* 93(2): 167–96.

Wright, M. J. (2007) *Religion and Film: An Introduction*, London: I. B. Tauris.

Filmography

Babette's Feast (1987, dir. G. Axel)
Dead Man Walking (1995, dir. T. Robbins)
From the Manger to the Cross (1912, dir. S. Olcott)
The King of Kings (1927, dir. C. DeMille)
The Lord of the Rings: The Return of the King (2003, dir. P. Jackson)
A Man for All Seasons (1966, dir. F. Zinnemann)
The Passion of the Christ (2004, dir. M. Gibson)
The Passion of Joan of Arc (1928, dir. C. Dreyer)
The Robe (1953, dir. H. Koster)
The Song of Bernadette (1943, dir. H. King)
Star Wars: Episode IV – A New Hope (1977, dir. G. Lucas)
Star Wars: Episode III – Revenge of the Sith (2005, dir. G. Lucas)
The Straight Story (1999, dir. D. Lynch)
Superman: The Movie (1978, dir. R. Donner)
Superman II (1980, dir. R. Lester)
Superman IV: The Quest for Peace (1987, dir. S. Furie)
Superman Returns (2006, dir. B. Singer)
The Ten Commandments (1923, dir. C. DeMille)
The Ten Commandments (1956, dir. C. DeMille)

Further reading

Historical and textual

Carnes, M. C. (ed.) (1995) *Past Imperfect: History According to the Movies*, New York: Henry Holt. (Treats *The Ten Commandments*, several Joan of Arc films, *A Man for All Seasons*, and other films with religious heroes.)

Wright, M. J. (2003) *Moses in America: The Cultural Uses of Biblical Narrative*, Oxford: Oxford University Press. (Comparative study that includes an extended chapter on DeMille's Moses compared to other American renditions.)

Thematic

Kinnard, R. and Davis, T. (1992) *Divine Images: A History of Jesus on the Screen*, New York: Carol Publishing. (A catalogue-type book that is comprehensive.)

Reinhartz, A. (2006) *Jesus of Hollywood*, New York: Oxford University Press. (A careful comparative study of Jesus rendered in significantly different ways.)

Dialogical

Jewett, R. (1993) *Saint Paul at the Movies: The Apostle's Dialogue with American Culture*, Louisville, KY: Westminster John Knox Press. (On dialogue between Paul and film as contributing insight to Pauline themes.)

—— (1999) *Saint Paul Returns to the Movies: Triumph over Shame*, Grand Rapids, MI: Eerdmans.

Myth/ideological criticism

Beal, T. K. and Linafelt, T. (eds) (2006) *Mel Gibson's Bible: Religion, Popular Culture, and* The Passion of the Christ, Chicago: University of Chicago Press. (Diverse critical responses to *The Passion of the Christ.*)

Forshey, G. E. (1992) *American Religious and Biblical Spectaculars*, Westport, CT: Praeger. (Portrays the bibilical spectacle as projection of American cultural themes.)

Humphries-Brooks, S. (2006) *Cinematic Savior: Hollywood's Making of the American Christ*, Westport, CT: Greenwood. (A study of heroic redemption in several major films.)

Lawrence, J. S. and Jewett, R. (2002) *The Myth of the American Superhero*, Grand Rapids, MI: Eerdmans. (Analysis of a persistent heroic model that runs through many strands of popular culture.)

Superhero commentaries

Galipeau, S. A. (2001) *The Journey of Luke Skywalker: An Analysis of Modern Myth and Symbol*, Chicago: Open Court. (Treats Luke Skywalker as model of healthy spiritual development.)

McDowell, J. C. (2007) *The Gospel According to Star Wars: Faith, Hope, and the Force*, Louisville, KY: Westminster John Knox Press. (A sympathetic exploration of spiritual themes.)

22
HORROR AND THE DEMONIC

Douglas E. Cowan

Introduction

We remember our monsters. Whether they come from under the bed or the tree outside our window, from long-ago camp fires or the screen at the local cineplex, the monsters that define so many of our fears are never far from the core of who we are as human beings. Dorothy and Toto may stand front and center in the larger history of *The Wizard of Oz*, but for millions of people who saw Victor Fleming's 1939 production, the Wicked Witch of the West and her vanguard of flying apes are at least as significant as the little girl who only wanted to go home. While 1973 saw the release of both *Godspell* and *Jesus Christ Superstar*, that year is marked for countless moviegoers by the experience of William Friedkin's *The Exorcist*. From the bug-eyed monsters (BEMs) of 1950s sci-fi horror to the latest crop of graphic "torture-porn" films, from fears of communist invasion and nuclear war (Jancovich 1996; Skal 1998) to the dread of random violence and the "vanishing hitchhiker" (Brunvand 1981; cf. Furedi 2006; Glassner 1999), scary movies ensure that our monsters are always close at hand, always ready to step from the darkness into the light. Indeed, as numerous commentators have pointed out, our monsters are relentlessly reflexive, telling us at least as much about ourselves as they do anything else (see, for example, Beal 2002; Bellin 2005; Carroll 1990; Creed 1993; Ingebretsen 2001). They demonstrate those aspects of ourselves we would far rather forget. They dig up those fears we would prefer to see buried, and in so doing encourage us to explore what we fear, why we fear, and who we are when we fear.

The technological progeny of ghost stories and the Grand Guignol, cinema horror has grown up with moviemaking. From Georges Méliès's fashionably gothic *Le manoir du diable* (1896) and J. Searle Dawley's *Frankenstein* (1910) lurching in front of Thomas Edison's Kinetoscope to the German expressionism of *The Golem* (1920), *Nosferatu* (1922), and *The Cabinet of Dr. Caligari* (1920), from Universal Studio's iconic movie monsters – *Dracula* (1931), *Frankenstein* (1931), and *The Mummy* (1932) – to Hammer's almost camp remakes in the decades following the Second World War, from mainstreaming the Devil in *Rosemary's Baby* (1968), *The Exorcist*, and *The Omen*

(1976) to a horde of satanic sequels and demonic imitators, cinema industries around the world have looked to horror for many of their most enduring stories (Boot 1993; Kalat 2007; Schneider 2003). Already occupying a solid place in literature and among other visual arts (Clemens 1999; Dijkstra 1986; Halberstam 1995; Ingebretsen 1996; Kendrick 1991; Kristeva 1982; Twitchell 1985), cinema horror has proven over the past century to be one of the big screen's most durable genres, rising anew each time critics confidently (and often derisively) predict its demise. This shouldn't surprise us, though. As psychologist Marvin Zuckerman points out, complex societies have rarely lacked a taste for vicarious violence or horrific entertainment, and "spectators at gladiatorial contests or public executions did not consider their recreation abnormal or perverted" (1996: 147). Neither do those who produce and consume cinema horror, something that quite naturally begs the question, "Why?"

Commentators have explained the popularity of cinema horror in a number of ways. Some argue that scary movies are a natural outlet for societal tension in times of crisis and uncertainty (e.g., Harrington 1950; Jancovich 1996; Skal 1994), while others locate the appeal in psychosexual development, arousal needs, and adolescent role performance (e.g., Lawrence and Palmgreen 1996; Twitchell 1985; Zillman and Weaver 1996). Still others consider cinema horror a reflection of society's ongoing ambivalence toward and often proactive denigration of women (e.g., Clover 1992; Grant 1996; Pinedo 1997; Waller 1987). While a few have tried to turn elements of cinema horror to religious advantage, arguing that they can be read as a kind of gospel in gruesome disguise (Leggett 2002; Paffenroth 2006), many conservative Christians mark horror movies as one more indication that "real" religion no longer occupies pride of place in society, that the appeal of horror implies the ongoing Edenic appeal of evil.

In the growing literature on the complex relationship between religion and film, however, comparatively little attention has been paid to cinema horror and its depiction of the demonic. There are a few essays or articles (e.g., Krzywinska 2000; May 1982; Telotte 1996), which are often subsumed under imprecise rubrics like "the dark side" (Butler 1969: 158–79) or "the problem of evil" (Hurley 1970; Zwick 1997), and an occasional book (e.g., Beal 2002; Cowan 2008), but this response seems out of proportion to horror's place both in the artistic, technological, and economic development of cinema and in the history, evolution, and systematization of human religious consciousness. While its budget may seem paltry by today's standards and its special effects rather dated, how many people know that when it was released The Exorcist was the most successful commercial motion picture to date? How many know that without the income a cash-strapped Twentieth Century Fox realized from Richard Donner's The Omen a young filmmaker named George Lucas would not have been able to finish a little picture he was working on called Star Wars (1977)?

On the other hand, the Roman satirist Petronius may have said that fear first brought the primal gods into being, but fear of hell (or hells), fear of hungry ghosts, angry spirits, and wrathful demons, fear that the gods are capricious at best and that the unseen order may not have humanity's best interest at heart have structured religious belief and practice throughout history. Religion and fear have been on intimate terms for millennia and, although that intimacy finds its natural creative reflection in cinema horror, it has been largely ignored by scholars. Two principal reasons explain this unfortunate lacuna: too narrow a vision of horror and too narrow a vision of religion.

Made for each other: rethinking religion and horror

Released in 1999, Rupert Wainwright's *Stigmata* was marketed as *The Exorcist* for an MTV generation. Rather than the careful, almost symphonic pacing of Friedkin's film, moviegoers were led to expect a rock video version of possession and exorcism. Many were disappointed, however, when they learned the movie was about the Bible, or, rather, books that didn't make it into the Bible due to early church intrigue. Frankie Paige (Patricia Arquette), a Philadelphia hairdresser, has become the unwilling vehicle for the spirit of a dead priest who, in life, had been entrusted to translate one of the oldest gospels excluded from the Bible – the Gospel of Thomas. As a result, Frankie has begun to manifest the stigmata. Sent to investigate, Father Andrew Kiernan (Gabriel Byrne) is astonished to learn she is an atheist. "I don't go to church because I don't believe in God," she says simply. "Officially, this is not a case for the Church," Kiernan replies, somewhat nonplussed. "To say that a self-confessed atheist exhibits the wounds of Christ is a contradiction in terms." Faced with the horror of Frankie's experience and the bleeding wounds in her wrists, his dismissal of her case echoes both aspects of the lacuna.

Founding editor of the *Journal of Religion and Film* Ron Burke begins his review of *Stigmata*, "You do not expect to find religion and spirituality in a horror film" (1999: par. 1). Notwithstanding such obvious examples as *Rosemary's Baby*, *The Exorcist*, and *The Omen*, if Burke has limited his understanding of horror movies to slasher films such as *The Texas Chain Saw Massacre* (1974), *My Bloody Valentine* (1981), or the seemingly endless sequelae (and the occasional crossover) of *Halloween* (1978), *Friday the 13th* (1980), and *A Nightmare on Elm Street* (1984), then his comment is understandable. They may be among the most culturally visible examples, but slasher films like these account for a relatively small proportion of the genre. Throughout its history, cinema horror is in fact replete with religion.

Ghost stories, for example, from *The Haunting* (1963, 1999) and *The Amityville Horror* (1979, 2005) to *The Fog* (1980, 2005) and *Poltergeist* (1982) are predicated on the possibility of life after death and the disposition of the soul or spirit, both principal components in religious thinking around the world. The various iterations of the *Frankenstein* story, from James Whale's 1931 Universal production to Kenneth Branagh's 1994 interpretation, explicitly challenge the notion that God is in control of creation and reinforce what many consider the basic Edenic paradox: we are created in God's image but we are prevented from becoming as God. Mummy movies, many of which retell the same tragic love story, require a popular perception of – and fascination with – Egyptian religion (Day 2006). Without these, the tortured shamblings of Boris Karloff and Christopher Lee lose all meaning, descending quickly from horror into slapstick. Witchcraft and modern Paganism, whether as subject (e.g., *Horror Hotel*

[1960] or *The Craft* [1996]) or object (e.g., *Witchfinder General* [1968] or *The Blair Witch Project* [1999]), posit an alternate religious reality that threatens the dominant order in significant ways. Nunsploitation films ranging from Sergio Grieco's *The Sinful Nuns of St. Valentine* (1974) to Bruno Mattei's *The Other Hell* (1980) and Lucio Fulci's *Demonia* (1990) rely on deeply embedded cultural ambivalences about the Roman Catholic Church for their power to shock and horrify. Neither should we forget to give the Devil his due: from Méliès onward, Satan has shown himself a cinema horror staple (Schreck 2000). In his study of nearly 1,000 British horror films released between 1931 and 1984, sociologist Andrew Tudor found that the first thematic line along which these movies divide is the supernatural/secular (1989: 8–12), what I have called the collision between nature and supernature (Cowan 2008), and that more than two-thirds rely on the supernatural in some form. What many commentators on cinema horror fail (or refuse) to recognize is that one person's superstition is another person's deeply held religious belief. This brings us to the second aspect of the lacuna: not that our vision of horror is too limited, but our vision of religion.

Deriving from the first, but indicating the lacuna more directly, the second aspect is epitomized by Christian missiologist Bryan Stone, who sees cinema horror as part of an ongoing denigration and popular rejection of religion in society. For him, scary movies are one more facet of a creeping secularization threatening the place religion has occupied in society for centuries. Writing in the *Journal of Religion and Film*, Stone argues that because "it offends, disgusts, frightens, and features the profane, often in gruesome and ghastly proportions, other than pornography, horror is the genre least amenable to religious sensibilities" (2001: par.3). Not unlike other critics, such as Michael Medved, who is virulently opposed to what he calls "the self-destructive nature of Hollywood's underlying hostility to organized religion" (1992: xviii), Stone concludes that "the mere fact that horror films rely heavily on symbols as mere conventions to scare the hell out of us does not make a case for religious vitality in our culture; in fact, their persistence eviscerated of any deeper connection to our lived questions may be a good example of the decline of the religious in our culture" (2001: par. 39). That is, if atheists cannot manifest the wounds of Christ, then cinema horror cannot disclose to us anything of value about religion.

This depends, of course, on what one means by "religion," something that scholars have argued about for so long and from so many different perspectives that there is not even an agreed-upon definition informing the discussion. Some define religion structurally – by what they think it is – others functionally – by what they think it does. Many define it theologically: religion means "my religion," and all others are relegated to the conceptual nether space of "cults" and "sects." Though, nowadays, William James is often either overlooked or treated as a historical footnote in this debate, in Lecture 3 of *The Varieties of Religious Experience* he offers what I consider one of the most useful definitions available. For James, "the life of religion" – because religion is a lived phenomenon or it is nothing at all – resides in "the belief that there is an unseen order, and that our supreme good lies in harmoniously adjusting ourselves thereto" (1999 [1902]: 61). Some scholars may consider this conceptualization unhelpfully broad, but James' definition has two principal advantages that suit it admirably to a discussion of religion and cinema horror.

First, the "unseen order" means simply that. It does not require the presence of one or another supernatural agent, nor adversion to a supreme deity. It does not deny belief in gods or goddesses, but it does say that lived religion around the world and throughout history cannot be limited to traditions informed by those kinds of beliefs. Neither does it adjudicate "religion" based on the dominance of one faith tradition over another (or all others). Those without cultural capital or social position worship no less fervently than those occupying the halls of political or religious power. The shadowy priests of Arkham keeping *The Mummy* alive through secret incantations or appeals to "the great god, Karnak"; Lady Sylvia Marsh (Amanda Donohoe) worshiping her savage pre-Christian deity in *The Lair of the White Worm* (1988); or Wilbur Whately (Dean Stockwell) trying to bring back the Old Gods in *The Dunwich Horror* (1970) – these present us with no less a vision of the unseen order than films lodged on more familiar theological ground. We may not think these visions reasonable or compelling in any offscreen sense, but that is not the point. As Mehemet Bey (George Pastell) says to John Banning (Peter Cushing) in Terence Fisher's 1959 Hammer remake of *The Mummy*, "You are intolerant. Because you are unable to experience the greatness of a deity, you dismiss it as of no consequence." Indeed, rarely has a single line of onscreen dialogue so concisely captured the off-screen reality for so many people around the world.

Second, and far more important for the discussion of religion and cinema horror, James' definition avoids what I have called elsewhere "the good, moral, and decent fallacy" (Cowan 2008: 15–16; Cowan and Bromley 2008: 10–14), the popular belief that religion is, has been, or should be a positive force in society. When I say, "John is a very religious person," many (arguably most) people interpret that to mean that he is good, moral, and decent, or that he strives to be on the basis of his religious belief. While John may be all those things, the problem is that there is little historical evidence that religion as a social phenomenon has been overwhelmingly a force for good – the millions of victims of any number of tribunals, inquisitions, crusades, and religious wars of conquest would beg to differ – and little sociological data supporting a causal relationship between ethical behavior and religious belief. Criticizing cinema horror for its depiction of religiously motivated torture or murder, for example, willfully ignores the abundant record of such behavior in human history. Blood sacrifices, whether human or not, have been a part of religious practice for thousands of years and animal sacrifice remains so in many traditions today. These rites form part of the relationship between the seen and unseen orders. They facilitate "harmonious adjustment" and negotiate for the "supreme good" of those who participate. As every first-year sociology student learns, concepts like goodness, morality, and decency are not absolutes, but are culturally constructed and socially reinforced. In this, then, religion and cinema horror seem made for each other.

Why religion, though? Given the abundance of real-life horror, from ethnic cleansing in Darfur to cultural genocide in Tibet, from the threat of renegade nuclear terrorism to the imperial terrorism of dominant nation-states, from fears of economic collapse to environmental catastrophe, why do filmmakers so often tell stories that either place religion center stage or use it to dress the set in significant ways? If movies are one of the principal lingua francas of late modern society, what are scary movies saying to us about religion?

Michael Medved and Bryan Stone think horror films celebrate the demise of religion in the late modern West, that they are, as it were, the flying apes of secularization. Certainly there are instances of this, but as a general phenomenon this explanation is wholly inadequate, if for no other reason than the limitations of vision I have just discussed. Put broadly, secularization is the belief that technologized societies are becoming less reliant on faith-based worldviews, less dependent on religion to explain the workings of the unseen order, and, often, more dependent on science for that which religion once provided. While there is certainly some evidence for this in parts of Europe, and in North America, especially the United States, religious belief remains remarkably high. We may tell ourselves that we are becoming more sophisticated in our approach to the universe, that we can explain its mysteries without reference to the gods and demons that ruled and haunted our less-informed forebears, but those gods and demons survive nonetheless. The issue is not one of secularization – that cinema horror discloses to us the abandonment of religion – but an overwhelming ambivalence toward the religious beliefs and practices, myths and ritual, doctrine and dogma by which we are continually confronted, in which we are often still deeply invested and distinctly unwilling to relinquish, but which we just as often only minimally understand. It is this ambivalence, and the various fears it both invokes and evokes, that cinema horror reveals.

The "fear factors" of cinema horror

When animals fear, a variety of physical responses are fairly standard across different species, including *Homo sapiens*: heart rate and respiration increase, pumping blood and oxygen to the muscles; pupils dilate slightly, perhaps to increase visual acuity; adrenaline is produced for the extra surge of energy on which survival may depend. What animals fear, however, and how they fear varies drastically across species, and for *Homo sapiens* across cultures and societies. Physical responses to fear may be similar, but the sources of fear differ widely. For over two decades now, many scholars have been looking at human fearing as a social phenomenon, rather than something limited to physical and/or psychological stimulus and response (cf. Cowan 2008; Scruton 1986; Tudor 2003). That is, we are subject to a range of *sociophobics*, that what we fear, why we fear, and how we manifest and resolve our fears are socially constructed, culturally conditioned, and integrally connected to who we are as communal animals. The cinema horror image of the zombie, for example, generates far different fear reactions in North American audiences than in either West Indian or Indian. An American audience may be titillated by the possibility of the walking dead, but in Haiti zombiism remains an important (if relatively minor) component of Vodou, while cremation as the standard method of corpse disposal in India renders the problem of the zombie slightly ridiculous. Small piles of ash creeping slowly across the ground are simply not that scary. Both religious socialization and secular enculturation ensure that we learn what we should fear, while a vast array of cultural products reflects, refracts, and reinforces those fears we have been taught. As I explore more fully in *Sacred Terror* (Cowan 2008), six basic themes emerge in a typology of religion and cinema horror. Though these should not be considered discrete categories and many films contain more than one sociophobic element, they are, in no particular order of importance: fear of a change in the sacred order; fear of sacred places; fear of death, of dying badly, and of not remaining dead; fear of evil externalized and internalized; fear of the flesh and the powerlessness of religion; and, finally, fear of fanaticism and the power of religion.

Fear of change in the sacred order

For hundreds of millions of people, religion is predicated on a sense of timelessness, a belief that their religious tradition has been and always will be. This is most obvious in triumphalist versions of Christianity that interpret every moment from the creation to the apocalypse as established in a divine plan to which they alone have access. Their god is *the* god, now and forever. Through what I call horrific metataxis – a fundamental change or shift in taxonomic categories (Cowan 2008: 67–8) – many horror movies challenge this most basic understanding of the universe. As Peter Berger points out in his classic work, *The Sacred Canopy*, "All socially constructed worlds are inherently precarious" (1967: 29). This is no less true for religious worlds than for any other kind, something cinema horror exploits in three particular ways: invasion, inversion, and insignificance.

Invasion narratives imagine the displacement of the dominant understanding of the unseen order by culturally unfamiliar religious traditions. Drawing on the complex mythology of the Old Ones developed by horror writer H. P. Lovecraft, for example, films such as *Dagon* (2001) and *The Dunwich Horror* present elder gods whose pride of place has been usurped by the younger deities of monotheism and who wait in the outer darkness for a chance to return. Analogous to alien invasion movies of the 1950s, these films highlight the instability of religious worldviews, contesting their inevitability in the same way UFOs challenged the dominance of the American social order in the years following the Second World War.

If invasion narratives represent the enemy, inversion stories use the concept of the traitor to challenge dominant religious understandings. Operating from within, trading on relationships of trust, traitors are far more dangerous than enemies. From satanic covens working within the Church to bring about the reign of the Antichrist (e.g., *Lost Souls* [2000]; *The Omen*; *To the Devil . . . a Daughter* [1976]) to the overthrow of heaven itself by those most trusted with its defense (e.g., *The Order* [2003]; *The Prophecy* [1995]), these films turn in many ways on Freud's concept of "the uncanny." A category that "belongs to the realm of the frightening, of what evokes fear and dread," the important point is that it "goes back to what was once known and had been long familiar" (Freud 2003 [1919]: 123, 124). In these cases, fear is a function of familiarity, of trust turned on its head.

Finally, there is insignificance, the fear that for all our belief, our prayers, and our devotion, our gods simply no longer matter. While *Hellraiser: Bloodline* (1996) is considered by fans one of the weakest of the franchise, the third mode of metataxis is epitomized by the main character, the Cenobite, Pinhead (Doug Bradley). "Oh, my God!" exclaims one of the human characters weakly when he encounters Pinhead for the first time. To which the Cenobite responds, "Do I look like someone who cares what God thinks?" Monsters, writes Timothy Beal, are continually "warning us to retreat into the established order of things" (2002: 161). What films like the *Hellraiser* (1987) franchise imagine is a world in which the established order no longer matters.

Fear of sacred places

"Place directs attention," writes Jonathan Z. Smith (1987: 103). That is, it directs our attention to something for some purpose. What cinema horror so often directs our attention to is the ambivalence we feel toward sacred places, the places set aside for our gods, where we conduct negotiations with the unseen order. Many horror movies, for example, use churches as places of first refuge, last resort, or final conflict (e.g., *28 Days Later* [2002]; *Children of the Damned* [1963]; *Resident Evil: Apocalypse* [2004]). Building on the horrific metataxis of a change in the sacred order, however, these putative sanctuaries often reveal themselves as the principal locus of challenge to the dominant religious under-standing. In *The Order*, the cavernous underground temple from which the onslaught of the Church will begin is located directly beneath the Vatican. In John Carpenter's *The Fog*, the old church on the hill is the last place to which townsfolk should flee since it was there that the original evil in the story was plotted. Cinema horror has an expansive range of settings, but three principal venues locate our fear of sacred places: buildings dedicated to the dominant religious order; the temples of other gods; and places of the dead.

First, religiously oriented cinema horror regularly features abandoned or desecrated churches. From *The Exorcist* and *Hellraiser III* (1992) to *Black Sunday* (1960), *Midnight Mass* (2003), and *Taste the Blood of Dracula* (1970), ruined and tainted sanctuaries have filled the silver screen for decades and reinforce the insignificance of the god in whose name they were originally constructed. Abandoned churches often indicate a truant God; they reflect a fear of God's absence. When a film's dénouement plays out in a dedicated sacred space, however (e.g., *Omen III: The Final Conflict* [1981]; *Bless the Child* [2000]; *End of Days* [1999]), these are the relatively rare occasions in cinema horror when a *deus ex machina*, whether by direct divine intervention or through divine agents, saves the day.

Second, the temples of other gods often highlight the socially constructed nature of religious fears, reinforcing the offscreen reality that what is a sacred site for one group is for others the architectural symbol of a threatening religious Other. The pyramids and temple complexes from which emerges *The Mummy* often signal the dangerous move from modern to premodern ways of thinking. Sacrificial altars and blood rites mark the places through which the elder gods seek to reenter our world.

Third, there are the places we set aside for the dead. Hundreds of millions of people around the world believe that the veil between the seen and the unseen orders is thinnest where the dead congregate. Graveyards, cemeteries, tombs, and mausolea haunt the vaults of cinema horror as they do our collective imagination, giving rise to the most memorable of movie monsters: *Dracula* rising from his crypt or *The Mummy* from his tomb; the graves robbed to give *Frankenstein*'s creation a semblance of life; zombies lurching from the ground in dread service or in search of their next meal. Religious sanctuaries and the numerous places of the dead they either house or protect are the quintessential liminal spaces between life and death, between the seen order of the living and the unseen order of the dead.

Fear of death, of dying badly, and of not remaining dead

"Though we know at any moment that we must die," writes Kurt Reizler, "we do not fear death all the time, except in some remote or dark corner of our mind" (1944: 490). It is into this dark corner that cinema horror so often shines its light, and though we may not fear death at any given moment, scary movies remind us that throughout human history we fear dying badly and not remaining dead. There is no *a priori* reason to believe that the dead feel any more or less animosity toward the living than they did when they were alive, but religious mythistory is filled with such beliefs. From pyramid complexes to crossroads and busy thoroughfares, elaborate burial rites work to ensure the dead remain on their side of the veil. Coins planted under the tongue pay for a soul's passage across the river Styx, while *mizuko kuyo* ensures the spirit of an aborted fetus or stillborn child will not return as a wrathful ghost. While the former finds its origin in Greek mythology and is rarely performed today, the latter is arguably the single most common religious ritual in Japan today. Most, if not all, cinema horror turns on the fear of death in one way or another, but religiously oriented horror preys on four particular sociophobic archetypes: entrapment, condemnation, bondage, and reanimation.

A pancultural staple, fear of entrapment, or the inability to move on, animates the ghost story. Whether a vengeful revenant (e.g., *The Fog*; *The Ring* [2002]), a haunted house (e.g., *The Haunting*; *13 Ghosts* [1960, 2001]), or men and women "caught dead" (e.g., *Carnival of Souls* [1962]; *The Sixth Sense* [1999]), ghost movies have generated box office receipts around the world for decades. Indeed, cross-cultural analysis of ghost movies – especially versions of the same film made for different audiences, such as *Ju-On* (2003) and *The Grudge* (2004), or *Ringu* (1998) and *The Ring* – reveals important details about the cultural construction of fear (Cowan 2008: 128–33). Condemnation, on the other hand, and the requirement to remain between life and death, is the cinematic domain of the vampire. Here, too, we see important differences in horror movies based on culturally specific sociophobics. North American audiences, for example, used to the cross-and-holy-water approach to dealing with the undead might be surprised to see the eight trigrams of the *I Ching* and elaborate Taoist magic employed in any number of Hong Kong vampire films. Whereas, in Hong Kong cinema, an inauspicious burial often results in the creation of a vampire (or a zombie, in some cases), numerous Western films have suggested that the Church itself bears responsibility for the undead (e.g., *Bram Stoker's Dracula* [1992]; *John Carpenter's Vampires* [1998]).

Although there are exceptions, the trope of the eternally lost love defines *The Mummy*, bound forever to protect the grave of the one he was forbidden to love in life.

Swathed in ragged grave-wrappings, the Mummy plods across the screen, its horror a function of the havoc it wreaks on those who have disturbed its rest. The real horror, though, so eloquently seen in Christopher Lee's eyes as the tomb door slowly closes, is tapophobia, the fear of being buried alive. Possessing neither the pancultural appeal of the ghost story, the potential eroticism of the vampire, nor the obvious pathos of the mummy, zombie movies have often been criticized as the poor second cousin of cinema horror. This is unfortunate since, whatever their origin – bioweapons research gone awry (*Resident Evil* [2002]), Vodou ritual (*White Zombie* [1932]), or extraterrestrial intervention (*Invisible Invaders* [1959]) – zombies represent the fear that, however we die, we cannot rest in peace. Rather than monsters, per se, they are us – our friends, our neighbors, our family, sometimes even our pets.

Fear of evil externalized and internalized

We externalize our fears in any number of ways: the bogeyman, the witch in the forest, and, throughout much of Christian history, the Devil. Although many forms of late modern Christian theology have relegated Satan to a metaphor, a psychological placeholder for those parts of ourselves we would prefer not to face, others are still deeply informed by belief in a literal devil. According to recent Gallup data, more than two-thirds of Americans say they believe in the Devil, a finding that cuts across all demographic boundaries (Robison 2003). Seventy percent of Americans believe in Hell, as do 50 percent of those who say they either never or only rarely attend church (Winseman 2004). In terms of the cultural stock of knowledge on which cinema horror draws, the importance of these statistics should not be underestimated.

For most of cinema horror's history, the Devil has been a standard character on the B-movie lot. Beginning in 1968, however, three films mainstreamed Satan in ways that brought to the surface fears that have been deeply embedded in Western culture for centuries. Excoriated by a number of feminist film scholars, one of whom called it "an odious fable of parturition" (Fischer 1992: 4), *Rosemary's Baby* remains one of the most popular films of post-Second World War horror cinema. Building on the belief in a "demon seed," the fear that evil grows within us, director Roman Polanski invites audiences to find in his film reflections of the fears they bring to the theater. For some, it is about the horror of birth; for others, it is the birth of horror. Once again, though, implicit in the birth is the potential for social chaos at the most profound level – God's unseen order traded for Satan's. If *Rosemary's Baby* attacks from within, then *The Exorcist* battles evil that invades from without. Called by many the scariest movie of all time, William Friedkin's story of a young girl possessed by a demon has become one of the enduring icons in the history of Western cinema horror. Relatively few in the technologized West may give credence to the existence of vampires, mummies, or zombies, but belief in the possibility of demon possession and the need for exorcism is firmly grounded in centuries of Christian theology. A thriving subculture of exorcism exists in both Roman Catholicism and fundamentalist Protestantism (Cuneo 2001), and for millions of Christian believers demons are no less real now than they were in the Middle Ages. Finally, building directly on Protestant dispensationalist obsession with the end times, Richard Donner's *The Omen* brought the

Antichrist to mainstream cinema. "I firmly believe," says producer Harvey Bernhard, "that the Devil didn't want us to make the film" (Zacky 2001). The film was made, however, and cinema horror has continued the mainstreaming of Satan ever since.

Fear of the flesh and the powerlessness of religion

Sex and fear couple in virtually all aspects of cinema horror (Hogan 1986), and religiously oriented scary movies are no exception. If horror is one axis of transgression across the cultural domains of religious belief and practice, when horror is eroticized its transgressive effect is significantly increased. From straightforward temptation narratives such as The Devil's Nightmare (1971) and Kiss Me, Kill Me (1973) to heterosexually and homosexually oriented tales of vampire lust (e.g., The Nude Vampire [1970] and Shiver of the Vampires [1971]), and from nunsploitation films to any of the seemingly endless, softcore Witchcraft (1988) series, the horrific and the erotic have shown themselves in intense, symbiotic relationship. Indeed, fear of witches and the sexual power of women goes back many hundreds, if not thousands, of years, finding its most potent religious expression during the late Middle Ages in works such as the Malleus Maleficarum and Compendium Maleficarum. Exploiting such a deeply rooted ambivalence, many horror movies focus on the woman's body as the object of fascination and desire, the site of repression and aggression, and, often, the locus of evil and catastrophe. As I note in Sacred Terror, for a significant number of these films, especially nunsploitation, "it is as though Augustine and Tertullian – two significant architects of Christian misogyny – sat in on the script sessions, costume meetings, and principal photography" (Cowan 2008: 237). The product of that most durable and misogynistic of Christian myths – that woman is a temptress at best and evil incarnate at worst – nunsploitation films are a late modern reflection of two powerful, linked obsessions that developed in many countries where the Roman Catholic Church established dedicated religious communities: fear based on what people came to believe took place behind convent walls and a fetishistic fascination with the women religious who live cloistered there.

Whatever other sins cinema horror discloses, in this particular sociophobic domain lust is the vehicle by which those who would challenge heaven seek to subvert the dominant social or religious order. In some cases, the victims are presented as ordinary people: men and women who experiment with the occult, who fall in with those who do, or who are simply offered up as victims. On the other hand, when religion is meant to provide a social space dedicated to spiritual development apart from the demands or responsibilities of the flesh, horror films reflect the fear that religious belief and practice will be powerless when those demands take center stage. When the devil comes then, he most often comes in the flesh.

Fear of fanaticism and the power of religion

When religion makes the news, few words galvanize public attention more than "cult," and few function so effectively as a lightning rod for social concern about the often terrifying force of religion. The secretive religious group plotting mayhem against an unsuspecting populace, the zealous followers of this or that charismatic leader expecting the end of the world in fire and death, the sinister coven carrying out rituals of blood sacrifice in the service of ancient gods – all these have featured in cinema horror and all have reinforced the fear of religious fanaticism and the power of the dangerous religious Other that lurks beneath our proud veneer of late modern religious pluralism. To be sure, throughout history religion has motivated believers to carry out horrific acts of violence and cruelty, but this reality is hardly limited to new or alternative religions, what are so often and so easily labeled "cults." Indeed, at any given time, there are thousands of small, alternative religious groups and only a tiny fraction of those ever turn violent in any way. Most pass all but unnoticed in society.

They live on in cinema horror, however, in films like *The Believers* (1987), which presents a skewed version of Santería, an Afro-Caribbean religion not dissimilar to Vodou, or *The Craft*, which turns fairly typical teenage angst into a pretense for modern Witchcraft, or *The Wicker Man* (1973), which, human sacrifice notwithstanding, many consider an accurate portrayal of modern Pagan revivalism. Herein lies the real power of cinema horror. Broadly speaking, it is axiomatic that most people don't know very much about religion, either historically or sociologically. They may know a tremendous amount about their own religion, or about the razor-thin slice of that religion in which they were raised. They may even have made an effort to learn about religions other than their own – for personal growth, to serve an apologetic agenda, or as a result of or precursor to conversion – but, historically speaking, these cases are relatively rare. Cinema horror capitalizes on this relative ignorance. Thus, films like *The Omen* and *Lost Souls* can use fabricated scripture as a plot device because writers and directors can count on the gravitas these references lend without worrying unduly that too many people will point out the obvious fakery (cf. Beavis 2003; Prothero 2007). When films such as *The Exorcist* or *The Exorcism of Emily Rose* (2005) are marketed as "based on real events," or the producers of *The Omen* advertise the story as "ripped from the pages of the Bible" (Zacky 2001), how many audience members are sufficiently knowledgeable to know where the line between fiction and reality is drawn? Thus, cinema horror becomes part of the bricolage of information informing the cultural stock of knowledge in which audiences participate and on which they draw.

Horror and the persistence of belief

However much we may want to believe we live in more sophisticated, more enlightened times, that science has replaced our need for God as a candle in the dark, the unseen order remains a cultural fixture. "Enough has been said," writes Gustav Jahoda in his seminal study of superstition, "to indicate that under the seemingly rational surface of modern society there is an unexpectedly widespread yearning for the mysterious and the occult we are supposed to have outgrown" (1969: 23). The important concept here is *yearning*. That is, not only do we continue to believe in the unseen order – in supernatural phenomena, in counterintuitive agencies such as gods and demons – but we retain an equally strong inclination to believe, an equally powerful desire that these things be true. However frightening they may be, like Fox

Mulder (David Duchovny) we want to believe. Though he wrote long before *The X-Files* first appeared in 1993, Jahoda's words were almost prescient. "Superstition," he argues, "is still very much with us, and it is even possible that some forms of it may be on the increase" (Jahoda 1969: 26). Between 1990 and 2001, for example, American belief in psychic or spiritual healing went from 44 to 54 percent. Belief in ghosts and haunting spirits rose from 25 to 38 percent, and a more general belief in the ability of the living to communicate with the dead from 18 to 28 percent (Newport and Strausberg 2001).

Terror, angst, and existential dread may not be the only engines of religious consciousness, but their role in the interplay between the unseen order and those who seek to harmoniously adjust themselves thereto cannot be denied. As Rudolf Otto pointed out in his seminal work, *The Idea of the Holy*, "It is this feeling which, emerging in the mind of primeval man, forms the starting point for the entire religious development in history" (1950 [1919]: 14). Whether Otto is correct or not, whether human religion finds its genesis in fear or fear is simply part of the cognitive and emotional apparatus we have developed along with religion, he points directly at the heart of sacred terror. "'Daemons' and 'gods' alike," he continues, "spring from this root, and all the product of 'mythological apperception' or 'fantasy' are nothing but different modes in which it has been objectified" (Otto 1950 [1919]: 15). Since the turn of the twentieth century, cinema horror has been one of the "different modes" in which this fear has been objectified, peeling away the skin of late modern sophistication and revealing the "daemonic dread" that still crawls beneath it. It has become our camp fire, our blanket and flashlight, our haunted house, the place to which our imaginations return when we confront our ambivalence about the unseen order and its relationship to us.

Bibliography

Beal, T. (2002) *Religion and its Monsters*, New York and London: Routledge.

Beavis, M. A. (2003) "Angels Carrying Savage Weapons: Uses of the Bible in Contemporary Horror Films," *Journal of Religion and Film* 7 (2). Online. Available HTTP: <http://www.unomaha.ed/jrf/vol7No2/angels.htm> (accessed 21 July 2008).

Bellin, J. D. (2005) *Framing Monsters: Fantasy Film and Social Alienation*, Carbondale: Southern Illinois University Press.

Berger, P. L. (1967) *The Sacred Canopy: Elements of a Sociological Theory of Religion*, New York: Anchor Books.

Boot, A. (1993) *Fragments of Fear: An Illustrated History of British Horror Films*, London and San Francisco: Creation Books.

Brunvard, J. H. (1981) *The Vanishing Hitchhiker: American Urban Legends and Their Meanings*, New York and London: W. W. Norton.

Burke, R. (1999) "Film Review: Stigmata," *Journal of Religion and Film* 3 (2). Online. Available HTTP: <http://www.unomaha.edu/jrf/Stigmata.htm> (accessed 21 July 2008).

Butler, I. (1969) *Religion in the Cinema*, New York: A. S. Barnes.

Carroll, N. (1990) *The Philosophy of Horror, or Paradoxes of the Heart*, New York and London: Routledge.

Clemens, V. (1999) *The Return of the Repressed: Gothic Horror from* The Castle of Otranto *to* Alien, Albany: State University of New York Press.

Clover, C. J. (1992) *Men, Women, and Chain Saws: Gender in the Modern Horror Film*, Princeton: Princeton University Press.

Cowan, D. E. (2008) *Sacred Terror: Religion and Horror on the Silver Screen*, Waco, TX: Baylor University Press.

Cowan, D. E. and Bromley, D. G. (2008) *Cults and New Religions: A Brief History*, Oxford: Blackwell.

Creed, B. (1993) *Monstrous Feminine: Film, Feminism, Psychoanalysis*, London and New York: Routledge.

Cuneo, M. (2001) *American Exorcism: Expelling Demons in the Land of Plenty*, New York: Doubleday.

Day, J. (2006) *The Mummy's Curse: Mummymania in the English-Speaking World*, London and New York: Routledge.

Dijkstra, B. (1986) *Idols of Perversity: Images of Feminine Evil in Fin-de-Siècle Culture*, New York and Oxford: Oxford University Press.

Fischer, L. (1992) "Birth Traumas: Parturition and Horror in *Rosemary's Baby*," *Cinema Journal* 31 (3): 3–18.

Freud, S. (2003 [1919]). *The Uncanny*, trans. D. McLintock, New York: Penguin Books.

Furedi, F. (2006) *Culture of Fear Revisited*, 4th ed., London: Continuum.

Glassner, B. (1999) *The Culture of Fear: Why Americans Are Afraid of the Wrong Things*, New York: Basic Books.

Grant, B. K. (ed.) (1996) *The Dread of Difference: Gender and the Horror Film*, Austin: University of Texas Press.

Halberstam, J. (1995) *Skin Shows: Gothic Horror and the Technology of Monsters*, Durham, NC: Duke University Press.

Harrington, C. (1950) "Ghoulies and Ghosties," *Quarterly of Film, Radio and Television* 7 (2): 191–202.

Hogan, D. J. (1986) *Dark Romance: Sexuality in the Horror Film*, Jefferson, NC, and London: McFarland.

Hurley, N. P. (1970) *Theology Through Film*, New York: Harper & Row.

Ingebretsen, E. J. (1996) *Maps of Heaven and Hell: Religious Terror as Memory from the Puritans to Stephen King*, Armonk, NY, and London: M. E. Sharpe.

—— (2001) *At Stake: Monsters and the Rhetoric of Fear in Public Culture*, Chicago and London: University of Chicago Press.

Jahoda, G. (1969) *The Psychology of Superstition*, Harmondsworth: Penguin Books.

James, W. (1999 [1902]) *The Varieties of Religious Experience*, New York: Modern Library.

Jancovich, M. (1996) *Rational Fears: American Horror in the 1950s*, Manchester and New York: Manchester University Press.

Kalat, D. (2007) *J-Horror: The Definitive Guide to* The Ring, The Grudge *and Beyond*, New York: Vertical.

Kendrick, W. (1991) *The Thrill of Fear: 250 Years of Scary Entertainment*, New York: Grove Press.

Kristeva, J. (1982) *Powers of Horror: An Essay on Abjection*, trans. L. S. Roudiez, New York: Columbia University Press.

Krzywinska, T. (2000) "Demon Daddies: Gender Ecstasy and Terror in the Possession Film," in A. Silver and J. Ursini (eds) *Horror Film: A Reader*, New York: Limelight: 247–67.

Lawrence, P. A. and Palmgreen, P. C. (1996) "A Uses and Gratifications Analysis of Horror Film Preference," in J. B. Weaver, III and R. Tamborini (eds) *Horror Films: Current Research on Audience Preferences and Reactions*, Mahwah, NJ: Lawrence Erlbaum: 161–78.

Leggett, P. (2002) *Terence Fisher: Horror, Myth and Religion*, Jefferson, NC, and London: McFarland.

May, J. R. (1982) "The Demonic in American Cinema," in J. R. May and M. Bird (eds) *Religion in Film*, Knoxville: University of Tennessee Press: 79–100.

Medved, M. (1992) *Hollywood vs. America*. New York: HarperPerennial/Zondervan.

Newport, F. and Strausberg, M. (2001) "Americans' Belief in Psychic and Paranormal Phenomena is Up over Last Decade." (8 June). Online. Available HTTP: <http://at www.gallup.com> (accessed 23 March 2004).

Otto, R. (1950 [1923]) *The Idea of the Holy*, trans. J. W. Harvey, London and Oxford: Oxford University Press.

Paffenroth, K. (2006) *Gospel of the Living Dead: George Romero's Visions of Hell on Earth*, Waco, TX: Baylor University Press.

Pinedo, I. C. (1997) *Recreational Terror: Women and the Pleasures of Horror Film Viewing*, Albany: State University of New York Press.

Prothero, S. (2007) *Religious Literacy: What Every American Needs to Know – And Doesn't*, New York: HarperSanFrancisco.

Reizler, K. (1944) "The Social Psychology of Fear," *American Journal of Sociology* 49 (6): 489–98.

Robison, J. (2003) "The Devil and the Demographic Details" (25 February). Online. Available HTTP: <http://at www.gallup.com> (accessed 23 March 2004).

Schneider, S. J. (ed.) (2003) *Fear Without Frontiers: Horror Cinema Across the Globe*, Godalming: FAB Press.

Schreck, N. (2000) *The Satanic Screen: An Illustrated History of the Devil in Cinema, 1869–1999*, New York: Creation Books.

Scruton, D. L. (ed.) (1986) *Sociophobics: The Anthropology of Fear*, Boulder, CO, and London: Westview Press.

Skal, D. J. (1994) *The Monster Show: A Cultural History of Horror*, New York: Penguin Books.

—— (1998) *Screams of Reason: Mad Science and Modern Culture*, New York and London: W. W. Norton.

Smith, J. Z. (1987) *To Take Place: Toward Theory in Ritual*, Chicago: University of Chicago Press.

Stone, B. (2001) "The Sanctification of Fear: Images of the Religious in Horror Films," *Journal of Religion and Film* 5 (2). Online. Available HTTP: <http://www.unomaha.edu/jrf/ sanctifi.htm> (accessed 21 July 2008).

Telotte, J. P. (1996) "Faith and Idolatry in the Horror Film," in B. K. Grant (ed.) *Planks of Reason: Essays on the Horror Film*, Lanham, MD, and London: Scarecrow Press: 21–37.

Tudor, A. (1989) *Monsters and Mad Scientists: A Cultural History of the Horror Movie*, London: Basil Blackwell.

—— (2003) "A (Macro) Sociology of Fear?" *Sociological Review* 51 (2): 238–56.

Twitchell, J. B. (1985) *Dreadful Pleasures: An Anatomy of Modern Horror*, New York and Oxford: Oxford University Press.

Waller, G. A. (1987) "Introduction," in *American Horrors: Essays on the American Horror Film*, Urbana and Chicago: University of Illinois Press: 1–13.

Winseman, A. L. (2004) "Eternal Destinations: Americans Believe in Heaven, Hell." Online. Available HTTP: <http://online at www.gallup.com> (accessed 8 April 2007).

Zacky, B. (dir.) (2001) *The Omen Legacy*, Fox Television.

Zillman, D. and Weaver, J. B. III (1996) "Gender-Socialization Theory of Reactions to Horror," in J. B. Weaver, III and R. Tamborini (eds) *Horror Films: Current Research on Audience Preferences and Reactions*, Mahwah, NJ: Lawrence Erlbaum: 81–101.

Zuckerman, M. (1996) "Sensation Seeking and the Taste for Vicarious Horror," in J. B. Weaver, III and R. Tamborini (eds) *Horror Films: Current Research on Audience Preferences and Reactions*, Mahwah, NJ: Lawrence Erlbaum: 147–60.

Zwick, Reinhold (1997) "The Problem of Evil in Contemporary Film," in J. R. May (ed.) *New Image of Religious Film*, Kansas City: Sheed & Ward: 72–91.

Filmography

The Amityville Horror (1979, dir. S. Rosenberg)
The Amityville Horror (2005, dir. A. Douglas)
The Believers (1987, dir. J. Schlesinger)
Black Sunday (1960, dir. M. Bava)
The Blair Witch Project (1999, dir. D. Myrick and E. Sánchez)
Bless the Child (2000, dir. C. Russell)
Bram Stoker's Dracula (1992, dir. F. Coppola)
The Cabinet of Dr. Caligari (1920, dir. R. Wiene)
Carnival of Souls (1962, dir. H. Harvey)
Children of the Damned (1963, dir. A. Leader)
The Craft (1996, dir. A. Fleming)
Dagon (2001, dir. S. Gordon)
Demonia (1990, dir. L. Fulci)
The Devil's Nightmare (1971, dir. J. Brismée)
Dracula (1931, dir. T. Browning)

The Dunwich Horror (1970, dir. D. Haller)
End of Days (1999, dir. P. Hyams)
The Exorcism of Emily Rose (2005, dir. S. Derrickson)
The Exorcist (1973, dir. W. Friedkin)
The Fog (1980, dir. J. Carpenter)
The Fog (2005, dir. R. Wainwright)
Frankenstein (1910, dir. J. Dawley)
Frankenstein (1931, dir. J. Whale)
Friday the 13th (1980, dir. S. Cunningham)
Godspell (1973, dir. D. Greene)
The Golem (1920, dir. C. Boese)
The Grudge (2004, dir. T. Shimizu)
Halloween (1978, dir. J. Carpenter)
The Haunting (1963, dir. R. Wise)
The Haunting (1999, dir. J. de Bont)
Hellraiser (1987, dir. C. Barker)
Hellraiser: Bloodline (1996, dir. A. Smithee [K. Yagher])
Hellraiser III: Hell on Earth (1992, dir. A. Hickox)
Horror Hotel (1960, dir. J. Moxey)
Invisible Invaders (1959, dir. E. Cahn)
Jesus Christ Superstar (1973, dir. N. Jewison)
John Carpenter's Vampires (1998, dir. J. Carpenter)
Ju-On (2003, dir. T. Shimizu)
Kiss Me, Kill Me (1973, dir. C. Farina)
The Lair of the White Worm (1988, dir. K. Russell)
Lost Souls (2000, dir. J. Kaminski)
Le Manoir du Diable (1896, dir. G. Méliès)
Mary Shelley's Frankenstein (1994, dir. K. Branagh)
Midnight Mass (2003, dir. T. Mandile)
The Mummy (1932, dir. K. Freund)
The Mummy (1959, dir. T. Fisher)
My Bloody Valentine (1981, dir. G. Mihalka)
A Nightmare on Elm Street (1984, dir. W. Craven)
Nosferatu (1922, dir. F. Murnau)
The Nude Vampire (1970, dir. J. Rollin)
The Omen (1976, dir. R. Donner)
Omen III: The Final Conflict (1981, dir. G. Baker)
The Order (2003, dir. B. Helgeland)
The Other Hell (1980, dir. B. Mattei)
Poltergeist (1982, dir. T. Hooper)
The Prophecy (1995, dir. G. Widen)
Resident Evil (2002, dir. P. Anderson)
Resident Evil: Apocalypse (2004, dir. A. Witt)
The Ring (2002, dir. G. Verbinski)
Ringu (1998, dir. H. Nakata)
Rosemary's Baby (1968, dir. R. Polanski)
Shiver of the Vampires (1971, dir. J. Rollin)
The Sinful Nuns of St. Valentine (1974, dir. S. Grieco)
The Sixth Sense (1999, dir. M. Shyamalan)
Star Wars (1977, dir. G. Lucas)
Stigmata (1999, dir. R. Wainwright)
Taste the Blood of Dracula (1970, dir. P. Sasdy)
The Texas Chain Saw Massacre (1974, dir. T. Hooper)
13 Ghosts (1960, dir. W. Castle)

13 Ghosts (2001, dir. S. Beck)
To the Devil . . . a Daughter (1976, dir. P. Sykes)
28 Days Later (2002, dir. D. Boyle)
White Zombie (1932, dir. V. Halperin)
The Wicker Man (1973, dir. R. Hardy)
Witchcraft (1988, dir. R. Spera)
Witchfinder General (1968, dir. M. Reeves)
The Wizard of Oz (1939, dir. V. Fleming)

23

JESUS AND CHRIST-FIGURES

Adele Reinhartz

In the days after his crucifixion, Jesus' followers were briefly able to see him alive once again. According to the Gospel of John, the newly resurrected Lord appeared first to Mary Magdalene, and then to the disciples. The disciples were overjoyed. But one of them, Thomas, was absent at the time, and refused to believe unless he could see and touch Jesus himself. Jesus returned a week later and offered Thomas the visual and tangible evidence he so desired: "Put your finger here and see my hands. Reach out your hand and put it in my side. Do not doubt but believe" (20:27). Thomas exclaimed: "My Lord and my God!" (20:28). Having seen, heard, and perhaps even touched Jesus, his faith was now complete. Despite his willingness to satisfy Thomas' deepest desire, however, Jesus did not entirely approve: "Have you believed because you have seen me? Blessed are those who have not seen and yet have come to believe" (20:29).

The longing to see Jesus has stimulated the creativity of countless artists in the two millennia since Jesus' death. The results of their efforts are on view in art galleries and live theaters throughout the world. But since the late nineteenth century, it is through film that Jesus is most readily visible to us. Hollywood, New York, and numerous international centers of cinema have portrayed Jesus directly – in the so-called "Jesus movies" about his life – and indirectly – in "Christ-figure films" that draw upon Christ-related images to tell a fictional story. This essay will provide an introduction to these two types of films, and some of the ways in which they have been interpreted, in order to consider to what extent and in what ways the cinema allows us, like Thomas, to see Jesus for ourselves.

Jesus movies

For most of us, the term "Jesus movies" calls to mind biblical epics which lavishly depict Jesus' life from birth to death (e.g., *The Greatest Story Ever Told* [1965]), or dramatize a particular period of his life (e.g., *The Nativity Story* [2006]; *The Passion of the Christ* [2004]).

Another vehicle for depicting scenes from Jesus' life is the "sword-and-sandal" movie, also known as the "peplum movie" (a reference to the loose-fitting clothing worn in these films) (Baugh 1997: 241). In these films, Jesus makes cameo appearances within a fictional story set in his lifetime (*Ben-Hur* [1959]) or after his death (*Demetrius and the Gladiators* [1954]). These films focus not so much on the details of Jesus' life but on the impact he, and the religious system in which he is worshiped as Messiah, had on others. The most famous scene in this style of film occurs in *Ben-Hur* in which a mysterious figure dressed simply in a brown robe offers water to the parched protagonist, Judah Ben-Hur. The gesture is then returned by Ben-Hur, when this mysterious man carries his cross toward Golgotha. At no point do we see the man's face, yet we recognize that he is Jesus.

A second type of film that embeds Jesus in a fictional frame narrative is the passion play film, which portrays a group of actors in the process of preparing a passion play. Some films of this type focus more or less equal attention on both the fictional frame and the passion play itself (*Jesus of Montreal* [1989]; *Master i Margarita* [*The Master and Margarita*, 1994]); some focus primarily on the passion play (*Jesus Christ Superstar* [1973]) and others exclusively on the frame narrative (Pasolini's *La ricotta* [1963]; *Celui qui doit mourir* [*He Who Must Die*, 1957]). Passion play films evoke the historical passion play tradition, in which a village or community stages an annual passion play, and the impact that the preparation and performance of the play have on the villagers or actors involved. The most famous and enduring example of the passion play has been staged in Oberammergau, Germany since 1634.

Brief chronology

Jesus was a favorite subject of filmmakers from the very beginning of the film era. The first known example of a Jesus movie was the nineteen-minute long *The Passion Play at Oberammergau* (1898). Despite its title, it was not filmed at Oberammergau, Germany but in New York (Kinnard and Davis 1992: 19–20). Other silent movies include *The Life and Passion of Jesus Christ* (1905), *From the Manger to the Cross* (1912), and *Christus* (1917). These films present living, if slow-moving, tableaux modeled after devotional paintings. They generally make little attempt to create a coherent storyline and presumed the viewers' familiarity with the story. The most interesting of these early films is D. W. Griffith's classic, *Intolerance* (1916). Griffith was the first to use the Jesus story to address a social issue in his period: he brought Jesus in to support his own case against the "Uplifters" of the Temperance movement who in his view exercised a moralistic and unChristian stranglehold on American society at the time.

By the 1920s, films began to develop particular themes and plot lines. The 1921 German film *Der Galiläer* (*The Galilean*) focused on the culpability of Jewish characters and made abundant use of antisemitic stereotypes. The 1923 film *INRI* provided a robust image of Jesus' mother, taking considerable liberties with the Gospel accounts by portraying her as having an active role in Jesus' life well beyond his infancy. The most famous silent Jesus film is Cecil B. DeMille's *The King of Kings* (1927). Like earlier silent movies, DeMille's work made use of inter-titles and creates scenes that imitate famous works of art. DeMille's narration, however, was much more sophisticated in that it developed a main plot and subplots the elements of which are linked through cause and effect. Furthermore, he used inter-titles not only to quote from scripture and provide background information, but also to convey original, and often witty, dialogue and to provide commentary that helped develop the plot and characters.

The King of Kings was enormously successful and highly influential. Indeed, for thirty-four years after its release, Jesus did not star in any major Hollywood film. This hiatus, however, was due only in part to the popularity of DeMille's epic. In 1930, Hollywood adopted the Production (Hays) Code. The code was a censorship system that restricted the ways in which films were permitted to deal with subject matter pertaining to religion, ethics, sexuality, and numerous other issues. It was forbidden to mock "ministers of religion"; Jesus could be represented only in the most reverential manner. The code continued to affect the Jesus movies even after it was officially lifted (Leff and Simmons 2001).

The early epics of the 1960s, Nicholas Ray's *King of Kings* (1961) and George Stevens' *The Greatest Story Ever Told* (1965), held to the reverential conventions of the Hays era by creating static and solemn Jesus figures who spoke very slowly and rarely smiled. In other respects, the epics were lavish and grand, featuring: large crowds, vivid color, majestic settings, and full orchestral music. Epics continued the trend toward complex plots held together by the principle of causality, and attempted to go beyond the Gospels in explaining, for example, why Judas betrayed Jesus, and what made Jesus such a threat to Jewish and Roman authorities alike.

One of the most acclaimed dramas from this, or any period of the Jesus movies, is Pier Paolo Pasolini's Italian film *Il Vangelo secondo Matteo* (*The Gospel According to St. Matthew*, 1964). While it belongs to the same era as the epics, Pasolini's film reflects a far different filmmaking tradition and sensibility. As the name suggests, this movie is based on the First Gospel. Indeed, the dialogue is taken entirely from Matthew's Gospel. The visuals, however, often import elements from other Gospels. For example, the Passion sequence is portrayed through the eyes of John, the "Beloved Disciple" of the Gospel of John. This film is intended as an allegory that reflects critically on the Italian state during and after the Second World War. Another Italian film that evokes the simple rural life and greatly expands the role of Jesus' mother is Roberto Rossellini's *Il Messias* (*The Messiah*, 1975). This film was never released in North America due to distribution difficulties.

The 1970s saw numerous Jesus films. Of these, the two musicals, *Jesus Christ Superstar* (1973) and *Godspell* (1973), stand out as attempts to bring the Jesus story to life in the rock opera medium. Both also transpose Jesus to a contemporary setting: the Negev desert in southern Israel filled with American hippies, in the case of *Superstar*, and the streets of a strangely silent New York City, in the case of *Godspell*. And both explore contemporary issues such as civil rights and the cult of celebrity.

The major English-language films from the 1970s and beyond include Franco Zeffirelli's lengthy made-for-TV series *Jesus of Nazareth* (1977), John Heyman's evangelical film *Jesus* (1979), Robert Young's miniseries by the same name (1999), and the British made-for-TV "claymation" (clay animation) movie *The Miracle Maker* (2000). These films, like the 1960s epics, present conventional narratives that harmonize all four Gospels and adopt a reverential attitude toward Jesus. Each has its own emphasis, however. Zeffirelli's film pays considerable attention to the Jewish context of Jesus' early life, and creates a fictional character, Zerah the scribe, as the devious mastermind behind the plot to have Jesus arrested, tried, and executed. The hero of Young's *Jesus* is an adolescent very attached to his father, Joseph. *The Miracle Maker* tells the story from the point of view of Jairus' daughter (see Mark 5:22–43) in order to appeal to a young audience. The overwhelming piety and conventionality of the epic genre helped to inspire a highly entertaining comedy, *Monty Python's Life of Brian* (1979). The film both makes use of and makes fun of the clichés of the genre by creating an accidental messiah, named Brian, whose life mirrors that of Jesus, while preserving the stereotypical representation of Jesus himself.

Two late twentieth-century dramas may also be seen as reactions or responses to the epic genre. Martin Scorsese's *The Last Temptation of Christ* (1988) differed from most of its predecessors in that it made no claims to historicity but rather presented itself as an adaptation of Nikos Kazantzakis' well-known novel. Here was a Jesus who is unsure of his identity and struggles to discern whether the voices that guide him belong to God or the devil. The film is iconoclastic in that it draws viewers into Jesus' subjective state, including his final dream, or perhaps hallucination, in which he marries, has a family, and works as an ordinary carpenter. The dream sequence created great controversy for many reasons, not the least of which were its depictions of Jesus making love with Mary Magdalene, and with Mary and Martha of Bethany (Medved 1992: 37–49; Tatum 2004: 188–92). Denys Arcand's *Jesus of Montreal* (1989), the principal Canadian contribution to the Jesus-film corpus, portrayed a group of actors that has been commissioned by the priest of St. Joseph's Oratory in Montreal to refresh the passion play that has been performed on the church grounds for decades. In the process of preparing and performing the play, the actors themselves take on the personas of the characters in the Gospel story; this blurring is actually typical of the passion play experience (Shapiro 2000). Arcand's film is the most thoroughly allegorical of the genre; it deconstructs Jesus' traditional biography in order to mount a trenchant critique of the Catholic Church in Quebec, and of other elements in contemporary society, including the debasement of art. Despite, or perhaps because of, its anti-ecclesiastical stance, the film succeeds, better than most Jesus films, in bringing us face to face with a Jesus who is humble, yet challenging and tremendously appealing.

The twenty-first century has thus far proven just as fruitful for the Jesus movie genre as the twentieth. Philip Saville's *The Gospel of John* utilized every single word of the Good News Bible's translation of the Fourth Gospel, appeared in 2003. It was soon overshadowed, however, by Mel Gibson's *The Passion of the Christ* (2004, 2005). Like *The Passion Play at Oberammergau*, *Golgotha* (1935), and *Jesus Christ Superstar*, Gibson's film is an account of Jesus' last hours. Months before its release, the movie created controversy with regard to both its heavy-handed violence and its negative representations of the Jewish authorities. While some viewers felt that the film brought them closer to the "true" Jesus, others found the film boring and shallow, and felt that it diminished Jesus rather than elevating him. Gibson took his inspiration from many sources, including the Gospels, the meditations of a nineteenth-century Catherine Anne Emmerich, and early Jesus movies. Like the early silent movies, the film is hard to follow for those who do not already know the story. One of its unusual features is the major role given to Satan, a disturbing figure who confronts Jesus in Gethsemene and slithers noiselessly but palpably through the Jewish and Roman crowds that seek Jesus' death.

Since Gibson's film, two feature films have appeared, both in 2006: Catherine Hardwicke's *The Nativity Story*, and Jean-Claude La Marre's *Color of the Cross*. *The Nativity Story* is a pleasant film about Jesus' birth and early childhood. The premise behind *Color of the Cross* is that Jesus was black, and was hated by the Jewish and Roman authorities alike due to the color of his skin. A BBC television miniseries, simply entitled *The Passion*, aired over Easter Week 2008. It is safe to say that Jesus movies will continue to be made for the foreseeable future.

Jesus movies as "biopics"

While most Jesus movies have been feature-length dramas, our survey shows that Jesus' story can be told in virtually any genre, including musicals, comedies, and animated children's films. Although all of these films rely on the Gospels as source texts, their plot structure and many other features are determined by the genre chosen. To give but one example, the animated version of the Jesus story, the 2000 BBC production *The Miracle Maker*, was clearly intended for an audience that included children. This film takes much of its material from Zeffirelli's *Jesus of Nazareth*, but also adds a frame narrative in that the action is seen through the eyes of Jairus' young daughter Tamar. This girl, who is not named in the Gospels, is resurrected from death or near death by Jesus (cf. Mark 5:41). She provides a lively perspective on the action. Other elements are toned down. For example, Mary Magdalene, often portrayed as the adulterous woman saved by Jesus in John 7:53–8:11, here is suffering from mental or emotional illness, not promiscuity.

Despite their variety, Jesus movies have many points in common with one another, as well as with other biographical films ("biopics"). Like other biographical films, and historical films more generally, the Jesus movies usually evoke a historical place and time: the Galilee and Judea of the early first century CE. In doing so, they make explicit use of primary sources. While some films, such as Pasolini's *The Gospel According to St. Matthew*, Heyman's *Jesus*, and Saville's *The Gospel of John*, base their accounts on a single Gospel account, most draw on all four canonical Gospels and harmonize their stories into a single linear narrative. Other sources, such as the apocryphal Gospels (Young's *Jesus*), and the works of first-century Jewish historian Josephus Flavius (utilized in Ray's *King of Kings*), are also used.

In claiming fidelity to scripture, most Jesus movies also claim to be true to the historical events of Jesus' life (Reinhartz 2007; 2006: 1–17). The 1912 silent movie *From the Manger to the Cross*, for example, announces itself as "a review of the Saviour's life according to the gospel-narrative." Cecil B. DeMille's 1927 classic *The King of Kings* also begins with a scrolled text that asserts the historicity of its account: "The events portrayed by this picture occurred in Palestine nineteen centuries ago, when the Jews were under the complete subjection of Rome – even their own High Priest being appointed by the Roman procurator." Similarly, the sonorous "voice-of-

God" narrative voice-over that opens the 1961 epic *King of Kings* (Orson Welles) begins with facts that are more or less based on Josephus' account but sound biblical in their formulation:

> And it is written, that in the year 63 BC the Roman Legions like a scourge of locusts poured through the east laying waste to the land of Canaan and the kingdom of Judea. Rome's imperial armies went unto the hills and struck Jerusalem's walls in a three-month siege. Reaching the gates, these legions laid the dust of battle in a shower of blood.

Yet at the same time as films explicitly claim to be historical, it is obvious that fictional elements abound. These include scenes, dialogue and characters, as well as lengthy subplots that have no foundation in the canonical Gospels. For example, DeMille's *The King of Kings* invents a backstory according to which Judas and Mary Magdalene were lovers until Judas was enticed away by the Carpenter from Nazareth. This subplot helps to explain how Mary Magdalene happened to meet Jesus (she went to pry Judas loose from Jesus' grip) and became a chaste, docile, and devoted follower of the Carpenter. In Pasolini's film, the holy family stops off for a picnic at the beach on their way back to Nazareth from Egypt; Young's *Jesus* invents a teenage romance between Jesus and Mary of Bethany.

Many of these innovations are the fruit of the filmmakers' imaginations; others, however, reflect the lengthy tradition of theological, narrative, liturgical, and artistic interpretation of Jesus' life story. The narrator in Ray's *King of Kings* recites lines from the Apostles' Creed. In *The Greatest Story Ever Told*, Jesus "borrows" from Paul's famous ode to love (1 Corinthians 13). Numerous films model the seating plan of the Last Supper upon Leonardo da Vinci's famous fresco. The Hallelujah Chorus from Handel's *Messiah* sometimes accompanies the resurrection of Lazarus (e.g., *King of Kings*). The Jesus films also borrow freely from one another. As we have already noted, *The Miracle Maker* uses scenes directly from Zeffirelli's *Jesus of Nazareth*. Gibson's Pilate strongly resembles the Roman governor of *The Greatest Story Ever Told*.

These observations suggest that the Jesus movies, like other biopics, are shaped by a conventionally accepted paradox: they declare their films to be authentic, historical, and faithful to scriptures, and simultaneously undermine that declaration through their creative activity. Further, if the films are authentic at all, it is to the problems, anxieties, social mores, and values, not of Jesus' time period, but of their own (Reinhartz 2007). Even films that resolutely maintain the aura of the first-century Judean outpost of the Roman empire betray their contemporary interests and anxieties. The epics of the 1960s, for example, are sensitive to the events of the Holocaust and the establishment of the State of Israel. Saville's 2003 film *The Gospel of John* puts Mary Magdalene at the Last Supper on the basis of contemporary feminist biblical criticism and theology (Reinhartz 1999: 56–69). *Color of the Cross* (2006) features a black Jesus and suggests that his crucifixion was an act of racism.

Despite the clearly fictional elements of the Jesus films, viewers frequently measure them against the claims to historicity made by the films and filmmakers themselves.

While audiences, including reviewers, grant these movies some artistic license – after all, films must flesh out the scant Gospel accounts, add visual details, and provide narrative continuity – they also expect these films to conform to the "facts" as they know them. This expectation was evident in many of the reviews and analyses of Gibson's *The Passion of the Christ*, which describe the historical "errors" of this film (cf. Fredriksen 2004).

Cinematic Christology

The main theme in the Jesus movies, as in the Gospels, is Christology. Until the 1980s, most films focused on Jesus' divinity. Because the role of an unseen God is so difficult to convey, these films tended to portray Jesus as static, unchanging, and aloof, though the occasional glimpse of humor and warmth was permitted (cf. deMille, *The King of Kings*). The films of the 1980s include a stronger focus on Jesus' humanity, no doubt out of recognition that it was rather difficult for audiences to feel attached to the relentlessly solemn Jesus of the silent movies and grand epics. More recently, Gibson managed to have it both ways; throughout his Passion, Jesus remains silent and impassive, even as he is being beaten to a pulp. In the flashbacks, however, he demonstrates warmth and even playfulness.

Even within these parameters, however, different portrayals of Jesus emerge. DeMille provides us with an empathetic Jesus, who uses his carpentry skills to mend a wooden doll for a young follower. At the other end of the spectrum is Pasolini's angry Jesus, the sole cinematic savior to recite Matthew's diatribe against the Pharisees (Matthew 23) in full. The epics present a Jesus who is extremely conscious of the Roman oppression of the troubled land into which he was born. He rejects the role of military or political messiah, to which others tried to hold him, and instead promises salvation of a higher, nobler sort than violence could bring. *Monty Python's Life of Brian* mocks this cliché by portraying Brian as a Jewish revolutionary who joins one of many liberation movements in order to bed the beautiful Judith. Young's *Jesus* is a North American-style adolescent who loves his father Joseph even as he chafes at Joseph's high expectations. Scorsese's Jesus is an emotionally volatile man who is consumed with uncertainty as to whether he is indeed the Son of God. Arcand's Jesus is a social critic whose death literally makes the blind see and the (nearly) dead live. The Jesus of *Color of the Cross* is the victim of racism; that of Gibson, the one who suffers beyond human endurance.

Judaism and anti-Judaism

Visually, the Jesus of the movies is almost always the light-haired, blue-eyed, slim savior of illustrated Bibles and Renaissance art. He bears absolutely no resemblance to the typical Semitic male of the first century as that image has been reconstructed based on archeological evidence (Wilson 2004). At the same time, most films acknowledge, at least nominally, that Jesus was a Jew who lived his life almost entirely within the Jewish societies of the Galilee and Judea. The Jewish Jesus became more prominent in the last quarter of the twentieth century, influenced at least in part by the so-called Third Quest of the Historical Jesus (Crossan 1991; Sanders 1985; Fredriksen 1999).

Zeffirelli, for example, paints a rich Jewish landscape and focuses on Jewish practices, life-cycle events, and synagogue rituals. This film is perhaps the only mainstream film to depict Jesus' circumcision, though a careful viewer will notice that the baby Jesus is also lightly sprinkled with (baptismal) water for good measure.

Despite increased awareness of Jesus' Jewishness, and the post-Holocaust sensitivity to anti-Judaism and antisemitism, even the best efforts to avoid anti-Judaism almost always come undone at the Passion sequence. As a narrative, the Passion dramatizes the tragic condemnation of an innocent man. As theology, the Passion confirms, for Christians, the hero's identity as the Messiah and Son of God. But for Jewish–Christian relations, the most pressing issue in the accounts of Jesus' Passion is responsibility: who was to blame for Jesus' condemnation and crucifixion?

From a historical perspective, responsibility lies with Pilate, the Roman governor of Judea. It is he who had the authority, on behalf of Rome, to prosecute capital crimes in Judea. But the Gospels themselves point the finger at the Jewish authorities, and, by extension, the Jewish people as a whole. Most famously, Matthew has Pilate wash his hands and declare his innocence of Jesus' death, while the Jews cry out: "His blood be on us and on our children" (Matthew 27:24–5). While mainstream churches have distanced themselves from the deicide charge, it has by no means disappeared. Jesus filmmakers are therefore faced with a serious dilemma. In order to remain faithful to the Gospel accounts, they must assign at least some responsibility for Jesus' death to the Jewish authorities of the time. This move, however, no matter how carefully done, will inevitably leave them vulnerable to the charge of antisemitism (Reinhartz 2007).

Approaches to the study of the Jesus movies

The Jesus movies have generated a long bibliography in the popular press, in journals, and in anthologies (cf. Beal and Linafelt 2006; Middleton 2005). Nevertheless, only a handful of book-length studies covering the genre as a whole have appeared to date. The most comprehensive listing of films through the 1980s, including brief descriptions, can be found in Kinnard and Davis, *Divine Images: A History of Jesus on the Screen* (1992). The book is an excellent guide to the history of the genre. Recent books such as those by Tatum (2004), Stern, Jefford, and DeBona (1999), and Staley and Walsh (2007) offer more detailed discussions of a selection of major films. Intended as viewers' guides, these books provide a brief synopsis of each film as well as comments about the director, actors, the context of its production, its reception by critics and the general public, and any other features of special note. Staley and Walsh specifically focus on the DVD versions of the best-known Jesus films.

In addition to these introductory survey texts, a small number of more specialized book-length studies have appeared. Most of these focus on a selection of films, and provide detailed discussion and analysis. Reinhold Zwick (1997) provides an overall introduction to the Jesus movies and then focuses on Pasolini, Rossellini, Zeffirelli, and Stevens, with special emphasis on their portrayal of the miracles and Christology. Richard Walsh (2003) brings a selection of films – *Jesus of Montreal*, *Godspell*, *The Gospel According to St. Matthew*, Ray's *King of Kings*, and *The Greatest Story Ever Told* – into an intertextual conversation with the Gospels. Babington and Evans (1993) focus particularly on the role of the epic in American society, for example as the locus of encounter between religion and secularism in twentieth-century America. Lloyd Baugh (1997) has a particular interest in theological issues, but he also considers historical accuracy, the relationship between art and film, the challenges specific to the Jesus film genre, and the ways in which the personalities of the filmmakers (e.g., Pasolini's homosexuality and Marxist convictions) and social context (the "Quiet Revolution" of the 1960s in Quebec) influenced the Jesus movies. Larry Kreitzer's *The New Testament in Fiction and Film* (1993) proposes to "reverse the hermeneutical flow." His hypothesis is that we might better understand the New Testament by analyzing contemporary literature and films that engage in dialogue with biblical texts. Indeed, he views cinema and literature as "hermeneutics in action" (Kreitzer 1993: 16). Examining films and novels provides insights that give a fresh perspective on the biblical texts themselves. The Jesus-related films treated are the peplum movies *Ben-Hur* and *Barabbas* (1961).

My own work on the Jesus movies, entitled *Jesus of Hollywood*, departs from previous works in that it takes a thematic rather than film-by-film approach. While it does not ignore chronology, the book looks at the movies as "biopics" and structures the discussion around the main characters of the Jesus movie genre rather than the main films. For this reason it includes a larger number of films, including several silent films currently unavailable in VHS or DVD format; it compares the films with their scriptural sources, considers extra-biblical influences, such as music, art, liturgy, and theology, and discusses the contemporary concerns that the films reflect.

Films and faith

In their different ways, the Jesus movies attempt to satisfy the desire to "see" Jesus, to the extent that this is made possible by the abilities of actors and all the others who shape the films we see on the screen. For Doubting Thomas, however, the need to see Jesus was not merely curiosity but a prerequisite for faith. Filmmakers sometimes insist that their Jesus movies are not merely entertainment but also a vehicle for faith. The 1923 silent film *INRI*, for example, declares at the outset that:

> INRI wants to speak in the simple language which appeals to all hearts. The teaching of Jesus is placed before everyone, rich and poor, great and humble; it is Love one another, even at the price of a great Sacrifice. It wants to lead the spectator's soul to the great aim which is common to all men and nations, the will to mutual help, the human love. Peace on Earth.

DeMille situates *The King of Kings* in the context of the Great Command (Matthew 28:19) that Jesus' message "be carried to the uttermost parts of the earth" and hopes that his film would "play a reverent part in the spirit of that great command." Heyman's *Jesus* is perhaps the most explicitly evangelical film. It concludes with a lengthy epilogue that urges viewers to confess their faith in Jesus, then and there. Even films that do not aim to propagate Christian faith generally portray believers in a positive light and may serve, if not to convert viewers, at least to reinforce their Christian faith.

Assessment of the Jesus film genre

Do the Jesus movies provide an adequate means of "seeing" Jesus in our day and age? The answer depends on the viewers' expectations and the criteria that they favor. As we have seen, no film scores highly from the point of view of historicity. Indeed, the paradoxical conventions of the biopic genre guarantee disappointment for viewers seeking historicity above all else. From a spiritual and emotional perspective, different films resonate with different viewers. There are many who love the epics such as *The Greatest Story Ever Told* or *Jesus of Nazareth* not so much for theological reasons as for nostalgic ones: these are the films that they watched as children at Christmas or Easter time. On the other hand, while many viewers disliked *The Passion of the Christ* because of its violence and negative portrayal of Jewish characters, others were powerfully moved by Gibson's graphic depiction of Jesus' suffering.

Aesthetically, the films use the techniques and technologies of their era, with varying levels of sophistication. Pasolini's film stands out from the others of his time. The fact that it is filmed in black and white rather than in color draws attention to the simplicity of Jesus' message and the starkness of the lives of the ordinary people. The use of hand-held camera creates a sense of immediacy and situates the viewer almost inside the frame. The scene of Jesus' trial before Pilate, for example, has the feel of a home movie taken by someone standing among the curious crowd and craning her or his neck in order to see what is going on.

From a narrative point of view, however, the Jesus movies face two almost insur-mountable difficulties: a main character who is the Son of God, and therefore perfect and unchanging despite his corporeal humanity, and a plot that is well known to virtually all viewers before they see the film. No wonder, then, that many films develop the characters of Judas and/or Mary Magdalene to a far greater extent than the Gospels would warrant. Judas is of interest as a disciple who becomes Jesus' betrayer. Mary Magdalene's aura of sexuality is alluring, and safe, as she undergoes a transfor-mation from prostitute to disciple (Reinhartz 2007: 125–9).

For viewers who do not come to these films with nostalgia for the films of their youth, or a prior faith commitment to a specific Christology, the ability of a film to engender a powerful emotional and spiritual response may well be in inverse relationship to its fidelity to scripture, tradition, and the conventions of the biopic genre. Certainly it is the films that stray the furthest from a literal depiction of the Gospels – *Monty Python's Life of Brian*, Scorsese's *The Last Temptation of Christ*, Gibson's *The Passion of the Christ* – that have engendered the most powerful public reaction.

As we have noted, however, all Jesus movies, even those that explicitly state that their main goal is to recreate the life and times of Jesus of Nazareth, also address a contemporary agenda. In some cases, this is done only indirectly, as when, for example, the presence of women at the Last Supper table hints at the changing role of women in Christian communities. In other cases, the Jesus story is told not so much for its own sake but for its allegorical utility, for example to criticize the Temperance movement (*Intolerance*), Italian fascism (*The Gospel According to St. Matthew*), or contemporary Quebec (*Jesus of Montreal*). By retelling Jesus' story, these films imply that their views have the support of Jesus, and God, themselves.

Christ-figure films

Prevalent as Jesus movies have been since the dawn of cinema, they are not the only type of film through which audiences can "see" Christ at the movie theater. Even more numerous than the Jesus movies are the so-called Christ-figure films. Indeed, it may be said, with only slight exaggeration, that Jesus Christ, or someone who resembles him, is on view at every Cineplex in North America at any given moment.

Whereas "Jesus figures" are representations of Jesus himself, "Christ-figures" are fictional characters who resemble Jesus in some significant way. As Baugh has pointed out, "From early in the development of cinema, filmmakers have told stories in which the central figures are foils of Jesus and in which the plot is parallel to the story of the life, death and, sometimes, the resurrection of Jesus, stories in which the 'presence' of Jesus is sensed and discerned in the person and struggle of the protagonist" (Baugh 1997: viii–ix).

Within the overall category of Christ-figures, Peter Malone further distinguishes between those that are redeemer figures, representing a character who takes on human burdens and sinfulness through suffering, and those that are savior figures, enacting Jesus' saving mission, whether with respect to humankind (as in apocalyptic films such as *Deep Impact* [1998]) or to individuals (e.g., *Sling Blade* [1996]). These two categories, however, are not mutually exclusive (Malone 1990: 17–18).

According to Lloyd Baugh, who has provided the most detailed discussion of the subject to date, Christ-figure films stand in a well-developed tradition of figurative or metaphorical approaches to concepts of divinity. Baugh points to the Hebrew Bible's frequent use of metaphors such as the gentle breeze, the mother hen, and the suffering servant, to represent aspects of God's self-revelation. The Gospels depict Jesus using metaphors and parables to speak of divine truths. Further, as Baugh notes, "from the very beginning the art of the Christian community created and developed visual metaphors to represent Jesus the Christ" (Baugh 1997: viii–ix). Hollywood's fascination with Christ-figures has not gone unnoticed. While all film critics agree that Christ-figures abound in popular film, there is no consensus as to the value of seeking them out, or on what to make of them once found. Even Anton Kozlovic, who has viewed enough Christ-figure films to be able to discern twenty-five characteristics, warns of viewer fatigue and deplores the tendency to see Christ-figures everywhere (Kozlovic 2004: 12–14). Clive Marsh refers to the quest for Christ-figures as a "tired and sometimes tiresome pastime, so that any character who helps another to come to some major realization about themselves can be seen as salvific, and thus Christ-like. This borders on triteness" (Marsh 2004: 48–9).

Nevertheless, many, including those who are sometimes critical of the enterprise, uphold the need for specific criteria in order to identify Christ-figures in film. Baugh lists eight important characteristics: mysterious origins, charisma (the ability to attract followers), commitment to justice, conflict with authorities, the providing of redemption, withdrawal to a deserted place, suffering, and post-death recognition. Most of these are features of the movie plot rather than character attributes. Anton Kozlovic proposes a list of twenty-five characteristics, including aspects of the character (e.g., divinely sourced, aged thirty, blue-eyed, an outsider) and plot elements (e.g., betrayal, death, and resurrection whether literal or figurative). Neither Baugh nor Kozlovic argues that every Christ-figure film must contain all the qualities in their respective lists. Nevertheless, my own observation is that two main characteristics suffice: a plot structure in which one character extends him or herself on behalf of another, and a visual image associated with Christ, such as the cruciform position, the wearing of a cross, and/or walking on, near, or in water.

The mere presence of a Christ-figure, however, does not necessarily denote a profound appropriation of theology, spirituality, Christianity, or any other Christ-related beliefs. While some films use Christ imagery in a way that deepens the meaning and increases the emotional impact (e.g., *The Shawshank Redemption* [1994]), others use it in a rather trivial, and trivializing manner (e.g., *Nell* [1994]).

Genres and examples

Every year sees new cinematic saviors who heal the sick, raise the dead, walk on water, and sacrifice themselves for the greater good. Christ-figures appear in films of virtually every popular theme in commercial cinema, and they can take numerous guises: saints, priests, women, clowns, fools, madmen, outlaws, children, and even actors who play Jesus in passion plays (Baugh 1997: 210ff.). The sheer number and variety of Christ-figure films preclude a chronological overview of the sort provided above for the Jesus movies. A brief list of genres and examples will suffice to indicate the broad range of films in which Christ-figures can be found.

Westerns

Westerns frequently include the motif of the mysterious stranger who rides into town, saves the hardworking folk from marauders, and rides off again into the sunset. He is usually excluded from the community he saves by his special status as well as his use of violence (e.g., *Shane* [1953], *Pale Rider* [1985], *The Good, the Bad and the Ugly* [1966]).

Boxing movies

Boxing appears often in cinema as a metaphor for the triumph over adversity. The fact that most of the protagonists come from the lower and poorer segments of society makes these films a good way to address issues pertaining to class and poverty (e.g., the *Rocky* series [1976–2006], *Million Dollar Baby* [2004], *Cinderella Man* [2005]).

Prison movies

Prison films are perennially popular both because of their subject matter and also because they symbolically draw attention to the ways in which we are all prisoners of institutions, communities, and customs which may be necessary to our lives but also limit our freedom. The Christ-figures in these films are often prisoners who manage to liberate themselves and/or others through acts of heroism (e.g., *The Shawshank Redemption*, *Cool Hand Luke* [1967], *The Green Mile* [1999], *Cape Fear* [1991], *Escape from Alcatraz* [1979], *Dead Man Walking* [1995], *A Man Escaped* [1956]).

Movies featuring the mentally impaired

Many movies feature heroes who are labeled as "simple," "crazy," or "retarded." In cases where these heroes are institutionalized, the films are similar thematically to prison movies. In others, the protagonist lives within the broader society, and either despite or because of her/his disability saves or liberates others. This type of film explores social attitudes toward those who are differently abled and contemplates the line between disability and sinless perfection (e.g., *Being There* [1979], *One Flew Over the Cuckoo's Nest* [1975], *Nell*, *Rain Man* [1988], *Sling Blade*).

Science fiction and "end of the world" movies

These films project into the future, whether they envision an alternative, often future, world (*The Matrix* [1999]), a world in which human beings have taken upon themselves the divine role of giving life and taking it away (*Frankenstein* [1931], *Blade Runner* [1982]), or one in which humans must cope with a catastrophe on a gigantic scale (e.g., *Deep Impact*, the *Star Wars* series [1977–2005], the *Terminator* series [1984–2009], *The Fifth Element* [1997], *Children of Men* [2006]).

Spy movies

Spy movies often involve heroes who, with all their imperfections, nevertheless save others, most often preventing massive destruction falling upon their own countries and/or other countries and the (Western) world order (e.g., *The Good Shepherd* [2006], *The Constant Gardener* [2005], *Walk on Water* [2004]).

Mafia movies

Movies about organized crime often make natural use of Christian, specifically Catholic, imagery. This is not surprising, given that the most famous mafia movies, *The Godfather I, II*, and *III*, focus on Italians with strong Catholic identities. More surprising is the fact that some of these mobsters take on Christ-like roles despite the fact that their activities are illegal and often lethal (e.g., *The Godfather* series [1972–90], *Goodfellas* [1990], *The Departed* [2006]).

Superhero movies

The heroes of these films have extraordinary powers which they usually use to save others; their exploits nevertheless involve some risk to themselves. Like Jesus, they often have mysterious parentage, eschew romantic relationships, and fight the forces of evil (e.g., *Superman Returns* [2006], the *Spider-Man* trilogy [2002–7], *The Incredibles* [2004]; cf. Lawrence and Jewett 2002; Garrett 2008).

Romantic comedies

Perhaps the most unlikely Christ-figure films are romantic comedies, in which a man or woman saves his or her romantic partner from loneliness, low self-esteem, a life of promiscuity, or some other negative emotional state. These films are often light entertainment and even frivolous; often one or even both protagonists are explicitly linked with Christ imagery (*About a Boy* [2002], *Music and Lyrics* [2007], *Pretty Woman* [1990]).

Animal movies

Often directed at children, films with animal protagonists often make use of the savior/redeemer plot structure in which the animal saves other animals (*The Lion King* [1994]) or humans (*The Chronicles of Narnia* series [2005–8], *Babe: Pig in the City* [1998], *Charlotte's Web* [2006]).

Finally, and perhaps most interesting, are the films that play with or even subvert the Christ-figure film category itself. While many viewers are unaware of the origins of some of the imagery and plot structures used in Hollywood movies, the same cannot be said of filmmakers. This is evident in the films that deliberately disrupt or subvert the Christ imagery and motifs. In *Stranger than Fiction* (2006), for example, the hero, predestined to die in the heroic act of saving a young child from death, is rescued when his "creator" deliberately breaks the narrative paradigm to which she had been committed for years.

Approaches to the study of Christ-figure films

Identifying Christ-figures is just a first step in the analysis of these films. Baugh suggests that Christ-figure films can be read on two levels: "the direct and the analogical, the literal and the figurative; and on the figurative or metaphorical level, they accept a reading that is biblical and christological." In this regard, argues Baugh, Christ-figure films are similar to Jesus' parables, which can be read literally as brief narratives of human experience, but which "fairly explode with theological or christological significance" when they are read metaphorically. He views Christ-figures as an example of metaphorical usage that is deeply embedded in Christian faith and doctrine. Specifically, he points to the incarnational nature of Christian faith, which "insists that God reveals God's-self in and through matter and in Christ – human matter – and not only once but in an ongoing way" (Baugh 1997: 109).

Christopher Deacy proposes to set aside the "quest for correlations" and to engage in a twofold conversation between theology and film. In his view, the identification of Christ-figures is unimportant and even illegitimate except "when that figure is no longer seen simply as a cipher who illuminates Jesus for the sole purpose of, say, making him accessible to a modern generation, but inspires or incites the viewer to engender a critical and productive theological conversation" (Deacy 2006: par. 13).

Other scholars are concerned not so much with the theological implications of these films but with their ideological messages. Bryan Stone argues that films not only depict a world, they also promote a world view (Stone 2000: 6). Joel Martin, for example, analyzes *Rocky* as a political and social text that employs Christological imagery for ideological ends (Martin 1995: 125–33).

The cultural studies approach looks closely at the social, political, and cultural context that produced these films. According to Margaret Miles, a cultural studies approach "refocuses attention from the film as a text to the social, political, and cultural matrix in which the film was produced and distributed" (Miles 1996: xiii). In her view, filmgoers will tend to interpret and discuss movies in relation to the social issues of the moment. For this reason,

> A spectator's impressions of a film ... are simultaneously informed by her education and life experiences and trained by film conventions and viewing habits. This does not mean that the strong feeling a film may elicit should be discarded or overlooked. Rather, the emotion a film evokes should be acknowledged and understood as the starting point for an exploration of the filmic strategies that elicited it. The purpose of paying serious attention to film is twofold. On the one hand, the ability to analyze filmic representations develops an individual's critical subjectivity. On the other hand, films reveal how a society represents itself. (Miles 1996: 10)

Melanie Wright's approach builds on that of Miles, but she draws more attention to the fact that these films have "specific histories of distribution and exhibition" and advocates dialogue with film theory, particularly aesthetics and reception (Wright 2007: 29).

Whereas others propose a dialogue between film and theology, film and ideology, film and theory, or film and society, Larry Kreitzer suggests that there is value in a dialogue between film and the biblical text. He argues that Christ-figure films, like Jesus movies, provide an opportunity to "reverse the hermeneutical flow." Studying movies can help to sensitize us to issues and features that can help us to better understand the biblical text as such (Kreitzer 1993: 12).

Virtually all of these approaches also incorporate a narrative approach to the Christ-figure films by considering the role that the Christ-figure plays in the film narrative. In discussing the figure of Superman, for example, Roy M. Anker suggests that

> *Superman* is far more than a pastiche of portentous allusions, pious claptrap, and melodrama, which are usually the results of Christians trying to make popular films or of pop-culture, myth-making movies such as *The Matrix*. In the case of the first two Superman films, which were shot simultaneously, Superman as a Christ figure is not a random allusion or image simply pasted over the top of displays of special effects or old-style heroism. Rather, in what is a rare accomplishment in Hollywood, the whole of the film serves to elucidate and impart the surprise, wonder, and delight of the fantastic possibility of an incarnation of divine love itself ... Most of this gleeful christomorphic "work" in *Superman* comes at pivotal moments in which the filmmakers borrow freely, and usually with great wit, from biblical usage and events to shape and deepen the history of Kal-El/Clark Kent/Superman. (Anker 2004: 251)

For Anker, then, the identification of Superman as a Christ-figure unlocks the meaning and power of the film.

Others propose variations on this approach. Bernard Brandon Scott views these films as myth, that is, as narratives that mediate fundamental conflict in indirect and allusive ways (Scott 1994: 11). Clive Marsh draws explicitly on reader-response criticism by emphasizing that a film's meaning is not determined solely by the filmmakers but rather is negotiated through the interaction between viewer and movie. Meaning therefore depends heavily on the identities, knowledge, and experiences both in the movie theater and in "real life" that viewers bring to their film watching (Marsh 2004: 37). William Telford lays out a comprehensive list of what film analysis entails. This includes the elements of film style and narration, including characters, plot, setting, camera work and editing; awareness of the historical and cultural context in which the film was produced, and knowledge of the biblical texts and characters to which reference or allusion is made (Telford 2005). My own essays on Christ-figure films follow this same general outline (Reinhartz 2003, 2008).

Assessment of the Christ-figure film

The explicitly fictional nature of the films and the metaphorical or symbolic (rather than literal or historical) use of Christ imagery affords more opportunity for character development and dramatic interest than do most Jesus movies. In cases where the Christ-figure exercises a salvific or redemptive function on behalf of others, these films may be just as effective, if less direct, in conveying the belief that Christ is the answer after all. On the other hand, there is something slightly insidious about the use of Christ imagery in films that are not about Jesus in any way whatsoever. In telling a fictional story according to a Christian narrative template, Christ-figure films almost always encode a Christian subtext.

Like the Jesus movies, the Christ-figure films point beyond themselves to the concerns and preoccupations of the society that produced them. And while Christ imagery itself has come under considerable scrutiny, little attention has been given to the broader questions raised by Christ's frequent if imperfect incarnation in the heroes and heroines of the silver screen. What does Christ's prominence in Hollywood say about our culture, about ourselves, and the increasingly diverse society in which we live? Even more important, why do commercial feature films continue to use Christ imagery in an era of global marketing and increasingly multicultural and multi-religious audiences at home, that is, in a context where many viewers belong to cultures in which Jesus does not play a central role, if any role at all?

Conclusion

The 2,000 years and many miles that separate us from the time and place of the historical Jesus do not prevent us from seeing Jesus, or rather, a facsimile of Jesus, whether as the historical figure or in his many Christ-like guises. Of course, it is not Jesus that has satisfied the desire for visual contact but rather filmmakers, actors, and the dozens of other people involved in the creation of each Jesus or Christ-figure film. Despite the fascination that Jesus movies and Christ-figure films hold for many viewers, it is still worth asking the question: just because we *can* see "Jesus" does it mean that we should? Were Jesus to have any comment on the matter, he might simply reiterate his gentle rebuke to Doubting Thomas: "Blessed are those who have not seen and yet believe," particularly in the multicultural yet globalized world in which we live today.

Nevertheless, the unabating production of Jesus and Christ-figure films testifies to the enduring power of this man and his story to go beyond Christianity as a set of beliefs, traditions, and institutions, to capture the imagination and to act as a vehicle to grapple with the issues of the times and the essential dramas of human existence.

Bibliography

Anker, R. M. (2004) *Catching Light: Looking for God in the Movies*, Grand Rapids, MI: W. B. Eerdmans.

Babington, B. and Evans, P. W. (1993) *Biblical Epics: Sacred Narrative in the Hollywood Cinema*, Manchester: Manchester University Press.

Baugh, L. (1997) *Imaging the Divine: Jesus and Christ-Figures in Film, Communication, Culture and Theology*, Kansas City, MO: Sheed & Ward.

Beal, T. K. and Linafelt, T. (2006) *Mel Gibson's Bible: Religion, Popular Culture, and the Passion of the Christ, Afterlives of the Bible*, Chicago: University of Chicago Press.

Crossan, J. D. (1991) *The Historical Jesus: The Life of a Mediterranean Jewish Peasant*, San Francisco: HarperSanFrancisco.

Deacy, C. (2006) "Reflections on the Uncritical Appropriation of Cinematic Christ-Figures: Holy Other or Wholly Inadequate?" *Journal of Religion and Popular Culture* 13. Online. Available HTTP: <http://www.usask.ca/relst/jrpc/art13-reflectcinematicchrist-print.html> (accessed 30 June 2008).

Fredriksen, P. (1999) *Jesus of Nazareth, King of the Jews: A Jewish Life and the Emergence of Christianity*, Berkeley: University of California Press.

—— (2004) "Gospel Truth: Hollywood, History, and Christianity," in P. Fredriksen (ed.) *Perspectives on the Passion of the Christ*, New York: Miramax.

Garrett, G. (2008) *Holy Superheroes!: Exploring the Sacred in Comics, Graphic Novels, and Film*, rev. ed., Louisville, KY: Westminster John Knox Press.

Kinnard, R. and Davis, T. (1992) *Divine Images: A History of Jesus on the Screen*, New York: Carol Publishing Group.

Kozlovic, A. (2004) "The Structural Characteristics of the Cinematic Christ-Figure," *Journal of Religion and Popular Culture* 8. Online. Available HTTP: <http://www.usask.ca/relst/jrpc/art8-cinematicchrist-print.html> (accessed 30 June 2008).

Kreitzer, L. J. (1993) *The New Testament in Fiction and Film: On Reversing the Hermeneutical Flow*, Sheffield: JSOT Press.

Lawrence, J. S. and Jewett, R. (2002) *The Myth of the American Superhero*, Grand Rapids, MI: W. B. Eerdmans.

Leff, L. J. and Simmons, J. (2001) *The Dame in the Kimono: Hollywood, Censorship, and the Production Code*, 2nd ed., Lexington: University Press of Kentucky.

Malone, P. (1990) *Movie Christs and Antichrists*, New York: Crossroad.

Marsh, C. (2004) *Cinema and Sentiment: Film's Challenge to Theology*, Waynesboro, GA: Paternoster Press.

Martin, J. W. (1995) "Redeeming America: *Rocky* as Ritual Race Drama," in J. W. Martin and C. E. Ostwalt (eds) *Screening the Sacred: Religion, Myth, and Ideology in Popular American Film*, Boulder, CO: Westview Press.

Medved, M. (1992) *Hollywood vs. America: Popular Culture and the War on Traditional Values*, New York: HarperCollins.

Middleton, D. (2005) *Scandalizing Jesus?: Kazantzakis's* The Last Temptation of Christ *Fifty Years On*, New York: Continuum.

Miles, M. R. (1996) *Seeing and Believing: Religion and Values in the Movies*, Boston: Beacon Press.

Reinhartz, A. (1999) "To Love the Lord: An Intertextual Reading of John 20," in F. Black, R. Boer, C. Kelm, and E. Runions (eds) *The Labour of Reading: Essays in Honour of Robert C Culley*, Atlanta, GA: Scholars Press.

—— (2003) *Scripture on the Silver Screen*, Louisville, KY: Westminster John Knox Press.

—— (2006) "History and Pseudo-History in the Jesus Film Genre," in J. C. Exum (ed.) *The Bible in Film – and the Bible and Film*, Leiden: Brill.

—— (2007) *Jesus of Hollywood*, New York: Oxford University Press.

—— (2008) "Playing with Paradigms: The Christ-figure genre in contempory film." Australian Religious Studies Review 21(3): 298–317.

Sanders, E. P. (1985) *Jesus and Judaism*, Philadelphia: Fortress Press.

Scott, B. B. (1994) *Hollywood Dreams and Biblical Stories*, Minneapolis: Fortress Press.

Shapiro, J. S. (2000) *Oberammergau: The Troubling Story of the World's Most Famous Passion Play*, New York: Pantheon Books.

Staley, J. L. and Walsh, R. G. (2007) *Jesus, the Gospels, and Cinematic Imagination: A Handbook to Jesus on DVD*, Louisville, KY: Westminster John Knox Press.

Stern, R. C., Jefford, C. N., and DeBona, G. (1999) *Savior on the Silver Screen*, New York: Paulist Press.

Stone, B.P. (2000) *Faith and Film: Theological Themes at the Cinema*, St. Louis, MO: Chalice Press.

Tatum, W. B. (2004) *Jesus at the Movies: A Guide to the First Hundred Years*, rev. and expanded ed., Santa Rosa, CA: Polebridge Press.

Telford, W. R. (2005) "Through a Lens Darkly: Critical Approaches to Theology and Film," in E. S. Christianson, P. Francis, and W. R. Telford (eds) *Cinéma Divinité: Religion, Theology and the Bible in Film*, London: SCM Press.

Walsh, R. G. (2003) *Reading the Gospels in the Dark: Portrayals of Jesus in Film*, Harrisburg, PA: Trinity Press International.

Wilson, G. (2004) "So What Colour Was Jesus?" BBC New Online Magazine (27 October). Online. Available HTTP: <http://news.bbc.co.uk/1/hi/magazine/3958241.stm>

Wright, M. J. (2007) *Religion and Film: An Introduction*, London: I. B. Tauris.

Zwick, R. (1997) *Evangelienrezeption im Jesusfilm: Ein Beitrag zur intermedialen Wirkungsgeschichte des Neuen Testaments, Studien zur Theologie und Praxis der Seelsorge 25*, Würzburg: Seelsorge-Echter.

Filmography

About a Boy (2002, dir. C. Weitz)
Babe: Pig in the City (1998, dir. G. Miller)
Barabbas (1961, dir. R. Fleischer)
Being There (1979, dir. H. Ashby)
Ben-Hur (1959, dir. W. Wyler)
Blade Runner (1982, dir. R. Scott)
Cape Fear (1991, dir. M. Scorsese)
Celui qui foit mourir (He Who Must Die; 1957, dir. J. Dassin)
Charlotte's Web (2006, dir. G. Winick)
Children of Men (2006, dir. A. Cuarón)
Christus (1917, dir. J. Anatamoro)
The Chronicles of Narnia series (2005–8, dir. A. Adamson)
Cinderella Man (2005, dir. R. Howard)
Color of the Cross (2006, dir. J. La Marre)
The Constant Gardener (2005, dir. F. Meirelles)
Cool Hand Luke (1967, dir. S. Rosenberg)
Dead Man Walking (1995, dir. T. Robbins)
Deep Impact (1998, dir. M. Leder)

Demetrius and the Gladiators (1954, dir. D. Daves)
The Departed (2006, dir. M. Scorsese)
Escape from Alcatraz (1979, dir. D. Siegel)
The Fifth Element (1997, dir. L. Besson)
Frankenstein (1931, dir. J. Whale)
From the Manger to the Cross (1912, dir. S. Olcott)
Der Galiläer (*The Galilean*; 1921, dir. D. Buchowetzki)
The Godfather series (1972–90, dir. F. Coppola)
Godspell (1973, dir. D. Greene)
Golgotha (1935, dir. J. Duvivier)
The Good, The Bad and the Ugly (1966, dir. S. Leone)
The Good Shepherd (2006, dir. R. De Niro)
Goodfellas (1990, dir. M. Scorsese)
The Gospel of John (2003, dir. P. Saville)
The Greatest Story Ever Told (1965, dir. G. Stevens)
The Green Mile (1999, dir. F. Darabont)
The Incredibles (2004, dir. B. Bird)
INRI (1923, dir. R. Wiene)
Intolerance (1916, dir. D. Griffith)
Jesus (1979, dir. J. Heyman)
Jesus (1999, dir. R. Young)
Jesus Christ Superstar (1973, dir. N. Jewison)
Jesus of Montreal (1989, dir. D. Arcand)
Jesus of Nazareth (1977, dir. F. Zeffirelli)
The King of Kings (1927, dir. C. DeMille)
King of Kings (1961, dir. N. Ray)
The Last Temptation of Christ (1988, dir. M. Scorsese)
The Life and Passion of Jesus Christ (1905, dir. L. Nonguet)
The Lion King (1994, dir. R. Allers)
A Man Escaped (1956, dir. R. Bresson)
Master i Margarita (*The Master and Margarita*; 1994, dir. Y. Kara)
The Matrix (1999, dir. A. and L. Wachowski)
Il Messias (*The Messiah*; 1975, dir. R. Rossellini)
Million Dollar Baby (2004, dir. C. Eastwood)
The Miracle Maker (2000, dir. D. Hayes)
Monty Python's Life of Brian (1979, dir. T. Jones)
Music and Lyrics (2007, dir. M. Lawrence)
The Nativity Story (2006, dir. C. Hardwicke)
Nell (1994, dir. M. Apted)
One Flew Over the Cuckoo's Nest (1975, dir. M. Forman)
Pale Rider (1985, dir. C. Eastwood)
The Passion (2008, prod. N. Stafford-Clark)
The Passion of the Christ (2004, 2005, dir. M. Gibson)
The Passion Play at Oberammergau (1898, dir. H. Vincent)
Pretty Woman (1990, dir. G. Marshall)
Rain Man (1988, dir. B. Levinson)
La ricotta (1963, dir. P. Pasolini)
Rocky series (1976–2006, dir. J. G. Avildsen)
Shane (1953, dir. G. Stevens)
The Shawshank Redemption (1994, dir. F. Darabont)
Sling Blade (1996, dir. B. Thornton)
Spider-Man trilogy (2002–7, dir. S. Raimi)
Star Wars series (1977–2005, dir. G. Lucas)
Stranger than Fiction (2006, dir. M. Forster)

Superman Returns (2006, dir. B. Singer)
Terminator series (1984–2009, dir. J. Cameron; J. Mostow)
Il Vangelo secondo Matteo (*The Gospel According to St. Matthew*; 1964, dir. P. Pasolini)
Walk on Water (2004, dir. E. Fox)

Further reading

Forshey, G. (1992) *American Religious and Biblical Spectaculars*, Westport, CT: Praeger. (A detailed treatment of the biblical epic genre.)

Solomon, J. (2001) *The Ancient World in the Cinema*, rev. ed., New Haven, CT: Yale University Press. (Treatment of a broad range of films about the ancient, including classical, world.)

Telford, W. R. (2005) "'His Blood Be on Us, and Our Children': The Treatment of Jews and Judaism in the Christ Film," in E. S. Christianson, P. Francis, and W. R. Telford (eds) *Cinéma Divinité: Religion, Theology and the Bible in Film*, London: SCM Press. (Discussion of anti-Judaism in the Jesus films.)

Wyke, M. (1997) *Projecting the Past: Ancient Rome, Cinema, and History*, New York: Routledge. (Focuses on films about ancient Rome.)

24
ICONOGRAPHY
Diane Apostolos-Cappadona

I felt like I was walking through a museum of Christian art when seeing your film; was that intentional?

Jay Leno to Mel Gibson (26 February 2004)

Introduction: the what and the how of seeing images in film

Without doubt, there has been, and continues to be, a viable relationship between religion and film not simply in terms of movie titles or themes, but perhaps more significantly in the little-discussed modes and methods of the *seeing* of images. Recent studies in biblical and art historical scholarship have raised our awareness to the modes of analyses identified as "reception history" and the study of the "afterlives" of biblical figures (Exum and Moore 1998; Hornik 2003a; O'Kane 2007). In past generations, art historians from Erwin Panofsky (1962) to Leo Steinberg (1983) would have identified this as the study of iconography, that is the visual readings of signs and symbols which both enhance the meaning of the image(s) and also present an organized code of visual literacy. Further, iconographic studies have been predicated upon the premise that these visual encoded "texts" are both multivalent and primary evidence for the so-called "doing of theology" and the historicity of religion, and that images while publicly identified as secondary had power – a power that could neither be ignored nor denied.

Again, recent studies in biblical studies, church history, and theology have recognized the primary significance of the visual even unto the admission into the "canon" of the Society of Biblical Literature (SBL) of a formal section identified as "Bible and Visual Arts," and the publication of significant texts such as the reception-history based *Blackwell Companion to the Bible and Culture* (Sawyer 2006) and the SBL series volume *The Bible, Popular Culture, and the Arts: Resources for Instructors* (Roncase and Gray, 2008). In fact, the SBL sections have expanded further to include "Art and Religions of Antiquity," "Bible and Cultural Studies," "Bible in Ancient and Modern Media," and "Bible and American Popular Culture." Such scholarly acknowledgment, then, is proof both of this specific trend toward acceptance of the principle of the importance of *seeing*, and of the growing recognition of images as primary evidence for the study of religion(s) and theology, and even the Bible. This "new" tendency to accept images on a par with text – thereby moving away from the logocentricism of Western culture since the Enlightenment, if not the Reformation – is affirmed further in the careful attention being given currently to the study of all images from the popular images/illustrations in the modern media as well as to those on the walls of museums.

More than a "catchall" or umbrella for the categories and concepts of images used and utilized in religion and film studies, whether so identified or not, iconography has been fundamental, albeit oftentimes unconscious, in the assessments of film analysis and the decisions of filmmaking. Iconography, especially in discussions of film, explains the how, what, and why images function as well as the integral role(s) of icons and images. The particular hermeneutics and methodologies for the understanding of how an image or an icon moves from one media, e.g., painting, to another, especially the multidimensional media of film, are a little-discussed issue in both film analysis, and religion and film studies. Iconography, perhaps better identified as iconology, can provide useful foundations for future directions in religion and film studies.

Definitions

A momentary aside for initial definitions of iconography and iconology is in order. Etymologically, these two words share the same first root word εἰκών which is the Greek word for icon, often characterized as an "original portrait." The second half of each term denotes the action(s) related to icons; that is "iconography" from the Greek εἰκών γ ραφία, or icon writing, which the *Oxford English Dictionary* identifies as, first, a description or illustration of any subject by means of drawings or figures, and second, as that branch of knowledge which deals with the representation of persons or objects by any application of the arts of design. Whereas, "iconology," from the Greek εἰκονολογία for icon and speaking of, signifies, first, that branch of knowledge that deals with the subject of icons (in any sense of the word), also the subject matter of this study, icons collectively, or as objects of investigations; and, second, symbolic representation or symbolism.

The disciplinary and methodological realities are such that whether one is a student, researcher, or scholar, iconography in art history and iconography in film studies have distinctive parameters and modes of analysis. Within the traditional art historical frame, iconography is distinguished either as having religious subject matter, that is Christian iconography, Buddhist iconography; or as having a chronological character, that is High Gothic iconography, Baroque iconography; or a geographic limitation, that is Chinese iconography, American iconography; or as concentrating on a specific motif, that is iconography of the Devil, iconography of dogs. The study or depiction of these multiple "iconographies" is dependent upon the ability of the artist and audience to "read" the signs and symbols encoded in works of art. Further, these signs and symbols are composed of animals, flora, vegetables, inanimate objects, colors, numbers, shapes, costume, and so forth; and will have a variety of interpretations predicated as much upon regional and historical attitudes as cultural and theological transformations. Not written in the proverbial stone but rather on the shifting sands of human development and cultural change, iconography corresponds to social and religious attitudes toward gender and race as well as to the developments in painting and sculpting techniques. For example, consider the Early Christian symbol of "the Good Shepherd" and its central significance for an agrarian and pastoral society as opposed to its reduction to a simple nurturing reference for twenty-first-century teenagers from any American inner city. Iconography provides both identifiable cues and narratives within a work of art, and art historians trained in reading these visual codes specialize in the interpretation of art as creative expressions of cultural and religious attitudes (Berdini 2003; Hornik 2003b).

The concept and the role of iconography in religion and film studies, however, is not singularly predicated upon the transposition of traditional religious signs and symbols from canvas or marble to the cinema screen. Just as iconography can have multidimensional foci for analysis of works of traditional art, so too for iconography in film. In fact, some of the earliest attempts by art historians and aestheticians to correspond a film(s) to the classic visual arts were characterized by the application of methods and vocabulary of analysis from one discipline to the other (Faure 1994; Panofsky 1996). For obvious reasons, these attempts are simply of historical significance in our attitudes toward the movies as "more" than simply entertainment. So while iconographic analysis in film can include discussions of the colors, forms, objects, and so forth, and their relationship in meaning to those same colors, forms, objects, etc., in a painting, the reality is that iconography in film encompasses much more.

Rather, for the role of iconography in film, several central issues arise here – how an image functions; how images garner meaning; and the history, if any, of this "power of images." In the first overt discussion of the transformative power and reception theory of images, art historian David Freedberg (1989) provided a cross-cultural and inter-class study of images which were both secular and sacred. Combined with his earlier studies on the history and meaning of iconoclasm, that is the "smashing" or destruction of images, Freedberg emphasized the unspoken-of, and little-examined, ability of images to communicate more than social, religious, and political ideas. Images, he countered, are capable of inspiring both fear and delight in those who encounter them. The fear, we can expect, is the most natural cause of iconoclasm, especially religiously inspired iconoclasm; while the delight inspires, soothes, or elevates the viewer. The communicative attributes of images include the fundamental elements of art, that is painting and sculpture – color, form, scale, and placement. Individuals respond to images, sometimes simultaneously, at other times independently, on at least two levels: the intuitive or affective, and the rational or effective.

Through its intuitive dimension, the visual arts communicate ideals and meaning through color and scale; while form and placement, perhaps better identified as composition, signify the modes of visual communication that are directed and responded to by rationality. The fundamental modality for these forms of communication is the act of *seeing* (Berger 1977). Throughout human history, regardless of class or geographic location, children learn to *see* before they are taught to read or write. The process of *seeing*, like the more primal, perhaps, tactile sense, is foundational to human development, and the singular place of the senses cannot be ignored. Our human quest for meaning, whether characterized as social, political, or religious, is predicated upon the communication accessed through image. We all come to art, to religion, to politics, or to film with a series of preconditioned experiences of *seeing*, especially of our individual and communal *seeing* of meaning through the signs and symbols.

The Gaze

Late twentieth-century scholarship on response theory, the concept of visual culture, and the redefining of gender have been predicated on the category of "*the* Gaze." Neither a protracted nor intensified mode of looking, the concept of "*the* Gaze" presumes that there is a right and a wrong way to look: intuitively, culturally, politically, religiously, and engendered. The lens through which each of us looks – at our daily encounters with other individuals, at the media, and at works of art including the movies – is predicated upon the communities, social, political, and religious, into which we have been socialized. A significant element of the socialization process is learning to look through a specialized lens and for specific visual cues or codes in signs and symbols, for symbols are the embodiment of those shared memories that are the foundation of, and the connectors between, past, present, and future for political, religious, and social community identity. While overtly unconscious, these socialized lenses conform to preconditioned interpretations and therefore to preexistent fashions. There is, then, no innocent eye but rather an eye shaped unconsciously to look for those figures, objects, and vistas that we identity as "authentic."

This socialized form of "*the* Gaze," especially in terms of our viewing of films that may be religious in theme or theological in nature, supports our acceptance or rejection of a particular interpretation of a scriptural narrative or figure as a success or failure – no matter how solid the actress's performance, the writer's script, or the composer's soundtrack. It becomes the recognizable history of shared memory and communal identity that grounds both the visual power of the film and our reception of it. The "shared history" of a religious or theological film is reinforced as both common religious and cultural histories become in the viewing of the film "our history" through the iconography which illuminates the screen before us.

The Bible in "high art"

As a society, we place a profound cultural value on the tradition of "high art," and what I have argued elsewhere (Apostolos-Cappadona 1992: 104-16) I believe is appropriate here also – that such a cultural valuing must combine successfully with the motif, narrative, or figuration in a religious film for it to be successfully received by the audience. I identified this mode of analysis as one predicated upon visual analogies, that is the relationship between the otherwise traditional iconography and iconology of a religious community and the representation of the story unfolding in color, sound, and light before the viewers. The majority of these visual analogies are predicated upon the works of the great masters of religious art, painters such as Rembrandt and sculptors such as Michelangelo.

While such works are indebted in their narratives and characters to the Bible or even to devotional texts such as *The Golden Legend*, it is the little-considered reality of what I have identified as "the space between" that has opened up the world that creates and sees the Bible in the arts, including film. Even in the most extensive biblical narrative, there are gaps, that is, "the space between." These occur in the story while physical descriptions of the central characters are absent; for example, in the well-known passage of the Resurrection narrative where Mary Magdalene encounters the Risen Christ (Apostolos-Cappadona 2006), there are "spaces between" their words and their actions, so exactly what does she see when she first encounters the gardener? What are the visual clues that lead Mary Magdalene to believe that the man before her is a gardener; his costume? the objects in his hands? his actions? What does the gardener do, as in how does he gesture and posture, when he encounters her? What does she do in "the space between" his calling of her by name and her recognition that he is NOT a gardener but the Risen Christ? How does she gesture or posture; what is her facial expression in the moment of this recognition? All of these most human of dimensions to the biblical narrative are the sources of interest for visual artists over the centuries, and their artistic responses result in a special visual vocabulary of postures, gestures, facial expressions, and dress that gives itself over first to Christian iconography and later to the visual analogizing of Christian art into the newer media of the movies, television, and video.

Visual analogies, then, lend an aura of both authenticity and reality to a film, especially a film with a biblical narrative as

> classical paintings have influenced the set and costume designs, character portrayals, and atmosphere of authenticity of those films recognized as "classics." A series of visual connectors registers in the viewers' subliminal and conscious minds as they watch these films. The assimilation of images from classical paintings has a dual result: first, they present the viewer with a sense of cultural ambience and authenticity; second, they allow for the principles of a painting masterpiece to be employed in a film. (Apostolos-Cappadona 1992: 105)

However, one of the greatest sources of our collective memory of what Jesus, Mary, and other biblical figures looked like, and of what the architecture, landscape, and setting of biblical narratives were, are Bible illustrations. In fact, this is how many people, untrained in art history or perhaps resident in places inaccessible to museums, came to know both their Bible stories and the great masters of Western art from Raphael and Leonardo to Rembrandt and Caravaggio. Many of the illustrations in Bibles printed from the time of Gutenberg onward incorporated prints or engravings of master painters such as Rembrandt's famed *Christ Healing the Sick* or those of Albrecht Dürer and Lucas Cranach the Elder, whose images were incorporated into Luther's many publications and his translation of the Bible into German. During the nineteenth century, a variety of artists, especially following the theological, and later public, interest in the so-called Quest for the Historical Jesus, emphasized biblical themes in their work; for example, the American artist Henry Ossawa Tanner whose paintings such as *The Savior* (Fig. 24.1) became recognizable images on prayer cards, and in Bibles and Sunday school texts. While often deemed as a form of popular culture,

Fig. 24.1 Henry Ossawa Tanner, *The Savior* (ca. 1900–5: Smithsonian American Art Museum, Washington, DC). Photo © Scala, Florence. Biblical illustrations premised on great paintings, such as Henry Ossawa Tanner's popular portrait of *The Savior*, created a visual ideal of what Jesus looked like. When this comforting image was transferred to the silver screen, the movie resonated with both familiarity and authenticity.

Bible illustrations as agents of both the transmission of the Christian faith and of the evolution of the Bible in the movies require our attention as a significant source of visual analogies.

The Bible of film, filming the Bible

The relationship between images and the Bible – first in the form of the Old Testament and then in the pre-canonical New Testament texts – has been one of intimacy even before the birth of Jesus and the establishment of Christianity as a legitimate religious entity in the fourth century. In a manner common to the indigenous, later identified as "pagan," religions of the Mediterranean basin in which Judaism and Christianity arose, images communicated to believers and nonbelievers alike the history, teachings, and practices of each religion. This religious imagery was inscribed on stone tablets, carved in sculptures, woven into tapestries, and depicted in mosaics, frescoes, and manuscripts as both an affirmation of a tradition and confirmation to those who were otherwise unable to access documents or texts.

In particular, Christianity has had a long tradition of biblically inspired art, especially from the third century with the recognition of the pedagogical significance of "pictures" to the majority of believers and those in the process of initiation as visual literacy was clearly dominant over textual literacy. Thus, those who were "children" – be they physically pre-pubescent or spiritually "young" – were taught the stories of the faith through the illustrations on the frescoes and sarcophagi in the catacombs, and eventually illuminated gospel and sacramentary books in churches and cathedrals. These images can be surveyed today as a mode of access to liturgical practices, cultural understandings of gender, and societal attitudes toward Christianity. This established a relational pattern between this faith tradition and the visual that has lasted into the twenty-first century, and that was transferred to film since the earliest silent films to the most recent biblical or biblically inspired epic. So what earlier generations came to know by looking at the pictures on their walls, altars, and Bibles, the present generations can learn by watching a movie for the interconnected frames that provide a narrative through sound, light, motion, and image (Apostolos-Cappadona 2004: 101). This connection between the "traditional" arts and film is most clearly expressed by the fact that movies have been identified as "moving pictures" for several generations.

Like art and literature, movies are the products of and inscribed with the attitudes, definitions, and prejudices of those cultures in which they arose, flourished, and survived. Awash with biblical images, motifs, vocabulary, and thought patterns, Western culture established a collective cultural memory grounded in the Bible. So intertwined were those biblical narratives with Western cultural history that the conflation of the reinterpretation of national epics and biblical narratives was a common, and perhaps unconscious, practice, thereby the identification of secular rulers with Solomon, of political leaders with Moses, and of the new nation with the "errand into the wilderness."

Similarly, each individual has both this cultural collective unconscious filled with signs and symbols, and the language and imagery through which we are socialized into our "communities" of faith, culture, and society. These verbal and visual vocabularies aid us in distinguishing reality from fiction, good from evil, and saint from sinner. In this way, every individual has a preconceived and "appropriate" mental image, if you will, of what Jesus looked like; so that when Cecil B. DeMille cast H. B. Warner, or Mel Gibson selected James Caviezel, to play the role of Jesus in their films, this decision was based as much on the actors' abilities as on how much they conformed to DeMille's or Gibson's image of Jesus (Higham 1973: 5; Bailey and Pizzello 2004). So while we recognize the primacy of *seeing* in the process of answering the epistemological question and in the formation of our individual and communal identities, we need to consider not simply how images work but what images work.

From childhood, each of us raised in Christian cultures has seen pictures of what Jesus and God, Moses, and Mary looked like, how they acted, gestured, and dressed, and "the heart" of their stories without ever questioning the racial, cultural, engendered, or physical characteristics of such images. Rather, these pictures were accepted as true almost unto the reality with which today we invest a photograph or unedited video record. These pictures garnered their sacrality as much from their placement on altars, church walls, or most especially in the Bibles we read in church or at home. Endowed with a "sacred authority" by their direct connection to those subjective and objective elements of religious tradition, we have come to empower and accept them as images with "authority," and thereby, a truth claim. So in many cases, we have no farther to look than the illustrations in our Bibles, on prayer cards, or on those religious greeting cards in our own homes. There we will see great works of art such as paintings by medieval and Renaissance masters such as Jan van Eyck's renderings of the Madonna and Raphael's famed *Madonna of the Chair*, Leonardo's *Last Supper*, and Michelangelo's *Pietà*.

These masterpieces of Christian art have shaped our religious consciousness, and simultaneously, despite our supposed distrust of the visual, have been invested with religious authority. Further evidence of these interconnections between the Bible and Western culture is the reality that so much art and so many artists have been inspired by and witnessed to biblical narratives, themes, and figures even unto the categorizing of those paintings and sculptures as masterpieces (Clark 1979). By labeling such works of art as "masterpieces," we empower those works, our viewing of them, and their influence on our collective memory even further, as I have suggested elsewhere:

> Images communicate authority and reality through what I have elsewhere identified as the process of visual analogy. Simply, enough, each new image presents a fresh and independent representation that is dependent upon an earlier classical image or traditional masterpiece on the theme of an individual or individuals of fame or power, or of an event that transformed history or ways of thinking. (Apostolos-Cappadona 1997: 114; referencing Apostolos-Cappadona 1992: 104–16).

Whether we consciously wish to admit it or not, ours is a culture premised upon images, a premise that has expanded its boundaries with the establishment of the modern media, television, film, and now even to the "icons" on our computers. We are bombarded in our daily lives by images and unconsciously determine the meanings of signs and symbols as harbingers of truth and values. Our collective internal warehouse of secular images combines with those collections of visual imagery into which we are each socialized to form our individual "warehouse" affecting our modes of being in the world (Apostolos-Cappadona 1997: 115). As the receptive partner in the process of seeing a movie, we bring with us these individualized encyclopedias of images, from family, friends, teachers, and public media, to help us in understanding both the story in the film and its relationship to each of us:

> A film is composed of "moving pictures" – frames that project both a series of recognizable images and a story. The narrative of the film tells us something about a person or persons, a place, an event. The images project both explicit and implicit messages to each viewer. The combination of the narrative and the images within a film is constructed by the filmmaker, but the actual "seeing" of them is dependent upon the viewer. (Apostolos-Cappadona 1997: 113)

For while images have power – the power to please, the power to shock, the power to educate, the power to convert, the power to transform – it is our "reading" of the images that results in their ability to communicate. However, we cannot "read" images as we read a written text. We need rather to recognize how images are distinct from text and how we therefore "read" them differently – that is, the rules of engagement and interpretation differ. By expanding our traditional "logocentric" sense of text to include the intuitive and experiential modalities by which images communicate, we can recognize the role of images and come, perhaps, to understand their ability to project meaning, value, and truth.

What we must remember here is that when we are considering the mode and method of iconography in religion and film, we are not limiting ourselves to that perhaps "irksome" categorization of art (read images) as illustration. Rather, we are referencing the symbolic nature of art, especially religious art. Martin O'Kane's reference to the "painting of the text" (2007) or Paolo Berdini's category of "visual exegesis" (2003) help us to recognize that even within the written text there are pauses, gaps, repetitions, ambiguities, and leaps in the telling of the story, in the descriptions of individuals, in the emphases on events, and in the descriptions of the scenes and settings. In an ironic "twist" to Gregory the Great's proclamation of Christian art as the *biblia pauperum* – usually translated as the "bible of the poor" – I would affirm that images whether painted, sculpted, or filmed come to fill in creative ways these "space(s) between" and thereby authenticate for the viewer the narrative, and at least one interpretation of its meaning, by coordinating image and text.

Further, this is no simplistic "one-to-one" relationship, as in "red means stop and green means go," but rather, the artistic imagination fills in that "space between" and so provides the viewer with both affirmation and the possibility of participation in identifying this image as meaningful. In the process of establishing the relationship between iconography in art and in film, and thereby between Christian art and religious film, I want to suggest that there are several modes of analysis: first, a careful re-rendering of recognizable art within a film; second, a substantive and intentional influence of the "ambiance" of recognizable art within a film; and third, *ekphrasis*, the intentional re-presentation of a work of art, that is a painting or a sculpture, within a film as idea, topic, theme, or narrative element. Significantly, all three of these "modes" can be characterized as forms of visual analogy as the viewer's conscious and unconscious knowledge of the referenced text or images is recognizable as being from within a long tradition of Christian art.

Given the fact that the majority of Americans have identified themselves as Christians, there is a potentially large and interested audience for movies that narrate the Bible. Traditionally, there has been an unwritten, and perhaps also unspoken, recognition among filmmakers and audience that biblically based films require an aura of both gravitas and respectability. This was seen as true at least into the 1970s; however, once Monty Python's *Life of Brian* (1979) captured the public's imagination one can argue gravitas and respectability went out the window. Nonetheless, the accessibility of "the Bible on film" was a powerful attraction especially in the 1950s and 1960s which were the decades of popular biblical epics ranging from *Samson and Delilah* (1949) to *The Robe* (1953).

The themes found especially in the Old Testament were exceptionally appropriate for those films identified as "biblical epics" which were sweeping in their visual effects such as detailed battle scenes, sword fights, natural disasters, and spectacular miracles while having as their basis a simple narrative premised on the eternal battle between good and evil. When we combine this "action formula" of the biblical epic with the central role played by seductive temptresses like Delilah, Bathsheba, Jezebel, and Salomé, the winning combination of sex and violence in the service of religion almost guaranteed a successful box office film.

While there was the added economic boost that the Bible is in public domain and thereby its stories and characters can be used freely by filmmakers, many of the films about Jesus made before the 1950s were funded by churches and shown to smaller audiences within the confines of a religious building (Lindvall 2001). However, from the 1950s onward, the financially and critically successful films organized in some way around the life and times of Jesus were based on biblical fiction rather than the Bible – that is, films such as *Demetrius and the Gladiators* (1954), *Quo Vadis* (1951), *Ben-Hur* (1959), and most recently *The Da Vinci Code* (2006). As the reading of the Bible both at home and at school became less frequent, images once again rose to prominence as the American populace lost surety in their knowledge of what Jesus said and did, but remained confident they knew what Jesus looked like – thanks in part to the illustrations in those otherwise unread Bibles and the great tradition of Christian art upon which they and biblical films were based.

While painters and sculptors have filled what I referred to as "the space between" in the narratives, passages, and physical descriptions of Biblical figures, filmmakers were able also to highlight or adapt the otherwise minimal characterizations, oftentimes without extensive public or critical dismay. Rather, these films like the religious art

449

that had preceded them became the basis over succeeding generations for the public understanding of the stories and characters of the Bible. With the growing seculari-zation and religious pluralism in the America of the late 1960s onward, viewers have come to learn "their Bible" and the stories of the Judeo-Christian tradition through the moving image in a fashion similar to and dependent upon the pedagogical influence of traditional Christian art, especially that from before the Reformation.

Cecil B. DeMille: "Painting the Bible on a big canvas"

Ann Graham Lotz witnessed the power of the visual presentation of the Bible on film when she affirmed that her own childhood conversion came as she watched a television showing of Cecil B. DeMille's *The King of Kings* (1927). Herself an inter-national preacher and Bible teacher, Lotz is the daughter of the renowned evangelist Billy Graham in whose household she would have been more than familiar with the Bible and the redemption promised through Christian faith. Yet, she came to conversion watching a movie. So the question quickly becomes, how did the viewing of a film bring the daughter of one of the world's greatest Christian evangelists to her moment of conversion? That is, why in the seeing of a film instead of the hearing (or reading) of the Word?

While Graham himself referred to DeMille as "a prophet in celluloid," it is his daughter's conversion experience that confirms the power of images because perhaps it was in the seeing of what she had otherwise heard or read that the reality of the Christian message became real. The irony of this, given the perceived connection between the producer and the scriptural narratives – even unto the near impossibility of mentioning his name without the epithet "master of the biblical epic" attached to it – is that only three of his films: *The Ten Commandments* (1923 and 1956), *The King of Kings*, and *Samson and Delilah*, were based on the Bible. To paraphrase Billy Graham, how and why was this famed director able to create some of the most significant and enduring depictions of the Bible on celluloid?

The son of a father who was a lay reader in the Episcopal Church and a Broadway playwright who read the Bible daily to his sons, and a mother who converted from Judaism, Cecil recognized from childhood the pedagogical power of the arts. "The two boys [Cecil and his brother, William] were constantly aware of religion from their earliest days, the walls of their bedroom lined with sacred texts and prints from the Bible" (Higham 1973: 5). However, it was not simply the text of the Bible, but his bedroom décor: "[he] loved the works of Gustave Doré: the most fingered book at Pompton Lake was the *Doré Bible Gallery*, a collection of illustrated sacred texts published by Belford-Clarke in 1891. Cecil loved to pore over pictures like *Ruth and Boaz*, *The Judgment of Solomon*, *The Sermon on the Mount* and *The Prodigal Son*. From these the whole visual inspiration of his great religious films sprang" (Higham 1973: 7–8).

The habits of his childhood became firmly rooted in his professional life as a filmmaker as Charles Higham attests that in the initial preparations for the filming of *The Ten Commandments*: "He [Cecil B. DeMille] sent a copy of the Bible to every single person on the Lasky payroll, with the words, 'As I intend to film practically the entire book of Exodus ... the Bible should never be away from you. Place it on your desk, and when you travel, stick it in your briefcase. Make reading it a daily habit'" (Higham 1973: 111–14). Even further:

> In mid-June 1926, DeMille summoned Jeanie [MacPherson] to his office and told her gravely that he was about to give her the most important assignment of her life. He handed her a text: the small, worn family Bible, dated 1874, which his father had used as a lay reader in the Episcopal Church in New Jersey, and instructed her to follow the great drama to the letter, impatiently dismissing her suggestion that she should use a modern story as a counter-balance. (Higham 1973: 160)

However, it was not simply the text of that Bible that was important, but the biblical illustrations and the masterpieces of Christian art upon which those illustrations were based; which evidences my theory of visual analogy as a mode of connectives of Christian art with biblical film, as well as the power of images as central to the art of the moving pictures. For example, in his detailed discussion of the making of *The King of Kings*, Higham advises that

> DeMille instructed the cameraman Peverell Marley to study hundreds of biblical paintings, examining precisely with what effects of light the old masters achieved their work. Two hundred and ninety eight paintings were fully reproduced in the film. Marley used seventy-five lenses as against his usual four, and seven different kinds of film stock, as well as special stock for the Technicolor sequences. For the crucifixion scene, based partly on DeMille's beloved Gustave Doré, partly on Rubens, he employed the most powerful sun arcs used up to that time, and two hundred fifty special lights set up around the hill of Calvary, fixed by a team of one hundred seventy-seven specialists, and giving out a strength of twenty-seven thousand amperes. (Higham 1973: 161)

Recognized by cinema professionals and the public alike as the great, if not the grand, master of the biblical epic, few of us are cognizant of DeMille's diligent study of Christian art as foundational to his creating on celluloid scriptural, religious, and emotional authenticity. By simply muting the sound – dialogue and music – coming from any of DeMille's biblical epics and watching only the detailed images (of scenery and characters) parade before our eyes, whether in the gradations of black-and-white in *The King of Kings* or the lushness of technicolor in *Samson and Delilah*, those images bring to life the emotions and meaning of the scriptural narrative. From the biblical illustrations of the *Gustave Doré Bible* memorized from childhood to his later encounter with James Jacques Tissot's illustrations for the special editions of *The Life of Christ* and the *Hebrew Bible* to his special commission from Arnold Friberg of fifteen paintings for the second version of *The Ten Commandments*, Cecil B. DeMille knew intimately the power of images which he sought to transfer to what he called "the big canvas."

Fig. 24.2 Gustave Doré, *Jesus and the Woman Taken in Adultery*, from the *Doré Bible Illustrations* for John 8:3–5. Courtesy www.creationism.org. Emphasizing the drama of the scriptural narratives through his depictions of both the figures and the settings, Gustave Doré's illustrations were immediately popular from the first printings in 1865 into the 1920s. A copy of one of the editions of *Doré's Bible Gallery* was one of the most read books in the childhood home of the movie producer Cecil B. DeMille.

The influence of biblical illustrators Gustave Doré and James Jacques Tissot

Two of the leading late nineteenth-/early twentieth-century artists specializing in biblical themes were the Alsatian illustrator Gustave Doré (1832–83) and the French painter James Tissot (1836–1902). Their scriptural images were recognized by connoisseurs and the general public alike, and their popularity was matched by their influence on artists, theologians, believers, and filmmakers including D. W. Griffith and, of course, Cecil B. DeMille. Tellingly, in the 1950s and 1960s, which were the peak years of biblical epics, Bibles illustrated with the work of Michelangelo, Rembrandt, and Tanner (see Fig. 24.1) flourished, while the end of the millennium ushered in not simply a renewal of interest in religion and religious films, like Mel Gibson's *The Passion of the Christ* (2004), but also a renewal of interest in the paintings of the Italian Baroque artist Michelangelo Merisi da Caravaggio.

Gustave Doré initially specialized in book illustration; however, his fame rests on the success and popularity of his depictions of biblical narratives. Along with the apprentices and artisans in his studios, Doré created hundreds of woodcuts and engravings that illustrated a variety of Old Testament and New Testament stories (Fig. 24.2). First issued in France in 1865, his Bible illustrations were eventually printed in German, English, and other language editions from the late 1860s to the present day. Presented in large-folio and multivolume formats featuring approximately 240 illustrations each, these publications were expensive and burdensome, so that smaller format editions were eventually published. Although the majority of Doré's illustrations were the same despite the various editions, he and his studio produced so many Bible illustrations that there were distinctive images used for specific language or format editions, even for the same scriptural text.

The public reception of Doré's illustrations was overwhelmingly favorable; as an example, records from the Art Institute of Chicago verify that over 1.5 million people saw the 1896 Doré exhibition. Further evidence of the significance of his Bible illustrations are the special smaller volumes of his biblical illustrations, often without biblical texts or only with excerpts, which were published under the rubric of the *Doré Bible Gallery* editions. A copy of one of these, we know, was in DeMille's childhood home and became one of his most read books. Whether it was his reliance upon earlier masterworks of Christian art or his ability to project an almost theatrical drama (see Fig. 24.2), Doré's artistry pervaded the frames and borders of the earliest biblical films, in particular those of D. W. Griffith and Cecil B. DeMille.

Perhaps better known for his elegant depictions of fashionable ladies and their society activities, James Tissot experienced a life-changing spiritual vision of Christ in the Église Saint-Sulpice, Paris, in 1886. Following a difficult four-year period of personal and professional crises initiated by the death of his beloved companion, muse, and model, Kathleen Newton, the French painter became involved in spiritualism and mysticism. However, following the 1886 vision, Tissot dedicated himself to illustrating the life of Christ and the Hebrew Bible. During this period of "the quest for the historical Jesus," the painter made two trips to the Holy Land in order to render the landscape and scenery with accuracy, and the figures – from body types to facial features and gesticulations – with his own form of vivid realism (Misfeldt 2008).

From 1886, Tissot completed over 700 works illustrating first *The Life of Christ* and then *The Hebrew Bible*. These works – oils, watercolors, gouaches, prints, and drawings – were popularly know as "Tissot's Bible." *The Life of Christ* was successfully exhibited and published, first in a 1896 "grande deluxe edition" in French, and then followed by a much acclaimed two-volume series in English. It was eventually printed in twenty-two editions between 1896 and 1909 alone. His *Hebrew Bible* paintings were exhibited posthumously and proved to be a financial disaster. Eventually purchased by

Fig. 24.3   James Tissot, *What Our Savior Saw from the Cross*, from *The Life of Christ* (1886–96: The Brooklyn Museum of Art, Brooklyn, NY/The Bridgeman Art Library). Tissot's singular image, *What Our Savior Saw from the Cross*, reverses our normal perspective, so that instead of looking up at the Crucified Christ, we look down with Jesus at the horde of humanity in a visual mode that would clearly influence cinematic presentations of this event.

the financier Jacob H. Schiff, these visual narratives of the Old Testament are today in the permanent collection of the Jewish Museum in New York City (Misfeldt 2008).

However, the initial presentation of approximately 350 gouaches dedicated to the life of Christ was a great success at the 1894 Paris Salon, with later expanded exhibitions including drawings, paintings, and watercolors in Paris (1896), London (1897), and thereafter throughout the United States (Tissot 1899). As a measure of the popularity of these exhibitions, the artist himself garnered an admission fees royalty of $100,000 in the US alone. Then the Brooklyn Museum in a rare and daring move purchased 5 oils, 345 watercolors, and 111 pen and ink drawings from Tissot's *Life of Christ* (Brooklyn Museum website). The significance of this purchase is recognized by the fact that the then enviable purchase price of $60,000 was raised by public subscription.[1] According to Judith Dolkart, current Brooklyn Museum Associate Curator of European Paintings and curator of a special 2009 exhibition of the *Life of Christ*, Tissot's works have never lost their popular luster – when exhibited they are among the most visited works in the museum, and the most requested for reproduction, study, and special access.

The visual theatricality of Tissot's depictions of the events in the life of Christ anticipates biblical epics like those by DeMille. Perhaps his most extraordinary image entitled *What Our Saviour Saw from the Cross* (Fig. 24.3) is remarkable both as a biblical illustration and as a visual omen of how filmmakers, like DeMille, and later twentieth-century artists, like Salvador Dalí, came to present the Crucifixion. In a moment of artistic inspiration, Tissot reverses the traditional perspective as the Crucified Christ considers the crowd spread out before him – from Roman soldiers to the anonymous mob and the crowds of followers. In the foreground is the identifiable faithful: first the anguished and crawling-forward figure of Mary Magdalene (a portrait of Mrs. Newton), Mary of Nazareth with hands clasped across her heart and supported by the other "holy women," and the white-robed John the Evangelist.

While the biblical illustrations of Doré and Tissot clearly influenced both DeMille and his audiences, perhaps the director's most intriguing visual analogy was his commission of Arnold Friberg to create fifteen paintings as the pictorial bases for the settings, costumes, and characters in *The Ten Commandments*. The master filmmaker had initiated an international search for an artist with both "the rare talent and inner vision to set down in paint, all of the power, the color, and the human drama" of a biblical narrative (Dall 2003). However, when prints of Friberg's biblical illustrations were sent to DeMille by a Swedish friend, the search was ended. At the time, the young artist/illustrator was teaching at the University of Utah and had been contracted by the Church of Latter Day Saints to illustrate the *Book of Mormon*. Given DeMille's earlier successful biblical epics, Friberg was granted a leave from that latter commission in order to work for DeMille who wanted the scenes, characters, and costumes "to look and feel authentic," not like typical "Hollywood costume design."

The artist moved his family to Hollywood to work with DeMille from 1953 to 1957 in this "turn around" from his earlier intimate dependence upon masterworks of Christian art and biblical illustrations. Friberg worked in close unison with the producer/director as their visualization of *The Ten Commandments* came to life through hundreds of his sketches, drawings, and paintings. In yet another reversal of the well-known and well-received art of

Doré and Tissot, this time the artist's works were put on view because of the movie. From 1956 to 1957, Friberg's paintings were exhibited throughout the world, and, at one point, DeMille announced that "when *The Ten Commandment* paintings toured the world, they were seen by more people than any other paintings except for some of the most celebrated masterpieces such as the *Mona Lisa, Nightingale,* and *The Last Supper*" (Dall 2003).

From Scorsese to Gibson: translating the chiaroscuro of Caravaggio to cinema

Beyond what may be considered as the primary mode of visual analogy in film, that is, the re-presentation of traditional Christian images as a confirmation that what one is *seeing* is authentic, there is a second mode by which a producer or director assimilates an artist's *oeuvre*, and translates it into his or her own visual style. Thereby such films project particular visual homologies by sharing in the visual vocabulary of the original artworks; for example, the films of Martin Scorsese or Mel Gibson's *The Passion of the Christ* reflect the aura and ambiance of the paintings of the Italian Baroque master Michelangelo Merisi da Caravaggio (Wolf 2005; Bailey and Pizzello 2004).

In a 2005 interview, Scorsese advised that "[t]here are touches of Caravaggio in *The Age of Innocence* (1993), and in *The Last Temptation of Christ* (1988)" (Wolf 2005). The director detailed the influence of the artist whose "use of light still has an influence on modern cinema" especially in terms of how that "light and shadow ... [deals with] the people" (Wolf 2005). Baroque art historians would affirm that the "dark light," or technically the *chiaroscuro,* that Caravaggio initiated to great effect is, as Scorsese emphasizes, "a dramatic light: it just lights the scene from one mysterious burst" (Wolf 2005). Combined with the intensity of his realism, this innovative use of a theatrical light emphasized the depth of the humanity in Caravaggio's characters who Scorsese describes as "obviously people from the streets" (Wolf 2005). Scorsese continued, "What hit us about his work was the extraordinary power of what seemed to be realism in that, say, you've got Judith beheading Holofernes, which is a difficult job, and you could see [it] in her face" (Wolf 2005). Perhaps there is more of Caravaggio in other Scorsese films, from *Raging Bull* (1980) to *Gangs of New York* (2002), in which a critic might also argue the sacred is camouflaged in the profane – in the drama of the light and shadows, the emotionally charged physicality of the action, and the intensity of human (read spiritual) depth of character.

Throughout the pre-release publicity for the 2004 release of Mel Gibson's *The Passion of the Christ,* both Gibson as producer/director and Caleb Deschanel as the cinematographer affirmed their mutual interest in and dependence upon Caravaggio's paintings. Deschanel repeated in interview after interview that he and Gibson looked for and looked at the Baroque artist's images to help them garner what they wanted for both the look and the feel of the film (Bailey and Pizzello 2004). Realistic, if not raw, presentations of what Scorsese identified as Caravaggio's "people from the streets" and the fervor of their interactions, combined with the compelling aura of his *chiaroscuro,* invest Deschanel with a visual vocabulary that translated into a cinematic milestone. Further, both Gibson and Deschanel, perhaps unconsciously once they assimilated the painter's vision into their own *seeing* of the film, orchestrated "visual

Fig. 24.4. Michelangelo Merisi da Caravaggio, *The Taking of Christ* (1602: Society of Jesus of Ireland on loan to the National Gallery of Ireland, Dublin). The paintings of Caravaggio, esteemed for his use of *chiaroscuro*, intense realism, and dramatic characterizations of "people from the streets," have influenced the films, especially the religious epics, of Martin Scorsese and Mel Gibson, to name just two.

quotes taken from Caravaggio's paintings, especially *The taking of the Christ*" (Fig. 24.4) (Apostolos-Cappadona 2004: 102). In fact, many reviewers and critics when writing about Gibson's film confirmed the filmmaker's own, now oft-quoted, sentiment to Deschanel, "Oh my God, it's a moving Caravaggio!" (Bailey and Pizzello 2004).

Of course, a crucial question for future study is "why Caravaggio?" Is the reality of his influence on filmmakers like Scorsese and Gibson as simple as the visual qualities of *chiaroscuro*? Is there for Gibson an affinity with Caravaggio's religious worldview? The Roman Catholicism of the sixteenth and seventeenth centuries can best be described as colored by the daily religious tensions wrought by the Reformation. The eventual response from Rome was the confirmation of what it meant to be Roman Catholic with a redefinition through the Council of Trent, the new spirituality of St. Teresa and others, and the establishment of the Jesuits. This "new" redefinition of the principles of Roman Catholicism rang as true for Gibson following his own conversion experience as it did for Caravaggio who lived in the turbulence and drama of Counter-Reformation Rome. Perhaps there is more than an aura of truth in Scorsese's assessment that, "If Caravaggio were alive today, he would have loved the cinema; his paintings take a cinematic approach" (Wolf 2005).

Fig. 24.5   Matthias Grünewald, *The Crucifixion*, central panel from *The Isenheim Altarpiece* (ca. 1515: Musée d'Unterlinden, Colmar). Photo © Scala, Florence. The greenish skin tones, pricked and open sores, and bodily distortions distinctive to Grünewald's masterful presentation of *The Crucifixion* are clearly influential to the presentation of this episode in William Wyler's *Ben-Hur* (1959). Created as a meditation on the sacred mystery of salvation, *The Isenheim Altarpiece* is Wyler's visual referent throughout this critical sequence in the movie.

Or as the Pope said to the painter, "When will you make an end?"

My third, and final, category of visual analogy in film is an expansion of the concept of *ekphrasis*, that is the literary or poetic representation of a painting or sculpture in verbal form, either as a description of the work, or an allusion to its meaning, or a reference to a particular element. When practiced between a work of art and a film, the original image takes on a life of its own through brilliant visual highlights, so a poem may portray a painting or an element in that painting such as a hand, a smile, or an object like a mirror. This form of *ekphrasis* between a film and a work of art is predicated upon the practice of visual codes in the development of a religious tradition and a cultural identity as evidenced in the following three examples.

Originally commissioned for the chapel of a hospice for patients suffering from terminal skin diseases, the central panel of Matthias Grünewald's *Isenheim Altarpiece* is one of the earliest depictions of the tortured, dead Christ on the cross (Figs 24.5, 24.6). Initially the viewer's eye is drawn to the drama of the crucified body – unnatural greenish skin tones, pricked and open sores, and the distortions of bodily joints from fingers to toes. It is a riveting and unforgettable image which becomes an *ekphrasis*

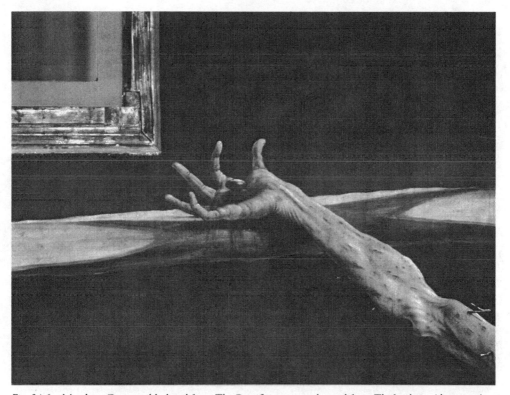

Fig. 24.6   Matthias Grünewald, detail from *The Crucifixion*, central panel from *The Isenheim Altarpiece* (ca. 1515: Musée d'Unterlinden, Colmar). Photo © Scala, Florence. The intercuts between the crucifixion of Christ and the healing of the leprosy of Miriam and Tirzah in Wyler's *Ben-Hur* (1959) visually authenticate the meaning of the scriptural message that the Christ will take on all the sins and illnesses of the world. From its opening overture throughout this film, there is a visual "play" on the theme of the healing touch, which culminates with the close-ups of the transfer of the physical distortions caused by leprosy from the damaged hands of Miriam and Tirzah to those of Jesus.

in the 1959 religious epic *Ben-Hur*. The action leading to the crucifixion scene concentrates on the return of Esther, Miriam, and Tirzah, to the Valley of the Lepers following Jesus' walk to Calvary. Waylaid by a sudden, violent storm, they find refuge in a cave as the sky darkens (as in Grünewald's painting):

> Wyler's sense of visual analogies and directorial genius take over in the next sequence of shots back and forth between the crucifixion scene proper and the three women in the cave. We see the mother and daughter slowly being healed of their ailment as their open sores and disfigurement are washed away by the torrential rains. Simultaneously we notice that the body of Jesus of Nazareth becomes distorted in a fashion similar to Grünewald's Christ as he takes on "all the sins [physical ailments] of the world." Wyler's most dramatic portrayal of these miraculous activities comes in the close-up of the distorted and diseased hands of Jesus and in the scene where Esther touches the now healed and whole hands of Miriam. (Apostolos-Cappadona 1997: 111)

Thereby, the *ekphrasis* of the body of Grünewald's Crucified Christ empowers the visual vocabulary of Wyler's film.

Similarly, Michelangelo's creation of the frescoes on the Sistine Chapel ceiling is both the narrative theme and the visual focus of the movie *The Agony and the Ecstasy* (1965). Perhaps an example of a double *ekphrasis*, this film is based on the Irving Stone novel which relates the trials and triumphs of the Renaissance genius Michelangelo, as the then Pope Julius II ordered him to stop working in sculpture and dedicate himself to the painting of the ceiling. What we have come to know about Michelangelo – either from reproductions of his work, illustrations in art history books or Bibles, and (since the 1980s) from the debates about the cleaning of these frescoes – is fundamentally visual knowledge of his art. This film struggles to capture the otherwise unimaginable imagery of spiritual inspiration and artistic creativity. Referencing what we know, the well-known ceiling frescoes come to life as the film emphasizes the artist's physical struggles, with the central motif being Michelangelo's renowned depiction of the *Creation of Adam*, which is also the opening and closing background for *Ben-Hur*.

Perhaps the best-known example of *ekphrasitic* simultaneity is the 2003 novel and the 2006 movie version of *The Da Vinci Code* which revolves visually around the art of Leonardo, most especially his version of *The Last Supper*. The opening sequences of the film, for example, intercut between two distinctive activities – the murder of Jacques Saunière in the Grand Gallery of the Musée du Louvre and Professor Robert Langdon's illustrated lecture on religious signs and symbols. Thereby, the esoteric environments of "holy museum" and "sacred academy" are juxtaposed under the scrutiny of one of the world's most recognizable paintings, Leonardo's *Mona Lisa*.

The game of visual codes is highlighted by the display of Saunière's lifeless corpse according to the pattern of Leonardo's esteemed drawing of *Vitruvian Man*. Extending the *ekphrasis* is Saunière's insertion of encoded riddles on Leonardo's renowned painting *The Virgin of the Rocks*. Well known to art lovers, museum-goers, and art students from their most fundamental studies to the most sophisticated of Renaissance art historians, these masterpieces create an initial comfort zone as the film begins.

We rely on our memories of these famous images to confirm the authenticity of the story as it unfolds cinematically over its two-hour running time. However, the first question we should be asking ourselves is "are the novelist's descriptions of these well-known works, beyond the mere mention of their titles, simply arbitrary or accurate?" By the time we reach the proverbial "moment of great awakening" in Sir Leigh Teabing's study, we have suspended our own visual knowledge and come to accept what we see projected on the movie screen; or, at least, what both the filmmaker and the novelist intend for us to see.

What then becomes the so-called resolution of the most extraordinary of riddles – the quest for the Holy Grail – is projected not by an *in situ* filming of Leonardo's masterwork in the Refectory of Santa Maria delle Grazie but rather on Teabing's extra-wide computer screen. The practice of *ekphrasis* is here taken to a new height as the elements of Leonardo's mural are reorganized as a computerized "cut-and-paste" is moved and reconfigured before our very eyes as a visual support of Teabing's theory. So we no longer ask ourselves in unison with Langdon and Sophie Neveu – "is there a woman in that painting?" – rather we question why we never saw her there before! Beyond the rhetorical argument of painting the text, this particular cinematic *ekphrasis* highlights the implications of iconography within works of religious art, and of iconography in film.

Conclusion

If a conclusion is a form of summation, then I can argue for a progression of ideas in this essay to show the recognition of the role of art and thereby iconography as central to more than the seeing of a movie but for the affirmation of the truth claim espoused by the filmmaker. This is especially true for religious films and their process of en-visioning the Bible, that is a text produced initially without images and more often than not without descriptions of key figures, places, or objects.

If, however, a conclusion is about the resolution of the thesis being argued within the text, then I am suggesting that as a fundamentally late nineteenth-century phenomenon, religious film is arguably central to film history and modern film studies. Thereby, the relationship I am suggesting between traditional works of Christian art and the images in religious film in the process of visual analogy, it seems to me, is as natural a progression as that of modern dance from ballet, or the Broadway musical from opera.

If, however, a conclusion is also an announcement of future directions for the study of iconography in religion and film, then, what I have been suggesting through my discussion of the three modes of visual analogy – a re-rendering of recognizable works of art; an intentional influence of the "ambiance" of recognizable works of art; and *ekphrasis* – needs to be incorporated into the current modes of analysis. Further, iconography and visual analogy alongside the equitably intriguing and promising category of movie music can lead us toward a fuller recognition of the "aesthetics of religious cinema," thus expanding the methodologies of film analysis by incorporating the "viewer's reception/response" with the filmmaker's intention, the story narration, and film technology.

Bibliography

Apostolos-Cappadona, D. (1992) "The Art of *Seeing*: Classical Paintings and *Ben-Hur*," in J. R. May (ed.) *Image and Likeness: Religious Visions in American Film Classics*, New York and Mahwah, NJ: Paulist Press: 104–16, 190–1.

—— (1997) "From Eve to the Virgin and Back Again: The Image of Women in Contemporary (Religious) Film," in J. R. May (ed.) *New Image of Religious Film*, St. Louis, MO: Sheed & Ward: 111–27.

—— (2004) "On Seeing *The Passion*: Is there a Painting in this Film? Or is this Film a Painting?," in S. B. Plate (ed.) *Re-Viewing "The Passion": Mel Gibson's Film and its Critics*, New York: Palgrave Macmillan: 97–108.

—— (2006) "The Saint as Vamp: Mary Magdalene on the Silver Screen," in D. Burstein and A. de Keijzer (eds) *Secrets of Mary Magdalene*, New York: CDS Books: 252–9.

Bailey, J. and Pizzello, S. (2004) "A Savior's Pain: [An interview with] Caleb Deschanel," in S. Pizzello and R. K. Bosley (eds) *American Cinematographer*. Online. Available HTTP: <http://www.theasc.com/magazine/index.htm?mar04/cover/index.html-main> (accessed 23 April 2004).

Berdini, P. (2003) "Jacopo Bassano: A Case for Painting as Visual Exegesis," in H. Hornik (ed.) *Interpreting Christian Art: Reflections on Christian Art*, Macon, GA: Mercer University Press: 169–86.

Berger, J. (1977) *Ways of Seeing*, New York: Penguin Books.

Clark, K. (1979) *What is a Masterpiece?* New York: Thames and Hudson.

Dall, R. D. (2003) "Lecture and Exhibition of his Paintings for the Motion Picture *The Ten Commandments*" from *Meridian Magazine*. Online. Available HTTP: <http://www.meridianmagazine.com/arts/030805arnold.html> (accessed 7 July 2008).

Exum, J. C. (1998) *Plotted, Shot, and Painted: Cultural Representations of Biblical Women*, Sheffield: Sheffield Academic Press.

Exum, J. C. and Moore, S. D. (eds) (1998) *Biblical Studies, Cultural Studies: The Third Sheffield Colloquium*, Sheffield: Sheffield Academic Press.

Faure, E. (1994 [1969]) "The Art of Cineplastics," in D. Talbot (ed.) *Film: An Anthology*, Berkeley: University of California Press: 3–14. Originally published in 1920.

Freedberg, D. (1989) *The Power of Images*, Chicago: University of Chicago Press.

Higham, C. (1973) *Cecil B. DeMille: A Biography of the Most Successful Film Maker of Them All*, New York: Charles Scribner's Sons.

Hornik, H. (2003a) *Illuminating Luke*, Harrisburg, PA: Trinity Press International.

—— (ed.) (2003b) *Interpreting Christian Art*, Macon, GA: Mercer University Press.

Lindvall, T. (2001) *The Silents of God: Selected Issues and Documents in Silent American Film and Religion, 1908–1925*, Lanham, MD: Scarecrow (see especially "Introduction": ix–xvi).

Lyden, J. (1997) "To Commend or to Critique: The Question of Religion and Film Studies," *Journal of Religion and Film* 1 (2). Online. Available HTTP: <http://www.unomaha.edu/jrf/tocommend.htm> (accessed 5 May 2007).

Miles, M. R. (1996) *Seeing is Believing: Religion and Values in the Movies*, Boston: Beacon Press.

Misfeldt, W. E. (2008) "Tissot, James." *Grove Art Online. Oxford Art Online*. Online. Available HTTP: <http://www.oxfordartonline.com.library.lausys.georgetown.edu/subscriber/article/grove/art/T085236> (accessed 29 July 2008).

Mulvey, L. (1989) "Visual Pleasure and Narrative Cinema," in L. Mulvey (ed.) *Visual and Other Pleasures*, Bloomington: Indiana University Press: 14–26

O'Kane, M. (2007) *Painting the Text: The Artist as Biblical Interpreter*, Sheffield: Sheffield Phoenix Press.

Panofsky, E. (1962 [1939]) *Studies in Iconology: Humanistic Themes in the Art of the Renaissance*, New York: Harper & Row.

—— (1996 [1994]) "Style and Medium in the Motion Pictures," in D. Talbot (ed.) *Film: An Anthology*, Berkeley: University of California Press: 15–32. Originally published in the *Bulletin of the Department of Art and Archaeology, Princeton University* (1934) and without revision in *Critique* 1 (3) (1947).

Plate, S. B. (forthcoming 2009) "Art, Bible in Film," in *Encyclopedia of the Bible and its Reception*, vol. 2, Berlin: Walter De Gruyter.

Roncase, M. and Gray, P. (eds) (2008) *The Bible, Popular Culture, and the Arts: Resources for Instructors*, Leiden: Brill.

Sawyer, J. (2006) *The Blackwell Companion to the Bible and Culture*, Oxford: Blackwell.

Steinberg, L. (1983) *The Sexuality of Christ in Renaissance Art and in Modern Oblivion*, New York: Pantheon Books.

Tissot, J. J. (1899) *The Life of Our Saviour Jesus Christ: Three Hundred and Sixty-Five Compositions from the Four Gospels*, New York: McClure-Tissot, 3 vols.

Wolf, M. (2005) "Interview with Martin Scorsese," *The Royal Academy Magazine*. Online. Available HTTP: <http://www.timesonline.co.uk> (Accessed 15 April 2005).

Filmography

The Age of Innocence (1993, dir. M. Scorsese)
The Agony and the Ecstasy (1965, dir. C. Reed)
Ben-Hur (1959, dir. W. Wyler)

The Da Vinci Code (2006, dir. R. Howard)
Demetrius and the Gladiators (1954, dir. D. Daves)
Gangs of New York (2002, dir. M. Scorsese)
The King of Kings (1927, dir. C. DeMille)
The Last Temptation of Christ (1988, dir. M. Scorsese)
Life of Brian (1979, dir. T. Jones)
The Passion of the Christ (2004, dir. M. Gibson)
Quo Vadis (1951, dir. M. LeRoy)
Raging Bull (1980, dir. M. Scorsese)
The Robe (1953, dir. H. Koster)
Samson and Delilah (1949, dir. C. DeMille)
The Ten Commandments (1923, dir. C. DeMille)
The Ten Commandments (1956, dir. C. DeMille)

Further reading

Conrad, M. T. (ed.) (2007) *The Philosophy of Martin Scorsese*, Lexington: University of Kentucky Press. (Collection of varied studies analyzing the interconnections between Scorsese's films and his aesthetic-philosophic-religious ideas).

Corley, K. E. and Webb, R. L. (eds) (2004) *Jesus and Mel Gibson's The Passion of the Christ: The Film, the Gospels and the Claims of History*, New York: Continuum. (A variety of perspectives on Gibson's 2004 landmark film from the multiple lenses of theologians, and scholars of the Bible and religious studies.)

Deacy, C. (2001) *Screen Christologies: Redemption and the Medium of Film*, Cardiff: University of Wales Press. (Informative analysis of film as both a religious activity and a locus for redemption with particular attention to the films of Scorsese.)

Fraser, P. (1998) *Images of the Passion: The Sacramental Mode in Film*, Westport, CT: Praeger. (Provocative study of overt and disguised Passion imagery as the sacramental model highlighted as a moral and religious code in secular and religious film.)

Horsfield, P., Hess, M. E., and Medrano, A. M. (eds) (2004) *Belief in Media: Cultural Perspectives on Media and Christianity*, Burlington, VT: Ashgate. (Collection of international scholars whose work deals with twentieth-twenty-first-century transformations in the interactions between the media – in all its manifestations – and Christianity as evidenced by a multi-year study with the International Study Committee of Media, Religion, and Culture.)

Kaminsky, S. M. with Hill, J. F. (1975) *Ingmar Bergman: Essays in Criticism*, New York: Oxford University Press. (Multiple views of the major films of the great Swedish filmmaker.)

Lyden, J. (2003) *Film as Religion: Myths, Morals, and Rituals*, New York: New York University Press. (Discussion of new modes of analyzing both religious and secular films through the lens of religious studies.)

McDannell, C. (ed.) (2006) *Catholics in the Movies*, New York: Oxford University Press. (Innovative essays organized around the theme of how Catholics are presented in the movies, whether religious or secular in theme.)

Malone, P. (ed.) (2007) *Through a Catholic Lens: Religious Perspectives of Nineteen Film Directors from around the World*, Lanham, MD: Sheed & Ward. (A collection of statements by and interviews with filmmakers on how religion – whether their own belief system or one they find appropriate to their story – has influenced their making of a film.)

Martin, J. (1995) "Introduction: Seeing the Sacred on the Screen," in J. W. Martin and C. E. Ostwalt, Jr. (eds) *Screening the Sacred: Religion, Myth, and Ideology in Popular American Film*, Boulder, CO: Westview Press: 1–12, 161–2. (Informative analysis of the basic approaches to religion and theology, and their applicability to film studies, highlighting the role of myth.)

May, J. R., (ed.) (1992) *Image and Likeness: Religious Visions in American Film Classics*, New York: Paulist Press. (Collected essays each focusing on a different American film classic, whether ostensibly religious or secular, through the lens of religious film analysis.)

—— (2001) *Nourishing Faith through Fiction: Reflections on the Apostles' Creed in Literature and Film*,

Franklin, WI: Sheed & Ward. (Well-presented study of how popular film and fiction can affect both our faith and our worldviews.)

May, J. R. and Bird, M. (eds) (1992) *Religion in Film*, Knoxville: University of Tennessee Press. (Classic collection of perceptive essays emphasizing the methodologies in the seeing and study of religion in film.)

Ostwalt, C. E. (1995) "Conclusion: Religion, Film, and Cultural Analysis," in *Screening the Sacred*, Boulder, CO: Westview Press: 152–9, 180–2. (Insightful discussion of the role of film studies in cultural analysis as for example in the analogies between the role of popular novels in nineteenth-century America and the role of film in twentieth-century America. Film has become the locus for both imagination and "otherness" in our daily lives.)

Peucker, B. (2007) *The Material Image: Art and the Real in Film*, Stanford: Stanford University Press. (Innovative discussion of "intermediality" as the locus where meaning is produced/experienced/known through the internexus of response theory, semiotics, and the psychology of the embodied spectator.)

Plate, S. B. (ed.) (2006) *Representing Religion in World Cinema*, New York: Palgrave Macmillan. (A wide spectrum of international scholars contributed to this cross-cultural and interdisciplinary collection of essays analyzing film as a venue for religion and the religious.)

Sanders, T. (2002) *Celluloid Saints: Images of Sanctity in Film*, Macon, GA: Mercer University Press. (Utilizing the category of saint and sainthood, the author provides both a clear lens and a new mode for the analysis of religion in film.)

Note

1 Conversation during research consultation with Judith F. Dolkart, then Assistant Curator, Department of European Painting and Sculpture, Brooklyn Museum of Art, on 21 July 2005. Dr. Dolkart led me through the original gouaches featuring Mary Magdalene in Tissot's original works.

25

SACRIFICE

Jon Pahl

Introduction

Any film with a death in it might be a sacrifice, since any death on a screen represents a surrogate or substitute whose killing or death can serve to compress the fears or desires of filmmakers and viewers, and displace such emotions onto an actor in a particular scene with whom viewers identify (Pahl 2009). Any screen death is a ritual death, in short, dramatized in ways that might be sacrificial. While scholars do not agree about what constitutes a "sacrifice," recent work might help us identify at least four key elements (Baumgarten 2002; Carter 2003). Sacrificial acts thus combine: selection of a victim or object to be offered; substitution (including metaphor or synecdoche) of a victim or object for a larger group; giving up (e.g., burning), expelling, or killing the victim or object; and catharsis – which includes identification with the victim or object *and* association of some emotion or attribute that serves as motive or rationale for the gift, expulsion, or killing (McClymond 2004). Classically, of course, catharsis is about purification (notably removing guilt). More accurately, however, sacrifices compress or channel fears and desires – including desires to dominate, associate, and flee, in ways that displace, purify, and legitimize desires through symbols or symbolic action. Such trust in symbols stabilizes social order *and* promotes transformation of societies, within bounds (Girard 1977). All in all, sacrifice includes both creative and destructive elements.

Given this definition of a "sacrifice" or of "sacrificial" representations on film, some movies obviously depict or comment on the origins and functions of sacrifice in more explicit ways than others. And yet the range of sacrifice as a topic in the history of cinema remains dauntingly broad. One might limit the field by studying only films that depict explicit, traditional ritual sacrifices, for instance of humans – with a victim on an altar and the killer with a knife and an assembled ritual entourage associated with a discrete religious or cultural tradition, such as in *Apocalypto* (2006). But such a narrow study, while interesting in its own right, might lose the forest of sacrifice for the trees of a particular tradition or practice, and thereby miss the collective significance of the many types of sacrifice that have been represented on a screen. Alternatively, one might study only self-sacrifice in film, whether literal physical self-sacrifice or ethical or psychological acts of renunciation (Milbank 1999). Here, one might look for cinematic representations of abnegation or self-denial in which an individual (or group) is represented for their self-selection as the offering, substitute, or catharsis-inspiring victim, such as in *Sophie's Choice* (1982). As a third approach, one might study films that depict communal sacrifices, where people offer a gift, token, or sign of respect, support, or reverence in ways that communicate some redemptive or significant meaning. One thinks, for instance, of the offering collected at the end of *It's a Wonderful Life* (1946), where the community of Bedford Falls gathers funds on Christmas Eve to fulfill the angelic prophecy that kept George Bailey (Jimmy Stewart) from killing himself. Finally, in a brief overview of what hardly constitutes a comprehensive range of the options, one might study sacrifice in politics or warfare (Strenski 2002; Frantzen 2003), where individuals are enlisted or serve as substitutes for the nation and die for the nation's causes, as in *The Birth of a Nation* (1915).

As this brief survey suggests, sacrifice would appear to be a major topic in the history of American cinema, so it is somewhat surprising how little theoretical, historical, or cultural analysis has been devoted to the topic (in the conclusion we will briefly discuss sacrificial depictions by filmmakers outside of the US). The essay that follows, which is an initial foray into the field, will consider broadly a range of sacrificial representations in the history of American cinema. This approach will allow us not only to study what filmmakers have had to say about the contours of specific ritual sacrifices (who gets selected, how the killing happens, for what purposes, and so forth), but also to explore what a variety of sacrifices depicted in American cinema might suggest about "America" itself. More specifically, it will become clear that the history of American cinema reveals a tension between two broad sacrificial trajectories: films that *critique* sacrifice as unnecessary or tragic violence, and those that *recommend* sacrifice as essential to create or uphold the social order, or as necessary to push forward "progress." In American films, the trajectory that *recommends* sacrifice – overtly or implicitly – has dominated the production of films from the origins of cinema to the present. As we shall see, such films have been routinely more popular than films critical of sacrifice. To be sure, even those films that appear to be pro-sacrificial might contain an undercurrent of criticism or contain awareness of a tragic component to any killing, expulsion, or offering. But a clear trajectory in American cinema is toward the increasingly vivid depiction of screen sacrifices to justify, glorify, celebrate, and recommend sacrifice as a way to assure American purity or innocence (including, of course, the innocence of the film industry).

Now, that this development within a domain of art correlates with the emergence of an American empire within the domains of economics and politics over the course of the twentieth century is probably no coincidence. But if American films from *The Birth of a Nation* to *Apocalypto* rather vividly reveal a tension between the glorious and tragic features of sacrifice, they also have tended to compress desires for domination and fears of enemies into entertainment that displaces, obscures, or selectively reveals the violence of American history in spectacles that more often than not seek to purify the nation or to assert its innocence (Brownlow 1990). Sacrifices gave birth to the nation, and the American people appear to require (or at least expect their artists to represent) repeated blood sacrifices that might function to help America maintain particular symbolic constructions of purity, progress, or dominance (Marvin and Engle 1999). Needless to say, this American fixation on blood sacrifices also reveals a problem that going to the movies, as ritual process, can hardly solve (Lyden 2003).

The birth of a notion: sacrifice in early American cinema

It is no exaggeration to say that the earliest American filmmakers were somewhat obsessed with the topic of sacrifice. No less than three-dozen films with the word "sacrifice" in the title appear in the *American Film Institute Catalog* covering the years between 1909 and 1920. For instance, Sidney Olcott explored traditional sacrifice in *The Aztec Sacrifice*, a 1910 film based on the 1843 book *History of the Conquest of Mexico* by William H. Prescott. Something of Olcott's interest in making a film about Aztec sacrifice might be evident from two of his other early films, which also treated religion. He was the first to direct *Ben Hur* (1907), based on the 1899 novel by Lew Wallace, *Ben-Hur: A Tale of the Christ*. And Olcott was the first to bring the story of Christ to the screen by filming on location in Palestine, in *From the Manger to the Cross: Jesus of Nazareth* (1912).

Self-sacrifices and sacrifice as communal gift were also popular themes in early American cinema. The theme of sacrifice as communal gift is evident in *The Family Honor* (1920). Directed by King Vidor (best known for his work on *Hallelujah* – the first film to use an African-American cast), the working title for *The Family Honor* was "The Battle of Youth." As the working title suggests, this film tracks how young people face choices that demand honesty and moral integrity as they come of age. The main character, Dal, goes to college because his cash-strapped family sees talent in him and supports him. But Dal is a wastrel youth. When he is falsely accused of murdering a detective who raids the saloon where Dal is drinking, it is up to a witness to come forward (thereby indicting himself) to protect Dal's tarnished honor and to keep him from jail. Only after this gift by a peer does Dal reform. His salvation, or at least maturation into moral responsibility, follows from the communal gifts of his family and a peer.

Another early film can exemplify the related theme of self-sacrifice. *The Divine Sacrifice* (1918) was directed by George Archainbaud and produced by William A. Brady. *The Divine Sacrifice* is the story of a complicated love triangle. In it, a scorned woman must choose to give up her resentment and give up her autonomy to do a selfless deed to help the next generation flourish. Like Sidney Olcott, William Brady had a consistent religious interest. In another of his early films, *The Perils of Divorce* (1916), Brady offered a moralistic defense of marriage (an alternative title was "The Tyranny of Love"). In *The Cross Bearer* (1918), Brady produced the story of Cardinal Mercier of Louvain, Belgium, who protected his people from the invading German army at risk to himself. In each film, in short, self-sacrifice approaches the border of the divine.

In the context of the First World War, however, it was perhaps not surprising that the theme of sacrifice for the nation received the fullest attention from early filmmakers, and none more (in)famously than D. W. Griffith in *The Birth of a Nation*.

Griffith had more than a passing interest in the topic of sacrifice. In 1909 alone he released five films whose titles, at least, touched on the topic: *A Convict's Sacrifice*; *The Renunciation*; *The Hindoo's Dagger* (which one might presume was about Hindu sacrifice); *The Sacrifice*, based on the short story "Gift of the Magi," by O. Henry; and *The Resurrection*, based on Tolstoy's novel. But it was *The Birth of a Nation* in 1915 that collected Griffith's most sustained and lasting meditation on our theme.

The Birth of a Nation presents at least three scenes that are explicitly sacrificial. As is well known, Griffith based *The Birth of a Nation* upon the novel *The Clansman*, published in 1905 by Thomas F. Dixon. The film, over three hours long, is in roughly two equal parts. Part I depicts scenes from the Civil War; Part II treats Reconstruction. Throughout, the film tracks the fates of two families – the Camerons, who are Southern cotton plantation owners, and the Stonemans, who are Northerners. The Cameron parents – identified only as Dr. and Mrs. Cameron – have five children: Ben (also called "The Little Colonel"), Margaret, Flora, Wade, and Duke. The Stoneman family is led by Austin, who is an ardent abolitionist and leader in the House of Representatives. Austin's wife never appears in the film, but the film does hint that he has a relationship with his mulatto housekeeper, Lydia Brown. Stoneman has three children – Elsie (played by Lillian Gish), Phil, and Tod. All of the children are youth or young adults. Over the course of the film, Phil Stoneman falls in love with and marries Margaret Cameron, and Ben Cameron falls in love with and marries Elsie Stoneman. These inter-regional romances are threatened, however, first by the rivalry of North against South in the war, and then by the rivalry of blacks (and white liberals) against whites (led by the Ku Klux Klan) during Reconstruction. Needless to say, the North wins the war, but the Klan wins Reconstruction. Both victories – which somehow become a "birth" for Griffith – are depicted as accomplished through sacrifice.

The first explicitly sacrificial scene in the film is in Part I. Duke Cameron and Tod Stoneman, who are depicted in early scenes of the film as fun-loving "chums" from their days together at a boarding school, meet on the battlefield. Duke is with a line of Confederate soldiers who charge toward a Union line. Duke is hit, along with many of his comrades, and falls to the ground. A Union soldier – Tod – rushes toward Duke with a bayonet, poised to stab him. But Tod refrains from the attack as he recognizes his old friend. Duke's wound, however, is mortal, and his body slumps still. Tod is then shot from behind, and he falls to the ground. He drops to lie down directly facing Duke, his arm first wrapped across Duke's chest, and then sliding up to an intimate embrace around the back of Duke's neck. The two "chums" lie face to face on the battlefield. The title board at the outset of the scene anticipates its intended meaning: "War claims its bitter, useless, sacrifice" (Lang 1992: 63). Griffith clearly claimed *The Birth of a Nation* to be an anti-war film. A very early title board put it bluntly: "If in this work we have conveyed to the mind the ravages of war to the end that war may be held in abhorrence," it reads, "this effort will not have been in vain."

In fact, however, Griffith undercuts his assertion of the "uselessness" of the sacrifice of Duke and Tod by including at least two other sacrifices that he depicts as more justified, if not necessary, in Part II (some might see the assassination of Lincoln –

which Griffith spends nearly six minutes depicting at the close of Part I – as another sacrificial scene). But the second explicit sacrifice in the film is the death of Flora, the youngest of the Cameron daughters. Flora comes of age in the course of the film, having been played in early scenes by a very youthful Violet Wilkey; in later scenes by a more mature Mae Marsh. Flora's efflorescence is not lost on the men around her, including "Gus," a black Civil War veteran who Griffith identifies in a title board as a "renegade." Like all of the major African-American characters in the film, "Gus" is played by a white actor in blackface. Griffith generally depicts Reconstruction as a time of chaos – with unruly blacks elected to the South Carolina Congress, and a power-driven mulatto, ironically named Silas Lynch, installed by the abolitionist Stoneman and elected Lieutenant Governor of South Carolina. These blacks join some whites to agitate for equal rights, including "equal marriage," Griffith informs viewers several times.

Gus takes the prospect of equal marriage seriously enough to pursue Flora as she goes for a walk in the woods. "You see, I'm a Captain now – and I want to marry," Gus says via a title card to Flora in the scene that begins the chase. Flora first looks agitated, then tries to flee, and finally slaps Gus – and the chase is on. "Wait, missie, I won't hurt yeh," Gus suggests through a title board – but the audience has been prepared by Griffith to sense otherwise as the chase leads Flora to a rocky outcropping over a cliff. "Stay away, or I'll jump!" a title board has Flora exclaim as Gus, foaming at the mouth, comes closer. Flora then jumps to her death. Ben, her brother, who became aware of Gus' intentions, arrives too late at the base of the rock. He embraces the still-living Flora in what is an unmistakably framed Pietà – her body drapes across his lap. Ben then takes the Confederate flag Flora had wrapped around her waist and uses it to wipe blood from her mouth. She dies after mouthing the name of "Gus," and the title board reads: "For her who had learned the stern lesson of honor we should not grieve that she found sweeter the opal gates of death" (Lang 1992: 120–3). This was not only a necessary sacrifice; it was noble, honorable, even "sweet."

That this scene was a sacrifice is made explicit as the denouement of the final sacrifice in the film – the lynching of Gus. Gus is captured by Ben, and brought before the Klan assembled in the woods. "The Trial," reads the title board. It takes about ten seconds. "Guilty," reads the next board. In an early version of the film, Griffith vividly depicted Gus' lynching (including his castration), but censors forced him to cut the scene (Salter 2004: 14). In the final theatrical release, Gus' body is simply shown astride a horse with the noose around his neck, and then, after a quick cut, his dead body is shown being dumped by five Klansmen on the steps of the home of Silas Lynch. Gus' body has pinned to it a piece of paper bearing the letters "KKK" and a picture of a skull and crossbones. After a quick scene in which Austin Stoneman is shown hastily leaving the South, Ben rallies the Klan, again in the woods. He holds up the Confederate flag from Flora's waist, and dips it in a basin of water. He baptizes the Confederate flag, while wearing his white robe inscribed with two red crosses on the chest. He then holds the baptized, blood-soaked flag aloft, and a title card reads: "Brethren, this flag bears the red stain of the life of a Southern woman, a priceless sacrifice on the altar of an outraged civilization." He then takes a burning cross from a Klansman standing behind him, and holds it and the flag aloft (Lang 1992: 124–8). From this point on, Griffith follows Dixon's novel to assert that the Klan will (re)establish a white, Christian America. The Klan will save the South from chaos, through necessary, and "just," even noble, sacrifice. Baptized in blood, the Klan will purify the nation and restore white supremacy (Weisenfeld 2000).

Now, how Griffith treats these three scenes of sacrifice reveals unmistakably both the racist and the nationalist dogmas at the core of the film – and establishes the predominant functions of sacrifice in American cinema ever after. The first sacrifice – of two white soldiers – Griffith depicts as "senseless." This associates Griffith with a noble, moralistic desire for peace – while also allowing him to depict the spectacle and drama of war with an unparalleled vividness and drama. Warriors remain heroes in Griffith's vision – as the ascension of Ben Stoneman, "The Little Colonel," to Klan savior and husband of the desirable Elsie, makes clear. The second sacrifice – of Flora – in contrast, is "priceless." Such hyperbole, and the attendant overt religious symbolism associated with the fetish object of the Confederate flag that she wore around her waist, renders this self-sacrifice of a woman to protect her virtue as noble, honorable – and necessary. But about the third sacrifice, of Gus, Griffith is simply mute, in denial, as if innocent. He does not recognize it other than as "The Trial," of a "Guilty" man. That Gus is "guilty," in fact, only of expressing the desire that white men will receive as their reward (and with which viewers are asked to identify) – to be married – matters not at all. Couched in the jargon of the courtroom, Griffith not only obscures but celebrates and exonerates the Klan's brutal execution, accompanied by ritual trappings, of an act of vengeance. An assembled mob of white men wearing robes and hoods is depicted as a pious, even Christian, agency of righteous justice.

And thus, after this "sacrifice" which was not a sacrifice, but an act of "justice," Griffith can imagine a new nation being "born." After two more chase scenes, in which Elsie and Dr. Cameron are both rescued from peril by the Klan on charging horses, Griffith depicts the South as the setting for a unified nation celebrating its common "Aryan birthright." A parade down the streets of Piedmont, South Carolina, led by the Cameron family and Stoneman boys, surrounded by Klansmen on horses, is met by cheering white townsfolk waving white handkerchiefs, as blacks run to the rear or offscreen out of fear. After "The Next Election" is announced in a title card, "overseen" by the Klan so that white power is restored, several final title cards bring home the tripartite domestic, religious, and political significance of all of this sacrifice. "The aftermath. At the sea's edge, the double honeymoon," reads the first. Margaret Cameron and Phil Stoneman sit on a couch together. After a fade, Ben Cameron and Elsie Stoneman sit together on a bluff, high above the sea. Ben turns toward Elsie, with the vastness of the sea as horizon, and the title card reads: "Dare we dream of a golden day when the bestial War shall rule no more. But instead – the gentle Prince in the Hall of Brotherly Love in the City of Peace." After another fade, a huge diaphanous image of Christ appears in the background of a large crowd of dancing and processing people. Another fade returns the viewer to Ben and Elsie on the bluff, and the final title cards appear shortly thereafter: "Liberty and union, one and inseparable, now and forever." And "THE BIRTH OF A NATION or 'The Clansman.' THE END" (Lang

1992: 155–6). Without exaggeration, the end of this film was only the beginning of its influence (Stokes 2007). It was wildly popular with white audiences (while protested by the just-emerging NAACP – National Association for the Advancement of Colored People). Even more, *The Birth of a Nation* established the basic notion of sacrifice in American film. It set the tension between senseless and necessary sacrifices, and clarified the basic conventions by which sacrifice would be depicted as necessary (or at least justified) along lines of race, gender, age, economics, and politics – that have largely endured, as we shall see, to the present.

King Kong and other purity and progress projects

In the forty years between 1915 and 1955, an average of one American film per year offered viewers some spectacle of human sacrifice, in titles such as *Aloha Oe* (1915), *South of Suva* (1922), *South of Tahiti* (1941), and *Miss Robin Crusoe* (1954). The last film, based on the Daniel Defoe novel but with a decidedly gender-bending twist, also features the theme of self-sacrifice. In it, Robin (played by Amanda Blake) is shipwrecked after a boat captained by her abusive father – to whom she served as a second mate – runs aground in a storm. Shortly after arriving on the island, Robin rescues a female "Friday" who is about to be sacrificed by natives. A third character, Jonathan – a British naval officer – is also shipwrecked on the island. Initially, Robin and Friday shun him. Eventually, a romance buds between Jonathan and Robin, but misunderstanding ensues and Jonathan ends up leaving the island on a longboat to seek to make it to the shipping lanes for rescue. He does so, and commandeers a ship to head back to the island for Robin and Friday. But the natives have returned, and Friday gives up her own life in an effort to protect Robin. Jonathan returns just in time to rescue Robin from the sacrificing savages. His loyalty proven, at the expense of Friday's self-sacrifice, their romance blooms anew.

Another better-known film from the time period on the theme of self-sacrifice is the 1937 *A Star is Born* (remade in 1954 and 1976). Framed by scenes at the Hollywood sacred place of Grauman's Chinese Theater, the plot tracks the diverging careers of Norman Maine (played by Fredric March) and Esther Victoria Blodgett, later known as Vicki Lester (played by Janet Gaynor). Esther's ambition becomes the counterpoint to Norman's self-sacrifice. He assists her career after they meet at a party, and she becomes a star after her first movie is a hit (Norman also appears, but his performance is panned by critics). The couple are married, but Norman's alcoholism leads him to lose work and find trouble with the law, while Esther's career takes off. Eventually, Norman overhears Esther tearfully telling her agent that she intends to quit work to stay with Norman. After telling Esther he's going for a swim in the ocean, and asking to look at her one more time (which is what he said to her when they first met), he then walks into the ocean and drowns. His self-sacrifice allows her to continue pursuing success. Other well-known films from this period with the mythic theme of self-sacrifice producing a "birth" might include titles such as *Bambi* (1942), where Bambi's Mom sacrifices herself to "man" to help Bambi become King of the Forest, and any number of war films – about which we will say more shortly.

On the theme of sacrifice as communal gift, we have already mentioned *It's a Wonderful Life* (1946), but a lesser-known film by King Vidor, the biblically entitled *Our Daily Bread* (1934), illumines the convention nicely. Mary Sims and her unemployed husband John (a couple featured in Vidor's 1928 masterpiece *The Crowd*), move to the country to try their hand at farming some fallow land. They gradually succeed, with the help of a quasi-communal co-op (including Swedish, Jewish, and Italian families) that John establishes. The cooperative flourishes, despite some trials, but seems unlikely to be able to overcome a severe drought. John, who has been tempted to leave the farm by a seductive single woman, Sally, experiences a vision while running away with Sally, turns around, and upon his return inspires the community to dig by hand a two-mile long irrigation ditch to draw water from the retention pond of the nearby power plant. The community balks, at first, but then pitches in over two continuous days and nights of intense labor (which took ten days to film). Their collective sacrifice succeeds, the farm is saved, and John and Mary renew their marriage. The film aptly captured the mentality of the New Deal, and President Franklin D. Roosevelt was given a private screening at the White House (Vidor 1972).

No film more successfully replicated the conventions of sacrifice as a purification project that *The Birth of a Nation* established, however, than *King Kong* (1933). Made in the wake of the successful *Tarzan: The Ape Man* (1932), which also included sacrifices, *King Kong*, like *The Birth of a Nation*, featured three sacrificial scenes. Also like *Birth*, *King Kong* included several exciting chases, repeated battles between Kong and various enemies, and several possible erotic pairings including, of course, the forbidden pairing of "beauty and the beast," a phrase invoked at least eight times in the script (Greenberg 1996). The first sacrificial scene takes place as the mercenary filmmaker Carl Denham arrives on "Skull Island" with his film crew. They have with them the "beauty" (Ann Darrow, played by Fay Wray) who Denham hopes to display as lead actress in his film. The Americans (identified as "whites" in the shooting script) approach the island with trepidation, hearing tribal drums in the distance. "What do you suppose is happening?" Ann asks. "Up to some of their heathen tricks," first mate Jack Driscoll answers, establishing the religious context for what comes next. What comes next is a scene of sacrifice. "Tribal" actors, some dressed in gorilla costumes – thus identifying Kong with a human surrogate – are preparing to sacrifice a woman on an altar. When the Americans are discovered, the ritual stops and the tribal chief requests Ann, "the woman of gold," as a replacement for the "sacrificial victim." Ann is to become the "bride of Kong." The sailors, led by Denham and Driscoll, manage to get Ann safely onboard ship, where "Charley," a native informer, identifies what was going on with the single word: "sacrifice" (*King Kong Shooting Script*: 32-9).

Later that evening, tribal members kidnap Ann. The next sacrificial scene follows shortly. Ann is now on the altar, as the tribal chief chants: "We call thee, Kong. O Mighty One, Great Kong ... Rama [Hindu god] Kong. Thy bride is here, O Mighty One, Great Kong." The tribe breaks into frenzied drumming, dancing, yelling, and torch-waving as Kong approaches. Ann screams, as the gorilla lifts her off the altar. She has been spared death, but the audience wonders what fate awaits her as the "bride of Kong." The chase through the jungle ensues, with Kong fighting off dinosaurs, sea monsters, and about a dozen sailors, until he reaches his lair – a cave in one of the eye-sockets of Skull Mountain. From this point, Kong (and the moviegoer) has an expansive panorama of the jungle and ocean. The view is good. It is, then, with this imperial gaze established that Ann's potentially monstrous fate is revealed. Slowly, Kong begins taking Ann's clothes off. Ann screams. When "the girl is almost naked," according to the filming script, Kong is distracted by the arrival near his lair of Driscoll, and by a pterodactyl. While Kong fights off the pterodactyl, Driscoll rescues Ann. Eventually, of course, *he* will marry her (*King Kong Shooting Script*: 47–85).

The third sacrificial scene in the film is its ending. Denham traps Kong and brings him to New York City. He is chained on stage (a vestige of an altar), but breaks through his chains and rampages through the city, carrying Ann with him. Eventually, as is well known, he winds up in another high place where the view is good: the Empire State Building. Phallic imagery aside, Kong's ascent with Ann cradled in one hand brings out the best military technology that America can muster – airplanes. The machine-gunners aboard the biplanes repeatedly buzz the gorilla – in a decidedly modern update of the chase scenario – and eventually the American warriors take down the beast. Kong falls to his death leaving Ann exhausted, if not ravaged, atop the tower. A cop offers what could be the final word: "Gee, what a sight. Well, the aviators got him." This would be the straightforward meaning of the sacrifice of Kong: American military prowess preserved progress and civilization over against the threat of the beast. But the film's last word even more directly invokes myth. "Oh no," Denham intones, "'twasn't the aviators. It was Beauty killed the Beast" (*King Kong Shooting Script*: 87–106).

Now, there are manifold ways to interpret these various sacrifices. The most salient, given the historical context in which the film arose, is that Americans during the Depression needed to be reminded to sacrifice the acquisitive, desire-laden animal in them in order to preserve "civilization." That "civilization" was defined, in the film, by markers of racial, sexual, and religious purity accompanied by technological mastery does not take much deciphering. Set in the context of the Depression and its corresponding expansion of Federal Government programs, one meaning of the sacrifices in *King Kong* is that the empire will continue to progress so long as greedy acquisitiveness is sacrificed on the altar of beauty. That this beauty depends, repeatedly, on gas bombs, guns, chains, airplanes, military prowess, and technological sophistication that reached to the highest places, does also not take much deciphering. Such a material reality of systemic violence, in short, is the terrifying flipside of the romantic sacrifices for purity and progress promoted by *King Kong* and many other films from this era, perhaps including, as Tina Chanter has recently argued, *Casablanca* (1942) (Chanter 2008: 180–215).

After all, the New Deal itself depended upon exactly the sort of rationalized, organized mastery that could build skyscrapers and imagine taming wild beasts. Not surprisingly, then, as the Second World War began to break in Europe, many filmmakers shifted the foci of cinematic sacrifices from internal purification of America to conquest over an enemy. Sacrifices for beauty, purity, or progress gave way to sacrifices for the nation. Not all filmmakers toed this nationalist line, of course. One interesting, early dissenting film with surprising religious overtones was the final feature film to be directed by the prolific silent film director Edwin Carewe, his 1934 *Are We Civilized?* The plot sets a father and son pair, Paul Franklin, Sr. and Jr. against an unspecified new political regime bent on censoring the press and burning books. In an effort to stave off the sacrifice of books (and the civil liberties they represent), Franklin Sr. offers an impassioned monologue that cites Moses, Buddha, Confucius, Jesus, and Muhammad, to name only a few, as advocates of what might be called an anti-sacrificial, pacifist religion. Franklin Jr. later reiterates, after his father has been mortally injured by a mob, the point of the monologue, namely that "mankind will never be truly civilized until all races become one in spirit, understanding brotherly love." The setting for the film could have been any modern state, but reviewers located it easily as Nazi Germany. In fact, however, as Sinclair Lewis' 1935 novel *It Can't Happen Here* suggested, and later events would prove repeatedly, there were also politicians in the US who were quite ready to dispense with civil rights and liberties.

There were also, in the years to come, filmmakers ready to demonstrate their patriotism in movies devoted to the topic of sacrifice for the nation. One of them, Harry Fraser, perhaps better known as the director of dozens of westerns (e.g., *Wagon Trail* [1935], *Gunsmoke Mesa* [1944]) and as screenwriter for *Captain America* (1944), offered an early entry in the sacrifice-for-the-nation genre with *Heroes of the Alamo* (1937), dedicated to "the memory of the immortal Texans." Many more such dedications would follow, before, during, and after US entry into the Second World War. *Adventure in Iraq* (1943) offered a distinctive twist, with Americans stranded in Iraq facing the prospect of human sacrifice at the hands of devil-worshiping militants. Apart from the more than 100 US Propaganda films commissioned between 1941 and 1945 (perhaps the most famous being Frank Capra's *Why We Fight* series), feature films such as the 1945 trio *Back to Bataan*, *God is My Co-Pilot*, and *The Story of G.I. Joe* demonstrated for ready viewers the sacrifices of US servicemen. After the war, one 1951 film, *Little Big Horn*, managed to snatch victory out of the worst military defeat in US history, claiming that Custer's loss was a sacrifice that helped give rise "to the greatest fighting force in the world today – The United States Army," to which the film was "respectfully dedicated." Throughout the Korean Conflict and postwar era, films such as *Sands of Iwo Jima* (1950) and *Battle Cry* (1955) perpetuated the links between war and sacrifice that seemed so certainly to have brought victory and prosperity to the US. Filmmakers had, to a large degree, done their part to cultivate and revive the civil-religious link between sacrifice on the battlefield and the security of the American nation, established by D. W. Griffith, now arrayed against almost any enemy.

Rebels with a cause: an empire of sacrifice?

After 1955, a different focus emerged to dominate American cinematic sacrifices, due perhaps to one film more than any other: *Rebel Without a Cause*. David Carrasco has proposed that sacrifice, in the context of the Aztec empire, was a tool for the indoctrination of youth. Those bloody rituals for which the Aztecs became infamous were, Carrasco suggests further, staged acts of performative violence to demonstrate the lengths the empire would go to preserve its power (Carrasco 1999). Without much of a leap, Carrasco's hypothesis might apply quite well to sacrifice in the recent history of American cinema, as well. For, since *Rebel Without a Cause* in 1955 to *Hostel* in 2005, the most prominent sacrifices in the American cinema have, indeed, offered up young people, represented in increasingly brutal ways.

Rebel features two sacrifices. The first is the most famous sequence in the film – the "chickie run." In it, two young men, Buzz and Jim – the latter played by James Dean – race two stolen cars toward a cliff. The scene is a rite of passage, a test of manhood, which becomes a sacrifice when Buzz inadvertently dies. The two youth are mimetic rivals – a common feature in myth and ritual, competing for status among a group of teenagers, and for the affection of Judy, played by Natalie Wood. After Buzz dies, Jim and Judy literally come together in a remarkable tableau as the soundtrack shifts from a minor to a major key, effacing "Plato" (played by Sal Mineo). This scene foreshadows the second sacrifice in the film. Plato is now the victim. He is gunned down by police on the steps of the D. W. Griffith Observatory outside of Los Angeles. Screenwriter Stewart Stern detailed that his intent in using the Planetarium setting was to remind viewers of "a Greek temple, like the Theater Dionysus ... where they did the sacrifices" (Pahl 2009). What critic Thomas Doherty calls Plato's "sacrificial snuff-out" is the counterpoint to Jim's attainment of masculine virtue: he gets the girl. Some youth must be sacrificed on the altar of American masculinity (Doherty 2002).

By *Halloween* (1978), this iconography of adolescent sacrifice took on an increasingly misogynist cast. Four victims, three of them female, fall in *Halloween*, which remains one of the most profitable independent films ever produced. The opening scene establishes that sacrifice seeks to purify or punish sin, which is associated especially with unfettered female desire. A young woman is supposed to be babysitting her brother, but instead is making out on a couch with her boyfriend. Unbeknownst to the couple, the brother, Michael, watches them through a window; a view shared by the audience through a first-person camera angle. The killer/viewer then observes the couple going upstairs to a bedroom. After an interlude in which the killer/viewer takes a large knife from a kitchen drawer, the camera ascends the staircase, as the young man rushes downstairs, adjusting his clothing. The viewer/killer then enters the bedroom to see the young woman sitting naked before a nightstand, brushing her hair in a mirror. The camera closes in on her naked breasts, as a knife slashes on the screen while the soundtrack represents repeated gashing noises of steel penetrating flesh. She has been sacrificed for her precocious sexuality. Three other killings follow in the ninety minutes of the film, all of them more or less sacrificial. The victims are all lust-driven adolescents, who are punished by Michael, a "messenger of God." Only Jamie Lee Curtis, the virginal "final girl," survives (Dika 1990). The success of the film spawned eight sequels, and countless imitators, many of which have become their own franchises, notably *Friday the 13th* (1980) and, more recently, the *Scream* trilogy (1996–2002). *Scream* updated the genre by making the eight youthful victims ironic participants in their own terror; much like the audience members who pay to be scared by these spectacles of sacrifice. Not surprisingly, *Scream*'s ironic playing with the conventions of the genre led to parody, in Keenen Ivory Wayans' *Scary Movie* (2000), which has now become its own franchise (Shary 2002).

With *Hostel* (2005), the sacrifices of youth turn to torture. Three young male backpackers on pilgrimage in Europe – two of them Americans – demonstrate "ugly American" stereotypes as they seek (and find) sex and drugs in Amsterdam. Upon a tip, they learn of a hostel in Slovakia where women are both cheap and easy. They find it. What they also find, however, is that torture of backpackers is big business. Clients of "Elite Hunting" pay for the "pleasure" of torturing and killing youth in an abandoned factory-turned-prison. One of the three backpackers escapes, after discovering that torturing Americans is the most lucrative business, and that American clients are charged the highest rates. Aside from the usual sacrificial instruments of knives, ropes, and guns, director Eli Roth has his ritual killers use chainsaws, electric drills, and various other tools. The United States Council of Catholic Bishops' review described *Hostel* in blunt terms as a "nauseatingly vile" attempt to package "dehumanizing brutality as entertainment." It earned $20 million in its first weekend, and a sequel, *Hostel II*, was released in 2007.

Now, this brief history of the sacrifices of young people in American cinema from *Rebel Without a Cause* to *Hostel* is hardly a self-evident trajectory, but it does rest on a consistent pattern to represent youth that has been replicated, and escalated, over recent decades. At the least, the profitability of these films might lead to some interesting questions in religious studies. Why have young people so frequently been depicted in cinematic spectacles of abjection and sacrifice? Even more, why have young people found these movies so consistently attractive? Here, John Lyden's emphasis on how film can function as religious discourse (myth) and ritual process (rite of passage) bears consideration. Such "shocking" images may assist young people to steel themselves to face the challenges living in a violent (even genocidal) era requires, and to survive in a culture where violence has become part of the everyday lived awareness of youth. Even more, that a film features scenes of torture just as US government policy officially sanctions torture should also not surprise. One can, of course, read into these films a moralistic *critique* of American sacrifices – and they do contain critical elements. More often, however, the cinema of adolescent abjection seems to exploit sadistic and masochistic desires for domination and degradation, compressing them into an artistic product to communicate in effect that violence is the only effective means to meet violence (Stone 1999). That this is a lesson quite consistent with the building or maintenance of an empire, as Carrasco suggested in a very different context, draws out the conclusion succinctly.

Conclusion

All in all, it may be surprising how often and in how many ways the theme of sacrifice has appeared in the history of American cinema. While a tension exists between films (and scenes within films) that represent sacrifice as necessary, on the one hand, and that critique sacrifice, on the other, the predominant trajectory we have traced has identified films that represent deaths or offerings on the screen in a way that justifies them for various projects of purity, progress, nation-building, or personal strength. Such films have tended, furthermore, to be detached from traditional religious discourses, practices, or communities in any substantive way. It is as if Hollywood has created an autonomous zone of cinematic sacrifice, with shifting allegiances to moral principles, the nation, notions of racial or gender purity, or other constructs, as needed. Institutional commitments to religious communities or traditions tend to be attenuated at best. This is true even of the one traditional sacrifice most frequently represented on the screen in a predominantly Christian culture, namely the death of Jesus of Nazareth. The sacrifice of Christ has within recent decades been far more a source of scandal or controversy than consensus, as in *The Last Temptation of Christ* (1988) and *The Passion of the Christ* (2004). Even *Dead Man Walking* (1995), which in its unforgettable final scenes portrayed capital punishment as a sacrificial crucifixion, also sought to "balance" that anti-sacrificial line of argument with sympathy for the victims and their families, who felt the killing was justified or necessary.

Interestingly, such tension has also marked, perhaps until very recently, war films that represent young people sacrificing for America. Explicitly anti-war films emerged in the wake of the Vietnam Conflict, in productions such as *Apocalypse Now* (1979), *Platoon* (1986), and *Born on the Fourth of July* (1989). More recently, *Saving Private Ryan* (1998) revived the glory (while also showing the gore and cost) of sacrifice for the nation. Most recently, films critical of the war in Iraq (e.g., *Jarhead* [2005]; *Redacted* [2007]; *Stop-Loss* [2008]) have largely failed to find audiences. These latter developments might suggest that the broad cinematic motif of sacrifice for the nation might have recovered from its post-Vietnam lack of popularity.

Other forms of cinematic sacrifice have also endured, while changing. The notion of sacrifices as necessary to preserve racial purity clearly underwent revision in the wake of the Civil Rights Movement. A film such as Spike Lee's *Malcolm X* (1992) depicts the death of Malcolm not as a justifiable purification or catharsis, but as a tragic loss. Similarly, John Singleton's *Boyz n the Hood* (1991), while unmistakably drawing on tropes from films that feature the sacrifice of youth as coming-of-age ritual, depicts the deaths of young black men in South Central Los Angeles as preventable through education and stronger families. Even *Mississippi Burning* (1988), for all of its historical problems, represented the sacrifice of civil rights workers as a crime, thereby cinematically reversing the glorification of the KKK established by *The Birth of a Nation*. Of course, films about traditional sacrifice (*Help!* [1965]; *Apocalypto* [2006]), self-sacrifice (*Thelma and Louise* [1991]; *Million-Dollar Baby* [2004]), and sacrifice as communal gift (*Gandhi* [1982]; *Schindler's List* [1993]) continue to be produced in ways that matched and extended previous conventions for their representation. How any of the above films featuring scenes of sacrifice relate to American ideals of personal identity and moral practices, consumerism, military adventurism, social activism, and commitment to traditional forms of religion, are all topics deserving further exploration. The meaning of any cinematic sacrifice, in short, remains contingent upon how individual films are read in their contexts, and upon individual viewers drawing upon broader patterns of discourses, practices, communities, and institutions across society.

Finally, something of the distinctively "American" cast to these notions of sacrifice in cinema might gain clarity by contrasting them with selected films on the topic made by filmmakers outside of the US. A film such as *Romero* (1989), produced by Paulist Pictures and directed by Australian John Duigan, depicts the sacrifice of the Salvadoran Catholic priest in a way that seeks to connect viewers not to the movie industry as much as to the tenets of liberation theology and to the long Catholic tradition. Similarly, two films on sacrifice from the Danish filmmaker Carl Theodor Dreyer, *La passion de Jeanne d'Arc* (1928) and *Ordet* (*The Word*) (1955), delve into the mechanisms of scapegoating and sacrifice to challenge systems of representation (including theologies) that multiply victims, seeking instead to find grace or even miracle in the midst of life. A surprising appearance of grace surely marks the sumptuous sacrifice in *Babette's Feast* (1987), yet another Danish production, and it is the possibility of grace as the counterpoint to destruction that draws the protagonist in Andrei Tarkovsky's *Offret* (*The Sacrifice*) (1986) to renounce the banal. There are, of course, many other films that could receive attention: Ingmar Bergman's *The Seventh Seal* (1957) which critiques the effort to use sacrifice to prop up the social order; Pier Paolo Pasolini's *Medea* (1969), which updated Euripides' tragedy in light of the durability of patriarchy and misogyny; and even Luis Buñuel's *The Exterminating Angel* (1962), which links human sacrifice to bourgeois repression and Christian dogma in Kafkaesque fashion. Quebec filmmaker Denys Arcand's *Jesus of Montreal* (1989) gives the conventional "Jesus sacrificed for us" meaning of the cross a powerful anti-capitalist (and non-supernatural) interpretation, and Monty Python's *Life of Brian* (1979) is simply a giddy anti-sacrificial parody in which viewers are encouraged to "always look on the bright side of death."

In whatever forms they take, then, films about sacrifice can raise profound and classical questions about the human condition, God, moral action, and cultural meaning. As Jeffrey Stout asks, writing about Lars von Trier's powerful and disturbing meditation on self-sacrifice and God, *Breaking the Waves* (1996): can films "disentangle" *agape* (self-giving love) "from the sadomasochistic fantasy and voyeurism that repeats itself endlessly in the rhetoric of sacrifice?" (Stout 2003: 221). Such a question drives to the heart of the problem posed by the presence of sacrifice in many of its representations in the history of cinema. In America, the problem is especially pointed by *policies* that have translated exploitative pornographies of sacrifice into national myths of redemptive violence, racial purity, misogyny, and more. And yet art not only imitates life; it can shape it. It can be expected, then, and perhaps even hoped, that filmmakers will continue to explore in increasingly sophisticated and wise ways the problems of destruction and possibilities of creation inherent in the manifold meanings of sacrifice.

Bibliography

Baumgarten, A. I. (ed.) (2002) *Sacrifice in Religious Experience*, NUMEN Book Series: Studies in the History of Religions, 93, Leiden and Boston: E. J. Brill.

Brownlow, K. (1990). *Behind the Mask of Innocence*, New York: Knopf.

Carrasco, D. (1999) *City of Sacrifice: The Aztec Empire and the Role of Violence in Civilization*, Boston: Beacon Press.

Carter, J. (ed.) (2003) *Understanding Religious Sacrifice: A Reader* (Controversies in the Study of Religion), London and New York: Continuum.

Chanter, T. (2008) *The Picture of Abjection: Film, Fetish, and the Nature of Difference*, Bloomington: Indiana University Press.

Dika, V. (1990) *Games of Terror: Halloween, Friday the 13th and the Films of the Stalker Cycle*, Rutherford, NJ: Farleight Dickinson University Press.

Doherty, T. (2002) *Teenagers and Teenpics: The Juvenilization of American Movies in the 1950s*, revised and expanded ed., Philadelphia: Temple University Press.

Frantzen, A. J. (2003) *Bloody Good: Chivalry, Sacrifice, and the Great War*, Chicago: University of Chicago Press.

Girard, R. (1977) *Violence and the Sacred*, trans. Patrick Gregory, Baltimore and London: Johns Hopkins University Press.

Greenberg, H. R. (1996) "King Kong: The Beast in the Boudoir – or, 'You Can't Marry that Girl, You're a Gorilla!,'" in B. K. Grant (ed.) *The Dread of Difference: Gender and the Horror Film*, Austin: University of Texas Press: 338–51.

King Kong (1933): Shooting Script. Story by M. C. Cooper and E. Wallace; Screenplay by R. Rose, and J. A. Creelman. Electronic edition. American Film Scripts Online, New York: Alexander Street Press, 2002.

Lang, R. (ed.) (1992) *The Birth of a Nation: D. W. Griffith, Director*, New Brunswick, NJ: Rutgers University Press.

Lyden, J. (2003) *Film as Religion: Myths, Morals, and Rituals*, New York: New York University Press.

McClymond, K. (2004) "The Nature and Elements of Sacrificial Ritual," *Method and Theory in the Study of Religion* 16: 337–66.

Marvin, C. and Engle, D. W. (1999) *Blood Sacrifice and the Nation: Totem Rituals and the American Flag*, Cambridge: Cambridge University Press.

Milbank, J. (1999) "The Ethics of Self-Sacrifice," *First Things* 91 (March): 33–8.

Pahl, J. (forthcoming, 2009) *Blessed Brutalities: The Religious Origins of American Empire*, New York: New York University Press.

Salter, R. C. (2004) "The Birth of a Nation as American Myth," *Journal of Religion and Film* 8 (October). Online. Available HTTP: <http://www.unomaha.edu/jrf/Vol8No2/SalterBirth.htm> (accessed 24 June 2008).

Shary, T. (2002) *Generation Multiplex: The Image of Youth in Contemporary American Cinema*, Austin: University of Texas Press.

Stokes, M. (2007) *D. W. Griffith's THE BIRTH OF A NATION: A History of "The Most Controversial Motion Picture of All Time,"* Oxford: Oxford University Press.

Stone, B. P. (1999) "Religion and Violence in Popular Film," *Journal of Religion and Film* 3 (April). Online. Available HTTP: <http://www.unomaha.edu/jrf/Violence.htm> (accessed 30 June 2008).

Stout, J. (2003) "Breaking the Waves," in M. L. Bandy and A. Monda (eds) *The Hidden God: Film and Faith*, New York: Museum of Modern Art: 215–22.

Strenski, I. (2002) *Contesting Sacrifice: Religion, Nationalism, and Social Thought in France*, Chicago: University of Chicago Press.

Vidor, K. (1972) *King Vidor on Film-Making*, New York: McKay.

Weisenfeld, J. (2000) "'For the Cause of Mankind': The Bible, Racial Uplift, and Early Race Movies," in V. L. Wimbush (ed.) *African Americans and the Bible: Sacred Texts and Social Structures*, New York: Continuum: 728–42.

Filmography

Adventure in Iraq (1943, dir. D. Lederman)
Aloha Oe (1915, dir. R. Stanton)
Apocalpyse Now (1979, dir. F. Coppola)

Apocalypto (2006, dir. M. Gibson)
Are We Civilized? (1934, dir. E. Carewe)
The Aztec Sacrifice (1910, dir. S. Olcott)
Babette's Feast (1987, dir. G. Axel)
Back to Bataan (1945, dir. E. Dmytryk)
Bambi (1942, dir. D. Hand)
Battle Cry (1955, dir. R. Walsh)
Ben Hur (1907, dir. S. Olcott)
The Birth of a Nation (1915, dir. D. Griffith)
Born on the Fourth of July (1989, dir. O. Stone)
Boyz n the Hood (1991, dir. J. Singleton)
Breaking the Waves (1996, dir. L. von Trier)
Captain America (1944, dir. E. Clifton and J. English)
Casablanca (1942, dir. M. Curtiz)
A Convict's Sacrifice (1909, dir. D. Griffith)
The Cross Bearer (1918, dir. W. Brady)
The Crowd (1928, dir. K. Vidor)
Dead Man Walking (1995, dir. T. Robbins)
The Divine Sacrifice (1918, dir. G. Archainbaud; prod. W. Brady)
The Exterminating Angel (1962, dir. L. Buñuel)
The Family Honor (1920, dir. K. Vidor)
Friday the 13th (1980, dir. S. Cunningham)
From the Manger to the Cross: Jesus of Nazareth (1912, dir. S. Olcott)
Gandhi (1982, dir. R. Attenborough)
God is My Co-Pilot (1945, dir. R. Florey)
Gunsmoke Mesa (1944, dir. H. Fraser)
Halloween (1978, dir. J. Carpenter)
Help! (1965, dir. R. Lester)
Heroes of the Alamo (1937, dir. H. Fraser)
The Hindoo's Dagger (1909, dir. D. Griffith)
Hostel (2005, dir. E. Roth)
It's a Wonderful Life (1946, dir. F. Capra)
Jarhead (2005, dir. S. Mendes)
Jesus of Montreal (1989, dir. D. Arcand)
King Kong (1933, dir. M. Cooper)
The Last Temptation of Christ (1988, dir. M. Scorsese)
Life of Brian (1979, dir. T. Jones)
Little Big Horn (1951, dir. C. Warren)
Malcolm X (1992, dir. S. Lee)
Medea (1969, dir. P. Pasolini)
Million-Dollar Baby (2004, dir. C. Eastwood)
Miss Robin Crusoe (1954, dir. E. Frenke)
Mississippi Burning (1988, dir. A. Parker)
Offret (1986, dir. A. Tarkovsky)
Ordet (1955, dir. C. Dreyer)
Our Daily Bread (1934, dir. K. Vidor)
The Passion of the Christ (2004, dir. M. Gibson)
La passion de Jeanne d'Arc (1928, dir. C. Dreyer)
The Perils of Divorce (1916, dir. W. Brady)
Platoon (1986, dir. O. Stone)
Rebel Without a Cause (1955, dir. N. Ray)
Redacted (2007, dir. B. De Palma)
The Renunciation (1909, dir. D. Griffith)
The Resurrection (1909, dir. D. Griffith)

Romero (1989, dir. J. Duigan)
The Sacrifice (1909, dir. D. Griffith)
Sands of Iwo Jima (1950, dir. A. Dwan)
Saving Private Ryan (1998, dir. S. Spielberg)
Scary Movie (2000, dir. K. Wayans)
Schindler's List (1993, dir. S. Spielberg)
Scream (1996, dir. W. Craven)
The Seventh Seal (1957, dir. I. Bergman)
Sophie's Choice (1982, dir. A. Pakula)
South of Suva (1922, dir. F. Urson)
South of Tahiti (1941, dir. G. Waggner)
A Star is Born (1937, dir. W. Wellman)
Stop-Loss (2008, dir. K. Peirce)
The Story of G.I. Joe (1945, dir. W. Wellman)
Tarzan: The Ape Man (1932, dir. W. Van Dyke)
Thelma and Louise (1991, dir. R. Scott)
Wagon Trail (1935, dir. H. Fraser)
Why We Fight series (1941–5, dir. F. Capra)

Further reading

American Film Institute, *American Film Institute Catalog*. Online. Available HTTP: <http://afi.chadwyck.com/home>. (This key-word searchable catalog documents the history of American films to 1972. It is especially helpful for plot summaries, cast and crew lists, and production notes.)

Considine, D. M. (1985) *The Cinema of Adolescence*, Jefferson, NC: McFarland. (Established the "genre.")

Durgnat, R. and Simmon, S. (1988) *King Vidor, American*, Berkeley: University of California Press. (The best biography of this underappreciated figure.)

McDannell, C. (2008) *Catholics in the Movies*, Oxford: Oxford University Press. (State-of-the-art essays on single films featuring Catholics and Catholicism.)

Pippin, T. (2002) "Of Gods and Demons: Blood Sacrifice and Eternal Life in *Dracula* and the Apocalypse of John," in G. Aichele and R. Walsh (eds) *Screening Scripture: Intertextual Connections between Scripture and Film*, Harrisburg, PA: Trinity Press International: 24–41. (Creatively locates sacrifice in vampire movies, and connects to apocalyptic motifs in scripture and American culture and policy.)

Sharrett, C. (ed.) (1999) *Mythologies of Violence in Postmodern Media*, Detroit, MI: Wayne State University Press.

26
ETHICS
Jolyon Mitchell

Introduction

At the heart of this essay on "ethics" is the question: To what extent can films be a site of ethical debate and a catalyst for moral reflection? The very fact that such a question is now regularly asked, and sometimes answered positively, illustrates how discussions about the place of ethics in film have evolved. Some of the early responses to cinema were characterized by anxiety about the supposed negative impacts that films have upon the morality of viewers. Far from being a site of ethical debate or a catalyst for moral reflection, films were deemed as promoting immorality, and therefore a danger to established ethical values or accepted norms. The good life depicted on the screen was believed by many religious leaders to be some distance from the life truly worth living. The result was that watching "inappropriate" movies was commonly described as a threat to an individual's morals and even to a whole society's morality.

John Rice's popular short book on *What is Wrong with the Movies?* (1938) provides a good example of this approach. Rice claims that the "movie is the rival of schools and churches, the feeder of lust, the perverter of morals, the tool of greed, the school of crime, the betrayer of innocence." The origins of his book, which ran to at least nineteen editions, are to be found in a sermon Rice preached on "The Sins of the Movies." The published text retains its homiletical tone with Rice declaiming how the movie: "glorifies impurity as love. It pictures murder as entertainment. It exalts nakedness and indecency as beauty. It shows drink, divorce, revelling, gambling, revenge, gun fights as proper and legitimate ..." Rice's polemic reflects a strong belief in the power of films to corrupt viewers: "They debauch the mind of children, inflame the lusts of youth, [and] harden the hearts of sinners" (Rice 1938: 14). As I have described in greater details elsewhere, Rice's polemic is by no means unique (Mitchell 2007a: 200–7). Other aptly named books, such as *The Devil's Camera* (Burnett and Martell 1932), also reveal a deep-rooted suspicion among some religious leaders about the impact upon a viewer's ethical life of watching sex and violence on the silver screen.

While many of these deeply critical texts reflect early twentieth-century American or British conservative evangelical views, it is also possible to find similar concerns articulated in Russian Orthodox pronouncements from the office of the Holy Synod in St. Petersburg (*On the inadmissibility of holy subjects being shown by means of the so-called "Living photography,"* 1898), in Papal Encyclicals from the Vatican in Rome (*Vigilanti Cura*, 1936), and among Marthomite families in southern India (Thomas and Mitchell 2005: 33). Nor are such attempts to criticize movies and control viewing habits confined to different Christian traditions. Shi'a imams in Iran and Sunni clerics in Saudi Arabia regularly express concern about the damaging impact of some films upon the moral and spiritual lives of viewers (Mitchell and Plate 2007: 9). At first sight these critical sources may appear similar, but a closer study reveals that they are by no means identical, rooting their criticism in different ethical foundations, divergent religious beliefs, or distinct communal practices. They are also not always exclusively critical voices as even the most negative detractors of film sometimes celebrate the unrealized potential of cinema.

Some religious leaders, scholars, and educators go further, arguing that many films actually do realize their potential and can be catalysts for reflecting upon what makes for genuine human flourishing. For example, Peter Malone, an Australian Jesuit scholar, believes that films can act as both a "moral and spiritual compass" (Malone 2005: 174). This is not a new line of argument. Over forty years ago a Dominican priest and academic, Anthony Schillaci, wrote a book on *Movies and Morals* (1968), in which his central thesis was "that motion pictures, rather than being an object of fear and suspicion as far as morals are concerned, are in fact a vital source of emotional maturity and sensitivity" (Schillaci 1968: 1). Through a number of examples he made a case for cinema performing the "role of morality play, cultural exorcist and moral sensitizer" (Schillaci 1968: 93). Malone's and Schillaci's work are examples of an increasingly common refrain found within recent discussions of the relation between religion and film (Johnston 2006: 226–8). In this body of work films are seen not only as a site for religious insight and ethical debate, but also as a catalyst for critical moral reflection.

This essay stands within that emerging line of scholarship. My aim is to demonstrate what a valuable resource film can be for those concerned with reflecting critically upon ethics and its implications for human flourishing. I am therefore attempting to provide neither a history of cinematic censorship nor a detailed account of the different debates over whether films can corrupt the morals of viewers, nor even a critical analysis of the moral failings of specific films. Instead, I provide an examination of two interconnected sets of cinematic practices: representing ethics and contesting ethics. A clearer understanding of these practices will further clarify the ways in which film can be a site of ethical debate and the extent to which movies can be a catalyst for moral reflection. In order to explore such questions I analyze how ethics is both represented and narrated, and viewed and contested, by discussing a range of films from various genres and periods.

Representing ethics

In this section I focus on how two contrasting ancient ethical traditions have been represented onscreen. By concentrating upon the depictions of ancient Greek and Hebrew ethics I am not suggesting that these traditions represent the world's dominant or only ethical foundations. Inevitably, my discussions are selective, though I will also consider noticeable absences. There are many other sources that could be discussed in detail, such as Indian epics, Chinese philosophy, or Iranian poetry. Nevertheless, the Greek and Hebrew traditions have interacted with all the world's main religions and provide useful insights for reflecting on how ethics is cinematically represented.

Representing the ancient Greek ethical traditions

Socrates onscreen

Many histories of the Western ethical tradition begin in ancient Greece, highlighting the work of Socrates (ca. 470–399 BCE), Plato (ca. 428/7–348/7 BCE) and Aristotle (ca. 384–322 BCE). The life and death of Socrates, along with the Socratic method of ethical reasoning, partly rooted in questioning, self-knowledge, and the belief that "the unexamined life is not worth living," is rarely explicitly depicted on the screen. There are three notable exceptions. First, Peter Ustinov played Socrates in George Schaefer's televised adaptation of Hillary Anderson's play *Barefoot in Athens* (1966). Socrates trudges the streets of Athens without footwear castigating the ethics of the ruling class, who in turn hatch a plan to bring about his final demise. By contrast in *Bill and Ted's Excellent Adventure* (1989) Socrates (mispronounced as "sow-crates") is depicted to greater comic effect. After an initial meeting in ancient Greece, Socrates is brought to modern-day California. Dressed in Hellenistic attire Socrates looks somewhat out of place in a busy twentieth-century shopping mall, though his garb doesn't prevent him from helping the two teenage protagonists pass their history exam.

This light-hearted imaginative fantasy stands in sharp contrast to Roberto Rossellini's *Socrates* (1971), which is primarily an abbreviated reenactment of the dialogues which Plato wrote in *Euthyphro, Apology, Crito,* and *Phaedo.* Daniel Migliore believes that: "The danger of this abbreviation is that the Socratic method may seem more like scoring points in a debate than assisting someone to achieve moral insight" (Allen *et al.* 1974: 200). Films commonly compress written texts and ethical reasoning. The processes leading up to a character making a choice or changing their mind is commonly hidden from the cinematic gaze. George Thomas is correct when he asserts that in Rossellini's *Socrates*: "The examples of the Socratic dialogue presented are too brief and fragmentary to show the movement of thought from false or superficial opinions at the beginning of a dialogue to a tentative conclusion at the end. And in the film Socrates usually seems to be expounding his own ideas in a brief lecture rather than searching for the truth through a real dialogue with others" (Allen *et al.* 1974: 200). The result of this compression is that the film, originally made for television, turns Socrates into an "excessively talkative, authoritarian, paternalistic, and oppressive" teacher (Allen *et al.* 1974: 203). For the *New York Times* film critic Vincent Canby, "the film is a series of rather proper, spoken tableaus that seldom erupt with spontaneity" (Canby 1971). The most memorable moment in the film is not the attempt at recreating the Socratic method of moral reasoning through questioning and dialogue, but rather the scene of Socrates, played by Jean Sylvère, pacing up and down his cell after he has taken the poison which was used to execute him. Here is a good example of one of the recurring themes of this essay: Film tends to portray dramatic action more effectively than rigorous moral reasoning. It is hard to recreate cinematically a sustained ethical debate. Nevertheless, as this portrayal of a dignified death illustrates, a dramatic scene or narrative can provoke viewers to embark upon their own ethical reflection. The way in which this representation of death elicited comments from both professional and amateur critics illustrates how such scenes can act as a catalyst for wider moral discussion.

Aristotle onscreen

Neither Plato's nor Aristotle's life ended so dramatically as that of Socrates, and their contributions to ethical reasoning are rarely, if ever, depicted explicitly. Aristotle (played by Barry Jones) appears in Robert Rossen's *Alexander the Great* (1956) encouraging Alexander (played by Richard Burton) to practice patience. He is effectively silenced by Alexander's response, that Zeus offered Achilles the choice of a long life and obscurity or a short life and glory. The inference is clear. Alexander is rejecting Aristotle's encouragement to embrace patience, preferring instead to take the more dangerous shortcut to glory. In Oliver Stone's *Alexander* (2004) Aristotle (played by Christopher Plummer) is depicted as a somewhat more forceful character. He is briefly presented teaching the young Alexander and his friends geography, politics, and the need for moderation. "Excess in all things is the undoing of all men ... Practice control of the senses." This exhortation resonates with Aristotle's well-known celebration of the golden mean, which is to be found between extremes. Alexander (played by Colin Farrell) is far from moderate in his approach to life and to conquest. Self-control is one of many virtues celebrated in the *Nichomachean Ethics*, which Aristotle believes are the way toward *eudaemonia* (often translated as "happiness," though "human flourishing" might be more accurate). Dramatic or epic films such as *Alexander* rarely celebrate the much debated "golden mean" or gentler virtues such as patience or self-control; instead they tend toward depicting moral extremes, partly as a way of driving the narrative forward while also maintaining the interest of the audience.

This is not to suggest that whenever ancient Greek philosophers are actually portrayed they are depicted as ineffectual moral agents or ethical teachers. On at least one occasion Aristotle and Plato make a cameo appearance in the same film: *The Story of Mankind* (1957). This Warner Brothers' film, directed by Irwin Allen, is based around a trial set in heaven to determine whether the human race is worth saving or whether the prematurely invented H-bomb should be allowed to be detonated and destroy humankind. The advocate for humanity (the Spirit of Man played by Ronald Colman) takes the prosecutor (the Devil or Mr. Scratch played by Vincent Price) to the Golden Age of Greece to see Socrates, Plato, and Aristotle, fine examples of the good in humanity's history; scholars who helped extend humanity's vision of reality. Along with Hippocrates and numerous other characters from different eras of history, they are each given a few seconds of screen time, effectively as witnesses for the defense. At the end of the film the judges conclude that humankind's good equals their evil, and they therefore postpone their judgment to a future unspecified date.

The absence and uses of ancient Greek ethics

The fact that the actual depictions of ancient Greek ethicists are cinematically sparse does not mean that their ethical insights have been relegated to the dustbin of history. Simply because there is no space for ethical nuance or abstractions, exemplified by the debates between different philosophical traditions or teachers, does not mean that cinematic narratives are devoid of ethical significance. Even films such as *Troy* (2004) or *300* (2006) celebrate specific Homeric virtues such as courage and loyalty. The viewer is offered a vision not merely of spectacular battles but also of comradeship and cunning embedded in the narrative and characterizations, resonating with many of the motifs found in the stories of *The Iliad* or *The Odyssey*. I shall return to consider in greater detail the significance of depicting virtues, but at this stage it is useful to observe how a film like *300* may celebrate friendship and bravery in the midst of the cut and thrust of skilled fighting, but it struggles to interrogate the value of such virtues when they are used to annihilate the Persian enemy. This dominant violent aspect of the narrative led some critics to interpret the film as a veiled encouragement to American audiences to distrust, to despise, and even to prepare to fight the descendents of Xerxes' Persian army in modern-day Iran. Whether this is a fair criticism or not, the moral insights embedded and promoted in narratives are worthy of careful consideration and criticism; and the ancient Greek ethical traditions provide resources for such an enterprise.

Over the past half century many contemporary ethicists have shown a renewed interest in the ethical thought of the ancient Greeks. For example, philosophers such as Alasdair MacIntyre and Christian theologians such as Stanley Hauerwas have drunk deeply at the well of Greek ethics, especially Aristotle's work on the virtues found in texts like the *Nichomachean Ethics*. This has contributed to a critical turn against "quandary ethics," in which scholars analyze difficult individual cases in order to derive ethical principles or foundations. In its place many ethicists now regularly highlight an approach to ethics rooted in the formation of virtuous character. The primary issue is not what the moral subject should do but rather what kind of person she or he should become. This has led scholars from widely divergent traditions to think further about the importance of nurturing virtues as a way toward human and global flourishing. Confucian ethicists tend to underline the importance of cultivating character which is like polishing a rough stone (*Analects* 1.15), thereby developing the virtuous human life. The recrudescence of virtue theory provides a valuable resource for reflecting critically upon the moral worlds presented in films.

The demands of creating a cinematic narrative which will hold viewers' attention ensures that filmmakers tend to prefer portraying a dramatic moment of decision, rather than the less dramatic daily habits which form the individual's or organization's character. Consider how the whistle-blower on the tobacco industry (played by Russell Crowe) in *The Insider* (1999) or the flawed but heroic attorney (played by George Clooney) in *Michael Clayton* (2007) make decisions to confront the corrupt individuals who control powerful organizations. Refusing to be intimidated, they choose to stand up against those who threaten them and the lives of others. Why do they make this courageous decision? Both appear to be partly motivated by personal attacks on their lives as well as by their concern for justice to be done. The daily habits and unseen influences which in real life help form a character, such as one who will risk much to reveal the truth, are often left outside the cinematic frame.

This is not surprising given how virtues are inculcated: gradually, imperceptibly, and through repetition. In the much quoted and often misattributed words, resonating with Aristotle's thought: "we are what we repeatedly do. Excellence, then, is not an act but a habit" (Durant 1991: 76). While physical training is represented in films as diverse as *Chariots of Fire* (1981) and *Kill Bill 1* (2003), the claim that the formation of character invariably happens through habitual repetitions is a valuable insight to be borne in mind when faced by film characters who are presented as making surprising decisions. Reflect on the risks taken by Rick Blaine (played by Humphrey Bogart) at the end of *Casablanca* (1942). They are somewhat surprising, given what is shown of him in the first half of the film: "I stick out my neck for no one." Equally surprising is his final encouragement of the woman (Ilsa Lund played by Ingrid Bergman) whom he loves to flee to safety with her husband (Victor Laszlo played by Paul Henreid), but the surprise heightens the power of the narrative. This is a good example of how filmmakers commonly depict characters making unexpected decisions and thus breaking with their habits of a cinematic lifetime. By overturning audience expectations, filmmakers not only attempt to keep their viewers' attention, but they also show how a virtue such as courage, or loyalty, or love can trump other less attractive character traits. In *Casablanca* Rick's renewed love for Ilsa appears to provide the resources for him to break free of his egocentric resentment, and act unexpectedly and altruistically.

Representing ancient Hebrew ethical traditions

While the ancient Greek ethical traditions have undoubtedly had a profound impact upon the development of both meta-ethics and applied ethics in the West, arguably the ancient Jewish traditions have proved as, if not more, formative. Compared to the limited film representations of the Greek traditions there is a much wider range of cinematic material to draw upon. Given the original dominance of Hollywood and other Western film-producing centers by filmmakers with Jewish or Christian backgrounds, it is not surprising that there is a more extensive repertoire of biblical epics than Greek tales. In this section I consider how the origins of a law-based or deontological approach to ethics have been represented. More specifically, I consider how the story of the Ten Commandments has been depicted. Up to this time there have been eight representations of the life of Moses, from Pathé's silent *Moses* in 1907 to Dreamworks' animated *The Prince of Egypt* in 1998. Two representations particularly stand out.

The Ten Commandments

Cecil B. DeMille (1881–1959) is commonly described as "one of the most successful filmmakers in Hollywood history." He directed over seventy films, between 1914 and 1956. He employed thousands of extras, creating vast cinematic spectacles. During his career DeMille produced two versions of *The Ten Commandments*. The first (1923) is a silent version and effectively divided into two halves. The first part depicts the story of Exodus, while the second portrays a modern morality tale of two brothers. One brother, John, is depicted as following the commandments and lives a humble but ultimately fulfilled life as a carpenter; while the other, Dan, succeeds at first, only for his success to tumble down around him. The church he builds with substandard concrete, to increase his profits, falls down crushing his mother. Dan then shoots his lover after finding out that she has infected him with leprosy. She is shot behind a shower-curtain, in a moment anticipating *Psycho*'s (1960) famous shower scene. He is finally killed himself as he tries to escape to Mexico in his speedboat named *Defiance*. He breaks every one of the Ten Commandments and is shown to be punished for his transgressions through being dashed to death on the rocks at sea.

The parting of the sea is one of the many memorable spectacles in the first half of the 1923 version. Several sequences were filmed in two-color Technicolor. The story of the Exodus is brought to life with the help of over 2,500 people and 3,000 animals, whom DeMille transported 200 miles up the coast into a desert space north of Los Angeles. The departure of the Israelites out of the Luxor-like vast temple, past the rows of sphinxes, and on through the Red Sea made for spectacular silent cinema. "Once Pharaoh's chariots are drowned, the picture cuts directly to its next tableau, upon Mount Sinai. Moses had already been ensconced there, waiting for the great explosion in which the words of the Commandments [are] thrust out of the screen towards the audience" (Louvish 2007: 220). Moses (played by Theodore Roberts) sculpts "the Law on the tablets at the direction of God," which like the 1956 version is "intercut with the apostasy of the Golden calf" (Babington and Evans 1993: 45). The opening titles reflect the moral behind this tale: "Our Modern World defined God as a 'religious complex' and laughed at the Ten Commandments as OLD FASHIONED." It is clear that this is not the view espoused by either of DeMille's cinematic renditions. As these titles make explicit: "The Ten Commandments are not rules to obey as a personal favour to God ... They are not laws – they are the LAW." As with his other biblical epics such as *The King of Kings* (1927) or *The Sign of the Cross* (1932) DeMille ensured that there was also plenty of "worthy sinning" to give the film mass appeal. The film was a box office success, leading to the production of other "ancient" movies through the 1920s.

Over thirty years later in 1956 DeMille returned to the same story, but created something even more spectacular and without the modern morality tale. It was DeMille's first and only widescreen production. Over 14,000 extras and 15,000 animals put this on an even grander scale than its silent predecessor. Costing over $13 million dollars to produce (the most expensive film up to that time) and lasting over three and a half hours, *The Ten Commandments* earned over $65 million in 1956 (equivalent to about $446 million today), making it the most financially successful religious epic ever made, until the release of Mel Gibson's *The Passion of the Christ* (2004). The film has also had a long life since its first release, with regular screenings often around Easter on national television in the USA and beyond. While this film ostensibly reflects the Exodus and the gift of the law to the Jewish people, it was rapidly appropriated by Christian groups in the USA, and like Gibson's *Passion* was put to different didactic and evangelistic uses by Christian groups when rereleased in 1989. This is not entirely surprising given the way in which the Exodus story is Christianized in the film (Wright 2007: 55–78). As Wright also suggests, the overwhelming power of the spectacle in the 1956 technicolor large-screen version was diminished when reduced for its regular broadcasts on the small screen of television.

This film reflects a vision of ethics which is rooted in divine revelation, but made memorable through dramatic special effects. The most famous is the parting of the Red Sea, which helped ensure it won an Oscar (its only one) for Best Visual Effects. In this version, the commandments are etched onto the stone by what looks like a laser beam or an acetylene torch emerging out of God's pillar of fire. In both versions these are not the product of Moses' over-ripe theological imagination, intent on controlling his people, nor are they the laws which have evolved over many generations of communal reflection. Instead they are depicted as laws revealed and given in a highly dramatic fashion by a deity with a deep and authoritative voice (claimed by Charlton Heston in the 2004 DVD version to be his own). The Divine law is given and is therefore to be obeyed. These laws are not immediately embraced. While the waywardness is made explicit through Moses' declamations and the narrator's commentary (DeMille used his own voice), the tablets of the law are hurled by Moses (played by Charlton Heston) at the Golden Calf. There is a flash and explosion, signaling God's displeasure with the orgy which has been carrying on at the foot of Mount Sinai while he has been giving Moses the commandments. Appropriate ethical behavior is enforced through violence, and inappropriate activities are punished with little obvious mercy. While this may be an attempt to revivify an interest in the ethics of Exodus, to underline the contemporary significance of the Ten Commandments, it is also a film produced during a time of revived puritanism and anxiety about communism. There is a sense in which the 1956 *Ten Commandments* provides the viewer with a window onto DeMille's attempt to reaffirm the ethical status quo in the USA. The irony is that the dramatic spectacle and narrative may also be promoting another kind of valuing, especially relevant to the context of Western capitalism: a valuing of how to maintain control over a people intoxicated by the consumption of freedom.

The Decalogue (Dekalog)

The cinematic worlds created in *The Decalogue* by the Polish director Krzysztof Kieślowski (1941–96), and his writing partner Krzysztof Piesiewicz, stand in sharp contrast to DeMille's spectacular *Ten Commandments*. Kieślowski's films portray everyday life in a large housing estate in 1980s Warsaw. These films were originally made for Polish television, though both *A Short Film about Love* and *A Short Film about Killing* were also produced in longer versions and released before the complete sequence in 1988. Kieślowski's English introduction to the script of *Dekalog* (*The Decalogue*, 1989) provides a rich resource for understanding the moral landscape out of which they emerged (Kieślowski in Mitchell and Plate 2007: 219–24).

In his introduction Kieślowski first describes his work as a young documentary filmmaker who discovered that his presence in courts with a camera during the early 1980s acted as a moral restraint upon judges. His feature film *No End* (1985, *Bez Konca*), which reflected his courtroom experiences, was perceived as unsympathetic toward the ruling authorities of the time. It received a critical reception in the Party newspaper (*Trybuna Ludu*), frosty comments by the political leaders, and criticism from the Catholic Church for its nudity. At this time Kieślowski "had the overwhelming impression that more and more I was seeing people who didn't really have a clear idea of why they were living" (Kieślowski in Mitchell and Plate 2007: 221). In the midst of this troubling context he was encouraged by his co-writer, Krzysztof Piesiewicz, to make a film on the Ten Commandments. As the idea evolved they decided to "find extreme, extraordinary situations for our characters, ones in which they would face difficult choices and make decisions which could not be taken lightly" (Kieślowski in Mitchell and Plate 2007: 222). They were clear that they had no wish "to preach" through these films, nor did they intend "to adopt the tone of those who praise or condemn, handing out a reward here for the doing of Good and a punishment there for the doing of Evil." The moral universe that they represent is more ambiguous, with characters not always making the wisest decision, and sometimes transgressing at least one if not more of the Commandments. In *The Decalogue*, unlike the 1956 version of *The Ten Commandments*, the law is not given supernaturally but is more like a faint shadow in the background of each of the individual stories.

Part of the power of these ten films is the representation of memorable moments in ordinary worlds: a child who falls through the ice, a teenager who encounters the women he has been spying upon, or a young man who kills a taxi driver for no apparent reason. The narrative of *A Short Film about Killing* becomes a cinematic site of ethical debate about the justice of execution, even as a punishment for a vicious murder. Kieślowski reasons first that: "Everyone knows that it is wrong to kill another human being yet wars continue and police forces the world over find dead bodies in cellars and parks with knives in their throats." He goes on to argue that: "One cannot put the question whether it is good or evil to kill without being suspected of naivety or stupidity. But it seems to me that one can put the question of why one human being may kill another without reason, especially if one voices doubts over whether the law has the right to punish one form of killing with another" (Kieślowski in Mitchell and Plate 2007: 223). This is exactly the question that Kieślowski brings alive in this short film. While he does not offer an answer to the question he does provide the viewer with a narrative that can at least frame the question. Their original hesitation about structuring their series of films around the Ten Commandments was overcome by the realization that from their perspective "all writers, painters, playwrights and filmmakers indirectly deal with themes which are central to the Commandments" (Kieślowski in Mitchell and Plate 2007: 224). This insight is useful to bear in mind when reflecting on how films may not explicitly represent the foundations of ethical traditions, but nevertheless do depict contrasting actions such as truth-telling and lying or loving and killing. DeMille's and Kieślowski's cinematic approach to this aspect of biblical ethics, as expressed in the Ten Commandments, is significantly different. For DeMille these are commands, literally etched into stone, that are to be obeyed, while for Kieślowski they are starting points for modern cinematic parables which explore through nuanced storytelling some of the ethical dilemmas faced in the late twentieth century.

Contesting ethics

Up to this point I have suggested that it is easier for filmmakers to represent a dramatic narrative in which ethical themes are embedded rather than an abstract theory in which ethics is dissected. I now consider, through a number of other cinematic examples, how film narratives are used to tease out ethical controversies and become a catalyst for ethical reflection.

Contesting virtues

The traditional vices of the Middle Ages, the so-called "seven deadly sins" such as anger, lust, or pride, appear to offer more scope than the "seven heavenly virtues" for filmmakers in search of stories which will sell and attract extensive audiences. Whether this is the case throughout all film genres and why this recurs in so many different world cinemas merit further investigation which is beyond the scope of this essay. What actually is a vice and a virtue is now commonly contested in different contexts, both cinematic and otherwise. Some ethicists claim, however, that there are universal principles, such as respect for human life, truth-telling, and justice, which are to be found across cultures (Christians and Traber 1997). Characters in recent films such as *No Country for Old Men* (2007) and *There Will Be Blood* (2007) intentionally ignore duties toward respect for life, telling the truth, or accepted codes of justice. This is by no means new or limited to Hollywood productions. The impoverished worlds of Brazilian *favelas* in *City of God* (2002), of South African townships in *Tsotsi* (2005), or dilapidated appartments in decaying Soviet Russia in *Cargo 200* (2007) provide the backdrop for cinematic explorations of what happens when life is not respected, deception is commonplace, and justice twisted. Loyalty to friends can take precedence over care for the "other" or the stranger. This behavior can be both scrutinized and even judged not only through the film's narration but also by the lively debates that such films can provoke online and beyond.

Nevertheless, the hidden or less dramatic virtues such as meekness or gentleness, celebrated in ancient texts such as the Sermon on the Mount (Matthew 5–7), are comparative rarities in most cinematic genres. Apparently, they make less attractive cinematic forms, or at least appear harder to portray. As I suggested earlier, the heroic virtues, such as courage or bravery celebrated in many different genres of ancient literature, such as Homeric tales, Icelandic sagas, Arthurian legends, or Hindi epics, tend to make more regular appearances in action, fantasy, and adventure films. Such virtues, "fragmented survivals from an older past" (MacIntyre 1981: 111), are commonly manifested through different kinds of violence. Many cinematic heroes fight "evil" adversaries wielding their weapons courageously: from Luke Skywalker's light saber in *Star Wars* to James Bond's Walther PPK to Aragorn's sword in *The Lord of the Rings* trilogy. Interpreters following in the footsteps of Nietzsche may perceive the gentler virtues as problematic or weak and their opposites as necessary for survival. "The will to power" (Nietzsche 1968: 127), as the struggle to survive, is commonly depicted in films and leaves little room for celebrating meekness. It is far more dramatic and probably cinematically simpler to depict Legolas loosing off his bow to kill yet another nameless Orc than to try to show a character attempting to nonviolently wage peace.

There are, of course, exceptions to this generalization. For example, consider how different actors have attempted to portray the central figure for Christian ethics, Jesus of Nazareth. While Mel Gibson's *The Passion of the Christ* (2004) minimized the ethical teaching of Jesus, many Jesus movies do attempt to depict aspects of Jesus' teaching, such as the Sermon on the Mount. In *King of Kings* director Nicholas Ray turned the Beatitudes into an open-air spectacle using a crowd of over 7,000 extras listening to Jesus' sermon. Nonetheless, these representations are generally far less memorable than the moments where Jesus heals, casts out evil spirits, raises the dead, breaks bread, shares wine, or boldly faces the violent aggression of the Roman empire. As with the depiction of Greek philosophers, we find that many filmmakers find it easier to portray dramatic action than complex moral ideas. This is shown in one of the most memorable scenes in Pier Paolo Pasolini's *The Gospel According to St. Matthew* (1964), when Jesus, played as an angry and revolutionary figure by Enrique Irazoquil, overturns the tables in the Temple.

Another character modeled on Jesus who exhibits his ethics in action is the hero of Denys Arcand's *Jesus of Montreal* (1989). Through a passion play staged in modern Montreal, Jesus (played by Lothaire Bluteau) is portrayed as a revolutionary figure who confronts the religious authorities of his time. In "modern-day life" the actor Daniel Coulombe, who plays Jesus, overturns tables at a sexually exploitative audition for a beer commercial. Later he is shown the city from a skyscraper by an advertising executive, who offers him the chance to become a powerful celebrity. He rejects the temptation. The life of Coulombe mirrors and eventually converges with the traditional narrative of Jesus. The story of Jesus is therefore enacted in at least two different settings, raising questions not only about the relation between the historical Jesus and the Christ of faith, but also about the contemporary ethical significance of Jesus' teaching, life, and violent death. His "postmodern" resurrection, with his organs being donated to give sight and life to others, raises both theological and ethical questions about his sacrifice and its value. In a different way the controversial representation in *The Passion of the Christ* of Jesus passively absorbing the extreme aggression meted out upon him raises questions not only about the ethical wisdom of nonviolent resistance, but also about the ethical value of depicting such unremittingly explicit violence. Many viewers objected to the extreme and prolonged violence of the film, but Gibson defended it as a representation of the extreme suffering of Jesus that he believes is essential to human salvation.

Contesting violence

I have argued elsewhere that it is more common for filmmakers to portray scenes of violence or revenge than scenes of peacemaking or forgiveness. This is partly because films tend to be more popularly appealing when the narrative is driven by dramatic violent moments, rather than slower, hidden processes of peacemaking (Mitchell 2007b: 13–19). Even films which appear to celebrate peaceful action regularly draw upon violent acts to highlight the value of peacemaking. Nonviolent leaders such as Gandhi and Romero have been the subject of cinematic biopics (*Gandhi* [1982] and *Romero* [1989]), which have not eschewed showing their central protagonists beaten, threatened, and finally killed. While not on the same level of explicit violence as Gibson's *Passion* the hero is depicted as contesting violence through passive resistance.

Film violence has provoked long and detailed controversy about the effects, the interpretation, and the censorship of such violence (Mitchell 2007a: 159–95). Filmmakers themselves also regularly reflect on the phenomenon. For instance, Kirby Dick's documentary *This Film is not yet Rated* (2006) interrogates the rating system in the USA, suggesting that it is biased toward large studio productions and is more lenient toward gratuitous violence than revealing sex. One of the contributors to this documentary argues that a film which shows the reality of violence (such as a war film like *Saving Private Ryan* [1998]) deserves a less restrictive rating than a film which glamorizes or trivializes the killing of others (such as a Bond film like *Die Another Day* [2002]). The debates about censorship and the consequences of depicting graphic violence invariably became heightened following well-publicized killings in real life such as at Dunblane in Scotland (1996), Columbine (1999) or Virginia Tech (2007) in the USA. While these debates look set to continue and to recur, there are an increasing number of attempts to go beyond the controversies surrounding the effects of viewing violent films (Mitchell 2007a: 159–229). In this context several films have recurred regularly in texts discussing film, religion, ethics, and violence, including: *Unforgiven* (1992), *The Shawshank Redemption* (1994), and *Dead Man Walking* (1995). These films are put to use in different ways, but are commonly used to reflect upon forgiveness, justice, or breaking the cycle of violence. Depictions of violence have provoked energetic interpretative discussions.

The Godfather trilogy has also received extensive attention within the emerging field of film and religion (e.g., May 1992; Lyden 2003; Mitchell 2005). There are at least three lines of interpretation. First, the baptism sequence in *The Godfather* (1972) is used to illustrate how films can depict the close relation between religion and violence rather than the way in which religious traditions can promote an end of violence (Stone 1999: 43). This line of interpretation has been both critiqued and developed. There are those scholars who see such cinematic portrayals as an actual challenge to theologians and ethicists who overlook how inextricably connected violence is with Christianity (Deacy and Ortiz 2008: 138–42) as well as with other religious traditions. Second, some writers argue that the intercutting between Michael's nephew's baptism and the premeditated killings of the other mafia bosses highlights the hypocrisy of Corleone's religious declarations in church. The result is that through this juxtaposition of the liturgical landscape with the world of the mafia murders, the ethics of Corleone are contrasted with the ethics of the Christian tradition (Anker 2004: 60–2). Through depicting violence in a critical way, films such as *The Godfather* can therefore promote peace. Third, other writers suggest that while the "cross-cutting" encourages the viewer to ask whether they "can go all the way with Michael in his protection of the family," the overall story lacks an "obvious 'moral' ... and to moralize its point is to simplify a complex text to which audiences will return precisely because it is both evocative and provocative of a range of values and concerns" (Lyden 2003: 161–3). The vigor and range of such interpretations illustrate how film, whatever the filmmaker's original intention, can be used as a site and catalyst for interrogating the ends of violence (see also the films *The End of Violence* [1997] and *A History of Violence* [2005]).

In this context it is worth considering other ways that film can depict contrasting approaches to violence. For example, in *Mongol* (2007) an incarcerated young Genghis Khan tells an old monk to murder one of his guards so he can escape. The monk, dressed in what looks like a Buddhist garb, refuses on the grounds that his religion does not permit killing. Temüjin (who later is known as Genghis Khan, leader of all the Mongols) retorts that his religion does. Again and again he kills to gain freedom, to liberate his wife, and to assert his "unifying" law (the *Jasagh*) over his people. The nonviolent ethical tradition of the monk does not, however, prevent him from going on an arduous quest, where he tries to take news of Temüjin's captivity to his family. This long, and ultimately fatal, walk may result in his monastery escaping the destructive ravages of the Mongols, but Temüjin's violence is given far more screen-time. His swordsmanship speaks more loudly than the faltering steps of an elderly monk. As with many other films the imperative for violent revenge is depicted with far greater cinematic skill than the complex criteria for waging a "just war" or the thoughtful and peaceable reflection often associated with pacifism.

Contesting injustice: vice unpunished and virtue unrewarded

Ethical debates are never far from the center of the comedic and dramatic work of Woody Allen (1935–). For over three decades Allen has cinematically explored the themes of love, sex, and death, and how they can sometimes interact with religious beliefs. He plays on his own Jewish heritage at several points (e.g., *Annie Hall* [1977]), shows signs of a search for faith at other points (e.g., *Hannah and Her Sisters* [1986]), and deals with deep, dark ethical quandaries in other films (e.g., *Crimes and Misdemeanors* [1989] and *Match Point* [2005]).

Crimes and Misdemeanors is a good example of one of his movies which has provoked extensive ethical debate. In this film a well-respected ophthalmologist, Judah, has his troublesome former lover Dolores murdered, but then gets away with the crime. Initially his conscience is troubled. He appears to feel guilt and is isolated during a lively family debate during an imaginary Passover seder, where his father Sol claims that if someone kills he will be punished. "Without compromising his critical detachment, Allen in *Crimes and Misdemeanors* seriously uses Jewish institutions and rituals as a means for discussing and debating the film's moral and philosophical concerns" (Girgus 2002: 130). As the film progresses, Judah's unease dissipates. He rejects the voices in his imagination (and beyond) which imply that there is an omniscient God and moral order in the universe. Unlike Raskolnikov in Dostoyevsky's *Crime and Punishment* (1866), Judah does not confess and face the reality of what he has done and so appears to escape the demands of justice. As Allen claims in an interview with the Swedish filmmaker and writer Stig Björkman (1938–): "We live in a world where there is nobody to punish you, if you don't punish yourself" (Mitchell and Plate 2007: 241).

In other words, the eyes of God, a recurring metaphor in the film, are not watching over an individual's moral life. Both Allen's and Judah's moral world are some distance from both Western and Eastern religious traditions which emphasize judgment on the basis of actions or belief. There is neither fear of an eschatological Last Judgment nor an expectation of reincarnation on the basis of ethical behavior. The life after death imagined in a film such as *What Dreams May Come* (1998), and redolent of Dante's *Divine Comedy* (ca. 1308–21), is debated elsewhere in Allen's *oeuvre* but certainly absent from Judah's final worldview in *Crimes and Misdemeanors*.

In such a world it is possible to live a life of epicurean hedonism driven by the desire for pleasure free of worry that there will be any judgment beyond this world. In other words, in a statement commonly misattributed to the Russian writer Dostoyevsky, a novelist that Allen greatly admires: "if there is no God, everything is permitted." In the denouement of *Crimes and Misdemeanors* this statement is enacted by showing Judah as a man who now looks set to enjoy a life free of guilt and apparently free of the consequences of being responsible for murder. Unlike Dan in the 1923 version of *The Ten Commandments* who comes to a sticky end on the rocks, Judah survives unharmed. Even though the story is full of moral ambiguity and some ethical debate, the ending underlines Allen's belief that "at best the universe is indifferent" (Mitchell and Plate 2007: 243). Judah may be worried about the consequences of his action insofar as he is concerned that he may be caught, but once it is clear that he has "got away with it," then he relaxes back into his old life where he is admired as a respected eye doctor and a pillar of the community. Behind this façade he appears to be free of the pangs of conscience. His duty is to himself and perhaps to his family, insofar as it is merely an extension of his own identity.

Religious existentialists may read the film differently. Although Judah does not appear to suffer, he has lost his authentic humanity in his decision to forego repentance and responsibility for his actions. In this way, he punishes himself, even if unknowingly, just as Socrates, according to Plato, held that those who neglect virtue first and foremost harm themselves: "If you kill such a one as I am, you will injure yourselves more than you will injure me" (*Apology* para. 57). Allen's work prompts much reflection and multiple ways of assessing the consequences of our moral actions.

Contesting duties and consequences

For some ethicists duty remains a highly significant category. It is commonly connected with the thought of Immanuel Kant (1724–1804) who underlined the importance of doing one's duty out of respect for the moral law, not on the basis of what the consequences might be. Duty is a theme which is common in film narratives, particularly war films. Consider, for example, Clint Eastwood's two films depicting the Second World War battle for the Pacific island of Iwo Jima (1945). The first, *Flags of Our Fathers* (2006), provides an American perspective on the battle and more specifically on the way the famous photograph of soldiers raising the flag was put to use in helping raise funds to finance the war effort. The duty of the three men to promote this cause on a fund-raising tour, even though they weren't the soldiers who raised the first flag, is a recurring motif throughout the film. The second film, *Letters from Iwo Jima* (2006), offers viewers an insight of the battle from the Japanese perspective. Toward the end of the film the Japanese capture and tend for a young, wounded American soldier. The Japanese officer, a former member of the equestrian team at the Los Angeles Olympics, chats with him and even reads words from the wounded soldier's mother's letter: "Do what is right because it is right." This imperative resonates both with him and his troops who see that here is not a demonic enemy but just another man, trying to do his duty, and far more similar to them than they had been led to believe. This scene, like many others in both films, through cinematic narrative reflects upon the nature of duty. On first viewing, these films appear to suggest that opposing armies may fight and kill each other even while they independently pursue their duty to their respective countries, and so they do no wrong. This invites questions about whether anyone can ever question "duty to country," or whether one may have a duty in some cases to consider a war unjust even if it is endorsed by one's native land and government. Pacifists and conscientious objectors would clearly have a different view of their duty in such situations than the one projected in these films by Eastwood.

Kant's approach to ethics is commonly characterized as "deontological," based upon duty and moral law. There is not space here to reflect in detail upon his widely quoted categorical imperative: "Act only according to that maxim whereby you can at the same time will that it should become a universal law" (Kant 1993: 30). This principle of universalizability is rarely, if ever, precisely stated or discussed in film, though it does provide a principle for reflecting on a film character's ethical consistency. For example, Michael Corleone in The Godfather expresses his unshakeable belief in the importance of loyalty to the family. This is his duty. It is not a hypothetical but a categorical imperative that must be followed; and yet he himself goes against this code when he deceives his wife, and orders the murder of his brother-in-law (The Godfather, 1972) and brother (The Godfather: Part II, 1974). Michael's "care" for his family resonates less with Kantian imperatives and more with a Confucian approach to ethics which emphasizes the importance of relational bonds and fidelity to those within your own family and friendship circle, even though this moral framework self-destructs as he will ultimately destroy his own family.

In contrast to a "deontological approach," films commonly embrace a more "teleological" approach to ethics which is rooted in concern about the consequences or ends of actions. Many documentaries employ this line of ethical reasoning (e.g., An Inconvenient Truth, 2006). Utilitarians such as Jeremy Bentham (1748–1832) and John Stuart Mill (1806–73) promoted an approach which sought to maximize happiness and minimize pain in the world. They both made "Utility, or the Greatest Happiness Principle ... that actions are right in proportion as they tend to promote happiness, wrong as they tend to produce the reverse of happiness" (Mill 1998: 55) the heart of their moral philosophy. Utilitarians therefore bring together a concern for maximizing pleasure and happiness while also reflecting upon the consequences of a particular course of action (Graham 2004: 128–61). This is a theme that can be traced in many films.

For example, Peter Weir's The Truman Show tells the story of Truman Burbank (played by Jim Carrey), who unbeknown to himself has been part of a reality television show since his birth. His life story, depicted daily on television, has given great pleasure to a huge global audience who watch his every move. Christof, the show's director, actively intervenes in an attempt to prevent Truman from escaping from the all-too-perfect world of Seahaven. For Christof, the ends justify the means. The happiness of his audience appears to be of greater value than the flourishing and freedom of Truman. Christof therefore ignores the consequences for the unknowing star of his reality TV show of controlling his life so closely. He appears to be more preoccupied with the consequences for his audience and for himself. This moral myopia is clear to discern in this modern morality tale, which satirizes different kinds of voyeurism. Utilitarianism's apparent preoccupation with promoting pleasure and happiness for the majority is an unquestioned given within many film narratives and rarely open to criticism. One can also question how genuine Christof is in his utilitarian argument, as it may be a cover for his own egoistic desire to safeguard his personal fame and fortune. After all, the viewers of the show root for Truman to escape, and when the show ends, they simply change the channel. This also suggests the impossibility of accurately predicting what will bring the greatest happiness to the greatest number, a perennial problem for utilitarians.

Conclusion

In this essay I have argued that film can be a site, a source, and a catalyst for ethical reflection and debate. In the first section, I proposed that ethical insights are more commonly represented through dramatic narratives and scenes than through depictions of abstract reasoning. In the second section, I analyzed four different spheres of contest which cluster around: virtues, violence, injustice, and duty and consequences. I have suggested that films can both provoke and illuminate ethical reflection around each of these themes. Films can be rich resources for reflecting on different aspects of the ethical life.

I have primarily, though not exclusively, confined my investigation to examples relating to the Western ethical tradition. Beyond the scope of this discussion is the significant topic of how bringing films into conversation with other film narratives might contribute to an inter-religious ethical dialogue (see Lyden 2003: 108–36). Compare, for example, the implied ethics found in the narratives of *Little Buddha* (1993), *Muhammad: The Last Prophet* (2002), and a Jesus biopic. It would be possible to highlight the discontinuities and dissimilarities, concluding that the enacted ethics are in diametrical opposition. A useful topic for future research, however, would be to identify and then go beyond points of contest to investigate ethical continuities in the films themselves. And on that basis one could go on to consider interpretative resources to be found both within the different cinematic narratives and religious traditions, and in the audience receptions that the films provoke.

Up to this point the role of the audience has remained in the background. As the novelist and philosopher Iris Murdoch suggested: "There is an important difference between learning about virtue and practising it, and the former can indeed be a delusive substitute which effectively prevents the latter. Even great art can be a potent source of illusion" (Murdoch 1993: 9). Films can indeed be a "potent source of illusion"; sometimes a wonderful escape, but sometimes an excuse to ignore the demands of the suffering other and a divided world. How can viewers develop a more "hospitable vision"? In other words how can audiences develop a way of looking at a film which "opens up space for otherness" (Miles and Plate 2004), and which sees clearly the difference between the world of fantasy and the world of reality? Many viewers are already skilled at this craft, but the habit of viewing wisely, both openly and critically, is rooted not in a constrained Platonic cave, but in communities of interpretation which will provoke audiences to look beyond the flickering and mesmerizing shadows to a fragile blue planet.

Bibliography

Allen, D., Thomas, G. F. , Hendry, G. S., Mulder, M. M., and Migliore, D. L. (1974) "Rossellini's *Socrates* – A Colloquy," *Theology Today* 31 (3) (October): 199–204.

Anker, R. (2004) *Catching the Light: Looking for God in the Movies*, Grand Rapids, MI: Eerdmans.

Babington, B. and Evans, P. W. (1993) *Biblical Epics: Sacred Narrative in the Hollywood Cinema*, Manchester: Manchester University Press.

Burnett, R. G. and Martell, E. D. (1932) *The Devil's Camera*, London: Epworth Press.

Canby, V. (1971) "*Socrates* Mirrors the Platonic Touch of Rossellini," *New York Times* (26 November). Online. Available HTTP: <http://www.nytimes.com/> (accessed 8 Dec 2008).

Christians, C. and Traber, M. (eds) (1997) *Communication Ethics and Universal Values*, Thousand Oaks, CA: Sage.

Deacy, C. and Ortiz, G. W., (2008) *Theology and Film: Challenging the Sacred/Secular Divide*, Oxford: Blackwell.

Durant, W. (1991) *The Story of Philosophy*, New York: Simon and Schuster.

Girgus, S. B. (2002) *The Films of Woody Allen*, 2nd ed., Cambridge: Cambridge University Press.

Graham, G. (2004) *Eight Theories of Ethics*, London and New York: Routledge.

Johnston, R. (2006) *Reel Spirituality: Theology and Film in Dialogue*, Grand Rapids, MI: Baker Academic.

Kant, I. (1993 [1785]) *Grounding for the Metaphysics of Morals*, 3rd ed., trans. by J. W. Ellington, Indianapolis: Hackett Publishers.

Louvish, S. (2007) *Cecil B. DeMille and the Golden Calf*, London: Faber and Faber.

Lyden, J. (2003) *Film as Religion: Myths, Morals, and Rituals*, New York and London: New York University Press.

MacIntyre, A. (1981) *After Virtue*, London: Gerald Duckworth.

—— (1998) *A Short History of Ethics*, 2nd ed., London and New York: Routledge.

Malone, P. (2005) *Can Movies Be a Moral Compass?* London: St. Pauls and WACC.

May, J. (ed.) (1992) *Image and Likeness: Religious Visions in American Film Classics*, New York and Mahwah, NJ: Paulist Press.

Miles, M. R. and Plate, S. (2004) "Hospitable Vision: Some Notes on the Ethics of Seeing Film," *Cross Currents* 54 (1) (Spring). Online. Available HTTP: <http://www.crosscurrents.org/MilesPlateSpring2004.htm> (accessed 8 Dec 2008).

Mill, J. S. (1998 [1871]) *Utilitarianism*, ed. R. Crisp, New York: Oxford University Press.

Mitchell, J. (2005) "Theology and Film", in D. F. Ford (ed.) *The Modern Theologians*, 3rd ed., Oxford: Blackwell: 736–59.

—— (2007a) *Media Violence and Christian Ethics*, Cambridge: Cambridge University Press.

—— (2007b) "Peacemaking in the World of Film", *Media Development* 4: 13–16.

Mitchell, J. and Plate, S. B. (2007) *The Religion and Film Reader*, London and New York: Routledge.

Murdoch, I. (1993) *Metaphysics as a Guide to Morals*, London: Penguin.

Nietzsche, F. (1968 [1895]) *Twighlight of the Idols* and *The Anti-Christ*, trans. R. J. Hollingdale, London: Penguin Classics.

Plato (1909–14) *The Apology, Phædo and Crito. The Harvard Classics*, vol. 2 Part 1, New York: P. F. Collier.

Rice, J. (1938) *What is Wrong with the Movies?* Murfreesboro, TN: Sword of the Lord Publishers.

Schillaci, A. (1968) *Movies and Morals*, Notre Dame, IN: Fides Publishers.

Stone, B. (1999) "Religion and Violence in Popular Film," *Journal of Religion and Film* 3 (1). Online. Available HTTP: <http://www.unomaha.edu/jrf/Violence.htm> (accessed 8 Dec 2008).

Thomas, S. and Mitchell, J. (2005) "Understanding Television and Christianity in Marthoma Homes, South India," *Studies in World Christianity* 11 (1): 29–48.

Waley, A. (trans.) (1938) *The Analects of Confucius*, London: George Allen & Unwin; reissue New York: Vintage (1989).

Wright, M. (2007) *Religion and Film: An Introduction*, London: I. B. Tauris.

Filmography

Alexander (2004, dir. O. Stone)

Alexander the Great (1956, dir. R. Rossen)

Annie Hall (1977, dir. W. Allen)

Bill and Ted's Excellent Adventure (1989, dir. S. Herek)

Cargo 200 (*Gruz 200*) (2007, dir. A. Balabanov)

Casablanca (1942, dir. M. Curtiz)

Chariots of Fire (1981, dir. H. Hudson)

City of God (*Cidade de Deus*) (2002, dir. F. Meirelles and K. Lund)

Crimes and Misdemeanors (1989, dir. W. Allen)

Dead Man Walking (1995, dir. T. Robbins)

The Decalogue (*Dekalog*) (1989, dir. K. Kieślowski)

Die Another Day (2002, dir. L. Tamahori)

The End of Violence (1997, dir. W. Wenders)

Flags of our Fathers (2006, dir. C. Eastwood)

Gandhi (1982, dir. R. Attenborough)

The Godfather (1972, dir. F. Coppola)

The Godfather: Part II (1974, dir. F. Coppola)

The Gospel According to St. Matthew (*Il Vangelo secondo Matteo*) (1964, dir. P. Pasolini)

Hallmark Hall of Fame: Barefoot in Athens (1966, dir. G. Schaefer)

Hannah and Her Sisters (1986, dir. W. Allen)

A History of Violence (2005, dir. D. Cronenberg)

An Inconvenient Truth (2006, dir. D. Buggenheim)

The Insider (1999, dir. M. Mann)

Jesus of Montreal (*Jésus de Montréal*) (1989, dir. D. Arcand)

Kill Bill 1 (2003, dir. Q. Tarantino)

The King of Kings (1927, dir. C. DeMille)

King of Kings (1961, dir. N. Ray)

Letters from Iwo Jima (2006, dir. C. Eastwood)

Little Buddha (1993, dir. B. Bertolucci)

The Lord of the Rings: The Fellowship of the Ring (2001, dir. P. Jackson)

The Lord of the Rings: The Return of the King (2003, dir. P. Jackson)

The Lord of the Rings: The Two Towers (2002, dir. P. Jackson)

Match Point (2005, dir. W. Allen)

Michael Clayton (2007, dir. T. Gilroy)

Mongol (2007, dir. S. Bodrov)

Muhammad: The Last Prophet (2002, dir. R. Rich)

No Country for Old Men (2007, dir. E. and J. Coen)

Moses (1907, dir. Pathé)

No End (*Bez Konca*) (1985, dir. K. Kieślowski)

The Passion of the Christ (2004, dir. M. Gibson)

The Prince of Egypt (1998, dir. B. Chapman, S. Hickner, and S. Wells)
Psycho (1960, dir. A. Hitchcock)
Romero (1989, dir. J. Duigan)
Saving Private Ryan (1998, dir. S. Spielberg)
The Shawshank Redemption (1994, dir. F. Darabont)
A Short Film about Killing (*Krótki film o zabijaniu*) (1988, dir. K. Kieślowski)
A Short Film about Love (*Krótki film o milosci*) (1988, dir. K. Kieślowski)
The Sign of the Cross (1932, dir. C. DeMille)
Socrates (aka *Socrate*) (1971, dir. R. Rossellini)
Star Wars Episode IV: A New Hope (1977, dir. G. Lucas)
The Story of Mankind (1957, dir. I. Allen)
The Ten Commandments (1923, dir. C. DeMille)
The Ten Commandments (1956, dir. C. DeMille)
There Will Be Blood (2007, dir. P. Anderson)
This Film is not yet Rated (2006, dir. K. Dick)
300 (2006, dir. Z. Snyder)
Troy (2004, dir. W. Petersen)
The Truman Show (1998, dir. P. Weir)
Tsotsi (2005, dir. G. Hood)
Unforgiven (1992, dir. C. Eastwood)
What Dreams May Come (1998, dir. V. Ward)

INDEX

Akkad, M. 137–8
Althusser, L. 280, 302–3
antisemitism 35, 81, 94–5, 97, 100, 110, 113, 427
apocalyptic films 119–20, 208, 322, 347, 368–383, 430
American Beauty 125, 317–8, 320, 343
Anker, R. 8, 318, 324, 331–50, 434–5, 493
Apocalypto 115, 465, 477
Aristotle 485
Armageddon 369, 371
atonement theories 352–3
audience response models 258–62; education 258; reinforcement 258–60; mediation 260–1; power relation 261–2

Babette's Feast 122, 312, 320–1, 392, 394, 478
Barker, M. 263–9
Baudry, J. 299–300
Baugh, L. 312, 335, 421, 428, 430–1, 433
Becket 56, 114, 320, 335
Bell, Book, and Candle 225–6
Believers, The 227–9, 414
Ben Hur (all versions) 19, 25, 28, 110–11, 148, 421, 428, 449, 458–60
Bergman, I. 56, 110, 122, 125, 259, 312, 333, 478
Bird, M. 333, 336
Birth of a Nation, The 110, 466–71 *see also* Griffith, D.
Bordwell, D. 331, 333
brainwashing 216–18
Breen, J. 32, 35–6, 38, 43, 45–6, 48
Bresson, R. 109, 113, 123–4, 322, 333, 337–41, 348

Caravaggio, M. 456–8
Carrasco, D. 474–5
Casablanca 473, 487
castration anxiety 292–8
censorship 2–3, 27, 32–51, 60, 68, 72–5, 77–8, 86, 138, 143, 283–4, 422, 483, 493
Chahine, Y. 137
Chaplin, C. 22–3
Chopra, Y. 157–8
Chronicles of Narnia, The 56, 312, 321, 341, 348, 433
circuit of culture 281–7
Color of the Cross 113, 424–6
Contact 372–3
Cowan, D. 8–9, 119, 220, 222, 224–5, 403–19
Craft, The 223–5, 414
Crime of Father Amaro, The 116, 191
Crimes and Misdemeanors 332, 345, 494–5

Cunningham, D. 317–8
Curse of the Voodoo 229–30

DaVinci Code, The 56, 460–1
Deacy, C. 8, 255, 263, 268, 276, 285, 287, 304, 316, 323, 351–67, 369, 433, 493
Dead Man Walking 336, 338, 348, 393–4, 432, 477, 493
Dekalog (Decalogue) 123–4, 346–7, 489–90 *see also* Kieślowski, K.
de-programming *see* brainwashing
DeMille, C. 21–2, 110–111, 120, 387–91, 421–2, 424–5, 428, 450–6, 487–9
see also Ten Commandments, The
Desai, M. 155–6
Detweiler, C. 4, 109–30, 321–2, 323–4
Doane, M. 239
Dogma 80–1
Doré, G. 453–6
dream tales 171–5
Dreyer, C. 58, 109, 113, 122, 322, 333, 391, 478

Eastwood, C. 117, 495–6
ekphrasis 458–61
Exorcist, The 119, 403–5, 410, 412, 414
Exum, C. 242

fable 341–2
Farley, E. 314
film noir 362–5
Fog, The 410
Ford, D. 315
From the Manger to the Cross 15, 110, 386–7, 421, 424, 467
Freud, S. 7, 239, 248, 277, 292–9, 301, 306, 409

Geertz, C. 285
Godfather, The (and sequels) 118, 331, 432, 493–4, 496
Godspell 112, 403, 422
Golden Compass, The 66–7
Gospel according to St Matthew, The (film) 52, 56, 111, 113, 335, 422, 492 *see also* Pasolini, P.
Gospel of John, The (film) 423–5
Graham, B. 42, 82
Gramsci, A. 214–16
Grand Canyon 316–8, 347
Greatest Story Ever Told 111, 335, 420, 422, 425, 427, 429
Greeley, A. 321

Griffith, D. 15–16, 94–5, 109–10, 241, 421, 453, 466–71; *see also Birth of a Nation, The*
Groundhog Day 168, 316
Grünewald, M. 458–60
Guadalupe 188–93

Hail Mary 112, 337
Haines Lyon, C. 257, 268–9
Halloween 475
Hart, W. 19
Hasidic Judaism 100–1
Haskell, M. 238, 243, 250
Hays, W. 3, 20, 27–8, 33–5, 43
Hays code 72–3, 78, 83, 422 *see also* Censorship; Breen, J.
Hellraiser: Bloodline 409–10
Hester Street 91–3
Hitchcock, A. 121, 239, 242, 301, 357
Holy Smoke 216–18
Hoover, S. 133, 256–7, 263, 269, 285
horror films 8, 68, 109, 119, 121, 149–50, 152, 205, 250, 269, 283–4, 301, 373, 376, 403–19
Hostel 476

Ice Storm, The 175
Israeli cinema 101–3
It's a Wonderful Life 120, 466

Jai Santoshi Maa 150–1
James, W. 406
Japanese Religion 195–8 *see also* Shinto
Jazz Singer, The 28–9, 94–5, 99
Jesus (1979) 83–5
Jesus Christ Superstar 112, 422
Jesus of Montreal 112, 421, 423, 427, 430, 478, 492
Jesus of Nazareth (1977) 97, 335, 422, 425, 429
Jewett, R. 8, 260, 317, 358–9, 364, 384–402, 432
Johnston, R. 7, 276, 310–328, 353, 483
Jump, H. 17, 310, 384

Kant, I. 495–6
Kaplan, E. 238, 248
Kapoor, R. 155
Khan, M. 153–4
Kiduk, K. 171–2
Kieślowski, K. 123–4, 344, 346–7, 489–90 *see also* Dekalog
King Kong (1933) 472–3
King of Kings (1927) 21, 25, 58, 95, 111, 388, 421–2, 424, 426, 428, 450–1, 488
King of Kings (1961) 111, 335, 422, 424–5, 427, 492
Kozlovic, A. 430
Kracauer, S. 348

Lacan, J. 295–8
Last Temptation of Christ 58, 65, 78–9, 86, 111–2, 322, 423, 426, 429, 456, 477
Lawrence, J. 8, 260, 384–402, 432
Laws of Eternity, The (Eien no hō) 207
Left Behind: The Movie 3, 83, 119–20, 284, 375, 377–9
Legion of Decency 32, 35–8, 42–9, 53–4, 57, 59, 64, 73; Protestant reaction to 38–40
Life of Brian 64–5, 112, 423, 426, 429, 449, 478
Lindsay, V. 17–8, 310
Lindvall, T. 2–3, 13–31, 37, 41, 121, 323, 449
Live Show 67
Lord of the Rings 120, 263–6, 341, 397–9, 491
Loughlin, G. 310, 316, 322–3
Lyden, J. 1–10, 85–6, 214, 275, 285, 304–5, 323–4, 356, 360, 362–3, 467, 476, 493–4, 497
Lynch, G. 6–7, 263, 275–91, 311, 323, 358, 365

Madeinusa 185–8
Magnolia 347
Mahayana Buddhism *see* Zen Buddhism
Malick, T. 110, 115, 333, 342–4
Malone, P. 3, 52–71, 117, 312, 319, 430, 483
Man For All Seasons, A 312, 335, 348, 391
Marsh, C. 6, 255–74, 276, 285–6, 304–5, 313, 316, 354–6, 360, 362, 365, 430, 435
Matrix, The 125, 168, 322, 341–2, 372–3, 375, 397, 432, 434
May, J. 57–9, 313, 317, 321
meditative narratives 342–4
Medved, M. 57–8, 311, 406, 408, 423
Mellencamp, P. 246–7, 251
Metz, C. 240, 280, 299–301
Mexican cinema 188–93
Miles, M. 29, 286, 311, 434
Miracle, The 43–5, 111
Miracle Maker, The 422–5
Miranda Prorsus 46–7
Mission, The 115, 312, 336, 338, 348
Mitchell, J. 9, 284, 315, 318, 323, 482–500
Mizoguchi, K. 173
Modleski, T. 239, 241, 251
Morgan, D. 288
mosaic narratives 344–7
Muhammed 131
Mulvey, L. 238–40, 244, 249, 278, 300–2
Mummy, The 407, 410–12
Murrow, E. 133

National Council of Churches 73, 77
Neon Genesis Evangelion 208
neo-paganism 219–22
Norbu, K. 168–9, 172–3

OCIC/SIGNIS 56, 59–64
Omen, The 119, 230, 403–5, 409, 412–14
Ortiz, G. 6, 237–54, 276, 284, 313, 316, 323, 354, 356, 359, 493
Ostwalt, C. 8, 275, 314–5, 368–383
Otto, R. 415

Pan's Labyrinth 120
parabolic narratives 340–1
Pasolini, P. 52, 56, 110–13, 335, 421–2, 424–9, 478, 492
Passion of Joan of Arc, The 58, 113, 122, 391–2
Passion of the Christ, The 7, 56, 64, 81, 95, 97, 110, 113, 158, 282, 284, 305–6, 312, 335, 348, 354, 384, 399, 420, 423–4, 426, 429, 453, 456–8, 477, 488, 492–3
Passion Play at Oberammergau, The 14–5, 110, 421
Pawnbroker, The 47, 54, 74, 98
Peruvian cinema 185–8
Phalke, D. 144, 146–7
Philippine Cinema 181–5
Pickford, M. 16, 19, 23–4
Plate, B. 113, 195, 284, 312, 318, 323, 483, 498
postfeminism 245–7
Practical Magic 226
Priest 65–6, 116
Production Code Administration 32, 35–6, 42–8
Projansky, S. 246, 250
Pulp Fiction 118, 312, 320, 345, 357, 365

Ramji, R. 135–6
Rapture, The 119, 375, 377–8
Ray, S. 153
realism, minimalist 338–40
realism, mundane 336–8
Rebel Without a Cause 474–5
Reinhartz, A. 9, 97, 109, 312, 335, 359, 420–39
Robe, The 111, 394–5, 449
Romero 114, 388, 478, 493
Rosemary's Baby 119, 230, 232, 403, 405, 412

sacrifice 9, 19, 95, 97, 117, 120–2, 147, 150, 154, 186, 190–1, 220–2, 227–31, 242, 340–1, 353–7, 371, 380, 385, 396–7, 407, 414, 428, 431, 465–81, 492
Santa Santita 181–5
satanism 230–2
Schrader, P. 58, 65, 109, 121–3, 125, 200, 322, 333, 338–41, 354
science fiction 109, 123, 163, 168, 250, 331, 368, 372–3, 376, 432
Scorsese, M. 58, 65, 78, 109, 112, 118, 121–2, 169, 238, 255, 316, 320, 322, 357, 423, 426, 429, 456–8

Serial Experiments: Lain 206
Seventh Sign, The 119, 375–7
Seventh Victim, The 230–2
Shaheen, J. 134–5
Shawshank Redemption, The 117–8, 340–1, 348, 358–60, 364–5, 431–2, 493
Shinto 197
Shoah 97–9
Socrates 484–5
Son of Man 113
spectacle, female as 239–40
spectatorship 6–7, 240–1, 249, 251, 279, 301–2
Spielberg, S. 98, 141, 333
Star Wars 318, 334, 341, 348, 388, 396–7, 399, 404, 432, 491
Stigmata 405
Stone, B. 3, 72–88, 317, 406, 408, 433, 476, 493
Straight Story, The 392–3
Sunshine 380–1
Superman 318, 341, 395–6, 399, 432, 434–5

Tanner, H. 445
Tarkovsky, A. 58, 109, 123–4, 168, 322–3, 333, 343, 478
Ten Commandments, The (1923, 1956) 21, 25, 95, 110, 387–92, 450–1, 455, 487–9 see also DeMille, C.
Tender Mercies 318, 334, 336–8, 348
Thelma and Louise 244–5
Thief in the Night, The 82–3
Thumim, J. 242
Tillich, P. 285, 312–4
Tissot, J. 453–6
Towelhead 138
Trial of Joan of Arc, The 113, 339 see also Bresson, R.
Truman Show, The 496–7

Vidor, K. 19–20, 467, 472
vodou 227–30

Waterworld 381
Wenders, W. 58, 110, 123–4, 333
westerns 18–9, 109, 117, 120–1, 368, 431, 474
Wicca 216, 219, 222–3, 230
Wicker Man, The (1973) 220–2, 414
Witchcraft 222–7, 230, 232, 405, 413–4
Wright, M. 4, 222, 276, 287, 304, 324, 385, 434, 489

Yiddish cinema 95–6

Zen Buddhism 165–7, 170

Related titles from Routledge

Film and Religion: The Reader
Edited by Jolyon Mitchell and S. Brent Plate

Edited by leading experts in the field, this is the first comprehensive reader to offer a survey of the subject to date. Film is now widely studied and researched in theology and religious studies departments; *The Religion and Film Reader* explores key topics including:

- early responses to film
- directors
- films and audiences
- cultural and social contexts
- Biblical connections
- theological approaches
- religious studies perspectives.

The reader brings together a huge amount of material in a student-friendly format and will be an invaluable resource for courses within both theology and religious studies.

ISBN10: 0-415-40494-0 (hbk)
ISBN10: 0-415-40495-9 (pbk)

ISBN13: 978-0-415-40494-5 (hbk)
ISBN13: 978-0-415-40495-2 (pbk)

Available at all good bookshops
For ordering and further information please visit:
www.routledge.com

Related titles from Routledge

The Routledge Companion to the Study of Religion
Edited by Professor John R. Hinnells

"A companion in the very best sense of the word: it provides the reader with excellent guides and mentors to walk alongside on the path to understanding... The result is an intelligent, fair-minded, thorough, and cutting-edge exploration of the field of religious studies." – *Wendy Doniger, Mircea Eliade Distinguished Service Professor of the History of Religions, University of Chicago USA*

"This is a very rich Companion to the Study of Religion. The survey of key approaches provides an excellent introduction for students and others, while the chapters show the reader why and where the study of religion is relevant to our contemporary situation." – *Willem B. Drees, Professor of Philosophy of Religion and Ethics, Leiden University, The Netherlands*

"The editor should be congratulated for bringing together such connoisseurs and seasoned observers to guide us... the lack of triumphalism only adds to the lustre of the book." – *Times Higher Education Suppliment*

The effective study of religion involves many disciplines and methods, from psychology to sociology, and from textual analysis to case studies in the field. It also requires an awareness of key thematic issues such as gender, science, fundamentalism, ritual, mysticism, and new religious movements.

Containing everything needed for a full understanding of theory and methods in religious studies, *The Routledge Companion to the Study of Religion*:

- surveys the history of religious studies and the key disciplinary approaches
- shows how to apply theories and methods to practical study
- highlights contemporary issues such as globalization, diaspora and politics
- explains why the study of religion is relevant in today's world

Beginning by explaining the most important methodological approaches to religion, including psychology, philosophy, anthropology and comparative study, the text then moves on to explore a wide variety of critical issues. Written entirely by renowned international specialists, and using clear and accessible language throughout, it is the perfect guide to the problems and questions found in exams and on courses.

978-0-415-33310-8 (hbk)
978-0-415-33311-5 (pbk)

Available at all good bookshops
For ordering and further information please visit:
www.routledge.com

Related titles from Routledge

Theology Goes to the Movies
Clive Marsh

By starting from issues explored in particular films, the book helps to ground theological debates in relation to human questions and experience. This really helps to bring the discipline of theology alive, and I wish this book had been available when I was a theology student.

Gordon Lynch, Senior Lecturer in Religion and Culture, University of Birmingham, UK

Marsh is correct! Theology is not just cognitive, but affective, aesthetic and ethical. And film has become a primary resource. Here is a helpful work-book for culturally-savy theology students and theologically-interested film-lovers.

Robert K. Johnston, author of Reel Spirituality: Theology and Film in Dialogue

Marsh never reduces the theological analysis of culture to an imposition of theological concepts onto culture; rather, theology is developed in critical engagement with popular culture, within "peaceful mutual critique." He accomplishes this task with clarity, open-mindedness, and grace.

John Lyden, Professor and Chair of Religion, Dana College

Theology Goes to the Movies is an introduction to understanding theology through film. Clive Marsh, an experienced teacher in the field, uses a range of contemporary films including *Touching the Void, Bruce Almighty, Notting Hill, 21 Grams, Legally Blond*, and *The Piano* to explain key theological concepts such as ideas of God, the church, eschatology, redemption, humanity and spirit.

Starting from the premise that film watching is a religion-like activity, the book explores the ways in which films require the viewer to engage at many levels (cognitive, affective, aesthetic and ethical) and argues that the social practice of cinema going has a religious dimension. This stimulating and entertaining book shows how theology through film can be both a method of reading the dialogue between film and Western culture, as well as a relevant and contemporary practical theology.

ISBN: 978-0-415-38011-9 (hbk)
ISBN: 978-0-415-38012-6 (pbk)

Available at all good bookshops
For ordering and further information please visit:
www.routledge.com

CPSIA information can be obtained
at www.ICGtesting.com
Printed in the USA
FFOW02n1300201115
18739FF